Rick Steves®

ICELAND

Rick Steves
with Cameron Hewitt & Ian Watson

CONTENTS

Post-Pandemic Travels: Expect a Warm Welcome...and a Few Changes
Research for this guidebook was limited by the COVID-19 outbreak, and the long-term impact of the crisis on our recommended destinations is unclear. Some details in this book will change for post-pandemic travelers. Now more than ever, it's smart to reconfirm specifics as you plan and travel. As always, you can find major updates at RickSteves.com/update.

Welcome to Rick Steves' Europe

Travel is intensified living—maximum thrills per minute and one of the last great sources of legal adventure. Travel is freedom. It's recess, and we need it.

I discovered a passion for European travel as a teen and have been sharing it ever since—through my tours, public television and radio shows, and travel guidebooks. Over the years, I've taught millions of travelers how to best enjoy Europe's blockbuster sights—and experience "Back Door" discoveries that most tourists miss.

This book offers a balanced mix of Iceland's glaciers, volcanoes, spectacular scenery, and fjordside villages. It's selective: Rather than listing every hot spring, I recommend only the best ones. And it's in-depth: My self-guided drives, town walks, and museum tours give insight into the country's unique geology, vibrant history, and today's living, breathing culture.

I advocate traveling simply and smartly. Take advantage of my money- and time-saving tips on sightseeing, transportation, and more. Try local, characteristic alternatives to expensive hotels and restaurants. In many ways, spending more money only builds a thicker wall between you and what you traveled so far to see.

We visit Iceland to experience it—to become temporary locals. Thoughtful travel engages us with the world, as we learn to appreciate other cultures and new ways to measure quality of life.

Judging by the positive feedback I receive from readers, this book will help you enjoy a fun, affordable, and rewarding vacation—whether it's your first trip or your tenth.

Góða ferð! Happy travels!

Rick Steves

ICELAND

Iceland, the land of the midnight sun and the northern lights, is equally famous for its magnificent glaciers and its active volcanoes. Magma bubbling up between tectonic plates formed this rugged island, leaving it stranded halfway between North America and Europe. Until recently a poor, backward Nordic outpost, today it's one of Europe's most expensive countries. Over the last few years, Iceland has vaulted from obscurity to become a can't-miss destination for curious travelers.

With its stunning natural wonders, kind people, and unique attractions, this little island stubbornly exceeds the lofty expectations of its many visitors. Most people's single biggest regret after visiting Iceland? They tried to squeeze it into just a day or two, instead of investing the time to see more of its striking landscape.

Iceland floats alone where the North Atlantic and Arctic oceans meet, just a smidge below the Arctic Circle. Its closest neighbors are Greenland, to the west, and the Faroe Islands, to the southeast. The remote island was uninhabited until the ninth century, when, at the height of the Viking Age, it was settled by farmers looking for a good place to graze their sheep. It remained a land of isolated farms for about a millennium. Up until the late 1800s, Iceland had no towns aside from Reyk-javík. If you stay in the countryside today, you can get close to the agrarian Iceland that existed for centuries. Some farms have a storied history, going back hundreds of years.

Social movements that sparked upheaval elsewhere—

Fields of lupine in Iceland's southeast corner; a monster truck gets you into the interior Highlands.

Christianization, Reformation, independence—arrived in Iceland with strangely little fuss. The country's Viking Age roots and its historic connections to Norway and Denmark give it an unmistakably Nordic aura, while the long-time presence of an American naval air base developed Iceland's affinity for all things Yankee. Today, Iceland feels like it has one foot in Europe, and the other in America.

About 300 miles across, Iceland is roughly the size of Kentucky and smaller than the island of Great Britain. More than half of the country is uninhabited tundra (in the interior Highlands). Almost all of its 340,000 residents live near the coastline, and more than half of Icelanders reside in the capital region of Reykjavík, on the southwest coast.

For the traveler, Reykjavík is the natural jumping-off point for exploring Iceland's dramatic countryside. It's an easy hop from Reykjavík to the inland Golden Circle route, studded with natural and historic attractions (from geysers to thundering waterfalls), or south to the famous Blue Lagoon thermal baths (on the Reykjanes Peninsula, near Keflavík Airport). Two hours away, the South Coast offers glaciers, black sand beaches, and a jagged volcanic landscape.

An hour's drive north of Reykjavík is the fjord-wrapped town of Borgarnes and the pastoral Reykholt Valley (with a premium thermal bath and tourable volcanic lava tube). Just

The Land of Fire and Ice

The country's name is "Ice-land," but that's only part of the story. This little island features a stunning diversity of landscapes—from frigid glaciers to boiling geysers, and from towering mountains to dreamy fjords. That's why, for most visitors, Iceland's raw, awe-inspiring nature is its biggest draw.

Iceland, which plugs the gap between the North American and Eurasian tectonic plates, was formed long ago by **volcanoes** (*eldfjöll,* "fire mountains")—and regular eruptions continue. The best known include those at Surtsey (1963), which added a new island off Iceland's South Coast, and on Heimaey (1973), which increased the size of that little island by a square mile. In 2010, the infamous Eyjafjallajökull volcano blew a column of ash four miles into the atmosphere that drifted east to Europe, halting air travel.

Odds are you won't witness an eruption during your visit; Iceland weathers about one every five years. Even so, it's impossible to come to Iceland without experiencing its volcanic landscapes: Keflavík Airport sits on a petrified lava flow. Things just get more interesting from there, from trapped-in-time sheets of lava, to giant burst bubbles of molten rock, to craters holding vibrantly colored (and still steaming) lakes.

Evidence of Iceland's power-ful natural forces: exploding geysers, gushing magma, and volcanic craters.

Iceland's highest volcanic peaks are capped by **glaciers** (*jöklar,* singular *jökull*)—frozen seas of ice. About 10 percent of the country is covered by glaciers, mostly along the South Coast and in the unpopulated Highlands in the island's center. All of them are melting; scientists predict Iceland's glaciers will largely disappear within the next two centuries. ▶▶▶

▶▶▶ For now, at Sólheimajökull, you can walk up and touch a glacier; at Jökulsárlón and Fjallsárlón, you can ride a boat on a glacier lagoon, circling bobbing icebergs calved off from an icy tongue; at various places, you can hike or snowmobile across the top of a glacier, or enter an ice cave within one.

After nearly 1,200 years of taming their volatile island, Icelanders have harnessed geothermal energy in ways both practical (to heat their homes and generate electricity) and hedonistic. To literally immerse yourself in Iceland's volcanic landscape, visit one (or, better yet, several) of its naturally occurring **thermal baths.**

Free hot springs and pools dot the island, attracting Icelanders year-round. Some are easy to reach by car, while others require a bit of a hike—but your reward is a long soak in toasty water surrounded by an incredible landscape. For a less rugged experience, visit a municipal swimming pool—with water naturally heated to around 100°F—or go to one of Iceland's well-advertised premium baths (such as the Blue Lagoon).

Hike to a glacier's edge; visit a geothermal plant; soak in a thermal bath.

Iceland's landscape is dramatic, but there are many ways to make it accessible. The Icelandic Experiences chapter is designed to inspire you with ways you can connect to Icelandic nature, then point you to the details elsewhere in this book. Enjoy! ◼

beyond that, Snæfellsnes offers a representative sample of Icelandic landscapes—fjords, scree slopes, lava rock, waterfalls, and a glacier—in an easy-to-navigate peninsula. And out at Iceland's northwest fringe are the Westfjords: a chain of jagged, sparsely populated inlets with far fewer tourists.

But the ultimate Icelandic thrill is an 800-mile road trip, circling the entire island on the Ring Road (highway 1). Give the Ring Road enough time, and it'll give you charming waterfront towns (Siglufjörður, Húsavík, and Seyðisfjörður), a pint-sized second city (Akureyri), simmering volcanic landscapes (near Mývatn), jagged fjords (the Eastfjords), and glaciers and glacier lagoons (on the southeast coast).

Iceland has a rich folklore and a strong connection between its heritage and its landscape. It seems every rock has a thousand-year-old name and a legend to go with it. With cinematic scenery and abundant opportunities to experience nature in its rawest form, Iceland exhilarates outdoorsy travelers. Snowmobile across a glacier. Zip over the waves on a rigid inflatable boat while scanning the horizon for breaching whales or puffins. Go for a ride on an Icelandic horse, hoping to feel the rhythm of its elusive "fifth gait." Scuba or snorkel in a tectonic rift flooded with crystal-clear glacial water. Hike from hut to hut, tracing the path of lava from a slumbering volcano.

For a quintessentially Icelandic experience, be sure to soak in one of the country's spring-fed thermal baths. The

Boat ride in Fjallsárlón's glacier lagoons on the southeast coast; small and strong Icelandic horses

Raufarhólshellir lava tube; beer-tasting flight near Dalvík

spa-like Blue Lagoon—with milky blue water filling a volcanic reservoir—is the most famous (and most expensive). But every village has its own municipal swimming pool filled with piping-hot water. Those who love the out-of-doors can find free and hidden opportunities for an al fresco soak throughout the countryside.

Iceland's natural splendors are what attract most visitors, but Icelanders are also worth getting to know. They have a gentle spirit and a can-do frontier attitude. They're also whip-smart (Icelandic scholars were the first to write down the legends and histories of the early Scandinavian people—collectively called "the sagas"). Enjoy meeting the easygoing Icelanders; in this little country, everyone's on a first-name basis.

Two often-repeated Icelandic phrases offer insight into the local psyche: *kærulaus* (loosely, "careless") describes the flexible, improvisational, sometimes inconsiderate way Icelanders move through life. And an Icelander facing an unexpected challenge might mutter, *"Þetta reddast"* ("It'll work out")...and in this mellow land, it usually does (with some major exceptions, like Iceland's economic crash in 2008).

Iceland has a rich cuisine scene. Trendy restaurants are enthusiastically organic—literally wallpapered with fish skin and serving gourmet delights on slabs of rock or rustic little planks. There are few places with fresher seafood: haddock, cod, arctic

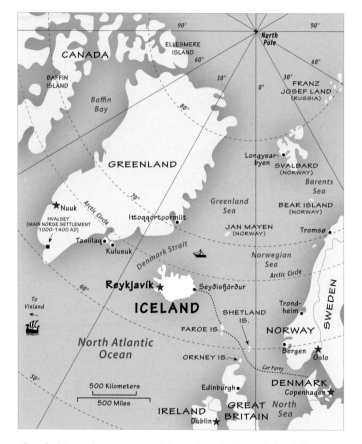

char, halibut, the controversial minke whale, and the delectable *humar* (langoustine). The rolling, green countryside teems with free-range sheep grazing on grass that seasons a tender and delicious meat. Vegetables are grown in hothouses, and a warming climate has allowed more farming of grains (barley, wheat, and rye). Soup is an Icelandic staple, and every grandma has her own secret recipe for *kjötsúpa* (lamb soup). And Icelandic *skyr*—a yogurt-like dairy food that's been around since Viking times—is newly trendy in American groceries.

Iceland is also famous for its notorious "hardship foods": an entire boiled sheep's head *(svið)*, jerky-like dried cod snacks *(harðfiskur)*, and the notorious *hákarl*—chewy, unbelievably pungent fermented shark. Locals scarcely eat these anymore, of course, but tourists do...usually on a dare.

Summer or winter, be prepared to bundle up (pack gloves, a fleece hat, sturdy boots, and a waterproof jacket). While conditions overall are surprisingly moderate for the latitude, frosty temperatures and bone-chilling wind can happen at any time of year. Icelanders use the term *gluggaveður* ("window weather") to describe weather that's pleasant to look at—from indoors. Blustery days arrive frequently, especially in winter, when strong low-pressure systems roll in regularly, whipping high winds across the whole island. It's not just a little unpleasant to be outside in high winds—you may literally not be able to walk, or open your car door.

Typically, two or three days of cloudy, drizzly skies alternate with two or three days of relatively sunny weather. The cloudy periods lengthen in winter, the sunny periods in summer. It rains often in Reykjavík, but pouring rain is infrequent. Lightning is rare enough to make the evening news.

Few places, especially one so remote and cold, have become so popular, so quickly. But Iceland's striking glaciers, craggy peaks, and steamy geysers—and the visible impacts of climate change—make this destination attractive to the inquisitive and the adventurous. Whether or not you can pronounce the names on its map, Iceland is a rewarding place to travel.

Iceland's Top Destinations

It's a small country, but there's a lot to see in Iceland. This overview breaks its top destinations into must-see sights (to help first-time travelers plan their trip) and worth-it sights (for those with additional time). I've also suggested a minimum number of days to allow per destination.

MUST-SEE DESTINATIONS

Iceland's capital, Reykjavík, is the natural hub for any visit, with an excellent assortment of accommodations, restaurants, shops, and nightlife. But, while Reykjavík easily has enough sights of its own to fill a day or two, with limited time, I'd spend my evenings in Reykjavík and my days in the country-side at these top choices:

▲▲▲Blue Lagoon (half-day)

This top-end thermal bathing complex, tucked in a volcanic landscape a 45-minute drive south of Reykjavík (and near Keflavík Airport), is relaxing and memorable, and a delightful toe-in-the-water dip into Iceland's thermal bathing culture.

▲▲▲Golden Circle (1 day)

Iceland's quintessential day trip is deservedly popular. You'll loop through eye-popping terrain, with stops at Þingvellir (site of Iceland's Viking Age gatherings, situated along a jagged tectonic fissure); Geysir (a steamy field that's home to the world's original "geyser"); and Gullfoss (a thundering waterfall). Along the way, you can tiptoe around the rim of a volcanic crater, visit Iceland's medieval religious center, and take your pick of thermal bath experiences.

▲▲▲South Coast (1 day)

This dramatic shoreline, shaped by volcanoes and glaciers, rivals the Golden Circle as Reykjavík's top day trip. You'll see spectacular waterfalls tumble over high cliffs, touch the tongue of a glacier, stroll along a black sand beach, and learn about the majestic power of volcanoes. Nearby, avid hikers can make the Þórsmörk nature reserve (nestled between three glaciers) a ▲▲ full day on its own.

Basalt columns at Reynisfjara (opposite); Þingvellir and Geysir, on the Golden Circle; Blue Lagoon; Þórsmörk

WORTH-IT DESTINATIONS

On a longer visit, these stops—rated ▲ or ▲▲—deserve consideration. All are within easy day-tripping distance of Reykjavík—except the Westfjords and the Ring Road, each of which demands several days.

▲▲Reykjavík (1-2 days)
An ideal home base for a visit of any length, Reykjavík is a worthwhile sightseeing destination in its own right. Its colorful, pedestrian-friendly downtown has fine museums, a stroll-worthy harbor, and a dozen thermal swimming pools, perfect for a rejuvenating soak among Icelanders. The capital's restaurants are surprisingly good, and its nightlife scene is legendary.

▲▲Westman Islands (1 day)
Reachable by a short ferry ride or flight, this little chain of 15 islands merits the effort. On Heimaey (the only inhabited island), you'll find towering seabird cliffs and the world's largest puffin colony (in summer), a busy harbor, two volcanoes (plus an excellent volcano museum), and an aquarium with a resident puffin and beluga whales.

▲▲Ring Road (5-10 days)
To really delve into Iceland, circle the island's perimeter on highway 1. It's a demanding drive (the entire circuit is 800 miles), but the scenic payoff is huge: breathtaking waterfalls and remote fjords, majestic mountains, volcanic cones and craters, otherworldly lava formations, rich birdlife, geothermal springs and geysers, glaciers, black-sand beaches, and windswept coastlines.

Colorful, quirky Reykjavík; harbor in the Westman Islands; lunar landscape near Mývatn, on the Ring Road; high-end "New Icelandic" cuisine

▲Borgarnes and Reykholt Valley (1 day)

This West Iceland area's subtle charms include the dramatically set town of Borgarnes (with a fine exhibit on Iceland's settlement and sagas) and the gentle Reykholt Valley, with lovely waterfalls, prolific hot springs, and a tourable lava tube, plus a traditional goat farm, premium thermal bath, and important religious site. Nearby is the hikeable Grábrók volcanic crater.

▲Snæfellsnes (1-2 days)

This peninsula, two hours north of Reykjavík, offers an "Iceland in a nutshell" loop past coastal scenery, bridal-veil waterfalls, chunky lava-rock landscapes, quirky museums, black-sand beaches, fjordside fishing towns, a lava tube, its very own glacier, and more. While doable as a (long) day trip, it's worth an overnight to settle in and escape from the capital-area crowds.

▲Westfjords (2-3 days)

For those wanting a remote, rugged corner of Iceland all their own—but who don't have a full week for a Ring Road drive—the Westfjords are a splendid compromise. Here a sawtooth coastline is peppered with few towns but ample stunning scenery and a poignant sense of the lonesome Icelandic frontier. You'll also find Iceland's finest bird cliffs (Látrabjarg) and one of its best waterfalls (Dynjandi).

Norwegian House in Snæfellsnes;
Dynjandi waterfall in the Westfjords

Planning Your Trip

To plan your trip, you'll need to design your itinerary—choosing where and when to go, how you'll travel, and how many days to spend at each destination. For my best general advice on sightseeing, accommodations, restaurants, and more, see the Practicalities chapter.

DESIGNING AN ITINERARY

As you read this book and learn your options...

Choose your top destinations.

My recommended itineraries in this chapter give you an idea of how to spend your time in Iceland—whether you've got one day or ten. Most visitors focus on the great outdoors: volcanic landscapes, waterfalls, thermal springs, and so on. Reykjavík is the natural home base, and on a very short visit, you can simply overnight there, spending your days side-tripping to nearby attractions (see the Beyond Reykjavík chapter for advice).

Decide when to go.

Your Icelandic experience will vary drastically depending on the time of year. Summer really is the best time to go—even if everyone else is there with you. From June through August, days are long and the weather is at its best. The country bustles and glistens under the bright sun; sightseeing attractions are open and in full swing. At these northern latitudes, from about June 1 to July 15, the sun dips below the horizon for only a few hours, and it never really gets dark. Icelanders take full advantage of these days of "midnight sun," and so should you. In

Iceland's Best Short Trips by Car

Iceland rewards a visit of any length. I've outlined two basic itineraries here: a whirlwind 24-hour visit and a more relaxed five-day stay (both can be modified for longer visits). I've provided additional multiday itineraries in the Beyond Reykjavík chapter. For my suggested Ring Road itineraries, see page 22 and the Ring Road chapter. For any itinerary, consider these factors:

Time of Year: My itineraries assume you'll visit in summer, when daylight is virtually endless and roads are clear. In the off-season, you'll want to stay closer to the capital.

Blue Lagoon Scheduling: The Blue Lagoon is located between Reykjavík and Keflavík Airport, so it's easy to combine a soak with your flight. These plans assume you'll arrive in the morning and stop at the Blue Lagoon on your way into town. But it works equally well to visit the Blue Lagoon on your departure day (if you have a late flight). Whenever you go, reserve the Blue Lagoon in advance.

Westman Islands Weather: Connections to the Westman Islands can be weather-dependent, so have a Plan B ready. Don't schedule a return from the islands the day of an onward flight from Iceland; give yourself at least a one-night buffer.

Without a Car: Base in Reykjavík and book day-trip excursions to the Golden Circle, Snæfellsnes, Blue Lagoon, South Coast, Westman Islands (by plane from Reykjavík), or Þórsmörk. It's also possible to fly from Reykjavík to Akureyri, a hub for tours in the north (Mývatn, Siglufjörður, whale watching) or to Höfn, near the glacier lagoons. See the Beyond Reykjavík chapter for more day-tripping details.

Iceland in 24 Hours

If one day is all you have in Iceland, here's how to pack it all in.

Morning:	Arrive, pick up car, head straight to Blue Lagoon and soak.
Midday:	Drive into Reykjavík for lunch and a few hours of browsing, then check into your hotel.
Afternoon:	Set out for Golden Circle loop trip—hitting just the highlights.
Evening:	Dinner in Golden Circle country.
Late:	Collapse at your hotel and sleep for a few hours. Fly out the next morning.

With 48 hours: Add a day trip to the South Coast.

With 72 hours: Spend more time exploring Reykjavík.

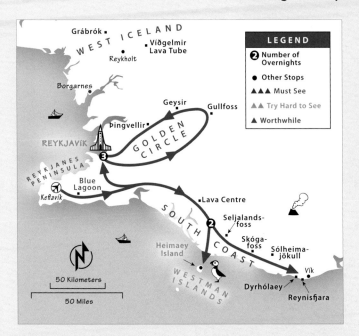

Iceland in 5 Days

Day	Plan	Sleep in
1	Arrive, pick up car, go to Blue Lagoon, then head to South Coast	South Coast
2	Westman Islands day trip	South Coast
3	South Coast sights, to Reykjavík	Reykjavík
4	Golden Circle	Reykjavík
5	Reykjavík (or excursions: whale watching, horseback riding, glacier hikes)	Reykjavík
6	Drop off car and fly out	

With 4 days: Spend less time in Reykjavík—see it in the two evenings, and on your morning of departure.

6 days: See the South Coast on Day 2, then overnight on the Westman Islands (Day 3) before heading to Reykjavík.

7 days: Head to Snæfellsnes, either as a long day trip or (even better) overnight.

8 days: Add another day in Reykjavík (and/or more excursions).

9 days: Day-trip from Reykjavík to Borgarnes and the Reykholt Valley, or spend some time here on the way up to Snæfellsnes. With more time, see my **10-day** itinerary on the next page.

Iceland's Best 10-Day Road Trip

With enough time, it's possible to see Reykjavík, drive the entire Ring Road route, including the South Coast, side-trip to the Westman Islands, and hit the Golden Circle highlights. The 10-day itinerary outlined here assumes you've rented a car (or campervan) and sets a fast pace, with several long driving days (and one-night stands) in a row. The more time you can devote to the Ring, the more relaxed and rewarding your circuit will be.

Day	Plan	Sleep in
1	Arrive, pick up car, go to Blue Lagoon on the way into Reykjavík	Reykjavík
2	Reykjavík	Reykjavík
3	Begin Ring Road: To Borgarnes, then Skagafjörður	Skagafjörður area
4	Drive the Tröllaskagi Peninsula (stopping in Siglufjörður and Akureyri), evening to Mývatn lake area	Mývatn
5	Mývatn area and Húsavík port town	Mývatn
6	To the Eastfjords (and Dettifoss falls)	Seyðisfjörður
7	Drive the Eastfjords to the southeast (Vatnajökull area)	Höfn, Jökulsárlón, or Skaftafell area
8	South Coast sights	South Coast
9	Westman Islands day trip	South Coast
10	Golden Circle highlights en route to Reykjavík	Reykjavík
11	Drop car and fly out	

July and early August, temperatures can climb into the 60s and even break 70. Icelanders take time off and Europeans arrive for camping vacations. After mid-August, it rapidly gets colder and darker, kids go back to school, and things quiet down.

May and September lack the vitality of summer but offer occasional good weather and minimal crowds. But in these months, snow and extreme weather can disrupt your plans, particularly on higher-elevation roads, and remote areas are inaccessible. April and October see harsher weather, with a good chance of snow and slippery roads anywhere outside Reykjavík.

Days are short from mid-October to mid-February—the

With 9 days: Spend only one night in Mývatn (and skip Húsavík). Or make Borgarnes your first overnight, and blitz Reykjavík and the Blue Lagoon at the end of your trip.

11 days: Add a Snæfellsnes detour, a day in Reykjavík, or overnight in Akureyri.

12-14 days: Add an excursion: Þórsmörk or Skaftafell hike, glacier visit, volcano tour, or whale watching.

Westfjords Alternative: If you don't have this much time to spare, but still want a taste of remote Iceland, consider a few days in the Westfjords; for a recommended itinerary, see page 325.

sun rises after 11:00 all December—and dusk will draw the shades on your sightseeing well before dinner. You can still enjoy a stopover in Reykjavík though, when music and film events liven up the darkness, and Christmastime activities offer a warm experience at a frosty time. Outside the city, roads ice over, and sights and accommodations are closed or have reduced hours. Bus trips to the nearby Golden Circle and South Coast are typically still possible (leave winter driving to the pros). Driving the Ring Road in winter is inadvisable at best, and impossible at worst.

One benefit of a winter visit is the chance to view the elusive northern lights, though whether you'll actually see them

is unpredictable. For weather specifics, see the climate chart in the appendix.

Connect the dots.

Many people drop into Iceland on the way to or from Europe; Icelandair typically allows a layover of up to several days for only a small charge.

Decide if you'll travel by car or rely on excursions, or a combination. A car or campervan rental is expensive, but offers maximum flexibility for side-tripping and exploring the countryside (for more on vehicle rentals, see the Practicalities chapter). Excursion trips make the island accessible to nondrivers, but are pricey, too—skipping the car rental doesn't necessarily save a lot of money.

To determine approximate driving times between destinations, study the driving map in the Practicalities chapter. Major roads are fairly good, but back roads are often unpaved. Be sure to tune into the peculiarities of Icelandic driving, including how to traverse city roundabouts and one-lane bridges and tunnels (for Icelandic driving tips, see page 513). Google Maps can help you navigate throughout most of Iceland, but even it has blind spots—be ready to supplement with printed maps if you'll be leaving well-traveled areas.

Write out a day-by-day itinerary.

Figure out how many destinations you can comfortably fit in your time frame. If you're energetic, you can take advantage of long summer days to cram in the maximum.

When planning your trip, allow enough time, and don't spend it all in Reykjavík. On a short visit, make Reykjavík your base, then devote your days to the nearby Golden Circle or South Coast. In summer you'll still have hours of evening sunlight by which to enjoy Reykjavík even after side-tripping (for more on day trips, see the Beyond Reykjavík chapter).

Decide whether you'll do everything as side trips from Reykjavík or divide your trip into multiple overnights (sleeping on the South Coast mixes in a little variety, and overlaps conveniently with the Golden Circle and Westman Islands). The Ring Road is a long, one-way trip...plan on lots of one-night stays. (To break it up, consider lingering in Mývatn in the north, or near the glaciers in the southeast.)

Check if any holidays or festivals fall during your trip—these attract crowds and can close sights (for the latest, visit www.inspiredbyiceland.com). If traveling outside of summer (Sept-May), be aware of potential weather-related road closures. Many sights and services in the countryside may be closed, and those in Reykjavík have reduced hours.

Give yourself some slack. Every trip—and every traveler—needs downtime for doing laundry, picnic shopping, people-watching, and so on. Pace yourself. Assume you will return.

Icelanders are easygoing and creative; horns or not—you'll want a warm hat.

Two-wheel drive is just right for the Ring Road in summer; budget accommodations; short-hop flights are handy for the Westman Islands or Akureyri; glacier walk.

Trip Costs Per Person

Run a reality check on your dream trip. You'll have major transportation costs in addition to daily expenses.

Flight: A round-trip flight from the US to Keflavík Airport costs about $700-2,000, depending on where you fly from and when.

Local Transportation: For a six-day trip using excursion buses and one intra-Iceland flight, allow $800 per person.

Car Rental: Allow roughly $350 per week (more for four-wheel drive), not including tolls, gas, parking, and insurance.

AVERAGE DAILY EXPENSES PER PERSON

$250
Applies to Reykjavík, about 10 percent less in the countryside

Lodging
Based on two people splitting the cost of a $250 double room with breakfast.
$125

Meals
$25 for lunch, $50 for dinner
$75

Sights and Entertainment
This daily average works for most people.
$50

Budget Tips

Iceland is one of Europe's most expensive destinations. Here are some strategies for keeping costs down.

Consider Airbnb. Airbnb and similar sites rent properties that are typically far cheaper than hotels. And if you're willing to forego hotel services (like a reception desk and daily cleaning), you'll get more space and amenities for your money. Air-bnb can also get you into more local neighborhoods; sleeping in a Reykjavík suburban home is both cheaper and more Icelandic than a touristy downtown hotel.

"Go" down the hall. Iceland's characteristic guesthouses typically offer basic rooms with a shared bathroom, which cost much less than rooms with en suite bathrooms. ▶▶▶

▶▶▶ **Have a big lunch and a small dinner.** Even the fanciest restaurants offer excellent-value lunch specials in the $25 range. Enjoy a high-end, sit-down meal for lunch, then picnic or grab cheap takeout for dinner.

Picnic. Cultivate the art of picnicking in atmospheric settings. Seek out Iceland's discount supermarket chains—Krónan and Bónus—and use them to stock up. Consider bringing a few staples from home: In a place where a basic takeaway coffee costs $5 a cup, packing some single-serving instant coffee lets you caffeinate cheaply.

Know what's included. Icelandic restaurants happily provide diners with a free carafe of tap water—just ask. Don't feel obligated to purchase a drink. If you've paid for unlimited soup and bread, don't be shy about going back for seconds. And if someone offers you free coffee, take it! Since Iceland has no tipping culture and taxes are included, you'll pay exactly the price you see on the menu.

Economize on alcohol. Alcohol is priced at a premium, particularly in bars and restaurants. Stock up at the airport duty-free store on arrival—with the lowest prices in Iceland—or at government-run liquor stores (called Vínbúðin). If you're going to a bar, go during happy hour.

Skip the Blue Lagoon. While famous and a highlight for many visitors, the Blue Lagoon costs ten times as much as Iceland's

many municipal thermal pools... which are also a more authentic experience. Reykjavík alone has more than a dozen municipal pools with water just as hot as the Blue Lagoon's. If visiting several pools, invest in a shareable multi-visit card.

Sightsee selectively. Icelandic museums are typically very good...but expensive ($12-38). If you'll be sightseeing a lot and hitting the thermal pools in the capital, consider a Reykjavík City Card. Fortunately, many of Iceland's best attractions—its natural wonders—are free.

Splurge where it counts. When you do splurge, choose an experience you'll always remember: If you're a naturalist, invest in a whale-watching tour; if you like to eat, take a culinary walk or dine out at one top-end restaurant; if you're an adventurer, spelunk through a lava tube or hike across a glacier. Minimize souvenir shopping—most shops sell things that are extremely expensive, produced outside Iceland, or both. (Plus, how will you get it all home?) Focus instead on collecting wonderful memories. ◾

BEFORE YOU GO

You'll have a smoother trip if you tackle a few things ahead of time. For more information on these topics, see the Practicalities chapter (and www.ricksteves.com, which has helpful travel tips and talks).

Make sure your travel documents are valid. If your passport is due to expire within six months of your ticketed date of return, you need to renew it. Allow six weeks or more to renew or get a passport (www.travel.state.gov). Check for current Covid entry requirements, such as proof of vaccination or a negative Covid-19 test result.

Arrange your transportation. Book your international flights. If you're planning on renting a car or campervan, do it in advance, and read up on the unique hazards of driving in Iceland. It's worth booking cheap domestic Iceland flights in advance. If you'll be taking your car on the ferry to the Westman Islands, book ahead for summer weekends.

Book rooms well in advance. Reserve your rooms as soon as you've pinned down your travel dates, particularly for Reykjavík and some places on the Ring Road (Mývatn and Höfn).

Book ahead for the Blue Lagoon. Make reservations at least several days in advance. With the exception of specialized experiences like ice caving or glacier hiking, other excursions can usually be booked a day or two beforehand.

Consider travel insurance. Compare the cost of the insurance to the cost of your potential loss. Check whether your existing insurance (health, homeowners, or renters) covers you and your possessions overseas.

Call your bank. Alert your bank that you'll be using your debit and credit cards in Europe. Ask about transaction fees, and get the PIN number for your credit card. You don't need to bring *krónur* for your trip.

Use your smartphone smartly. Sign up for an international service plan to reduce your costs, or rely on Wi-Fi in Iceland instead. Download any apps (or bookmark websites) you'll want to access on the road, such as maps, translators, road conditions, weather forecasts, and Rick Steves Audio Europe (see sidebar).

Pack light. I travel for weeks with a single carry-on bag and a daypack. Use the packing checklist in the appendix so you're sure to include a few important extras for Iceland. Pack an insect head net if you plan to visit Mývatn. In winter, consider strap-on ice cleats if you plan to do much outdoor walking.

Rick's Free Video Clips and Audio Tours

Travel smarter with these free, fun resources:

Rick Steves Classroom Europe, a powerful tool for teachers, is also useful for travelers. This video library contains over 400 short clips excerpted from my public television series. Enjoy these videos as you sort through options for your trip and to better understand what you'll see in Europe. Check it out at Classroom. RickSteves.com (just enter a topic in the search bar to find everything I've filmed on a subject).

The Rick Steves Audio Europe app makes it easy to download audio content to enhance your trip. Use the app to listen to audio tours of Europe's top sights, plus interviews from my public radio show with experts from Europe and around the globe. Find it in your app store or at RickSteves.com/AudioEurope.

Travel Smart

Iceland is famously spectacular, and it's hard to have a bad time here. But it's easy to underestimate the changeable weather, blow through too much money, or waste time by not making a good plan. If you equip yourself with good information (this book) and expect to travel smart, you will.

Read—and reread—this book. To have an "A" trip, be an "A" student. Note opening hours of sights, closed days, crowd-beating tips, and whether reservations are required or advisable. Check the latest at www.ricksteves.com/update.

Be your own tour guide. As you travel, get up-to-date info on sights, reserve tickets and tours, reconfirm hotels and travel arrangements, and check weather forecasts. Upon arrival in a new town, lay the groundwork for a smooth departure; confirm the road conditions and route to your next destination.

Outsmart thieves. While theft is rare in Iceland, some pickpockets are arriving with the tourist crowds. Keep your backup credit cards, passport, and big bills secure in a money belt tucked under your clothes; carry one credit card and a little cash in a wallet in your front pocket. Don't set valuable items down on counters or café tabletops, where they can be quickly stolen or easily forgotten.

Minimize potential loss. Keep expensive gear to a minimum. Bring photocopies or take photos of important documents (passport and cards) to aid in replacement if they're lost or stolen. Back up photos and files frequently.

Be budget-conscious. Fully experiencing Iceland is worth paying a lot for...but it's not necessary to break the bank.

Smart, organized travelers can avoid overpaying. For suggestions, read and heed my "Budget Tips," earlier.

Be flexible. Even with a well-planned itinerary, expect changes, closures, howling winds, sore feet, and so on. Your Plan B could turn out to be even better.

Attempt the language. Most Icelanders—especially in the tourist trade—speak English. But if you learn even just a few Icelandic phrases, you'll get more smiles and make more friends (see the Survival Phrases near the end of this book).

Connect with the culture. Interacting with locals carbonates your experience. Enjoy the friendliness of the Icelandic people. Ask questions; most locals are happy to point you in their idea of the right direction. Set up your own quest for the best fish-of-the-day, volcanic crater, thermal swimming pool, or mountain pass. When an opportunity pops up, make it a habit to say "yes."

Iceland...here you come!

ICELANDIC EXPERIENCES

Iceland is a small land that packs in a lot of experiences. From gazing into a volcanic crater lake to descending into the underground magma chamber of a dormant volcano, from exploring glaciers and geysers to luxuriating in an outdoor pool filled with earth-warmed water, Iceland offers adventures and activities that you can't do anywhere else (not easily, at least).

Many of these experiences require going through a tour operator (even if you have a car). I've listed some established outfits. A good one-stop resource is Guide to Iceland, a for-profit consolidator of travel providers (www.guidetoiceland.is). They charge no additional commission and will match a better price if you find one. They work with some, but not all, tour providers in Iceland, so it's smart to also do your own research (for instance, the "Things to Do" reviews on TripAdvisor can offer a helpful roundup of tour companies and the latest experiences).

Note that while Reykjavík is generally a good home base, many excursions head to farther away destinations involving higher prices and long hours in a bus. Consider booking tours that are closer to where you're staying, even if it means home-basing outside of Reykjavík. For example, if you're interested in glacier activities, consider spending a night or two on the South Coast or in Southeast Iceland.

As you join the hordes of international visitors who treat Iceland as a newly discovered playground, do so considerately. Respect the land. The nature on display may seem raw and powerful, but it's also extremely fragile. Nobody yet knows precisely what long-term impact the recent influx of tourism will have on this special place. To be part of a sustainable long-term prosperity, treat Iceland as a precious treasure...because that's what it is.

The Many Ways Iceland Can Kill You

Several times a year, Iceland is captivated by a full-scale land and helicopter search for travelers sucked out to sea by a wave, separated from their snowmobile tour group, or lost in the wilderness. More so than in any other country in Europe, in Iceland nature can threaten your very survival.

To encourage safe travel, Iceland operates the SafeTravel.is website with detailed advice and up-to-the-minute alerts. Their "112 Iceland" app is free; they also staff a counter at the What's On TI in Reykjavík at Bankastræti 2. For help in English, dial 112, the national emergency number.

Travel smart and keep the following risks in mind. For specific driving hazards, see page 518.

Wind: The signature feature of Icelandic weather is wind. For Icelanders, good weather means no wind or a light breeze; bad weather means it's blowing hard. Even in summer, you'll likely encounter winds that are uncomfortable or dangerous to walk or drive in. On a recent trip, when picking up my rental car, I was talked into a $20-a-day insurance supplement for "wind damage and sandstorms." And later, while I was standing on a rock to snap a photo, a freakish gust nearly blew me into the sea. Check the forecast at the Icelandic weather service's website (https://en.vedur.is). If it's windy and icy at the same time, take extra care.

Slips and Falls: In winter, Reykjavík's sidewalks generally aren't cleared or salted, and are very slippery and icy. Falls are common. Paths in the countryside ice over, too. Cautious travelers visiting from December through February can pack a pair of ice cleats to strap over their shoes.

Exposure and Getting Lost: When traveling in less inhabited parts of the country, be prepared for the unexpected. Your car could break down or run out of gas, or you could take a wrong turn. Travel with extra clothing (even summer days can turn cold and windy, especially at higher elevations) and keep your phone charged (bring a portable charger; reception is good all around the Ring Road). Carry a paper map as a backup. Before heading into wilderness areas, upload your itinerary to SafeTravel.is.

Glaciers

More than one-tenth of Iceland's surface is covered with glaciers (*jökull*)—mainly along the southern coastline and in the desolate interior. Glaciers are most accessible at so-called tongues, where a slow-motion river of ice flows down a valley.

Below are several glacier-related experiences you can do on your own. For more options, join a guided excursion. If you won't be venturing beyond Reykjavík, the Wonders of Iceland exhibit at

Sneaker Waves: Iceland's South Coast has some very dangerous beaches with strong waves that regularly pull unsuspecting tourists out to sea. Those breathtaking black sand beaches can suddenly become dangerous. Obey all signs, and stay *much* farther from the water than you think is safe.

Trail Hazards: There are very few ropes, guardrails, or warning signs in Iceland—but if you see any, take them seriously. Step carefully, and watch out for loose stones, crevices, and sharp lava rocks.

Scalding Thermal Water: The water in Iceland's geothermally active areas can be boiling hot, and the danger is often unmarked. Every year or two a tourist falls in and gets severely burned, typically in a less-visited geothermal area without ropes or walkways.

Avalanches: Icelanders have taken this danger more seriously since 1995, when two avalanches in the Westfjords killed 34 people. Wintertime travelers may encounter avalanche warnings in any settled area close to a steep mountain slope.

Volcanoes: On average, a volcano erupts in Iceland every five years. Some eruptions can be viewed from a safe distance, but others melt glaciers, let loose streams of boiling lava, give off poisonous gases, or spew ash and boulders that will damage you or your car. Volcanic eruptions and their consequences can and regularly do interfere with travel plans. The Icelandic weather service website posts regular updates on eruptions (and earthquakes).

Angry Birds: While not life-threatening, angry birds can be a nuisance. In late spring and early summer, Arctic terns *(kríur)* will dive-bomb your head if you get too close to their breeding grounds. Obey any closure signs near major nesting areas.

the Pearl has a simulated ice cave and glacier, and exhibits that focus on Iceland's glacial geology.

Glacier Sightseeing

There are several accessible glacier tongues along Iceland's southern coast, from near Skógar in the west to near Höfn in the east. If traveling on your own, you can **hike close to the tongue of a glacier** in two places: at the Skaftafell wilderness area, where you can walk to a branch of Iceland's largest glacier, Vatnajökull (see page 426); or at Sólheimajökull, along the southern coast closer to Reykjavík (page 227).

In Southeast Iceland, Jökulsárlón and Fjallsárlón are two **glacier lagoons** within minutes of each other, where a glacier tongue terminates in a beautiful pool of water, and icebergs calve off and float around. At either, you can pull over to view the lagoon, or take a boat trip between bobbing icebergs. Near Jökulsárlón is another enchanting glacial sight, the so-called **Diamond Beach,** where chunks of shimmering ice from the nearby lagoon wash up on a black sand beach. This is a grand look at the final stage of glacial ice's very long, very slow journey to the open ocean. (For more on all three of these sights, see page 434.)

Guided Glacier Tours

For more extreme glacier adventures, you'll need to go with a guided tour.

Glacier Walks: Equipped with cold-weather gear, crampons, and ice axes, you and your group will be tied together for an amble across the ice. The most popular places for this are Sólheimajökull and Skaftafell in Southeast Iceland, and Snæfellsjökull on the Snæfellsnes Peninsula. Companies offering glacier walks include the big Reykjavík Excursions and Gray Line, along with smaller, more specialized operators, such

as Icelandic Mountain Guides (www.mountainguides.is), Arctic Adventures (www.adventures.is), Troll Expeditions (www.troll.is), Glacier Guides (www.glacierguides.is), Glacier Journey (www.glacierjourney.is), and Extreme Iceland (www.extremeiceland.is).

Snowmobiling: The Mountaineers of Iceland offers a variety of snowmobile trips across Langjökull, near the Golden Circle ($250-450, www.mountaineers.is; or try Glacier Journey). At the Snæfellsjökull glacier (at the tip of the Snæfellsnes Peninsula), you can join a **snowcat tour** (essentially a big van on tank treads; for details, see page 301). You can even go on a **dogsled trip** across a glacier (consider Extreme Iceland).

Ice Caves: Visitors can explore three ice caves burrowed into glaciers ($160-250, 3-4 hours). Into the Glacier takes visitors to an artificial cave in Langjökull in West Iceland—the only ice cave open year-round (www.intotheglacier.is; see page 284). The glacier atop the Katla volcano in southern Iceland has a natural cave that's open from June to December—but it's melting quickly, so could close soon (tours depart from Vík; try Katlatrack, www.katlatrack. is). In the winter (Nov-March), Vatnajökull has a natural cave that you can explore with a tour that departs from the Jökulsárlón glacier lagoon (companies include Arctic Adventures, Extreme Iceland, and Glacier Journey; you'll pay more for pickup in Reykjavík).

Volcanoes

Travelers come to Iceland hoping for a glimpse of a volcano. When the volcano called Eyjafjallajökull spewed ash into the atmosphere in 2010—bringing European air travel to a halt—it grabbed the imagination of many. While you probably won't see any spewing ash or flowing lava while you're here, there is a variety of volcanic sights where you can learn more about the island's unique geology.

Volcanic Landscapes

Because much of Iceland is plainly shaped by volcanic activity, lava landscapes are common. Here are a few of the most dramatic and accessible (all are described in detail elsewhere in the book).

Westman Islands: This archipelago, just off the South Coast, is the most interesting volcano-related sight in Iceland, and a pilgrimage for those with serious interest. The Westman Islands saw some of Iceland's most spectacular volcanic activity in recent times. First, from 1963 to 1967, the islet of Surtsey literally rose from the Atlantic Ocean; while it can't be visited, on a clear day you can see the islet from the main island, Heimaey. Then, in 1973, the town of Vestmannaeyjar was rudely awoken in the middle of the night by a surprise eruption on the adjacent hillside. Residents were evacuated, and the flowing lava gradually swallowed the eastern part of the town. Today, streets dead-end at steep walls of volcanic rock, and a few lucky houses are surrounded on three sides by jagged cliffs. The still-warm crater hovers above it all. And the Volcano Museum in town is literally built around a house buried by lava—letting you peek into a family home forever trapped in rock.

Reykjanes Peninsula: As you'll see as you're flying into Iceland, the area around Keflavík Airport is covered with jagged lava fields. The nearby Blue Lagoon is situated in this same rocky world. Closer to Reykjavík, the suburb of Hafnarfjörður is nicknamed the "Town in the Lava" because it sits on a lava flow.

Mývatn: This North Iceland lake is ringed by a variety of otherworldly features, from the "pseudocraters" at Skútustaðir (where giant bubbles of steam burst through molten rock) to the jagged

Iceland's Volcanoes

Iceland is one of the most volcanically active places in the world, with roughly one eruption every five years. Aside from liquid lava, Iceland's volcanoes eject gas, ash, cinders, and solid rock (like pumice). The biggest rocks are sometimes called "volcanic bombs." Volcanic eruptions can last from a couple of days to several years.

Grímsvötn, a hard-to-reach volcano under the Vatnajökull glacier (in Southeast Iceland), is currently Iceland's most active; it last erupted in May 2011. Bárðarbunga, another volcano under the same glacier, began rumbling awake as recently as late 2017. The more famous Eyjafjallajökull, on the South Coast, made news in 2010—costing airlines more than $1 billion in disruptions. Other well-known Icelandic volcanoes include Hekla (once nicknamed the "Gateway to Hell"), Krafla, Askja, and Katla, which has the most potential for a damaging eruption (it threatens coastal hamlets with flooding; Katla erupts about once a century—the last time in 1918—so many think it's due).

Of the roughly 130 volcanoes in Iceland, the most common type is the stratovolcano—the classic cone-shaped peak with explosive eruptions that form a crater in the very top (such as Hekla and Katla). There are also a few dormant shield volcanoes—with low-profile, wide-spreading lava flows (one called Skjaldbreiður is near the Golden Circle). Eruptions from fissure vents (long cracks in the earth's crust) are also common in Iceland, such as the Holuhraun eruption of 2014 or the destructive Laki eruptions in the 1780s.

Iceland's entire surface is made of volcanic rock, most of it basalt—the rock that forms when lava cools. Iceland's towering cliffs and jagged islands and skerries are all made of basalt. When basalt cools in particular ways, it forms the hexagonal rock columns that you see at Reynisfjara (on the South Coast), near Dettifoss (in the north), and other places.

At the lake called Mývatn, in North Iceland, you can see pseudocraters (also called rootless cones), which form after lava flows over a pond or marsh. The water beneath the lava boils and a giant bubble breaks through the lava, leaving a crater-like depression.

New lava is shiny and oily-looking, while old lava loses its gleam. Old lava fields—recognizable by their unique, bumpy ap-

formations along the lake's eastern shore, at Dimmuborgir, and at the huge, climbable Hverfjall crater. For more, see the Ring Road chapter.

South Coast: All along the South Coast, you'll see plenty of volcanoes—but you may not realize it, since they're currently dormant and covered with thick glaciers. The most famous, under

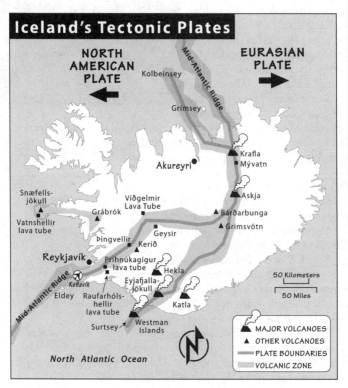

Iceland's Tectonic Plates

NORTH AMERICAN PLATE ←

EURASIAN PLATE →

Kolbeinsey

Mid-Atlantic Ridge

Grímsey

Krafla
Mývatn

Akureyri

Askja

Snæfells-jökull

Viðgelmir Lava Tube

Grábrók

Bárðarbunga
Grímsvötn

Vatnshellir lava tube

Geysir

Þingvellir
Kerið

Reykjavík

Þríhnúkagígur lava tube

Hekla

Eyjafjalla-jökull

50 Kilometers

50 Miles

Keflavík

Eldey

Raufarhóls-hellir lava tube

Katla

Mid-Atlantic Ridge

Surtsey

Westman Islands

N

North Atlantic Ocean

▲ MAJOR VOLCANOES
▲ OTHER VOLCANOES
▬ PLATE BOUNDARIES
▬ VOLCANIC ZONE

pearance—are often covered with a fuzzy layer of Icelandic moss.

So why does Iceland have so many volcanoes? The answer lies beneath the surface. Iceland is located on the long, mostly underwater Mid-Atlantic Ridge—the meeting point of the Eurasian and North American tectonic plates. As the two tectonic plates move apart, magma from the earth's mantle rises to the surface (we start calling it "lava" when it erupts). Iceland is located on a mantle plume, where magma is especially close to the surface, which explains why land formed here and not elsewhere along the tectonic ridge.

Eyjafjallajökull, blew its top in 2010. Several other large glaciers, such as Mýrdalsjökull and Vatnajökull, have volcanoes underneath. For a hike with the best views of glacier-topped volcanoes, head to **Þórsmörk,** where a huff up to the Valahnúkur viewpoint affords you panoramas over three volcanoes.

Climbable Craters: Several craters around Iceland invite you to climb up onto their rims for spectacular views. One of the finest, **Grábrók,** is alongside the Ring Road in West Iceland, just before the pass to the north. **Kerið,** along the Golden Circle route, requires almost no climbing and has a lovely lake inside. On Snæfellsnes Peninsula, Saxhóll crater has a staircase to the

top. Near Mývatn, in the north, you can hike to the top of **Hverfjall** or drive just over the mountains and up the Katla Valley to reach **Víti** ("Hell"), a rugged crater encircling a deep-blue lake.

Volcano Museums

To learn more about volcanoes, visit one of these museums (for details, see the listings in their chapters).

Westman Islands: Iceland's best explanation of volcanic activity is here, at the Volcano Museum.

South Coast: The high-tech Lava Center in Hvolsvöllur is both entertaining and educational. A short drive up the road is the more modest Katla Geopark Visitor Center, which has exhibits and shows a dramatic video of the 2010 Fimmvörðuháls and Eyjafjallajökull eruptions.

Reykjavík: The Volcano House shows films about two of Iceland's most famous eruptions (Westman Islands and Eyjafjallajökull). At the Pearl, visitors feel and hear the power of volcanoes and earthquakes in the Wonders of Iceland exhibit.

Snæfellsnes Peninsula: Stykkishólmur's Volcano Museum collects artistic depictions of volcanoes from cultures around the world.

Volcanic Underground Tours

Iceland offers several opportunities for subterranean volcanic exploration. While pricey (especially the first option), they're definitely memorable experiences and worth at least ▲▲ for those interested in an up-close look. The first two can be done as excursions from Reykjavík.

Þríhnúkagígur ("Inside the Volcano" Tour)

At this cinder cone in the Bláfjöll mountains southeast of Reykjavík, you have the chance to descend into the magma chamber of a dormant volcano that erupted about 4,000 years ago. When the magma drained out, it left a cavity so big that it could contain the Statue of Liberty. The first explorer entered in 1972. Today, visitors can ride a lift through the opening at the volcano's top and 400 feet down into the vast chamber. At the bottom you're free to wander around a rocky floor that's the size of three basketball courts.

Cost and Hours: 44,000 ISK, includes lunch and shuttle transfer from Reykjavík hotel, tours run several times a day mid-May-Oct, 4-6 hours, 20-person max, tel. 519-5609, book ahead at www.insidethevolcano.com. Wear sturdy shoes and bring extra layers for the chilly chamber.

Visiting the Volcano: The tour starts at a ski lodge a half-hour from Reykjavík (take their shuttle from town or drive there your-

self) with a brisk 45-minute hike to the "base camp" hut at the foot of the volcano. Along the way your guide points out features of the otherworldly volcanic terrain. At base camp you'll get a briefing on the journey, and be fitted with a hard hat and a harness (for safety when boarding the lift). From here a lift operator will take you to the top of the cone, help you board the open lift (eight people max), and—down you go.

During the seven-minute descent, your lift operator stops to describe the fascinating features of the chamber walls. Lamps illuminate the chamber, bringing out its pastel colors. On the bottom, you have about 30 minutes to explore. No more than 16 people are on the floor at one time, so it's an intimate experience.

Once back outside, you'll head down to base camp for an included lunch, and then hike back to the lodge.

Raufarhólshellir ("The Lava Tunnel" Tour)

The fourth-longest known lava tube in Iceland, Raufarhólshellir was created 5,000 years ago during a lava flow that extended to

the South Coast and Reykjavík. The tube formed as the flowing river of molten rock began crusting over, causing the lava to burrow deeper. When the eruption ceased, the lava drained out, leaving behind an extensive tunnel covered in colorful formations. In 2017, the tunnel was closed to the public and converted into a private attraction—infuriating local spelunkers, as well as partyers who were trashing the place.

Cost and Hours: Basic one-hour tour costs 6,900 ISK (11,900

ICELANDIC EXPERIENCES

Pool Rules: Visiting an Icelandic Thermal Swimming Pool

Icelanders love going to their local swimming pools, which are heated with natural thermal water. These aren't elaborate water parks, but more like municipal swimming pools back home. (Not so long ago, it was common for Icelanders to live in apartments with no shower or bathtub—instead, they had an annual pass for the pool and went daily.)

Of course, the big draw of Icelandic pools is the naturally steamy water, which is pumped right out of the ground. Even the lap pools stay at a warm temperature (around 85°F), while "hot pots" (smaller hot pools) are in the 100°F range. Bigger pools have more facilities, which can be indoors, outdoors, or both. Very windy or cold weather makes indoor bathing attractive. But if it's not too bad out, there's something cozy about submerging yourself in hot water while the wind ruffles your hair and snowflakes settle on your nose.

Iceland's public bathing culture has its own set of customs, which locals take very seriously. You'll quickly get the hang of the system. Just follow these steps.

1. Bring a swimsuit and towel (rentals are available but expensive). Also bring any other gear you need: bathing cap, goggles, flip-flops (although most Icelanders don't bother with them), or toys for children (you can bring a bag into the pool area and stow it discreetly). There's no need to bring soap or shampoo—there are liquid soap dispensers in the showers.

2. Pay. Most towns have a shareable 10-visit discount card, which can save money with as few as five adult entries. At some pools, you'll be issued a locker key or an electronic wristband that will open a locker; at others, keys are in the locks.

3. Change. Changing rooms are sex-segregated. Young children may go with a parent of either sex. Before entering the locker area, take off your shoes. (Many Icelanders leave them on public shoe racks, but I put mine in my locker.) Find an available locker, disrobe and lock your clothes inside, and carry your swimsuit and towel with you to the shower area.

ISK with Reykjavík bus transfer), tours depart daily every hour between 9:00 and 17:00—best to book ahead, 30-person max. "Adventure" tour costs 19,900 ISK (more with transfer), lasts 3-4 hours, and goes deeper into the tunnel. Tours run year-round; bring warm clothing—the temperature in the tunnel is 38 degrees. Mobile 760-1000, www.thelavatunnel.is.

4. Shower. Store your towel in one of the cubbyholes and keep your swimsuit handy. Soap down and shower thoroughly. Yes, you're expected to shower naked: Icelanders are relaxed about nudity, and showering is considered a (required) sanitary issue. (Only the touristy Blue Lagoon has some frosted-glass stalls for bashful foreigners.) Note: Iceland's water is extremely soft. You don't need much soap, and it can take a long time to wash it off.

5. Swim and soak. After showering, slip on your swimsuit and head for the pool area. Typically, people start out in the warm pools (usually a lap pool for swimmers, a shallower pool for recreation, and a wading pool for kids; these are typically around 29°C/85°F). Then they finish off with a soak in the hot tubs or a visit to the sauna. Each tub is marked in Celsius, and you'll quickly find your own comfort range. (For reference, 38°C is 100°F, 40°C is 104°F, 42°C is 108°F, and 44°C is 111°F.) Stay as long as you want; if you feel dizzy or uncomfortable, take a break outside or in a cooler pool. Drink water even if you're not thirsty—when you're in hundred-degree water, dehydration can sneak up on you.

6. Finish up. When you're done, return to the shower room, take off your swimsuit, shower again, and retrieve your towel. Towel off *before* returning to the locker area (they like to keep it as dry as possible). Many pools have a centrifuge to wick the water out of your suit—find it and use it. Back at your locker, get dressed, but don't put your shoes on until you exit the locker room. Return any keys or armbands to the counter.

7. Refuel. Most pools have tables and chairs in the entry hall where you can eat a packed lunch or snack. Most also have vending machines, snack counters, or even full-fledged cafés.

Note: At the pool, Icelanders usually just talk to the people they came with and generally leave strangers alone. Everyone is polite and helpful, but don't expect long conversation. At some times of day, groups of local "regulars" (often senior citizens) may seem to take over one of the hot pots, but you're welcome to squeeze in, too.

No Phones or Photos: Phones and cameras are strictly prohibited anywhere near the pool and dressing rooms. Just relax, and enjoy the experience.

Visiting the Tunnel: The tour starts at the visitors center about 40 minutes from downtown Reykjavík (take their shuttle or drive there yourself), roughly on the way to the South Coast. There you'll meet your guide and receive a hard hat.

After a quick briefing, you'll enter the tunnel, passing beneath several "skylights" where the tunnel's ceiling had completely collapsed. Then, it's into the intact lava tube, which is as big as a railroad tunnel in most places. There's some uneven ground, but the route is mostly easygoing on boardwalk and stairs. Subtle lighting brings out the tube's variety of colors. At the turnaround point, you'll have the chance—if the group is willing—to experience a few minutes of total darkness when the guide shuts off the lights.

Other Volcanic Caves

Víðgelmir ("The Cave" tour): Located in West Iceland, this cave is newer than Raufarhólshellir (about 1,000 years old rather than 5,000) and more extensive, but also more remote (about a 2-hour drive north of Reykjavík, or an hour east of Borgarnes). With a guide, you can walk about a half-mile into a lava tube (for details, see page 283).

Vatnshellir: This lava tube, near the tip of Snæfellsnes Peninsula in the national park, is similar to but less impressive than the ones mentioned above; still, if you're going to Snæfellsnes, it's convenient and satisfying (for details, see page 305).

Thermal Waters

Iceland's volcanic activity goes hand-in-hand with naturally heated water—which Icelanders have cleverly harnessed in a number of ways, from thermal baths to sources of electricity and heat.

Thermal Baths and Pools

Iceland has a wide range of options for enjoying its relaxing (and, yes, slightly stinky) thermal waters. Some bathing experiences cater primarily to tourists, chief among them the heavily advertised "premium baths." While those baths have big marketing budgets and attract lots of international visitors, they're rarely frequented by Icelanders—who know that you can bathe in equally luxuriant 100°F water for a fraction of the price at one of the country's many thermal swimming pools.

Touristy Baths

The most famous of these is the **Blue Lagoon** near Keflavík Airport (see the Blue Lagoon & Reykjanes Peninsula chapter); a similar (if smaller) version is **Mývatn Nature Baths** in North Iceland—a must for those doing the Ring Road. A less impressive premium bath is **Fontana,** in Laugarvatn and handy to the Golden Circle route. Smaller, more upscale baths include **Krauma** at Deildartunguhver (west of Borgarnes) and **Geosea** in Húsavík, to the north of Mývatn. Another tourist-oriented bathing experience is the **Secret Lagoon,** a simple but cleverly marketed bath a short drive from the Golden Circle route at Flúðir.

Swimming Pools

Every community of even a few hundred people seems to have scraped together the funds for their own well-maintained pool complex, often with a (warm) lap pool and at least one or two smaller hot pools (called "hot pots"). Many have a wide variety of pools, saunas and steam rooms, and colorful waterslides for kids. In addition to being affordable, these pools *(sundlaug)* provide a pleasantly authentic Icelandic experience, allowing you to rub elbows with locals who come home from work or school, grab a towel, and head to the pool. I've listed several of these in the Reykjavík area, and throughout the country—including in Borg, right along the Golden Circle; in a remote corner of West Iceland, at Húsafell; in Patreksfjörður, in the Westfjords; in tiny Hofsós, just off the Ring Road, with an infinity pool overlooking a fjord; and in Iceland's second city, Akureyri.

Up-to-date opening hours for each pool are on the website of each town, but you usually have to hunt for them a bit amid the other municipal services. These websites also won't show temporary closures (for special events, maintenance, etc.), so it's wise to confirm opening hours by telephone before making a trek to a distant pool.

For a list of Iceland's thermal pools, try https://sundlaugar.is. Or you can simply keep a lookout for the international "pool" symbol—a swimmer's head poking out above

waves—anywhere you go. Even though the clientele is mostly Icelandic, visitors are welcome (just follow the rules—see sidebar).

Natural Thermal Springs

Iceland has a few opportunities to (carefully) bathe in natural thermal springs. Above the town of Hveragerði, near the end of the Golden Circle route, you can hike an hour to soak in the thermal river of Reykjadalur (see page 209). There are a couple of these on the Westfjords—one near the town of **Tálknafjörður,** and the other on a remote road along the Reykjafjörður **between Bíldudalur and Dynjandi waterfall** (see the Westfjords chapter). In the Highlands, Landmannalaugar ("The People's Pools") has a famous natural thermal area, which takes quite some effort to reach (described later, under "Other Outdoor Experiences"). It's important to note that tourists regularly wind up in the burn unit of Reykjavík's hospital after being scalded at natural thermal areas. Watch your step, keep on marked trails, and bathe only where you see others doing so safely.

Thermal Sights

Wandering through a steaming, bubbling, colorful, otherworldly thermal landscape is a uniquely Icelandic treat. For such a small island, Iceland has a remarkable variety of these locations. Just watch your step—always stay on marked trails, as a thin crust can cover a boiling-hot reservoir—and be ready for some intense sulfur smells.

The most visited is **Geysir,** on the Golden Circle. But, while it's unique in offering the chance to watch a geyser spurt high into the air, it's crowded. For more interesting and varied thermal landscapes, consider the following options.

Perhaps the best thermal area is at **Námafjall,** just over the hills from Mývatn, in North Iceland. Much closer to Reykjavík, the **Seltún** geothermal area on the Reykjanes Peninsula is quite striking. "Honorable mentions" go to the sputtering shore of **Laugarvatn** lake, along the Golden Circle route; the bubbling spring at **Deildartunguhver,** in West Iceland; and the steaming valley of **Reykjadalur,** above the town of Hveragerði (just off the Golden Circle route). See "Thermal Bath Hikes," later.

To see how Iceland has harnessed the substantial power of its thermal waters, stop by a geothermal plant. **Hellisheiðarvirkjun** sits amid a lunar landscape just outside Reykjavík, on the way to the Golden Circle and South Coast day trips, and boasts Iceland's most extensive visitors center about its geothermal energy industry. **Krafla,**

with a modest information center, fills a dramatic valley in the north, near Mývatn.

Whales, Birds & Horses

Whale Watching

Many come to Iceland hoping to catch a glimpse of the elusive whales of the North Atlantic. The waters here are home to 23 different varieties of gentle giants. On a typical whale-watching trip, you're most likely to see white-beaked dolphins, harbor porpoises, and mid-sized minke whales (the species also listed on local menus). With luck, you may spot a breaching humpback whale (often seen from ports in North Iceland, such as Húsavík and Akureyri) or a black-and-white orca (Keiko, the late killer whale of *Free Willy* fame, was captured in Iceland). On very rare occasions, some get a glimpse of one of the two biggest mammals on the planet: the blue whale or the fin whale.

Whale-watching trips generally last 3-4 hours and cost about 11,000 ISK (twice that much for smaller tours in RIBs, described below). While Icelanders say that the best place to whale-watch is in North Iceland (in the tiny town of Húsavík, and Iceland's second city of Akureyri; both described in the Ring Road chapter), if you don't have time, you can also do whale-watching tours in Reykjavík. (Or, at the very least, stop by the Whales of Iceland exhibit near Reykjavík's harbor; all described in the Reykjavík chapter).

Be aware that most whale sightings will be from a distance. Multiple boats often converge on the same whale, taking turns getting closer. Also, boats are only allowed to get so close with their engine on; at a certain distance they must drift, and you can only hope that the whales get curious and come to you.

When to Go: Ideally, don't book your whale-watching trip too far in advance. Track the weather and choose a summer day that's as sunny and windless as possible; like you, whales and dolphins enjoy nice weather and are most likely to surface then. The best months are May through August, when whales are attracted to the small creatures feeding near the sun-warmed surface of the water. It's best to avoid whale watching in winter (Nov-Feb) and in windy weather, when seas can be rough, seasickness can get bad, and it's unlikely you'll see much wildlife. At any time of year, dress warmly.

Types of Boats: Most companies use fairly **large boats** with a comfy, heated, indoor seating area and a simple on-board café. In bad weather, some companies offer coveralls for those who want to be out on the deck the entire time. There's typically a naturalist guide on board, who describes the types of whales in Iceland and points out wildlife.

Some outfits offer whale-watching trips in **RIBs** (rigid inflatable boats; sometimes billed as a "premium" trip). These small, open boats zip across the water in search of whales and offer no indoor cover (all passengers get coveralls). In bad weather, the trip can be pretty miserable. In good weather, you get two fun experiences in one: a high-speed RIB trip, plus whale watching.

Birds and Birding

Birders find plenty of seabird species to get excited about in Iceland. For a one-stop look at (taxidermy-style) examples of all Icelandic bird species, head north to Sigurgeir's Bird Museum near Mývatn (see page 399).

Puffins

Adorable, chubby little puffins—with their black-and-white markings and cartoonish beaks—are fun to watch. They usually arrive in Iceland in April/May, then take off again at summer's end—making the window for seeing them quite short. (For more on puffins, see the sidebar.)

The biggest puffin populations are in the Westman Islands (with about half of Iceland's estimated 10 million puffins—and one-fifth of the world's puffins); along the South Coast (particularly around the Dyrhólaey promontory, and farther east, at Ingólfshöfði cape); and along the Westfjords (at Látrabjarg, Hornbjarg, Hornstrandir, and Breiðafjörður). The islet called Lundey ("Puffin Island")—with a relatively small population of about 20,000 puffins—is ideally situated just a short boat trip from downtown Reykjavík, and a handy destination for a puffin cruise from the Old Harbor.

Other Birds

Along with puffins, the auk family includes the guillemot, the murre, and the razorbill (all of which have a black body and white belly, but lack that cute orange beak). Arctic terns are sleek flyers—gray on top, white on bottom, with a black crown and a reddish beak. They're notorious for aggressively dive-bombing tourists who wander too close to their nests, then pulling up at the last second. Arctic terns have the longest migration in the animal kingdom: They spend their summers in the Arctic...and then, come fall, fly to the "southern summer" in the Antarctic (over its life, an Arctic tern

Puffins

Iceland's unofficial mascot is the Atlantic puffin *(Fratercula arctica)*—that adorably stout, tuxedo-clad seabird with a too-big orange beak and beady black eyes. Some 10 million puffins summer in Iceland—the largest population of any country on earth.

Puffins live most of their lives on the open Atlantic, coming to land only to breed. They fly north to Iceland in April/May and lay their eggs (usually by June). Puffins mate for life and typically lay just one egg each year, which the male and female take turns caring for. A baby puffin usually leaves the nest by mid-August and is called—wait for it—a puffling. Puffins return to the ocean by early September.

To feed their pufflings, puffins plunge as deep as 200 feet below the sea's surface to catch sand eels, herring, and other small fish. Their compact bodies, stubby wings, oil-sealed plumage, and webbed feet are ideal for navigating underwater. Famously, puffins can stuff several small fish into their beaks at once, thanks to their agile tongues and uniquely hinged beaks. This evolutionary trick lets puffins stock up before returning to the nest.

Stocky, tiny-winged puffins have a distinctive way of flying. To take off, they either beat their wings like crazy (at sea) or essentially hurl themselves off a cliff (on land). Once aloft, they beat their wings furiously—up to 400 times per minute—to stay airborne. Coming in for a smooth landing on a rocky cliff is a challenge (and highly entertaining to watch): They choose a spot, swoop in at top speed on prevailing currents, then flutter their wings madly to brake as they try to touch down. At the moment of truth, the puffin decides whether to attempt to stick the landing; more often than not, it bails out and does another big circle on the currents...and tries again... and again...and again.

Each August, the puffins head south at night, following the moon. On the Westman Islands, pufflings are often distracted by the town lights and crash-land on streets and rooftops. It's a tradition for local children to collect and help release them into the wild to try again.

In addition to seeing puffins along the summer coastline, you may occasionally see them on restaurant menus. With such abundant numbers, Iceland doesn't protect the puffin. Considered by some Icelanders to be a delicacy, puffin tastes like salty, smoked chicken...but cuter.

might fly as many as 1.5 million miles). Rounding out the flock are seagull-like fulmars and kittiwakes.

But there's more: Iceland is very proud of its eider ducks, which produce a down that's very useful in this frigid climate. You may also see oystercatchers and golden plovers.

Icelandic Horses

Icelandic horses are small, strong, and docile, and descend from the ponies originally brought to Iceland in the Settlement Age. (Viking Age settlers carefully selected only the strongest horses for the journey—small enough to fit on their ships, but capable of working hard once in Iceland.) After an early attempt to crossbreed these horses failed, the Alþingi (parliament) stopped horse imports to the island altogether in 982—so every Icelandic horse

you see is a purebred. Today, there are about 60,000 horses on the island.

Icelandic horses are renowned for their unique gaits: In addition to the typical walk, trot, and gallop, Icelandic horses employ the *tölt*, which is fast and extremely smooth, and the *skeið*, a high-speed "flying pace." This "five-gaited" status is their claim to fame.

Horseback Riding

Horseback riding is big business, and dozens of farms all over Iceland offer rides for travelers—including a cluster just outside Reykjavík.

Near Reykjavík: From Reykjavík, the experience takes about a half-day (either morning or afternoon). This includes a ride to and from the farm and about an hour and a half on horseback (about 12,000-19,000 ISK, includes helmet and riding gear, some tours come with lunch, check for lower prices if you drive out yourself). Browse and book on company websites: Íslenski Hesturinn (The Icelandic Horse, tel. 434-7979, http://islenskihesturinn.is), Viking Horses (mobile 660-9590, www.vikinghorses.is), Laxnes (tel. 566-6179, www.laxnes.is), and Íshestar (tel. 555-7000, www.ishestar.is).

Elsewhere in Iceland: Options include some in dramatic surroundings, including in the broad valley of Skagafjörður, through the glacial rivulets of Þórsmörk, along the beaches of the South Coast, and so on. Wherever you ride, check the weather forecast before booking.

Other Horse Sights

For just a glimpse of an Icelandic horse, watch for roadside paddocks all around the island. Or head to the Reykjavík Family Park and Zoo (see page 115), ideally at feeding time. On weekends, the zoo lets little kids trot around the horse paddock, accompanied by a keeper.

Hiking

Iceland is a wonderland for hikers, whether you're taking an easy stroll from your car to a waterfall, or embarking on a grueling but dramatic multiday trek.  Before heading out on a challenging hike, make sure you have proper equipment, water, maps, and advice from an experienced local. Be aware of current weather conditions—and don't underestimate the impact of Iceland's howling winds and bone-chilling (even in summer) temperatures. Read "The Many Ways Iceland Can Kill You" sidebar (earlier in this chapter).

Easy Hikes

Throughout this book, I've focused on easy hikes that offer a big reward for minimal effort—mainly starting from a parking lot and looping through an accessible slice of Icelandic scenery. More details on each of these are given in the individual chapters. Some of my favorite easy car hikes include the loop through Þingvellir along the Golden Circle route; the hikes up to the South Coast glaciers at Sólheimajökull and Skaftafell; the hike up to the lighthouse at Dyrhólaey promontory, on the South Coast; and walking up to Eldfell volcano on the Westman Islands.

Along the Ring Road is a variety of enjoyable options around Mývatn lake—including the pseudocraters at Skútustaðir, the forested peninsula at Höfði, and the lava pillars at Dimmuborgir. Other Mývatn hikes include the Námafjall thermal field and adjacent hill-climb just over the mountains from the lake, and the hike out to the volcanic cone at Leirhnjúkur. Also consider the crater hikes described in the "Volcanoes" section, earlier.

Each of the great **waterfalls** I've described in Iceland comes with a hike—some short, some long—and often an opportunity to climb up to a higher vantage point: Gullfoss on the Golden Circle, Seljalandsfoss (and its neighbor Gljúfrabúi) on the South

Coast, Skógafoss on the South Coast, Hraunfossar and Barnafoss in West Iceland, Dynjandi in the Westfjords, and along the Ring Road—Goðafoss and Dettifoss in North Iceland, and Svartifoss in the southeast.

Thermal Bath Hikes

To combine a hike with a natural thermal bathing experience, you can walk about an hour up the valley called **Reykjadalur,** just above the town of Hveragerði (an hour from Reykjavík and on the route of both the Golden Circle and the South Coast day trips). Your reward is a thermal river where you can recline in warm, rushing water. Less of a hike, and less rewarding, is **Seljavallalaug,** a tepid pool tucked into the side of a mountain about a 15-minute hike from the South Coast road. At both, expect minimal, grubby changing areas and plenty of adventurous hikers.

Serious Hikes

For serious hikers, Iceland offers dozens of premier hiking destinations—many in the Highlands, and inaccessible with a standard car. The two below (Þórsmörk and Landmannalaugar) are perhaps the best known; for either you'll need a high-clearance four-wheel drive vehicle, or you can ride in a specially equipped excursion bus.

Perhaps the best combination of quality hiking and accessibility is **Þórsmörk,** a volcanic landscape with glorious mountain, valley, and canyon walks; the moderately challenging hike up to Valahnúkur is spectacular. Þórsmörk is a short detour from the South Coast, but most people get there via excursion bus from Reykjavík (5 hours each way; for more on Þórsmörk, see the South Coast section). More remote is **Landmannalaugar,** in the Highlands, with lots of good hiking (described below, under "Other Outdoor Experiences").

Both Þórsmörk and Landmannalaugar are key stops along a variety of popular multiday hikes (with overnights in staffed huts) that traverse the glacial landscape of the south. One of the most popular routes, called **Laugavegur,** takes three to five days (34 miles over challenging terrain) and connects Þórsmörk and Landmannalaugar. Another favorite is the two-day, 14-mile **Fimmvörðuháls** hike, from Þórsmörk south, over the saddle between Eyjafjallajökull and Mýrdalsjökull, to Skógar on the South Coast—right over the site of the first stage of the 2010 Eyjafjallajökull eruption.

For something closer to the capital, you could ascend **Esja**—the big, long ridge that looms just north of Reykjavík. The most popular hike here is the four-mile round-trip to Steinn ("The Stone"), with an elevation gain of 650 feet (don't attempt this in cold weather).

For details on these, and good overall information about hiking, see the websites of FÍ (the Iceland Touring Association, www.fi.is) and NAT (Nordic Adventure Travel, www.nat.is). Companies offering guided hikes in Iceland include Icelandic Mountain Guides (www.mountainguides.is) and Trek Iceland (www.trek.is).

Other Outdoor Experiences

Land Tours

To reach spectacular scenery without the climb, you can choose from a variety of wheeled tours. Tours by **mountain bike,** by **ATV,**

or by **"Super Jeep"** (a generic term for any monster 4x4 vehicle that can go just about anywhere) give you access to some of the more remote areas mentioned earlier.

Landmannalaugar ("The People's Pools"): This remote area, 120 miles east of Reykjavík in the Highlands—and only reachable via off-road vehicle—offers vivid landscape, a famous natural thermal area, and a variety of hikes. This area is striped with volcanic hues and features a petrified lava field from 1477 that butts up against pointy peaks. Excellent hiking trails abound, and you'll encounter some natural thermal pools. You could trek to the crater lake called Ljótipollur ("Ugly Puddle"); huff your way up the extremely colorful Brennisteinsalda, with high-altitude views and an optional detour to the Stórihver thermal area near the top; or opt for an easier walk to the big lake called Frostastaðavatn.

To reach Landmannalaugar, you'll need a 4x4 vehicle, or—better—join a guided excursion (only in summer, around 25,000 ISK, offered by various outfits, includes pickup and drop-off in Reykjavík). You can also take a bus operated by Iceland On Your Own (www.ioyo.is), Trex (www.trex.is), or Iceland By Bus (www.icelandbybus.is). Much of the route is on difficult-to-traverse, gravel-and-rock roads (about 4.5 hours one-way). While you can get a glimpse of the area in a very long day trip from Reykjavík, serious hikers overnight at the Landmannalaugar hut/campground.

Water Activities

Various companies offer **rafting and kayaking tours,** either in the canyon just below Gullfoss (the thundering waterfall on the Golden Circle), or in North Iceland on two rivers that drain the Hofsjökull glacier, south of Sauðárkrókur in the Skagafjörður region. Companies include Arctic Adventures (www.adventures.com) and Viking Rafting (www.vikingrafting.is).

For divers, **scuba diving or snorkeling at Silfra**—a fissure flooded with crystal-clear glacial water, at Þingvellir on the Golden Circle—is a highlight (see the Golden Circle chapter).

Northern Lights

The northern lights are a magical, occasional, serendipitous sight on clear, crisp nights in Iceland from about the end of August to the middle of April. You can't really plan to see the northern lights—they don't always appear, and when they do, are often obscured by cloud cover. While often visible in Reykjavík, the northern lights stand out better farther from the center of town and in the countryside, where there's less light pollution. All things being equal, spending a night or two in a more remote area could increase your chances.

The dreamy northern lights images that you see are done using long exposures and sometimes Photoshop (tweaking the aurora colors to a Kermit-the-Frog green). What you'll actually see will probably be closer to the color of a Thai green curry—more coconut milk than Kermit.

With all the interesting things to do in Iceland, it would be a shame to spend your energy chasing after the northern lights every evening. I suggest planning your trip as if you won't see them, and considering it a bonus if you do. Whether you'll see the lights or not is mostly out of your control, but consider the tips below to improve your odds.

Come during aurora season. Visit Iceland in aurora season

Nature's Light Show

The northern lights arc across Iceland's wintery sky, primarily in shades of green. The lights are caused by charged particles from the sun that collide with the earth's upper atmosphere and cause it to glow. The earth's magnetic field deflects most of these particles (which, if they hit the earth's surface, would cause catastrophic radiation), but near the poles, where the field is weakest, some can seep through, creating the northern lights. They are strongest along a ring-shaped band that crosses Iceland, Greenland, northern Canada, Alaska, Russia, and northern Scandinavia, and diminish as you move farther north toward the magnetic pole. Their intensity varies with the sunspot cycle; the last maximum was in 2013, and the next will be in 2025.

While Iceland is relatively easy to get to and a good place to see the northern lights, it's not the best because of its frequent cloudy weather. So if you're planning a trip specifically to see the lights, your best bet are places that have more reliably clear winter weather and are closer to the center of the band, such as the northern parts of Norway, Finland, and Sweden (especially spots where the weather is continental and dry).

(from a little before the fall equinox to a little after the spring equinox). Some say that September/October and February/March are the best months. At the least, they have longer days and nicer temperatures, so you can enjoy regular sightseeing more. If you're planning to rent a car, go in fall, when the road conditions are better.

Maximize your chances. It's easy to miss the northern lights simply by not bothering to look for them.

On any clear, dark night, go outside and scan the sky every half hour or so up until bedtime. You can follow the aurora and cloud-cover forecast on the Icelandic weather service's English-language website (https://en.vedur.is; click on "Weather," then "Aurora forecasts"). The American aurora forecasts at www.swpc.noaa.gov also cover Iceland.

See the lights without a car. If you're staying in Reykjavík and you don't have a car, consider taking a northern lights bus tour (4,500-9,000 ISK). Tours only run when conditions look good—call around dinnertime to find out. You'll leave town at 21:00 or 22:00 and you won't be in bed until almost four hours later. Read a few reviews before you go, and remember that even if the forecast is good, you may see nothing at all. (If so, the bus company will likely give you a voucher for another trip—not much help on a short visit.) For some, the trip is a nice chance to snuggle up with a travel partner on a bus and listen to an entertaining tour guide who serves hot cocoa. For others, it's a disappointing few hours of yawning and wishing they'd turned in early.

See the lights with a car. If you're staying in Reykjavík and have a car, you could put together your own northern lights tour by driving out into the suburbs or a little way into the countryside. Þingvellir (see the Golden Circle chapter) and Kleifarvatn (see the Blue Lagoon & Reykjanes Peninsula chapter) are plenty dark and within a 45-minute drive of town. If you stay within greater Reykjavík, drive out to the end of Seltjarnarnes (to the parking area facing the little island called Grótta) or to the tip of Álftanes (by Bessastaðir, the presidential residence), where city lights are a little dimmer.

"See the lights" without actually seeing the lights. Two museums in Reykjavík offer the chance to "see" the aurora and learn the science behind it: the 20-minute "Áróra" planetarium show at The Pearl and Aurora Reykjavík, near the harbor in Grandi (for detailed descriptions of these exhibits, see the Reykjavík chapter). While nowhere near as thrilling as seeing the real thing, they're visual and informative.

REYKJAVÍK

REYKJAVÍK

Reykjavík, the tiny capital of a remote island-nation, is unexpectedly cosmopolitan, with an artistic, bohemian flair. It lacks world-class sights, yet manages to surprise and delight even those who use the city mostly as a home base for exploring Iceland's natural wonders.

The city's downtown streets are lined with creative restaurants, quirky art galleries, rollicking bars serving everything from craft beer to designer cocktails, and shops selling stuffed puffins, local knitwear, and Gore-Tex parkas.

Reykjavík is a colorful enclave in a stark landscape: It seems every wall serves as a canvas for a vibrant street-art mural, and each corner is occupied by a cozy, art-strewn, stay-awhile café. In the old town center, colorful timber-frame houses clad in corrugated metal sheets huddle together amid a sprinkling of landmarks—such as the striking Hallgrímskirkja church, which crowns the town's highest point.

Like the rest of the country, Reykjavík has old roots. Viking Age farmers settled here in the ninth century. Until the 1750s, this area remained nothing more than a sprawling farm. As towns started to form in Iceland, Reykjavík emerged as the country's capital. Today, the capital region is a small city, home to two out of every three Icelanders—a population similar to that of Berkeley, California, or Fargo, North Dakota. The northernmost capital city on earth—which straddles the European and American hemispheres—feels more New World than Old.

With the recent tourism boom, these days Icelanders tend to work, live, and shop in the suburbs, and make fun of Reykjavík's downtown core with all its "puffin shops" selling souvenirs. But that doesn't mean you should avoid downtown: Visitors find just about everything they need in this small, walkable zone. You can take in the vibe of this pithy city in a leisurely two-hour stroll, and it's an enjoyable place to simply hang out. While museums aren't a priority here, those seeking sights can easily fill a day or two.

Step into Hallgrímskirkja's serene church interior. Learn about this little nation's proud history at the National Museum and the Maritime Museum, and about the city's humble Viking Age roots at the Settlement Exhibition—built around the surviving walls of a 10th-century longhouse. Art lovers can visit a half-dozen galleries highlighting Icelandic artists (early-20th-century sculptor Einar Jónsson is tops). Naturalists can go on a whale-watching cruise, or ride a ferry to an island. Modern architecture fans can ogle the award-winning Harpa concert hall, then walk along the shoreline to the iconic *Sun Voyager* sculpture.

Or head out to the suburbs to see the Pearl, the domed building designed to check off many Icelandic targets in one go—with exhibits on whales, puffins, glaciers, volcanoes, and the northern lights, plus panoramic city views.

Plenty of family-friendly activities—open-air museum, zoo, botanic garden—are just beyond the city center. To recharge, the capital area has plenty of relaxing—and very local—thermal swimming pools.

But don't focus too much on Reykjavík. Instead, use the city as a springboard for Iceland's glorious countryside sights, taking advantage of its accommodations, great restaurants, and lively nightlife. Even on a longer visit, drivers may prefer sleeping at a distance, dropping into town only for occasional sightseeing, strolling, and dining. To save money and have a more local experience, consider sleeping in suburban Reykjavík—which has fewer hotels, but ample Airbnb options.

REYKJAVÍK

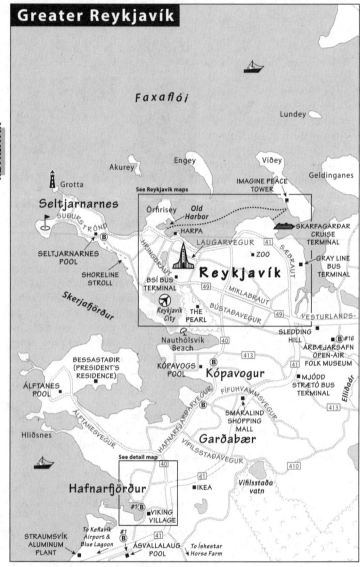

Greater Reykjavík

Faxaflói

Lundey

Engey

Akurey

Viðey

Geldinganes

Grotta

IMAGINE PEACE
TOWER

Seltjarnarnes

See Reykjavik maps

Örfirisey

*Old
Harbor*

SKARFAGARÐAR
CRUISE
TERMINAL

SUÐURSTRÖND

HARPA

LAUGARVEGUR 41

SÆBRAUT

Reykjavík

HRINGBRAUT

ZOO

GRAY LINE
BUS
TERMINAL

SELTJARNARNES
POOL

BSÍ BUS
TERMINAL

49

SHORELINE
STROLL

MIKLABRAUT

VESTURLANDS-

Skerjafjörður

Reykjavík
City

BÚSTAÐAVEGUR

49

THE
PEARL

SLEDDING
HILL

B #16

Nauthólsvík
Beach

40

ÁRBÆJARSAFN
OPEN-AIR
FOLK MUSEUM

BESSASTAÐIR
(PRESIDENT'S
RESIDENCE)

513

41

B

KÓPAVOGS
POOL

Kópavogur

MJÓDD
STRÆTÓ BUS
TERMINAL

ÁLFTANES
POOL

FÍFUHVAMMSVEGUR

Ellidaár

413

SMÁRALIND
SHOPPING
MALL

Hliðsnes

ÁLFTANESVEGUR

HAFNARFJARÐARVEGUR

VÍFILSSTAÐAVEGUR

Garðabær

410

See detail map

40

*Vífilsstaða
vatn*

Hafnarfjörður

41

IKEA

#1 B

VIKING
VILLAGE

STRAUMSVÍK
ALUMINUM
PLANT

To Keflavík
Airport &
Blue Lagoon

#1
B

41

ÁSVALLALAUG
POOL

To Íshestar
Horse Farm

PLANNING YOUR TIME

On a short visit, savor Reykjavík's strolling ambience in the morning and evening, maybe drop into one or two sights early or late, and use your precious daytime hours to tour sights in the countryside (see the Beyond Reykjavík chapter for an overview of your options). My self-guided Reykjavík Walk offers a helpful town ori-

entation (and crash course on Iceland) that can be done at any time of day or night.

On a longer trip—or in winter (when countryside options are limited)—Reykjavík warrants more time. The following schedule is designed to fill two full days in Reykjavík itself. With less time, mix and match from these options. My plan ignores weather—in practice, let the weather dictate your itinerary. If it's blowing hard and drizzling, prioritize indoor sights. When the weather's good, get outside.

Day 1: Start with my self-guided walk around downtown, and (if the line's not too long) ride up the tower of Hallgrímskirkja church. Find a nice lunch in the Laugavegur/Skólavörðustígur area. Walk down to the *Sun Voyager* sculpture for a photo op, then follow the shoreline to the Harpa concert hall (peek in the lobby, and stop by the box office to survey entertainment options). Follow the moored boats around to the Old Harbor, where you can comparison-shop whale watching and other boat tours for tomorrow. Then continue along the harbor to the Grandi area, where you can drop into your choice of exhibits: Whales of Iceland, Saga Museum, Maritime Museum, Aurora Reykjavík, or FlyOver Iceland. Return to the downtown area for dinner and after-hours strolling. Before or after dinner, unwind with the Icelanders in one of Reykjavík's thermal swimming pools.

Day 2: Begin your day at the Settlement Exhibition. If that compact exhibit whets your appetite for Icelandic history, take a walk along the Pond (the city's little lake) to the National Museum. After lunch, take your pick of activities: boat trip (either whale or puffin watching, or simply a ride out to Viðey Island); suburban sights, including the Pearl (with its many high-tech exhibits, and a grand city view), the sights in Laugardalur (botanic garden, zoo), and/or Árbær Open-Air Museum; or explore the city's many art museums. Consider another dip in a thermal pool before enjoying a food tour or dinner in the center.

If you're in town on a weekend, squeeze in a visit to the Kolaportið flea market, downtown.

Orientation to Reykjavík

Reykjavík's population is about 125,000, but the entire capital region stretches to about 216,000. The compact core of Reykjavík radiates out from the main walking street, which changes names from Austurstræti to Bankastræti to Laugavegur as it cuts through the city. You can walk from one end of downtown Reykjavík (Ingólfstorg square) to the other (the bus junction Hlemmur) in about 20 minutes. Just northwest of downtown is  the mostly postindustrial Old Harbor zone, with excursion boats, salty restaurants, and a few sights.

Greater Reykjavík is made up of six towns. Hafnarfjörður

("harbor fjord"), to the south, has its own history, harbor, and downtown core. Kópavogur and Garðabær, between Reykjavík and Hafnarfjörður, are 20th-century suburbs. Mosfellsbær, once a rural farming district along the road running north from Reykjavík, has turned into a sizable town of its own. And Seltjarnarnes is a posh enclave at the end of the Reykjavík peninsula. While I haven't recommended specific hotels or restaurants in these neighborhoods (except in Hafnarfjörður), finding an affordable Airbnb in one of these areas can provide a local home base.

TOURIST INFORMATION

Reykjavík has four tourist information offices (TIs), called **What's On,** sprinkled along the main east-west tourist axis, from Laugavegur to the Old Harbor (see the "Reykjavík Walk" map). Each offers mostly the same services (including baggage storage, excursions, and tour bookings) and has similar hours (generally daily 9:00-20:00, shorter hours Sun and in winter, tel. 551-3600, www.whatson.is). You'll find offices at Laugavegur 54, Laugavegur 5, Bankastræti 2 (set back from the street, closed Sun), and in the Volcano House at Tryggvagata 11. Bus passes are only available at the Bankastræti location; this location also has a **Safe Travel** counter, which offers advice about driving, weather, and other concerns while on the road or out in the backcountry (www.safetravel.is). There's also a lounge with tables where you can sit and enjoy free coffee while you ponder your options.

The TI's free and helpful monthly entertainment guide, *What's On*, is distributed at their offices and at hotels.

Alternatively, **Visit Reykjavík,** the city-run TI, offers info online at www.visitreykjavik.is.

The *Reykjavík Grapevine,* a free informative English-language paper and website, provides a roundup of sightseeing hours, music listings, helpful restaurant reviews, and fun insights into local life (www.grapevine.is). The local blog IHeartReykjavik.net also has helpful insights about both the capital region and all of Iceland.

Sightseeing Pass: The **Reykjavík City Card** may make sense for busy museum sightseers on a longer stay, but is not worth it for a short visit. It covers bus transport, city-run museums, Reykjavík swimming pools, and some other attractions (24 hours-3,900 ISK, 48 hours-5,500 ISK, 72 hours-6,700 ISK; sold at participating museums, TIs, hotels and hostels, and at City Hall; www.citycard.is).

ARRIVAL IN REYKJAVÍK

International flights use Keflavík Airport, a 45-minute drive from downtown Reykjavík (the Reykjavík City Airport is for domestic flights). For information on getting between Keflavík and down-

REYKJAVÍK

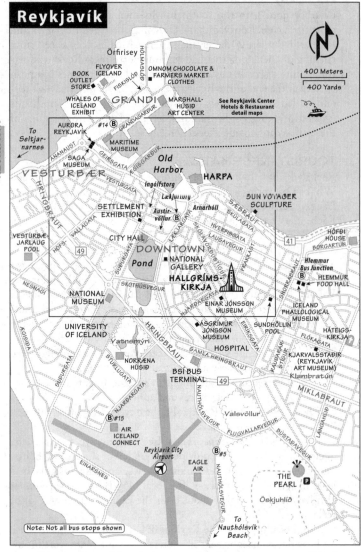

Reykjavík

Örfirisey

BOOK OUTLET STORE
FLYOVER ICELAND
OMNOM CHOCOLATE & FARMERS MARKET CLOTHES

WHALES OF ICELAND EXHIBIT
GRANDI
MARSHALL-HÚSID ART CENTER

See Reykjavík Center Hotels & Restaurant detail maps

400 Meters
400 Yards

AURORA REYKJAVÍK
#14 (B)

To Seltjar-narnes

MARITIME MUSEUM

SAGA MUSEUM

Old Harbor

HARPA

VESTURBÆR

Ingólfstorg

SUN VOYAGER SCULPTURE

SETTLEMENT EXHIBITION
Lækjartorg
Austur-völlur (B)
Arnarhóll

HÖFDI HOUSE

VESTURBÆ-JARLAUG POOL
49
CITY HALL
DOWNTOWN
Pond

NATIONAL GALLERY

41

Hlemmur Bus Junction

NESHAGI
HALLGRÍMS-KIRKJA

(B) HLEMMUR FOOD HALL

NATIONAL MUSEUM
EINAR JÓNSSON MUSEUM

ICELAND PHALLOLOGICAL MUSEUM

UNIVERSITY OF ICELAND
Vatnsmýri
ÁSGRÍMUR JÓNSSON MUSEUM
SUNDHÖLLIN POOL
HÁTEIGS-KIRKJA

NORRÆNA HÚSID
HRINGBRAUT
GAMLA HRINGBRAUT
HOSPITAL
KJARVALSSTADIR (REYKJAVÍK ART MUSEUM)
Klambratún

BSÍ BUS TERMINAL
49
MIKLABRAUT

(B) #15
AIR ICELAND CONNECT

Valsvöllur

Reykjavik City Airport
(B) #5
EAGLE AIR

THE PEARL
P

EINARSNES
Öskjuhlíd

Note: Not all bus stops shown
To Nauthólsvík Beach

town Reykjavík, and for getting to other destinations around Iceland, see "Reykjavík Connections" at the end of this chapter.

HELPFUL HINTS

Money: Remember, you'll use credit cards more than cash in Iceland. If you do need cash, several big banks downtown have ATMs. The downtown branch of Landsbankinn at Austurstræti 11 is convenient and along my self-guided walk.

Useful Bus App: If you'll be using public buses, use the **Strætó**

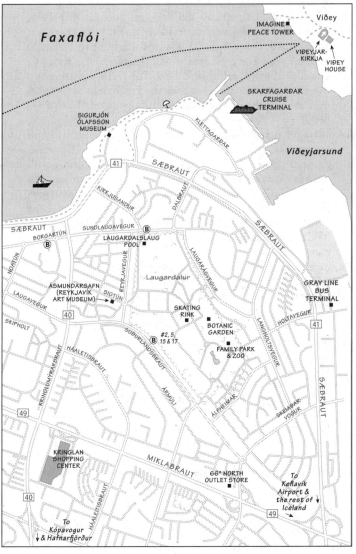

app to avoid having to carry exact bus fare. Download the app, then change the default language to English under "Settings." At the prompt to enter your mobile number, include "+1" for the US country code. You'll receive a PIN number on your mobile phone—once you enter the PIN, you can enter your credit card details to buy bus tickets. The app also has a real-time route planner, which lets you track your bus to be confident of your stop.

Pharmacy: Downtown pharmacies are at Austurstræti 19 (Mon-

Fri 9:00-18:00, Sat 11:00-16:00, closed Sun, tel. 552-4045, www.lyfja.is) and Laugavegur 46 (Mon-Fri 9:00-19:00, Sat 10:00-16:00, closed Sun, tel. 414-4646, http://islandsapotek. business.site). For a pharmacy with longer hours, try Lyfja Granda in Grandi at Fiskislóð 3 (tel. 512-3770) or, farther out, the Lyfja at Smáratorg 1, under the Læknavakt after-hours medical service near the Smáralind shopping mall (tel. 564-5600).

Laundry: A handy full-service laundry, **Úðafoss,** is located just off Laugavegur at Vitastígur 13. They promise same-day wash/dry/fold service if you drop off before 11:00, otherwise it's next-day service (Mon-Fri 8:00-18:00, closed Sat-Sun, tel. 551-2301). The downtown **Laundromat Café** has four self-serve washers and dryers in its basement (long hours daily, Austurstræti 9, tel. 587-7555). It's also a popular comfort-food restaurant (described later in this chapter)—turning your chore into a fun night out.

Baggage Storage: All What's On TIs offer baggage storage for 1,000 ISK/bag per day—just be sure to note the closing time.

Bike Rental: For quality bikes, **Reykjavík Bike Tours** rents from its location on the pier in the Old Harbor (3,500 ISK/4 hours, 4,900 ISK/24 hours; in summer daily 9:00-17:00, in winter by appointment; Ægisgarður 7, mobile 694-8956, www.icelandbike.com). They also run tours (see "Tours in Reykjavík," later).

Taxis: The two long-established companies are **Hreyfill** (tel. 588-5522, www.hreyfill.is) and **BSR** (tel. 561-0000, www.taxireykjavik.is). Both offer flat rates to Keflavík Airport. For early-morning rides, call the evening before to reserve. Icelanders usually order taxis by phone, but there are a few taxi stands downtown and at major transportation hubs. In general, though, taxis are expensive—even a short ride in Reykjavík will cost 2,000 ISK—so use them only when there's no better option (cabbies expect payment by credit card but not a tip). Ride services such as Uber and Lyft don't operate in Reykjavík.

Online Translation Tips: A few of the websites I list in this chapter are in Icelandic only. To view them in English, use Google's Chrome browser (for automatic translation) or paste the URL into the translation window at Translate.google.com. When searching for Icelandic words on a website, omit all the accent marks and use *th, d,* and *ae* instead of *þ, ð,* and *æ.*

GETTING AROUND
By Car
North Americans will feel at home in Reykjavík, as it's largely a

car city. If you'll be renting a car to explore the countryside, you may want to keep it for part of your time in Reykjavík. Several important sights are outside of downtown (where parking is generally free and easy).

That said, you don't need a car to enjoy your visit. And if you're staying in the center (inside the street called Hringbraut) and visiting only downtown sights, a car can be a headache. If you plan to have your own wheels in town, consider looking for accommodations with free parking a little outside the center.

Parking: Downtown, on-street parking is metered (Mon-Fri 9:00-18:00, Sat 10:00-16:00; free outside these times). Pay with credit cards or coins at machines (look for the white and blue "P" sign), and display your ticket on the windshield. Parking in the P1 zone is the most expensive (370 ISK/hour); parking in P2 through P4 costs about 190 ISK/hour. You can prepay for an entire day, so even if overnighting in the center, you don't have to worry about returning to feed the meter. Check along Garðastræti and its side streets, just a couple of blocks above Ingólfstorg. A few coin-only parking meters may still survive.

There are several small public parking garages downtown (check up-to-the-minute availability at www.bilastaedasjodur. is/#bilahusin). The following all charge 240 ISK for the first hour, then 120 ISK/hour after that, and are open daily 7:00-24:00. The Traðarkot garage at Hverfisgata 20 is the best option and close to the end point of my Reykjavík Walk. Progressively closer in, but typically full on weekdays, are the Kolaport garage, near the Harpa concert hall at Kalkofnsvegur 1; the Ráðhúsið garage, underneath City Hall at Tjarnargata 11; and—closest to my Reykjavík Walk's starting point—the Vesturgata garage at Vesturgata 7 (on the corner with Mjóstræti). Another very central choice is the private garage at the Hafnartorg building (enter on Steinbryggja, from the main harborfront road Geirsgata).

You can also park just outside downtown in a neighborhood with free on-street parking, such as behind Hallgrímskirkja church or near the BSÍ bus terminal. A free parking lot is along Eiríksgata at the top of the hill by Hallgrímskirkja church, but it's often full. There's also plenty of free parking in the Grandi box-store zone to the far side of the Old Harbor.

By Public Transportation

Greater Reykjavík has a decent bus *(strætó)* system. In this late-rising city, buses run from about 6:30 on weekdays, 8:00 on Saturdays, and 10:00 on Sundays, with last departures between 23:00 and 24:00. Service is sparse on evenings and weekends, when most buses only run every half-hour.

Bus routes intersect at several key points, notably Hlemmur,

Reykjavík at a Glance

▲▲▲**Thermal Swimming Pools** Bathe with the locals at more than a dozen naturally heated municipal pools. See page 118.

▲▲**Laugavegur** Eastern stretch of Reykjavík's main drag, a delight to stroll any time of day. See page 96.

▲▲**Hallgrímskirkja** Iconic Guðjón Samúelsson-designed Lutheran church, with crushed-volcanic-rock exterior, serene and austere interior, and bell tower with sweeping views. **Hours:** Daily 9:00-21:00, tower until 20:30; Oct-April until 17:00, tower until 16:30. See page 97.

▲▲**Einar Jónsson Museum and Garden** Talented sculptor's house and studio, with free back garden decorated with his works. **Hours:** Tue-Sun 10:00-17:00, closed Mon. See page 98.

▲▲**National Museum of Iceland** Well-curated Icelandic artifacts that illustrate the nation's history. **Hours:** Daily 10:00-17:00, mid-Sept-April closed Mon. See page 99.

▲▲**Harpa** Boldly modern harborfront concert hall, with a fun-to-explore lobby and regular schedule of cultural events. **Hours:** Lobby open daily 9:00-22:00. See page 103.

▲▲**The Pearl (Perlan)** Domed building in the suburbs with fine views over Reykjavík's skyline and the Wonders of Iceland exhibit. **Hours:** Daily 9:00-22:00. See page 112.

▲**The Settlement Exhibition** Modern museum showcasing the actual ruins of a millennium-old Viking Age longhouse. **Hours:** Daily 9:00-18:00. See page 92.

at the eastern end of Laugavegur, Reykjavík's downtown shopping street; Lækjartorg, at the western end of Laugavegur; Mjódd, in the eastern Reykjavík suburbs; and Fjörður, in the town of Hafnarfjörður. The English journey planner at Straeto.is makes using the system easy, and recognizes addresses without Icelandic characters (you can omit all the accent marks and use *th, d,* and *ae* instead of *þ, ð,* and *æ*). To get help from a real person, call 540-2700.

You can pay for the bus in cash (470 ISK), but few do this, and drivers don't give change. Instead, buy a pass, a shareable perforated strip of paper tickets, or use the Strætó app (described in "Helpful Hints," earlier; one-day pass-1,800 ISK; three-day pass-4,200 ISK; 20 tickets-9,100 ISK and more than most visitors will need).

▲**Kolaportið Flea Market** Lively market hall just off the Old Harbor, with fun food section. **Hours:** Sat-Sun 11:00-17:00. See page 93.

▲*Sun Voyager (Sólfar)* Modern harborfront sculpture by Jón Gunnar Árnason evoking Iceland's earliest settlers. See page 102.

▲**Old Harbor** Modern harbor with waterfront eateries and sightseeing cruises. See page 104.

▲**Aurora Reykjavík** Modest but enjoyable exhibit on the northern lights, starring a mesmerizing film of the aurora borealis. **Hours:** Daily 9:00-21:00. See page 107.

▲**Whales of Iceland** Pricey exhibit with life-size models of the gentle giants in Icelandic waters. **Hours:** Daily 10:00-17:00. See page 110.

▲**FlyOver Iceland** Stunning virtual flight over the country in a simulator, capturing all the senses of the landscape. **Hours:** Daily 9:00-21:00. See page 111.

▲**Viðey Island** An easy ferry ride to a smattering of attractions, including the John Lennon Imagine Peace Tower (lit in fall). Ferries depart daily in season from the Old Harbor (none off-season) and Skarfagarðar (off-season Sat-Sun only). See page 114.

▲**Árbær Open-Air Museum** Collection of old buildings in the suburbs, offering a glimpse of traditional lifestyles. **Hours:** Daily 10:00-17:00, Sept-May 13:00-17:00. See page 116.

Buses are also covered by the Reykjavík City Card (described earlier).

Tickets and passes are sold at 10-11 convenience stores, the TI at Bankastræti 2, most swimming pools, information desks at the Kringlan and Smáralind shopping malls, and at the Mjódd bus junction (but not from bus drivers). Without a pass, ask the driver for a free transfer slip if you need to change buses.

Tours in Reykjavík

While you'll see bus tours advertised in Reykjavík, I wouldn't take one. The city is easy and enjoyable by foot and lends itself to walking tours.

Walking Tours

CityWalk is a group of young, fun-loving locals who give chatty two-hour walks of the town center at least three times a day (in season). The cost: whatever you think it's worth. Tours start in front of the parliament building. While my self-guided town walk covers more standard information on essentially the same route, these walks fill the time with fun local insights (mobile 787-7779, www.citywalk.is, citywalk@citywalk.is). Their website explains other options, like a Walk the Crash tour with journalist/historian Magnús Sveinn Helgason, who gives the inside story of the 2008 financial crash (magnus@citywalk.is).

Funky Iceland runs a variety of tours with an irreverent spirit, including a Reykjavík Highlights Walk (7,000 ISK, 2.5 hours, daily at 14:00); a Funky History Walk that includes lunch (6,000 ISK, 2.5 hours, daily at 10:30); and a Funky Food and Beer Walk (14,000 ISK, includes 5 craft beers and stops at 5 restaurants, 3 hours, nightly at 17:00). Get details, learn about their other tours, and book ahead on their website (www.funkyiceland.is).

Food Tours

To learn more about Icelandic cuisine and cooking—from traditional dishes to modern interpretations—you can take a three- to four-hour guided walk with stops at a half-dozen local eateries. Show up with an appetite, as it amounts to a big mobile feast.

Wake Up Reykjavík Food Tour (www.wakeupreykjavik. com) and **Your Friend in Reykjavík** each offer good food tours for around 14,000 ISK. Your Friend in Reykjavík's tour mixes local history, fun, and classic traditional dishes (smoked puffin, lamb soup, hot dog, shark, whale, *skyr;* daily at 11:00, 13:00, and 17:00, RS%—use code "RICKSTEVES" for 10 percent discount, 2-12 people, mobile 655-4040, www.yourfriendinreykjavik.com). **Funky Iceland,** listed above, does a similar food tour.

Bike Tours

Reykjavík Bike Tours takes you on a 2.5-hour, fairly flat guided bike tour that starts on the Old Harbor pier and does a circuit through downtown and all the way over to the university and residential areas on the other side of the peninsula. This is a nice way to get to know more of the city than the downtown core (7,500 ISK, mid-May-Sept daily at 10:00, confirm times in advance, Ægisgarður 7, mobile 694-8956, www.icelandbike.com, Stefan Valsson).

Private Guides

I Heart Reykjavík, run by Auður and Hrannar, offers private walking tours (2.5 hours, 35,000 ISK, tel. 511-5522, www. iheartreykjavik.net, hello@iheartreykjavik.net).

City Walks and **Reykjavík Bike Tours** (see earlier listings) also offer private walks for roughly the same cost.

Reykjavík Walk

This self-guided walk, rated ▲▲▲, introduces the highlights of downtown Reykjavík, as well as some slices of local life, in about

two hours. While a few indoor sights may be closed early or late, the walk can be done at any time—allowing you to fit it in before or after your day trips. The walk starts at one of Reykjavík's central squares, Ingólfstorg, and finishes at Hallgrímskirkja, the big, landmark church on the hill. As Reykjavík is likely your first stop in Iceland, I've designed this walk as a crash course not only for the city, but for the whole country—introducing you to names, customs, stories, and themes that will come in handy from here to the Eastfjords.

• *Begin on the modern, sunken square called...*

❶ Ingólfstorg (Ingólfur's Square)

While this somewhat dreary square isn't much to look at, it packs a lot of history and myth. Ingólfstorg is named for Ingólfur Arnarson who—according to the Icelandic sagas—settled at Reykjavík in 874. You can think of him as Iceland's version of the Pilgrims.

In the middle of the square, look for the two nondescript **stone pillars** (one of them marked *874*). These recall the much-told legend about Ingólfur: As he sighted the southeast coast of Iceland, he followed an old Scandinavian custom and threw the two carved wooden pillars from his "high seat" (belonging to the head of the household) overboard—vowing to establish his farm wherever they washed ashore. In the meantime, he set up a temporary settlement on the South Coast and sent two of his slaves on a scavenger hunt all over the island. Three years later (in 874), they discovered the pillars here. Ingólfur called this place Reykjavík, meaning "Smoky Bay"—likely for the thermal vapor he saw venting nearby.

While the details of this story are a mix of fact and legend (see the "Sagas of the Icelanders 101" sidebar in this chapter), archaeologists confirm that the original Reykjavík farm was just a few steps

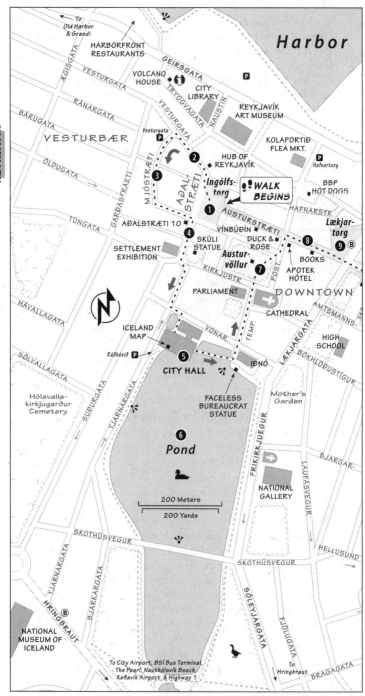

REYKJAVÍK

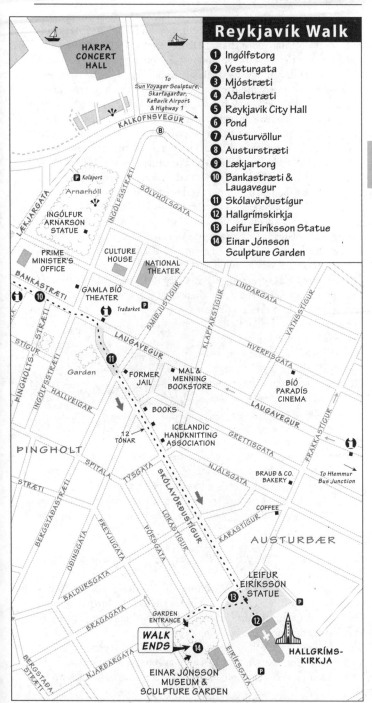

Reykjavík Walk

1. Ingólfstorg
2. Vesturgata
3. Mjóstræti
4. Aðalstræti
5. Reykjavik City Hall
6. Pond
7. Austurvöllur
8. Austurstræti
9. Lækjartorg
10. Bankastræti & Laugavegur
11. Skólavörðustígur
12. Hallgrímskirkja
13. Leifur Eiríksson Statue
14. Einar Jónsson Sculpture Garden

REYKJAVIK

from where you're standing. And for most of its history, Reykjavík remained nothing more than a farm—set between the sea and a pond a few hundred yards inland (we'll go there in a few minutes). But in the 18th century, Reykjavík gradually emerged as the country's dominant town and the logical seat of Iceland's government.

Ingólfstorg was not an open space until 1944, when a big hotel that used to stand here burned down. The lot was left vacant and became a seedy hangout where Reykjavík teens would drink, smoke, and do other things they didn't want their parents to know about. Locals called it Hallærisplan (which means, roughly, "Messed-Up Square"). Only in 1993 was it cleaned up, redesigned, and respectably renamed. Today, this square is designed for skateboarders, and hosts outdoor concerts and performances in summer. Lining the square are cafés and fast-food joints where you can pick up a hot dog, a slice of pizza, a toasted sub sandwich, or an ice cream (or even a decadent *bragðarefur*—a giant cup of soft serve with mix-ins, like a supersized McFlurry).

The big, glass-fronted, **eight-story building** that dominates the square represents the latest chapter in Reykjavík's story: its recent tourism boom. Long the  headquarters of Iceland's biggest newspaper, those offices recently moved out to the suburbs, and the building is now a hotel. A generation ago, downtown Reykjavík was mostly offices, government institutions, cheap housing, and lots of students. But with the flood of tourism over the last decade, most of these have been replaced by hotels, bars, restaurants, shops, and tour operators; the number of Icelanders who actually live downtown has dropped sharply.

• *Let's take a little loop through the back streets. Facing that big building, angle to the right and walk to the end of the square. The street leaving the square is...*

❷ Vesturgata, Reykjavík's Original Shoreline

This lovely lane (literally "West Street") is lined with colorful buildings from the early 20th century. The **yellow building** (today the Restaurant Reykjavík) was once the base of the town pier, back when the waterfront came all the way up to this point. The entry to the pier ran under the building's tower (beneath the round window). In 1874, when the king of Denmark visited Iceland, his fleet anchored in the harbor, and he came ashore on a little boat right here. Around 1910, land reclamation created the modern harborfront zone, just beyond the yellow building. Today, this so-called Old Harbor area has some appealing sights (see page 104).

In the sidewalk immediately in front of the yellow building, notice the brass plaque marking the **"hub of Reykjavík"**—both

the symbolic gateway to the city and the spot from where the city's address numbers radiate.

Around the left side of the yellow building, you can spot faint remains of the **original wharf,** and a little tidal pool that's still connected underground to

the harbor (for a better look, cross partway over the little footbridge and look down). Several recommended restaurants are on or near this square (see "Eating in Reykjavík," later).

• *Now continue along Vesturgata. Just after the bright red building on the left corner, turn left onto...*

❸ Mjóstræti, Back-Streets Reykjavík

Even in the bustling downtown of Iceland's capital, you're never more than a block or two away from a sleepy residential area. Stroll a couple of blocks along Mjóstræti ("Narrow Street"), appreciating some slices of Reykjavík life.

As you walk along Mjóstræti, notice, by a bench, one of Reykjavík's distinctive **fire hydrants**—painted in garish, McDonald's-esque red and yellow. Residents embrace these cheery hydrants, some embellished with faces, as a sort of local symbol.

Moving on, you'll see houses sided with vertical **corrugated iron** (despite the name, it's usually steel, galvanized with zinc).

Since the late 19th century, corrugated metal sheets have been widely used for siding and roofing in Iceland. Many cover older wooden walls. Wood, which needed to be imported on this treeless island, didn't do well when exposed to the harsh weather. Corrugated iron, meanwhile, stands up well to

the punishing wind and sideways rain, it doesn't burn, it's easy to maintain, it's cheap and easy to transport to Iceland, and can dress up renovated old houses as well as new ones. Many locals prefer to use brightly saturated hues, perhaps to help cheer them through the gloomy winters. Around town, you may also notice a few houses with boring gray metal: Newer siding needs to weather for a few years to get rough enough for primer and paint to adhere.

As you stroll, notice lots of **propped-open windows.** Icelanders mostly heat their homes with geothermal hot water—harnessing the substantial natural power of their volcanic island. There are radiators in every room, but typically no central thermostat. Heating costs are low, so when things get too warm or stuffy indoors, Icelanders just open the window to create a cross-breeze. For tourists, opening a window also helps vent the sulfur smell that accompanies the city's scalding-hot tap water, which is piped in directly from boreholes in the countryside. (Residents are used to the smell and don't even notice.)

Another way Icelanders use all that hot water is to heat **swimming pools.** Every Iceland town has a municipal thermal pool complex where locals swim laps, relax, and socialize—particularly appealing in the cold and dreary winter months. These basically feel like your hometown swimming pool...except the water is delightfully warm-to-hot year-round. Tourists are welcome to join in the fun, and many find it the most local-feeling experience they have in Iceland. (For more about visiting pools, see "Experiences in and near Reykjavík," later.)

Any **cats** roaming around? Reykjavík has a relaxed, small-town vibe, and people tend to let their cats wander free by day. Watch for clever little cat doors built into windows and doors. You won't see many dogs, though; until 1984 they were banned in the city for health reasons (for the whole story, see page 463), and condo owners still need permission from their neighbors to keep a dog.

• *After another block, Mjóstræti dead-ends into someone's driveway. Turn left on Brattagata and head downhill. You'll pop out back at the bottom of Ingólfstorg square, on...*

❹ Aðalstræti, Reykjavík's First Street

While today it feels more like an alley, this "Main Street" (as its name means) was Reykjavík's first thoroughfare.

The **one-story black house** on your right (at Aðalstræti 10) was originally built around 1760 for the textile industry. The current version is a complete rebuild (only the location of the walls is original), but faithful to the original style. The hand pump across the street (under the arcade) is a reminder that,

until 1910, locals used pumps like this one as their sole source of drinking water.

Turn right down Aðalstræti. A few doors down on the right is the Hótel Reykjavík Centrum. When this hotel was built in 2001, workers unearthed the ruins of a 10th-century Scandinavian longhouse—part of the original Reykjavík farm. Today it's the excellent **Settlement Exhibition,** where you can step down into the cellar and walk around the ancient structure (enter at the corner; museum described later, under "Sights in Reykjavík").

Opposite the hotel, a statue of **Skúli Magnússon** stands in a small square with a few trees. Skúli was an Enlightenment-era entrepreneur whose enterprises seeded settlement at Reykjavík in the mid-1700s—finally transforming it from a farm into a real town, and setting the stage for its eventual capital status. While Ingólfur may have settled in Reykjavík, Skúli put it on the map. The little square was the village cemetery until 1838.

• *Directly in front of Skúli is a lane called Tjarnargata (between two yellow houses). Follow this for a long block to Vonarstræti, where you'll see, on your left, a large, modern concrete building with a curved roof and a mossy pond in front. This is the...*

❺ Reykjavík City Hall (Ráðhús Reykjavíkur)

Enter the blocky, curved-roofed, concrete-and-glass building using the door at the inner corner of the fountain (Mon-Fri 8:00-18:00, Sat from 10:00, Sun from 12:00, free WCs and free smartphone charging kiosk). The city council meets

upstairs, but most city offices are outside the center, and this "City

Hall" is more of a ceremonial hall for the city's residents. Its ground-floor space, normally open to the public, is rented out for concerts, exhibitions, and other cultural events.

A huge wooden **relief map of Iceland** is sometimes displayed in front of the large windows overlooking the little lake known as the Pond. The towns on the map are not labeled, but it's easy to find Reykjavík and the Reykjanes Peninsula: Look for the airport. Pick out the island's major landforms: Fjords ruffle the coastline in the northwest (the Westfjords), the east coast (the Eastfjords), and the far north (Skagafjörður and Eyjafjörður, flanking the mountainous Tröl-laskagi—"Troll Peninsula"). Glacier-covered volcanic peaks loom ominously above the South Coast, while the desolate Highlands cover the middle of the country. Trace your own route through Iceland; spotting the roads and towns around the country is absorbing. Topographic maps help you identify fjords, mountains, and rivers.

• *Exit the building to the left from where you entered, and walk across the pedestrian bridge that runs along...*

❻ The Pond (Tjörnin)

This miniature lake feels just right for this small capital of a small country. On sunny days, parents bring small children to feed the ducks and swans that live in the Pond. In the winter, if the temperatures drop to a safe range (generally several days a year), snow on the Pond is cleared away to make a skating rink. It's a pleasant one-mile walk all the way around.

At the far end of the pedestrian bridge, you're greeted by a quirky statue of a **faceless bureaucrat.** The period building next to him is Iðnó, Reykjavík's old theater, which now houses a café.

Gaze out to the far end of the Pond, where you'll see some of the **University of Iceland** buildings (that's the science center with the curved glass roof). The country's oldest and largest university, with a total enrollment of around 13,000, was founded in 1911. Before that, students had to go abroad for college (mostly to Denmark)...a reminder of just how recently this country came into its own.

Farther right, rising a couple of stories above the rooftops, is the brown tower of the recommended **National Museum,** where a thoughtfully explained collection of artifacts tells the story of Iceland (described under "Sights in Reykjavík"). Along the right side of the Pond are fine homes built by wealthy families a century ago.

On the left of the Pond is the historic **Free Church of Reykjavík,** a Lutheran congregation that broke from the state church over a difference in social issues.

• *Standing next to the "faceless bureaucrat," turn your back to the Pond, cross the street, and walk straight up Templarasund. You'll arrive at a lovely little park with a big statue in the middle. Stand by the statue and get oriented to...*

❼ Austurvöllur, Iceland's Parliament Square

Translated roughly as "Eastern Field," Austurvöllur is the political center of this small country. With your back to the statue, the

big, stone building facing the square is Iceland's parliament, the **Alþingi** (pronounced, roughly, "all-thingy"). While Icelanders like to call the Alþingi the "world's oldest parliament," this is an exaggeration. The Alþingi that met at Þingvellir in the centuries after settlement was very different from a modern democratic parliament. From about 1400 to 1800, it was an appeals court, not a legislature. Then there were 45 years when the Alþingi didn't meet at all. It was reestablished in Reykjavík, in a totally new and different form, in 1845. In 1874, Iceland received a constitution that gave the Alþingi real decision-making power—even though Iceland remained fully part of Denmark.

On the building's gable, notice the crowned 9, which represents King Christian IX (the Danish ruler in 1881, when the building was erected). Engraved over four of the upstairs windows of the Alþingi, notice the mythical "four protectors of Iceland"—dragon, eagle, giant, and bull—which also appear on Iceland's coat of arms and many Icelandic coins. (As if to drive home Iceland's closeness to the sea, the flipsides of the coins feature cod, dolphins, crab, and lumpfish.) Imagine Iceland when this was built, in 1881, its people so excited to have at least some self-rule. One of the poorest countries in 19th-century Europe, it's said that this single building cost a third of the entire country's national income.

There are no public tours of the Alþingi, but if parliament is in session visitors are welcome to sit in the gallery (the 63-member parliament is on vacation June-mid-Sept; otherwise confirm session times at www.althingi.is—typically Mon and Wed at 15:00, Tue at 13:30, Thu and sometimes Fri at 10:30). The gallery entrance is around the back of the building, by a fine little walled garden that's open to the public.

Now turn your attention to the statue on the pillar: **Jón Sigurðsson** (1811-1879) was the 19th-century scholar and politician who successfully advocated for Iceland's increased autonomy under the Danish crown. Jón spent most of his life in Denmark, where he politely but forcefully pressed the case for freer trade and a constitution that would reduce the king's power. At the time, many other Europeans were agitating for the same kinds of things, and often took up arms. But Icelanders achieved their goals without firing a shot—thanks largely to the articulate persistence of this one man. The parliament building was finished just a couple of years after Jón's death. In Jón's honor, his birthday—June 17—became Iceland's National Day.

Look around the **square.** Early each summer new turf is laid and flower beds are filled in preparation for National Day ceremonies and speeches. But it was quite a different scene in the winter of 2008-2009: Thousands of Icelanders gathered here to demand the government's resignation in the wake of the country's financial collapse. Protesters banged pots and pans with wooden spoons, and pelted politicians with eggs and tomatoes (hence the protest's nickname, the "Kitchenware Revolution"). New elections were called, and the prime minister was censured for failing in his responsibilities. Ólafur Þór Hauksson—a small-town cop who became the unyielding special prosecutor for financial crimes—emerged as something of an international folk hero. A good number of bankers were tried, convicted, and in a few cases jailed for their role in the crisis.

Then, in spring 2016, thousands came to this square again after it was revealed that Iceland's then-prime minister had kept some of his considerable family wealth in an offshore account in Panama. Again, new elections were called.

To the left of the Alþingi is Reykjavík's **Lutheran Cathedral** (Dómkirkjan; generally open Mon-Fri 10:00-15:00, closed Sat-Sun except for services, occasional concerts—look for posters, www.domkirkjan.is). Surprisingly small, it was built in the 1790s and expanded in the 1840s. The city now has larger churches, but the cathedral is still regularly used for weddings, funerals, and the opening of parliament. If you  go inside, you'll find a beautifully tranquil interior, with an upstairs gallery and finely painted ceiling. The centerpiece—directly in front of the main altar—is a marble baptismal font by renowned

19th-century Danish sculptor Bertel Thorvaldsen, whose father was Icelandic.

At the right end of the Alþingi, notice the **statue of a strong woman** on a pillar: Ingibjörg H. Bjarnason (1867-1941), who was elected Iceland's first female member of parliament in 1922. Iceland has an impressive tradition of honoring women's rights. On October 24, 1975, 90 percent of Icelandic women went on strike to drive home their importance to society. The country ground to a halt. (Icelandic men—who very quickly learned their lesson—gave the protest the tongue-in-cheek nickname "The Long Friday," which is also what Icelanders call Good Friday.) In 1980, Iceland became the first modern, democratic nation to elect a female head of state, when single mother Vigdís Finn-

bogadóttir became president. She served for four terms (16 years) and remains a beloved figure today.

Facing the Bjarnason statue, at the corner of the park, notice the chunk of rock split in half by **"The Black Cone."** This monument to civil disobedience was placed here (somewhat controversially) in 2012—when memories of those 2009 protests were still fresh and, for some, painful.

• *Exit the square behind Jón Sigurðsson's left shoulder, and go one short block up the street called Pósthússtræti ("Post Office Street"). Pause at the intersection with Austurstræti ("Eastern Street"), in front of Apotek Hótel.*

❽ Austurstræti, Reykjavík's Main Street

Reykjavík's main drag begins about a block to your left (at Ingólfs-torg, where we started our walk) and continues about a mile to your right, changing names as it runs through town.

Looking straight ahead, on your right is the red former **post office** building. Across the street on the left, the old-meets-new building is **Landsbankinn,** founded as Iceland's national bank in 1886. It was privatized around 2000, failed spectacularly in 2008, and then continued operations under a slightly altered name. Past that, at the end of the block, you'll see a white, boxy building that houses the **Kolaportið flea market** on weekends—a fun browse, even for nonshoppers (see page 93).

Tucked away kitty-corner from the flea market (just down this street and on the right, a block away but not quite visible from here) is Reykjavík's most famous **hot dog stand.** (You can side trip

there now, or come back later.) It's been serving weenies to an enthusiastic local following since 1937. In 2004, Bill Clinton was in Reykjavík to speak at a UNICEF event. When the proprietor of this stand offered him a free frankfurter, Clinton—a notorious connoisseur of junk food—couldn't say no. Camera shutters clicked...and suddenly, eating at Bæjarins Beztu Pylsur—"The City's Best Sausages"—became *the* thing to do when visiting Reykjavík. Now people stand in long lines to shell out 600 ISK for what is, by any honest assessment, a fairly average weenie. On the street corner by the stand, you can fill up your water bottle for free at the red dispenser.

Back on Austurstræti, look up at the Art Deco-style facade of the **Apotek Hótel.** This was designed by Guðjón Samúelsson, Iceland's best-known 20th-century architect, who's responsible for many of the major landmarks around town—including his masterpiece church, Hallgrímskirkja.

Facing the hotel, across the street, is a restaurant called **Duck & Rose.** Look up at the relief on the pediment-like gable, from the 1920s, which shows an imagined scene from the settlement of the country: An established settler—standing in front of his pack animals—shakes hands with a new arrival, whose crew is taking down the mast of his longship. While you may sometimes hear the word "Viking" used to describe those early Icelandic settlers, that's not quite right. They were contemporaries (and actually relatives) of the Vikings, but had a different modus operandi: Rather than pillage, plunder, and rape, the first Icelanders were mostly farmers in search of good grazing land.

Now look up the street past the Duck & Rose (back toward Ingólfstorg). On the left side of the street (next to the English pub), notice **Vínbúðin**—one of the unobtrusive state-run liquor stores. Only weak beer can be bought at supermarkets; every other kind of alcohol can be purchased only here. While nationalized liquor stores are fairly standard in Nordic countries, Iceland has at times taken a particularly hard line against alcohol. From 1915 all the way until 1989—in an attempt to curtail everyone's favorite, cheap "gateway drug"—

beer with an alcohol content over 2.25 percent was illegal. Iceland-ers compensated by mixing spirits—which were, oddly, perfectly legal—with light beer, creating a super-alcoholic faux-brew. Today, as if making up for lost time, Iceland has a vibrant microbrew culture (see recommendations, including many within a few steps of this walk, on page 130). Also look for the Icelandic firewater called *brennivín*. In another anti-alcohol crusade, originally the *brennivín* bottle came with a health warning in the form of a black skull. While that's long gone, today the drink still carries the tongue-in-cheek nickname "Black Death" *(svartidauði)*. Pop in to survey the liquor store if you like. The only cheap way to try the interesting array of local beers is to buy them here—a fun, affordable cultural experience. Single cans and bottles cost about 300 ISK each.

From the Duck & Rose, turn right and walk up Austurstræti. After a few steps, on your right, look for one of the city center's three main **bookstores** (this one is run by Eymundsson—Iceland's answer to Barnes & Noble). Books are clearly valued here: A high percentage of Icelanders are published authors, and every Icelandic living room has shelves of books on display. Books also play a key role in Christmas gift exchanges: The Iceland publishers' association mails a catalog of the year's new releases each fall, just in time for holiday shopping lists.

Just past the bookstore, notice "The Hot Dog Stand"...taking full advantage of its prime location to hijack hungry tourists looking for the famous place around the corner.

• *Across the street from the bookstore is a 10-11 convenience store, useful for bus tickets or a bus pass. (But it's much more expensive for groceries.) At the end of the street, you'll emerge into a square fronting a busy street. Stop here to survey the scene.*

❾ Lækjartorg (Creek Square)

This square and the adjacent, busy street (Lækjargata) are named for a creek *(lækur)* that ran from the Pond (to your right) down to the sea (to your left) in Reykjavík's early days. It still flows, but was buried in an underground culvert more than a century ago.

Look across the street at the white stone building with the five upstairs windows. As Reykjavík grew in the mid-1700s, the first building constructed of materials more permanent than turf or timber was not a church or palace but a prison, built across the creek from the village center. Today it's the **office of Iceland's prime**

Icelandic Names: From Magnússon to Gunnarsdóttir

Traditionally, Icelanders' last names were patronymics, formed from the father's name plus "son" or "dóttir." So if you meet a man named Gunnar Magnússon, you know his father's name was Magnús. If Gunnar has a son Jón, he'll be named Jón Gunnarsson. A daughter María will be María Gunnarsdóttir. Get it? (This system was the norm all over Scandinavia until just a few hundred years ago.) Women keep their name at marriage.

Around 1900, fashions changed, and Icelanders started to assume family names and pass them down from generation to generation, like we do in the US. Then the pendulum swung back: In 1925, family names were banned as un-Icelandic, but people who had already taken one were allowed to keep it. (You may run into a few of these today.) Things went so far that for a few decades, immigrants who wanted to take up Icelandic citizenship had to abandon their foreign surname and choose an Icelandic patronymic (this requirement was abolished only in the 1980s). Today, with immigration rising, and many marriages between Icelandic women and immigrant men, family names are on the increase in Iceland again.

These days, Icelanders can choose to form their children's last name from either parent's first name. So, if Gunnar and Katrín have a son, they could give him the last name Katrínarson. But the country's Personal Names Committee still controls what first names parents can give their children (from a list of 3,500 autho-

minister. The *no parking* sign out front indicates the spot reserved for the prime minister.

But no matter how high you rise in Icelandic society, you're called by your first name—so President Guðni Jóhannesson is known to Icelanders simply as "Guðni." That's why, in this book, I'm on a first-name basis even with big-name historic Icelanders. This isn't necessarily because Icelanders are more casual than the norm—it's because of the unique way they form their last names. (For more on this tradition, see the "Icelandic Names" sidebar, above.)

Flanking the prime minister's office are two streets: **Bankastræti** (on the right) runs uphill for a couple of blocks, and then changes its name to Laugavegur. This has long been the main

rized names). While this seems oppressive, it's largely a grammatical concern—to ensure that names will work within the structure of the Icelandic language. Recently, politicians have moved to abolish the committee. Stay tuned.

All Icelanders address each other by first names, which may seem strangely informal. But in Icelandic, using a person's full first name actually has a ceremonial ring to it. Most Icelanders go by a nickname among family and friends, so Magnús's old schoolmates probably call him "Maggi." But strangers wouldn't dare call him anything less than Magnús. There's no real equivalent of "Mr." or "Ms." in Icelandic.

It's traditional for Icelandic parents to reveal their children's names only when the child is christened (usually a few weeks after birth, but the law lets them wait for up to six months). Many parents choose the name before the birth, but still follow custom and keep it a secret. Others appreciate the chance to get to know their child before deciding. In the meantime, parents use nicknames for their baby, like "The Short One."

What children do get within minutes of birth is a 10-digit identification number, based on their birth date, which follows them through life. This number, called the *kennitala,* is almost like an alternative name, and Icelanders use it very openly and casually to identify themselves to schools, banks, or the power company. Anyone can look up anyone else's ID number and address. This shocks Americans, who are used to keeping their Social Security number secret. Despite—or perhaps because of—this openness, identity theft in Iceland is practically unknown.

By the way, many Icelandic first names are comically hard for tourists to pronounce, something locals have fun with. (And locals in the tourist trade generally have an easy-to-remember nickname.)

downtown shopping street; we'll head up this way soon. **Hverfis-gata** (on the left), a more heavily trafficked commercial street, is where city buses run on their way between the two main bus stops downtown: Lækjartorg (where you're standing) and Hlemmur (just under a mile to the east).

On the hill to the left of Hverfisgata are many government offices, including Iceland's supreme court, ministry of finance, and central bank.

Cross the busy street. Before you head straight uphill on Bankastræti, look back on your left by the harbor. The dark, glassy, boxy building is called **Harpa**—Reykjavík's concert hall and conference center. Don't trek out to Harpa now; at the end of this

REYKJAVÍK

walk, you can head to Harpa to enter the hall's futuristic lobby for a good look at its multicolored windows.

• *Now, walk uphill on Bankastræti (passing the prime minister's office on your left).*

⓾ Bankastræti/Laugavegur, More of Reykjavík's Main Drag

By the end of the 19th century, Reykjavík had expanded, and most people lived on this side of the town's little creek. This stretch became the city's main shopping and business street. Today, most locals shop at malls and in the suburbs, and services along Laugavegur are geared toward tourists.

A half-block up on your left, notice another old stone building (marked with the *Stella* sign). This was Iceland's first bank building, built in 1882, which gave Bankastræti its name. To the right, tucked back from the street, is one of three TIs sprinkled along the main drag (generally daily 9:00-20:00, shorter hours Sun and in winter).

Continuing up Bankastræti, notice the moveable **traffic barriers** (including some shaped like bicycles). In the summer, some stretches of this street are closed to cars to promote strolling.

Keep your eye out—both along this main strip, and in the residential side streets—for big **street-art murals.** This isn't eyesore

graffiti, but quite the opposite: Locals have found that if you supply a blank canvas, it'll be tagged. But if you decorate it yourself, taggers leave it alone. So government and private property owners commission murals like these. Many of the most renowned Icelandic street artists are women. The back lanes are even more highly decorated than the main streets we're seeing on this walk—be sure to explore later.

After two short blocks, pause at the lively intersection where Skólavörðustígur splits off to the right (dead-ending at Hallgrímskirkja, crowning the bluff). This is also where the street changes names to **Laugavegur** (roughly LOY-ga-VEH-grr, Hot Springs Road)—once the walking route for those going to do their laundry in the Laugardalur hot springs east of downtown. We won't walk the length of Laugavegur right now, but you'll certainly find plenty of excuses to explore it while you're in town—many of the city's best restaurants, shops, and bars are on or within a few steps of this street. About 10 minutes' walk away, at Laugavegur's far end, is Hlemmur, the main city bus junction (with a trendy food hall and the Phallological Museum—see "Sights in Reykjavík," later). While the entire drag is commercialized, the farther you go up Laugavegur, the less it feels like a tourist circus.

• *From here, dogleg right and head uphill on the rainbow-painted street toward the distant church steeple. This street is called...*

REYKJAVÍK

⓫ Skólavörðustígur Street

This street (SKO-la-vur-thu-STEE-grr, "School Cairn Lane") leads up to Hallgrímskirkja church. The street got its name from a pile of rocks that Reyk-javík schoolchildren set up long ago atop the hill, near where the church is now. Like Laugavegur, this street is lined with cafés, restaurants, and bookstores. As it's a bit less congested, and capped with a lovely church stee-  ple, this street is a favorite place to stroll in Reykjavík.

Just a few steps up Skólavörðustígur at #4 (on the right), notice the tiny gap between the buildings. From the gate, peek discreetly into an adorable, private little **garden** facing a bright red house—a tranquil parallel world to the bustle just a few steps away. Many downtown blocks have an interior garden, shared among the surrounding houses. Sometimes, like here, little houses are tucked behind other houses. This was a good way to increase the capacity of your lot in this city of chronic housing shortages (and loosely enforced building regulations).

Back on Skólavörðustígur, continue a block uphill. A few steps up on the left is **Mokka Café.** The first place in town to do fancy Italian-style coffee (since 1958), it's long been a writers' hangout and retains its old atmosphere. Farther up on the left, you'll see another **old stone building.** It looks a bit like the historic jail we saw earlier—and yes, it's another former jail, built in 1874 (after the city had expanded, and this area was just outside town). This remained in use until summer 2016. Run your fingers over the chunky, volcanic rock in the building's facade.

Just past the jail, also on the left, the boxy three-story building at #11 was a bank, until the financial crisis, and now houses a branch of the Eymundsson bookstore chain.

While the lower end of the street is dominated by big, glitzy shops (like Geysir, with modern Icelandic fashion, or the venerable Rammagerðin handicraft shop), as you continue uphill the shops become smaller, more characteristic boutiques. Ceramic and jewelry shops—often with a small workshop in the back—are popular along here. At #15 (on the left), 12 Tónar is Reykjavík's most beloved music store, specializing in Icelandic tunes. Browsers can listen in their sampling lounge and enjoy a free cup of coffee. A few doors up at #19 (with the metal balcony) is the Handknitting Association of Iceland's shop, a co-op where you can browse expensive but top-quality handmade Icelandic sweaters and other woolens. For more recommendations, see "Shopping in Reykjavík," later.

• *The last couple of blocks on the street are increasingly residential. It's fun to explore the side streets in this neighborhood, where you'll find more corrugated metal siding, propped-open windows, street art, hidden gardens, and cats. But for now, continue straight uphill until you run right into...*

⑫ Hallgrímskirkja Lutheran Church

After Reykjavík's Catholic minority built their church atop the hill west of downtown in 1929, Lutheran state church leaders felt they needed to keep up. They hired the same well-known architect, Guðjón Samúelsson, and commissioned him to build a taller, bigger response on the higher hill to the east of downtown. His distinctive Hallgrímskirkja (HAHTL-greems-KEER-kyah) was designed in the 1930s, with construction beginning in 1945, but was not completed until the 1980s. On New Year's Eve, this square is where locals gather to watch fireworks.

Exterior: The basalt-column motif soaring skyward on the facade recalls Iceland's volcanic origins—and evokes the cliffs you'll see around the country. In the winter, as you look up from Skólavörðustígur, light shining out through the windows makes the top of the 250-foot tower glow like a giant jack-o'-lantern.

Guðjón Samúelsson (1887-1950)—an Icelander who trained in Denmark—was Iceland's most influential architect. Arriving back home after finishing his studies in 1919, he was hired as the government's in-house building designer—a plum post that he kept until his death. These were good years for architects, as Iceland urbanized and the availability of concrete opened up new design possibilities. Guðjón's favored aesthetic was the functionalist style typical of the 1920s and 1930s. He attempted to forge a distinctly Icelandic architectural style...and, because he designed so many buildings here, you might say he succeeded. In Reykjavík alone, he designed this church, the main university building, the original National Hospital building, the National Theater, the Sundhöllin swimming pool, the Apotek Hótel we saw earlier, and the Hótel Borg across the square from the parliament building.

Hallgrímskirkja is named for the 17th-century Icelandic poet Hallgrímur Pétursson, who wrote a well-known series of 50 hymns retelling the story of the Passion of Christ.

Interior: Step inside (free, daily 9:00-21:00, Oct-April until 17:00). Temporary art installations fill the entry foyer. Strolling down the church's dramatically austere nave, you're immersed in a sleek space culminating in classically Gothic pointed arches—with virtually no adornments. The glass is clear, not stained, and the main altar is a simple table. Notice how the ends of the pews echo the stair-step steeple outside.

Turn around and face the massive organ, which was "crowdfunded" in 1991; people paid to sponsor individual pipes. (To the right of the door you came in, notice the collection box shaped like an organ pipe—donations for the instrument's upkeep.) The church is a popular venue for organ and choral concerts (look for posters, and see page 127). If the organist is practicing (most likely in the morning), sit down and enjoy a little musical break.

Notice that the pews are reversible—the seat backs can be flipped over to face the organ. Not only is this in keeping with Lutheranism—where the most important aspects of worship are the sermon (pulpit) and the music (organ)—but it's also very practical. In smaller towns, you can't have both a church and a concert hall— so one building has to do double-duty.

Before leaving, consider riding the elevator (plus 33 steps) to the top of the **tower,** with a fine view over the rooftops (1,000 ISK, daily 9:00-20:30, Oct-April until 16:30). If there's a long line for the small elevator, consider coming back in the evening.

• *Head back outside. Prominently displayed in front of the church is a...*

® Leifur Eiríksson Statue

Known as Leif Erikson (c. 970-1020) to Americans, this Viking Age explorer was—if we can trust the sagas—the first European

to set foot on the American continent. The sagas weave a colorful tale of Leifur's outlaw-family lineage and his clan's explorations. His grandfather, Þorvaldur Ásvaldsson, was exiled from Norway to Iceland, and his father, Eiríkur Þorvaldsson (Erik the Red), was in turn exiled from Iceland—establishing the first settlements on Greenland. Leifur carried on farther west, seeking a mysterious land that had been spotted by another Nordic sailor when he was blown off course.

Around five centuries before Christopher Columbus, Leifur and his crew landed in the New World, very possibly at L'Anse aux Meadows, in today's Newfoundland, where there are ruins of a Viking Age complex. Norsemen may have established more settlements in this area—which they called *Vínland* (meaning either "Land of Wine" or "Land of Meadows") for its relatively lush climate—but if so, they did not last. On his way home, according to the sagas, Leifur rescued the crew of another ship that had been stranded on a small island, and after that he was dubbed "Leifur heppni" (Leif the Lucky). The US government donated this statue to mark the Alþingi's 1,000th anniversary in 1930. The inscription delicately acknowledges Leifur as the "discoverer of Vínland"—but not of America.

If it's summertime, in the park flanking Leif the Lucky, look for three types of **flowers** that grow abundantly in this otherwise inhospitable land: the vivid purple Nootka lupine (from Alaska, introduced to Iceland in the mid-20th century to combat erosion); bright yellow European gorse, an alpine shrub with a pungent herbal fragrance in the early summer; and...dandelions. All three are considered weeds in much of the world, but most Icelanders don't remove them. As one local explained, "We're just happy when *anything* grows here."

• *We'll finish our walk with one more hidden sight. With the church at your back, turn left and head toward the bunker-like mansion. You'll curl around the right side of this building, passing a fun little metal cut-out that lines up perfectly with the jagged roofline of the church—turn around and try it. Just past the cutout, watch for a gate on the left and enter the...*

⑭ Einar Jónsson Sculpture Garden

Of Iceland's notable artists, Einar Jónsson (1874-1954) was one of the first and most significant. After studying in Copenhagen and Rome, Einar made his name working in big European capitals. But, like so many Icelanders, after half a lifetime of living abroad he felt drawn back to his homeland. Einar struck a deal with the Alþingi (much like the sculptor Gustav Vigeland did in Oslo): If they built him a mansion and studio, he'd move back to Reykjavík and bequeath all that he produced to the city. He designed and built this house back when this was a naked, largely uninhabited hilltop (not even the church was built yet), seeding what has become a desirable neighborhood.

Linger over the 26 bronze works in the sculpture garden (free to enter, open late). Einar's statues—with universal human themes—are taut with tension and angst. Einar was a fearful man, yet also very spiritual; his work suggests glimmers of hope in frightening times. You'll see motifs from Norse mythology and references to Iceland's "hidden people" (elves and the like). The men are mighty warriors, and the women (whose faces are modeled after Einar's wife, Anna) are protectors. Einar and Anna lived in a small, cozy, wood-paneled penthouse apartment at the top of the building's tower. To learn more about Einar, see some plaster casts of his work, and walk through his apartment, you can pay to enter the building (today the **Einar Jónsson Museum**—described on page 98, entrance facing the church).

• *Our walk is over. Both of the two downtown shopping streets— Skólavörðustígur and Laugavegur—are lined with eating options. To quickly get down to Laugavegur (and the Hlemmur bus junction), head down Frakkastígur, which runs to the left as you face the church from the top of Skólavörðustígur; on your way to the main drag, you'll pass several good places to take a break—including top-end coffee shop Reykjavík Roasters, and the "destination" bakery Brauð & Co (other options are described later, under "Eating in Reykjavík").*

If you follow Frakkastígur down to Laugavegur, then cross it and continue straight downhill through an uninviting condo zone (near the recommended Kex Hostel café, a block to the right down Skúlagata), you can cross a busy street to reach the city's iconic Sun Voyager sculpture. From here, it's an easy five-minute walk (with the water on your right) to the Harpa concert hall. The Old Harbor zone is just beyond.

Sights in Reykjavík

In addition to its fine state- and city-run museums, Reykjavík has an assortment of pricey private museums (including Whales of Iceland, Saga Museum, Aurora Reykjavík, and the Phallological

Museum). You might expect these to be tourist traps, but (while expensive) they're thoughtfully presented.

DOWNTOWN REYKJAVÍK
Near Parliament and Laugavegur

These sights are all within a short walk of the city's main artery. They're listed roughly from west to east.

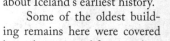

▲The Settlement Exhibition (Landnámssýningin)

During downtown construction work in 2001, archaeologists discovered the remains of a 10th-century longhouse from the original Reykjavík farmstead. These ruins were carefully pre-served, and a small, modern, well-presented museum was built around them. This is the most accessible (and most cen-tral) place in Reykjavík to learn about Iceland's earliest history.

Some of the oldest build-ing remains here were covered by tephra material from a volcanic eruption; carbon dating has nar-rowed the time of the eruption to AD 871...give or take a couple of years. (That's why you see "Reykjavík 871±2" around town.) It's worth paying admission to see what's left of the old Viking Age house and the modern, well-presented exhibits that surround it.

Cost and Hours: 1,700 ISK, covered by Reykjavík City Card, free for kids 17 and younger, daily 9:00-18:00, Aðalstræti 16, tel. 411-6370, www.settlementexhibition.is.

Tours: Admission includes an audioguide (ask for it) and a guided 45-minute tour in English—worth planning your visit around (June-Aug Mon-Fri at 11:00, no tours on weekends or off-season).

Visiting the Museum: You'll descend to cellar level and walk around the stone-and-turf wall that survives from the 65-by-26-foot longhouse. A circle of high-tech exhibits on the surrounding walls explains the site. You'll learn how Scandinavians first settled the Reykjavík area a little before a volcanic eruption that took place around AD 871. This house dates from later (around 930) and may have belonged to the grandson of Reykjavík's semi-legendary founder, Ingólfur Arnarson (famous for throwing carved pillars overboard to select a building site). The house of a fairly prosperous farmer, it held an extended family of about 10 people. It had a sod roof and a big hearth in the middle. The house was abandoned after only a few decades—around AD 1000— perhaps due to damage from a spring that still runs beneath it. Exhibits explain the landscape, flora, and fauna of this area in that era, suggesting why it was an attractive place to establish a farm. You'll see actual items excavated here: a spindle whorl with runic inscriptions, and primitive tools such as keys, fishhooks, arrowheads, and ax heads. A model and a virtual, interactive reconstruction of the longhouse further illustrate the lifestyles of these earliest Icelanders.

▲Kolaportið Flea Market

Reykjavík's flea market, open only on weekends, takes up the dingy ground floor of the old customs building. While you'll see plenty

of tourists, the market is still aimed largely at locals. It's fun to rummage through the stalls of used books and music, clothing (including knockoff Icelandic sweaters), and collectibles.

Cost and Hours: Free entry, open Sat-Sun 11:00-17:00, closed Mon-Fri, closed or varying hours on major holiday weekends, Tryggvagata 19, tel. 562-5030, www.kolaportid. is.

Visiting the Market: The food section serves as a crash course in Icelandic eats. Several stalls offer free samples. Look for the different kinds of smoked fish: *silungur* is trout, *bleikja* is arctic char, and *lax* is salmon. If you're a bit bolder, there's *harðfiskur* (air-dried, skinless white fish that's been pounded flat—eaten as a snack with butter), crunchy fish chips, or dried seaweed (which might be labeled *hollustusnakk*—"health snack"). And if you're even more daring, you can buy a tiny 200-ISK tub containing cubes of the notorious fermented shark, *hákarl* (you'll never eat more than this amount, and the rare restaurant that serves it charges much more). Occasionally you may be offered a free sample of *hákarl*—which is ideal, since you'd never want to buy more (for the reason why, see page 497).

Also look for other unusual Icelandic eats: horsemeat and horse sausage, and in summer, seabird eggs (typically from guillemots or other *svartfuglar*—birds in the auk family, which also includes puffins and murres). Look in the freezers for cod *(þorskur)*, haddock *(ýsa)*, and plaice *(rauðspretta)*, which are all Icelandic, as well as Asian imports such as pangasius (catfish), mussels, and squid. To cleanse your palate, grab some samples at the bakery counter (they might have a layer cake with frosting or jam), or taste-test the many different varieties of chocolate-covered licorice.

REYKJAVÍK

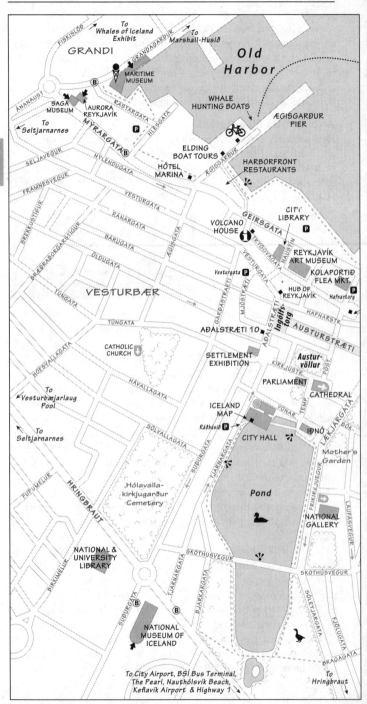

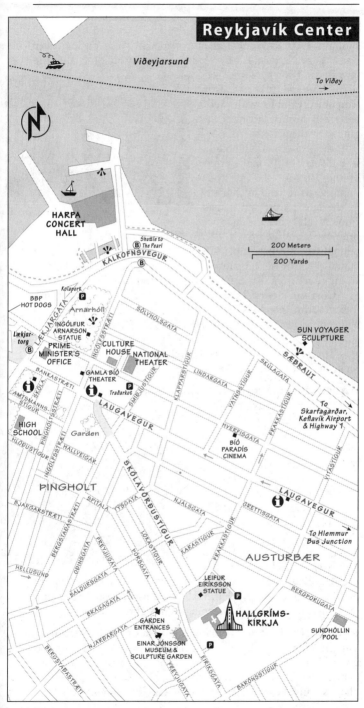

REYKJAVÍK

REYKJAVÍK

Culture House (Safnahúsið)

Built in 1909 to house Iceland's National Museum, and later home to the National Library, today this stately building holds the downtown branch of the National Museum. It hosts mostly temporary exhibits with well-described historic artifacts arranged by theme.

The collection's highlight is a display of 14 manuscripts of the *Jónsbók*—the law code imposed on Iceland by Norway in the late 1200s, and named "Jón's Book" after the man who compiled it. The earliest is the priceless *Skarðsbók* from 1363, an illuminated manuscript painstakingly written on vellum (calfskin). As the original Icelandic saga manuscripts are not on public view, this is as close as you'll get to seeing pages from that era. It's a very big deal to Icelanders.

Cost and Hours: 2,000 ISK, covered by Reykjavík City Card, includes admission to National Museum, daily 10:00-17:00, closed Mon off-season, Hverfisgata 15, tel. 530-2210, www.culturehouse. is.

Tours: The audioguide (which you can rent, or browse on your phone using the free Wi-Fi) is worthwhile for history buffs.

▲▲Laugavegur, Reykjavík's Main Drag

The city's main walking street is a delight to stroll—particularly its eastern stretch, Laugavegur. While far from "local" (you'll rarely spot an Icelander here who doesn't work in the tourist trade), it's enjoyable to wander and browse, with characteristic old houses, vivid street art, tempting cafés and bars, and—yes—plenty of touristy puffin shops. Many visitors wind up doing several laps up and down Laugavegur, picking out new details with each pass. I've described a short stretch of Laugavegur on my self-guided "Reykjavík Walk," and listed several businesses along here in the Eating, Shopping, and Nightlife sections.

Icelandic Phallological Museum (Hið Íslenzka Reðasafn)

This gimmicky museum near the Hlemmur bus junction (at the far end of Laugavegur) is a one-room collection of preserved animal penises that can be seen in 15 minutes, plus various depictions of phalluses in folk art. It's impossible to describe (or visit) this place without juvenile jokes, so here goes: You'll see more wieners than you can shake a stick at—preserved, pickled peckers floating in jars of yellow liquid. You'll see a seal's schlong, a wolf's wang, a zebra's zipper trout, a fox's frankfurter, a giraffe's gherkin, a dog's dong, a badger's baloney pony, a squirrel's schwanz, a coyote's crankshaft, a horse's hardware, a reindeer's rod, and lots of whale willies. If you can't get through this description without giggling, maybe you should visit. If you're about to set down this book and write me an angry letter...don't.

Cost and Hours: 1,700 ISK, daily 10:00-18:00, Laugavegur 116, tel. 561-6663, www.phallus.is.

Hallgrímskirkja Area

This hilltop zone is marked by the prominent tower of Reykjavík's landmark church.

▲▲Hallgrímskirkja Lutheran Church

Reykjavík's most recognizable icon is the stairstep gable of this fine, modern church, designed in the 1930s by state architect Guðjón Samúelsson. It boasts a sleek interior and a tower with grand views. For more on the church, see my "Reykjavík Walk," earlier. In the summer, there are regular performances on its booming organ (see "Entertainment in Reykjavík," later).

For a fine photo op, view the church from atop the steps of the Einar Jónsson Museum across the street.

Cost and Hours: Church—free; tower—1,000 ISK, 100 ISK for kids under 15. Church open 9:00-21:00, tower until 20:30; Oct-April church until 17:00, tower until 16:30. The church sometimes closes for special events. Tel. 510-1000, www.hallgrimskirkja.is.

Tower: The 250-foot-tall tower offers a commanding view of the city. A six-person elevator takes you up to the belfry, where you can look down on the city's colorful roofs amidst the clang of the church bells (cover your ears at :00 and :30 past the hour). Straight ahead, look down over the colorful roofs lining Skólavörðustígur street, which stretches toward the harbor. In the distance, if it's clear, you may see the snow-capped Snæfellsjökull peak at the end of the Snæfellsnes Peninsula, 50 miles away. The closer mountain, looming to the right, is the 3,000-foot Mount Esja, a popular destination for local hikers. And to the right, the island you see is Viðey, reachable on an easy cruise (see page 114). Ponder that well over half of Iceland's population lives in view of this church. Lines for the elevator can be long—if there's a crowd, swing back later in the day.

▲▲Einar Jónsson Museum and Garden (Listasafn Einars Jónssonar)

The former home of gifted sculptor Einar Jónsson (1874-1954)—facing Hallgrímskirkja church—has a free sculpture garden out back (described in "Reykjavík Walk," earlier). For a more intimate look at the artist, tour the museum (entrance at the front, facing the church). Inside, you'll see his home, and several large- and small-scale plaster casts for Einar bronzes that decorate the city.

Cost and Hours: 1,000 ISK, Tue-Sun 10:00-17:00, closed Mon; English language info sheets available; Eiríksgata 3, tel. 551-3797, www.lej.is.

Visiting the Museum: Stepping into the grand **entry hall,** immediately on your right is *Outlaws* (*Útlagar,* 1901). This break-

through work, completed while Einar was a student in Denmark, is one of his trademark pieces. It depicts a convicted man who takes his wife's lifeless body to a cemetery before escaping with his child to live in the Highlands. (As many original Icelandic settlers were themselves outlaws—exiled from Norway—this theme is particularly poignant.) Just beyond that, *Dawn* (*Dögun,* 1906) illustrates a scene from an Icelandic folk tale, in which a girl tricks a troll by keeping him talking until the sun rises. He sweeps her up in his arm at the very moment the sun freezes him in stone, and he shakes his fist defiantly.

In the red room, down the spiral staircase, the striking *Rest* (*Hvíld,* completed in 1935) is an eerie, oversized bust of a young man whose face is half-covered by reptilian basalt columns. Beneath his chin stands a sculptor leaning against a giant hammer, taking a break. This recalls the notion (dating back to Michelangelo) that the sculpture already exists within the stone; it's the artist's job to chip away and reveal it. In *The Spell Broken* (*Úr Álögum,* completed 1927), a St. George-like knight—protectively cradling a woman—slays a dragon by driving his sword through its head. In the green room, the evocative *Remorse* (*Samviskubit,* completed 1947) shows a man tormented by tiny, conscience-like beings. One holds his eyes open, the other recites a litany of wrongdoings in his ear, and both ensure he can't escape whatever's wracking him with guilt.

For a peek at the life of the artist himself, climb the tight spiral staircase to the top floor to see the intimate **apartment** that Einar and his wife Anna shared—a cozy, human-scale contrast to the beefy building and Einar's dynamic works.

Beyond the Pond
▲▲National Museum of Iceland (Þjóðminjasafnið)

The National Museum presents a thoughtful and manageable look at the history of this island nation, making excellent use of artifacts and a top-notch audioguide that brings meaning to the exhibits. The collection is well laid out and strikes just the right balance, presenting enough information to satisfy those with a reasonable attention span while not going overboard. There's also a pleasant café and a classy gift shop.

Cost and Hours: 2,000 ISK, covered by Reykjavík City Card, includes admission to Culture House; daily 10:00-17:00, mid-Sept-April closed Mon; Suðurgata 41, tel. 530-2200, www. thjodminjasafn.is.

Tours: You can rent an audioguide for 500 ISK—or download it for free via the museum's Wi-Fi.

Getting There: The museum is near the far end of the Pond, a pleasant 10-minute walk from City Hall along Tjarnargata; you can also take bus #1, #3, #6, or #12 to the Háskóli Íslands stop. If walking between the harbor area and the museum, you can short-cut along Garðastræti and through Hólavallakirkjugarður, the city's oldest cemetery.

Visiting the Museum: The permanent exhibit fills the two long floors upstairs, telling the story of Iceland. The exhibit is loosely chronological and well-explained in English.

From the ticket desk, head upstairs to begin. You'll see a few objects from the Settlement Age, including candle holders and gorgeous, oversized brass "dome brooches." Much of this floor is dominated by medieval church art, created after the island's conversion to Christianity around 1000. The darkened room in the center displays vestments, statues, altar tapestries, and bells that were all imported from Europe—a reminder that early Icelanders were hardworking frontier farmers who had to order their luxury goods from "back east." Two locally made exceptions are wooden panels

(side margin) REYKJAVÍK

from a c. 1100 *Judgment Day* painting, and a carved crucifix from c. 1200. Nearby, examine the exquisite wood-carved door from the church in Valþjófsstaður (in eastern Iceland), illustrating the story of a knight who slew a dragon to save a lion. Like many precious Icelandic objects, this door was taken to Denmark for safekeeping; the Danish government returned it in the 1930s, as part of a gift to Iceland in honor of the millennial celebration of the Alþingi.

Near the end of this floor, look for Guðbrandur's Bible—the first-ever Bible in Icelandic (1584). The Protestant Reformation, which began in Europe, also spread to Iceland, and to this day, the majority of Icelanders are Lutheran. The landing at the far end of the hall quickly covers the period of Danish rule and has an exhibit on the church in Iceland.

The exhibit continues upstairs, covering the 17th century through the present. Look for the drinking horn by Brynjólfur Jónsson, painstakingly carved with Bible scenes (1598). Following the Reformation, the Danish king also headed the Lutheran Church of Iceland, giving him tremendous power. While absolute rule by the king limited his subjects' freedom, it spurred efficiency and economic progress. Exhibits explain how, in 1703, Iceland conducted the world's first census that recorded every person's name (allowing us to know with precision that, in that year, Iceland was home to 50,358 people—99 percent of them farmers and farm workers).

Other exhibits explain how Danes maintained a monopoly on trade in Iceland. Starting around 1750, first the Enlightenment and then the wave of nationalism and democracy that swept Europe also reached these shores—with diverse effects, from the reconstitution of the Alþingi in 1845, to the creation of an Icelandic national costume by a local artist in 1860 (Sigurður Guðmundsson's *skautbúningur*). Meanwhile, the humble people of Iceland toiled along on chilly, smelly farms in the countryside—peer inside a typical farmhouse living room (called a *baðstofa*). They also lived off the sea—fishing from basic, small, open rowing/sailing boats, like the one on display, all the way up to the advent of motorized vessels.

Soon Iceland was primed for self-rule, and you'll see the desk of the man who worked hardest to make it happen: Jón Sigurðsson, who loudly agitated in Copenhagen for a national constitution and an end to the trade monopoly. Nearby, look for "The Blue and White"—an early, unofficial Icelandic flag (missing the current red cross). In 1913, a young Icelander flew the flag from his small boat in Reykjavík harbor, until a Danish coast guard ship seized the "unauthorized" colors. Furious Icelanders demanded that the issue

be resolved, and it eventually caught the attention of the Danish king—who agreed that Iceland deserved its own banner. Viewing tests from a distance showed that the blue-and-white flag was too easy to confuse with Sweden's, so the red cross was added. The flag was made official in 1915. Iceland became a sovereign state in 1918, and a fully independent republic in 1944.

The exhibit finishes with a look at modern Iceland. Look for the giant, white trawl wire cutters—a weapon used in the "Cod Wars" between Iceland and the UK (1958-1976), when the two countries squabbled over fishing rights (rather than torpedoing each other, they cut fishing nets). Finally, an airport conveyor belt displays various trappings of modern Icelandic life.

REYKJAVÍK'S ART MUSEUMS

This small community has a busy arts scene, and the six local museums described next proudly show off Iceland's 20th-century artists. Iceland's artistic tradition goes back only a century or so; most Icelandic artists (even today) traveled abroad to get a solid education. The Reykjavík City Card covers all six branches, but I wouldn't dedicate much time here: These museums have a hard time competing with all the nearby natural beauty and interesting history.

National Gallery of Iceland (Listasafn Íslands)

The National Gallery has three branches, each with separate costs and hours (you can get a 2,000 ISK combo-ticket that covers all three). The **main branch** is near the Pond, with five gallery spaces showing off a continually changing selection of pieces from their permanent collection of mainly modern Icelandic artists. They also have a few international pieces—including works by Picasso and Munch—but these are not always on display (2,000 ISK, daily 10:00-17:00, off-season Tue-Sun from 11:00, closed Mon; café, Fríkirkjuvegur 7, www.listasafn.is).

The **Ásgrímur Jónsson Collection** highlights a rotating selection of works by this early-20th-century painter who specialized in Impressionistic landscapes of his homeland, dynamic illustrations of the sagas, and some later Expressionistic Munch-like pieces (1,000 ISK, daily 13:00-17:00; in his former home at Bergstaða-stræti 74—a few blocks southeast of the main branch and Pond).

The **Sigurjón Ólafsson Museum** showcases the heavily stylized, sometimes abstract works of this mid-20th-century sculptor, who studied under both Einar Jónsson and Ásgrímur Jónsson (1,000 ISK, daily 13:00-17:00; northeast of downtown near the Skarfagarðar cruise terminal, at Laugarnestangi 17).

Reykjavík Art Museum (Listasafn Reykjavíkur)

This institution has three branches, each with changing exhibits focusing on modern art (for the latest lineup, see www.artmuseum.is). The **Hafnarhus main branch,** right downtown and near the Kolaportið flea market at Tryggvagata 17, has an eclectic range of temporary exhibits, and sometimes highlights works by Pop artist Erró—Iceland's answer to Roy Lichtenstein. The **Kjarvalsstaðir** branch exhibits some works by idiosyncratic modern painter Jóhannes Sveinsson Kjarval, who blended Icelandic landscapes with abstract and surreal flourishes (it's a 10-minute walk south of the Hlemmur bus junction, in the Klambratún park at Flókagata 24). And the **Ásmundarsafn** branch, in the eastern neighborhood of Laugardalur, highlights work by the mid-20th-century, mostly abstract, Miró-like sculptor Ásmundur Sveinsson, displayed in his architecturally striking former home (on Sigtún, near the corner of Reykjavegur).

Cost and Hours: All three museums are covered by an 1,800-ISK ticket for 24 hours, covered by the Reykjavík City Card, and open daily 10:00-17:00. The main branch stays open until 22:00 on Thu, and Ásmundarsafn has shorter hours off-season (13:00-17:00; www.artmuseum.is).

ALONG THE WATERFRONT

These sights are spread along a lengthy stretch of the city waterfront. I've listed them roughly from east to west.

Just Below the Main Drag

These sights are just downhill from Bankastræti/Laugavegur streets.

▲Sun Voyager (Sólfar)

This popular outdoor stainless-steel sculpture is shaped like an old Viking boat, pointing northwest in the direction of the setting sun in summer. This ode to the sun is a good place to watch the sea, take a selfie, and ponder the promise of undiscovered territory

that brought Scandinavians to Iceland more than a thousand years ago—and the impulses that pushed them farther west, to Greenland and Canada. The sculpture, by Icelandic artist Jón Gunnar Árnason, is a few blocks along the shore past Harpa, at the base of Frakkastígur street, about a five-minute walk below Laugavegur; drivers on the westbound waterfront highway will find a handy pullout right at the sculpture.

▲▲Harpa Concert Hall

One of Reykjavík's newest landmarks, this cutting-edge performing arts and conference center almost feels too big for such a small city. That's because the ambitious building was conceived during Iceland's banking mania. When the crash came in 2008, construction had already begun. (Some cynics proposed that it be left half-built, as a monument to the greed and excess of unbridled capitalism.) By the time Harpa was opened in 2011, the hall was hemorrhaging money and was kept alive thanks only to huge subsidies (which some Icelanders felt would be better spent elsewhere). Despite the woes, Reykjavík wound up with a fine performance space, and the city is growing into it. In 2013, the building (designed by the Danish Henning Larsen firm) won the EU's prestigious Mies van der Rohe Award—achieving the goal of putting Iceland on the world architectural map. And in 2019, a once-shelved plan for a massive new residential and commercial quarter next to it was finally under construction.

Harpa's honeycombed facade, designed by Danish-born Icelandic artist Ólafur Elíasson, is the most-loved part of the building: In summer the windowpanes reflect the light in patterns, and in winter they're illuminated in pretty colors. The choice of location, parroting the harborside opera house cliché that started in Sydney, unfortunately separates Harpa from the rest of downtown across a busy four-lane road. But photographers drool over the building, and find lots of great angles to shoot. Don't miss the view from the far end of the pier that extends to the right of the building; from there, the facade is reflected in the harbor along with sailboats.

Be sure to step inside, where you're bathed in the light of those many windows. The dominant interior materials are black concrete and red wood, evoking the volcanic eruptions that have shaped Iceland. To enjoy the building's full effect, catch a performance (see options under "Entertainment in Reykjavík," later) or take a tour.

Cost and Hours: Lobby free to enter, daily 9:00-22:00; box office open daily 12:00-18:00; café and gift shops, tel. 528-5000, www.harpa.is.

Tours: In summer, a 30-minute guided tour for 1,750 ISK runs hourly 11:00-16:00. Some tours include a musical performance in the concert hall in an exclusive viewing area. For a brisk intro to Iceland's natural and human diversity, watch *Iceland in a Box,* an immersive video projected on four walls (1,500 ISK, every half-hour daily 10:00-17:30, 15 minutes).

Old Harbor Area

Reykjavík's Old Harbor—about a 10-minute walk west of Harpa—isn't a creaky, shiplap time capsule, but an industrial-feeling port. Tucked around the busy berths and piers are a few seafood restaurants, kiosks selling boat trips, and (at the far end) a smattering of museums. To get here, walk out from downtown (10 minutes), or take bus #14 to the Mýrargata stop.

▲Exploring the Harbor

To get your bearings at the harbor, stand on the seaward side of the turquoise-colored sheds (which house some recommended restaurants) and face the bobbing boats. This "old" harbor was built only in the 1910s, on reclaimed land. (For much of its history—back when Reykjavík was a farm, then a small town—there was good anchorage, but no real harbor.) Today, heavy traffic has moved to the newer container terminal farther along

the peninsula. The harbor serves a mixture of excursion boats, small craft, the coast guard (notice the hulking gray ships with red-and-blue trim), and a few fishing trawlers that bring their catch to processing plants. A single small cruise ship can also moor in the harbor (larger ones use the cruise terminal farther out of town).

On your left is the Ægisgarður pier, lined with ticket offices for several whale-watching tours (described next), as well as bike tours. On your right, across the harbor, you can see the angular, glass facade of the Harpa concert hall. And the dramatic mountain rising up straight ahead is Esja—six miles away and 3,000 feet high.

Stroll out to the end of the **Ægisgarður pier** to comparison-shop excursion boats, and to get a good look at the hodgepodge of vessels that call this harbor home. At the beginning of the pier, an anti-whaling organization would love to talk you out of sampling whale meat. At the far end (on the left), you'll see part of Iceland's whale-hunting fleet moored (look for the black-and-white boats called *Hvalur 8* and *Hvalur 9*)—an odd juxtaposition with the whale-watching industry all around you.

Back at the base of the pier, in front of Hótel Marina, is a slip where boats are hauled up to be painted (one of the remaining vestiges of the maritime industry here). To extend your visit to the nearby Grandi area—with several sightseeing attractions and eateries—simply follow the footpath between the harborfront and Hótel Marina. For more on this area, see "Grandi," later.

Whale Watching and Other Boat Trips

Whale watching out in Faxaflói bay is a popular Reykjavík activity. While it can be enjoyable to get out on the water—and catching a glimpse of a whale is undoubtedly exciting—it's a substantial investment of time and money, particularly given that you may see nothing at all. Before deciding to go on a whale-watching cruise, read the description on page 47. As an alternative to a pricey whale-focused trip, consider a faster and cheaper boat trip—such as to the island of Viðey (see later). And if you want to be assured of seeing "whales"—very up-close—you may prefer a visit to the Whales of Iceland exhibit, a short walk away (described later, under "Grandi," later). If you're traveling around Iceland, be aware there are also whale-watching opportunities in the north, in the Akureyri area and in Húsavík (both covered in The Ring Road chapter).

The many boat-tour companies with ticket booths along the Old Harbor's Ægisgarður pier are fiercely competitive, offer-

ing much the same experience. For the latest prices, schedules, and details, check each company's website, look for brochures locally, or stop by the sales kiosks. The most established outfit is **Elding** ("Lightning," described later); others in-

REYKJAVÍK

clude **Whale Safari** (www.whalesafari.is), **Special Tours** (www.specialtours.is), and **Ambassador** (www.ambassador.is). While Elding is typically the most all-around reliable choice, check the latest online reviews to survey the pros and cons of each one. For comparison's sake, I've outlined Elding's offerings here. Prices are typically a bit cheaper if you prebook directly online, where you'll usually find special offers.

Whale Watching: The **classic** whale-watching trip is three hours and runs daily all year, weather permitting (from 6/day mid-June-Aug to 1/day Dec-Jan; adults 11,000 ISK, children 7-15 pay half-price, children under 7 free; Ægisgarður 5, tel. 519-5000, www.elding.is). You'll pay about double for a **"premium"** option on a "RIB"—a rigid inflatable boat that also includes a high-speed zip across the waves. You'll be issued a warm coverall and goggles for this two-hour thrill ride (22,000 ISK, April-Oct only).

Other Boat Trips: Elding and their competitors also run other seasonal boat trips. The **puffin-watching** cruise (May-mid-Aug only) is shorter (1 hour) and cheaper (6,500 ISK adults) than whale watching—so if you're most interested in riding a boat, it's a reasonable alternative. Cheaper still is Elding's 20-minute ferry service to **Viðey Island** (1,600 ISK round-trip, 2/day, mid-May-Sept only; for more on what to do on the island, see page 114). In the early winter (early Oct-early Dec), when the **Imagine Peace Tower** on Viðey Island is illuminated, Elding offers a two-hour cruise for a closer look (8,500 ISK). Anglers enjoy the **sea-angling** trips (3 hours trying your luck catching cod, haddock, mackerel, and catfish, with an on-board grill party at the end, May-mid-Sept only, 15,000 ISK). And in the dark months, you can take a two-hour, late-evening cruise in hopes of viewing the **northern lights** from the water (11,000 ISK, Sept-mid-April at 21:00 or 22:00).

Volcano House

This attraction, a block off the Old Harbor, is just a small theater that shows two volcano videos—it's 50 minutes of fire and fury (including clips of Iceland's most famous recent eruptions: the Westman Islands in 1973, which swallowed up part of the town of Heimaey; and Eyjafjallajökull in 2010, which halted European air traffic). The movies are interesting, particularly if you're not getting beyond Reykjavík and are curious about Iceland's famous volcanoes, but it's pricey. The building also contains a branch of the What's On TI, which has a display of volcanic rocks, crystals, and other stones.

Cost and Hours: 1,790 ISK, daily 9:00-22:00, showings on the hour starting at 10:00, last film begins at 21:00, Tryggvagata 11, tel. 555-1900, www.volcanohouse.is.

Grandi

The long, broad peninsula that juts out beyond the far end of the Old Harbor is an up-and-coming district called Grandi. This former sandbar, built up with landfill, is an odd assortment: A spread-out strip of old warehouses and new big-box stores, but with a lively little waterfront zone (along Grandagarður) where you'll find some excellent eateries, and several sights (which I've listed in the order you'll approach them, if walking from the Old Harbor). At the far tip of the peninsula—a 15-minute walk or short drive away—is a trendy little cultural zone, anchored by the Marshall-húsið arts center.

Saga Museum

The Saga Museum is your best bet for an experience focused on the stories of the early Norsemen who turned Iceland's wilderness into a European community (even the National Museum covers the sagas only tangentially). This place does a valiant job of telescoping the sagas into an educational 35 minutes. The included audioguide takes you on a 17-stop tour of Iceland's Settlement Age, through 17 mannequin scenes—each one rooted in textual evidence from the sagas. While the audioguide is academic enough that it might bore younger or less interested visitors, a treat for kids of all ages awaits at the end: a chance to dress up in Viking garb for a photo.

Cost and Hours: 2,200 ISK, 800 ISK for kids 6-12, includes audioguide, daily 10:00-18:00, Grandagarður 2, mobile 694-3096, www.sagamuseum.is.

▲Aurora Reykjavík: The Northern Lights Center

Many visitors come to Iceland and spend lots of time and money failing to see the northern lights. But this little museum offers a sure-fire, no-risk solution. You'll walk through some sparse exhibits, including one on legends and superstitions that attempted to explain these once-mysterious dancing lights. Then you'll learn a bit about the science of the phenomenon. But the main attraction is a lounge-like theater playing an extremely soothing 38-minute widescreen film on a loop, featuring time-lapse footage of the aurora borealis at points around Iceland, photographed over eight years of cold nights. In the gift shop, enjoy a free coffee, then slip on a pair of virtual-reality goggles and spin around in a chair, tracking the lights as they flutter through the sky. (For more on the northern lights, and how to see them yourself, see the Icelandic Experiences chapter.) Note: If you're heading out to the Pearl, consider spending less to watch the excellent 20-minute Áróra planetarium show there instead (described later).

Cost and Hours: 1,800 ISK, daily 9:00-21:00, Grandagarður 2, mobile 780-4500, www.aurorareykjavik.is.

Sagas of the Icelanders 101

As with tales of Beowulf, King Arthur, and Robin Hood, scholars don't know how much of the Icelandic sagas are historically based and how much are fictionalized. But all agree that the sagas are an essential resource for understanding both Iceland's history and the cultural heritage it shares with mainland Scandinavia.

Icelanders have strong narrative traditions. Before they had a written language, legends and laws were passed down orally. With Christianity around AD 1000 came the Latin alphabet, which Icelandic scribes used to document their history, writing mostly in their own language.

These historical narratives, known collectively as "the sagas," were written on precious vellum (calfskin) mainly in the 13th and 14th centuries. It was the Icelanders who first wrote down the dynamic stories of the early Norsemen—from myths of Norse gods like Óðinn (Odin) and Þórr (Thor) to early histories of Scandinavian warriors and kings. Like the epic poems of the ancient Greeks, the sagas provide a cultural foundation for the Nordic people, stretching all the way through history to the present.

Here's a simplified overview of some of the most famous or influential sagas and other early writings:

The **Book of Settlements** (Landnámabók)—not strictly a "saga"—documents the earliest ninth- and tenth-century settlers in Iceland. This chronicle tells the story of Hrafna-Flóki (the Raven) Vilgerðarson, who followed a bird to Iceland after he'd been blown off course on his way to the Faroe Islands; and the story of Ingólfur Arnarson, who threw two carved pillars overboard and built his settlement where they washed up (Reykjavík). Remarkably, the Book of Settlements lists more than 400 different families, where each one settled, their family tree, and vivid stories of what they encountered here. The much shorter **Book of Icelanders** (Íslendingabók), written by Ari fróði ("the Wise") Þorgilsson in the early 12th century, gives a concise summary of the history of Iceland up to Ari's own time, including the establishment of the Icelandic Commonwealth and the conversion to Christianity.

The **Saga of Erik the Red** (Eiríks saga rauða) and the **Saga of the Greenlanders** (Grænlendinga saga), known together as "the

Vínland sagas," tell of how Eiríkur rauði ("the Red") Þorvaldsson (950-c. 1003)—banished from Norway, then Iceland—founded a Norse settlement in Greenland; and how his son, Leifur heppni ("the Lucky") Eiríksson, explored what we now know as North America.

Egill's Saga *(Egils saga Skallagrímssonar)* tells the story of Egill Skallagrímsson (c. 904-c. 995). Egill is a fascinatingly complex figure: Swarthy and ugly, he was both a fearsome champion warrior and a tender-souled poet. When he was just seven years old, after losing a game, a furious Egill buried his ax in the head of his opponent—claiming his first of many victims. And yet, Egill composed his first poem at the tender age of three, and went on to author some of the loveliest verse in Icelandic literature (after two of his children died, Egill composed the heartbreaking "Lament for My Sons"). Egill's Saga tells of his tortured relationship with his equally short-tempered father, Skalla-Grímur ("Grímur the Bald"); his friendship and rivalry with his dashing brother, Þórólfr; his relationship with his foster sister, turned-sister-in-law, turned wife, Ásgerður; his run-ins with the powerful witch Gunnhildur; and his clashes with his nemesis, King Harald Fairhair of Norway.

Njál's Saga *(Brennu-Njáls saga)* tells the story of wise Njáll Þorgeirsson and his best friend, the gallant Gunnar Hámundarson. Things take a tragic turn—as they always do in the sagas—as early Iceland's penchant for escalating blood feuds spirals out of control, culminating in several tragic deaths. (Spoiler: The protagonist is also known as Brennu-Njáll—"Burning Njáll.")

Icelanders also recorded mythic histories much older than the settlement of Iceland. **Völsunga Saga,** which may have roots in the fifth-century conquests of Attila the Hun, is a sprawling, epic tale of the Völsung clan, including Sigurðr Fáfnisbani ("Slayer of the dragon Fáfnir"), which has inspired artists from Richard Wagner to J. R. R. Tolkien. The two Eddas—the anonymous **Poetic Edda** and Snorri Sturluson's **Prose Edda**—contain ancient poetry that records the myths of the Germanic pagan religion.

Snorri Sturluson (1179-1241)—who also wrote **Heimskringla,** the history of the Norwegian kings—was himself a dynamic figure whose life is described in **Sturlunga Saga.**

For a hefty (and I mean hefty) sample of some of the better-known sagas, pick up *The Sagas of the Icelanders,* a good, brick-like English translation edited by Robert Kellogg. If you're headed to Snæfellsnes, see the sidebar in the Snæfellsnes Peninsula chapter for the many sagas specific to that area.

Reykjavík Maritime Museum (Sjóminjasafnið í Reykjavík)

This exhibit covers Reykjavík's connection to the sea, tracing its history from remote farm to bustling capital—partly thanks to its role as a fishing, shipping, and maritime center. You'll see plenty of well-described artifacts telling the story of the seafood industry and the evolution of the harbor, models of fishing vessels, and vintage fish-processing machinery. You'll learn why stockfish (naturally dried in the cold Reykjavík wind) was so important on early voyages, how boats gradually evolved from rowing and sailing to industrial trawlers, and how radios and navigational technology improved over time.

Cost and Hours: 1,700 ISK, daily 10:00-17:00, Grandagarður 8, tel. 411-6300, www.borgarsogusafn.is.

▲Whales of Iceland

Tucked unassumingly in a box-store zone a five-minute walk beyond the museum strip, this attraction fills a cavernous warehouse with life-size models hanging from the ceiling of the whales found in the waters around Iceland. The models are impressively detailed, bathed in a shimmering blue light, and painted on Styrofoam.

Cost and Hours: 2,900 ISK, 1,500 ISK for kids ages 7-14, free for kids under 7, includes audioguide, daily 10:00-17:00, Fiskislóð 23, tel. 571-0077, www.whalesoficeland.is.

Getting There: The exhibit is a little tricky to find. From the Maritime Museum and recommended Grandi restaurants along Grandagarður, walk to the end of the first long, white-and-turquoise warehouse building with eateries and boutiques, then turn left on Grunnslóð and walk one long block. You can also take bus #14 to the Grunnslóð stop, or drive (free parking right in front).

Visiting the Museum: Get the included audioguide and, as you walk one species at a time, enjoy the serious 30-minute education on these amazing creatures—all with the additional audio backdrop of gleeful children around you.

Begin with the smaller marine mammals: dolphin, narwhal, orca. Then step into a vast space to ogle the majestic giants: pilot whale, humpback whale, sei whale, bowhead whale, minke whale (the one you'll see on local menus—fittingly suspended above the museum café), *Moby Dick*-style sperm whale, and the largest specimen, the blue whale—which can grow up to 110 feet long and (they say) has a tongue as big as an elephant. While this is very expensive considering the brief amount of time most visitors spend here, it's legitimately educational and scratches your Icelandic-whale itch.

▲FlyOver Iceland

A block beyond Whales of Iceland, this attraction offers a thrilling virtual flight over stunning Icelandic scenery. You'll be strapped into a flight simulator, then lifted off your feet toward a big wrap-around screen, where you'll have the sensation of soaring over Iceland's volcanoes, coastline, farmlands, and islands. You'll be spritzed by "clouds" and smell the flowers and the sulfur. (It's very similar to the popular "Soarin'" attraction at Walt Disney theme parks.) The whole experience lasts about 30 minutes, including 20 minutes of setup and a nine-minute "flight." While it's quite expensive—and the "Icelandic history" lessons that precede the ride are silly (lacking the substance of other Reykjavík attractions)—as a thrill ride, it's pretty thrilling. (If you're prone to motion sickness, give it a miss.)

Cost and Hours: 4,000 ISK, 2,000 ISK for kids 12 and under, daily 9:00-21:00, Fiskislóð 43, www.flyovericeland.com.

Marshall-húsið Art Center

Filling a converted fish factory at the far tip of the pier (and of interest mainly to art lovers with a car), this arts center hosts several galleries. The big draw is the gallery of Ólafur Elíasson, the renowned Icelandic artist who was born in Denmark and keeps a (private) studio upstairs here. Ólafur—who helped design Reykjavík's Harpa concert hall—specializes in large-scale, multimedia pieces that combine technical precision with intangible elements like light, water, wind, temperature, and movement. The building also has two other artist-run gallery spaces (The Living Art Museum, www.nylo.is; and Kling & Bang, www.this.is/klingogbang) and La Primavera, an appealing **$$$** café/restaurant facing the harbor (generally same hours as galleries, tel. 519-7766).

Cost and Hours: All galleries are free, Tue-Sun 12:00-18:00, Thu until 21:00, closed Mon, Grandagarður 20, bus #14 to Fiskislóð stop.

Nearby: This far tip of Grandi has attracted some trendy businesses. Across the street in a nondescript warehouse zone, you'll find the flagship store of the Farmers Market brand—called **Farmers & Friends**—with updated Icelandic fashion (open daily, www.farmersmarket.is; city-center branch described later, under "Shopping in Reykjavík"), and **Omnom,** a boutique chocolate factory (closed Sun, www.omnomchocolate.com).

OUTSIDE THE CENTER

You'll need a car, a bus, or a boat to reach the sights in this section. Driving is quick and a breeze, and parking is free and easy at all these sights.

Just South of Downtown
▲▲The Pearl (Perlan)

This attraction, housed in the city's former water-storage tanks, ticks off several sightseeing boxes at once: a fine view of the city skyline; engaging high-tech ex-

hibits extolling Iceland's abundant natural wonders; and a top-floor café, also with a stunning view. Seemingly designed to keep tourists happy in bad weather, it's well done and worth the short drive. A visit here is a great primer before you head out to the Golden Circle or Ring Road—or a satisfying substitute if you're only visiting Reykjavík. It's pricey, but even if you skip the museum, the views from the café are worth the short detour.

Cost and Hours: Museum and view deck—3,990 ISK, 1,950 ISK for kids 6-15; museum, view deck, and Áróra planetarium show—4,490 ISK, 2,450 ISK for kids; view deck only—890 ISK; daily 9:00-22:00, last entry one hour before closing, www.perlanmuseum.is.

Seeing the Pearl for Free: It's free to see the basement photo exhibit, and to enjoy the top-floor café, shop, and view from inside. To go outside to the view deck, however, you'll need to pay.

Getting There: For drivers, the Pearl is 100 yards off highway 40, the main drag into town; there's a big, free parking lot. If you're without a car, you can catch an hourly shuttle bus from the Harpa concert hall (typically leaves Harpa at the top of the hour, and the Pearl at the bottom of the hour; 890 ISK for the shuttle also includes the view deck, or your shuttle fare can be applied to a ticket for the exhibits).

Visiting the Pearl: Read the descriptions below before you enter to decide which ticket you want. If there's a line, look for the ticket machines.

The **Wonders of Iceland exhibit** features a variety of informative displays about Iceland's unique environment. The curators have cleverly designed interactive displays to satisfy your curiosity about this volatile island. The volcano exhibit—nearly as good as the Lava Center on the South Coast—vividly teaches about Iceland's cracked-eggshell pastiche of tectonic plates. In the atrium stands a

towering re-creation of the Látrabjarg seabird wall of the Westfjords; aim the binoculars to learn about the many species that call
Iceland home. Nearby is a small whale-watching exhibit and the
entrance to the ice cave—an artificial, 300-foot-long cave actually
made of ice brought in from a glacier, designed to teach chilly visitors how glaciers hold clues to a thou-
sand years of history (such as stripes of
ash from various volcanic eruptions). At
15°F, the ice cave is a frigid highlight
for many (don't worry—they provide
jackets). Climbing up through the ice
cave, you reach an exhibit on glaciers,
with a 180-degree immersive video
screen that lets you "stand on top" of
Iceland's biggest glacier, plus poignant
time-lapse videos of the world's great
glaciers receding. Also on this floor is a
detailed exhibit about aquatic creatures
that live in Iceland's seas and rivers.

The 20-minute **Áróra planetari-
um show** explains the northern lights with a sweeping after-dark
tour of Icelandic landmarks. With eye-popping visual effects and
an engaging mix of science and folklore, it offers a thrilling introduction to the aurora borealis for summertime visitors (or disap-
pointed wintertime cloudy-day visitors) who won't have the chance
to see it in person. It plays on the ground floor on the half-hour,
usually in English (confirm at the desk).

After touring the museum, climb to the top floor for the dome
and the **view.** Under the dome on the top floor is **$$ Kaffitár café,**
with a short menu of good food, as well as the posh **$$$$ Út Í
Bláinn** ("Out in the Blue"), serving pricey modern Icelandic food.
One floor down is a branch of the Rammagerðin gift shop (free
to ogle the view from its windows), and the door to a 360-degree
panorama of the city and surrounding countryside, well-explained
by orientation tables. From here, Reykjavík lines up on its hilltop
around the spire of the Hallgrímskirkja church, while in the op-
posite direction, you'll see the downtown airport that connects the
capital to far-flung Icelandic outposts.

Nearby: Around the Pearl is the forested **Öskjuhlíð** hill, with
walking paths, WWII ruins (signboards explain them), many rab-
bits, the temple for Iceland's revived pagan religion (the "first Norse
temple built here in a thousand years," www.asatru.is), and a large
cemetery (Fossvogskirkjugarður).

Southwest of Downtown
Seaside Stroll

For a break from sightseeing (if the weather's nice), join the locals for a stroll along the paths on the south side of the Reykjavík peninsula. There are plenty of diversions and good places for a picnic, especially at low tide, when you can walk down onto the rocks and sand. Start near the streets called Ægisíða and Faxaskjól (take bus #11; see the "Greater Reykjavík" map at the beginning of this chapter).

Northeast of Downtown
▲Viðey Island

On a nice day, spend an afternoon enjoying the views of the sea and the mountains from this island a few hundred yards offshore. It's a relaxing escape from the crowds in the city, though it takes a little work to reach. But, it gets you into the Icelandic outdoors inexpensively and without a trip out of town. Viðey's rich bird life is readily evident—watch your step—and bird-watchers may spot golden plovers, godwits, snipe, greylag geese, and oystercatchers. The island also has an interesting history that dates back to the 10th century. An Augustine monastery stood on Viðey during the Middle Ages, and during the early to mid-20th century, the island was home to a bustling port.

Getting There: You have two options for reaching Viðey (schedules below). From the Old Harbor in the city center, Elding runs a direct but infrequent ferry (2/day, mid-May-Sept only, 20 minutes). Or—for a more frequent and much shorter connection—go to the Skarfagarðar ferry dock, right next to Reykjavík's cruise-ship terminal, where a small passenger ferry makes a five-minute crossing to the island (take bus #16 from the Hlemmur bus junction—look for the stop hidden behind the white building with the red, peaked roof—and ride six stops to Skarfagarðar). Drivers park for free by the Skarfagarðar dock. Grab a free island map on board the ferry.

Cost and Hours: The ferry is 1,600 ISK round-trip from either the Old Harbor or Skarfagarðar, and is covered by the Reykjavík City Card; sights on the island are free. You have the option of cruising to the island from one harbor and returning to another, if you wish. Ferries from the Old Harbor leave daily mid-May-Sept at 11:50 and 14:50 (none off-season); last return from island at 17:30. Hourly ferries from Skarfagarðar leave mid-May-Sept daily 10:15-17:15, last return from island at 18:30; Oct-mid-May Sat-Sun only 13:15, 14:15, and 15:15, last return from island at 16:30. Ferry info tel. 519-5000, www.elding.is.

Visiting the Island: Above the island's dock, the large, restored **house** from the 1750s is the oldest in the capital area. It was originally built for Iceland's Danish governor, but he chose to live in Reykjavík instead. Inside is a modest **$** café, a free exhibit about the island, and a free WC. Next door, look into the small, traditional church, which is almost as old (from the 1760s).

From where you land, you can stroll to either end of the island in about 25 minutes. To the left, the west part of the island is empty grassland except for a series of columnar basalt statues by American sculptor Richard Serra. To the right, the road through the east part of the island leads to an **abandoned village** that, in the 1920s, had a port almost as important as Reykjavík's. You can enter the old village school (its last class was in 1941) to view a photo exhibit on the island's history—and use the WC.

A five-minute walk to the left of the café is the **Imagine Peace Tower**—paid for by Yoko Ono, the widow of murdered Beatle John Lennon. The cylindrical white pedestal, inscribed with "Imagine Peace" in several languages, launches a powerful vertical pillar of light each year from October 9, Lennon's birthday, until December 8, the day he died (www.imaginepeacetower.com).

In Laugardalur, East of Downtown

Though modest by international standards, the Laugardalur (LOY-gar-DA-lurr) valley makes a pleasant outing on a nice day and lets you hang out with Icelandic families and their kids. You pay to enter the zoo and amusement area (the adjacent botanic garden is free). A lovely café in the gardens serves meals, and there's also an indoor ice rink. Nearby are the big, excellent Laugardalslaug swimming pool (described later) and the Reykjavík Art Museum's Ásmundarsafn branch (see listing, earlier).

Getting There: Take bus #2, #5, #15, or #17 to the Laugardalshöll stop and walk 10 minutes downhill to the parking lot and entrance.

Family Park and Zoo (Fjölskyldu- og Húsdýragarðurinn)

The park and zoo combines animal exhibits, amusement-park rides, and a giant playground area. You'll see Icelandic farm animals—pigs, cows, horses, sheep—plus a seal pool, birds, reindeer, rabbits, and a small aquarium. The website lists feeding times (click on "Program"). The park is open all year, but in winter it's a bit desolate, especially on weekdays, and most rides are closed.

Quick Icelandic horse rides for little kids are offered year-round (Sat-Sun at 14:00). If you're hungry, you can grab a meal at the nondescript café, or stop by one of the hot-dog or ice-cream stands and enjoy a picnic at the outdoor tables with grills.

Cost and Hours: 1,900 ISK, covered by Reykjavík City Card, less for kids; rides cost about 250-750 ISK, or buy a day pass for 2,300 ISK, free parking; daily 10:00-18:00, mid-Aug-May until 17:00; Múlavegur 2, 411-5900, www.mu.is (yes, that's the Icelandic word for "moo").

Botanic Garden (Grasagarður)

Next to the Family Park and Zoo, the city-run botanic garden showcases local trees, herbs, flowers, and other plants. Dotted with ponds and small white bridges, it's a soothing place for a stroll. And buried in the garden is the excellent **$$ Flóran café** (described later, under "Eating in Reykjavík"), which makes a visit worthwhile even on a rainy day (free, daily 10:00-22:00, Oct-April until 15:00, tel. 411-8650, www.grasagardur.is).

Nearby: Follow the parkland five minutes downhill from the gardens (past the ponds and bridges) to an open grassy area. Here you can see the remains of the washing troughs and channels where city residents used to do their laundry in hot spring water, all the way up to the 1970s. Outdoor posters tell the story, and give you a feel for how fast the country has modernized.

Ice Rink (Skautahöllin)

Next to the parking lot for the zoo and gardens is the city's indoor ice rink with public skating most afternoons—a useful bad-weather option (entry including skate rental-1,500 ISK, less for kids; closes for several weeks in summer, confirm current hours on website; Múlavegur 1, tel. 588-9705, www.skautaholl.is).

FARTHER EAST OF REYKJAVÍK

The Árbær Open-Air Museum is just on the outskirts of town, while the **Halldór Laxness House** is farther east, roughly on the way to or from the Golden Circle loop. If you're efficient, you may be able to squeeze one of these into your Golden Circle day trip. Or you can consider these as easy side-trips from the capital—each is about a 30-minute drive from downtown.

▲Árbær Open-Air Museum (Árbæjarsafn)

Reykjavík's open-air museum is a modest collection of old buildings and farm animals—meant to help visitors envision Icelandic life in the 1800s. Homes hold period furnishings and reward those with the patience to poke around and ask questions; while everything is described in English, exhibits seem designed for Icelandic families. At the far edge of the property, the four attached houses (one with a

sod roof) are the only ones that were originally located here; walking through them, you can see how each successive generation added its own wing. The grounds—tucked next to a subdivision, with a highway rumbling along the horizon—are underwhelming, especially if you've visited the lush open-air museums elsewhere in northern Europe. But the exhibits compensate.

Try to time your visit to coincide with the 13:00 hour-long guided tour (included in admission). In the weeks before Christmas, the museum opens with a holiday spirit on Sundays from 13:00 to 17:00.

Cost and Hours: 1,700 ISK, covered by Reykjavík City Card, free for kids under 17. Museum open daily 10:00-17:00, Sept-May 13:00-17:00. Café (waffles and snacks) open June-Aug daily 11:00-17:00 and on the Sundays before Christmas. Kistuhylur 4, tel. 411-6300, www.borgarsogusafn.is.

Getting There: The museum is at the end of the street called Kistuhylur, just off busy highway 49. The easiest bus connection from downtown is #16 from Hlemmur to the Strengur/Laxakvísl stop.

Nearby: Very close to the open-air museum is one of the capital region's best neighborhood swimming pools, **Árbæjarlaug** (described later). If you're considering trying this Icelandic custom, bring your swimsuit and go for a dip after your museum visit.

Halldór Laxness House (Gljúfrasteinn)
Iceland's most famous author, Nobel Prize winner Halldór Laxness (1902-1998), lived in a house called Gljúfrasteinn ("Canyonstone"). The house has been preserved as a museum; an audioguide explains each room. The backyard borders on a rushing stream.

Cost and Hours: 1,200 ISK, daily 9:00-17:00; shorter hours off-season and closed Mon; Nov-March closed Sat-Mon; tel. 586-8066, www.gljufrasteinn.is.

Getting There: It's one of the last houses on the right as you drive up the Mosfellsdalur valley on highway 36, about 25 minutes from downtown Reykjavík. You can easily combine Laxness's house with a visit to Þingvellir, but doing the house plus the whole Golden Circle in a day is too much.

Background: Born in Reykjavík, Halldór Guðjónsson was the eldest son of parents who started life poor. His father worked in road construction, and bought a farm at Laxnes in Mosfellsdalur when Halldór was three. Halldór grew up in the valley and started to write as a teenager. Like many Icelanders of his time, he took a surname (based on the farm where he grew up) instead of using his traditional patronymic. In the 1920s and 1930s he traveled in Europe and America, and converted to Catholicism. In 1945, he settled at Gljúfrasteinn, close to where he grew up, with his second wife. Here he lived comfortably, but not lavishly.

Over his lifetime, Laxness wrote more than a dozen novels, some brilliant...and others barely readable. *Independent People* (in Icelandic, *Sjálfstætt fólk*) is the best known. He also wrote short stories, plays, poetry, travel books, memoirs, and other nonfiction. In his writing, Laxness concerned himself strongly with social justice and the struggles of working people. Icelanders on the political right forbade their children to read his books, and cringed when he received the Nobel Prize; those on the political left loved him and felt he told the truth. In the end, no one could deny that he was a gifted writer and a person of insight and compassion.

Experiences in and near Reykjavík

▲▲▲Thermal Swimming Pools

The vast majority of tourists head straight for the Blue Lagoon, but never consider diving into Iceland's many thermal swimming pools. That's a shame, because—while they lack the atmospheric lava-rock landscape and opaque water—these pools are more authentic and local...and they're much cheaper. They offer a relaxing way to unwind from a busy day of sightseeing, and warm you up in cold weather. You can still visit the Blue Lagoon, but consider complementing it with a swim in a community pool.

There are more than a dozen pools to choose from in the greater Reykjavík area, each one run by the local municipality. The more recently built pools in the suburbs are typically more spacious, with more elaborate waterslides and at least one weatherproof indoor pool—making them well worth a short drive or bus ride. Of the ones I list below, only the first two are within walking distance of downtown. (If doing day trips by car, swing by a pool for a relaxing dip at the end of a long day.) Any Icelander you ask will have a favorite pool and can rattle off its advantages and disadvantages. The recommended pools below are definite winners.

How to Visit: As they're designed for Icelanders, these pools do come with some special etiquette and can be intimidating to outsiders. Read the "Thermal Waters" section on page 44, and you'll have a smooth, comfortable visit.

Cost: Pools in Reykjavík charge 1,000 ISK. The pools in Seltjarnarnes and Hafnarfjörður provide the same experience for a little less—950 and 600 ISK, respectively. In Reykjavík, a shareable 10-entry ticket costs 4,650 ISK, which saves money with only five entries (for example, a couple visiting three times). These are adult rates—kids get in for less. You can bring your own towel, or rent one for 600 ISK; swimsuits are also available for rent or sale.

Hours: On weekdays, most swimming pools in the capital area open early in the morning (before 7:00) and stay open until 22:00. On weekends, pools open a little later (around 8:00 or 9:00) and may close earlier in the evening (often 18:00 or even earlier)—confirm hours online at www.reykjavik.is/en/swimming-pools. Note that most pools close on national holidays. Pools are most crowded after work and school, in the late afternoon; during the day, it's mostly kids and retirees.

▲▲Sundhöllin

Reykjavík's oldest swimming pool—designed by state architect Guðjón Samúelsson in 1937—is the only one within the downtown zone. Parts of the complex retain a classic, antique feel, though the newer outdoor section (from 2017) feels modern and engaging. For nondrivers, the central location makes it an easy choice for sampling a thermal pool. From the windows by the ticket desk, look down over the outdoor section, with city sprawl beyond. From here, the old-fashioned, tiled men's changing rooms are to the left along with a couple of hot pools and a sauna. To the right are both women's changing rooms and additional ones for men, and a variety of pools to choose from. The two sections—indoor and outdoor—are connected by a staircase or elevator; if you enter near one section, don't miss the other (Barónsstígur 45a, 5-minute walk from Hlemmur bus junction or Hallgrímskirkja, limited free street parking in front, tel. 411-5350).

▲Vesturbæjarlaug

This compact 1960s-era pool, in a somewhat posh neighborhood near the university, is a good all-around choice for those staying downtown (20-minute walk, or take bus #11, #13, or #15). While nothing fancy, it offers a look at a typical suburban pool; it's close enough to the center to catch a few tourists, but has a predominantly neighborhood feel. It's outdoor-only, with a  small lap pool, a wading area, hot pots, a steam room, and a sauna (corner of Hofsvallagata and Melhagi, free parking in front or on the street nearby, tel. 411-5150).

Nearby: The burger/hot dog stand immediately in front of the pool is a local favorite. For something classier, the recommended Kaffihús Vesturbæjar café is across the street. And next door is a branch of the delicious Brauð & Co bakery. After your soak and meal, you can explore the neighborhood—a mellow coastal walk is just a couple of blocks away.

▲▲Árbæjarlaug

Farther from the center, this complex wins for nicest modern design (from the 1990s)—and may be the most appealing all-around choice. A soaring glass dome covers its small indoor section, from which you can swim right outside to an interconnected series of pools, including a lap pool, large warm pool with bubbles and waterfalls, modest water slide, several hot pools, and a steam bath. While there's a lot of variety, it's compact and manageable, and looks out over a wooded valley with the sprawl of Reykjavík on the horizon (Fylkisvegur 9, tel. 411-5200). It's a 20-minute drive from downtown, or take bus #5 or #16 to the Fylkisvegur stop. Árbæjarlaug is just off highway 1—convenient for those coming back from Golden Circle or South Coast day trips. It's also handy to combine with a visit to the nearby Árbær Open-Air Museum.

▲Laugardalslaug

The country's largest pool is a bit industrial-feeling and long in the tooth, but it's big enough to offer a wide variety of entertaining options. As you step out of the locker room, the left side is all business (including a pool of seawater that's pumped in from the coastline) and the right side is all fun (with a thrilling waterslide tower). A short bus ride east of the center, Laugardalslaug is next to the official Reykjavík youth hostel and sports complex. It's a good option if you're staying nearby, if you want to go swimming late on a weekend evening, or on major holidays like Christmas or New Year's Day, when it's typically the only pool open (Sundlaugavegur 30, bus #14 to Laugardalslaug stop, big free parking lot on Reykjavegur just before the pool complex, tel. 411-5100).

▲Sundlaug Seltjarnarnes

This small, cozy residential pool is frequented mainly by locals (10-minute drive or bus ride from the center on #11, or a 40-minute walk). It's outdoor-only, and has easy parking, nice views, a modest water slide, and a cozy wading and lounging area (on Suðurströnd in Seltjarnarnes; bus #11 to Íþróttamiðstöð Seltjarnarness stop, tel. 561-1551, www.seltjarnarnes.is).

▲Ásvallalaug

The best indoor pool in the capital area, and arguably the best family pool overall, is on the outskirts of Hafnarfjörður (the bedroom community south of Reykjavík, which you'll drive through on the way in from the airport). From downtown Reykjavík, it's a 20-minute drive or a long 45 minutes by direct city bus. Opened in 2008, it has a full-size lap pool, a large wading pool, a large and shallow family pool, a good water slide, and hot pools; the only outdoor facilities are two small hot pools. It's a great bad-weather destination with a big parking lot (Ásvellir 2, Hafnarfjörður, bus #1 to Ásvallalaug stop, tel. 512-4050, www.hafnarfjordur.is). You could stop in downtown Hafnarfjörður to eat afterward (see recommendations later in this chapter), or drive to the cheap cafeteria at IKEA, which is on the way back to Reykjavík.

Heated Beach: Nauthólsvík

Nauthólsvík, maintained by the city of Reykjavík, is an artificial beach *(ylströnd)* in a sheltered part of the shoreline, where you can bathe in an area heated with excess geothermal water from the city's heating system. This can be fun on a nice summer day, although you'll find better facilities and services at the regular pools (free, possible charge for changing facilities; daily 10:00-19:00, limited hours and 650 ISK charge mid-Aug-mid-May, off Nauthólsvegur, bus #5 to Nauthóll/HR stop, free parking, or walk from here to the Pearl, tel. 511-6630, www.nautholsvik.is).

Also Consider...

Lágafellslaug, a large, new pool in the town of Mosfellsbær (about 9 miles northeast of downtown Reykjavík), has a small indoor section. It's convenient if driving between Reykjavík and the Golden Circle (Þingvellir) or the north (toward Akureyri; Lækjarhlíð 1a, Mosfellsbær, mobile 617-6080, www.mosfellsbaer.is).

Álftaneslaug, with a high waterslide and the country's only wave pool, is in the formerly separate town of Álftanes (on the peninsula due south of Reykjavík). This pool cost so much to build that the town went bankrupt and merged with neighboring Garðabær (Breiðmýri, Garðabær, tel. 550-2350, www.gardabaer.is).

Sundlaug Kópavogs, an older pool in the town of Kópavogur, is handy for those staying nearby (Borgarholtsbraut, Kópavogur, tel. 570-0470, www.kopavogur.is).

More Experiences

The following activities are described in more detail in the Icelandic Experiences chapter.

Horseback Riding

Several horse farms on the outskirts of Reykjavík run riding tours for tourists.

Volcanic Underground Tours

Two pricey subterranean excursions exploring Iceland's volcanic origins are close to Reykjavík. At the very expensive Þríhnúkagígur ("Inside the Volcano"), you're lowered 400 feet into a vast chamber inside a 4,000-year-old dormant volcano (4-6 hours including pickup from Reykjavík hotel). More affordable is **Raufarhólshellir** ("The Lava Tunnel"), where you are guided through a 5,000-year-old lava tube (1-hour basic tour, 3-4 hour "adventure" tour, about 45 minutes from Reykjavík). See page 37 for more info and other volcanic-exploration opportunities.

Shopping in Reykjavík

While you'll find plenty of shopping opportunities, don't expect any bargains: Iceland has almost no manufacturing industry of its own, so many items are imported and quite expensive. My shopping advice emphasizes items that are produced or at least designed in Iceland.

Store Hours: Most shops are open at least Mon-Fri 10:00-18:00; on Saturdays, many close earlier. Sundays are unpredictable—larger or tourist-oriented shops remain open, while others close. In general, touristy shops on the main shopping streets downtown (Laugavegur and Skólavörðustígur) have longer hours in the evening and on Sundays.

WHERE TO SHOP

Downtown Reykjavík seems designed for shoppers—you'll find plenty of temptations as you window-shop along the main drag, **Laugavegur.** Dozens of stores along here run the gamut from gaudy "puffin shops" to high-end craft and design boutiques; a few highlights are mentioned in the next section.

Don't be so mesmerized by Laugavegur that you miss **Skólavörðustígur,** the charming street leading up from Laugavegur to Hallgrímskirkja. It's lined with more authentic-feeling small boutiques. I've listed some of my favorites in the next section, but here's a quick rundown: Near the bottom are large branches of Geysir (fashion), Rammagerðin (top-end souvenirs), and Eymundsson (books). Farther up—especially

around the intersection with Týsgata—you'll find an enticing assortment of one-off boutiques, including the 12 Tónar record shop and the Handknitting Association of Iceland.

Jewelry is a popular item along here, including at **Orrifin** (with funky style, at #17A) and **Fríða** (#18). This street also specializes in ceramicists; look for **Stígur** (a collective showcasing the work of seven artists, at #17B) and **Kaolin** (at #5). It also has some eclectic fashion boutiques, such as **Yeoman** (at #22B). **Nikulásar-kot** features delicate, handmade dolls and ornaments infused with Icelandic folk culture (at #22). Many of these stores have their own little workshops attached, where you can watch artisans at work.

WHAT TO BUY
Sweaters and Other Icelandic Fashion

At the top of many shopping lists is a handmade Icelandic wool sweater *(lopapeysa)*. Knitting is a major pastime in this nation where

sheep outnumber people, and where hobbies get you through the dreary winter months. Traditional Icelandic designs—often with classy one- or two-tone patterns radiating from the neck—are both timeless and stylish. A good, handmade sweater starts at around $200; they tend to be bulky, so you'll need room in your luggage.

Classic Sweaters: The best place for a traditional sweater (as well as other knitwear and yarn) is the cozy little **Handknitting Association of Iceland** (Handprjónasambandið) shop; browse their website before you go (Mon-Fri 9:00-22:00, Sat until 18:00, Sun 10:00-18:00, Skólavörðustígur 19, tel. 552-1890, www.handknitted.is).

Secondhand Sweaters: For a quality sweater at a lower price (closer to $100-120), consider buying secondhand. For a big, well-stocked vintage clothing shop, stop by **Spúútnik** on the main drag (Laugavegur 28) or their second location, **Fatamarkaður** (at the Hlemmur bus junction, Laugavegur 126). Or, to support a good cause while you shop, the **Red Cross** charity shop has three very central locations (at Laugavegur 12B, Laugavegur 116, and Skólavörðustígur 12). Note that these places line up conveniently—allowing you to comparison-shop easily in about a 10-minute stroll along Laugavegur. There's also a **Salvation Army** (Hertex) branch at the corner of Garðastræti and Ránargata. You'll find plenty of sweaters at the **Kolaportið flea market**—but don't expect top quality there (Sat-Sun only, see listing on page 93).

Stylish Sweaters (and Other Fashion): Icelandic designers enjoy updating traditional sweater designs. **Farmers & Friends** has a full range of fashionable Farmers Market-brand clothes, including sweaters (www.farmersmarket.is). Their downtown outpost is at Laugavegur 37, while their flagship store is at the far end of the Old Harbor's Grandi pier (near the Marshall-húsið arts center) at

Hólmaslóð 2. **Geysir**—another modern Icelandic fashion designer with several branches downtown (including at Skólavörðustígur 7 and Skólavörðustígur 16, www.geysirshops.is)—also has contemporary sweater styles, as do various one-off boutiques along Laugavegur.

Other Clothes: 66°North, Iceland's best-known outerwear brand, is *the* place to buy waterproof shells and puffy vests. Two convenient locations are right on the main drag (Laugavegur 17 and Bankastræti 5). For a better deal, drivers can head to their suburban outlet store with deep discounts—typically about half off (buried in the back of the Skeifan shopping zone, Mon-Fri 9:00-18:00, Sat from 10:00, Sun from 12:00, Faxafen 12, bus #5 to Fen stop, tel. 535-6676, www.66north.is).

Icelandic Souvenirs

Visitors enjoy browsing for keepsakes emblazoned with the Icelandic flag, or an outline of the country. Other popular items include stuffed puffins, whales, cheesy Viking-themed trinkets, and polar bears (they don't live in Iceland, but every now and then, a stray bear drifts across from Greenland on an iceberg). Laugavegur and adjoining streets seem to specialize in tacky souvenir outlets; most of what you'll find is overpriced and made in China. Here are a few better options for more authentically Icelandic souvenirs.

Locally produced and inexpensive, edible souvenirs may be your best bet. **Icelandic candy** is unusual and hard to get outside of Iceland, but easily found at discount grocery stores (Bónus and Krónan), which are generally cheaper and have a better selection than the duty-free airport shops. Cooks on your shopping list might enjoy some of the wide variety of flavored **Icelandic sea salts** (including birch-smoked, seaweed, black lava, and arctic thyme).

Gift shops at the **National Museum** and the **Harpa** concert hall are a little more sophisticated than the norm (see listings in "Sights in Reykjavík").

Rammagerðin, a venerable, high-end boutique, offers extremely expensive but good-quality Icelandic handcrafts and design (www.rammagerdin.is). The main branch—with a row of taxidermy puffins looking out the window—is in the heart of the main shopping zone at Skólavörðustígur 12; other branches are just up the street at Skólavörðustígur 20, at Bankastræti 9, at the Pearl, and at the airport ("Iceland Gift Store").

Iceland, like other Nordic countries, has a knack for clean, eye-pleasing design. **Hrím Eldhús** has a fun selection of upscale kitchen gadgets and housewares—a mix of Icelandic and international (Laugavegur 32); their sister shop just up the street, **Hrím Hönnunarhús,** has a more eclectic selection (Laugavegur 25, www.hrim.is). Also check out **Epal Icelandic Design** (Laugavegur 70); and **Hjarta Reykjavík,** with colorful images of the city's cute houses (Laugavegur 30, www.hjartareykjavikur.com).

Bookstores
Some English-language books on Iceland are available much more cheaply back home; others are hard to find outside the country.

Mál og Menning, along Laugavegur, is Reykjavík's most enjoyable-to-browse bookstore. In the big atrium, tables are piled with intriguing choices, including many English books and travel guides, and there's a tiny café upstairs (Mon-Fri 9:00-22:00, Sat-Sun from 10:00, Laugavegur 18, tel. 580-5000, www.bmm.is).

Three downtown branches of **Eymundsson,** Iceland's answer to Barnes & Noble, are at Austurstræti 18, Skólavörðustígur 11, and Laugavegur 77 (similar hours to Mál og Menning, www.penninn.is).

Those with a car or bike can visit the **publishers' outlet store** in the Grandi neighborhood beyond the Old Harbor, which has a large selection of books, maps, and posters offered at a 15 percent discount (Mon-Fri 10:00-18:00, Sat 11:00-16:00, closed Sun, Fiskislóð 39, tel. 575-5636, www.forlagid.is).

Other Ideas
12 Tónar, downtown at Skólavörðustígur 15, is a local institution. Their shop specializes in Icelandic music, and they run their own label—making this a beloved outpost for indie music lovers. You're welcome to listen to whatever you like over a free cup of coffee (Mon-Sat 10:00-18:00, Sun from 12:00, www.12tonar.is).

Greater Reykjavík's two big **shopping malls** (Kringlan and Smáralind) are convenient for drivers and give you a nontouristy look at Icelandic commercial life.

REYKJAVÍK

Entertainment in Reykjavík

PERFORMANCES AT HARPA

Iceland's cutting-edge arts center (described earlier, under "Sights in Reykjavík") has several venues, big and small, that offer entertainment options every night of the year. Three serious musical ensembles are based at Harpa: the **Iceland Symphony Orchestra** (Sinfóníuhljómsveit Íslands, http://en.sinfonia.is), the **Icelandic Opera** (Íslenska Óperan, http://opera.is), and the **Reykjavík Big Band,** a large jazz ensemble (Stórsveit Reykja-

víkur, www.reykjavikbigband.com). All three regularly perform in the 1,800-seat main hall, called Eldborg. Harpa's smaller halls (200-1,100 seats) host many types of performances. Check the schedule for a chance to combine a show with a visit to the most architecturally exciting building in Iceland (box office open daily 12:00-18:00, often later during performances, http://en.harpa.is).

Among the shows at Harpa are likely to be the following tourist-oriented options (all designed for an English-speaking audience). While these may change, each one has been running for several years (though sometimes only in summer). All are entertaining and (aside from the first and last) designed to give visitors insights into Icelandic culture.

Reykjavík Classics is a daytime concert offering a 30-minute presentation of some "greatest hits" of classical music (Mozart, Beethoven, etc.) performed by a smaller ensemble from the symphony. As it's short and nearly always in the main hall, it's an affordable way to experience Harpa without investing too much time and money...but there's very little Icelandic about it (2,600-3,300 ISK, usually at 12:30, http://en.harpa.is).

Pearls of Icelandic Song presents a collection of traditional tunes sung by operatically trained soloists with piano accompaniment. The formal presentation of these informal songs may not be to everyone's taste, but it's authentically Icelandic (3,900 ISK, usually at 18:00 in the main hall, www.pearls.is).

Icelandic Sagas: The Greatest Hits is a frenetic two-person show that attempts to compress centuries of deep and complex Icelandic heritage into 75 minutes, with plenty of humor and costume changes. Though more entertaining than educational, you'll come away with a somewhat better appreciation for Iceland's history (4,900 ISK, usually at 19:30 in the Northern Lights Hall, www.icelandicsagas.com).

How to Become Icelandic in 60 Minutes is a breezy, irreverent, and sometimes naughty one-man comedy show that's a 15-step lesson on what it takes to live like a local on the "biggest little island in the world" (4,850 ISK, usually at 19:00 in the smaller Kaldalón, www.h2become.com).

Múlinn Jazz Club hosts weekly jazz performances in an intimate setting (2,500 ISK, typically Wed and Fri at 21:00, www. facebook.com/mulinnjazzclub).

OTHER PERFORMANCES

The Gamla Bíó theater—a classic old cinema in the heart of town—periodically presents **Saga Music 101.** A contemporary songwriter has written music designed to tell some of the saga stories with English lyrics (4,700 ISK, occasional Wed at 20:00, www. sagamusica.com). The theater hosts other performances, too (check www.gamlabio.is), and its recommended rooftop bar—Petersen Svítan—is a fine venue for a before- or after-show drink.

Various **churches** around Reykjavík present low-key concerts. The big, landmark Hallgrímskirkja offers concerts (mainly on their huge organ) about four times weekly in summer (late June-late Aug, as part of the "International Organ Summer"), and sporadically at other times of year (www.hallgrimskirkja.is). And the cathedral—the modest building next to the parliament, downtown—hosts occasional concerts in its intimate, lovely space (www.domkirkjan.is).

Movies: Bíó Paradís, a beloved art-house cinema just off the main drag downtown, shows international films in their original language with Icelandic subtitles, as well as Icelandic films with English subtitles. Locals kick off weekend revelry at their throwback film series every Friday night—camp classics, '80s movies, interactive screenings (like the *Rocky Horror Picture Show*), and so on. Their bar/café is a popular hangout. The movie lets out just as things get rolling outside (Hverfisgata 54, tel. 412-7711, www. bioparadis.is).

NIGHTLIFE

Reykjavík is renowned for its crazy nightlife. It's pretty simple: Just go downtown any Friday or Saturday night and hit your choice of bars and clubs. Typically, Icelanders come here only on weekends. Many young Icelanders drink at home first (less expensive) before heading downtown between 23:00 and midnight. Higher-end drinking places—hotel cocktail bars, craft-beer specialists, and the like—tend to close on the "early" side...which, in Reykjavík, means midnight on weeknights and 1:00 in the morning on weekends. Harder-partying places stay open until 3:00 or later.

I've recommended some well-established watering holes (see the "Reykjavík Center Restaurants" map, later)—but this scene

Icelandic Music

For centuries, there were few instruments in Iceland, and it was hard to organize an ensemble in a land with difficult travel and no towns or villages. What little music Icelanders had was mostly vocal, using simple melodies in minor keys and lyrics from old ballads and verses, sometimes accompanied by primitive string instruments. At Christmastime, Icelanders danced holding hands in a line while singing traditional verses. When the Pietist movement gained ground among Lutherans in the mid-1700s, music and dance were frowned upon.

But over time, that changed—especially in the 20th century, as Icelanders became wealthier and better tied into European culture. Young Icelanders started to take music lessons, sing in choirs, and play in bands, and both classical and popular music blossomed. Today, Icelanders love to sing along to local folk songs at birthdays or Christmas parties.

The best-known modern Icelandic musician is Björk Guðmundsdóttir—known worldwide by her first name alone. Born in 1965 in Reykjavík to two politically active parents (her father was the head of the Icelandic electricians union for years), Björk sang in choirs as a child. She gained fame as the lead singer of the Sugarcubes, then struck out on her own in 1993. Björk is known for her eclectic musical style, unique voice (which strikes some ears as discordant), energetic performances, and avant-garde fashion sense (most famously, the swan-shaped dress she wore to the 2001 Oscars). Björk has also dabbled in acting, taking home the Cannes Best Actress prize for her lead performance in the 2000 Lars von Trier film *Dancer in the Dark*. While Björk's music

changes quickly. For a more timely take, pick up the latest issue of the *Reykjavík Grapevine* (or read it online at www.grapevine. is) to find what's in, what's on, and which bands or DJs are playing where. The *Grapevine* also publishes a list of best happy hours—good to know about in this pricey city.

If you want company, go on a **guided pub crawl** such as the one offered by CityWalk (2,500 ISK, Fri-Sat at 22:00, mobile 787-7779, www.citywalk.is).

Upscale Cocktails

These options are for those who'd prefer a more sophisticated scene, and don't mind investing in a pricey (2,000-2,500 ISK) but well-crafted cocktail in a memorable setting.

Sophisticated Art Deco Vibe: Right in the heart of town, **Apotek** fills the ground floor of a landmark hotel by renowned architect Guðjón Samúelsson. This stuffy place loves to brag about its many "best cocktails" awards and generous happy-hour deals (half-price drinks 15:00-18:00). More sedate than the rowdy party scene

is not for everybody, her fans are devout. To get a taste for Björk, some of her early albums in Icelandic are available for free on YouTube and well worth listening to. Try *Gling-Gló* (roughly, "Ding Dong"), with accessible but typically idiosyncratic interpretations of jazz standards. Later in her career, Björk moved to England, but still spends a lot of time in Iceland.

Over the last decade or so, other Icelandic bands have become known internationally. Sigur Rós and, more recently, Of Monsters And Men specialize in soaring, bombastic soundscapes (fitting for their dramatic homeland) that often turn up in Hollywood epics. Singer-songwriter Ásgeir is attempting to become the next Icelander to break out in a big way.

Icelandic music fans may enjoy the Icelandic Museum of Rock 'n' Roll, a five-minute drive from Keflavík Airport (see page 180). The 2013 book *Blue Eyed Pop* is also good (buy it at the museum, or from the website of the author, Gunnar Lárus Hjálmarsson, better known as Dr. Gunni; http://blueeyedpopdotcom1. wordpress.com).

Two annual festivals showcase the latest in Icelandic pop music. Iceland Airwaves takes place in Reykjavík in late October/ early November (www.icelandairwaves.is). Aldrei Fór Ég Suður (which loosely translates as "I never moved to Reykjavík") fills Ísafjörður, the largest town in the Westfjords, with young visitors for a few days at Easter (www.aldrei.is). There's also Eistnaflug, a heavy metal festival each July in the eastern town of Neskaupstaður (www.eistnaflug.is), and the famous Þjóðhátíð music festival in the Westman Islands (www.dalurinn.is).

all around it, this is a popular choice for a genteel drink. They also serve a full menu of food—including a decent lunch special—but better restaurants are nearby; come for the drinks and the ambience (daily 11:30-late, Austurstræti 16).

Rooftop Bars: To reach **Petersen Svítan** ("The Petersen Suite"), you'll slip through a side door next to the classic Gamla Bíó theater, then ride the elevator up to a rooftop deck. You can sit in the Old World interior, but the main draw is the large outdoor area, overlooking city rooftops—a delight on warm evenings. Don't miss the spiral stairs up to an even higher deck (open daily from 14:00, happy hour until 20:00, Ingólfsstræti 2a).

The recommended **Loft Hostel** runs a convivial rooftop bar perched above the Bankastræti action, with a city-view deck that's as much a draw for locals as visitors (daily until 23:00, happy hour 16:00-20:00, Bankastræti 7, take elevator to the fourth floor).

By the Harbor: Slippbarinn ("Dry Dock Bar") is one of the best places in town for quality, creative cocktails. The menu is vividly described and fun to peruse, with a few mainstays and lots of seasonal concoctions. A mellow hangout by day, at night it's a big, boisterous, and colorful party. It sprawls through the spacious, creative, industrial-mod lobby of the Icelandair Hótel Marina, right along the harborfront, facing the namesake dry dock (daily 11:30-late, also serves food, occasional DJs or live music, Mýrargata 2).

Craft Beer

Iceland has a burgeoning craft beer scene, including high-end bars where you can focus on sampling local brews. While some proudly feature Icelandic beer, most acknowledge the limits of local brewers and make a point to also offer a carefully curated range of imports. Most craft-beer bars have several taps and a chalkboard listing what's on today. Figure on paying 1,000-1,800 ISK for a pint.

Skúli Craft Bar, named for the statue of the original Reykjavík developer on the downtown square it faces, has a great section of Icelandic craft beers. The prices are high, but the glassy, modern, aboveground space feels inviting and attracts a few locals along with the tourists. At the bar—in front of an illuminated wall displaying bottles like trophies—you can choose between Icelandic brews (marked with red-and-blue stripes) and imports. They also have pleasant outdoor tables (Mon-Thu from 15:00, Fri-Sat from 14:00, Sun from 16:00, happy hour until 19:00, Aðalstræti 9, tel. 519-6455).

MicroBar fills a straightforward cellar with happy drinkers (mostly tourists, thanks to its main-drag location) enjoying an even wider selection of microbrews. They specialize in Icelandic beers—with 14 on tap, and more than 100 in bottles—and is the only craft beer place I saw that offers 5- or 10-beer sampler boards; this being Iceland, you'll pay dearly for each sip (daily from 16:00, happy hour 17:00-19:00, Vesturgata 2, mobile 865-8389).

Ölstofa Kormáks og Skjaldar ("Kormákur and Skjöldur's Tavern") is a nice hybrid of the beer-geek places mentioned earlier. Because it's tucked away from Laugavegur, it feels more local, with a *Cheers* vibe and a table often filled with regulars. While they do have taps and bottles from local brewers, their draft selection is limited (all from the same brewery, Borg Brugghús); visit for the atmosphere, not a deep dive into Icelandic brews (daily from 15:00, Vegamótastíg 4, tel. 552-4687).

Session Craft Bar pours mostly Icelandic microbrews from its 16 taps in a modern space, one floor above the tourist parade at the intersection of Laugavegur and Skólavörðustígur (daily from 12:00, Bankastræti 14, above the Subway sandwich shop, mobile 690-1938).

Lively Late-Night Bars

These places really get rolling late at night on weekends (though you're welcome to stop by earlier in the evening, when they can already be quite crowded on weekends). Come for Reykjavík's famous social weekend experience, not the drinks.

Kaffibarinn is a classic dive bar right in the center. It's a local institution that still attracts a largely Icelandic clientele. Filling an old house, it can feel crowded and gets pretty wild on weekends; for a mellower visit, check it out on a weeknight (daily from 15:00, good happy-hour deals before 20:00, live DJ at prime times, Bergstaðastræti 1, tel. 551-1588).

Right along the busiest stretch of Laugavegur, you can't miss **Lebowski Bar,** with neon lights, a Dude-Walter-and-Donny bowling theme, 16 versions of white Russians...and, one would assume, owners very nervous that the Coen Brothers' legal team will catch on. It's rollicking, rowdy, and popular with young Americans (open long hours daily and nightly, Laugavegur 20b, tel. 552-2300).

A block from Ingólfstorg toward the harbor is a cluster of rowdy, hole-in-the-wall bars for late-night revelry. **Húrra** is the all-around favorite, with a big dance floor and great DJs and live music (Tryggvagata 22, tel. 571-7101). **Paloma** is a late-late-late-night weekend option with a dance floor and a vaguely nautical vibe; it's bigger than most, so it feels less claustrophobic (Naustin 1, above The Dubliner). And **The Dubliner** is the city's most central Irish pub (daily from 12:00, Naustin 1, below the Paloma).

In addition, several of the places listed under "Eating in Reykjavík," later, can be good places to grab a drink, including the hipster café **Kaffi Vínyl** and **Kex Hostel.**

Sleeping in Reykjavík

Reykjavík is an expensive place to spend the night. With its spike in tourism, the city is bursting at the seams, demand is soaring, and lots of new places are opening up (or old places expanding) each year—some of them great, others not.

I've focused my listings on relatively established hotels offering good value. Given how pricey Reykjavík's hotels are (especially in the center), I'd also give guesthouses and private rentals (such as on Airbnb) a serious look; youth hostels are especially good for solo travelers. Real hotels are very expensive, especially in the center, and can easily cost $400 a night in summer. Guesthouses (figure $200 a night) and Airbnb (closer to $100 a night) give you more value for the money and a more local experience.

Whatever you do, book any accommodations well in advance, as the best places sell out early for the peak summer months, or if your trip coincides with a major holiday.

In Iceland, prices drop a lot if you are willing to share a bathroom. If a place has the option of a shared bathroom, I've noted

REYKJAVÍK

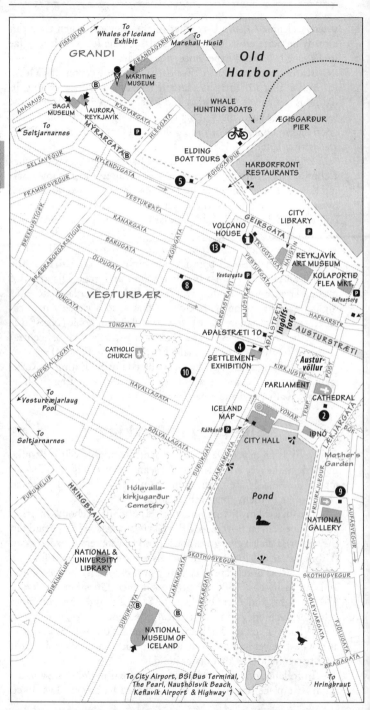

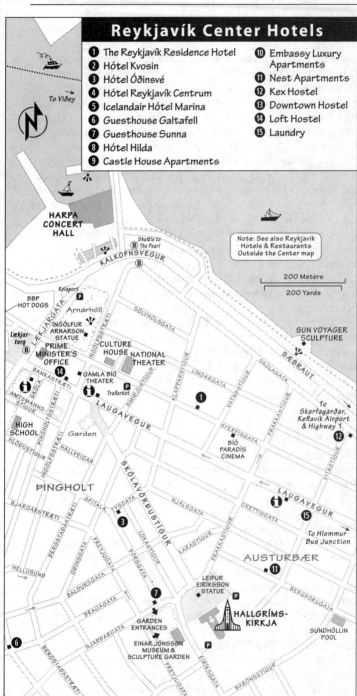

Reykjavík Center Hotels

1. The Reykjavík Residence Hotel
2. Hótel Kvosin
3. Hótel Óðinsvé
4. Hótel Reykjavík Centrum
5. Icelandair Hótel Marina
6. Guesthouse Galtafell
7. Guesthouse Sunna
8. Hótel Hilda
9. Castle House Apartments
10. Embassy Luxury Apartments
11. Nest Apartments
12. Kex Hostel
13. Downtown Hostel
14. Loft Hostel
15. Laundry

REYKJAVÍK

To Viðey

HARPA CONCERT HALL

Shuttle to The Pearl

KALKOFNSVEGUR

Note: See also Reykjavik Hotels & Restaurants Outside the Center map

200 Meters
200 Yards

BBP HOT DOGS
Kolaport
Arnarhóll
INGÓLFUR ARNARSON STATUE

SUN VOYAGER SCULPTURE

Lækjartorg
PRIME MINISTER'S OFFICE
CULTURE HOUSE
NATIONAL THEATER

LÆKJARGATA
HVERFISGATA
SÖLVHÓLSGATA
INGÓLFSSTRÆTI
KLAPPARSTÍGUR
LINDARGATA
VATNSSTÍGUR
SKÚLAGATA
FRAKKASTÍGUR
SÆBRAUT

BANKASTRÆTI
GAMLA BÍÓ THEATER
Traðarkot
SMIÐJUSTÍGUR

To Skarfagarðar, Keflavík Airport & Highway 1

AMTMANNS-STÍGUR
SKÓLA
PÓSTHÚSSTRÆTI
LAUGAVEGUR
HVERFISGATA

HIGH SCHOOL
Garden
HLÖÐUSTÍGUR
INGÓLFSSTRÆTI
HALLVEIGAR

BÍÓ PARADÍS CINEMA

ÞINGHOLT

SKÓLAVÖRÐUSTÍGUR

LAUGAVEGUR
GRETTISGATA
VITASTÍGUR

BJARGARSTRÆTI
BERGSTAÐASTRÆTI
SPÍTALA
TYGGATA
ÓÐINSGATA
FREYJUGATA
ÞÓRSGATA
LOKASTÍGUR
NJÁLSGATA
KÁRASTÍGUR
FRAKKASTÍGUR

To Hlemmur Bus Junction

HELLUSUND
BALDURSGATA
BRAGAGATA

AUSTURBÆR

GARDEN ENTRANCES
LEIFUR EIRÍKSSON STATUE

BERGÞÓRUGATA

NJARÐARGATA
EINAR JÓNSSON MUSEUM & SCULPTURE GARDEN

HALLGRÍMS-KIRKJA

SUNDHÖLLIN POOL

EIRÍKSGATA
FREYJUGATA
BARÓNSSTÍGUR

that in the listing—a shared bath often knocks down the price considerably.

Without a car, stay downtown. It's more convenient for restaurants, nightlife, much of the worthwhile sightseeing, and bus-excursion pickups (though if noise is an issue, request a quiet room, as it can get loud on weekend nights). With a rental car, it can make better sense to stay outside the downtown core—where lodgings cost less and parking is easy. There are fewer hotels and guesthouses in the suburbs, but Airbnb and other rentals are abundant.

For car travelers, the outlying community of Hafnarfjörður is a nice compromise. It has its own little downtown core and quaint old houses, but free parking and less noise and traffic than Reykjavík. It's strategically situated for those driving to and from the airport, the Golden Circle, the Blue Lagoon, and the South Coast.

City buses run to every corner of the metropolitan area, although some parts are a long ride (with a transfer) from downtown. When scoping out a place to stay, check bus access by plugging the address into the journey planner at www.straeto.is and seeing how long it takes to get to the main downtown stops (Lækjartorg and Hlemmur).

I rank accommodations from $ budget to $$$$ splurge. To get the best deal, contact small hotels and guesthouses directly by phone or email. If you go direct, the owner avoids a roughly 20 percent commission and may be able to offer you a discount. For more information and tips on hotel rates and deals, making reservations, finding a short-term rental, and chain hotels, see the Practicalities chapter.

AIRBNB AND OTHER RENTAL SITES

I've intentionally listed fewer hotels and guesthouses than I normally would for a city of Reykjavík's size. That's because here, even more than elsewhere, I find Airbnb and other short-term rentals to be a much better value than hotels. The bottom line: Iceland is expensive, and staying in nontraditional accommodations can have the single biggest impact on your travel budget.

Airbnb lists plenty of options in the downtown core, and is handy for finding less-expensive suburban accommodations (easier for drivers), while providing a more authentic look at Icelandic life. A search for "Reykjavík" may turn up some of these, but for more options, search for the name of the separate town: Hafnarfjörður, Garðabær, Kópavogur, Mosfellsbær, or Seltjarnarnes.

EXPENSIVE DOWNTOWN HOTELS

If you're going to spend a lot of money, you might as well do it with class. These hotels each offer something special.

$$$$ The Reykjavík Residence Hotel rents out studios,

suites, and apartments in five buildings located within minutes of each other along or near Hverfisgata (a block off Laugavegur). The most notable building, next to the National Theater, was once a private home built in 1912 by a local bigwig who later became prime minister. When the king of Denmark visited in 1926, this is where he stayed. It's been converted into 10 top-end suites, each with a kitchenette. For the best value, ask for the "economy studio," which costs the least, comes with a kitchenette, and is more spacious than most standard doubles you'll find in Reykjavík (includes breakfast, laundry service, Hverfisgata 45, tel. 561-1200, www.reykjavikresidence.is, info@rrhotel.is).

$$$$ Hótel Kvosin, across the street from parliament and the cathedral in a building from 1900, has 24 big suites with full kitchenettes and fine art on the walls (breakfast extra, Kirkjutorg 4, tel. 571-4460, www.kvosinhotel.is, desk@kvosinhotel.is).

$$$$ Hótel Óðinsvé, with 50 modern, stylish rooms and 10 apartments in a blocky shell, sits in a pleasant residential area a short walk from the lively Skólavörðustígur shopping and dining street (breakfast extra, Þórsgötu 1, recommended Snaps Bistro on-site, tel. 511-6200, www.hotelodinsve.is, odinsve@hotelodinsve.is).

$$$ Hótel Reykjavík Centrum boasts a great location, in view of the parliament, in a modernized building with a period facade and 89 rooms. The Settlement Exhibition on Reykjavík's early history is in the basement, centered on archaeological ruins found when the hotel was built in 2001 (breakfast extra, Aðalstræti 16, tel. 514-6000, www.hotelcentrum.is, info@hotelcentrum.is).

$$$ Icelandair Hótel Marina is at the Old Harbor in a long, skinny building that spent many years as the post office's sorting facility. This hotel's location is more interesting and convenient than the other Icelandair hotel, the Natura, and it's also home to the recommended Slippbarinn cocktail bar (includes breakfast, Mýrargata 2, tel. 560-8002, www.icelandairhotels.com, marina@icehotels.is).

GUESTHOUSES AND SMALL HOTELS

These smaller, less expensive properties are generally in converted residential buildings without elevators. Most of these listings give you the option of sharing a bathroom, which brings down the price substantially. When comparing prices, remember to factor in breakfast and parking costs.

Closer In

$$$ Guesthouse Galtafell offers 11 rooms on a quiet street in a handsome neighborhood close to the Pond—and is a convenient five-minute walk from both downtown and the BSÍ bus terminal.

REYKJAVÍK

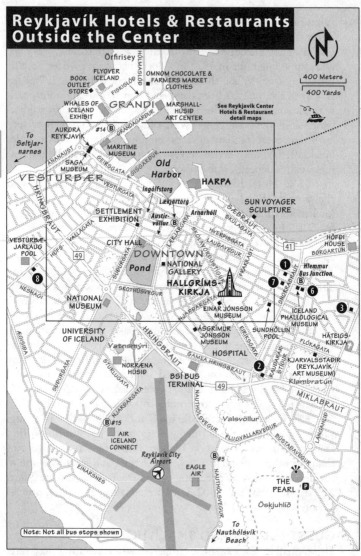

Reykjavík Hotels & Restaurants Outside the Center

One of Iceland's richest merchants and fishing magnates built this attractive house with its crenellated roof in 1916. Breakfast, which costs extra, is served in a cozy, art-filled dining room in the main house (free parking, Laufásvegur 46, mobile 699-2525, www. galtafell.com, info@galtafell.com).

$$$ **Guesthouse Sunna,** just down the street from the big Hallgrímskirkja church, is big and feels more like a hotel than a guesthouse. It offers a range of rooms with shared or private bath—some with kitchens—and some with lots of stairs. There's limited

REYKJAVÍK

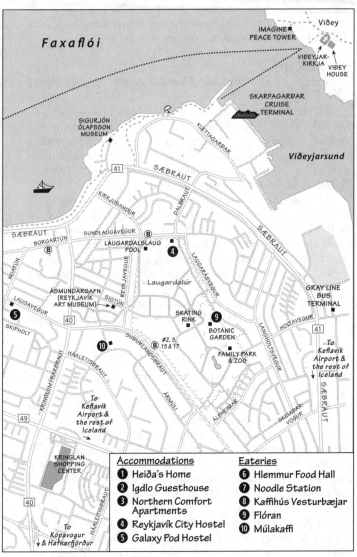

Faxaflói

Viðey

IMAGINE PEACE TOWER

VIÐEYJAR-KIRKJA

VIÐEY HOUSE

SKARFAGARÐAR CRUISE TERMINAL

Viðeyjarsund

SIGURJÓN ÓLAFSSON MUSEUM

KLETTAGARÐAR

41

SÆBRAUT

SÆBRAUT

KIRKJUSANDUR

DALBRAUT

SÆBRAUT

BORGARTÚN

SUNDLAUGAVEGUR

LAUGARDALSLAUG POOL

❹

Laugardalur

LAUGARÁSVEGUR

NÓATÚN

REYKJAVEGUR

SIGTÚN

ÁSMUNDARSAFN (REYKJAVÍK ART MUSEUM)

GRAY LINE BUS TERMINAL

LAUGAVEGUR

❺

SKIPHOLT

40

SKATING RINK

❾

BOTANIC GARDEN

HOLTAVEGUR

41

To Keflavík Airport & the rest of Iceland

SUÐURLANDSBRAUT

#2, 5, 15 & 17

❿

HÁALEITISBRAUT

FAMILY PARK & ZOO

LANGHOLTSVEGUR

ÁRMÚLI

ÁLFHEIMAR

KRINGLUMÝRARBRAUT

To Keflavík Airport & the rest of Iceland

SÆBRAUT

SKEIÐAR-VOGUR

49

KRINGLAN SHOPPING CENTER

HÁALEITISBRAUT

40

To Kópavogur & Hafnarfjörður

Accommodations
❶ Heiða's Home
❷ Igdlo Guesthouse
❸ Northern Comfort Apartments
❹ Reykjavík City Hostel
❺ Galaxy Pod Hostel

Eateries
❻ Hlemmur Food Hall
❼ Noodle Station
❽ Kaffihús Vesturbæjar
❾ Flóran
❿ Múlakaffi

free parking in their courtyard (includes breakfast, Þórsgata 26 at the corner of Njarðargata, tel. 511-5570, www.sunna.is, sunna@sunna.is).

$$$ Hótel Hilda, a lesser value, has 15 rooms, many quite small and tight—but all with private baths. Upper rooms can be stuffy, so ask for one on the first two floors. It's in a pleasant, fairly quiet residential neighborhood just a five-minute walk west of downtown. Pay for street parking in front, or look for free spots a block or two away (includes skimpy breakfast, Bárugata 11, tel. 552-3020, www.hotelhilda.is, info@hotelhilda.is).

Farther Out

For locations, see the "Reykjavík Hotels & Restaurants Outside the Center" map.

$$ Heiða's Home rents 14 tight double rooms (no sinks), all but one with shared bathrooms. It's close to the Hlemmur bus junction, occupying an older building along a busy urban-feeling street at the east end of downtown (no breakfast, shared kitchen facilities, pay on-street parking, lots of stairs, Hverfisgata 102, mobile 692-7654, heidashome@gmail.com).

$ Igdlo Guesthouse (the name is Greenlandic for "igloo") is on the outskirts of downtown, about a 5- to 10-minute walk from the BSÍ bus terminal, in a converted small apartment building on a dead-end street near a busy road. It's a bit hostel-like—all rooms share a bathroom, and most rooms have multiple beds. The exterior and location are ho-hum, but prices are low, downtown is a 15-minute walk away, and there's usually plenty of free on-street parking (kitchen, laundry facilities, rental bikes, family rooms, Gunnarsbraut 46, tel. 511-4646, www.igdlo.com, booking@igdlo.com).

APARTMENTS

These apartments are good for a longer stay, or if you want your own kitchen.

$$ Castle House Apartments at Skálholtsstígur 2a and **Embassy Luxury Apartments** at Garðastræti 40 offer a dozen well-appointed, mostly one-bedroom apartments with kitchenettes in two super downtown locations well-described on their shared website. They also have cheaper studio apartments dubbed **Northern Comfort** in a lesser location at Skipholt 15, a bit outside downtown (pay on-street parking, tel. 511-2166, www.hotelsiceland.net, 4@4.is, see map on page 136).

$$ Nest Apartments rents four units in a three-story building in a quiet spot not far from Laugavegur. The basement is generously called the "ground" floor (2-night minimum, cheaper if you stay a week, pay on-street parking, Bergþórugata 15, mobile 893-0280, www.nestapartments.is, nest@nestapartments.is).

HOSTELS

¢ Kex Hostel ("Cookie")—filling an old cookie factory—is a popular choice for backpackers. While a bit pricey, it's big, close to downtown, and has a popular café that's frequented even by non-guests (lots of stairs, pay on-street parking, Skúlagata 28, a 7-minute walk from the Hlemmur bus junction—see map on page 133, tel. 561-6060, www.kexhostel.is, info@kexhostel.is).

"Official" HI Hostels: These three ¢ listings belong to the Hostelling International network (website for all: www.hostel. is). **Reykjavík City Hostel** is a 45-minute walk or easy bus ride from downtown, conveniently next to the Laugardalslaug swimming pool and close to the Family Park and Zoo (private rooms available, bike rental, playground, free parking, Sundlaugavegur 34—see map on page 136, bus #14 to Laugarásvegur stop, tel. 553-8110, reykjavikcity@hostel.is). **Downtown Hostel** is better suited to travelers without a car (private rooms available, Vesturgata 17—see map on page 133, bus #14 to the Mýrargata stop, tel. 553-8120, reykjavikdowntown@hostel.is). **Loft Hostel** is even more urban, occupying a couple of floors in a downtown building just uphill from the prime minister's office (recommended rooftop bar, elevator, Bankastræti 7—see map on page 133, near the Lækjartorg bus stop, tel. 553-8140, loft@hostel.is).

¢ **The Galaxy Pod Hostel** offers something different: Guests sleep in individual capsules, which give a little privacy and space to lock up valuables. The capsules are a good value for solo travelers, but two people traveling together will do better in a two-bed room at one of the HI hostels listed earlier. It's in an uninteresting neighborhood above a Mitsubishi Motors showroom, a half-hour's walk or short drive from Parliament (elevator, breakfast optional, free parking, Laugavegur 172—see map on page 136; bus #2, #5, #14, #15, or #17 to Gamla Sjónvarpshúsið; tel. 511-0505, www. galaxypodhostel.is, bookings@galaxypodhostel.is).

OUTSIDE REYKJAVÍK, IN HAFNARFJÖRÐUR

If you're renting a car and using Reykjavík as a base for day trips to sights in the countryside, you may find it easier to stay outside downtown in the southern suburb of Hafnarfjörður (HAHP-nar-FYUR-thur). While calling this area "charming" is a stretch, it does get you into a car-friendly zone away from the crowds (parking is easy), and gives you a glimpse of an

authentic Icelandic neighborhood, with restaurants and services in walking distance. And it's strategically located between downtown Reykjavík and points south: the airport, the Blue Lagoon, and the Golden Circle and South Coast.

While I've listed a few traditional accommodations (hotel,

Hafnarfjörður

To Reykjavík

To Reykjavík

8

VÍÐISTAÐA CHURCH

4

To 2

HJALLABRAUT

HERJÓLFSGATA

FLATAHRAUN

40

41

300 Meters

300 Yards

NORÐURBRAUT

VESTURGATA

REYKJAVÍKURVEGUR

To IKEA, Reykjavík, Highway 1 & Ring Road

N

3

HELLISGATA

VESTURBRAUT

Hellisgerði

B

LINNETSSTÍGUR

MAIN HIGHWAY

HISTORY MUSEUM

1

6

Shore Walk

FJARÐARGATA

P

P

B

Thors-plan

HVERFISGATA

AUSTURGATA

Harbor

STRANDGATA

B

LÆKJAR-GATA

HRINGBRAUT

LÆKJARKINN

CHURCH

Hamarinn

Bus to Keflavík Airport

B

VIKING VILLAGE

7

SELVOGSGATA

ÓLDUGATA

BÁRUKINN

41

STRANDGATA

1

5

SUÐURGATA

HRINGBRAUT

HVAMMABRAUT

KALDAKELSVEGUR

SUÐURBÆJARLAUG SWIMMING POOL

Cemetery

ÁSBRAUT

To Ásvallalaug Swimming Pool & Keflavík Airport

MAIN HIGHWAY

41

Accommodations
1 Viking Village Hotel
2 To Hlíð Hótel
3 Edda's Farmhouse in Town
4 Lava Hostel

Eateries
5 Von & Pallett
6 Súfistinn Kaffihús
7 Fjörukráin
8 Noodle Station

B&B, and hostel), you'll often get a better value via Airbnb. Before booking anything with a Hafnarfjörður address, check a map to make sure it's near downtown, rather than in the industrial zone to the east.

Getting There: Downtown Reykjavík is a 15-minute drive away, or a 25-minute ride on bus #1; airport buses stop in the center, but don't offer door-to-door pickup.

If you stay here and drive the Golden Circle or South Coast

day trips, Breiðholtsbraut (highway 413) is a useful shortcut from Reykjanesbraut (highway 41) over to highway 1 in the direction of Selfoss. Your GPS or map app will guide you; otherwise, from highway 41, follow the signs for highway 413 toward highway 1.

$$ Viking Village Hótel, part of the cheesy Viking-themed Fjörukráin restaurant complex, has Viking-esque common areas, but most of its 41 rooms are straightforward, on the small side, and full of heavily varnished wooden furniture; some feel a bit tired. They also have bunk-bedded cabins that sleep up to six (with private baths)—potentially cost-effective for families or small groups. There's a free sauna and hot pots, and the airport bus stops nearby (Strandgata 55, tel. 565-1213, www.fjorukrain.is, booking@vikingvillage.is). Their "Fishermen's Village" annex, called **$$$ Hlíð Hótel,** is a little compound of woody, waterfront cabins on a rustic, sparsely populated point just north of Hafnarfjörður (a 15-minute drive from the main hotel; 20 minutes from downtown Reykjavík). It feels remote, yet is still close to the city (same contact information).

$ Edda's Farmhouse in Town, in a charming and historic residential zone a short walk from town, has three rooms with a shared bathroom, though it may be closing. It's a "farmhouse" because Edda has cats, dogs, and rabbits (Vesturbraut 15, tel. 565-1480, mobile 897-1393, ekaritas@simnet.is).

¢ Lava Hostel, a 15-minute walk north of town, is smaller and more intimate than the hostels in Reykjavík. This nonprofit hostel raises funds for the local Boy Scout troop; they also manage the adjacent campsite. As the name suggests, it's in the midst of an old lava flow (free parking, Hjallabraut 51, tel. 565-0900, www.lavahostel.is, info@lavahostel.is).

HOTELS NEAR THE AIRPORT

It usually makes better sense to stay in Reykjavík (even when arriving or departing at odd hours). Still, given the 45-minute distance between the city and the airport, staying out here does make arrival and departure quicker: Late-night arrivals won't have to blearily pick up a rental car, or wait for an airport bus to slowly fill and rumble into town. Hotels and Airbnb lodgings in Keflavík and Njarðvík, the towns near the airport, are also a bit cheaper than in Reykjavík. But basing yourself out here makes for a much longer drive to the sights on your full days in Iceland, and drastically reduces your choice of bus tours if you're not using your own wheels. A taxi from the airport into Keflavík town can cost as much as 5,000 ISK, so figure that into your budget. For locations, see the "Keflavík Airport Area" map near the end of this chapter.

$$$ Hótel Aurora Star, a hundred yards from the terminal, is the only hotel right at the airport, with 72 rooms. It's undistinguished but gets the job done; has family rooms, free parking, and a restaurant...and starts serving breakfast at 5:00. Prices are less expensive than downtown Reykjavík hotels, but still pricey by international standards (Blikavöllur 2, Keflavík, tel. 595-1900, www. hotelairport.is, airport@hotelairport.is).

$$$ Hótel Keflavík, near the harbor in the center of the town of Keflavík, also offers breakfast from 5:00 and free transport to (but not from) the airport. They have in-house laundry that even nonguests can use. If you arrive on an early-morning transatlantic flight and get a rental car, you could have breakfast here and watch the town wake up (Vatnsnesvegi 12, Keflavík, tel. 420-7000, www. kef.is, stay@kef.is).

Eating in Reykjavík

Iceland's tourist boom has equipped Reykjavík with a surprisingly good range of dining options. You'll dine well here—and it's easier than you might think to eat out without emptying your wallet. My best budget tip is to have your main meal at lunch: If you stick to free drinking water (that's the accepted default), you can come away from a near-gourmet seafood lunch downtown only about $25 poorer. Then, for dinner, save by pic-

nicking, having a light meal at a café, grabbing a cheap takeout or fast-food meal, or finding a restaurant that doesn't increase its prices in the evening—they do exist. For a few specific leads on cheap eats, see the "Budget Bites" sidebar in this section.

I rank restaurants from $ budget to $$$$ splurge, based on average main-course dinner prices; many restaurants also offer a few cheaper items (like burgers or pizza). That said, you get what you pay for—in my experience, a $40 dinner is substantially better than a basic $25 dinner. For a memorable meal, consider splurging on a fixed-price, multicourse dinner (8,000-10,000 ISK). For more advice on eating in Reykjavík, including ordering, tipping, and Icelandic cuisine, see the "Eating" section of the Practicalities chapter.

DOWNTOWN RESTAURANTS
Reykjavík's restaurants—from mom-and-pops to swanky splurges—serve weekday lunch specials for about 2,000-3,000 ISK (this may be a fixed "fish of the day," but sometimes you can choose among several options). Many places close for lunch on week-

ends—or, if open, have a pricier menu. Fancier restaurants become more expensive (sometimes *much* more expensive) at dinnertime.

Given the large tourist crowds, virtually any downtown restaurant (particularly in the $$$ or $$$$ price range) can book up during the busy summer months. In peak season, it's always smart to book ahead; in shoulder season, it's a good idea on weekends.

Fine Dining in Central Reykjavík

These are my favorite places for a classy splurge in the town center. Make reservations if you're going for dinner (all are more affordable at lunch).

$$$$ **Dill** is one of Iceland's finest restaurants (and its only Michelin-star recipient). They serve up high-end, New Nordic-inspired dishes at prices that aren't drastically higher than many other "upper-midrange" places in this pricey town. They often book up weeks or months ahead—reserve as early as possible (Wed-Sat 18:00-22:00, closed Sun-Tue, Laugavegur 59, second floor—above Bónus supermarket, tel. 552-1522, www.dillrestaurant.is).

$$$$ **Grillmarkaðurinn** (The Grill Market) has a rustic-mod, two-story setting, with big split-log counters and a lively

energy. The architecture, furnishings, and food sing a chorus of Iceland; the action at their busy charcoal grill mixes with the smart clientele to create a winning conviviality. Creative dishes allow curious travelers to sample traditional Icelandic "nov-

elty foods" in a modern, palatable way. The slider trio features a few bites each of puffin, minke whale, and Icelandic lobster *(humar)*, and the grilled minke whale steak comes on its own little hibachi. The service is helpful and without pretense (enticing tasting menus worth the high price, Sun-Thu 17:30-22:30, Fri-Sat until 23:00, Lækjargata 2a, tel. 571-7777, www.grillmarkadurinn.is).

$$$$ **Fiskmarkaðurinn** (The Fish Market) is a stylish adventure in Icelandic cuisine, with inventive and artful takes on traditional fare such as fish, shellfish, whale, puffin, lamb, and beef. Or, venture something from their fine selection of sushi. The upstairs and downstairs dining rooms, in an elegant old wooden building, ooze a subtle Asian ambience and have a friendly, attentive staff. This is justifiably a hot spot with locals and travelers, so reservations are smart (Sun-Thu 17:30-22:30, Fri-Sat until 23:00, Aðalstræti 12, tel. 578-8877, www.fiskmarkadurinn.is).

$$$ **Fiskfélagið** (The Fish Company) is a classy splurge, el-

REYKJAVÍK

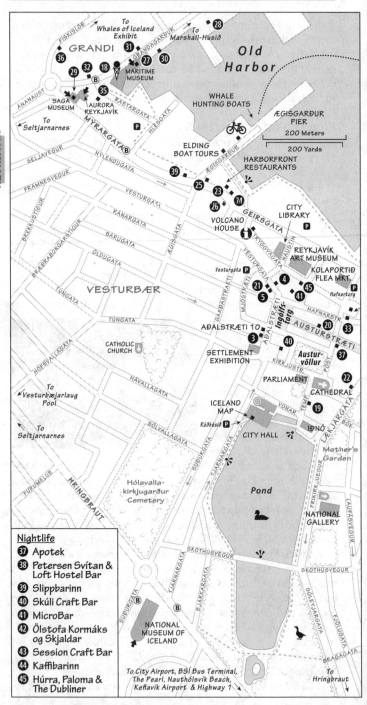

To Whales of Iceland Exhibit

To Marshall-Húsið

GRANDI

Old Harbor

FISKISLÓÐ
GRANDAGARÐUR
ANANAUST
MÝRARGATA
RASTARGATA
HLÉSGATA

MARITIME MUSEUM

SAGA MUSEUM

AURORA REYKJAVÍK

To Seltjarnarnes

WHALE HUNTING BOATS

ÆGISGARÐUR PIER

200 Meters
200 Yards

SELJAVEGUR
FRAMNESVEGUR
BREKKUSTÍGUR
BRÁÐRABORGARSTÍGUR
NÝLENDUGATA
VESTURGATA
RÁNARGATA
BÁRUGATA
ÖLDUGATA
ÁGÍSGATA

ELDING BOAT TOURS

ÆGISGARÐUR

HARBORFRONT RESTAURANTS

CITY LIBRARY

VESTURBÆR

TÚNGATA
TÚNGATA
HOFSVALLAGATA
HÁVALLAGATA
SÓLVALLAGATA

CATHOLIC CHURCH

To Vesturbæjarlaug Pool

To Seltjarnarnes

VOLCANO HOUSE

GEIRSGATA
TRYGGVAGATA

REYKJAVÍK ART MUSEUM

KOLAPORTIÐ FLEA MKT.

Vesturgata

Hafnartorg

MJÓSTRÆTI
GARÐASTRÆTI
AÐALSTRÆTI
VESTURGATA
HAFNARSTR
AUSTURSTRÆTI
PÓSTH.
HAFNARSTR.

AÐALSTRÆTI 10

Ingólfstorg

SETTLEMENT EXHIBITION

Austur-völlur

KIRKJUSTR.

PARLIAMENT

CATHEDRAL

ICELAND MAP

Ráðhúsið

CITY HALL

VONAR
TEMP
LÆKJARGATA
LÆKJARBOK

IÐNÓ

Mother's Garden

Hólavalla-kirkjugarður Cemetery

SÚÐURGATA
TJARNARGATA

Pond

NATIONAL GALLERY

FRÍKIRK.-VEGUR
LAUFÁSVEGUR

FÚRUMELUR
HRINGBRAUT

SKOTHÚSVEGUR
SÓLEYJARGATA
FJÖLNISVEGUR

B
SÚÐURGATA
TJARNARGATA
BJARKARGATA
BRAGAGATA

NATIONAL MUSEUM OF ICELAND

To City Airport, BSÍ Bus Terminal, The Pearl, Nauthólsvík Beach, Keflavík Airport & Highway 1

To Hringbraut

Nightlife
- 37 Apotek
- 38 Petersen Svítan & Loft Hostel Bar
- 39 Slippbarinn
- 40 Skúli Craft Bar
- 41 MicroBar
- 42 Ölstofa Kormáks og Skjaldar
- 43 Session Craft Bar
- 44 Kaffibarinn
- 45 Húrra, Paloma & The Dubliner

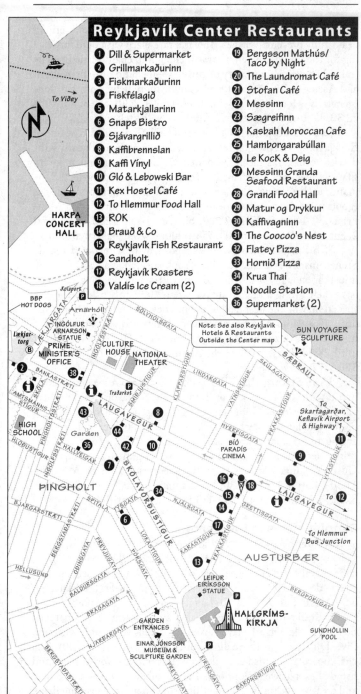

Reykjavík Center Restaurants

1. Dill & Supermarket
2. Grillmarkaðurinn
3. Fiskmarkaðurinn
4. Fiskfélagið
5. Matarkjallarinn
6. Snaps Bistro
7. Sjávargrillið
8. Kaffibrennslan
9. Kaffi Vínyl
10. Gló & Lebowski Bar
11. Kex Hostel Café
12. To Hlemmur Food Hall
13. ROK
14. Brauð & Co
15. Reykjavík Fish Restaurant
16. Sandholt
17. Reykjavík Roasters
18. Valdís Ice Cream (2)
19. Bergsson Mathús/ Taco by Night
20. The Laundromat Café
21. Stofan Café
22. Messinn
23. Sægreifinn
24. Kasbah Moroccan Cafe
25. Hamborgarabúllan
26. Le KocK & Deig
27. Messinn Granda Seafood Restaurant
28. Grandi Food Hall
29. Matur og Drykkur
30. Kaffivagninn
31. The Coocoo's Nest
32. Flatey Pizza
33. Hornið Pizza
34. Krua Thai
35. Noodle Station
36. Supermarket (2)

Note: See also Reykjavik Hotels & Restaurants Outside the Center map

REYKJAVÍK

egantly filling the dark, stony cellar of a historic house and serving beautifully presented dishes. This is a rare place with outdoor seating for the rare day when it's warm enough to enjoy. Their French-trained chefs meld a variety of cuisines—including Mediterranean and Asian—with a respect for Icelandic ingredients and traditions (generally Mon-Fri 11:30-14:30 & 17:30-22:30, Sat-Sun 17:00-22:30, Vesturgata 2a, tel. 552-5300, www.fiskfelagid.is).

$$$ Matarkjallarinn (The Food Cellar) manages to be one of Reykjavík's most popular restaurants despite being in a nearly windowless cellar. It's nicely decorated and feels more contemporary than its neighbor Fiskfélagið—with live piano adding to the romance each evening. They serve Icelandic and international dishes (good-value fixed-priced meals and daily fish combo, open Mon-Fri 11:30-14:30 & 17:00-23:00, Sat-Sun 17:00-23:00, Aðalstræti 2, enter from Vesturgata, tel. 558-0000, www.matarkjallarinn.is).

$$$ Snaps Bistro is Parisian-posh, with a menu of mostly French-inspired dishes. The lively, sophisticated, glassed-in setting is just far enough off the main drag to attract locals alongside tourists. Their filling and artfully prepared 2,000-ISK fish-of-the-day special may be the best deal in town. They accept reservations only until 18:30, and it's busy at dinner—reserve to eat early, or plan to wait a bit (jazz club downstairs, Sun-Thu 11:30-23:00, Fri-Sat until 24:00, Þórsgata 1, in the recommended Hótel Óðinsvé, tel. 511-6677, www.snaps.is).

$$$$ Sjávargrillið (The Seafood Grill) is a respected seafood house with a corner location right along Skólavörðustígur where Chef Gústav Axel Gunnlaugsson grills up delicious fish, lobster, puffin, and lamb. They have a nice selection of lighter main courses and sushi for smaller appetites...and budgets. The cozy, tight interior is decorated with Icelandic driftwood gathered during Chef Gústav's culinary travels (blowout fixed-price dinners, Mon-Thu 11:30-14:30 & 17:00-22:30, Fri-Sat until 23:00, Sun 17:00-22:30, Skólavörðustígur 14, tel. 571-1100, www.sjavargrillid.is).

Simpler Meals in the Center

$ Kaffibrennslan, a café and bar owning a prime spot on Laugavegur, offers a tasty selection of sandwiches, baked goods, coffee drinks, Icelandic beer, and wine. Eat in or grab a seat on their streetside patio for prime people-watching (Mon-Fri 8:00-late, Sat 9:00-13:00, Sun 9:00-21:00, Laugavegur 21, tel. 511-5888).

$ Kaffi Vínyl has a hipster-chic ambience, with mismatched furniture, old record players, and an extensive record collection (live DJs spin mostly mellow tunes Wed-Sat after 20:00). The chalkboard menu lists an eclectic selection of flavorful meat and fish dishes, plus vegan options. They also have a full bar with beer and creative cocktails, making this a cozy spot for an evening drink (order food at the bar, Mon-Fri 15:00-23:00, Sat-Sun from 11:00, Hverfisgata 76, tel. 537-1332).

$ Gló, a local vegan favorite, is a smart choice for a quick, inexpensive, healthy meal in the center. It's a cafeteria with an inviting space filling the upstairs of a characteristic old Reykjavík house just off the main street (daily 11:00-22:00, Laugavegur 20b).

$$ Kex Hostel runs a big café open to all, serving breakfast, burgers, lunch specials, and reasonably priced dinners, plus beer, wine, and cocktails in an ex-industrial space with lots of couches and a water view (daily 7:00-10:30 & 11:30-23:00, close to Hlemmur and the *Sun Voyager* sculpture at Skúlagata 28, tel. 561-6060).

$$ Hlemmur Food Hall (Hlemmur Mathöll): This food hall—with 10 trendy eateries filling a former bus depot—is worth the short walk to the end of Laugavegur. You'll find a variety of food stands, a *smørrebrød*-and-aquavit bar, and a branch of the delectable bakery Brauð & Co. Anchoring the scene is Skál!, a cocktail bar serving small plates of delicately prepared modern Scandinavian fare (a good choice if you just can't decide). There's ample shared seating, or pull up a stool at one of the bars. It feels urban and urbane, yet affordable and easy (daily 8:00-23:00, at the Hlemmur bus junction, Laugavegur 107, www.hlemmurmatholl.is).

Frakkastígur Street

For a small-plates lunch or dinner, or a pastry-and-coffee break, head to hip Frakkastígur street. Between Hallgrímskirkja and Laugavegur you'll find some of Reykjavík's most appealing little eateries separated by a grungy but colorful square, with my favorite fish-and-chips joint close by.

$$ ROK, filling a black house with a grass roof across from Hallgrímskirkja, is a hip, lively joint buzzing with energy. Serving small, stylishly presented plates featuring fish, meat, and vegetarian options, the menu lets you try a variety of imaginative dishes for a reasonable price. Dine in the two-story, wood-beamed interior or out on the cozy patio with a church view (lunch specials, daily 11:30-23:00, Frakkastígur 26A, tel. 544-4443).

$ Brauð & Co (Bread & Co.) is an artisanal bakery with a storefront slathered with a wild graffiti mural. Inside, the pastry chefs work like clockwork—churning out hot-from-the-oven cinnamon rolls *(snúðar)*, danish *(vínarbrauð)*, croissants, sourdough loaves, and seasonal pastries. While the to-go pastries are the

REYKJAVÍK

hot item (literally), they also sell simple sandwiches and have two stools at the window. If you get takeaway, there's a little square with benches just up the street (daily 6:00-17:30, Sat-Sun until 17:00, Frakkastígur 16, mobile 776-0553). Understandably popular, this bakery is expanding, with locations in the Hlemmur Food Hall (described earlier), and in the suburbs. Keep an eye out.

$ Reykjavík Fish Restaurant feels like a fish restaurant in Reykjavík should—rustic with a cool young staff, cranking out basket after basket of fresh fish. It's a tough choice: the best fish-and-chips or *plokkari* (also known as *plokkfiskur*)—a traditional hash of shredded cod, potato, and onion (daily 11:30-22:00, Frakkastígur 12, tel. 578-5656).

$$ Sandholt, around the corner on Laugavegur, is a refined, upscale-feeling bakery. At the front counter they offer a fine selection of great pastries (including croissants and danish), and serve breakfast and light meals at tables in the back (daily 7:30-21:00, Laugavegur 36, tel. 551-3524).

Coffee: Reykjavík Roasters is the city's best, top-end gourmet coffee shop, where each grind of beans is weighed to ensure a perfect pull. Flip through their vintage record collection while you wait, or just hang out in the bohemian-chic interior (Mon-Fri 8:00-17:30, Sat-Sun until 17:00, intersection of Frakkastígur and Kárastígur, tel. 517-5535).

Ice Cream: Valdís, set back from the street just down from the Reykjavík Fish Restaurant, slings fresh ice cream flavors by the scoop (daily 11:30-23:00, Frakkastígur 10).

Near Ingólfstorg

$ Bergsson Mathús is a favorite with local office workers. Inviting and cozy, it has a healthy hippie feel and serves mostly vegan dishes, with some fish and vegetarian options (daily 7:00-16:00, a block off the Pond, behind the cathedral at Templarasund 3, tel. 571-1822). During the summer, Bergsson turns into a Mexican food joint—**Taco by Night**—in the evening, specializing in tacos and Mexican refreshments.

$$ The Laundromat Café is more café than launderette, and a handy place to enjoy comfort food (burgers, sandwiches, and fish) whether or not your laundry is spinning downstairs. The open-feeling space—decorated with photographs of laundromats around the world, big maps, and a bookshelf bar—is understandably popular with travelers. There's also a children's play area in the basement (Mon-Fri 8:00-23:00, Sat-Sun from 9:00, Austurstræti 9, tel. 587-7555).

$$ Stofan Café ("Living Room") is straightforward, central, and popular, with a warm living-room vibe that caters to coffee drinkers playing chess or cards. Overlooking a colorful (and touristy) slice of Reykjavík, it's a tempting place to escape the drizzle for a soup or sandwich (daily 10:00-22:00, Vesturgata 3, tel. 546-1842).

$$ Messinn, in a bright space on busy Lækjargata, has a pleasant, woody, Westfjords ambience. It features an appealing menu of fish and seafood, including "fish pans" served in sizzling skillets. You're welcome to share the large 4,400-ISK fish pan, making a budget meal for two (lunch specials, daily 11:30-14:00 & 17:00-22:00, reservations smart, Lækjargata 6b, tel. 546-0095, www.messinn.com).

IN THE HARBOR AREA

These eateries are a short walk north of downtown.

$ Sægreifinn (The Sea Baron) is a local institution beloved for its affordable lobster soup. A few decades back, commercial fisherman Kjartan Halldórsson began cooking out of his boathouse by request. His reputation grew, and his little fish joint became a harborfront fixture. Kjartan recently died, but one of his employees now runs the place, keeping the same easygoing, keep-it-simple spirit. (A wax statue of Kjartan is under the stairs in the back dining room.) There's no real menu: It's lobster soup or grilled seafood—whatever's in the display case, clearly labeled and priced (including potatoes and sample-size servings of minke whale). They also have fermented shark appetizers—just ask. Line up at the register, order your soup and/or seafood skewers, then find a seat at a shared table in the sprawling interior (squeeze past the bar to find more tables). There's a children's play area and outdoor seating with a windbreak in the back (daily 11:30-22:30, Geirsgata 8, tel. 553-1500).

$$ Kasbah Moroccan Cafe brings a slice of North Africa to the North Atlantic, serving traditional Moroccan fare such as *briouat* (stuffed pastries), *tagine* (slow-cooked meats and vegetables), couscous, *tangia* (stew), *pastilla* (meat pie), and tea. Dine in the comfy, atmospheric interior or out on the patio (daily 11:00-23:00, Geirsgata 7B, tel. 588-8484).

Burgers: $ Hamborgarabúllan is a fun little 1950s-style, street-corner hamburger joint, with a clutter of stools and service set to classic rock (daily 11:00-22:00, Geirsgata 1, tel. 511-1888). **$$ Le KocK**—just across the street—is a hipper, pricier place that regularly wins local "best burger" awards (daily 11:30-23:00, Tryggvagata 14); attached to that is **Deig** bakery, with bagel sandwiches (Sun-Fri 7:00-19:00, Sat from 12:00).

At the Far End of the Harbor, in Grandi

The peninsula called Grandi—which defines the far (western) end of the harbor area—has sprouted some good eateries that are worth the extra walk from the center.

$$ Messinn Granda Seafood Restaurant, at the Reykjavík Maritime Museum, has a big, comfortable dining hall with harbor views. They offer a quality 2,800-ISK seafood lunch buffet (11:30-14:00), with seven kinds of fish, as well as vegetables, soup, bread, and coffee (daily 11:30-17:00, Grandagarður 8, tel. 562-1215).

$ Grandi Food Hall (Grandi Mathöll) is an edible festival of Icelandic dishes filling a former fisherman's hall (Sjávarklasinn, "Ocean Cluster House") with eight small bars and restaurants. It's youthful and creative, very local, and family-friendly, with shared tables and big windows overlooking the harbor. It's easy to find something for any taste here. You could go for traditional Icelandic or choose from one of several more modern international choices (Sun-Wed 11:00-21:00, Thu-Sat until 22:00, Grandagarður 16, mobile 787-6200, www.grandimatholl.is). Hiding down a hallway is a lounge where you can peek into the actual fish processing floor where the day's catch is sorted and sold; you can even watch the fish auction take place every weekday at 13:00.

$$$ Matur og Drykkur (Food and Drink), inside the Saga Museum, prides itself on time-tested recipes that others might dismiss as old-fashioned. Here, chefs update those traditional dishes for modern tastes. For starters, give the fish-skin chips or fried cod tongues a nibble. Then consider the trademark "halibut" soup (not made with halibut—which is illegal, for complicated reasons), cod's head (more delicious than you'd imagine), or arctic char smoked over burning sheep's dung (ditto).

You'll also find lots of barley and seaweed. Despite the casual, rustic bistro ambience, the food is high-end (Wed-Sun 17:00-23:00, closed Mon-Tue, reservations smart, Grandagarður 2, tel. 571-8877, www.maturogdrykkur.is).

$$ Kaffivagninn (The Coffee Cart) perches on a pier overlooking bobbing boats. The understated nautical decor is charming, and its seaward glassed-in patio is tempting on a sunny day. The main dishes are Icelandic home-cooking classics like fish cakes, *plokkfiskur* (fish hash), and cod, plaice, and arctic char filets; on weekdays, soup and coffee are included (Mon-Fri 7:30-21:00, Sat-Sun from 9:00, Grandagarður 10, tel. 551-5932, www.kaffivagninn.is).

$ The Coocoo's Nest is a somewhat trendier-feeling café just across the street from the Reykjavík Maritime Museum, and lacks its view. But it does have a cozy, split-level, stay-awhile interior and a tempting, brief menu—ideal for escaping the elements and enjoying soup, salad, or sandwiches. It serves a rotating menu—tacos one night, pizza the next, then Italian (Tue-Sat 11:00-22:00, Sun until 16:00, closed Mon, Grandagarður 23, tel. 552-5454).

$$ Flatey fires up delicious, Neapolitan-style pizzas in a trendy modern atmosphere. If you want pizza a step above Domino's, this is the place (Mon-Fri 11:00-22:00, Sat-Sun from 12:30, Grandagarður 11, tel. 588-2666).

Ice Cream: Valdís, a couple of doors down, is a local favorite offering creative flavors. The name is a pun—it's a woman's first name, but can also be read as "Power Ice Cream" (daily 11:30-23:00, Grandagarður 21).

OUTSIDE DOWNTOWN
These places are best for drivers (all have free parking) but can also be reached by bus.

In Vesturbær, West of Downtown
$ Kaffihús Vesturbæjar, an inviting neighborhood café across the street from the Vesturbæjarlaug swimming pool, is the kind of place that makes you want to hang out and pretend you live here. They serve good lunches and dinners from a small menu chalked on the board. Choose a table, then order at the counter—but don't come if you're in a hurry (Mon-Fri 8:00-23:00, Sat-Sun from 9:00, hot food served 11:30-15:00 & 17:00-21:00, at Melhaga 20 at corner of Hófsvallagata, walk or take bus #11 to Melaskóli or #15 to Vesturgarður, tel. 551-0623, www.kaffihusvesturbaejar.is).

Near the Botanic Garden
For locations, see the map on page 136.

$$ Flóran, the relaxing café inside Reykjavík's botanic garden, has an eclectic, inventive menu, with main dishes and meal-sized salads. Eat outdoors on a nice day, or in the warm, greenhouse-like interior. They grow some of their own vegetables and herbs (daily 10:00-22:00, early May and Sept until 18:00, closed Oct-April; take bus #2, #5, #15, or #17 to the Laugardalshöll stop and walk 10 minutes downhill to the parking lot and garden entrance; tel. 553-8872).

$ Múlakaffi serves old-style Icelandic cuisine with all the polish of a 1970s school lunchroom. You can stuff yourself for about 2,000 ISK, even at dinnertime. Choose a main dish at the counter—it might be fish cakes, cod cheeks, or pasta with meat sauce—then help yourself to as much soup, salad, bread, and coffee as you like (dishes are listed at www.mulakaffi.is). This place has been here—in a commercial zone amidst office blocks and strip malls—for decades. You'll see tradespeople here on a midday break and older men who meet to chat and read the papers together (Mon-Fri

Budget Bites

Hot dog stands are the Icelandic "hamburger joint." They all sell the same dogs for about 600 ISK. While you can find hot-dog stands on squares just about anywhere, many make a pilgrimage to **Bæjarins Beztu Pylsur** ("The City's Best Sausages") on Pósthússtræti by the flea market (described in my "Reykjavík Walk"). It's been in the same family since 1937 and was a fixture here long before Bill Clinton made it famous with his 2004 visit. Clinton ordered his weenie with mustard only, creating his own menu item. Locals go with everything—especially fried onion.

Pizza is a bad value at lunch but competitive at dinner, when a 2,500-ISK one-person pizza starts to look cheap compared to a 5,000-ISK entree at a sit-down restaurant. Pizza joints downtown include **$$ Hornið** (at Hafnarstræti 15, close to Parliament and Lækjartorg), or, for a cheaper meal, locals call **$ Domino's,** with multiple outlets (including a central one at Skúlagata 17, near Hlemmur; easy ordering in English online or call 581-2345, locations and offers at www.dominos.is).

Just like back home, Reykjavík's suburban **IKEA** store has a handy and very cheap **$ cafeteria.** Local families pack in for inexpensive (if small) main dishes, including Swedish meatballs and Icelandic *plokkfiskur* (fish gratin or hash). Downstairs by the cash registers are Reykjavík's least-expensive hot dogs and soft-serve ice cream. IKEA is just off the main route from Reykjavík to the airport, the Blue Lagoon, and the Ásvallalaug swimming pool (daily 9:00-20:30, Kauptún 4 in the suburb of Garðabær, bus #21 to the IKEA stop—catch it at Mjódd or in Hafnarfjörður).

As in other expensive European cities, **international food** can be a good value here. **$ Krua Thai,** a couple of blocks downhill from Hallgrímskirkja church, has a wide selection and a bright upstairs dining room (daily 11:30-21:30, Skólavörðustígur 21a—see map on page 145, tel. 551-0833). **$ Noodle Station,** a small local chain, serves just one dish: big portions of a vaguely Vietnamese noodle soup, with your choice of beef, chicken, or vegetables. There's a location close to the Hlemmur bus junction (Laugavegur 103—see map on page 136), another near the Old Harbor (next to Aurora Reykjavík), and another in a strip mall on the main road through Hafnarfjörður.

Of course, the absolute cheapest option is to assemble a picnic at a **supermarket.** Discount supermarket **Bónus** has a downtown branch at Laugavegur 59 and one in Grandi at Fiskislóð 2 (daily, at least 10:00-18:00). Bónus is much less expensive than the various 7-Eleven-type convenience stores. There's also a **Super 1** grocery at Hallveigarstígur 1, a block off Skólavörðustígur (daily 10:00-22:00).

7:30-20:00, Sat 10:00-14:00, closed Sun, Hallarmúli 1, bus #2, #5, #15, or #17 to Nordica stop, tel. 553-7737).

Farther Out, in Hafnarfjörður

This bedroom community, about a 15 minutes' drive south of Reykjavík, isn't worth going out of your way for a meal. However, if you're sleeping in Hafnarfjörður—or passing through on your way to the airport or back from a day trip—it can be easier to grab a bite here than to look for parking downtown. See the "Hafnarfjörður" map for locations.

$$ Von (Hope) is the top choice. This small, ambitious restaurant serves modern fish and meat dishes and is proud of their seafood and ox cheek. Local office workers come for the good-value weekday lunch specials, listed on the chalkboard as you enter (reservations recommended for dinner, Mon-Fri 11:30-14:00 & 17:30-21:00, Sat 16:00-22:00, closed Sun, Strandgata 75, along the water at the south end of downtown, past the fake stave church, tel. 583-6000, www.vonmathus.is).

$ Pallett, an inviting hangout café in the same building as Von, is run by an Icelandic-British couple. They serve great coffee, affordable soups and sandwiches, and—on weekends—a full traditional English breakfast at midday (Mon-Thu 8:00-23:00, Fri until 18:00, Sat 10:00-18:00, Sun 11:00-23:00, Strandgata 75, tel. 571-4144).

$ Súfistinn Kaffihús is a simple, two-story coffeehouse and café offering soups, salads, sandwiches, cakes, and a short list of hot dishes for dinner. It's on the old main street, close to the town library (Mon-Fri 8:00-23:30, Sat from 10:00, Sun from 11:00, Strandgata 9, tel. 563-3740).

$$$ Fjörukráin (The Waterside Tavern) is a Viking-themed dinner-only restaurant, often busy with groups (you can't miss it—look for the Norwegian stave-church-like roof). It's kitschy and the prices are high for what you get, but the interior is a work of art and there's occasional live Viking-style entertainment, so a visit can be fun (daily 18:00-22:00, Strandgata 55, tel. 565-1213).

Reykjavík Connections

BY PLANE
Keflavík Airport (International Flights)

Keflavík Airport (pron. KEP-la-VEEK, code: KEF, www.kefairport.is) is Iceland's only real international airport and the center of Icelandair's hub-and-spoke operation that carries thousands of passengers a day between North America and Europe. Keflavík is a particularly reliable airport thanks to its star-shaped design. (It originated as a US military airbase in World War II, and its various runways allow planes to land against any wind. Given its windy and remote location, so far from any alternative airport, it needed this flexibility...a blessing for approaching pilots to this day.)

The airport's status as a transfer point gives Icelanders a much broader range of flight options, all year long, than they would otherwise have in this small country. During summer months, the airport gets very crowded.

Arrival and departure areas are both on the ground floor, on opposite sides of the main terminal building. You'll find a café and a convenience store, car rental offices, a tax-refund desk (facing the car-rental desks), and ATMs, but no TI. A 24-hour bank is located inside (after security) where you can change any leftover Icelandic crowns when you leave the country—they're hard to exchange outside Iceland. The airport has free Wi-Fi.

If you're flying Icelandair or another budget carrier, you'll have to buy (measly and overpriced) meals on board; savvy travelers buy something more enticing ahead of time and bring their meal onto the plane.

Nearby Gas Stations: When returning a rental car be aware that the airport has only a couple of teeny self-serve pumps hidden near the car-rental return. It's smarter to fill up at the handy **ÓB gas station** just outside the airport entrance, on the corner of Aðalgata and highway 41 (self-service, accepts US credit cards with chip). Or fill up in downtown Keflavík.

Breakfast Near the Airport: Many flights from the US arrive early in the morning. Hótel Keflavík, near the harbor in the town of Keflavík, offers a buffet open to nonguests (no reservations needed, 2,800 ISK, daily 5:00-10:00, Vatnsnesvegi 12, tel. 420-7000). The Viking World museum on the Reykjanes Peninsula also does a breakfast buffet that includes admission (see page 181).

Getting Between Reykjavík and Keflavík Airport

The airport is about a 45-minute drive from downtown Reykjavík (30 minutes from Hafnarfjörður). For details on renting a car, see the Practicalities chapter. Without a rental car, your options are

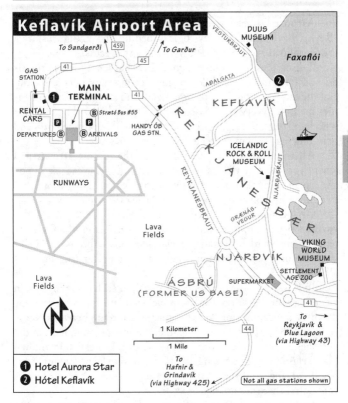

Keflavík Airport Area

To Sandgerði — 459
To Garður
GAS STATION
41 — 45
MAIN TERMINAL
41
RENTAL CARS — Strætó Bus #55
P — P
DEPARTURES — ARRIVALS
HANDY ÓB GAS STN.
RUNWAYS
REYKJANESBRAUT
Lava Fields
Lava Fields

DUUS MUSEUM
VESTURBRAUT
Faxaflói
AÐALGATA
KEFLAVÍK
❷
REYKJANES
ICELANDIC ROCK & ROLL MUSEUM
NJARÐARBRAUT
GRÆNÁS-VEGUR
NJARÐVÍK
BÆR
VIKING WORLD MUSEUM
SETTLEMENT AGE ZOO
ÁSBRÚ
(FORMER US BASE)
SUPERMARKET
41
To Reykjavík & Blue Lagoon (via Highway 43)

N

1 Kilometer
1 Mile
44
To Hafnir & Grindavík (via Highway 425)
Not all gas stations shown

❶ Hotel Aurora Star
❷ Hótel Keflavík

REYKJAVÍK

private airport buses, door-to-door van service, taxis, or an infrequent public bus.

Don't worry about making an early flight: The whole system is designed for people to get from Reykjavík with plenty of time to make a 7:00 or 8:00 departure. Buses, shuttles, and taxis are ready to go by 3:00 or 4:00 in the morning.

By Airport Bus: Three companies—Reykjavík Excursions, Gray Line, and Airport Direct—run buses between Reykjavík and the airport. Buses run whenever there are flights, even at odd hours. From the airport, buses typically depart when full, which can mean a wait. From Reykjavík, buses depart according to a schedule that varies depending on the flight density.

Reykjavík Excursions runs the **Flybus** (tel. 580-5400, www.flybus.is) between the airport and the company's terminal in Reykjavík (called BSÍ, at Vatnsmýrarvegur 10, about a 10- to 15-minute walk from downtown).

Gray Line runs **Airport Express** buses (tel. 540-1313, www.airportexpress.is) to and from their terminal at Holtavegur 10, next to a Bónus supermarket in a distant part of Reykjavík.

Airport Direct has a similar service, departing from their "Reykjavík Terminal" a few blocks behind the Hallgrímskirkja (Skógarhlíð 10, tel. 497-8000, www.airportdirect.is).

Taking these buses makes good financial sense for solo travelers and for families, as children ride free or at a sizable discount. But the buses can be slow, disorganized, and stressful. The companies try to fill every seat. At busy times, the aisle will be crowded with hand bags, the luggage compartment will be jammed full, and boarding may be a mob scene.

All three companies have desks in the airport arrivals hall where you can buy tickets (about 3,000 ISK); you can also book and pay in advance online. A round-trip ticket (ranging from 5,400 to 6,300 ISK) sometimes saves you a little over two one-ways.

Gray Line's regular price is a tad cheaper, but Reykjavík Excursions tickets are discounted if you buy them from the flight attendant on board Icelandair. (Icelandair mostly promotes Reykjavík Excursions, with which they have a longstanding business alliance.)

In Reykjavík, the buses stop primarily at each company's main transfer point, but Gray Line also picks up and drops off at a few downtown locations for no extra charge. En route between Reykjavík and the airport, both companies' buses stop on request at the bus shelter across from the Viking Village Hótel in downtown Hafnarfjörður (at Strandgata 55). If you need to be picked up there, pay in advance and reconfirm with the company, as buses bypass this stop if there are no requests.

Door-to-(almost)-Door Service: For about an extra 1,000 ISK each way, each company will tack on the transportation between their transfer point and stops at or near major hotels and hostels in central Reykjavík. This usually involves a separate minibus trip between the transfer point and a drop-off point close to your hotel or Airbnb, and takes about 30 extra minutes. It's cheaper than a taxi, and easier than taking the city bus. The transfer procedures can be confusing (you'll need to carry your luggage from one bus to the other). If you're staying in an Airbnb, put in a nearby hotel or bus stop as your pickup and drop-off point, then walk between that point and your lodgings. If you're staying way out in the suburbs, the transfer service may not serve any point near you.

By Shared Shuttle: To pay a little bit more for door-to-door service, but without having to transfer between a bus and a van, you can use **Airport Direct**'s "premium" service. A smaller shuttle van will take you directly to (or from) your hotel without the intermediate transfer—though they will spend a little extra time circling the city to drop off and pick up other passengers (5,990 ISK one-way, 10,990 ISK round-trip, see contact information earlier).

By Private Shuttle: A more expensive option is **Back To Ice-**

land Travel's private door-to-door minibus servic
stop nearest your accommodation) for 20,000 ISK
gers). You can tack on a visit to the Blue Lagoon for an e.
ISK—lagoon admission not included (mobile 846-3837, w.
btitravel.is).

By Taxi: Groups of at least four adults (who can split the cost) save time and pay only a little more to take a taxi to or from the airport. Reykjavík's two main taxi companies both offer fixed-price service to and from the airport for about 15,500-16,500 ISK (1-4 passengers) or 19,500-22,000 ISK (5-8 passengers). If you reserve in advance, they'll wait for you at the airport with a sign. When reserving, tell them your destination and ask their advice; if your starting or ending point is in the southern part of the capital area (for example, in Hafnarfjörður), using the meter may be cheaper than these fixed rates. Contact **Hreyfill** (tel. 588-5522, www. hreyfill.is) and **BSR** (tel. 561-0000, www.taxireykjavik.is). Other smaller taxi and transfer companies may offer slightly lower rates.

By Public Bus: Strætó, the public bus company, runs buses (#55) between downtown Reykjavík and Keflavík Airport every 1-2 hours, taking about 70 minutes. At some times of the day and on weekends, they run only between the airport and the Fjörður stop in Hafnarfjörður, where you change to bus #1. The public bus is meant more for commuters than for international travelers and goes infrequently, but it's the cheapest way into town and has space for luggage. As it's considered a long-distance route, you can pay the bus driver with a credit card (1,880 ISK one-way; connecting city buses are free if you ask the driver for a transfer slip). For schedules, see www.straeto.is (enter the airport as "KEF" in the journey planner).

The Strætó bus stop is out in the open air along row A of the car-rental lot. To find it, walk out from the arrivals side of the terminal under the roofed walkway, then hang a left and look for the tiny "S" sign (it's not signposted from inside the arrivals hall).

Reykjavík City Airport

Reykjavík's domestic airport (code: RKV) is just south of downtown. Planes landing from the north fly directly over Parliament at a height of only a few hundred feet. While the runways are long enough to land an Icelandair 757, the airport is only used for smaller planes flying domestic routes and to the Faroe Islands and east Greenland. Check-in at the pint-sized terminals feels informal; arriving even an hour early feels like overkill, and there's no security checkpoint for domestic flights.

It's important to know that the airport has two terminals on *opposite* sides of the runway. If you go to the wrong terminal, you'll have to take a taxi to get to the other (you can't walk). Air Ice-

.d Connect uses the larger main terminal on the *west* side of the runways (take bus #15 to the Reykjavíkurflugvöllur stop). If you're flying on Eagle Air—for example, to the Westman Islands—you'll go from a separate, smaller terminal on the *east* side of the runways (take bus #5 to the Nauthólsvegur stop; the terminal is behind the Icelandair Hótel Reykjavík Natura and the control tower). Parking is free at both terminals.

To make an early-morning domestic flight, before buses start running, call a taxi (reserve the night before; see the taxi recommendations earlier, under Keflavík Airport). Figure about 2,000 ISK for a taxi between downtown and either terminal (or between terminals). When you get in the taxi, remember to specify which airline/terminal you're heading to.

BY BUS

Reykjavík has several bus stations. Buses run by **Reykjavík Excursions,** including all of their excursion buses and the scheduled Fly-Bus to the airport, use the old **BSÍ** bus terminal at Vatnsmýrarvegur 10, about a 10- to 15-minute walk from downtown (or take bus #1, #3, #5, #6, or #15 to BSÍ). Two smaller companies, Sterna Travel and TREX, also use BSÍ for their scheduled and excursion buses.

Buses run by **Gray Line** use their terminal at **Holtavegur 10,** in the Reykjavík suburbs near the container-ship harbor. Gray Line runs minibuses to hotels around town to pick travelers up and shuttle them to the terminal. You can get within a five-minute walk of the terminal by public bus (#12 or #16 to the Sund or Holtagarðar stops), but it's easier to use their shuttles.

Long-distance buses run by **Strætó,** Iceland's public bus service, depart from the Mjódd bus terminal in the eastern Reykjavík suburbs. It's next to a small indoor shopping mall, also called Mjódd (MEE-ohd). Many city bus routes stop at Mjódd, including #2, #3, #4, #11, #12, #17, #21, and #24 (no extra charge for transfer ticket).

Strætó's downtown city bus junction at **Hlemmur** doesn't serve long-distance routes, but is a good place to catch a bus to the long-distance terminal at Mjódd.

BY CRUISE SHIP

There's no scheduled boat service from Reykjavík, but cruise ships frequently stop here in summer. The cruise-ship terminal is at Skarfagarðar, a five-minute drive east of downtown; by bus, take #16 to the Klettagarðar/Skarfagarðar stop. Smaller cruise ships occasionally use a berth in the Old Harbor, just steps from downtown. The weekly ferry from Iceland to Denmark leaves from Seyðisfjörður, in eastern Iceland (see the "Transportation" section of the Practicalities chapter).

BEYOND
REYKJAVÍK

BEYOND REYKJAVÍK

BEYOND REYKJAVÍK

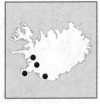

Reykjavík is a great city, but most visitors to Iceland want to get out into the countryside. Fortunately, some of the most beautiful places in Iceland are within striking distance of downtown. Many of the destinations in the following chapters are doable as day trips from Reykjavík, either with a rental car or with an excursion.

Two of the best side trips for experiencing Iceland's dramatic landscape are the Golden Circle, a classic loop trip featuring an impressive gorge, waterfalls, and an active geyser; and the volcano-rich South Coast, where you can hike up to the face of a glacier, stroll along black sand beaches, and walk behind a thundering waterfall.

There's also the famous Blue Lagoon spa—a serene, milky-blue oasis in a volcanic landscape—and the eclectic region around Borgarnes. The Snæfellsnes Peninsula, beyond Borgarnes, offers a little bit of everything that's made Iceland famous.

My favorite "Back Door" destination is the Westman Islands, just off Iceland's South Coast. There you can see the effects of a recent volcanic eruption and enjoy front-row views of the country's cutest bird, the puffin. The Westfjords, far to the northwest, are another relatively untouristed Back Door, but they're too distant for day-tripping (unless you fly into and out of Ísafjörður).

My advice here skews toward either driving yourself or joining an excursion. Public transportation—a godsend for budget travelers in most places—is sparse in Iceland. While suburban buses can help you reach points very close to Reykjavík, there's no practical way, for example, to use cheap public transit to link up the sights of the Golden Circle or South Coast on your own.

While most of this chapter (and the chapters that follow) focus on day trips from Reykjavík, travelers wanting to delve into a scenic slice of Iceland without committing to the full Ring Road can choose from several appealing multiday itineraries. See the end of this chapter for suggestions.

DAY-TRIP PLANNING TIPS

For visitors, Iceland is a bit like a giant cruise ship, with thousands of passengers overwhelmed by the choices about what they can do on shore. Take the time to sort through your options (group tour, private tour, do-it-yourself with a rental car) and make the right choice for your interests, time, budget, and appetite for adventure and travel challenges.

These tips will help maximize your Icelandic experience:

Summer Daylight Bonus: In summer you'll enjoy very long hours of daylight; from early June to mid-July it never really gets dark. You can pack a day full by sightseeing close to your home base in the morning, then set out on a side trip in the late afternoon. In

Decoding Icelandic Place Names

Most Icelandic place names are simply a pileup of geographical features. For example, the word for the famous tongue-twister volcano Eyjafjallajökull can be broken down into three smaller words meaning "Island-Mountain Glacier." You can learn a lot about a place simply by decoding its name (and often just its suffix). For example, if you see *fjörður*, expect a dramatic seaside setting; *vík* is on the water, but less thrilling; *fjall* is mountainous; and *hver* means things could get steamy.

These place-name elements recur throughout the country, and in a few cases entire names are recycled (for instance, there's a Reykholt near Borgarnes in western Iceland, and another near Geysir along the Golden Circle). When that happens, the place name might get an add-on modifier for clarity. The town of Vík ("Bay"), on the South Coast, is called Vík í Mýrdal (Bay in Marshy Valley) to distinguish it from other less-visited Víks around the country. And if you're heading for Borgarfjörður Eystri (literally the "more eastern Borgarfjörður"), don't follow your GPS to plain old Borgarfjörður...nearly 400 miles to the west.

Here are the basic building blocks:

á: river, stream	*braut:* avenue
akur: field	*brú:* bridge
ár: river, stream	*bú:* estate, farm
austur: east	*dalur:* valley
bær: town, farm	*eldfjall:* volcano
bjarg: cliff	(fire mountain)
borg: outcrop, fortification	*ey:* island

the peak of summer, for example, it's possible to leave Reykjavík for the Golden Circle as late as 16:00, see most of the sights along that route, and be back in town before the sun goes down.

Winter Wake-Up: Winter is a rotten time to explore Iceland's countryside. Daylight is brief (as few as four hours), and it can be dreary and icy. Weather permitting, though, you can still join organized bus trips from Reykjavík to a few outdoor attractions; this makes good use of the few hours of light and leaves winter driving to pros. One popular way to get into the countryside in the winter is to join a northern lights tour—turning the darkness into an asset. If you do decide to drive in Iceland in winter, be alert to weather conditions, as roads may close due to snow, high winds, or ice. If roads are clear, it's smart to leave Reykjavík in the dark and time your arrival at the first attraction for sunrise.

Cost Considerations: Although a car rental may seem pricey (roughly $350 for a one-week rental in summer, plus insurance, fuel, tolls, and parking), consider this: Per person, the bus transfer

eyja: island
eyri: point, spit
fell: hill, mountain
fjall: mountain
fjara: beach, shore
fjörður: fjord
fljót: large river
flói: gulf, bay
flúðir: rapids
foss: waterfall
gata: street
gerði: fence, hedge
gígur: crater
gljúfur: canyon, gorge
grænn: green
heiði: treeless highland, heath, sometimes "pass"
hellir: cave
hlíð: mountainside, slope
holt: hill
höfn: harbor
hraun: lava
hús: house
hver: hot spring
hvítur: white

jökull: glacier
krókur: hook, river bend
laugar: hot spring, pool
lækur: creek
lón: lagoon
mýri: swamp, marsh
nes: promontory, headland
norður: north
reykur: steam, smoke
sandur: sandy area
skagi: peninsula
skarð: mountain pass
skógur: forest
staður: place, farm, town
stígur: trail
stræti: street
strönd: coast, sandy beach
suður: south
svartur: black
tún: hay field
vatn: lake (also "water")
vegur: road
vestur: west
vík: bay, inlet
völlur: field, plain (plural *vellir*)

BEYOND REYKJAVÍK

to and from the airport is $50, you'll pay at least $60 for a basic Golden Circle excursion, and $90 for the South Coast. If you're in Iceland for three nights, and take two day-trip excursions, you'll spend close to $200 (double that for a couple). Suddenly that "expensive" rental car seems reasonable, considering the freedom it affords.

DAY-TRIPPING WITH A CAR

More than any other country I can think of, road-tripping is a big part of the joy of exploring Iceland. For one thing, it's hard to get lost: Even on little branch roads, you'll find signs showing what's out there. And at most points of interest, a handy pullout with an information board explains all the upcoming roadside attractions.

For travelers day-tripping on their own by car, the following chapters outline detailed self-guided driving tours with suggested schedules and opinionated descriptions to help you assess your options and plan your drive.

My driving directions assume you're starting from Reykjavík. But if you're staying outside the city, you can drive to these day-trip destinations from a home base anywhere in the southwestern part of the country—for example, from along the South Coast; from the Reykjavík suburb of Hafnarfjörður; or from Keflavík, near the international airport.

Before heading out, be sure to read the tips on driving in Iceland in the Practicalities chapter.

DAY-TRIPPING WITH AN EXCURSION

A variety of companies offer excursions around Iceland. These are great if you want to sit back, enjoy the scenery, and learn from a knowledgeable guide (or, in a few cases, a well-produced recorded commentary). With careful planning, you can cobble together several half- and full-day excursions that will get you to many of Iceland's top sights.

Excursion Destinations

The most popular excursion destinations are the Golden Circle, the Blue Lagoon, the South Coast, and the Snæfellsnes Peninsula.

In winter, you'll find evening trips in search of the northern lights. Some tours run all year, but winter offerings are generally sparser.

Most excursions start in Reykjavík, but there are also options from Ísafjörður in the Westfjords, and Akureyri, Mývatn, and other small towns around the Ring Road (see the Westfjords section and Ring Road chapter for specific recommendations).

You may see tours advertised for the glacier lagoons and Skaftafell National Park in Southeast Iceland; while these are amazing sights, they're too far from Reykjavík for a reasonable day trip (at least 10 hours round-trip)—you'll spend far more time on the bus than at your destination. Save these for a drive around the Ring Road or add an overnight or two in the southeast and do it right.

Choosing an Excursion Company

Sorting through the numerous excursion options can be overwhelming. For starters, look at each company's brochure and website. As the offerings are constantly in flux, check reviews on TripAdvisor (in the "Things to Do" section) for recent firsthand accounts. All branches of Reykjavík's TI (called What's On, www.

whatson.is) have a booking desk for excursions that can help you find and book a tour.

You can also turn to one of Iceland's travel-company consortiums, such as Guide to Iceland (www.guidetoiceland.is), which can be a good online source. You'll pay the same whether you book direct or use a booking service—they get their commission from the tour companies.

Tour Companies: The two biggest players are Reykjavík Excursions (www.re.is, owned by Icelandair and promoted on their flights) and Gray Line (www.grayline.is). Their offerings are slick and consistent, but the 50-seat buses are typically jam-packed (though Gray Line offers some minibus departures). An advantage, though, is predictability and price; what these tours lack in intimacy they make up for in efficiency and lower ticket costs.

Several smaller outfits are more personal, generally use smaller vehicles, and can be pricier. Well-established and respected companies include family-run Nicetravel (www.nicetravel.is); environmentally focused Geo Iceland (www.geoiceland.com); small-bus, small-group Iceland Horizon (www.icelandhorizon.is); and pricey, boutique Season Tours (www.seasontours.is).

Add-On Options: Beyond the standard sightseeing loops, excursion companies offer a wide variety of optional activities such as hiking, caving, horseback riding, snorkeling, glacier walking, and snowmobiling. Among the possibilities: You can do the Blue Lagoon on the way to the airport; add the Fontana baths in Laugarvatn, snorkeling, or an ATV ride to a Golden Circle trip; or visit *Game of Thrones* shooting locations.

Prices: Excursions run from about $60 to $250 (more for boutique experiences). For example, an express, seven-hour Golden Circle tour starts at around $60; a 10-hour South Coast tour starts at around $90; and a bus trip to the Blue Lagoon, including admission, runs about $125.

When to Book: For standard tours—such as the Golden Circle or South Coast—you generally don't need to book a seat more than a day or two in advance, so you may want to wait until you arrive in Iceland and know what the weather will be doing. One exception is the Blue Lagoon, which can fill up faster than other excursions. Your hotel may be happy to book these tours for you (be aware that they get a commission).

More specialized tours (ice caving, glacier hikes) can book up;

for these, keep an eye on online booking calendars, which typically count down the number of slots available for each tour. If it looks like they're selling fast, book yours before it's too late.

Unguided Excursions to More Remote Destinations

A number of private companies run regularly scheduled buses throughout Iceland's countryside—offering transportation to otherwise difficult-to-reach, remote areas, but without any guiding. Developed primarily to get hikers to trailheads, some of these buses can also work for independent travelers who want to put together day trips on their own.

For example, the worthwhile but difficult-to-reach Icelandic **Highlands** in the center of the country are served by specially equipped excursion buses. Two rough dirt roads (the Kjölur and Sprengisandur routes) cross the Highlands, but can only be driven in a sturdy four-wheel drive vehicle, and only from roughly the end of June to the first snows. You can take a bus from Reykjavík into the Highlands to the geothermally active Landmannalaugar, a base for hikers a short detour off the Sprengisandur route (see page 53). Similar buses cross the island from Reykjavík to Akureyri via the Highland route (see the "Transportation" section of the Practicalities chapter).

MULTIDAY ITINERARIES

The recommended itineraries in this book's introduction focus on two types of travelers: short-timers ("layover" visitors squeezing in a day trip or two) and long-haul road-trippers (devoting a week or more to the entire Ring Road). But for those whose available time falls somewhere in between, it is possible to get beyond the capital region without driving the full 800 miles of the Ring Road. Thinking creatively about domestic flights and one-way car rentals can help you make the most of your time.

Air Iceland Connect has fast and affordable flights from Reykjavík's small and easy downtown airport to Akureyri (in the north), Ísafjörður (the Westfjords' main town), Egilsstaðir (on the Eastfjords), and more (www.airicelandconnect.com). Flights run in the $100 range (if you book ahead) and tend to be quick (an hour or less), easy (there's no security checkpoint), and outrageously scenic.

Most car rental companies let you drop off a car elsewhere in Iceland. This usually comes with an extra fee, but it's often worth the time and money you'll save by not retracing your drive back to Reykjavík.

Intermediate-Length Itineraries

Here are some suggested itineraries that get you farther afield in just two to five days.

Snæfellsnes in 2 Days: Of all the day trips in this book, Snæfellsnes is the one most deserving of an overnight, which lets you spread the driving and sightseeing over two days. That chapter's "Planning Your Time" section has advice for both one- and two-day versions.

The North in 2-3 Days: The Mývatn area is one of Iceland's natural treasures. Unfortunately, it's a tedious six-hour drive from the capital. To be efficient, you could fly from Reykjavík to Akureyri, pick up a rental car, and drive around a bit (including Mývatn and/or the scenic Tröllaskagi Peninsula, with the lovely town of Siglufjörður). From there, you could drop off your car and fly or take the bus back to Reykjavík—or keep your car (and pay the one-way fee) to drive the Akureyri-Reykjavík segment of the Ring Road.

The South in 2-4 Days: Simply drive down to the South Coast and find a countryside hotel to settle into before taking in the sights. You could spend a day hiking in Þórsmörk (meeting the monster-truck bus in Hvolsvöllur); do a side trip to the Westman Islands; or visit the Golden Circle as a loop from here instead of from Reykjavík (each of these takes about a day). If you'd like to linger in glacier country and have time for Skaftafell National Park, you could drive a couple of hours farther east, adding an overnight in Southeast Iceland.

The Westfjords in 2 Days: The remote and rustic Westfjords are the best place in Iceland to get away from the crowds. For a targeted visit, fly in and out of Ísafjörður, doing a day or two of excursions (either with tour companies or on your own with a rental car). Better yet...

Snæfellsnes Plus the Westfjords in 5 Days: These two areas in northwestern Iceland pair perfectly for several wonderful days of sightseeing. Do the Snæfellsnes loop (ideally with an overnight), then take the ferry to the southern Westfjords. From there, you can loop around the Látrabjarg Peninsula and head north (via Dynjandi Waterfall) to the Ísafjörður area. From Ísafjörður, you can drive six tedious hours back to Reykjavik...or, for maximum efficiency, drop your car and fly back to the capital. This plan is outlined in the "Planning Your Time" section of the Westfjords chapter.

BLUE LAGOON & REYKJANES PENINSULA

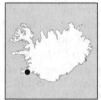

The Blue Lagoon—arguably Iceland's most famous attraction—is tucked into a jagged volcanic landscape in the middle of nowhere, about a 45-minute drive south of downtown Reykjavík and not far from the international airport. People flock here from around the globe to soak, splash, and bob in the lagoon's thermal and, yes, milky-blue waters. While many visitors consider the Blue Lagoon a must, it's not everyone's cup of tea—it's pricey, time-consuming, and not ideal for small kids.

The Blue Lagoon and Keflavík Airport both sit on the Reykjanes (RAYK-yah-NESS) Peninsula, which extends into the sea south of Reykjavík. A few low-impact sights are scattered around the volcanic terrain beyond the Blue Lagoon—including Kleifarvatn lake; the thermal fields at Seltún; Grindavík, a humdrum town with some good lunch options; and Keflavík, the peninsula's main town. While the scenery is more impressive in other parts of the country, a quick drive around Reykjanes provides those on a tight timeframe with an efficient glimpse of the Icelandic landscape.

PLANNING YOUR TIME

The Blue Lagoon requires reservations—you can't just show up and hope to slip in. Day-of openings are rare. To have your choice of slots, book several days ahead.

Blue Lagoon Strategic Strike: Given the Blue Lagoon's proximity to the international airport, a smart, time-saving strategy

Blue Lagoon: To Visit or Not to Visit?

Travelers are split on the Blue Lagoon. For some, a visit to this iconic thermal pool is the highlight of their time in Iceland. For others, it's outrageously expensive and overrated.

Pros: The Blue Lagoon is a unique and memorable travel experience, thanks to its stunning volcanic setting, silky-blue water, and luxury-spa class. While you can splash in hot water at any municipal swimming pool in Iceland, the Blue Lagoon is as refined as those are functional—it is, in a sense, the ultimate expression of Icelandic thermal bathing. And it's simply fun: sipping a drink, smearing fancy mud on your face, and feeling pebbles under your feet as 100°F water ebbs your stress away. As a bonus, it's easy to reach on the way to or from the airport.

Cons: The Blue Lagoon is expensive (absurdly so to Icelanders), crowded with an almost exclusively touristic clientele, grossly commercial, not great for young kids, and inconveniently located for those staying in Reykjavík. The reservation requirement is cumbersome, and minerals in the water can wreak havoc on your hair. If you believe that one big pool of hot water is pretty much the same as any other, you can pay one-tenth of the price to enjoy one of Reykjavík's many municipal swimming pools—and enjoy a far more authentic cultural experience.

is to schedule your visit to coincide with your flight: If arriving on a morning flight, hit the Blue Lagoon on your way into Reykjavík. Or if you're flying out in the afternoon, soak in the Blue Lagoon on your way to the airport. With a several-hour layover, it may not be worth the trouble to go all the way into Reykjavík—but a visit to the Blue Lagoon (or sights in the town of Keflavík) makes a far better alternative to hanging out at the airport. Luggage storage is available at the lagoon parking lot.

Blue Lagoon and Reykjanes Peninsula Loop: If you're staying longer in Reykjavík and want to make a day of it, book your Blue Lagoon reservation for 13:00 and follow this plan. For details, see page 175.

10:00	Leave Reykjavík for Kleifarvatn lake (45 minutes)
11:00	Visit Kleifarvatn and Seltún geothermal field
11:30	Drive to Grindavík (30 minutes) and have lunch
12:45	Drive to the Blue Lagoon (10 minutes)
13:00	Soak in the Blue Lagoon—*aaah*
16:00	Return to Reykjavík—or, before heading home, take in one of the museums in the town of Keflavík

Blue Lagoon

While Iceland has a wide variety of thermal baths, the Blue Lagoon's setting amid rocky, moss-covered lava fields makes it unique. Bathing at the wildly popular Blue Lagoon is, for some travelers, the ultimate Icelandic experience, and worth ▲▲▲.

The Blue Lagoon (Bláa Lónið) has a don't-miss-it reputation and prices to match. Over 3,000 people visit each day. Reservations are required, and some slots sell out days in advance. (The bottleneck isn't the lagoon itself, but the number of lockers.) The reservation requirement keeps the lagoon from getting too congested—even on the busiest days, you can find pockets of hot water where you can escape the tour groups.

The Blue Lagoon is a steamy oasis—a sprawling hot-water playground for grown-ups. Chunky rocks disappear beneath the opaque water, where they're coated with white silica slime. The naturally heated water is thoroughly relaxing. You'll smear mineral deposits on your face, while giggling at your fellow silica-masked bathers. The hardest "work" you'll do is keeping your Icelandic microbrew or *skyr* smoothie above the water, as you behold the surrounding rocks hissing like teakettles.

GETTING THERE

With a Car: The Blue Lagoon is very easy by car. It's about 45 minutes from downtown Reykjavík, and only 15 minutes from Keflavík Airport, off highway 43, on the way to the town of Grindavík. Some highway signs use only the Icelandic name: *Bláa Lónið*. It's free to park in the lagoon's huge parking lot.

By Excursion Bus: The lagoon runs its own hourly bus service, **Destination Blue Lagoon,** from Reykjavík and Keflavík Airport (5,500 ISK round-trip; each leg 2,750 ISK one-way, i.e., airport to lagoon or lagoon to Reykjavík; sold separately or as an add-on to lagoon admission, www.bluelagoon.com).

Reykjavík Excursions sells packages that include standard "comfort" admission and round-trip travel between Reykjavík and the Blue Lagoon for about 15,000 ISK. You can use your return ticket to continue to Keflavík Airport instead of going back to Reykjavík. Buses run hourly between Reykjavík and the lagoon, but less frequently between the lagoon and airport—check schedules carefully and plan ahead (tel. 580-5400, www.re.is).

Gray Line offers a pricey, four-hour private round-trip shuttle

from Reykjavík starting around 27,000 ISK, including "comfort" admission (longer, more expensive packages also available; tel. 540-1313, www.grayline.is).

Note that excursion companies have access to the same time slots for the Blue Lagoon as individuals—if the lagoon is sold out in one place, it'll be sold out everywhere.

ORIENTATION TO THE BLUE LAGOON

Cost: The basic "comfort" package costs 7,000 to 12,000 ISK (depending mostly on how far in advance you buy your ticket) and includes entry, locker, towel, a drink from the lagoon bar, and a dollop of silica white mud for your face. The lagoon's website explains fancier packages that get you slippers, Champagne, in-water massage, and access to the luxury Retreat Spa. Bring your own suit or rent one there (700 ISK).

Hours: Daily 8:00-22:00, June-Aug 7:00-23:00 or 24:00, Oct-Dec 8:00-21:00, last entry one hour before closing. You need to leave the water at closing time, but have another 30 minutes after that to dress.

Information: Tel. 420-8800, www.bluelagoon.com.

Reservations: Book far in advance for the widest selection of times. Evening entries are often cheaper and less likely to be sold out.

The Origin of the Blue Lagoon

The Blue Lagoon dates only from the early 1970s, when the local power authority drilled for hot water to heat homes on the Reykjanes Peninsula. They hit a good high-temperature source, but as often happens, the water wasn't suitable for piping directly into home radiators—it was salty (due to sea-water intrusions) and had a high mineral and clay content. Instead, they set up a heat-exchange system where the geo-thermal water was used to heat fresh, cold water that could then be piped to homes. After running through the system, the partly cooled geothermal water was simply dumped into the lava field near the plant.

Within a few years, locals realized this was a great place for a free dip and started to bathe in the water. Silica clay gives the water its milky texture, and sunlight gives it a blue appear-ance. (The name "Blue Lagoon"—borrowed from the notori-ous 1980 Brooke Shields movie—was originally used in jest.) Authorities caught on, fenced off the lagoon, built a changing shed, and started to charge admission, which at first was no more than at a local swimming pool. Word spread, and within a few years the lagoon had become a major tourist attraction. The power authority privatized  the lagoon, controversially selling it to a group of local politi-cians. They raised capital and did an admirable job developing and marketing the lagoon, adding cosmetics lines, a gift shop, a hotel, and a fancy restaurant.

Today, almost all the Blue Lagoon's guests are tourists; only a small percentage are Icelanders, who now find the fa-cility too expensive. Meanwhile, more premium pools have sprung up across Iceland: **Fontana** (at Laugarvatn, on the Golden Circle); **Krauma** (at Deildartunguhver, in West Iceland), and **Geosea** and the **Mývatn Nature Baths** (along the Ring Road, in the north).

If your preferred date is sold out, check back closer to that day: Big excursion companies may release a block of unsold tickets. The website explains cancellation and change fees.

Arrival and Luggage Storage: You must enter within an hour of your selected entry time. You may be let in early depending on the locker availability—just ask; a half-hour early is often no problem.

The lagoon's parking lot is connected to the main building

by a 100-yard path cut through the lava field. A small building near the parking lot has a WC, pay luggage storage, and a
waiting room for those taking buses from the lagoon.

Eyewear and Jewelry: Avoid wearing eyeglasses if you can—they
fog up, and you won't find them in the opaque water if they
fall off (a strap can help). Clay can scratch delicate lenses; rinse
glasses in fresh water when you leave the pool. On a bright day,
cheap sunglasses can make the lagoon more pleasant. Because
the water is opaque, there's no need for goggles. Leave jewelry
in your locker to avoid tarnishing or losing a ring in the pool.

Hair Concerns: The minerals in the Blue Lagoon can leave hair
dry and brittle. The effect goes away within a day or two. Don't
stress about this too much—the lagoon is more fun if you relax
and let your hair get wet. Still, especially for those with long
hair, it's smart to slather on the free conditioner (from dispensers in the shower stalls) before and after you bathe, or keep
long hair tied up and out of the water. A bathing cap offers
the best protection. In addition to conditioner, the lagoon provides free body wash and the use of hair dryers.

Kids: Children under age two are not allowed in the Blue Lagoon,
and the facility is not designed for kids (no slides, kiddie pools,
or play areas). The water is opaque, so if a child goes under, you
won't be able to see him or her. The same goes for toys, glasses,
goggles...and anything else that might slip out of little hands.

Eating: The main building has an appealing **$ self-service caf-
eteria** (with prepackaged sandwiches), plus the expensive, sit-
down **$$$$ Lava Restaurant** (reservations recommended,
same contact info as lagoon). In the luxury Retreat Hotel next
door, the **$$$$ Moss Restaurant** offers elegant dining with a
view (reservations recommended, tel. 420-8700). Better-value
eateries are in Grindavík, a 10-minute drive away (described
later in this chapter).

Sleeping: The lagoon runs the nearby **$$$$ Silica Hotel** and the
preposterously expensive **Retreat Hotel.** You'll find lower
prices in Keflavík and Grindavík (see "Hotels near the Airport" in the Reykjavík chapter).

Free Peek: If you just want a glimpse at the dreamy setting, you
can park, enter the main building, and visit the Blue Lagooon's
gift shop, cafeteria, and restaurant without a ticket. There's a
good view of the pools from the cafeteria and the open deck
between the cafeteria and the restaurant. A path from just outside the main entry leads through the non-bathing section of
the lagoon. Also, as you drive toward the complex, there's a
point where water from the power plant comes right up to the
road; you could get out for a photo—if you can pull over without blocking traffic.

BLUE LAGOON & REYKJANES

VISITING THE BLUE LAGOON

The procedures for a visit to the Blue Lagoon are basically the same as at other Icelandic pools (see the "Pool Rules" sidebar on page 42). Watch the helpful video on the website (www.bluelagoon.com), which walks you through a visit.

Entry Procedure: When you pay, you'll get an electronic **wristband** that serves as your locker key (and lets you charge drinks, face mud, and other extras—pay when you leave).

Once in the **changing area,** find an available locker. To lock the locker, touch your wristband to the light-up panel (if you forget, your locker will pop open after you leave—oops!). You can use your wristband to reopen your locker as often as you like (making it easy to enjoy the experience without your camera, then get a few shots when you're finished soaking). If you forget your locker number, touch your wristband to the panel and it will remind you.

Once you've changed and showered (in a private cabin, if you prefer), head out to the **lagoon.** Review the chart above the main door as you leave the indoor area. It locates everything (bar, mud shack, waterfall, sauna, steam rooms, etc.) and shows the temperature of various hot spots. If you get turned around, bath attendants are standing by to answer questions and point you in the right direction.

In the Pools: The lagoon is *big*. The towel situation is chaotic. I don't even bother tracking mine: It's easy to just ask for another.

Once you're in, be aware that the water ranges from waist to chest deep. The temperature varies more than in a regular swimming pool, with hot and cool spots—the average is around 100°F. For safety, the original scalding hot springs are contained in **"hot boxes"** (never over 105°F). While the water is not chlorinated, new water continually circulates into the lagoon—refilling the entire pool about every 40 hours. Bathers congregate by the warm spots where the hot water enters. Lifeguards love to talk and are full of fun facts.

Splish and splash around, exploring the hidden nooks and crannies of the interconnected **pools,** including a little roofed grotto, and several areas with benches that resemble hot pots at the municipal baths. The farther out you go, the quieter the pool becomes. Find the hot, thundering **waterfall** and give your shoulders a pounding. From there you can access the steam room, steam cave, and sauna.

Don't forget to find the **swim-up bar**—everyone gets

one free drink. Water fountains under the bridges help you stay hydrated.

At the **mud station,** there are three options. Every bather gets a free ladleful of the white silica mud that collects in the lagoon. Smear this exfoliant on your face, let it set for about 10 minutes, then wash it off. Bathers with a higher-end ticket (or who pay extra for a dollop) get a blob of greenish algae, which supposedly reduces wrinkles and rejuvenates the skin (same procedure: wear for 10 minutes, then rinse). Or try a black "lava scrub" face wash. While it adds to the experience, all that mud is really just a sales pitch for the spa products for sale inside.

Leaving the Bath: After you've showered and dressed, you'll pay for any extras you indulged in. At the exit turnstile, touch your wristband to the panel, then insert it in the slot. The machine eats it, and you're on your way. Now comes the hard part: Try to keep your relaxed body awake on the drive back to your hotel or the airport.

Reykjanes Peninsula

The Reykjanes Peninsula has enough sights to fill a day trip, and it's easy to combine with a visit to the Blue Lagoon. This is not the most scenic or historic part of Iceland—don't visit here at the expense of more dramatic scenery only a bit farther away, such as the Golden Circle or South Coast. But Reykjanes is handy for those who don't have time to venture far beyond the airport area. My plan for the drive from Reykjavík to the Blue Lagoon assumes you'll tour the peninsula first and then visit the Blue Lagoon, but it works just fine in reverse, too.

I've also listed a short yet scenic loop drive around the northern tip of the peninsula—a pleasant, less-touristed introduction to Iceland or fine way to kill time if you're picking up or returning a rental car at Keflavík Airport.

Reykjanes and Blue Lagoon Loop

This 90-mile loop route is fairly straightforward. From Reykjavík, you'll drive about 45 minutes across the Reykjanes Peninsula to the rugged Kleifarvatn lakeshore, with some interesting natural features (especially the Seltún geothermal field). Then you'll loop along the peninsula's south coast to Grindavík (about 30 minutes), a harbor town with some appealing lunch options. From there, it's a 10-minute drive to the Blue Lagoon. When you're done bathing, you can head straight back to Reykjavík (45 minutes), or consider a quick detour to some of the museums in Keflavík.

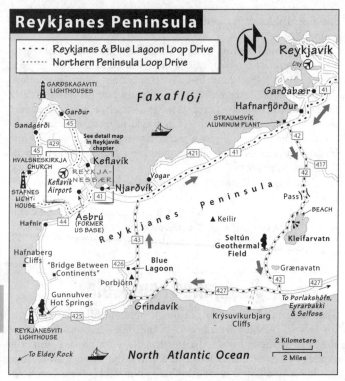

BLUE LAGOON & REYKJANES

Reykjanes Peninsula

- - - Reykjanes & Blue Lagoon Loop Drive
- - - - Northern Peninsula Loop Drive

Reykjavík
City

GARÐSKAGAVITI
LIGHTHOUSES

Faxaflói

Garðabær 41

Hafnarfjörður

Garður
Sandgerði 45 STRAUMSVÍK
ALUMINUM PLANT 42

See detail map
in Reykjavík
chapter 421 41 417
45 429
HVALSNESKIRKJA Keflavík 42
CHURCH REYKJA- Vogar
NESBÆR
STAFNES Keflavík Njarðvík Pass
LIGHT- Airport 41 BEACH
HOUSE
Ásbrú Keilir Kleifarvatn
Hafnir 44 (FORMER Seltún
US BASE) Geothermal
Hafnaberg 43 Field
Cliffs Grænavatn
"Bridge Between 426 Blue 42 427
Continents" Lagoon
Þorbjörn 427 To Þorlákshöfn,
Gunnuhver Eyrarbakki
Hot Springs Grindavík & Selfoss
425 Krýsuvíkurbjarg
REYKJANESVITI Cliffs
LIGHTHOUSE 2 Kilometers
To Eldey Rock North Atlantic Ocean 2 Miles

• *Leaving the city, drive south on highway 41 through* **Hafnarfjörður**—
following the route toward the airport.

Hafnarfjörður

This harborfront suburb of Reykjavík feels like a small town and
has some good eateries (see page 153). It doesn't have much in the
way of sights, but there are some nice places to stroll (such as its
pedestrianized core and Hellisgerði, a small park off Hellisgata),
and a surprisingly good little town history museum (Vesturgata 6,
http://museum.hafnarfjordur.is).

As you crest the hill at the end of Hafnarfjörður, notice the
red-and-white towers of the massive **aluminum plant** at Straumsvík. This was Iceland's first metal smelter, opened in 1969.

• *Before you reach the smelter, follow the signs for* Krýsuvík *and turn
left on highway 42. Continue as it makes several turns through an industrial area.*

*The forbidding-looking mountains ahead of you enclose your desti-
nation, the lake called Kleifarvatn. A low pass winds through the mountains to the lake; for these few miles, the road isn't paved—drive slowly
as you dodge potholes.*

Kleifarvatn Lake

Kleifarvatn (CLAY-vahr-VAHT) lake offers a nice sample of Iceland's distinctive volcanic scenery. In good weather, you can walk

along the black sand beach and even dip your toes in the water. There's something peculiar about Kleifarvatn: It has no outlet (it's fed by underground springs, and the water level varies). The area around the lake is totally undeveloped, and is a good (if lonely) place to look for the northern lights on clear, dark nights. There's a small parking lot near the end of the first long stretch of sandy beach, as well as parking lots at the overlooks from the headlands a little farther on. Don't drive off-road here.

• *A little past the end of the lake, take the turnoff to the right and park to explore the...*

▲Seltún Geothermal Field

This steaming, bubbling, boiling (and very smelly) landscape hints at the geothermal power just underfoot. A boardwalk and marked

paths take you on a 15-minute circuit through the field. Stay on the path, as the water and steam here are boiling hot. Partway through the loop, you can climb steeply up to a hilltop viewpoint overlooking the entire area, with Kleifarvatn lake just

beyond—but the up-close boardwalk stroll through the steam zone is plenty satisfying. The environment here is not just natural, but also the product of botched attempts to exploit the geothermal field for energy—first in the 1750s, and most recently in the 1940s. In 1999, one of the boreholes from the last attempt got plugged up and exploded violently, creating a 30-foot crater now filled with water (at the first overlook). There are picnic benches here, and a WC (in summer).

Just after leaving Seltún, watch on the left for the Grænavatn parking lot. **Grænavatn** (Green Lake), a small lake that formed inside a volcanic crater, is worth a quick stop to gaze at its vivid color (from algae) and the surrounding jagged hilltops.

• *Continue south on highway 42 until it tees at highway 427, where you'll turn right. About 10 minutes from Seltún, you'll see a dirt road*

BLUE LAGOON & REYKJANES

History of the Reykjanes Peninsula

The Reykjanes Peninsula is geologically new and active, and the extensive lava fields here have at most a thin layer of vegetation. (Looking at it from an approaching plane, or on Google Maps, you'll see lots of brown.) During Iceland's early centuries, when farming was the mainstay of the economy, few people lived here. But the peninsula was a good base for rich offshore fishing grounds. As fishing became more important, the temporary settlements on the peninsula became permanent. Villages sprang up, particularly at Keflavík and Njarðvík on the north side, and at Grindavík in the south. Many of the people who settled here were poor and landless, and today's Icelanders, perhaps wrongly, still think of the peninsula as a proletarian region with little "old money" wealth—no sheep, no fine churches.

During World War II, military planners realized that the broad, flat wastelands near the town of Keflavík were an ideal place for an air base. Planes crossing the Atlantic could refuel here efficiently, and there was space for very long runways (long enough to land a space shuttle). After the war, the US military established a base next to the airport. Until 2006, when the base was closed, up to a few thousand Americans lived there, in a mostly self-contained community. The military base and the airport became the peninsula's largest employers, and the towns of Keflavík and Njarðvík grew.

branch off to the left, signposted Krýsuvíkurbjarg. *This road (too rough for two-wheel-drive cars) leads out to a high coastal cliff with a large seabird colony. Hikers not in a hurry could park along the shoulder of the dirt road and walk out (about 2.5 miles each way).*

Highway 427 continues through attractive, moss-covered lava fields and then traverses a dark, inhospitable upland before arriving in the town of Grindavík.

Grindavík Town

Unassuming Grindavík is important for its harbor, which was improved in the 20th century and is one of the few usable ports on Iceland's southern coast. Follow *Höfnin* signposts to reach the harbor, where you'll see fishing boats moored and large fish-processing factories. If you like, spend a few minutes driving around this windswept town of 2,000; keep an eye out for the old church, the new church, the

police station, the primary school, and the municipal swimming pool.

Sights in Grindavík: The town museum, **Kvikan** (Saltfish Museum), backs up to the harbor. It has exhibitions on the town's history (including life-size dioramas of the fishing industry); the history of salted cod (once the backbone of the local economy); Icelandic geology and geothermal energy; and novelist Guðbergur Bergsson (b. 1932), who was born here but spent much of his life in Spain. The building also serves as the local TI, with maps and brochures, and a contemporary art exhibition space upstairs. While nicely presented, the museum is worth visiting only if you have time to kill before your Blue Lagoon appointment (1,500 ISK; mid-May-Sept daily 10:00-17:00, Sat-Sun only off-season, Hafnargata 12a, tel. 420-1190, www.grindavik.is/kvikan).

Eating in Grindavík: The cozy **$ Bryggjan** café at the harbor specializes in lobster soup, served with bread and butter, as well as sandwiches and cakes. Decorated with fishing gear and memorabilia from Iceland and the Faroe Islands, it attracts both locals and travelers (daily 8:00-22:00, Miðgarður 2, tel. 426-7100). **$ Hjá Höllu** (Halla's Place) is a popular local lunch joint with a small, inventive, ever-changing menu that includes vegetarian options—ask them to translate. It's on the town's main road, in the tiny mall next door to the Nettó supermarket, which also houses a liquor store, pharmacy, and hair salon—enter from inside the mall (Mon-Fri 8:00-17:00, Sat from 11:00, closed Sun, Víkurbraut 62, tel. 896-5316, www.hjahollu.is). For something more formal, try the **$$ Salthúsið** sit-down restaurant, a block behind Nettó, with a spacious, woody interior and a deck that's inviting on a nice day (daily 12:00-22:00, off-season until 21:00, Stamphólsvegur 2, tel. 426-9700, www.salthusid.is).

Onward to the Blue Lagoon

The Blue Lagoon is a 10-minute drive north of Grindavík: Hopefully you've timed things so that you arrive promptly for your reservation. Even if you're not getting wet at the Blue Lagoon, you can park for free at the complex and have a look around.

• *Road signs direct you to* **Bláa Lónið** *along highway 426, which winds through the lava around the west side of the mountain called Þorbjörn.*

Alternate Route: It's also fine to take highway 43, going north past the Svartsengi geothermal plant, which feeds the lagoon. The plant is not open to the public, but you can make an unmarked turn off highway 43 and drive up as far as the visitor parking lot, getting a view of the red-painted water pipes that deliver hot water to area communities, and the turbine halls that generate electricity. (To actually visit a geothermal power plant, plan a trip to Hellisheiði, between Reykjavík and Selfoss; see page 210.)

Skip the Southwest: From Grindavík you may be tempted to drive around the desolate southwestern tip of the Reykjanes Peninsula. Be warned that the route is much less interesting than it looks on the map. Although the Reykjanesviti lighthouse and the nearby headland would seem to promise great views, in practice the lighthouse is set on a hill far, far from the shore, and the view of the coast from it or the headland path doesn't merit the effort. The Gunnuhver geothermal area is interesting, but Seltún is better; and the bridge over a tectonic fissure, which claims to let you "walk between continents," is a lame gimmick. I'd skip this circuit.

Blue Lagoon back to Reykjavík (or Detour to Keflavík/Njarðvík)

From the Blue Lagoon, most travelers get back on the road to Reykjavík. Alternatively, you can detour to Keflavík and Njarðvík, with a few good museums.

• *Head out to highway 43 and head north. After about 10 minutes, highway 43 tees into highway 41, the main road between Keflavík and Reykjavík. Turn right to head straight back to* **Reykjavík** *(about 45 minutes from the Blue Lagoon), or left to stop in* **Keflavík** *and* **Njarðvík** *(about a 15-minute drive from the Blue Lagoon).*

Keflavík and Njarðvík (Reykjanesbær)

The peninsula's main settlement (pop. 15,000) isn't a must-see, but has some attractions that can easily fill a few hours. Once separate towns, Keflavík and Njarðvík have grown together; in the 1990s they merged governments under the new name Reykjanesbær.

In 2006, the town expanded even more when the US military left its base near the airport and turned the area over to civilian use. That neighborhood is now called **Ásbrú;** if you're curious, you can follow signs into it and drive around (turning off highway 41 at a roundabout). The streets still have English names and you can drive past the old military PX, the base's theater, and the yellow-painted housing blocks.

Keflavík and Njarðvík have several museums that can be a good end to this driving tour. To reach them, turn off highway 41 and head into town, following signs for the museums. For a map of this area, see the end of the Reykjavík chapter.

Icelandic Museum of Rock 'n' Roll: Chronicling Icelandic pop music from the 1930s to the present, this museum fills a large space in the local music school and concert-hall complex. Exhibits cover the biggies

(Björk, Sigur Rós, and Of Monsters and Men), as well as lesser-known Icelandic musicians. Visitors can sample music and video clips; visit the Sound Lab to add their own vocals to tunes and try out drums, guitars, and keyboards; and watch documentary films in a small theater. The museum sells coffee and candy, but doesn't have a real café (1,500 ISK, daily 11:00-18:00, Hjallavegur 2, Reykjanesbær, tel. 420-1030, www.rokksafn.is).

Viking World: This museum houses the *Icelander*, a replica of the medieval Scandinavian ship unearthed at Gokstad, Norway in the 1880s (the original is in Oslo). While the boat itself is worth seeing, the rest of the attraction— with a few artifacts, some conceptual exhibits, and a Viking dress-up area— lacks substance. The museum is useful though for its early opening time and

breakfast buffet (museum-1,500 ISK, museum and breakfast-2,500 ISK, daily 7:00-18:00, breakfast until 10:00, Víkingabraut 1, tel. 422-2000, www.vikingworld.is). More interesting is the **Settlement Age Zoo** (Landnámsdýragarður) just across the parking lot—a cute (and free) petting farm, with animals living in miniature sod-roofed huts (early May-July daily 10:00-17:00).

Duus Museum: At the northwestern end of Keflavík, this local history and art museum has a collection of more than 100 model boats made by a retired local sea captain (1,000 ISK, daily 12:00-17:00, Duusgata 2, tel. 420-3245, http://sofn.reykjanesbaer. is/duusmuseum). A **TI** is next to the museum (Mon-Fri 9:00-17:00, Sat-Sun from 12:00, tel. 420-3246).

• *To head back to Reykjavík, it's a straight 45-minute shot along highway 41.*

Northern Peninsula Loop Drive

For a short and sweet drive that samples an uncrowded stretch of coastal Iceland, take a spin around the northern tip of the Reykjanes Peninsula. My counterclockwise route takes you to a pair of lighthouses on a windblown point, an old church built of lava rock, and a short, pleasant walk to another scenically set lighthouse. It takes less than an hour to drive the 27 miles, but be sure to allow time to linger along the way.

• *From Keflavík Airport, take highway 45 following the coastline through the tiny town of Garður. You'll come to a pair of lighthouses and a parking lot at Garðskagi Point, the northernmost tip of the Reykjanes Peninsula.*

Garðskagi Point

The short red-and-white lighthouse on the water is the old Garðskagi lighthouse. Built in 1897, it's the second oldest lighthouse in Iceland. No longer in service, it now houses the tiny, three-table **$ Old Lighthouse Café** in the former keeper's quarters (serves coffee, cakes, sandwiches, beer, and their *ástarpungar* (love balls)—like a pair of dense doughnut holes with raisins; daily June-Aug 8:00-18:00, closes in nasty weather). You can climb the five ladder-like sets of stairs to the top of the lighthouse for breezy views of some of Iceland's most treacherous waters, and to Reykjavík in the distance (500 ISK, or spend that amount in the café for free admission).

The big lighthouse you see inland, **Garðskagaviti,** was built in 1944 and is Iceland's tallest at just over 90 feet. Because of coastal erosion, this replacement for the old lighthouse was built well away from the shoreline. Inside its doorway is a plaque presented by survivors of the US Coast Guard cutter *Alexander Hamilton*—torpedoed by a German U-boat in January 1942—to the crews of Icelandic fishing boats who came to their rescue.

In the white building beyond the lighthouse is a small **maritime museum** (1,000 ISK, includes admission to Garðskagaviti lighthouse, daily 13:00-17:00) and the **$ Röstin Restaurant** (burgers and fish and meat dishes, daily 12:00-20:30, closed Mon in winter, tel. 422-7220).

Aside from the lighthouses, Garðskagi Point is a fine spot for birdwatching and catching sunsets or the Northern Lights.

• *From the point, it's about 7 miles to our next stop. Head south on road 402 (part of it gravel) until you join up with highway 45, and turn right. Continue on this lightly traveled road through the sleepy fishing port of Sandgerði, by small hay farms and pastures, until you see a dark stone church on a rise off to the right. Turn off at the* Hvalsnes *sign and drive to the walled cemetery and park.*

Hvalsneskirkja Church

Hvalsneskirkja, standing solidly against the elements, dates to 1887. It was built of local basalt, with an interior partially finished using driftwood collected from the nearby shores. Famous Icelandic poet Hallgrímur Pétursson, who wrote 50 hymns telling the story of the Passion of Christ, served as pastor from 1644 to 1651 at a previous church that stood here (the iconic Hallgrímskirkja in Reykjavík is named after him). It's a serene setting, with the church watching peacefully over wide-open fields spreading out under even wider skies.

Before driving on, visit the sweet cemetery, with lovingly tended graves decorated in summer with pots of colorful flowers braving the breeze.

• *Continue south on highway 45 another three miles until you see a sign for* Stafnes, *where you'll turn off to the right. Drive a short distance past some farmhouses to the parking lot at the end of the road.*

Stafnes Lighthouse (Stafnesviti)

The plaque in the parking lot memorializes the 1928 wreck of the trawler *Jón Forseti*, in which 15 crewmembers perished (and 10 survived). Just past the plaque, a grassy path leads out to the orange-colored Stafnes Lighthouse. Built in 1925 of concrete, today it's automated (and not open to visitors). The lighthouse itself may not be all that remarkable, but it does strike a colorful  pose. Walking past the lighthouse toward the sea (if the surf allows) you can't miss the curiously pockmarked lava rock stretching along the shore. It's quiet here, and even on a sunny day you'll likely have this place to yourself, with nothing but the North Atlantic between you and Greenland.

• *From Stafnes it's a 10-minute drive through lava fields and blue lupines (in season) to the junction with highway 44. Turn left, and follow it to highway 41 where, at the roundabout, you can go right for Reykjavík, or left for Keflavík Airport and Keflavík town.*

GOLDEN CIRCLE

The Golden Circle is Iceland's classic day trip. If you have just one day to see the Icelandic countryside from Reykjavík, this route offers the most satisfying variety of sightseeing and scenery per miles driven. And you'll be in good company: Travelers dating back to the Danish king Christian IX, who visited Iceland in 1874, have followed the same route outlined in this chapter.

The Golden Circle loop includes this essential trio of sights: Þingvellir, a dramatic gorge marking the pulling apart of the Eurasian and North American tectonic plates (and also the site of the country's annual assembly in the Middle Ages); Geysir, a bubbling, steaming hillside that's home to Strokkur, Iceland's most active geyser; and Gullfoss, one of Iceland's most impressive waterfalls.

You can round out the trip by adding any of several minor sights, taking a dip in a thermal bath, having lunch on a dairy farm, or sipping a Bloody Mary in a tomato-filled greenhouse. This chapter explains your options and links them with driving directions. As nearly everything lies along the simple loop road, navigating is easy.

Note that the Golden Circle loop is well trod and extremely touristy. Long lines of tour buses and rental cars follow each other around the route each day, but despite the crowds the attractions hold their appeal.

On Your Own vs. Taking an Excursion: Driving the Golden Circle on your own is completely doable and offers maximum flexibility, but some find it more relaxing to join an organized bus trip. If you have the time, full-day tours are best (see the Beyond Reykjavík chapter for options). Half-day tours cost only slightly less and rush you through the sights.

Golden Circle Drive

The entire 150-mile Golden Circle circuit involves about four hours of driving, not including stops. The basic self-guided route is simple: From Reykjavík, the first leg of the drive is a scenic hour to Þingvellir. After touring Þingvellir, it's about an hour to the thermal fields at Geysir, then 10 minutes farther to the gushing Gullfoss waterfall. From there, you'll backtrack to Geysir and

circle back to Reykjavík in about two hours, passing a slew of lesser roadside attractions. My suggested route goes clockwise—starting with Þingvellir—but it can also be done in the other direction.

PLANNING YOUR DRIVE

Here's a suggested plan (with stops) for those wanting to get an early-ish start and be home in time for dinner:

9:00   Leave Reykjavík and head for Þingvellir national park, taking the scenic Nesjavallaleið route (1 hour)

10:00   Visit Þingvellir

11:30   Drive from Þingvellir to the village of Laugarvatn (30 minutes); have lunch here or nearby

13:00   Head to Geysir geothermal field (20 minutes) and watch Strokkur erupt a couple of times

14:00   Drive to Gullfoss (10 minutes) and visit the waterfall

15:00   Head in the direction of Selfoss (1 hour), stopping briefly at Skálholt Church and Kerið crater (or other sights along the way that interest you)

16:30   Return to Reykjavík (about 1 hour from Selfoss)

Golden Circle Tips

This drive is peppered with additional sights and activities; you can easily alter my suggested plan to suit your interests. Before setting out, review your options, prioritize, and make a plan that hits what you want to see in the time you have. Here are some things to consider.

Dealing with Crowds: The number of visitors to Iceland has grown in recent years, but so have facilities to handle them. You'll make the same "big three" stops (Þingvellir, Geysir, Gullfoss) as everyone else. You won't be alone in enjoying the wide-open wonders...but there's a joyful mood, and the crowds are part of the fun. Most people blitz through, seeing little more than those

three—which leaves the rest of the route fairly crowd-free. Frankly, I wouldn't worry about it. But if you're set on avoiding crowds, an early start keeps you ahead of the rush (bus tours generally go clockwise, leaving Reykjavík at 9:00 to arrive at Þingvellir at 10:00); in summer, when days are long, you could instead do this trip late in the day. Or, better yet, spend the night along the route so you can visit the top sights outside of peak tourist hours—see "Sleeping on the Golden Circle" at the end of this chapter.

Activities: Several activities along the Golden Circle require extra time—and in some cases, reservations. The Silfra fissure, at Þingvellir, provides top-notch **scuba or snorkeling** opportunities (book well in advance—see details on page 197). Several horse farms are just outside Reykjavík, making it easy to incorporate **horseback riding** into your Golden Circle spin (again, this should be prearranged—see page 50). There are also several **thermal baths** along the way (see sidebar later in this chapter). If you plan to see the geothermal exhibit at the **Hellisheiði Power Plant,** note that it closes at 17:00.

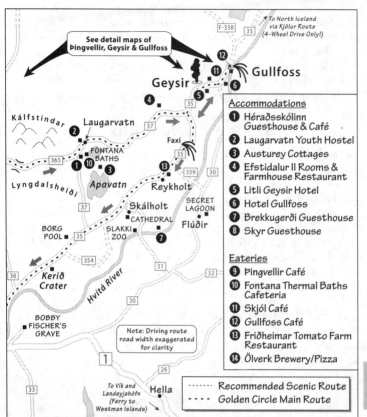

GOLDEN CIRCLE

Evening Options: In the summer, some intrepid travelers—determined to wring the absolute maximum travel experience out of every moment—set out on this loop in the late afternoon...making the most of the abundant daylight. And since the major Golden Circle sights (Þingvellir, Geysir, Gullfoss) don't technically "close," you can visit them anytime—plus, they're less crowded in the evening (some of the lesser sights and thermal baths do have closing times). Another fine evening activity is to have a memorable dinner in the countryside at one of my recommended restaurants—stretching your day and allowing a late return to Reykjavík.

Weather and Road Conditions: The route crosses three mountain passes (Mosfellsheiði or Nesjavallaleið, then Lyngdalsheiði, and finally Hellisheiði). These passes can be icy and slippery, especially from October to April. Check the road-conditions map at Road.is before you start off. In treacherous conditions, take a bus tour and leave the driving to pros. If you do drive the Golden Circle in winter, it's smart to set off from Reykjavík an hour before sunrise to get maximum value from the daylight hours.

Fill 'Er Up: Gas stations are few and very far between (going clockwise, the first one you hit is in Reykholt). Fill up before you start this road trip.

Name Note: Be aware that there are two Reykholts in Iceland: one here on the Golden Circle (with all the greenhouses), and the other about 100 miles away, east of Borgarnes (no vegetables).

Golden Circle Loop

Below, I've linked the main stops with driving directions. Let's get started.

REYKJAVÍK TO ÞINGVELLIR

There are two ways to get from Reykjavík to Þingvellir: the scenic Nesjavallaleið road (1 hour on highway 435) or the Mosfellsheiði road (40 minutes on highway 36). Nesjavallaleið is my preferred route—but, because of its high elevation, it's open only from May to September. If it's closed, it will appear in red on the road-conditions map at Road.is. The Mosfellsheiði route stays open all year.

Scenic Route via Nesjavallaleið

This rugged one-hour route climbs high up (to about 1,500 feet) over a craggy mountain range, descends steeply past the Nesjavel-lir geothermal plant, and then hugs the shore of Þingvallavatn lake. Most of Nesjavallaleið (NESS-ya-VAHT-la-layth) was built as a service road for a giant hot-water pipe that feeds Reykjavík's heating system.

Start out by leaving Reykjavík south on highway 1 toward Selfoss and the South Coast. As the town thins out into countryside, turn left, following small signs for highways 431 *(Hafravatn)* and 435 *(Nesjavellir)*; highway 431 becomes 435 on the way. Just after leaving the main road, you'll pass a maximum-security prison. (In a country with, on average, fewer than two murders a year, it's small—only about 40 cells.)

The road crosses the giant **hot-water pipe,** then curves around to follow straight along it. You'll drive (through a lava field from an eruption a thousand years ago) parallel to the pipe—and some high-tension wires—for quite some time. The road rises and eventually hits a ridge, part of a volcanic system called Hengill; from here the road climbs in a series of bends. Before the crest, you can stop at a pullout in the small, mountain-ringed **Dyradalur valley,** with signboards and picnic benches; an important path for travelers once led through the gully you see at the end of the valley (called Dyrnar, The Doors).

As you come over the ridge, you'll see the **Nesjavellir geothermal power station** far below you. This plant, built in the early

1990s, sends 250 gallons of boiling water through the pipe to Reykjavík every second, and also generates electricity. For a better look, take the lane to the right; it dead-ends at a tiny viewpoint parking lot. The igloo-like structures mark places where a borehole was drilled. Each little pipe feeds into a bigger pipe. Steam marks little hot springs. (Another power plant, on the Hellisheiði heath near the end of this tour, has a real visitors center.)

From here the road descends steeply into the valley. At the T-junction with highway 360, turn left toward *Þingvellir*. (Note that if you're doing the Golden Circle in reverse, highway 435 is signposted here only as *Hengilssvæði*.)

Now the road winds tightly along the shore of **Þingvallavatn** lake, with fine views, no guardrails, and several narrow, blind summits. You'll pass some nice summer homes, built before construction was banned here. Eventually, the road leaves the lake, passes a lone farm (sheep, potatoes, hay, and horses) and ends at a junction with highway 36. Turn right. From here, it's 4 miles to Þingvellir.

Alternative Route via Mosfellsheiði

If Nesjavallaleið is closed due to bad weather (typically Oct-April), take the main Mosfellsheiði route instead. While less scenic and less interesting, it's more direct.

Start this 40-minute route heading north out of Reykjavík on highway 1 toward Borgarnes and Akureyri, then turn right on highway 36 just past the town of Mosfellsbær, following the *Þingvellir* signs. This leads up through Mosfellsdalur (Moss Mountain Valley) and over a low, broad pass (900 feet above sea level) to Þingvellir.

The Mosfellsdalur valley is still rural, with several horse farms. As you drive through, look left up the hillside (or turn up the side road called Mosfellsvegur) to see the unusual church called **Mosfellskirkja**, designed

GOLDEN CIRCLE

Thermal Bathing Along the Golden Circle

To pack the maximum Icelandic experience into your Golden Circle day, add a visit to a thermal bath. This loop drive passes near four extremely different options (all described in this chapter). Skim these options before you depart, to strategize where you might squeeze in a dip...and remember to bring your swimsuit and towel (or rent one—available at all listed here except Reykjadalur).

Fontana Thermal Bath, in Laugarvatn, is the upscale choice. While not nearly as ritzy as the Blue Lagoon, it's a "premium" option that feels a notch up from standard municipal swimming pools.

The Secret Lagoon, in Flúðir (a 10-minute detour from the main Golden Circle route, near Reykholt), is a big, rustic outdoor pool packed with young travelers unwinding after a busy day of sightseeing. This is the only bathing experience on this route where it's smart to reserve ahead.

Borg swimming pool is a municipal facility right along the main road between Reykholt and Selfoss—nothing fancy, but cheap, handy, and the most authentically Icelandic of the options on the Golden Circle.

Reykjadalur—the "Smoky Valley" above the town of Hveragerði—is the adventurous choice. It's a remote, steaming, natural thermal river that requires a one-hour hike each way.

Of course, if you're heading home to Reykjavík at the end of your Golden Circle day, you can have your pick of the capital area's many **public swimming pools** (options described on page 118); two good suburban pools, Lágafellslaug and Árbæjarlaug, are convenient to the Golden Circle route.

Before visiting any of these, get up to speed by reading the "Pool Rules" sidebar on page 42.

by architect Ragnar Emilsson in the 1960s. It's full of triangular shapes—including the bell tower and roof—as a reference to the Trinity.

Note that this route passes by the former home of Iceland's most famous author, **Halldór Laxness** (open to tourists; for details see page 117). Otherwise, it's a (fairly dull) straight shot to Þingvellir. When you begin to see **Þingvallavatn lake**—Iceland's largest—on your right, you know you're getting close.

▲▲▲Þingvellir

The gorge at Þingvellir (THING-VET-leer), dear to all Icelanders, is both dramatic and historic. It's dramatic because you can readily see the slow separation of the North American and Eurasian tectonic plates—the earth's crust is literally being torn apart. And it's historic because, about a thousand years ago, it was here at "Assembly Plains" (as its name means) that chieftains from the different parts of Iceland began gathering annually to  govern themselves (at a meeting called the Alþingi). Today the area has been preserved as a national park. Visitors can walk along the rifts created by the separating plates, stand at the place where the original Icelanders made big decisions, hike to a picturesque waterfall, see a scant few historic buildings, and even go for a snorkel or scuba dive into a flooded gorge.

Orientation to Þingvellir

Cost and Hours: The natural site is always open and free, but you'll pay 750 ISK to park. The visitors center features a skippable high-tech interactive exhibit explaining the geology, history, and nature of Þingvellir, and has free WCs and a gift shop/café (exhibit-1,000 ISK, visitors center open daily 9:00-18:00, tel. 482-3613, www.thingvellir.is). Free one-hour guided tours in English depart daily at 10:00 and 15:00 from the Þingvellir church.

Arrival at Þingvellir: You can park on either the upper (west) or the lower (east) side of the Öxará river. The two sides are no more than a half-mile apart if you use the footbridges over the river, but it's a five-mile drive by car.

The first turnoff you'll reach is for the main lot, **P1** (sometimes called *Hakið* on maps). I prefer to park here because this is where the facilities are clustered. Farther along (on road 361, beyond the intersection with the park offices/café) are several **smaller parking lots** on the lower side: P2, P4, P5, and Silfra. These parking lots can be handy for hikers, divers, and picnics. If P1 is full and you're with a group, consider having the driver drop everyone off at P1; the driver can park at one of the lower lots and hike back up to meet you.

A camera records your license-plate number as you drive in; at **pay machines** (P1's is in the visitors center), punch in your license-plate number, then insert your credit card.

Length of This Visit: For a quick visit, you can enjoy the overview, hike the gorge, and see the Law Rock in less than an hour. Add a half-hour to hike up to the waterfall (about a mile one-way from P1), and a half-hour to cross the river to the church (least interesting and skippable).

GOLDEN CIRCLE

GOLDEN CIRCLE

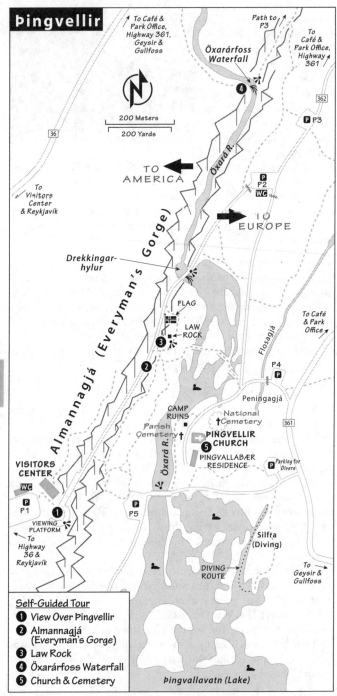

Þingvellir

To Café &
Park Office,
Highway 361,
Geysir &
Gullfoss

Path to
P3

Öxarárfoss
Waterfall

To
Café &
Park Office,
Highway 361

N

200 Meters

200 Yards

36

362

P P3

TO
AMERICA

Öxará R.

P
P2
WC

To
Visitors
Center
& Reykjavík

TO
EUROPE

Drekkingar-
hylur

FLAG

LAW
ROCK

Flosagjá

To Café
& Park
Office

P4
P

CAMP
RUINS

Peningagjá

National
Cemetery

361

Parish
Cemetery

Öxará R.

PINGVELLIR
CHURCH

VISITORS
CENTER

ÞINGVALLABÆR
RESIDENCE

Parking for
Divers
P

WC

P
P1

VIEWING
PLATFORM

P
P5

To
Highway 36 &
Reykjavík

Silfra
(Diving)

DIVING
ROUTE

To
Geysir &
Gullfoss

Þingvallavatn (Lake)

Self-Guided Tour
1 View Over Þingvellir
2 Almannagjá
(Everyman's Gorge)
3 Law Rock
4 Öxarárfoss Waterfall
5 Church & Cemetery

Almannagjá (Everyman's Gorge)

Eating: In good weather, Þingvellir is a nice place for a picnic. There are benches, wooded areas, and free portable WCs near P2. The visitors center (at P1) has a basic **$ café** selling premade sandwiches, ice cream, snacks, and hot and cold drinks. Otherwise, the only eatery nearby is the small **$ café** at the national park office a couple of miles away, at the junction of highways 36, 361, and 550 (daily 9:00-22:00, Sept-May until 18:00).

Self-Guided Tour

This plan assumes that you're parking at the upper P1 lot. The visitors center is helpful for geological and historical context, but is skippable.

• *From P1 and the visitors center, walk a few steps to the overlook with the railing.*

❶ **View Over Þingvellir:** Look down at the lake and the land that's subsided to its north. You can see how the Öxará (Ax River)

empties into the lake. Þingvellir's church (and some ruins of the old chieftains' encampments) lies just across the river below you. The five-gabled farm building dates from 1930.

Directly below you is Þingvellir's **great fissure;** look at how the North American and Eurasian tectonic plates are moving apart. Imagine pulling a big, chewy cookie apart very slowly; you'd start to see cracks in the dough, and eventually crumbs would start to slide into the gap. Here, you can see long, narrow fissures in the earth, running roughly north-south. The lake itself sits in the largest fissure of all. The lake bed (and the land to the north and south) basically has slid into the gap between the plates. It's deep. In fact, the deepest parts of the lake bed are actually below sea level.

• *Follow the boardwalk as it switchbacks down between the cliffs, descending through the little side channel that leads into...*

❷ **Almannagjá** (Everyman's Gorge): As you walk, you're tracing the boundaries of continents. To your left is America. To your right is Europe. (A geologist might say it's not quite that simple, but would agree that Iceland is half in Europe and half in America—and this is where they meet.)

On the left, the vertical cliff face is original

rock as it was laid down by volcanic eruptions and compressed over the eons. On the right, you can see how the rock—once even with the cliff on your left—has fallen away into the gap due to the subsidence that also created the lake. On the right (fallen) side of the gorge, you can scramble out to various walkways and viewpoints.

• *As you approach the valley floor, follow the boardwalks to the right to stand in the area just below the flagpole. This marks the likely location of...*

❸ **The Law Rock** (Lögberg): Within about 60 years of the first settlements, Iceland was home to roughly 15,000 people—almost

all of them farmers, scattered across the island on isolated homesteads. In about AD 930, local chieftains began to gather at an annual meeting called the Alþingi ("all-thing"), which took place more or less where you're standing. For this reason, Þingvellir can be thought of as Iceland's first capital. Today, this site remains important for Icelanders—it's their Ancient Agora, their Roman Forum, their Independence Hall.

Gaze over the marshy delta below you, and time-travel back a thousand years. It's the middle of June, and you're surrounded by fellow chieftains, some having traveled on horseback more than two weeks, over challenging terrain, just to be here. Each chieftain has brought along an entourage of *þingmenn* (assemblymen). The field below you is dotted with temporary turf huts—like a festival grounds, set up only in summer.

The meeting is about to begin, and you're immersed in a hairy mosh pit of hundreds—maybe thousands—of unwashed Norsemen (and Norsewomen). The collective body odor is overwhelming. But for two weeks, you've all agreed to set aside your grudges and work together to find consensus on critical issues of the day. This is your one chance all year to learn the latest news and gossip. And while everyone's here, there are sure to be some big parties, business wheeling and dealing, marriages arranged...and, quite likely, some duels. Merchants, tradesmen, and panhandlers are milling about, trying to drum up a little business. The whole event has a carnival-like bustle.

Iceland's Conversion to Christianity

In AD 1000, the Alþingi had its most important session. Iceland's longtime ally Norway—whose king had recently converted to Christianity—was exerting tremendous pressure on Iceland to follow suit. When Norwegian missionaries failed to convert the entire island, the impatient king took several Icelandic traders hostage. Losing its primary trade partner would have been devastating to Iceland, and at the next summer's Alþingi, all hell broke loose between the pro- and anti-conversion factions. Civil war was in the air.

Eventually, both sides agreed to let the law speaker, a pagan named Þorgeir Ljósvetningagoði, make the decision for all of Iceland. According to the sagas, Þorgeir covered himself with a fur pelt and slept on it (literally) for one night and one day. Upon emerging, he addressed the assembly with his decision: Iceland was now Christian, but Icelanders could still worship their pagan gods privately, and continue a few key pagan practices (including the consumption of horse meat, the infanticide of unwanted children, and animal sacrifices to the old gods). And so, in one fell swoop, Þorgeir brought Iceland into the Christian fold, and averted a conflict with Norway that could well have wiped out the island's still-fragile civilization. This stands as one of the most peaceful mass religious conversions in history.

The crowd quiets with the appearance of the *allsherjargoði* (grand chieftain)—a direct descendant of Ingólfur Arnarson (who was, according to the sagas, the first Icelandic settler of Reykjavík). As the high priest of the Norse pantheon, the *allsherjargoði* calls the assembly to order, and sanctifies the proceedings before the gods. Then the "law speaker" *(lögsögumaður)* takes his position at the Law Rock and recites the guidelines for the assembly, outlines the broad strokes of Icelandic law, and recaps the highlights of last year's session. The acoustics created by the cliff behind him help bounce his voice across the throngs; other speakers, strategically located at the back of the crowd, carefully listen to, then repeat, whatever the law speaker says.

As the Alþingi continues, the law speaker also presides over the Law Council *(Lögrétta)*, on the opposite riverbank. A more select group of chieftains reviews and debates existing legislation, and weighs in on legal disputes, and the law speaker is responsible for memorizing whatever is decided. Eventually, Christianity brings literacy and the Latin alphabet, and the law speaker's role gives way to that of a sort of "high attorney"—*lögmaður*.

The Alþingi gatherings took place as long as Iceland was independent. But things changed after 1262, when the chieftains entered into union with Norway—pledging fealty to the Norwegian king under an agreement called the Old Covenant. The Alþingi still convened annually at Þingvellir, but morphed into an appeals court; it continued this way until 1798.

Þingvellir became a national park in 1930, to celebrate the millennial anniversary of the first Alþingi. And in 1944, the modern, independent Republic of Iceland was proclaimed right here. The stands below the flag are for official ceremonies; one of the information boards at the railing displays photographs of some of these ceremonies.

By the way, those original settlers couldn't possibly have known that the place they selected for their gathering also happened to straddle America and Europe. They chose this site mainly because Þingvellir is fairly central (relatively accessible in summer from every corner of Iceland) and had ample water, grazing lands, and firewood to supply the sprawling gatherings. Its location along the cusp of continents is just one of those serendipities of history.

• *Follow the wide, gravel path straight ahead, and cross the river on a small bridge over a waterfall (the bottom end of Öxarárfoss, which we'll visit next). To your left is Drekkingarhylur (Drowning Pool), where women accused of witchcraft were drowned between the late 16th and mid-18th centuries.*

If you're short on time, you could turn back here. Otherwise, continue along the path. After about 300 yards, just before reaching parking lot P2, branch off on the small path to your left. Follow it for a few minutes as it crests the rise to your left. Then, a hundred yards to your left is the large waterfall called...

❹ Öxarárfoss: This is where the river—which rises up on the plateau—plunges over the cliff face into the valley. Old sagas say that the early settlers changed the course of the river to improve the water supply at Þingvellir, but no one is exactly sure whether this is true and how that might have been done.

• *You've already seen the most interesting parts of Þingvellir—you can head back the way you came (past the P2 lot). With more time, cross the footbridges on your left (below the Law Rock) to reach the...*

❺ Church and Cemetery: The current **church** was built in 1859, but churches have stood here for centuries. The original church was supposedly built using timbers sent to Iceland by Norway's St. Olaf (King Olav II, 995-1030). If the church is open, step inside to see the humble, painted interior (generally closed Sept-May). Local parishioners lie in the small cemetery in front of the

church. The multi-gabled house just beyond it, called **Þingvallabær,** was built in 1930 as a residence for the local priest, who was also the park warden. It's now used for ceremonial functions.

Behind the church, the round, elevated area up the stairs is a **cemetery** lot. This was planned as a resting place for national heroes, but the idea never took off, and only two people (well-known writers) were ever buried there.

Along the riverbank near the church, the **mounds** contain the remains of the temporary dwellings that were set up here each year for the annual assembly. From here, looking back the way you came, enjoy great views of the sheer cliff that defines the fissure.

• *Between the church and the river, a waterside path allows further exploration. Following this path takes you to the P5 lot, where a steep shortcut (on a rocky path through the woods) leads back up to the P1 lot and the high viewpoint where you started. Also nearby is Silfra, a favorite destination of divers—described next. For an easier route back to P1, backtrack along the river, take the bridge on your left to reach the Law Rock, and then hike back up through Everyman's Gorge.*

Silfra Snorkel or Dive Trip

One of the many fissures at Þingvellir, Silfra is renowned among snorkelers and scuba divers for its water clarity. Thanks to the purity of the glacial water that fills it, you can see underwater for more than a hundred yards.

To snorkel or dive in Silfra, you'll need to join a tour (such as those offered by Dive.is, the largest operator—book well in advance). Snorkelers must be relatively fit and comfortable in the water, while divers need to be certified and experienced. There have been a few fatal accidents at Silfra in recent years (even involving snorkelers)—don't overestimate your abilities.

The water is a constant 35-39°F, so you'll be outfitted with some serious gear: a neoprene dry suit, hood, gloves, fins, mask, and snorkel. (Some companies have basic changing cabins in the parking lot; otherwise, there's limited privacy.) The suit keeps your body warm

GOLDEN CIRCLE

enough, but expect your face to go numb and your hands to get cold. After changing into your gear, you'll walk a few minutes to the entry stairs and descend into the fissure with your guide. A gentle drift current slowly takes you along the fissure and into a lagoon, where you'll need to kick against the current to U-turn to the metal exit stairs. You'll be in the water for about 30-40 minutes.

Cost: 20,000 ISK for guided snorkeling, extra 5,000 ISK for pickup in Reykjavík; 35,000 ISK for package that includes pickup, Silfra, and bus tour of Golden Circle; more for divers; tel. 578-6200, www.dive.is.

Getting There: Silfra is at the lakeshore near the east bank of the river. The entry point to Silfra is between parking lots P4 and P5. Follow the directions to Þingvellir and turn off onto road 361 to reach this area; look for the designated parking lot.

ÞINGVELLIR TO GEYSIR AND GULLFOSS

This section of the drive circles around the far end of the lake, where you can clearly see the intercontinental rift—as if a giant dropped his hoe and dredged out a tidy furrow between America and Europe.

• *Leaving Þingvellir, return to highway 36 and continue east for about 10 minutes around the lake's north shore, crossing smaller fissures, and passing fishermen hoping to hook one of the lake's famously big trout. Soon you'll pass the intersection with road 361 (a right turn here takes you back to Þingvellir's lower parking lots) and, immediately after that, the national park office, with a café.*

Continuing along the east side of the lake, you'll reach a point where highway 36 turns off to the right. Stay straight toward Laugarvatn on highway 365. This road crosses an upland heath called Lyngdalsheiði (altitude: about 700 feet; if it's closed, use highways 35 and 36).

On your left, enjoy some otherworldly, craggy mountain scenery— the Kálfstindar ridge. A half-hour after leaving Þingvellir, you leave the heath, and descend to a village on a lake. At the roundabout, follow signs onto route 37 toward Geysir (not Selfoss) and enter sleepy, unassuming Laugarvatn.

Laugarvatn

Set by a small lake of the same name, Laugarvatn was long the home of Iceland's college for sports teachers (the program has now been moved to Reykjavík), and it's in a region popular with local vacationers. As you drive you'll see many summer cottages owned by the country's labor unions for member use. Driving into the village, take the exit (right) by the recommended Héraðsskólinn Guesthouse and head down to the fancy, thatched Fontana Thermal Baths. There are hot springs in and around the lake, and Fontana, a nicely designed premium bath, makes good use of them.

▲Fontana Thermal Baths

Sitting right along the Laugarvatn lakeshore and built atop a natural hot springs, Fontana is one of Iceland's handful of premium baths—a step up in comfort (and price) from municipal swimming pools, and a bit more tourist-oriented. For some, Fontana may be a good alternative to the Blue Lagoon—it's cheaper, smaller (easier to navigate), less pretentious, much less crowded, and

doesn't require reservations. But it's also more functional than spa-like, and lacks the Blue Lagoon's romantic, volcanic setting.

Beyond the visitors center—with ticket desk, changing rooms, and a good cafeteria—is the outdoor bathing area, overlooking the lake. The complex has three modern, tiled pools, artfully landscaped with natural boulders, as well as a steam room (where you can hear the natural hot spring bubble beneath your feet) and a dry sauna. To cool off or for a change of pace, bathers are encouraged to take a dip in the lake.

Cost and Hours: 3,800 ISK, daily 10:00-22:00, Sept-May from 11:00, tel. 486-1400, www.fontana.is.

Thermal Bread Experience: Fontana follows the Icelandic tradition of baking sweet, dense rye bread right in the thermal

sands at its doorstep. Twice daily, you can pay to join the baker as they dig up a pot of bread, then taste it straight out of the ground (1,500 ISK, daily at 11:30 and 14:30). But note that you can eat the very same bread as part of their regular lunch buffet.

Nearby Thermal Beach: The lake in front of Fontana—heated by natural hot springs—is free to bathe in. Facing the lake, head right to find a small, black sand beach next to the fenced-off geothermal area (keep well clear of this area of boiling-hot water). The water near the springs is warm, but it gets colder as you go deeper. At a minimum, consider rolling up your pants and dipping your feet. On the wooden walkway between the geothermal plant and the lakeshore, notice—but don't touch—little boiling pools in the mud.

Eating in Fontana

In addition to three very good lunch options listed here, there's an "art café" at the far end of town and a grocery store next to the N1 gas station.

$$ Fontana Thermal Baths cafeteria is in the bath's entrance lobby, and open to the public (no bath entry required). You can order from the menu or spring for their full 2,900-ISK lunch buffet or 3,900-ISK dinner buffet (daily from 12:00, last lunch served at 13:45, dinner 18:00-21:00).

$$ Héraðsskólinn Café, at the recommended Héraðsskólinn Guesthouse, serves an inexpensive lunch of soups, salads, and sandwiches, and dishes up fish, meat, pizza, and vegetarian plates for dinner. The spacious dining room is filled with light and fun mid-century furniture (daily 11:00-16:00 & 18:30-21:30, breakfast available, Laugarbraut 2, tel. 537-8060).

$$ Efstidalur II Farmhouse Restaurant, 10 minutes beyond Laugarvatn, is on a large family-run dairy farm (with a recommended hotel) just off highway 37. Downstairs, a counter serves homemade ice cream. The upstairs restaurant, with windows overlooking the cows in the barn, specializes in burgers and pricier main courses. It's a popular, bustling place—family-friendly and often crowded with groups. Their 2,000-ISK special of soup, bread, fancy spreads, and coffee is fast, affordable, and delicious (daily 11:30-21:00, mid-Sept-mid-May until 20:00, well-signposted up a gravel driveway, tel. 486-1186, www.efstidalur.is). Even if you're not hungry, Efstidalur II is worth a stop for a peek at an Icelandic farm.

• *From Laugarvatn, highway 37 leads 20 minutes onward to the geothermal field at Geysir. On the right, just past Efstidalur II, notice the small farm that's augmenting its income by harnessing geothermal power (just as wind turbines generate electricity on US farms). Soon, the road changes numbers to highway 35.*

▲▲Geysir Geothermal Field

When people around the world talk about geysers, most don't realize they're referencing a place in Iceland: Geysir (GAY-seer), which literally means "the gusher." While the original Geysir geyser is no longer very active, the geothermal field around it still steams, boils, and bubbles nonstop, regularly punctuated by a dramatic eruption of scalding water from the one predictably active geyser, Strokkur.

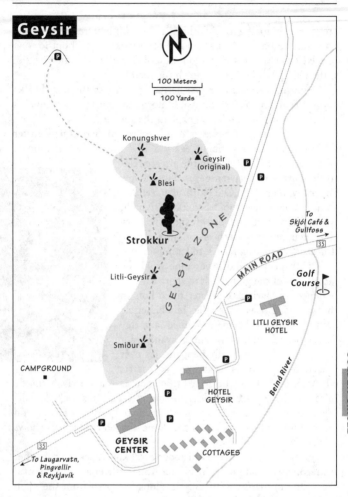

This stop is pretty simple: Watch Strokkur erupt a couple of times, look at the rest of the field, and then continue on.

Cost and Hours: Free and always open.

Safety Warning: Make sure to keep young children close. Impress upon them that they should not touch any of the water, which is boiling hot, and that they must stay behind the ropes. At Strokkur, standing upwind will keep you out of any spray.

Arrival at Geysir: Approaching Geysir, you'll see the geothermal field on your left, and a visitors complex with parking lots on your right. Park as close to the geothermal field as you can (if you drive 100 yards past the hotel and take the lane to the left, you'll find the spots closest to the geyser action).

Services and Eating: Across the road from the geothermal area is a strip mall with a clothing and souvenir store, free WCs, a golf course, a hotel, and a handful of restaurants. (I'd opt for one of the Laugarvatn eating options described earlier, or wait for Skjól Café, about 2 miles farther down the road.)

Visiting Geysir: The geothermal field lacks the boardwalks and other maintenance you would normally expect at a sight this popular. Outdoor signboards explain the geology.

The area's centerpiece is a geyser called **Strokkur** (Butter Churn), which erupts about every 5-10 minutes. The eruptions, which shoot about 50 feet in the air, are rela-tively short—in every sense—and won't wow anyone who has seen Old Faithful at Yellowstone. What's nice about Strokkur, though, is the short wait between gushes and how close you can get. Each eruption is a little different. It's surreal to stand around in a field with people who have come from the far reaches of the globe, just to share this experience...of staring at a water-filled hole in the ground. Everyone huddles in a big circle around Strokkur, cameras aimed and focused, trigger fingers twitching, waiting for the spurt. When it finally happens, it's over in a couple of seconds, as abruptly as it start-ed. After each show, the crowd thins out, and new arrivals shuffle in to take their place, shoulder-to-shoulder, cameras cocked, wait-ing...waiting...waiting. (To record the entire spurt on video, stand on the high end and watch for the dome-shaped bubble that shows a second before it blows.)

Just a few yards up the hill above Strokkur, check out the other **fumaroles and hot pools,** including Konungshver and the colorful Blesi. The miniature Litli-Geysir, along the path from the main parking lot, bubbles and boils but doesn't erupt.

Steaming uneasily off to the side is the **original "great" Gey-**

sir. This was the only one known to medieval Europeans, and is the origin of the word geyser. It was dormant for most of the 20th century, but after a nearby earthquake in 2000 it started erupting occasionally. It blows higher and longer than Strokkur, but rarely and unpredictably, so don't expect to see anything.

For a commanding view over the Geysir area, continue past Konungshver, climb over the stile, and make your way 10 minutes up to the top of one of the rocky outcroppings that overlook the geothermal field and surrounding terrain. Snowy glaciers loom to the east.

• *From Geysir, continue to the Gullfoss waterfall, a straight shot 10 minutes onward along highway 35. Along the way you'll pass $ Skjól Café (connected to a hostel and campground, serving good, affordable, split-table pizzas, burgers, and fish-and-chips; June–Aug daily 10:00–15:00 & 18:00–23:00, shorter hours off-season; mobile 899-4541, www. skjolcamping.com).*

▲▲Gullfoss Waterfall

The thundering waterfall called Gullfoss (GUTL-foss) sits on the wide, glacial Hvítá river, which drains Iceland's interior. The name means "Golden Falls" and gives this "Golden Circle" its name. The waterfall has two stages: a rocky upper cascade with a drop of about 35 feet, and a lower falls where the water plummets 70 feet straight down into a narrow gorge. Somewhat unusually for a  waterfall, the gorge runs transverse to the fall line, effectively carrying the water off to the side. Dress warmly: Cold winds blow down the valley, and the spray from the falls can soak you. Winter visitors should watch for slippery areas. If you have ice cleats, this is a good place to put them on.

Cost and Hours: Free and always open, tel. 486-6500, www. gullfoss.is.

Arrival at Gullfoss: Two viewing areas—connected by a metal staircase—let you admire the falls; each has its own free parking lot and viewpoints. Both are equally worth seeing, but if you're short on time, focus on the lower one, where you can get up close and feel the spray. To park there, watch for a blue *P* sign as you approach, and take the right turn to the lower parking lot. With more time, continue to the upper parking lot, with a huge tourist complex housing a pay WC, café, and massive gift shop (with free WCs for customers).

GOLDEN CIRCLE

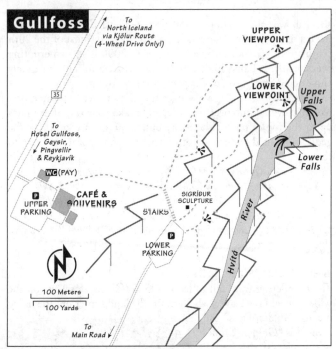

Gullfoss

To
North Iceland
via Kjölur Route
(4-Wheel Drive Only!)

UPPER
VIEWPOINT

LOWER
VIEWPOINT

Upper
Falls

35

To
Hotel Gullfoss,
Geysir,
Þingvellir
& Reykjavík

Lower
Falls

WC (PAY)

P
UPPER
PARKING

CAFÉ &
SOUVENIRS

SIGRÍÐUR
SCULPTURE

STAIRS

Hvítá
River

P
LOWER
PARKING

100 Meters
100 Yards

To
Main Road

GOLDEN CIRCLE

Eating: The large **$ café** at the upper parking lot serves soup, salad, and sandwiches (daily 9:00-21:30, Sept-May 10:00-18:00).

Visiting the Waterfall: From the upper parking lot, boardwalks lead along the edge of the plateau, high above the falls, to two good **upper viewpoint** spots. On a clear day, you can see glaciers in the distance. The view upriver gives a sense of Iceland's vast and lonely interior Highlands.

From here, stairs lead down to the **lower viewpoint.** This area gets you close to the falls. It's closed in winter, when ice can make it dangerous (don't try it). A narrow trail leads through the spray from the falls to a level area between the upper and lower stages of the waterfall.

It would be easy to dam or divert the river above the falls for electricity generation. In the early 1900s, British investors tried to buy the waterfall and do just that, but their plans fell through. The government acquired the land and the falls have been left in their natural state. Near the base of the staircase, look for the relief sculpture of **Sigríður Tómasdóttir,** a local farmer who helped thwart plans for the dam.

Near Gullfoss: Leaving Gullfoss, look to your right, where you'll see the **Langjökull glacier** in the distance and get a sense of Iceland's vast interior. This no-man's-land, uninhabited and without roads, stretches over a hundred miles to Iceland's north coast. After a couple of minutes (just past the Skjól Café), a farmer has created a little **horse-petting experience** (complete with a shack that sells "horse candy"—corn goodies to feed as you make friends with young Icelandic horses).

GULLFOSS BACK TO REYKJAVÍK

You've seen the main three sights on the Golden Circle. This last stretch features a grab bag of interesting stops to consider on the way back to Reyjavík—waterfall, thermal pool, tomato farm, church, petting zoo, crater, and thermal river—but if you're in a hurry, these are all skippable. It's about two hours back to Reykjavík (direct) but, even on a quick trip, I'd give it four hours with stops of your choice.

• *The following sights are all on (or are short detours from) highway 35/ highway 1 and the main Golden Circle route. From Gullfoss, return to highway 35 and pass by Geysir again. Shortly after Geysir, make a left turn to stay on highway 35 toward Reykholt and Selfoss.*

The first sight, the Secret Lagoon, is a 10-minute drive off the main Golden Circle route. From highway 35, just before the village of Reykholt, turn left at highway 359, signed Flúðir. Follow this about 5 miles into the small village of Flúðir, watching on your left for the turnoff to Hvammur and Gamla Laugin. The Secret Lagoon is tucked amid the big greenhouses, on your right.

Secret Lagoon (Gamla Laugin)

Claiming to be the oldest swimming pool in Iceland (from 1891), the Secret Lagoon is a big, rustic, three-foot-deep, 100°F pool in front of a dilapidated old house (with a modern entrance/changing facility; 3,000 ISK, daily 10:00-22:00, Oct-April 11:00-20:00, last entry one hour before closing, tel. 555-3351, www.secretlagoon. is). The pool is surrounded by an evocative thermal landscape; a boardwalk leads around the pool, past steaming and simmering crevasses. Greenhouses stand nearby. Compared to the over-the-top-romantic Blue Lagoon, or even Reykjavík's municipal swimming pools, this is a very straightforward experience: Its proximity to the Golden Circle and clever marketing make it more popular than it probably should be. On the other hand, the bathers here seem very happy—sipping drinks, bobbing on colorful pool noodles, happy to enjoy this après-Golden Circle hangout. Far from "secret" (it's included on several day tours from Reykjavík), the pool can get quite crowded with a younger clientele. It's smart to reserve ahead online—when it's full, it's full.

• Return to highway 35 heading southwest toward Reykholt.

Faxi Waterfall

Just before Reykholt you'll see a tiny sign for *Faxi Camping and Restaurant* on the left. Exit and enter the upper parking lot, where you'll pay 700 ISK (park in the lower lot closer to the falls). Faxi is a lovely waterfall, but nothing on the scale of Gullfoss. Notice the fish ladder built alongside it for the convenience of spawning salmon. A small café with a view deck perches along the road from the upper lot.

Reykholt—the Greenhouse Town

With Iceland's long dark winters and lack of fertile topsoil, the only way to grow anything well (other than hay) is in greenhouses. Reykholt is known for its man-made fertility. Greenhouses here grow strawberries, cucumbers, peppers, herbs, flowers—and at the Friðheimar farm (described next, open to non-diners) it's all about tomatoes.

$$ The Friðheimar Tomato Farm Restaurant, a very popular, borderline-pretentious tomato farm and eatery, offers lunch daily (12:00-16:00). You'll dine right in the greenhouse, with a muggy warmth, surrounded by rows of tomato plants, with pots of fresh basil on each table. The brief menu is all tomato: tomato soup with bread, fresh pasta with tomato sauce, and tomato ice cream or cheesecake with green tomato sauce. If you want just a quick bite or drink (or don't have a reservation), you can enjoy the bar, which serves a creative array of Bloody Marys and more. As the farm is popular with big bus groups, reservations are smart (along highway 35, in the village of Reykholt, tel. 486-8894, www.fridheimar.is).

Even if not eating at the farm restaurant, you're welcome to read their info boards and wander into the tomato-filled greenhouse. The Friðheimar farm has been in the family, growing tomatoes in greenhouses, since 1946. Today they claim to produce about a fifth of all tomatoes in Iceland, shipping a ton of tomatoes to

Reykjavík each day. Taking advantage of a hot spring above town, the greenhouse walls are lined with heat-radiating water pipes. This off-the-grid farm uses geothermal energy to produce electricity to power its lights, providing a kind of synthetic sunshine in the darkness of winter. And the greenhouse cleverly corrals all that goodness, nursing its sweet vegetables.

• *To reach the next two sights a few minutes southwest of Reyhkolt, detour left onto highway 31, following Skálholt signs. The church is just over the hill, overlooking a lake-and-mountain panorama.*

Skálholt Church

This church was the old seat of the bishopric of southern Iceland. The current church was built in the 1960s and is flanked by a retreat center run by Iceland's Evangelical Lutheran state church. This low-key site is worth a few minutes if you want to mix something nongeological into your day.

Cost and Hours: Church entry—free, crypt—500-ISK donation requested; daily 9:00-18:00, pay WC in complex next to church.

Visiting the Church: As you drive up, you can see how the rich farmland around the church was able to support a medieval religious community and imagine how, in the 1700s, this was one of the most densely populated—and most powerful—places in Iceland.

It's peaceful here, with no tourist crowds. Almost nothing is left of the original buildings, many of which were destroyed by earthquakes in the late 18th century. The **church** is simple, with locally designed stained-glass windows and a thousand years of bishops listed on the back wall.

Downstairs, the **crypt** has a small exhibit of historical and archaeological artifacts, including a bishop's stone coffin dating to at least the 14th century. There's also a period sketch of the 18th-century church, which survived the earthquakes but was torn down soon after. From the crypt, you can exit directly outdoors (open the door in the right-hand corner) through the only original part of the building, a short tunnel. An old-style, turf-roofed wooden chapel on the grounds is usually open (often with temporary exhibits).

Slakki Zoo

Slakki (about a mile past Skálholt Church along highway 31) is designed for little kids. It's a combination petting zoo and indoor mini-golf complex, housed partly in cute buildings meant to look like a typical old-style Icelandic farm. There's a decent café, tiny playground, and good photo ops, and kids can get to know a big, noisy green parrot.

Cost and Hours: 1,300 ISK, kids-700 ISK, daily 11:00-18:00 in summer, May and Sept Sat-Sun only, closed Oct-April, off Skál-holtsvegur in the hamlet of Laugarás, tel. 486-8783.

• *Backtrack to highway 35 and continue southwest to the town of Borg.*

Borg Public Swimming Pool

In the tiny town of Borg (at the junction of highways 35 and 354), a simple community pool offers about the least touristy and most basic Icelandic swimming opportunity available. Look for the water slide just past the main turnoff into Borg (1,000 ISK; Mon-Fri 10:00-22:00, Sat-Sun until 19:00; late Aug-May Mon-Thu 14:00-22:00, Sat-Sun 11:00-18:00, closed Fri; tel. 480-5530, www.gogg.is).

• *After passing Borg, watch for the little Kerið sign, which comes up very quickly (look for an Icelandic flag and people hiking along a ridge on your left as you approach).*

▲Kerið Crater

The Kerið (KEH-reethe) crater is a volcanic cone from an eruption about 6,500 years ago that collapsed and filled with water—creat-

ing a tiny crater lake. It's right next to highway 35, but you'll see nothing without paying to climb the little hill. The crater is vividly colorful: red walls draped with green vegetation, overlooking deep aquamarine-blue water. You can see it in a single glance, take a half-hour to walk around the rim, or descend 150 feet down a set of stairs to the surface of the lake (400 ISK when staffed, not staffed at night or in darkness, mobile tel. 823-1336, www.kerid.is).

• *Continue southwest from Kerið crater toward Selfoss on highway 35.*

Kerið Crater to Highway 1

Just before crossing a river, there's a popular pizza joint on the right. After the river, you'll drive past a dramatic slope on your right. Look at the mountainside to see the huge boulders that have tumbled down the slope over the ages—and see if you can spot the one lonely summer house taking its chances among them.

• *When you finally reach highway 1, turn right for Reykjavík. (You're skirting the town of Selfoss, known for having the grave of chess master Bobby Fischer (described on page 219). It's about an hour's drive from here back to Reykjavík.*

Road safety is an issue here. Notice the road sign with wind direction and speed along with temperature. After that is a speed-camera warning...then the camera. On the left you'll see 52 white crosses at the base of a conical hill. These commemorate motorists and pedestrians killed on this busy, poorly lit road—statistically one of Iceland's most dangerous—between 1972 and 2006. Consider this a sobering reminder to drive with extra caution. (Farther along you'll see two smashed cars with an indication of how many deaths there have been on Icelandic roads so far this year.)

▲Reykjadalur Thermal River

At the town of Hveragerði is the exit for this aptly named natural thermal area—literally "Steamy Valley." For outdoorsy hiker/bathers, Reykjadalur (RAYK-yah-dah-lrr) is worth ▲▲. The hike to the river is just over two miles one way along a well-maintained path, with a 600-foot el-evation gain (allow at least three hours total for this experience).

Stepping out of your car at the end-of-the-road parking lot, you're surrounded by steaming hillsides. From here, cross the bridge, then hike approximately one hour up the valley. Eventually you'll reach some basic changing cabins next to a hot stream. The water is shallow—you'll need to lie down to be submerged—but wonderfully warm. Reykjadalur is far from undiscovered, so you'll likely have plenty of company. Relax and enjoy the experience...but remember it's an hour's hike back down to your car.

Warning: Stay on marked paths at all times. This entire area is very geologically active, and anyone wandering off the path could end up stepping into a hidden, underground pool of boiling water.

Eating in Hveragerði: Other than the river, the main reason to visit nearby Hveragerði is to eat at **$$ Ölverk** (Beerworks), a friendly little microbrewery/pizzeria tucked in a dreary strip mall a couple of blocks into town. In addition to a chalkboard menu of their own beers, and others by local brewers, they dish up decent pizzas from a brick oven. Casual and family-friendly, it works well for an easygoing dinner on your way back to Reykjavík (lunch specials, daily 11:30-23:00, take the main road through Hveragerði and watch for the pizzeria on your right at Breiðumörk 2b, tel. 483-3030, www.olverk.is).

• *Past the small town of Hveragerði, the road climbs steeply in a series of wide bends to a high upland plateau (1,200 feet above sea level) called Hellisheiði. This plateau separates southern Iceland from the Reykjavík area. About halfway across the plateau (the turnoff is clearly marked Hellisheiðarvirkjun), you'll see pipes and steam from a geothermal plant that welcomes visitors.*

Hellisheiði Power Plant (Hellisheiðarvirkjun)

This is the only one of Iceland's seven geothermal energy plants where visitors can get a good look at the powerful turbine machin-

ery at work. The hot water from the ground (which is piped to homes for heating) drives the turbines that generate electricity.

In the geothermal exhibit, you can see turbine rooms through big windows, read posters on how geothermal energy works, and watch a couple of films. Included guided tours run several times a day (last tour at 15:00, see details at their website).

Cost and Hours: 1,750 ISK, Mon-Fri 8:00-17:00, Sat-Sun from 9:00, confirm hours in advance, tel. 591-2880, www.geothermalexhibition.com.

• *From the power plant, it's less than 30 minutes—across a lunar landscape—to Reykjavík. Your Golden Circle loop is finished.*

Sleeping on the Golden Circle

For locations, see the map near the beginning of this chapter.

In Laugarvatn: $$ Héraðsskólinn Guesthouse is hard to miss as you drive into Laugarvatn from Þingvellir, with its green gables and prominent location on a bluff above the lake (just above the Fontana Thermal Baths). This historic 1928 schoolhouse, designed by Guðjón Samúelsson of Hallgrímskirkja fame, is filled with light and offers generous, warmly decorated public areas and a recommended in-house café. Its bright, clean rooms come with views (breakfast extra, family rooms, cheaper rooms with shared baths, hostel-style dorm in the basement, laundry, elevator; Laugarbraut 2, 25 minutes to Geysir, 35 minutes to Gullfoss; tel. 537-8060, www.heradsskolinn.is, booking@heradskolinn.is).

¢ **Laugarvatn Youth Hostel,** on the main drag, offers basic, economical accommodations (breakfast extra, family rooms,

GOLDEN CIRCLE

private rooms with baths available, laundry facilities, Dalbraut 10, tel. 486-1215, www.laugarvatnhostel.is, laugarvatn@hostel.is).

Near Laugarvatn: $$ Austurey Cottages are six modern, one-bedroom cabins plopped on a sheep farm owned by the same family since 1926. Here you'll find peace and quiet (except for the occasional bleating sheep) and floor-to-ceiling windows offering wide-open vistas that, on a clear day, include volcanoes Hekla and Eyjafjallajökull (indoor kitchenettes, gas grills outside; located at Austurey 1, south of Laugarvatn near the shore of lake Apavatn in Bláskógabyggð; 5 minutes to Laugarvatn town and grocery store, 30 minutes to Geysir, 40 minutes to Gullfoss; tel. 773-0378, www. austurey.is, austureycottages@gmail.com).

$$$ Efstidalur II, home to the recommended Farmhouse Restaurant, is a fine place to get a hint of what life is like on a real Icelandic farm—with horses, cows, and dogs. They rent 15 rooms in two buildings with either private or shared baths; several rooms come with views over the valley (family room, farm scents, horse rental, free parking, 10 minutes east of Laugarvatn on highway 37; 15 minutes to Geysir, 25 minutes to Gullfoss; tel. 486-1186, www. efstidalur.is, info@efstidalur.is).

In Geysir: $ Litli Geysir Hotel, tucked away from the Geysir tourist hubbub, is a straightforward one-story hotel offering 22 tidy, modern rooms a short walk from the geothermal action. When booking, don't mistake the good-value Litli for its big sister, the brash and pricey new Hotel Geysir by the shopping center (well-regarded restaurant, look for parking lot on the right after you pass the shopping zone, 10 minutes to Gullfoss, tel. 480-6800, www.hotelgeysir.is—choose Litli Geysir, geysir@geysircenter.is).

Near Gullfoss: $$ Hotel Gullfoss offers comfortable, good-size, modern rooms just minutes from its namesake falls. From the outside this family-run hotel doesn't exude a ton of charm, but inside everything's bright and fresh (off highway 35 a few minutes past Skjól Café, tel. 486-8979, www.hotelgullfoss.is, info@hotelgullfoss.is).

Near Skálholt: $ Brekkugerði Guesthouse offers nine simple yet modern rooms in a quiet, woodsy setting amid pastures above the Hvítá river (flowing from Gullfoss upstream). Helpful and friendly host Haraldur is happy to answer questions and offer tips (cheaper rooms with shared bath, shared kitchen, garden area in back, free parking; at Austurbyggð 26—from highway 35 take the Skálholt exit to highway 31, pass the Skálholt Church, turn left onto Skúlagata, then right onto Brekkugerðisvegur, which leads straight onto Austurbyggð; 30 minutes from Geysir, tel. 779-7762, www.brekkugerdi.is, brekkugerdi@brekkugerdi.is).

In Hveragerði: $$ Skyr Guesthouse, charmingly occupying a former *skyr* factory, is convenient to the Reykjadalur thermal river. The decor of its 13 warm rooms swings between vintage and modern; some come with a private bath and all share a shower (cozy dining room and café, Breiðamörk 25, just up the street from the recommended Ölverk microbrewery, tel. 481-1010, www.skyrgerdin.is, info@skyrgerdin.is).

SOUTH COAST

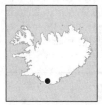

To bask in a land of mountains, glaciers, and rugged coastal scenery, head for Iceland's South Coast. Within a 2.5-hour drive of Reykjavík, you'll find black sand beaches, dramatic promontories, gushing waterfalls, glacial tongues just finishing their slow-motion 500-year journey, museums on folk culture and volcanoes, and rolling green farm fields dotted with sheep, cows, and Icelandic horses.

The towns here are humble, with sparse sights and services. Vík—at the far end of this day's drive—has a beautiful setting and several nice restaurants. Þórsmörk—accessible only via specially outfitted 4x4s or public buses equipped with monster-truck tires—rewards hikers with stunning, panoramic views over cut-glass peaks and ruddy valleys. All of this sits in the shadow of two glacier-topped volcanoes: Eyjafjallajökull and the even more powerful Katla.

PLANNING YOUR TIME

The South Coast rivals the Golden Circle and Snæfellsness Peninsula as Reykjavík's best side-trip: It's arguably even better for outdoorsy types, offering more nature activities and a top hiking destination, the mountain region called Þórsmörk. However, unlike those loop trips, unless you're doing the South Coast as part of the Ring Road, you'll head home the way you came—making the scenery a rerun.

As a Day Trip: You can do the South Coast on your own, following the **driving tour** outlined in this chapter—or with a **bus excursion**—in a single long day (about 10-11 hours) from Reykjavík. Various companies offer full-day guided excursions year-round (prices range from about 12,000 ISK to 19,000 ISK based on the group size; see the Beyond Reykjavík chapter for a list of tour companies). These don't pack in as many stops as this chapter outlines, but some tours offer the option of adding on a glacier hike or other activities.

As an Overnight: While many people visit this area as a day trip from Reykjavík, the South Coast is well worth an overnight. It can be used as a home base from which to explore this part of the country (see recommendations later in this chapter, under "Sleeping on the South Coast"); it's a logical last stop if doing the long, clockwise Ring Road route; and it's easy to add on to the Golden Circle drive from Reykjavík (instead of looping back to the city, end that drive here on the South Coast, where you can spend a night or two—and head straight to Keflavík Airport for your departure flight, without returning to Reykjavík).

Spending two full days here opens up more sightseeing options. You can day-trip from Landeyjahöfn to the Westman Islands (see that chapter). Or you can devote a day to the trails at Þórsmörk, which presides over a volcano-ringed glacial valley (described later in this chapter).

South Coast Drive

This drive links up the main attractions along the South Coast, in the order you'll reach them from Reykjavík. (Those ending their clockwise Ring Road drive will see these sights in the opposite order. Just hold the book upside down.) It's about a 2.5-hour, 115-mile drive one way between Reykjavík and the far point of this area, the town of Vík. Adding in time for a few necessary side roads, plan on at least six hours behind the wheel, plus about five hours to visit sights along the way. Figure on about 11 hours for the full round-trip experience.

The basic plan: From Reykjavík, make good time on highway 1 across the desolate Hellisheiði plateau, then through the towns of Hveragerði, Selfoss, Hella, and Hvolsvöllur (with the Lava Center volcano exhibit). Just beyond—1.5 hours after leaving the capital—you'll cross the river called Markárfljót and enter the most striking part of the drive. The stops along this stretch are captivatingly Icelandic: Hike behind the thundering Seljalandsfoss waterfall, ogle the glacier-capped volcano called Eyjafjallajökull, and pause in Skógar to see another tower-

ing waterfall and a wonderful folk museum. Next, hike up close to the icy tongue of Sólheimajökull glacier, enjoy the views from the Dyrhólaey promontory, and stroll along the black sand beaches at Reynisfjara. Just beyond those sights, the village of Vík has a big gas station and restaurants, offering a good pit stop before starting the 2.5-hour return drive back to Reykjavík.

PLANNING YOUR DRIVE

This plan is designed to efficiently link the highlights of Iceland's South Coast:

9:00	Leave Reykjavík and head for your first stop: the Seljalandsfoss waterfall (1.75 hours)
10:45	Visit Seljalandsfoss waterfall
11:15	Drive to Skógar (30 minutes) to visit the waterfall and folk museum, and have lunch
14:00	Head for Sólheimajökull (15 minutes from Skógar) to see a glacier
15:15	Drive to Dyrhólaey promontory (15 minutes); with time and energy, hike (or drive) to the lighthouse
16:00	Depart for Reynisfjara (25 minutes) and walk the black sand beach, then take a quick look at Vík, the town at the end of this drive
17:00	Start the drive back toward Reykjavík, stopping in Hvolsvöllur (1 hour)
18:00	Tour the Lava Center in Hvolsvöllur (open until 19:00)
19:00	Drive back to Reykjavík (1.5 hours), and consider stopping for dinner en route

South Coast Tips

There are a number of adjustments you can make to this suggested plan. Consider the following:

With Less Time: Read ahead and decide which stops to prioritize. To make it a shorter day, skip the Lava Center and Dyrhólaey. (Exhibits at the worthwhile Lava Center are open until 19:00—getting back before it closes can feel like a rush).

With More Time: If you're willing to leave earlier, get back later, or spend two days, your South Coast experience will be more leisurely. For example, rather than driving straight back for a late dinner in Reykjavík, consider having dinner in Vík and taking your time enjoying the lack of crowds and evening light as you retrace your route back to Reykjavík. Alternatively, you could enjoy a countryside dinner on your way back (for ideas, see "From Vík Back to Reykjavík," at the end of the drive).

If overnighting on the South Coast, you can add more sights: Stop at the Hellisheiðarvirkjun geothermal power plant, check out

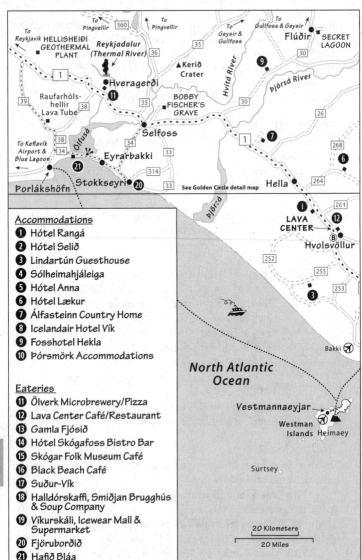

Accommodations
1. Hótel Rangá
2. Hótel Selið
3. Lindartún Guesthouse
4. Sólheimahjáleiga
5. Hótel Anna
6. Hótel Lækur
7. Álfasteinn Country Home
8. Icelandair Hotel Vík
9. Fosshotel Hekla
10. Þórsmörk Accommodations

Eateries
11. Ölverk Microbrewery/Pizza
12. Lava Center Café/Restaurant
13. Gamla Fjósið
14. Hótel Skógafoss Bistro Bar
15. Skógar Folk Museum Café
16. Black Beach Café
17. Suður-Vík
18. Halldórskaffi, Smiðjan Brugghús & Soup Company
19. Víkurskáli, Icewear Mall & Supermarket
20. Fjöruborðið
21. Hafið Bláa

Bobby Fischer's grave, see the Gljúfrabúi waterfall, or day trip by ferry to the Westman Islands.

Enjoy the Viewpoints: There's generally a pullout with picnic benches at any great viewpoint. Stop for a snack, read the information boards (in English), and take time to savor the views.

Photographers: The sun shines on the Seljalandsfoss waterfall in the afternoon; in the mornings the mountain shadows it. For the

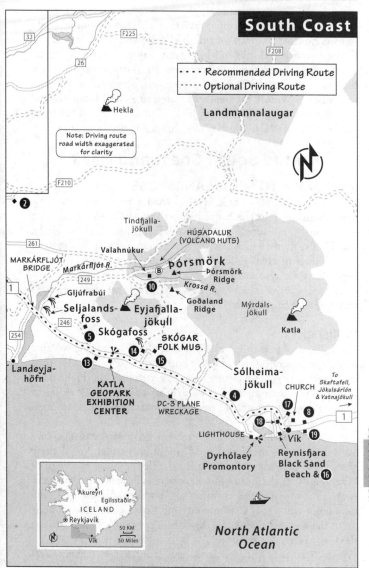

best light, consider visiting in the afternoon, on your way back to Reykjavík.

Hiking at Þórsmörk: The mountain ridge and valleys of Þórsmörk are a hiker's delight, but take the better part of a day to experience. If sleeping along the South Coast, you can catch a bus to Þórsmörk from Hvolsvöllur. Þórsmörk is also possible as a very long day trip from Reykjavík.

Weather Warnings: Visiting waterfalls and glaciers can be cold and wet; dress warmly and bring waterproof clothing and footwear. Also, be aware of the risk of blowing sand (which can damage your rental car's finish, at your expense). There is a small sandy patch (just a few hundred yards long) at the bridge where highway 1 crosses the Markárfljót river, just before the Seljalandsfoss waterfall. Check the weather before you go (at en.vedur.is) and consider alternative plans if very high winds are forecast. For more information, see "Driving Hazards" in the Practicalities chapter.

To the South Coast and Back

REYKJAVÍK TO SELJALANDSFOSS

Once you've left Reykjavík, it's less than a two-hour drive east along highway 1 to the Seljalandsfoss waterfall. Along the way, you'll pass some functional towns—Hveragerði, Selfoss, Hella, and Hvolsvöllur—which have a few minor sights, including the Lava Center in Hvolsvöllur. You could see it on your way out, or save it for your return drive.

• *Just a few minutes after leaving Reykjavík's suburban sprawl on highway 1, you'll find yourself at...*

Hellisheiði

The 1,200-foot pass called Hellisheiði is a starkly desolate volcanic landscape, where you could easily encounter bad weather in April or October. If you have time, consider a stop at the **Hellisheiði Power Plant,** with an exhibit on geothermal energy (it closes at 17:00, so stop at the start of your trip if you're interested; see page 210).

Soon after the plant, you reach the edge of the plateau and drop down on a switchback road. In good weather, you'll enjoy great views over the southern lowlands. Below you is the town of **Hveragerði,** at the head of an evocative valley misty with steam vents. (The town's name, aptly, means "hot spring enclosure.") The top end of this valley is where intrepid bathers can hike an hour up to the thermal river at **Reykjadalur** (get details before leaving Reykjavík; see page 209).

• *About 10 minutes past Hveragerði, you'll reach the large town of Selfoss (population 7,000), with a full range of services. If you don't want to stop, stay on highway 1, which crosses a river and then heads east as it skirts the northern edge of Selfoss (follow signs toward Vík and Hella).*

But if you're intrigued by American chess grandmaster Bobby Fischer, you may want to consider a brief detour to see his grave. At the east end of Selfoss (the far end, if coming from Reykjavík), a sign for Laugardælakirkja points north along a side road. Turning off here and driving less than a mile brings you to a small church at the Laugardælur farm (you'll practically drive through the farmyard).

Bobby Fischer's Grave

American chess champion Bobby Fischer was buried here after his death in Iceland in 2008. His gravestone is easy to find, just inside the churchyard gate. When the eccentric,

reclusive Fischer came to Iceland in 1972 to face Russian grandmaster Boris Spassky for the world chess championship, he struck up a friendship with Sæmundur Pálsson, the policeman assigned to chauffeur him around. In 2004, Fischer landed in prison in Japan and was due to be extradited to the US on tax-evasion charges. (He was in trouble with the IRS for playing chess in Serbia during the Yugoslav wars.) Sæmundur and a small group of friends arranged for the Icelandic parliament to grant Fischer citizenship and chartered a plane to pick him up in Japan. They brought him to Reykjavík, where he lived quietly until his death. This basically merciful act eased the last years of an ill and elderly man. Some think that the American government silently condoned the operation to avoid the discomfort of putting Fischer on trial.

If you're interested in seeing Fischer memorabilia, visit the tiny information center about him on the main street in Selfoss (1,000 ISK, daily 13:00-16:00 & 19:30-21:30, closed mid-Sept-mid-May, Austurvegur 21, mobile 894-1275, www.fischersetur.is).

• *From Selfoss, follow highway 1 east across a lush plain, eventually passing through two small towns, Hella and Hvolsvöllur (KVOLS-vurt-lur). Each town has about 1,000 people, a grocery store, a couple of places to eat, a thermal swimming pool, and gas stations with WCs (you'll also find several recommended accommodations nearby). Right along the main road through Hvolsvöllur is the Lava Center (described next). Even if not touring the center, it makes a handy coffee-and-WC stop—the lobby (with some informative exhibits) is free to enter.*

▲Lava Center

This state-of-the-art attraction rivals the excellent Volcano Museum in the Westman Islands and uses clever exhibits to explain Iceland's volcanic heritage. While expensive, it's well-presented and enjoyable for all ages and interest levels. As it's open fairly late, consider stopping here on your way back to Reykjavík.

Cost and Hours: 3,590 ISK includes exhibit and film, 1,400 ISK for just the film, daily 9:00-19:00, can't miss it along highway 1 at the western edge of Hvolsvöllur, tel. 415-5200, www. lavacentre.is.

Eating: The Lava Center has a **$** café (with an affordable soup buffet, and takeaway salads and sandwiches) and a cafeteria-style **$$ restaurant.** You can eat here even if you're not visiting the museum (both open until 20:00—later than the exhibit).

Visiting the Museum: In the free-to-enter **lobby,** you'll find a large virtual map of Iceland identifying minor earthquakes over the last 48 hours. Smaller screens cycle through recent eruptions. Check out the cross-section of soil excavated at this site, striped with ash and tephra deposits from eruptions over time. (The lobby also has free WCs, a coffee counter, and a branch of the Rammagerðin gift shop.)

After buying your ticket, head down a long pulsing **timeline** corridor, pinpointing significant eruptions over Iceland's geologic history. Reaching the **exhibit,** you'll walk around a towering, glowing mantle plume (representing a "hot spot" of molten rock gushing upward to Iceland from the Earth's core) and manipulate eerie and mesmerizing simulated lava flows on tabletops. Throughout, touchscreens and video walls invite you to learn more, and darkened corridors between the rooms add to the experience—with simulated ash clouds, noisy eruptions, and trembling floors. In the "Volcano View" room, you'll stand in the middle of wraparound, wall-to-ceiling virtual footage of what eruptions in this area would look like.

In the **cinema,** a 12-minute film playing three times an hour shows off high-definition footage of spitting and flowing lava; historic photos and videos of past eruptions; and aerial eye-candy scenery of volcanic landforms around Iceland. (Check in the lobby for the next planned show time.)

• *From Hvolsvöllur (famous only as the home of the Icelandic hot-dog factory on the left), it's about a 15-minute drive to the bridge over the Markárfljót river. Directly after the bridge, turn left onto highway 249, and then take the first right into the pay parking area for the Seljalandsfoss waterfall (with a basic café and WCs).*

▲▲Seljalandsfoss Waterfall

Seljalandsfoss (SELL-yah-lahnds-foss) tumbles over its cliff into a pool, with a cave-like walkway just behind it. The 210-foot-high falls aren't that powerful—but they are handsome. The water comes from the glacier Eyjafjallajökull, atop the volcano that erupted in 2010. In good weather, a one-way path lets you walk around the back of the waterfall; in icy conditions, skip it (it's closed in winter). If you do walk the path, it's safer to go counterclockwise. Wear a waterproof jacket and good shoes—the path is damp and uneven, and you'll be sprayed steadily.

Before starting off, visually trace the entire path around this one-way loop to be sure you're up for it. The easy part is circling down around behind the cascade. The return trip is the hard part, as it requires climbing up steep rocks and tiptoeing through deceptively deep mud puddles to the top of an old staircase that allows an easy drop down to street level.

Cost and Hours: Seljalandsfoss is free to visit and open all the time—come during off-peak hours for a more peaceful experience. There's a pay-and-display parking lot (700 ISK) and a little coffee shop to serve the crowds.

Optional Add-On: A 30-minute side-trip takes you to another waterfall called **Gljúfrabúi** (GLYOO-vrah-BOO-ee, lit-

erally "Canyon Dweller"). This waterfall, much smaller than Seljalandsfoss, drops into a hollow within the rock and then exits (as a stream) under a tall, narrow, natural archway. To catch a glimpse, walk 10 minutes on the gravel path left of Seljalandsfoss past several minor cascades. From outside, you can only see the very top of the falls. To see a little more, hike up to the archway (on a challenging trail with handholds). It's possible to get close to the falls by wading several yards, at your own risk, along the normally shallow but swift-flowing stream as it exits the arch (you'll want high rubber boots and full rain gear). On a typical day trip from Reykjavík, Gljúfrabúi isn't really worth it, but nature lovers or those with more time may enjoy it.

SELJALANDSFOSS TO VÍK

This stretch—less than an hour's drive without stops—is lined with attractions and detours that can easily fill the rest of your day.

• *Leaving Seljalandsfoss, return to highway 1 and continue east. If the coast is clear, look out to sea, where the horizon is fringed with the jagged cliffs of the* **Westman Islands** *rising up just offshore. These islands were formed by volcanoes, including a dramatic eruption in 1973 that consumed a third of the main town's houses and expanded the island's size by about 20 percent. Aside from the eruption, the Westman Islands* *are known among Icelanders for their fishing industry, seabird colonies (including lots of puffins in the summer), and folk music. The terminal for the Westman Islands ferry (a 40-minute trip) is a few miles to the south of highway 1 (see the Westman Islands chapter). About 15 minutes' drive beyond Seljalandsfoss you'll reach the...*

Eyjafjallajökull Area

Eyjafjallajökull (the famous "E15") is the name of the glacier that tops the volcanic mountain peak you're driving under (the mountain itself is called Eyjafjöll). This volcano thrust Iceland onto the world stage for a week in April 2010, as the ash it ejected high into the atmosphere settled over Europe, halting international air travel. (For details, see the sidebar.)

Once a fjord, the land around here was filled in over the ages with glacial debris. Looking inland, you can imagine the cliffs plunging into the sea here 10,000 years ago. Farther inland is the vast natural preserve called Þórsmörk (covered at the end of this chapter), tucked in between three glacier-topped volcanoes: Eyjafjöll, Katla (with Iceland's fourth-largest glacier, Mýrdalsjökull), and the smaller Tindfjöll.

Venerable farms dot the countryside. Until 1900 most people on the island lived in turf homes on country farms like these. These days, it's tough for farms to be profitable. Hay is the main crop here—used to feed sheep, cows, and Iceland's unique breed of horses. Once part of the local diet, Icelandic horses are now raised more as a hobby, for tourism, and for export to enthusiasts worldwide.

• *If you're hungry by now, look for the gray metal building with a rusty sign of a cow attached to it.*

Eating near Eyjafjallajökull: Located at this roadside farmstead, **$$ Gamla Fjósið** (Old Cowshed) specializes in simple but satisfying dishes made with beef raised right here—delicious steak sandwiches, burgers, and soup. From the outside it doesn't look like much, but inside is a rustic and cozy setting, with mismatched furniture under open rafters. If you avoid the spendy fish and seafood dishes, it's a decent value. Their "Volcano" soup (beef goulash) makes a hearty and affordable lunch, and seconds are free (daily 11:00-21:00, Hvassafell, tel. 487-7788).

• *About three minutes after passing the restaurant, you'll come to the modest...*

Katla Geopark Visitor Center: Exhibits and a dramatic 10-minute video detail the Fimmvörðuháls and Eyjafjallajökull

Eyjafjallajökull: The Volcano that Stopped Europe in Its Tracks

The Icelandic volcano called Eyjafjallajökull (EH-ya-FYAH-tla-YUR-kutl) erupted in the spring of 2010, famously disrupting airline flights all over Europe.

The first, short stage of the eruption started late on the night of March 20, 2010, at Fimmvörðuháls, the saddle between the Eyjafjallajökull and Mýrdalsjökull glaciers (where the hiking path crosses between Skógar and Þórsmörk). Tongues of red-hot lava, some as much as 600 feet high, shot up along a short fissure. This was a real "tourist eruption:" The curious could view the show by helicopter, or even hike up toward it, in relative safety.

The Fimmvörðuháls eruption died down within a few weeks, and for all anyone knew the whole thing was over. But then came the eruption's second stage, much more violent and dangerous, as the earth opened right in the middle of the glacier. On April 14, a column of black soot and smoke shot four miles into the sky, meltwater rushed down the slopes, and ash rained over the downwind countryside—covering fields, cars, and roofs. The ash blocked out the sun and put livestock in danger. Flights across Europe were canceled because of the fear that windborne ash would disable jet engines. Paradoxically, Iceland's Keflavík Airport (upwind of the volcano) mostly stayed open throughout the entire eruption.

The second stage lasted until late May, and by August, the volcano was dormant. Thankfully, despite its international infamy, the Eyjafjallajökull eruption caused little real damage—other than dumping a considerable amount of ash on the nearby countryside. Its main legacy was confronting the world with how difficult long Icelandic words are to pronounce. If you'd like to master the pronunciation of Eyjafjallajökull, several YouTube videos offer a tutorial...or you can use its nickname: "E15" (that's E followed by 15 letters).

Eyjafjallajökull had an even bigger impact on tourism. Some experts believe that those headlines in 2010 reminded the world not only that Iceland exists, but that it's a geologically fascinating place. They credit Eyjafjallajökull, in part, for the recent spike in international visitors.

So, when's the next eruption on the South Coast? Historically, eruptions of Eyjafjallajökull have been followed by eruptions of Katla (under Mýrdalsjökull)—which last blew its top in 1918 and, according to volcanologists, is overdue. Stay tuned...

SOUTH COAST

eruptions, and the friendly staff is happy to explain the region's volcanic history and the geopark's mission to promote the protection and sustainable development of geologically significant areas in south Iceland. There are also WCs, coffee, and a gift shop (exhibit-500 ISK, Mon-Fri 10:30-18:00, closed Sat-Sun). Right behind the building, a path cuts through a field to a scenic view of Eyjafjallajökull looming over the Þorvaldseyri farm.

• *Driving past the visitor center, look for a pullout with picnic benches and informational plaques (next to the Þorvaldseyri farm's driveway).*

Thermal Bath Detour: Hardy bathers can consider a detour to **Seljavallalaug,** a very rustic thermal swimming pool (from 1923) built right into the side of a mountain slope. Some people enjoy the pool's scenic and remote location, which requires a 15-minute hike up a desolate valley. Don't expect a sleek and sanitary experience: The pool is unstaffed and has very limited services (grubby changing rooms), and the water is warm rather than hot. But backpackers and campers looking to take a memorable dip enjoy the detour. (From highway 1, just beyond the Gamla Fjósið restaurant and Katla Geopark Visitor Center, watch on the left after the bridge for road 242 to *Raufarfell,* then follow signs for *Seljavellir* to the end of the road, where you can park and hike.)

• *Continuing along highway 1, watch on the left. After about four miles, you'll see rustic old buildings embedded into the sides of massive rocks.*

Cave Houses: These huts were built to shelter animals and warehouse supplies, but they're a good reminder that, well into the 1800s, Icelanders lived in dwellings much like these.

The first rock house—**Rútshellir**—has a handy roadside pullout and an information board. The structures you see grafted onto the stone are just the entrances to the sprawling, hand-carved cave.

Drive a bit farther to find the second house down a short driveway at the farm called **Drangshlíð II.** While it's private property, you're welcome to park and discreetly walk over for a closer look (donations are accepted; entering the structures is off-limits).

While I'm not much for Iceland's "hidden people" legends (see sidebar), these sights are intriguing enough to warrant some fantastical stories. The cowsheds are said to be peopled by elves who look after the livestock...and prefer to do it without human interference. According to legends, the farmer would leave hay and an empty milk bucket outside the sheds. And then later, he'd discover that the cows had been fed and milked.

• *Soon after Drangshlíð II, watch on the left for a dramatic waterfall (our next destination) and then the turnoff to a small settlement called...*

Skógar

Skógar (SKOH-ar, Woods) was originally the site of a local district school. There are two main attractions here: the Skógafoss

Iceland's Hidden People *(Huldufólk)*

Icelandic folk tales often speak of "hidden people" *(huldufólk)*—mystical sprites, elves, and other little creatures who inhabit a parallel universe.

According to legend, these hidden people look, dress, and live much like humans, only smaller. They're farmers and fishers, and typically live inside rocks and hillsides. Hidden people are invisible to normal humans—unless they choose to be seen.

No Photo Available

Most hidden people have no interest in humans, they sometimes need our help, and they aren't shy about retaliating if disturbed. (After experiencing mysterious equipment malfunctions, construction projects have been known to reroute a road or carefully move a boulder—or even consult a mystic to negotiate with the hidden people.) And some mischievous hidden people take advantage of humans. For example, a truculent elderly elf might be switched out for a human baby as a changeling—to make him some poor Icelander's problem.

Tales of Icelandic hidden people date back to the earliest years of the Settlement Age. It's no coincidence that the stories told in this rugged, sparsely inhabited land feature many instances where showing generosity to a stranger is richly rewarded—promoting a "we're all in this together" ethic essential for survival in this challenging environment.

You may see polls suggesting that most Icelanders believe in hidden people (or at least refuse to rule out their existence). A few Icelanders even claim, matter-of-factly, to have seen an elf walking across their lawn. But many Icelanders—particularly younger ones—roll their eyes at talk of hidden people. In their view, these "beliefs" are exaggerated by the media, by local tour guides, and in guidebooks like this one.

Yet even if today's Icelanders don't really believe in elves, some may sense concentrated pockets of mysterious energy here and there. Tales of hidden people remind Icelanders to fear and respect nature—and on this island of volcanoes, earthquakes, and steaming geysers, nothing could be more rational.

In the 19th century, a pair of Brothers Grimm-style scholars—Jón Árnason and Magnús Grímsson—collected Iceland's tales of hidden people. To read a variety of vivid folk stories, search for "hidden people folktales" at www.grapevine.is; for a more scholarly compendium, books in English include J.M. Bedell's *Hildur, Queen of the Elves: And Other Icelandic Folk Tales*. For a concise overview, see Alda Sigmundsdóttir's *The Little Book of the Hidden People* or *Icelandic Folk Legends*.

(SKOH-gah-foss) waterfall (which you can't miss, on your left) and the Skógar Folk Museum (to the right).

▲▲Skógafoss Waterfall

This waterfall, on a river that drains down from Eyjafjallajökull, is much broader and more powerful than Seljalandsfoss. And yet it's less spectacular, and you can't walk behind it. Park in the free lot (with pay WC) and gaze up at the water plunging over the side. A stairway climbs all the way up to the top of the falls (about 500 steps); it offers another perspective on the falls and lets you see the river up top. Skip the stairs if you're in a hurry or just not up for the climb. The stairway is actually the start of a long, popular trail that continues all the way up over the saddle between the Eyjafjallajökull and Mýrdalsjökull glaciers, and over to Þórsmörk (requires good preparation; for more on the Þórsmörk area, see the end of this chapter).

Eating at Skógafoss: Of the cluster of restaurants near the falls, **$$ Hótel Skógafoss Bistro Bar** is the best. The dining room and outdoor deck have a nice view, and they have a fine menu of lamb, fish dishes, burgers, and soup (daily 11:00-21:00, until 22:00 in summer, tel. 487-8780).

▲▲Skógar Folk Museum

This large and impressive collection, with both indoor and outdoor areas, is worth the entry price for those who'd like to mix some museum-going into their scenic South Coast day.

Cost and Hours: 2,000 ISK, daily 9:00-18:00, Sept-May 10:00-17:00, tel. 487-8845, www.skogasafn.is. The museum has a café with a good soup deal and sandwiches (closes one hour before museum).

Visiting the Museum: The site has two exhibit halls and an open-air museum, with most exhibits described in English. The ticket desk is in the building with the excellent **regional history museum.** Its three floors showcase old household goods, farm implements, local archaeological finds, an 1855 fishing boat with a photo of its crew, a whale vertebra made into a bucket, and more artifacts that give a rare and vivid look at Iceland in the 19th century. Compared to similar museums, the sheer volume of stuff here impresses. Where other such museums might have one spinning wheel, Skógar has a dozen, all in a row. Displays in the basement include a large collection of stuffed Icelandic wildlife.

The adjacent building contains the café and a **transport and**

communication museum. A one-way route snakes through a huge hall cluttered with artifacts. Exhibits explain how Iceland entered the modern age (showing how, for example, in the early 1900s, a phone line was strung across the island and a cable laid to Europe). In addition to lots of shined-up old cars and rescue equipment, you'll wander past neatly arranged piles upon piles of all kinds of devices—like radio transmitters—and entire walls lined with first-generation cell phones.

In the field behind the two buildings is a small **open-air museum** with original buildings moved here from elsewhere in Iceland, including two sod-roofed farmsteads (with stone walls and labyrinthine passages), an old timber house (from 1878, built of driftwood and wood salvaged from a French shipwreck), and a school building—each traditionally furnished. The little

church itself is not old—it was built here in the 1990s—but the furnishings inside are centuries-old originals, salvaged from other churches in the region.

• *From Skógar, your next stop is Sólheimajökull, a glacier tongue that spills downhill from the much larger Mýrdalsjökull. To visit the glacier, continue on the main road. Less than 10 minutes past Skógar, (just past the bridge) look for signs to Sólheimajökull. Turn off the main road, slalom through the glacial debris for five minutes along paved highway 221, then park in the lot at the end of the road.*

▲Sólheimajökull Glacier

Sólheimajökull (SOHL-HAY-ma-YUR-kutl, Sun-homes Glacier) is one of Iceland's most accessible places to get close to a glacier. Allow about an hour for a quick visit.

From the parking lot (pay WCs in the Icelandic Mountain Guides building), walk about 15 minutes toward the glacier. (The walk gets longer each year as, like nearly all glaciers, this one is retreating with climate change.) At first you walk on a wide, rocky gravel track. You'll then see a sign telling you not to proceed farther. There are several reasons for this: Melting ice under sand can create a quicksand-like phenomenon, poisonous volcanic gas can be released from under the glacier, ice calving off the glacier can create small tidal waves on the lagoon, rock can slide down the slope, and people can simply slip and fall into the cold lagoon.

Despite these dangers, most visitors choose to keep going, walking across uneven ground to the glacier itself. If you continue past the sign, use common sense, stay near other visitors, and keep in mind that the snout of the glacier is always moving and changing, along with ice and meltwater conditions. In recent years, it's been easy to walk right up to the ice and give it a loving pat. But rock falls or rushing streams may force you to stay back. (You'll likely notice helmeted glacier-hiking groups actually walking on the glacier with their guides.)

If you've never seen a glacier before, you may be surprised at how dirty it is. Brilliant whites alternate with sections where the

surface is covered in black grit. You can watch a good time-lapse sequence of its receding extent at www.extremeicesurvey.org.

Something else to ponder: A generation ago, the glacier reached all the way to the parking lot (saving visitors a long

hike). Politicians may squabble over climate change, but Icelanders will tell you that there's no question their glaciers are receding. In western Iceland, the Okjökull glacier receded to the point that it lost its glacier status—now it's just called "Ok." That's not OK.

Guided Hiking on the Glacier: For most visitors, just looking at the glacier is a fine experience. But if you want to climb on

it, you must be properly outfitted and travel with a group for safety's sake. Many companies offer excursions of varying lengths and difficulty that take you up on Sólheimajökull. Some companies offer glacier hikes as a day trip from Reykjavík, but you can also join an excursion on-site.

Icelandic Mountain Guides runs guided glacier hikes several times a day from a building next to the parking lot. Their 3.5-hour glacier walk (worth ▲▲) takes you past the iceberg-filled lagoon to the glacier's snout, where you attach crampons to your boots for the climb through spooky canyons of ice and black ash up to the smoother surface on top of Sólheimajökull. Along the way your guide explains how glaciers form and behave, where those mysterious cones of coarse black ash come from, how massive sinkholes appear, and how climate change is killing the glacier (as evidenced by the vast amount of water flowing on and through the ice).

Groups go out rain, wind, or shine—or in all three. Wear

sturdy hiking boots and dress in layers, and have waterproof Gore-Tex-style outerwear and gloves handy (you can rent some of these items here before setting out).

While you can just drop in and see what's available, it's best to book in advance (2+ hours-9,500 ISK, 3.5 hours-15,900 ISK, 3.5-hour glacier hike with ice climbing-21,500 ISK; boot rental-1,000 ISK, rain pants/jacket rental-1,000 ISK each; tel. 587-9999, www.mountainguides.is). For more about glacier hikes, see the "Glaciers" section of the Icelandic Experiences chapter.

Nearby: You might hear about **Sólheimasandur,** a desolate beach where you can see the remains of a DC-3 plane that crash-landed in the 1970s (everyone survived). The corroded fuselage lies close to the sea on the sandy wastes near the turnoff to Sólheimajökull. But unless you're an aviation nut, skip it: It's a dull 2.5-mile hike each way from the trailhead parking lot at the highway, and there's nothing to see besides the empty fuselage.

• *Back on highway 1 continue east 10 minutes, then turn right onto highway 218. In five minutes you'll cross the causeway to the Dyrhólaey Promontory. The left fork (signed Lágey) takes you to the lower parking lot, viewpoint, and trail to the lighthouse. The right fork (signed Háey) is a steep, rutted gravel lane leading to the upper parking lot, lighthouse, puffin-watching, and more impressive views.*

Note that the lighthouse lane is signed for four-wheel drive vehicles only; in practice, drivers in smaller cars should be able to make the short trip (and the views are worth the effort), but the rutted-in-some-parts gravel road may intimidate less confident drivers.

▲Dyrhólaey Promontory

Dyrhólaey (DEER-hoh-la-AY) is a promontory set above a nature reserve with a lighthouse, natural sea arches, and picturesque off-shore rocks. At the lower parking lot (free parking, pay WC), short paths lead up to several overlooks.

To the right is the highlight for most visitors: a longer path that takes you all the way to the summit of the bluff and the lighthouse. You'll hike up along the cliffs about a half-mile to the lighthouse capping the bluff—just follow the signs. As you make your way up, stay back from the cliff edge and heed the warning signs, as rock falls have taken a few tourists with them over the past several years. It can also be quite windy here.

From the top, you'll enjoy sweeping views in both directions:

black sand beaches as far as the eye can see, with the open Atlantic on one side and glacier-capped volcanoes on the other. From the lighthouse parking lot, a brief, gradually uphill walk—to the far side of the lighthouse—offers views down on some massive rocks with caves excavated by thundering surf. In the early summer, the cliffs around you teem with seabirds (including, often, puffins)... birders love Dyrhólaey. Note, however, that from early May to late June, part or all of Dyrhólaey may be closed to car traffic (and maybe even to hikers) to protect nesting birds. While they typically keep it open during daylight hours, it depends on nesting conditions. Even if the area is open, avoid getting too close to nests; Arctic terns aggressively dive-bomb tourists who accidentally wander near their eggs.

"**Mirror Beach**": Depending on the time of day and conditions, you may enjoy an added attraction on the causeway to Dyrhólaey (on the left as you approach from the mainland). At low tide, the sunlight sometimes reflects off the black sand just below a very thin layer of water, turning the bay into one big mirror. If you see cars parked along the causeway, pull over and join in the fun of "walking on water."

• Next up: the black sand beach of Reynisfjara. Return to highway 1 and continue east almost 10 minutes, then turn right onto paved highway 215, following signs for Reynishverfi (the settlement next to the beach). Along the way you'll drive through a broad, lush, green farmland delta. In the pastures, cows moo contentedly—a relatively rare sight in Iceland, where they're mostly kept indoors. Another 10 minutes brings you to a big parking lot with pay WCs and a beach café. From the parking lot, it's a couple minutes' walk to...

▲Reynisfjara Black Sand Beach

Tucked under grassy mountains, at the far end of the bay from Dyrhólaey, Reynisfjara (RAY-nis-fyah-rah) is worth ▲▲ on a nice, calm day. The long stretch of **beach** and adjacent cliffs were created when lava flowed into the ocean and slowly cooled. The beach itself—more small black pebbles than fine sand—changes frequently with the ocean currents. The sand can bank up higher, or be partially swept away. The tide has an ef-

fect, too. In exceptional conditions, a very high tide can flood the parking lot. In winter, all but a thin strip of black sand may be covered by snow.

Looking out to sea, on your left you'll see dramatic **basalt for-**

mations—splintered hexagonal columns of volcanic rock, evocative of the famous Giant's Causeway in Ireland. Kids enjoy scrambling up the uneven stair-steps formed by the splintered rock of this pyramidal cliff, known as the Garðar (Stronghold). Scan the grassy areas above the basalt columns for nesting puffins. If the tide is out, circle around to the left to explore shallow caves framed by even more fantastical formations—columns thrust at unlikely angles and rock cascading in paper-thin layers.

Just beyond the basalt caves are the jagged **Reynisdrangar sea stacks**—the sea-eroded remnants of an ancient basalt cliff. Scanning the horizon to the right, you'll see all the way to the Dyrhólaey promontory with its dramatic arch.

Caution: The beach here is inviting...but dangerous. It's fine to walk along the black sands, but stay well back from the water—*much* farther back than you think is safe—and never turn your back to the sea. Make sure that children also understand the rules. The sea is strong here, with an undertow, and tourists have drowned. Frequent sneaker waves—huge, unexpected surges of water—swamp areas of the beach that looked dry a minute before.

Eating at Reynisfjara: The cafeteria-like **$ Black Beach Café,** also known as Svarta Fjaran, serves simple grill meals (daily June-Aug 11:00-21:00, Sept-May until 18:00, tel. 571-2718, www.blackbeach.is). There's also a tiny hot-dog food truck.

• *If you're tired or short on time, head back to Reykjavík now—you've seen the best of the South Coast. Otherwise, continue on to one more town to refuel and refresh for the 2.5-hour return trip.*

Vík

A 10-minute drive over a low pass beyond the Reynisfjara turn-off, Vík (pop. 300) is Iceland's southernmost village and the end-point of this drive. Vík enjoys a stunning setting—huddled up against a craggy cliff, with green pastures all around and a pointy steeple overlooking the town center from its plateau perch. But the town itself is more practical than charming. Most

people use it simply as a turnaround spot for a rest and a bite to eat before returning to Reykjavík.

Vík Church Viewpoint: Entering town, turn left (on the road marked *Suðurvíkurvegur*) and drive uphill to the village church's parking lot for a grand view of Vík, adjacent cliffs, jagged dragon's-teeth sea stacks just offshore, and long stretches of the South Coast.

"Downtown Vík": Continuing into town, turn right off the main road onto Víkurbraut street. Two blocks down on the right, the Brydebúð building dates from the 19th century (with an 1831 storefront moved here from the Westman Islands; open daily May-Aug 10:00-20:00, Sept-April 12:00-18:00, at #28, tel. 487-1395). It hosts the **TI,** a free exhibit on the local volcano (Katla), a nice gift shop, a WC, and a lively recommended café.

Old Ship Museum: Across the street from the TI, the little Skaftfellingur Museum is a dusty warehouse displaying the rickety remains of a beloved local ship (500 ISK, pay at TI, June-Sept daily 10:00-20:00, shorter hours off-season). The *Skaftfellingur* was built in 1918, served during World War II, and was decommissioned in 1963. The museum works hard to spin nostalgic stories about Vík's town heritage. One exhibit identifies the many shipwrecks that have occurred in the treacherous waters off Iceland's South Coast.

Vík Beach: Vík has no harbor. Before the road arrived (in the 1940s), provisions came in via tough boats beaching here on the black sand. From the Skaftfellingur Museum, follow Víkurbraut street as it curves left and comes to a T; then turn right and look for the turnoff (on the left) that leads to a couple of beach parking lots. This remote and windy beach has a breakwater (to prevent erosion) and some blustery picnic benches, and offers nice walks.

Eating in Vík: For Vík's version of finer dining, **$$ Suður-Vík,** up the road near the church (go left at the fork), has a fun, cheery, attic-like space. Their à la carte menu is pricey but their good pizzas are cheaper (daily 12:00-22:00, Suðurvíkurvegur 1, tel. 487-1515).

The rest of these restaurants are **$** choices. **Halldórskaffi,** a busy, convivial café sharing the Brydebúð building with the TI, serves reasonably priced meals from an enticing menu (fish, lamb, pizza, daily 12:00-21:00, tel. 487-1202).

Smiðjan Brugghús (Old Smithy Brewhouse) sells brew-pub grub and a good selection of craft beers—including its own (hamburgers, BBQ ribs, daily 12:00-24:00, Sunnubraut 15, tel. 571-8870).

Soup Company is a modern and efficient eatery serving up several good soups, including a spicy meat soup called "Red Hot Lava" (daily 12:00-21:00, Víkurbraut 5, tel. 778-9717).

Víkurskáli is a cheap, grubby, roadside grill good for burgers and fried fish (daily 11:00-19:30, Austurvegur 18—at the N1 gas station on the main road at the east end of town, tel. 487-1230).

For **groceries,** a big Krónan supermarket is in the made-for-tourists Icewear Magasín mall at the east end of town, by the N1 gas station. Here you'll also find a restaurant, café, wool products, a huge souvenir shop, an ATM, and free WCs (daily 8:00-21:00).

VÍK BACK TO REYKJAVÍK

It's about 2.5 hours—back the way you came on highway 1—to return to the capital. While I like eating in Vík and then enjoying the evening light on the drive home, you could break up the drive by eating on the way back to Reykjavík.

Dinner Options

Along the way, consider dinner at one of these restaurants (listed in the order you'll reach them as you drive back):

In the Eyjafjallajökull Area: For burgers and other beef dishes, **Gamla Fjósið** is a good place to stop (see listing on page 222).

In Hvolsvöllur: If you're stopping at the **Lava Center** on the way home, it's easy to grab a basic bite in their café/restaurant (see page 219).

Lobster Detour near Selfoss: These places, each about 15 minutes south of Selfoss and an hour from Reykjavík, highlight *humar* (a.k.a. langoustine or Norway lobster). While pricey, these are very local—a good place for a when's-the-next-time-I'm-gonna-be-in-Iceland blowout feast. In Selfoss, head south on highway 34 (at the main roundabout, turn off for *Þorlákshöfn, Eyrarbakki,* and *Stokkseyri*) to find these two places along the coast. From this area, it's less than an hour's drive back to Reykjavík (follow highway 33/34 west, then north on highway 39 to rejoin highway 1 near the Hellisheiðarvirkjun power plant).

$$$$ Fjöruborðið (The Water's Edge) is a venerable, nautical-themed lobster house with simple but good dishes. It's not cheap—a meal-sized bowl of lobster soup is 3,650 ISK, or you can pay (dearly) by weight for a sizzling skillet of *humar* tails. But it's a memorable way to sample this coastal delicacy. Despite its name and waterside location, there's no view (daily 12:00-21:00, reservations recommended, Eyrarbraut 3a, Stokkseyri, tel. 483-1550, www.fjorubordid.is). To reach it from highway 34, when you hit the coast, turn left (east) on highway 33, to the village of Stokkseyri. The restaurant is in the back of the parking lot next to the big red Art Hostel.

$$$ Hafið Bláa (The Blue Sea) is perched scenically on a ridge by the beach. The food is slightly cheaper than at Fjöruborðið, with more non-lobster dishes. And while it's not as well-regarded, the setting is far more striking: From the airy, modern dining room, you look north into the delta of the Ölfusá river, and south over crashing waves and a

SOUTH COAST

black sand beach that's good for a stroll before or after dinner (daily 12:00-21:00, Óseyrartangi, between Porlákshöfn and Eyrarbakki, tel. 483-1000, www.hafidblaa.is). It's at the Ölfusá Bridge: Follow the directions above, but stay right (west) on highway 34.

In Hveragerði: Consider dinner at the satisfying **Ölverk** microbrewery/pizzeria (see the end of the Golden Circle chapter).

In Hafnarfjörður: An efficient option is to stop off in Hafnarfjörður for dinner on your way through Reykjavík's suburban sprawl (see recommendations in the Reykjavík chapter).

Sleeping on the South Coast

For locations, see the "South Coast" map, earlier in this chapter.

Near Hvolsvöllur: Named after the river it backs up to, **$$$$ Hotel Rangá** is a classic-feeling, high-end luxury resort with 51 woody, rustic, and unpretentious rooms and inviting, lodge-like public spaces. They also have an observatory and offer a "northern lights wake-up service" in case of any late-night light shows. You'll find a hot tub to relax in, a pricey restaurant, and a comfy bar with overstuffed leather chairs and reasonable prices. If you're looking to splurge on the South Coast, this is the place (5 minutes west of Hvolsvöllur on highway 1 at Suðurlandsvegur, tel. 487-5700, www. hotelranga.is, hotelranga@hotelranga.is).

$$ Hótel Selið (Summer Pasture), remote and restful with views of snowy peaks, has eight modern rooms attached to a big red barn. It's up a gravel road from highway 1, between Hella and Hvolsvöllur (about 15 minutes from either). Owner Irena runs the place with care and will show you the path to a lovely view of a cascade-draped gorge (simple dinners available for guests with half-hour notice, on road 264—watch for turnoff from highway 1 close to Hotel Rangá, tel. 487-8790, www.hotelselid.is, selid@hotelselid.is).

$$ Lindartún Guesthouse, an unassuming place set amid horse and sheep pastures, offers eight modern yet cozy rooms (six with bath). Friendly host Kristín runs a tidy ship and provides a hearty breakfast in her light-filled dining room (breakfast included, shared kitchen, take road 255 exit off highway 1, drive 5 minutes and guesthouse will be on the left, tel. 552-5060, http://lindartun. is, info@lindartun.is).

Near Skógar: My favorite accommodation in this area, **$$ Sólheimahjáleiga** is a country-classy gem. This working farm—conscientiously run by the same family since 1875—is a tidy little compound with 300 sheep and 20 rooms split between new and old buildings. There's a shared kitchen for guests to use, and dinner is available (family room, cheaper rooms with shared bath, just off the main road between Skógar and Vík, tel. 864-2919, www.solheimahjaleiga.is, booking@solheimahjaleiga.is).

$$ Hótel Anna, roughly midway between Seljalandsfoss and Skógafoss, has seven good-size, warmly decorated hotel rooms, plus 10 well-appointed apartments with kitchenettes. Set in the foothills below Eyjafjallajökull, it's a friendly, family-run place that also has a full restaurant (includes breakfast, sauna and hot tub, a couple of minutes off highway 1—coming from Seljalandsfoss, take the second road 246 exit signed *Ásólfsskáli*, tel. 487-8950, www. hotelanna.is, hotelanna@hotelanna.is).

Near Hella: Once an abandoned farm, **$$ Hótel Lækur** has 21 rooms filling a renovated old barn and a modern annex, and four cottages that each sleep six. The owners have created a cheery, relaxing place where you can enjoy big-sky vistas and wander a grassy path along the creek (family room, sauna and ice bath, full restaurant, 15-minute drive down a gravel road north of main highway connecting Hella and Hvolsvöllur, near village of Hróarslækur, tel. 466-3930, www.hotellaekur.is, laekur@hotellaekur.is).

$ Álfasteinn Country Home is a sod-roofed guesthouse that oozes atmosphere. The main house has several (cheaper) rooms with shared bath, and two cottages with private baths. Ágúst Rúnarsson—the well-traveled host—is a wealth of information who understands travelers' needs and also guides mountain adventures (5.5 miles west of Hella—turn off at the *Ásamýri* sign,

then take the first right, tel. 772-8304, www.icelandmagic.is, icelandmagic@icelandmagic.is).

Big Chain Hotels: Along the South Coast, you'll also find large, tour group-oriented hotels operated by big chains: **$$$ Icelandair Hotel Vík** (44 rooms, tel. 487-1480, www.icelandairhotels. com, info@icehotels.is) and **$$ Fosshotel Hekla,** just north of highway 1 between Hella and Selfoss (42 rooms, tel. 486-5540, www.fosshotel.is, bookings@fosshotel.is).

Þórsmörk

Þórsmörk (THORS-murk)—literally "Thor's Woods"—includes a rugged mountain ridge and valleys immersed in a dramatic glacial landscape. This is one of Ice-

land's premiere hiking destinations, with a well-marked network of trails that let you gain elevation for thrilling views over volcanoes, glaciers, and valleys.

Þórsmörk is tucked in between three volcanoes topped by glaciers— Eyjafjallajökull, Mýrdalsjökull, and the small Tindfjallajökull. It's flanked by the wide Markárfljót river valley to the north, and the Krossá river valley to the south. The mountain ridge just south of the Krossá (near the Básar hut/bus stop) is called Goðaland—but in practice, the entire area is known as Þórsmörk.

For most visitors, half the fun of Þórsmörk is getting there: It's accessible only on gravel roads that ford several rushing rivers and streams. While intrepid drivers (with specially equipped 4x4s) can attempt visiting Þórsmörk on their own, for the rest of us, jacked-up buses on monster-truck tires provide a memorable journey.

Þórsmörk requires the better part of a day. Many visitors do it as a long day trip from Reykjavík, while others do it from a home base on the South Coast. The information here is designed to help travelers doing Þórsmörk in one busy day—with an emphasis on its most rewarding hike, to the stunning Valahnúkur viewpoint (with 360-degree panoramas). While not time-consuming, this hike is moderately challenging and staircase-steep in parts. If you're not physically up for the climb, you may want to skip Þórsmörk; although the bus ride in and out is fun, and the area is scenic, there's not much for nonhikers to do.

GETTING THERE

By Car: Drivers who have a full-size 4x4 vehicle, and really know what they're doing, can attempt to drive to Þórsmörk—but before you do, check current conditions (www.safetravel.is), watch some YouTube videos to fully understand what you're committing to, and be sure your car-rental company is OK with the idea.

To reach Þórsmörk, turn off highway 1 north on road 249, pass the Seljalandsfoss waterfall (buses stop here for a photo op and to pick up passengers), then continue north to where the road turns to gravel. From there, the route hooks east and goes under several streams as it works its way along—and eventually through the middle of—the Krossá river to Þórsmörk. Throughout its course, the river splinters and remerges, and the flow can vary dramatically; the drive into Þórsmörk is never the same twice.

By Bus: The one-way journey from Reykjavík to the Þórsmörk Volcano Huts takes up to five hours. Three companies run very

expensive bus services to Þórsmörk (summer only): **Iceland On Your Own** (part of Reykjavík Excursions; 3/day June-Aug, 1/day in May and Sept, www.ioyo.is); **Iceland by Bus** (1/day late June-early Sept, www.icelandbybus.is); and **Trex** buses (2/day mid-June-late Sept, www.trex.is). Buses begin in Reykjavík and make a few stops on their way to and from Þórsmörk. (If you're overnighting along the South Coast, you can catch the bus at the N1 gas station in Hvolsvöllur.) Figure around 15,000 ISK round-trip from Reykjavík. While you can theoretically just hop on the bus, it's smart to book a day or two ahead (once you're confident that the weather is good enough to justify the trip).

Stops Along the Way: On the way into Þórsmörk, some buses stop for a stretch-your-legs photo op at **Gígjökull,** a glacial tongue of Eyjafjallajökull. In the 2010 erup-

tion, melted glacier water came pouring down Gígjökull, flooding this area and silting up what had been a dreamy glacier lagoon. Look for a gigantic rock split cleanly in half—a reminder of the geological power at play here.

Buses may stop at various points on the route to pick up additional passengers—if seats are available. The primary bus stop is **Húsadalur** (also known as the **Volcano Huts**), facing the broad Markárfljót valley, with a little café, shop, and information point. It's a popular launch pad for day hikes—the challenging Valahnúkur hike and the easier saddle hike to Langidalur both begin here.

The other stops are in the narrower, adjacent Krossá valley: **Stakkholtsgjá,** a stop made by request only, is where you can hike up a scenic canyon. **Langidalur,** just over the ridge from Húsadalur, faces the Krossá valley and the Goðaland ridge. It's home to the Skagfjörðsskáli hut, from where you can cross over Þórsmörk either on the steep Valahnúkur route, or on the easier saddle trail. The **Básar/Goðaland** hut is the end of the line, at the base of the

Goðaland ridge, on the opposite side of the Krossá from Langidalur.

HIKING IN ÞÓRSMÖRK

This section focuses on hikes for day-trippers. Those overnighting have many more options—get information at the various huts
and invest in a good hiking map
(available at huts for 1,000-
1,500 ISK). Þórsmörk is also a
stop along several multiday hiking routes. Come prepared and
check trail conditions before
heading out.

Hiking Tips: Most people
hop off the bus at Húsadalur,
hike from the Volcano Huts
over Valahnúkur, descend to Langidalur, then return on the easy
saddle trail back to Húsadalur. With more time, consider riding
the bus all the way to Básar, hiking across the Krossá to Langidalur, then summiting Valahnúkur and descending to Húsadalur for
your return bus at the Volcano Huts; you'll miss the wooded saddle
hike, but the variety gained by hiking across the river valley more
than makes up for it. Stakkholtsgjá is a fine hike, but bus schedules
can make it hard to combine with others in the area. See below for
more details on each of these options.

▲▲▲Valahnúkur (Moderately Challenging with Spectacular Scenery)

The main reason to come to Þórsmörk is for this glorious hike, offering stunning views in every direction. But the trail makes you
earn it: While the hike isn't long (less than
one mile from either valley to the summit),
it's extremely steep in stretches (with an elevation gain of about 900 feet). The footing
varies—stone steps, wooden steps, gravel—
but it's mostly stable. You can hike to Valahnúkur from the Volcano Huts (Húsadalur) or from Langidalur. Either way, follow
the well-marked *Valahnúkur* trail up, up, up,
enjoying higher and higher views. Near the
summit, the ladder-like trail has been known
to cause vertigo—take plenty of breaks.

From the top, scan the horizon for the
three glacier-topped volcanoes that surround
Þórsmörk, the adjacent Goðaland range, and glacial valleys that
fan out into the horizon. The smaller valley just to the right of the

Krossá is the Hvanná. Look just above this, to the saddle of land between the two big glaciers (Eyjafjallajökull and Mýrdalsjökull); this is Fimmvörðuháls, where the first stage of the big 2010 Eyjafjallajökull eruption took place. A directional sign points out these and other distant landmarks. On the steep trail back down, watch your footing and take your time. Figure about 1.5 hours to summit Valahnúkur and make it back down the other side.

▲Saddle Trail Between Húsadalur and Langidalur (Easy)

The easiest ascent over the Þórsmörk ridge connects two low-lying valleys: Langidalur (Long Valley) and Húsadalur (House Valley). The terrain is pretty but mostly wooded, without dramatic views. Hikers use this trail mainly for an easy return to the Volcano Huts after tackling Valahnúkur, but it's also a nice option for those seeking an easier hike (figure 45 minutes or less, one-way). Along Húsadalur, among the jagged volcanic formations just above the Volcano Huts, a side trail leads to Snorraríki—a cave burrowed into a wall that's carved with modern names and old runic inscriptions (to reach the cave itself, you'll need to scale a wall with stone footholds).

▲Rocky Stroll Across the Krossá River (Easy)

The Krossá river carves its way through a rocky landscape between Básar (at the base of the Goðaland ridge) and Langidalur (at the base of the Þórsmörk range). This is the same river you'll crisscross on your way to and from this area, but the 30-minute hike across this valley gives you a closer look. As you walk across the desolate expanse, keep an eye out for two or three movable bridges, which are strategically placed to help hikers cross (marked with yellow arrows). The footing is uneven but walkable—a mix of sand, pebble, and ankle-twisting rock of every color.

▲▲Stakkholtsgjá Canyon Hike (Moderate)

This narrow valley, with walls up to 300 feet high, cuts a mossy mile-and-a-quarter deep into the cliff. Plan on 1.5 hours round-trip for this hike. While mostly level, the footing is uneven, and the canyon's river is always in flux—you'll likely have to step, or even jump or wade, across a swift current (wear proper footwear). Where the stream forks, bear left. The ever-narrowing canyon culminates at a cave-like enclosure with a gushing waterfall. For a closer look, you'll have to scramble up some slippery rocks. Unfortunately, this hike's location—not easily walkable to the other trailheads—makes it tricky to combine with other hikes in the area. Stakkholtsgjá is a good compromise for reasonably hardy hikers who don't mind uneven footing and want a scenic walk, but aren't up for the steepness of Valahnúkur. The real challenge is finding a way to do this hike if you're getting around by bus. Buses stop here by request only—and you may not be able to catch a returning bus for many hours. Before getting off, clearly establish the return bus time with your driver. (Probably the most certain way to do this hike, and then visit other parts of Þórsmörk, is to take a private—and pricey—"super jeep" tour.)

SLEEPING AND EATING IN ÞÓRSMÖRK

Serious hikers enjoy settling in for a few days to explore Þórsmörk. Your options are the ¢ **Volcano Huts** at Húsadalur, with a variety of private rooms, dorms, cottages, and camping (www.volcanohuts. com); the ¢ **Skagfjörðsskáli** hut, at Langidalur, with dorms, camping, and a private cottage (www.fi.is); and ¢ **Básar,** with dorms and camping across the valley from Skagfjörðsskáli in the Goðaland foothills (www.utivist.is).

Services are sparse in Þórsmörk. The only real restaurant is the $ **cafeteria** at the Volcano Huts. It's smart to bring a picnic to enjoy at your leisure—there are plenty of glorious viewpoints.

WESTMAN ISLANDS

Vestmannaeyjar

The Westman Islands are my favorite "Back Door" destination in Iceland: a highly scenic, relatively undiscovered island experience. On clear days, the islands' sharp cliffs hover like a seductive mirage just offshore from the touristy South Coast. Those who make the trip discover that this pint-sized archipelago packs in an appealing variety of experiences: a dramatic approach by air or sea, a gorgeously set small town with engaging museums and good restaurants, an up-close look at a recent volcanic eruption, and craggy sea cliffs teeming with birds (including puffin colonies in the summer). The islands are a bit of a project to reach, but worth the trouble for travelers spending more than a few days in Iceland. You can get there by ferry from the South Coast or by plane from Reykjavík.

Among Icelanders, the Westman Islands (Vestmannaeyjar, VEST-mah-nah-AY-ar) have various claims to fame: They're known for their recent volcanic activity (and excellent Volcano Museum), busy fishing industry, large populations of seabirds, and musical traditions celebrated in a huge annual festival. Puffins are an unofficial mascot for all of Iceland, but (in summer) they are particularly abundant here on the Westman Islands.

The "Westman" Islands, which actually lie south of the mainland, are named for a trio of Irish slaves who fled to the islands after killing their owner, according to the sagas. In Old Norse, the Irish were called *Vestmenn* (Westmen), so a better translation might be the "Irishmen's Islands."

Only one island—called Heimaey (HAME-ah-AY)—is inhabited, and that's the one you'll be visiting.

PLANNING YOUR TIME

Consider whether you'll stay the night or visit Heimaey as a day trip, and whether to walk or drive on to the ferry.

Overnight or Day Trip?: An **overnight** in the islands gives you the flexibility to go later in the day. Staying two nights is over-kill if you're spending less than a week in the country. Note that an overnight on the Westman Islands works well in conjunction with a visit to the South Coast; the Landeyjahöfn ferry dock is about a 15-minute drive south of the Seljalandsfoss waterfall.

You can **day-trip** here from Reykjavík—or from the South Coast—in a rushed but still worthwhile visit. If home-basing on the South Coast, ideally budget two days; use the day with nicer weather for your Westman Islands trip. To go by **boat,** drive or ride a bus to Landeyjahöfn harbor to catch the **ferry** first thing in the morning, and reverse the trip in the evening. By **plane,** take a morning flight out and a late afternoon flight back. Note that flying from Reykjavík works best Monday through Friday (flight schedules make day-tripping difficult to impossible on Sat-Sun).

Walk On or Drive On?: On a short visit, it's easy to see the main sights in town by foot. To see the rest of the island, you can either bring your car on the ferry, or join a recommended bus tour (see "Helpful Hints," later). Drivers walking onto the ferry can park their cars for free at the Landeyjahöfn port.

Ferry Day-Trip Plan: Take the earliest ferry over and the last one back. (It's 40 minutes each way.) Outside of festival weekends, walk-ons can almost always return on an earlier ferry if they like. To really see the island, take an island tour (2 hours, late morning or early afternoon departures). Budget an hour apiece for sights in Vestmannaeyjar and another hour for my self-guided town walk. To save time en route, the ferry has a basic, fairly priced cafeteria with meals (breakfast or dinner) ready to go.

Plane Day-Trip Plan: If flying from Reykjavík on a weekday, you'll arrive in the wee hours (before 8:00) and have time to kill before the island's museums open (10:00 or later). This is a good time to explore the town and orient yourself with my self-guided walk. Hop on the 9:30 bus trip around the island with Eyja Tours, have lunch, then visit the Volcano Museum before heading back to the airport for your return flight (departures generally Mon-Fri at 16:30).

GETTING TO THE WESTMAN ISLANDS

Flying is pricey, but it's quick and handy for those looking for an efficient side-trip from Reykjavík. The ferry makes sense for those spending time on the South Coast. Both options are equally scenic, and are more or less equally weather dependent.

WESTMAN ISLANDS

By Plane from Reykjavík

Take a 19-seat turboprop plane with **Eagle Air,** which flies from Reykjavík City Airport, near downtown—*not* the international Ke-
flavík Airport (about $170  each way, cheaper online fares sell out quickly, 2-3 flights/day Sun-Fri, 1/day on Sat June-Aug only, 25 minutes, tel. 562-4200, www.eagleair.is). A day trip on Eagle Air is the most efficient way to see the islands, but if the
morning departure is cancelled due to bad weather, you've lost your only shot at going (they'll normally refund the entire round-trip fare).

At Reykjavík City Airport, the Eagle Air terminal is on the *east* side of the runways, behind the Icelandair Hotel Reykjavík Natura and the control tower. (Don't confuse it with the Air Iceland Connect terminal that serves most domestic flights.) To reach Eagle Air by public transport, take bus #5 to the Nauthólsvegur stop. For early-morning flights, take a taxi (best to arrange taxi the night before). As there's no security check, you can show up 30 minutes before departure (if sleeping in downtown Reykjavík, have the taxi pick you up about an hour before your flight).

Luggage Limits: Eagle Air permits just 15 kilos (33 pounds) of luggage; you may need to leave some of your gear in Reykjavík.

By Ferry from Landeyjahöfn

The tiny harbor at Landeyjahöfn is just 10 minutes south of high-way 1 on the South Coast. Except in winter, you'll use this port for the 40-minute ferry ride to the Westman Islands. The port is a two-hour drive east from Reykjavík; turn south onto highway 254 just before the bridge over the Markarfljót river.

A handy bus from Reykjavík connects with two ferries per day. Take bus #52 from Reykjavík's Mjódd terminal (4,400 ISK, first bus departs Reykjavík about 8:00, last bus departs Landeyjahöfn about 20:40, 2.5 hours, tel. 540-2700, www.straeto.is).

Sailing from Landeyjahöfn: The short, inexpensive crossing to the islands is a pleasure (1,600 ISK/person, 2,320 ISK/car, book online at www.herjolfur.is). In summer there are typically seven sailings a day in each direction. Reserve your ferry ticket in advance, especially for cars (morning departures from Landeyjahöfn and evening departures from Vestmannaeyjar can sell out). A few days in advance is usually enough, but if your itinerary is rigid

WESTMAN ISLANDS

or you're visiting during festival times (see later, under "Helpful Hints"), make ferry reservations as soon as your itinerary is set.

Passengers are expected to check in 30 minutes before sailing, so plan to arrive in Landeyjahöfn with enough time to find parking and walk to the tiny ferry terminal (with WCs, a small waiting area, and vending machines). To check harbor conditions, visit www.herjolfur.is (to talk to a real person, call 481-2800). In Vestmannaeyjar, the boat ticket office is at the harbor (open whenever boats sail).

Canceled Landeyjahöfn Ferry? The ferry from Landeyjahöfn can be canceled due to harbor and weather conditions, especially in winter. If the ferry can't dock at Landeyjahöfn, it will use the older Þorlákshöfn harbor instead. Þorlákshöfn is closer to Reykjavík but a two-hour drive from Landeyjahöfn (see details below). To minimize inconvenience to drivers parked in Landeyjahöfn, the ferry company always provides a bus back to that port in the event of a detour.

Back-Up Sailing from Þorlákshöfn: It's a three-hour trip (3,420 ISK/person, 3,420 ISK/car), which makes a day trip to Westman Islands impractical—it really only works if you stay overnight. Þorlákshöfn is a 45-minute drive from Reykjavík. To reach Þorlákshöfn by public transportation, take bus #51 to Hveragerði, and then change to bus #71 for Þorlákshöfn (around 1.5 hours, 2,200 ISK).

Heimaey Island

Your visit is limited to Heimaey (Home Island), the only inhabited island. Although its lone town, Vestmannaeyjar, is humble, its setting is dramatic: buildings huddle up along the harbor, facing a busy industrial port and steep, scenic cliffs. From here, Vestmannaeyjar climbs gradually uphill, filling a broad plateau between the cliffs to the west and the volcanoes to the east. The roughly dozen smaller islands surrounding Heimaey

have a wet, warm, and windy climate—by Icelandic standards. Icelanders refer to this area as simply "the islands," and people from here as "islanders."

WESTMAN ISLANDS

Orientation to Heimaey Island

The only town on Heimaey shares the name of the archipelago: **Vestmannaeyjar.** Its main commercial street, called Bárustígur, runs up from the harbor and holds many of my recommended eats and sleeps. Puffin-head sign-posts scattered around town direct you to the various museums and other landmarks.

Tourist Information: The Sea Life Trust Visitor Center, at the harbor end of the main drag at Ægisgata 2, serves as the local TI (daily 10:00-17:00, shorter hours off-season, tel. 488-2555, www.visitvestmannaeyjar.is).

ARRIVAL IN VESTMANNAEYJAR

By Plane: From the airport, you can take a taxi into town (1,700 ISK—ask the airport staff to call one for you or try Eyjataxi at mobile 698-2038); ask your hotel to pick you up; make friends with a local from the flight and ask for a ride; or on a nice day, and without luggage, walk 1.5 miles from the airport downhill into town (go left from airport, around west side of Helgafell mountain, 35 minutes). To return to the airport, take a taxi instead of walking uphill.

By Boat: If arriving on foot by ferry, follow the blue stripe painted onto the pavement. This leads you to the ticket kiosks for various boat and bus tours. The main drag (and the start of my self-guided walk) is uphill from the harbor, roughly behind the Krónan supermarket, about two blocks to the left (look for the Eymundsson bookshop).

HELPFUL HINTS

Puffin Viewing: The best time to see puffins is from roughly late May to mid-August. They actually arrive around the end of April, but spend only a brief time cleaning their burrows before they go out to sea to mate. In recent years, the number of puffins nesting here has declined, perhaps due to the warming ocean around the islands.

Festivals: On the first weekend in August, the islands host the massive **Þjóðhátíð** (National Festival) in Herjólfsdalur, a picturesque valley near town (fireworks, bonfires, and singing; must buy festival ticket and book accommodations and transport to islands well in advance; www.dalurinn.is). The week-

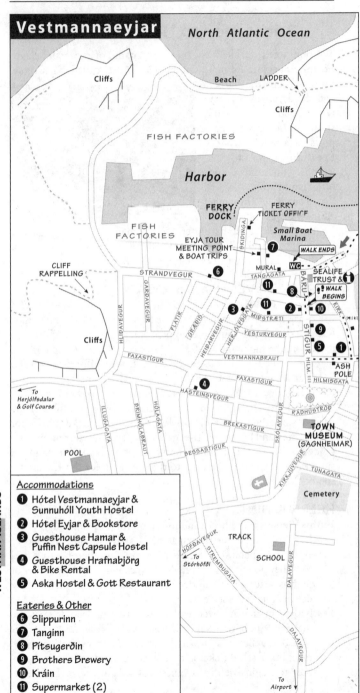

Vestmannaeyjar

North Atlantic Ocean

Cliffs

Beach

LADDER

Cliffs

FISH FACTORIES

Harbor

FERRY DOCK

FERRY TICKET OFFICE

FISH FACTORIES

Small Boat Marina

EYJA TOUR MEETING POINT & BOAT TRIPS

CLIFF RAPPELLING

STRANDVEGUR

7

6

MURAL

WALK ENDS

WC

SEALIFE TRUST &

1

TANGAGATA

11

8

WALK BEGINS

GARÐAVEGUR

FLATIR

GREÐIS

HEIÐARVEGUR

HERJÓLFSGATA

3

11

2

10

MIÐSTRÆTI

9

Cliffs

HLIÐAVEGUR

VESTURVEGUR

5

1

STÍGUR

HILM

KIRK

FAXASTÍGUR

VESTMANNABRAUT

ASH POLE

To Herjólfsdalur & Golf Course

HÁSTEINSVEGUR

4

FAXASTÍGUR

HILMISGATA

HÓLAGATA

ILLUGAGATA

PRIMHÓLABRAUT

BREKASTÍGUR

SKÓLAVEGUR

RÁÐHÚSTRÖÐ

TOWN MUSEUM (SAGNHEIMAR)

ÞESSASTÍGUR

POOL

TÚNAGATA

Cemetery

KIRKJUVEGUR

TRACK

To Stórhöfði

HÖFÐAVEGUR

STREMBUGATA

SCHOOL

DALAVEGUR

DALAVEGUR

To Airport

Accommodations

1 Hótel Vestmannaeyjar & Sunnuhóll Youth Hostel

2 Hótel Eyjar & Bookstore

3 Guesthouse Hamar & Puffin Nest Capsule Hostel

4 Guesthouse Hrafnabjörg & Bike Rental

5 Aska Hostel & Gott Restaurant

Eateries & Other

6 Slippurinn

7 Tanginn

8 Pítsugerðin

9 Brothers Brewery

10 Kráin

11 Supermarket (2)

WESTMAN ISLANDS

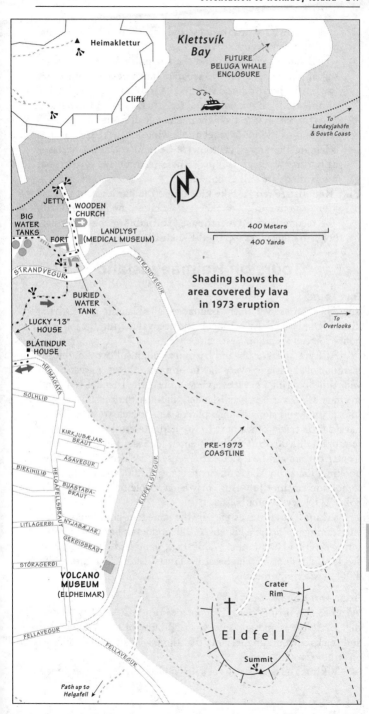

Heimaklettur

Klettsvík Bay

FUTURE BELUGA WHALE ENCLOSURE

Cliffs

To *Landeyjahöfn & South Coast*

JETTY

WOODEN CHURCH

BIG WATER TANKS

FORT

LANDLYST (MEDICAL MUSEUM)

400 Meters

400 Yards

STRANDVEGUR

STRANDVEGUR

Shading shows the area covered by lava in 1973 eruption

BURIED WATER TANK

To Overlooks

LUCKY "13" HOUSE

BLÁTINDUR HOUSE

HEIMAGATA

SÓLHLÍÐ

PRE-1973 COASTLINE

KIRKJUBÆJAR-BRAUT

ÁSAVEGUR

BIRKIHLÍÐ

HELGAFELLSBRAUT

BÚASTAÐA-BRAUT

LITLAGERÐI

NÝJABÆJAR

GERÐISBRAUT

STÓRAGERÐI

VOLCANO MUSEUM (ELDHEIMAR)

Crater Rim

FELLAVEGUR

E l d f e l l

FELLAVEGUR

Summit

Path up to Helgafell

end is known for drunkenness and other rowdy behavior, and everything books up.

School-age athletes and their families fill the island for soccer tournaments on two separate June weekends: **Pæjumót** (girls, https://tmmotid.is) and **Orkumót** (boys, www. orkumotid.is). Book hotels and ferry tickets well in advance.

The **Goslok** festival commemorates the end of the 1973 eruption of Eldfell (weekend following July 3). Islanders also celebrate the annual nationwide **Seamans' Day** enthusiastically (first weekend in June). These festivals are smaller, but reservations are still essential.

Bike Rentals: A **rent-a-bike kiosk** is at the harbor next to Eyja Tours (mountain bikes and electric bikes, mobile 896-3340). The recommended **Guesthouse Hrafnabjörg** above the harbor also rents bikes (4,300 ISK/half-day).

Tours on Heimaey Island

Bus Tours

These bus tours cover all the points described later in my "Driving Tour of the Island." Eyja Tours is the best value...and the best two hours you can spend on Vestmannaeyjar.

At **Eyja Tours,** Ebbi and Iris run a delightful two-hour minibus tour of the island every day in summer. This is a great use of your time, offering a good overview of the entire island, lively commentary from a gregarious islander, and just the right balance of information and stops to snap photos and stretch your legs. They have a little ticket office next to the harbor, across from Tanginn restaurant (8,900 ISK, includes entry to Sea Life Trust Visitor Center but not any boat ride, RS%—use code "Rick Steves" when booking; tours run May-mid-Sept at 9:30, 12:00, and 14:30; smart to book in advance July-Aug, may be available off-season, mobile 852-6939, www.eyjatours.is).

Viking Tours does essentially the same two-hour tour with an entertaining guide on a big bus. While it doesn't have the minibus intimacy, it's a good option (7,000 ISK, daily mid-May-mid-Sept at 14:00, does not include Sea Life Trust Visitor Center, tel. 488-4884, www.vikingtours.is).

Boat and Kayak Tours

Weather permitting, several companies run boat and kayak tours that circle the island and give you a glimpse of the smaller islets and stacks surrounding it. Note that these are commonly canceled on windy days.

Viking Tours uses a larger ship (7,400 ISK, departures generally mid-May–mid-Sept at 11:00 and 16:00, 1.5 hours, tel. 488-4884, www.vikingtours.is).

Ribsafari runs more expensive, bumpy tours on small RIBs—rigid inflatable boats (17,900 ISK, 2 hours, mobile 661-1810, www.ribsafari.is). Neither trip visits Surtsey (the island that erupted from the sea in the mid-1960s), as it's too distant from Vestmannaeyjar and landing there is not allowed.

Kayak & Puffins leads guided 1.5-hour kayak tours from the small boat harbor (6,000 ISK, must be 14 years old, 2/day in summer, generally at 13:30 and 16:30, 2-person minimum, mobile 861-3090, https://kayakandpuffins.is).

Vestmannaeyjar Town Walk

This one-hour walk is designed to give you a handy ▲▲▲ overview of the island's only town—Vestmannaeyjar—with views from atop the lava that swallowed up several houses, and a stroll past its scant historic landmarks and along its busy harborfront. The walk begins in front of the Eymundsson bookstore on the main street.

• *Stand with your back to the water, looking up the street called...*

Bárustígur: This is the little main street of a little town on a little island. The bookstore staff are helpful, and can answer your questions between ringing up book sales and pulling espresso shots. Look up the street to find the gray, blocky building at the far end (above the set of black steps)—it houses the town history and culture museum (called Sagnheimar and described later).

• *Walk two blocks up Bárustígur, taking note of the town's handful of restaurants and shops. When you reach Vestmannabraut, turn left and head toward the hill in front of you. Across the street from Hótel Vestmannaeyjar, find the black...*

Ash Pole: Standing here today, it's hard to imagine this entire street buried in pumice and gravel-like ash for months following the 1973 eruption. These poles, scattered throughout the east part of Vestmannaeyjar, show just how high the ash reached, providing a tangible scale of the destruction.

• *Continue straight, toward the hill, crossing over Kirkjuvegur. A half-block up on the left (just after the house labeled Lagafell 1905), turn onto the path leading to a reconstructed white facade.*

Blátindur House: Although this house was almost entirely swallowed by the newly formed hillside, its facade remained standing, becoming a symbol of the island people's resilience. When the original facade eventually gave way decades later, funds were raised to rebuild it. More striking than the house itself are the photos on display chronicling the home pre- and post-eruption. A short slideshow plays inside the window, explaining the history of the house and its owners. You can walk around the side of the reconstruction to see the actual ruins.

• *Return to Kirkjuvegur and turn right. We're heading for the stair-case up the side of a bluff. Before climbing up, notice the brown wooden chalet-type house to the right: The lava—now the grassy bank between you and it—stopped just in time to save the house. Its street number? Lucky number 13.*

Climb to the top of the stairs, then take a hard left with the trail and follow it out along the edge of the bluff to a cross and a small stone monument a few steps beyond.

Vestmannaeyjar Viewpoint Spin-Tour: Get oriented with this 360-degree visual tour. First, look out over the **harbor,** where

boats big and small are shel-tered by two steep cliffs with rounded, green tops. Vestman-naeyjar's excellent natural har-bor became even more sheltered by cooled lava after the huge eruption in 1973 (see sidebar). A significant share of Iceland's total fish exports comes from here, even though the island has only a little more than 1 percent of Iceland's population. The whole northern side of the harbor is given over to fish processing, and the community tends to vote for Iceland's conservative party, which works to protect fishing interests. The harbor is too tight for big cruise ships...which is a good thing for independent travelers.

Just to the left of the harbor is a towering **cliff,** home to some of the island's many birds. The Westman Islands are rich with bird

life—puffins, of course, but also fulmars, guille-mots, and kittiwakes. This cliff is also where local kids learn the age-old climbing and rappelling skills needed to collect seabird eggs on the jag-ged outlying islands—a practice called *sprangan.* If you have great vision (or binoculars), you may be able to spot a knotted rope dangling to the left of the birds. Starting around age eight, children learn how to free-climb their way up steep cliff faces and swing on strategically placed ropes. (Better to learn here, where at worst they might fall on the soft sod, rather than the sharp rocks and cold surf at the base of a sea cliff.)

Tucked around the far side of that cliff (not visible from here) is Herjólfsdalur, a natural amphitheater where this teensy island hosts a gigantic music festival each summer.

Now pan left, over Vestmannaeyjar's **rooftops.** This is not a cutesy tourist town, but a no-nonsense working community. For centuries, no more than a few hundred people lived here. The island boomed between 1900 and 1920 with the rise of motorized fishing, and much of the downtown zone dates from that era. Today, the 4,300 islanders still live off fishing, plus a little tourism. Living out on the islands comes with compromises: Errands often require a trip to the mainland, and many expectant mothers travel to Reykjavík to give birth at the larger hospital there. If the houses look a little ragtag, keep in mind that maintaining property on a little island is a challenge. Despite the islands' volcanic activity, there's no geothermal water source, so this is one of the parts of Iceland where homes are heated with electricity and oil.

Turning farther left, find the two looming **volcanic peaks** on the horizon. The one on the right, with the classic volcanic dome shape, is the dormant Helgafell, which last erupted 6,000 years ago. The lower-lying, reddish one to its left, Eldfell, was born in the 1973 eruption—when, for six months, a slow and steady flow of lava gradually consumed this corner of the island.

Continue looking left, across a **rocky landscape.** The entire "hill" upon which you stand—all the land between here and that volcano—is less than 50 years old. You're standing on a now-solidified molten river of liquid rock that's 50 feet deep. (Remember that staircase you climbed up?) All around you, notice the wood-carved "street signs," bearing the names of streets that now lie deep underfoot. Keep an eye out for plaques memorializing former landmarks (Kiwanis club, electrical plant, and so on). Looking down from this vantage point it's easy to see where present-day dead-end streets once continued directly below you. The low-lying, rust-colored, boxy building that sits between the V formed by the two volcanoes is the excellent **Volcano Museum,** called Eldheimar; a visit here is an essential Westman Islands experience (described later).

Hiking paths and gravel roads crisscross this area. It's fun to wander around the **lava rocks,** which are blanketed in fuzzy moss and (in early summer) enlivened by colorful wildflowers. If you have time and energy, you can hike all the way up to the volcano summit (see "Climbing up Eldfell Volcano," later).

• *Now continue along the gravel path, with the lava on your right and the harbor on your left. When the path reaches an asphalt road, cross it to the bench and look down over historic **Skansinn Cove**. Walk down the steep steps to the remaining walls of an old fortress with a lone cannon.*

Fortress (Virkið): In 1586, the Danish king built this to enforce Danish power against the British, who wanted to trade with the islands. The fortress saw action only once, during perhaps the only dramatic event in local history until the 1973 eruption: In 1627, pirates (often misidentified as "Turkish") raided the island and carried off most of its inhabitants to slavery in Algeria. The island's priest, Ólafur Egilsson, was one of the few who managed to return. He wrote a book about his experiences, which you can buy in English translation. More of the fortress's history is on the information board.

Just past the fortress, embedded in the bluff on the right, look for the white, semicircular **water tank**—or what's left of it, as

more than half of the structure was consumed by lava. Built in 1932, this was a seawater tank that helped local fishermen keep their catch fresh. It also fed a big swimming pool—which is now under the lava (see photos of happy swimmers on the nearby information boards). For centuries, the Westman Islands suffered from a lack of fresh water, with just two wells and the rainwater that residents collected from their roofs. In 1968, a pipeline was completed that brought water from the mainland, which is now stored in the huge white tanks between here and the harbor.

• *Continue past the water tank and the big mast mounted in the ground, to the old house on the right.*

Landlyst: Relocated here in 2000, this building is the oldest residence on the island and the former home of Iceland's first maternity hospital. Information boards explain how neonatal tetanus

The Westman Islands Eruption of 1973

In the middle of the night on January 21-22, 1973, a volcanic eruption started along a fissure just above the town of Vestmannaeyjar. Most of the islanders were immediately evacuated, but the eruption went on for months—destroying a third of the town. This event is still fresh in many islanders' minds, and tourists usually spend part of their visit understanding it and seeing its consequences—including the many bits of buried homes still sticking out of the lava all around the eastern side of town.

Lava from the newly formed volcanic cone, named Eldfell, gradually encroached on local homes, even as it expanded the island's footprint by about 20 percent. Meanwhile, the volcano ejected massive volumes of tephra (volcanic particles) into the air, blanketing much of the island's northern half under a thick layer of ash and rock. A small crew stayed on the island to observe the eruption and wrap up the evacuation, and when possible, they retrieved valuables from houses before they were buried by ash or set alight by hot lava bombs. Ultimately the eruption destroyed 400 homes, displacing 1,500 residents. One person died (from toxic gases that built up where he was sleeping).

By June, after six terrifying months, the eruption was finally over. Some islanders moved back home, but about a third never returned—they'd forged new lives on the mainland, or they didn't want to live in fear of another eruption.

Although the volcano caused great disruption, it also had some positive effects. Geothermal heat from the earth allowed the islanders to heat their water for a few years, with pipes running underneath the new lava (these days, they're back to electricity and oil). Tephra from the eruption was useful for road building and paving. Most importantly, the eruption didn't close off the island's harbor, but did helpfully narrow the harbor mouth enough to make it a much more sheltered anchorage. For better or for worse, the 1973 eruption shaped the Westman Islands that you're visiting today.

killed three-quarters of all babies born on the Westman Islands in the mid-19th century...a problem solved only when an islander went to Copenhagen to train as a midwife. Today the building houses a delightful little medical museum (looks closed when it's open, free, daily 11:00-17:00).

• *Continue downhill a few yards to the...*

WESTMAN ISLANDS

Wooden Church: Just below the old house, you can't miss the small black wooden church, donated by Norway in 2000 to mark a millennium of Christianity in Iceland (free to enter). While lacking a tall steeple, it's typical of humble Norwegian village churches (and designed as a replica of a circa-1170 church in Trondheim, Norway).

• *Walk out to the end of the stubby...*

Jetty (Hringskersgarður): This helps protect the harbor from the churning sea. Looking right, you'll see the narrow passage ships use to access Vestmannaeyjar's port —and you can clearly see how the harbor became even more protected by the

1973 lava flow, which came as far as this jetty. Islanders were terrified that the lava would seal off the harbor entirely, which would have turned Vestmannaeyjar into a ghost town with no industry. With the help of the US military, locals pumped seawater on the lava to try to cool sections of it and divert the flow away from the town and harbor. Opinions are divided about whether this had any real effect, but the islanders like to think it did. American writer John McPhee wrote a good account of this effort (*The Control of Nature*, 1989).

The pontoons in the small cove across from you, Klettsvík Bay, mark an **underwater pen** built to house two beluga whales brought to Heimaey in 2019 (for details, see the "Sea Life Trust Visitor Center" listing, later). This cove has been home to a whale before: Keiko, the orca made famous by the movie *Free Willy*, was held here from 1998 to 2002.

Now gaze up at the 930-foot-tall cliff that rockets up across the harbor—called **Heimaklettur.** Seabirds love to nest in the craggy horizontal walls, and you may spot some surefooted sheep grazing at the top. Hardy islanders race each other to the top of this cliff, using specially placed ladders; the record is 13 minutes. For us mortals, it's more like 45 minutes up, 25 minutes down...but only if you're in great shape—it's fearsomely steep and only for adventurous, dedicated climbers.

• *Let's head back into town. Retrace your steps back up to and through the fortress. Past the lonely cannon, a small lane leads down to the big, white water tanks. Walk around the tanks to the right, go down the stairs, and then head left, along the water, back into town to...*

Vestmannaeyjar's Harbor: Stroll along the busy waterfront, peering into warehouses and onto ship decks. After the blue warehouse, you'll bear left, then right, to circle around the inner harbor, where smaller boats moor. This area, called Bæjarbryggjan

(Town Wharf), was built in 1907, around the time motorized fishing arrived in the Westman Islands. It was later expanded, and eventually modern docks were built on the far side of the harbor.

Soon you'll reach a little skate park under a mural, with WCs and benches nearby. The Sea Life Trust Visitor Center and the main drag, Bárustígur, are to your left. Straight ahead are the sales kiosks for various bus and boat tours (see "Helpful Hints," earlier). The ferry dock back to the mainland is just a couple minutes' walk past the kiosks.

• *Our walk has come nearly full circle. From here, you can browse tour options, head back up into town for lunch, or visit your choice of Vestmannaeyjar's museums, described in the next section.*

Sights on Heimaey Island

Vestmannaeyjar has two charming homegrown museums worth your time plus the underwhelming and overpriced Sea Life Trust Visitor Center. Save walking by seeing the town museum (Sagnheimar) and the Volcano Museum consecutively; extend this trip farther by walking from the Volcano Museum up the path to the summit of Eldfell volcano.

▲▲Volcano Museum (Eldheimar)

This modern museum tells the story of the 1973 Eldfell eruption, which destroyed half the town and has been an inseparable

part of the islands' image ever since. The vivid exhibits are well described by the included audioguide. The centerpiece of the museum is an actual house, half-immersed in lava rock.

Cost and Hours: 2,300 ISK, includes audioguide; daily 11:00-18:00; mid-Oct-April Wed-Sun 13:00-17:00, closed Mon-Tue, or by arrangement; Gerðisbraut 10, tel. 488-2700, http://eldheimar.is.

Getting There: The museum is about a 20-minute, moderately uphill walk from the harbor; follow the red lampposts, and look for the boxy, rust-colored building on the hillside. It's about 10 minutes uphill from Sagnheimar, the town museum; to walk between the two, take the street called Birkihlíð.

Visiting the Museum: Before going inside, to the right of the entry, a staircase leads to the ruins of a house immersed in lava. The museum itself is built over the excavated remains of a house that was buried (but didn't burn) in the eruption. Guðni Ólafsson and Gerður Sigurðardóttir and their three young sons lived in the one-story, ranch-style house, which had just been finished two years before. Their home—now windowless, with its roof propped up by steel supports, and its contents left in disarray as they were found—is the highlight of the museum. You can't go in the ruin, but joysticks and monitors allow you to control cameras and investigate remotely. The oft-heard label "Pompeii of the North" is a bit of an exaggeration, but it's definitely a one of-a-kind sight.

From there, the audioguide takes you around the seven stages of the exhibit in about 20 minutes. You'll learn about the town before, during, and after the eruption, with striking photographs and gripping (if grainy) television footage. Island residents retell the exhausting excavation of the town—mountains of tephra (2.2 cubic tons) were shoveled and trucked away. If you have time, there's also a 25-minute documentary film. Upstairs, you'll find good views over the house stuck in lava, a coffee shop, and a less engaging exhibit on the Surtsey eruption of 1963-1967.

▲▲Town Museum (Sagnheimar)

This endearing museum has an eclectic array of exhibits that give context to your island visit. It's well done, insightful, and worth seeing if you have time.

Cost and Hours: 1,000 ISK; daily 10:00-17:00; Oct-April Sat only 13:00-16:00, closed Sun-Fri; Ráðhúströð, at the upper end of the Bárustígur main drag, on the second floor in the same building as the town library; tel. 488-2045, www.sagnheimar.is.

Visiting the Museum: Head upstairs, buy your ticket, then make a counterclockwise loop through the circular floor plan. First you'll learn about the 1973 eruption, including before-and-after photos and video interviews with local residents (English subtitles). The next section has photos of the roughly 200 islanders who converted to the Mormon Church in the mid-1800s and emigrated to Utah, and an illustrated retelling of the 1627 "Turkish Raid" on the islands (in which pirates kidnapped over 200 islanders and took them away to slavery in Algeria). On the left, a room tells the story of women on the island, including one of the island's first midwives, Sólveig Pálsdóttir. Next you'll learn about the Danish governor who started a local militia in the 1850s—in this country without an army—to defend the islands against further attacks. The far wall displays photos of notable island athletes.

The back of the museum features an exhibit about the history of the annual Þjóðhátíð National Festival held in August, including one of the tents locals set up for the festival and some of the outrageous costumes the revelers wear. Then you'll loop around to a fun section on puffins (with a birders cabin and interesting video clips). Next is an exhibit about the fishing industry that is at the heart of Westman Island life, with a reconstructed 1924 town pier, a 1970s fishermen's dorm, a poignant "in memoriam" wall honoring fishermen who have been lost at sea, and a seasickness-inducing video showing a fishing trawler navigating insanely rough seas, practically going airborne as the crew struggle to haul in their catch. The last room, on the left, displays examples of Iceland's national costume, developed as the country sought independence.

Climbing Up Eldfell Volcano

It's relatively straightforward to walk up to the summit of Eldfell (ELD-fehtl), the volcano that emerged in the 1973 eruption. The

simplest way is to follow the short path that starts a bit above the Volcano Museum (20-30 minutes up), by a small parking lot. You can also walk directly through the lava from downtown, starting at the stairway up into the lava from the end of Miðstræti (at the corner of Kirjustræti; this area is also described on my self-guided walk). The ground at the summit gets a bit cooler every year, and it's no longer easy to boil an egg or bake potatoes in holes dug in the lava. However, locals report that you can still bake Icelandic rye bread in it.

Sea Life Trust Visitor Center

Big business came to Vestmannaeyjar in 2019 with the opening of the Sea Life Trust Beluga Whale Sanctuary and Puffin Rescue Center on the harborfront (a.k.a. the Sea Life Trust Visitor Center). The center replaced the town's longtime homey aquarium and ad hoc puffin center, and coincided with the arrival of two beluga whales. Townspeople welcomed the new tourist attraction, and have worked to keep the community aspect of puffin rescue—but the center can feel more commercial than educational. (Sea Life Trust is a partner charity of the British firm behind Legoland and Madame Tussaud's Waxworks.)

The big stars are Little Grey and Little White, two female beluga whales native to Russia who spent most of their lives in an aquarium in China. Shipped to Heimaey by plane in 2019, they're currently being held in a "care pool" within the aquarium. This section is not always open to the public—ask before you decide to pay for entry. Eventually the whales will be moved to a 350,000-square-foot enclosure across the harbor in Klettsvík Bay, where you'll be able to view them by boat. The whales won't ever be released into the wild, but it's hoped they'll learn to fish for themselves and enjoy greater freedom.

Cost and Hours: Aquarium/puffin rescue—3,500 ISK, family pass—10,000 ISK; combined aquarium/puffin rescue and boat trip—8,500 ISK, boat trip only—6,000 ISK—boats will run once the whales have been moved; daily 10:00-17:00, facing the small boat marina at the corner of Bárustígur and Ægisgata, Ægisgata 2, https://belugasanctuary.sealifetrust.org. Entry to the aquarium/puffin rescue is included in the Eyja Tours bus tour; this is a better value than paying to enter the aquarium separately.

Visiting the Center: Your visit starts with a display about the whales and their journey to Vestmannaeyjar, and tanks holding fish and other sea life from the harbor. The next room is the puffin rescue center, home to Hafdís—the center's unofficial puffin mascot—along with a handful of other resident puffins. Puffins nest in burrows on steep grassy slopes just above the island's cliff edges. Every August, when the baby puffins raised on the island

that summer are ready to take flight for the South Atlantic, some become distracted by the lights of the town and land in the streets. Island children collect the pufflings (that's right, a baby puffin is called a puffling) and bring them to the rescue center, which keeps them overnight and then releases them at an appropriate spot by the sea. Cute photos show local kids with the pufflings they rescued. Hafdís was once one of these birds, but her feathers didn't generate the right waterproofing, making it impossible for her to survive in the wild.

Finally, you may be able to peer through windows into the pool holding Little Grey and Little Blue and rooms where aquarium workers go about their tasks.

Driving Tour of the Island

With a car, you can take an easy spin around the island of Heimaey. The entire loop (which is what the island bus tours do) takes about a half-hour with no stops, but allow an hour or two at a leisurely pace, with plenty of photo stops for views of Westman islets and happy, roaming sheep grazing on scrubby groundcover. Once you leave town, you won't see much civilization. Heimaey once had several working farms, but the sheep and horses you see now are raised more as a hobby.

• *From town, loop west to...*

Herjólfsdalur: This valley, in a collapsed volcanic crater, is the site of the Þjóðhátíð (National Festival) held each August.

There's not much to do at other times, but it's a dramatic setting. Look for the stage (which faces the cliff and benefits from the acoustics of the mountain bowl) and the pulpit-like spot where bonfires are lit. Between the amphitheater and road sits a reconstruction of the first Westman Island settler's farmhouse.

What looks like two separate dwellings is actually connected; in winter, animals were housed on the left to share their warmth with the family's living space on the right. The area also has a golf course and a campsite. The cliffs over the little jagged inlet on the western side of the meadow (which famously look like an elephant) are a good place to look for puffins in the summer. If you have time, a lovely walking path leads south from Herjólfsdalur along the island's western shore.

• *Drive south toward the island's southern point, Stórhöfði. Along the way are some prime...*

Offshore Island Views: The best views of the 15 other (uninhabited) Westman Islands, worth ▲, are from the road that runs

south between Herjólfsdalur and Stórhöfði. Nobody lives on any of these islands full-time, but island men join together in fraternity-like clubs that own them. Each club builds and maintains a hut on its island—and some huts are quite elaborate. Locals go to the outer islands mostly to harvest seabird eggs.

WESTMAN ISLANDS

The most distant of the smaller islands—which you can just barely see on the horizon, on very clear days—is Surtsey, which rose from the sea in a long eruption, lasting from 1963 to 1967, that attracted attention from around the world. Surtsey has been left alone and it's illegal for the public to land there, although scientists visit it regularly to follow along with the plants that colonize it and the wave erosion that makes it a little smaller each year.

• *About 10 minutes after leaving Herjólfsdalur, you'll reach...*

Stórhöfði: This hilly knob of land was a separate island before the Helgafell eruption created the isthmus several thousand years ago. The first pullout along the road up to the lighthouse, on a hairpin bend, has a small parking area and short path to a bird-watching blind. Here you can get a good view of the cliffs where puffins nest in the summer (not visible from the road; be sure to close the windows, door, and gate when you're finished).  The second pullout, just below the lighthouse, has the best views. You're standing in line with three volcanoes: On the coastline to the north you can see Eyjafjallajökull (erupted 2010), on the island itself stands Eldfell (1973), and behind you (not visible, off-shore), is Surtsey (1963). The lighthouse has a weather station that regularly records the strongest winds in Iceland...and that's really saying something.

• *From here it's just 10 minutes back to town. Or, to drive right into a volcano, turn right on Strembugata (above the school playfield) then left on Fellavegur, following it around to an unmarked gravel road that crosses the lava field (see the map).*

Eldfell: You're driving into the new land created by the 1973 eruption. While devastating, the eruption made the island 20 percent bigger, gave the harbor more protection, and provided a land barrier to break the harsh wind that until then barreled from the open sea right into town. The gravel road leads to a cross below the summit that marks the center of the volcano. From here, it's possible to climb a steep path to the crater rim. Notice the different colors of volcanic rock, and the slow-growing scrub grass planted to keep the volcanic dust from blowing into town.

Sleeping on Heimaey Island

HOTELS AND GUESTHOUSES

These options are within a 10-minute walk of the harbor. Except for Hótel Vestmannaeyjar, big hotels here are plain and tatty.

$$$ Hótel Vestmannaeyjar, the only large, well-established hotel in town, is a few short blocks away from the harbor, with 43 business-class rooms, an upscale on-site restaurant, and an indoor sauna and hot tubs in the basement that Austin Powers might appreciate; they're free for guests (elevator, generous breakfast buffet, Vestmannabraut 28, tel. 481-2900, www.hotelvestmannaeyjar.is, booking@hotelvestmannaeyjar.is).

$$$ Hótel Eyjar (Islands) is loosely run, but has a good location a block from the harbor. More of a guesthouse than a true hotel, it fills the two floors above the Eymundsson bookstore with 15 rooms with private baths (some kitchenettes, very pricey for what you get, RS%—ask for Rick Steves discount, lots of stairs, no reception but the owner is usually around, Bárustígur 2, tel. 481-3636, www.hoteleyjar.is, info@hoteleyjar.is).

$$ Guesthouse Hamar, closer to the harbor, has 14 basic rooms with private bath at reasonable prices (Herjólfsgata 4, tel. 481-3400, www.guesthousehamar.is, info@guesthousehamar.is).

$ Guesthouse Hrafnabjörg, on the hill above the harbor, has eight crisp white rooms in two buildings, all with shared bath. This is your best budget option (shared kitchen and living room, no breakfast, bike rentals, Hásteinsvegur 40, mobile 858-7727, https://guesthousehrafnabjorg.is, solbakkablom@simnet.is, helpful Hrefna).

HOSTELS AND PODS

You can save substantial money by going with Airbnb or one of these hostels, where a bed costs about 7,000 ISK.

¢ The Sunnuhóll Youth Hostel, with 17 beds, is actually the back wing of the Hótel Vestmannaeyjar. Not really a hostel, as they don't rent single beds in shared rooms, it's just a simple annex—woody and modern—with four cheap twin rooms and four family rooms with facilities down the hall and a kitchenette (same contact info as Hótel Vestmannaeyjar).

¢ Aska Hostel, with 38 beds in rooms of two to eight beds each, is a homey place that feels a bit like a college dorm run by two friendly brothers. It's central and offers a kitchenette and a big comfy lounge (reception next to Gott restaurant, Bárustígur 11, mobile 662-7266, www.askahostel.is, info@askahostel.is).

¢ The Puffin Nest Capsule Hostel feels like a garage filled with 40 white spaceship-like pods with a shared bath, kitchen, and living room. The pods are futuristic, private cocoons about twice as big as a coffin, with high-tech gadgetry to make them sleepable (individual TVs and air-con, same location and contact info as Guesthouse Hamar).

WESTMAN ISLANDS

Eating on Heimaey Island

The Westman Islands are a good place to eat. Most mid-price restaurants generally charge the same prices at lunch and dinner, and you can easily get a good, square meal for 2,700-3,200 ISK at any time of day. At nicer restaurants, it's smart to reserve for dinner. The island's restaurants don't serve puffin (breeding populations are low) or other seabirds.

$$$ Slippurinn (The Shipyard) is the town's top restaurant and a mecca for foodies—offering Reykjavík quality at Reykjavík prices. Run by a respected chef who prides himself on mingling authentic traditions with modern cookery, it has a tempting menu of perfectly executed classic dishes. Its long, well-worn tables and other funky mismatched furniture fill a big, open, industrial-mod space a block above the harbor. It's most affordable at lunch, with a fish of the day for under 3,000 ISK, but prices rise substantially at dinner—when you might want to splurge on a blowout fixed-price dinner. Reservations are recommended (May-mid-Sept daily 17:00-22:00 plus Wed-Sun 12:00-14:00, above the harbor at Strandvegur 76, tel. 481-1515, www.slippurinn.com).

$$ Gott (Good), on the little shopping street, is small, tasteful, and casual (but with table service). They do fish, chicken, burgers, and healthy bowls at competitive prices (vegetarian and vegan options, Sun-Thu 11:00-21:00, Fri-Sat until 22:00, Bárustígur 11, tel. 481-3060).

$$$ Tanginn (The Spit), at the harbor, has a great view of the cliffs and the fishing boats—which means it gets crowded and servers can be overwhelmed at busy times. The menu is predictable: fish of the day, ribs, a whale steak, and less-expensive burgers, soup, and salad (kitchen open Sun-Thu 11:30-14:00 & 18:00-21:00, Fri-Sat until late, Básaskersbryggja 8, tel. 414-4420).

$$ Pítsugerðin (Pizza Garden), at the base of the little shopping street, is the town pizza joint (daily 11:30-21:30, Bárustígur 1, tel. 551-0055).

Local Craft Beer: With a convivial tap house on the main street, **Brothers Brewery** makes their own microbrews right here on Heimaey (no food, tasting flight-2,000 ISK, Sun-Wed 14:00-21:00, Thu-Sat until late, Bárustígur 7, tel. 571-5510).

Cheap Eats: Find budget takeaway options at **Kráin,** which fries up "fresh fast food" on Bárustígur (daily 10:00-21:00). Two supermarkets near the harbor are open daily: **Bónus,** a few blocks up at Miðstræti 20, and **Krónan,** right along the harbor.

Breakfast: Most planes from Reykjavík land before restaurants open. For a breakfast on arrival, **Hótel Vestmannaeyjar**'s buffet is your best bet (2,100 ISK for nonguests, served 7:00-10:00 daily, see listing earlier).

BORGARNES & REYKHOLT VALLEY

One hour north of Reykjavík sits the fine fjordside town of Borgarnes, which anchors a region offering a convenient slate of engaging attractions. This is farming country: more sedate and less crowded than some of the more famous day-trip destinations, and a good choice for those seeking less driving and a mellower pace.

The town of Borgarnes packs its peninsula with picturesque beaches, a fine little museum about the early Icelandic settlers and their sagas, and grand views of scree slopes that rise up across the bay. Just 30 minutes north, Grábrók crater is one of Iceland's most satisfying to climb—earning you sweeping views over a desolate, frozen-lava landscape.

Inland from Borgarnes is the pastoral Reykholt Valley—which stretches from the waters of Borgarfjörður past thousand-year-old lava flows to Iceland's second-largest glacier, Langjökull. The village of Reykholt was home to Iceland's most important Settlement Age scribe, and remains a draw for historians today. The Deildartunguhver thermal springs steam and bubble, keeping the classy Krauma Geothermal Nature Baths piping hot. And Víðgelmir lets you spelunk through a lava tube—a cave with walls made of petrified molten rock. The Reykholt Valley also has easy-to-visit waterfalls, charming country hotels and restaurants, and a lovable family-run goat farm.

Many people simply zip through this region (on their way around the Ring Road, or to Snæfellsnes and the Westfjords). But travelers who explore Borgarnes and the Reykholt Valley are rewarded with vivid memories. This chapter ties everything together in one manageable day-trip drive from Reykjavík, but also lets you mix-and-match based on your itinerary.

As a Day Trip: You can visit Borgarnes and the Reykholt Valley on your own by car (following the drive outlined in this chapter), or with a bus excursion. The major excursion bus companies offer day trips to the Víðgelmir lava-tube cave that include many of the sights listed in this chapter (see list of tour companies on page 164).

As an Overnight: Accommodations in this area tend to be reasonably priced. I recommend staying in one of three areas: in Borgarnes, near Grábrók crater, or in and near Reykholt.

Sleeping here is particularly smart if you're continuing farther north along the Ring Road and want to see the region in depth. Some people stay in this part of West Iceland on their first night in Iceland—bypassing Reykjavík and getting a head start on their trip around the Ring. (Borgarnes is about 1.5 hours by car from Keflavík Airport.)

As a Stopover: Borgarnes makes a good pit stop on the way north to Snæfellsnes (and by extension, to the Westfjords).

Name Note: Pay attention if you are using GPS to navigate: Iceland has two towns that go by the name of Reykholt—one here in West Iceland, and the other about 100 miles away, near the Golden Circle.

Borgarnes and Reykholt Valley Drive

This itinerary assumes you're seeing this region's highlights as a day trip from Reykjavík. You'll go north to the town of Borgarnes for some sightseeing, detour up to Grábrók crater, then continue over to the area around Reykholt, where you'll do a circuit of the area's sights, before heading back to Reykjavík.

PLANNING YOUR DRIVE

The following plan is minimalistic; it assumes that you'll just visit the town of Borgarnes, Grábrók crater, and a few easy sights in the Reykholt Valley. To adjust this plan, see the tips in the next section.

9:00	Drive north from Reykjavík to the town of Borgarnes on highway 1 (1 hour)
10:00	Walk around Borgarnes; tour the Settlement Center
11:30	Head to Grábrók crater (30 minutes) and climb to the top and back; have a picnic lunch there or eat at the nearby Hraunsnef country hotel
13:30	Drive to Deildartunguhver hot springs (30 minutes) for a quick look (allow more time if you go for a soak at Krauma)
14:15	Drive from the hot springs to Hraunfossar and Barnafoss waterfalls (20 minutes); see the falls
15:00	Take scenic highways 520 and 47 back to Reykjavík, arriving back a little after 17:00

Borgarnes and Reykholt Valley Tips

This region offers plenty to see beyond my suggested plan above. You can mix and match, depending on your interests, and the weather and road conditions. Historians can focus on the good museums in Borgarnes as well as the modestly interesting church complex at Reykholt. Outdoorsy travelers can hike through an underground lava-tube cave at Víðgelmir (book ahead). Hot-spring enthusiasts will want to spend time at the Krauma thermal bath. Families can add a visit to the kid-friendly Háafell Goat Farm. All of these are covered in this chapter; for even more suggestions, see the helpful tourism website www.west.is. You'll need to allow extra time for any of these—especially the Víðgelmir lava tube. You can shave off a half-hour by returning on highway 1 instead of the scenic route.

Doing the Route in Reverse: It's worth considering doing this drive in the reverse direction from what I've described. Indoor sights here open at 10:00; if you're getting an early start (i.e., leaving Reykjavík around 8:00), you might as well take the scenic route on your way up, while you're fresh.

Weather and Road Conditions: As elsewhere in Iceland, check the weather forecast and road conditions before you head out—strong winds occasionally close highway 1 between Reykjavík and Borgarnes. Note that the scenic route from the Reykholt area back to Reykjavík (highways 520 and 47) is more difficult to drive, with long stretches curving around dramatic fjords, and short stretches on rough, unpaved roads—including one over a low mountain pass. Hurried and faint-hearted drivers should stick to highway 1. Before you go, double-check road conditions at Road.is.

To the Reykholt Valley and Back

We'll head north from Reykjavík on highway 1 to Borgarnes, sightsee the town, then drive farther north for an optional hike up the Grábrók crater. Next, we'll head east to the Reykholt Valley. From here, it's an easy trek to the waterfalls of Hraunfossar and Barnafoss, or farther east to the Víðgelmir lava tube. Backtracking to Reykholt, we'll head south on highways 520 and 47 (a slower but more scenic return) to Reykjavík. Recommended sights, restaurants, and hotels along this driving route are described later in the chapter. Budget about 10 hours (about half of that is driving). This drive covers about 200 miles in total—100 miles out to Víðgelmir with the Grábrók detour, and another 100 back to Reykjavík. For a route overview, see the map on page 268.

REYKJAVÍK TO BORGARNES

It's a bit over an hour's drive to Borgarnes.

• *Leave Reykjavík on highway 1 to the north, following signs for* Borgarnes, Akureyri, *and* 1n.

As you leave the city, you pass under **Esja,** the mountain that shadows the city to the north, and you'll see the parking lot for hikers climbing the peak. As you round the mountain, you'll see some of the city's chicken hatcheries to your left. A little farther on, an intriguing stone structure is actually just the retaining wall for a pig farm. You'll pass the small community of Kjalarnes. Strong winds are frequent along the road here.

Soon after, you'll enter the two-lane, 3.5-mile-long **Hvalfjörður tunnel** that passes beneath the fjord. (If you prefer to take the scenic route around the fjord—highways 47 and 520—on your way up, turn off to the right just before the tunnel entrance.)

Finished in 1998, this tunnel cut travel time from Reykjavík to all points north. Before that, you had to drive all the way around the fjord (on what is now scenic highway 47; we'll come back that way).

While the tunnel area is not actively volcanic, it lies across a geothermal vent, and the undersea rock is warm (up to 135°F near its south end). If your car's dashboard shows the outside temperature, you'll notice the south end of the tunnel is several degrees warmer than the north end. Watch your speed in the tunnel: The speed limit is 70 km/hour and monitored by cameras (for tunnel info, see www.spolur.is).

• *At the roundabout just after the tunnel, go right, following signs for* Borgarnes *and* Akureyri. *(Going left would bring you to Akranes, a relatively large but skippable town of 6,000 people, many of whom work in the fish-processing industry or in the nearby metal smelters.)*

In a few minutes, you'll pass three huge **metal smelters** at Grundartangi. The green-and-brown one produces ferrosilicon, the blue one makes aluminum. A third smelter, producing silicon for the solar-power industry, is under construction. Smelters need to be along the coast, as ships bring in the raw ore (such as bauxite for making aluminum) and carry the finished product to market. This is an efficient way of putting Iceland's electricity surplus to use, and the smelters create jobs (though they require a relatively small crew).

You'll now cross a low-lying, thinly settled plain between two mountains: **Akrafjall** on your left, and **Hafnarfjall** (HAHP-nahr-FYAHTL) to your right. Farther west is another mountain, **Skarðsheiði,** which under snow cover looks like a meringue chopped into great wavy peaks. On a clear day, you might be able to see the mountains of the Snæfellsnes Peninsula far ahead of you.

The road curls around the left side of Hafnarfjall; this stretch is subject to frequent high winds. Soon you're driving along the base of vast gravel slopes that tumble down from Hafnarfjall. You'll see many small islands in Borgarfjörður, the fjord to your left.

Eventually the town of **Borgarnes** will come into view, and the road will bend left and cross a causeway and bridge into the town (for more on the town, see "Borgarnes," later).

BORGARNES TO THE REYKHOLT VALLEY

When you're ready to continue toward the Reykholt area, you have three route options (described in greater detail below): In good weather, hikers will want to drive up to the Grábrók volcanic crater, then loop back down toward Reykholt. (All together, Grábrók adds about 1.5 hours, including the drive and time to hike up to the crater, but not lunch.) If the weather's too cold or windy to hike the crater, you could skip Grábrók and take the scenic route to the Reykholt area over the old bridge called Hvítárbrú. Or take the quicker route through Baulan.

Each of these options takes you to Deildartunguhver hot springs—the first of the Reykholt-area sights described later in this chapter. Notice that no single route connects all of your choices in the Reykholt area; you'll make one or more loops to connect them, via paved highway 518 and unpaved highways 519, 523, and 550. The recommended Brúarás GeoCenter Café, more or less at the center of the Reykholt sights, is a great all-purpose stop for a snack, drink, or meal; they're also happy to answer questions about this area.

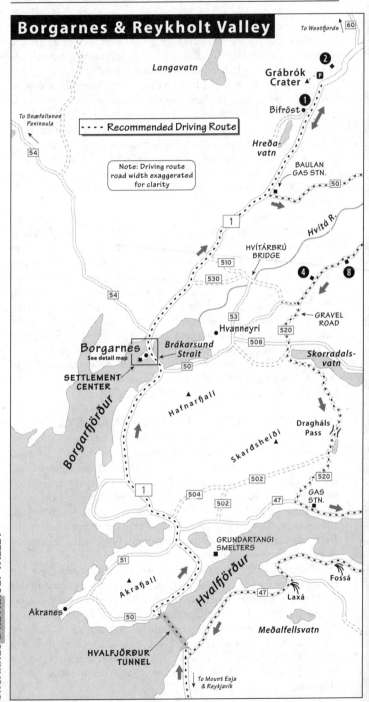

Borgarnes & Reykholt Valley

To Westfjords — 60

Langavatn

Grábrók Crater ▲

2

1

Bifröst

To Snæfellsnes Peninsula

54

- - - - Recommended Driving Route

Hreða-vatn

Note: Driving route road width exaggerated for clarity

BAULAN GAS STN.

50

Hvítá R.

1

HVÍTÁRBRÚ BRIDGE

510

530

4   8

GRAVEL ROAD

54

53

520

Hvanneyri

508

Skorradals-vatn

Borgarnes
See detail map

Brákarsund Strait

SETTLEMENT CENTER

50

Borgarfjörður

Hafnarfjall ▲

Draghals Pass

Skardsheiði ▲

502

520

GAS STN.

1

504

502

47

GRUNDARTANGI SMELTERS

Fossá

51

Akrafjall ▲

Hvalfjörður

47

Laxá

Akranes

50

Meðalfellsvatn

HVALFJÖRÐUR TUNNEL

To Mount Esja & Reykjavík

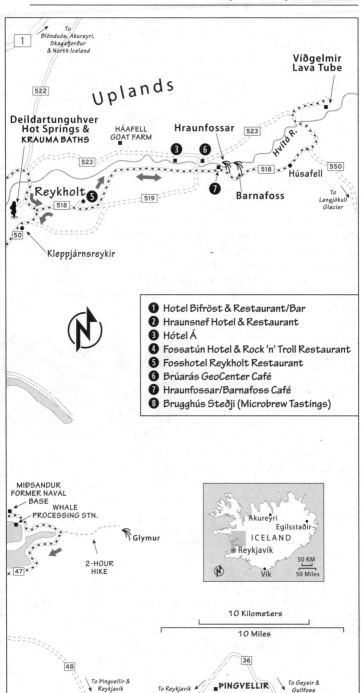

Víðgelmir Lava Tube

Uplands

To Blönduós, Akureyri, Skagafjörður & North Iceland

1

522

523

Deildartunguhver Hot Springs & KRAUMA BATHS

HÁAFELL GOAT FARM

Hraunfossar

523

Hvítá R.

3

6

518

518

Húsafell

550

7

Barnafoss

To Langjökull Glacier

519

Reykholt

5

50

Kleppjárnsreykir

1. Hotel Bifröst & Restaurant/Bar
2. Hraunsnef Hotel & Restaurant
3. Hótel Á
4. Fossatún Hotel & Rock 'n' Troll Restaurant
5. Fosshotel Reykholt Restaurant
6. Brúarás GeoCenter Café
7. Hraunfossar/Barnafoss Café
8. Brugghús Steðji (Microbrew Tastings)

MIÐSANDUR FORMER NAVAL BASE
WHALE PROCESSING STN.

Glymur

2-HOUR HIKE

47

ICELAND

Akureyri

Egilsstaðir

Reykjavík

50 KM
50 Miles

Vík

10 Kilometers

10 Miles

48

To Þingvellir & Reykjavík

To Reykjavík

36

ÞINGVELLIR

To Geysir & Gullfoss

For any of these, you'll begin by heading north from Borgarnes on highway 1, following signs toward *Akureyri*.

Detour to Grábrók Crater (50 minutes): From Borgarnes, head up highway 1 about 30 minutes; you can't miss the crater, on the left side of the road. After visiting, return south and backtrack on highway 1 about 10 minutes; look for a small ÓB gas station (called Baulan). Turn left here onto highway 50, then drive another 15 minutes until you see a small turnoff to the right marked *Deildartunguhver*. (If you get to the junction with highway 518, you've gone a half-mile too far.)

Skipping Grábrók, via Hvítárbrú Bridge (40 minutes): This pleasant route crosses bridges that don't allow trucks or buses. From Borgarnes, drive north along highway 1 for about 10 minutes, turning right on highway 510 (signposted *Hvanneyri*), a potholed gravel road. (If you're using Google Maps, note that it mislabels this road as highway 53.) Drive slowly. Soon you'll cross a stream on wooden bridges and pass a farm called Ferjukot.

Then the old bridge called **Hvítárbrú** comes into view. This arched concrete bridge was built in 1928. The main route between Reykjavík and Borgarnes passed over it until the Borgarfjörður causeway was finished in 1983. The bridge has one narrow lane; before driving over, scan the far bank to make sure no one is coming toward you.

After crossing, follow signs for *Reykholt*, continuing along highway 510 and then turning north onto highway 50. Along the way, you'll pass **Fossatún** (with the recommended Rock 'n' Troll restaurant; described later) and the **Brugghús Steðji** ("Anvil") microbrewery (5 tastes-1,500 ISK, no meals, ask about their whale beer, Mon-Sat 13:00-17:00, closed Sun, also rents 2 "brewery bungalows," tel. 896-5001, https://stedji.com). Just after the greenhouse village of **Kleppjárnsreykir,** near the junction of highways 50 and 518, turn left to stay on highway 50. After a minute or two, turn left at the sign for *Deildartunguhver*.

Easier Route, via Highway 1 and Highway 50 (30 minutes): The simplest route is to drive north from Borgarnes about 20 minutes along highway 1 to the junction with highway 50, at the Baulan ÓB gas station; turn right here and drive 15 minutes until you see the small turnoff to the right marked *Deildartunguhver*.

REYKHOLT VALLEY TO REYKJAVÍK

To head back south to Reykjavík, you have two choices. Off-season, or in doubtful weather, play it safe and loop back south along highway 50 to return the way you came: on highway 1, past Hafnarfjall and Akrafjall mountains, and through the tunnel (about 1.5 hours).

In decent weather (generally May-Sept), I'd take the scenic route down highways 50 and 520 via the Draghals pass and Hvalfjörður. From Reykholt, this adds about 30 minutes to your trip (2 hours to Reykjavík). It comes with some unpaved stretches (including a gravel pass that rises to several hundred feet above sea level). But the payoff is that Hvalfjörður feels more off-the-beaten-track than other day-trip destinations from Reykjavík, and comes with many fine views.

• *From Reykholt, drive south on highway 50, then turn off onto gravel highway 520.*

This road parallels **Skorradalsvatn,** a good fishing lake where you'll see many summer cottages. Then it climbs over the low **Draghals** pass to the east of the Hafnarfjall moun-  tain system. Drive slowly and carefully, watching for potholes. Skirting a couple of small lakes, the road ultimately descends to **Hvalfjörður** (Whale Fjord), which you earlier traversed by undersea tunnel.

• *Where the road tees, you'll hit paved highway 47. Turn left, passing a tiny gas station (called Ferstikla) with a café that may be open in summer.*

Take highway 47 all the way around the fjord. After about five minutes, you'll pass the old Allied naval installation at **Miðsan-**  **dur** (the only signpost you'll see reads *Hjálmsstaðir*). The Nissen huts and camp here are Iceland's best-preserved WWII-era buildings. The fjord here is quite deep. As the oil tanks on the far hillside suggest, this was a refueling station for ships, especially those traveling from North America to Murmansk in northern Russia. They could dock at two piers on either side of the camp.

After the war, the naval station was converted into a whale-processing facility. Today, slaughtered whales are still brought ashore at the eastern pier and processed in the buildings against the hillside. Iceland's whaling company also owns the camp area. Everything is fenced off and signs make it clear that they don't want you poking around (the station has been a target of animal-rights activists).

Highway 47 reaches the east end of the fjord (a small road here leads to the beginning of a challenging two-hour hike to a high, pretty waterfall called Glymur). Next, the road doubles back along the south shore of the fjord. It crosses two rivers with fine waterfalls: **Fossá** (with a tiny, old stone sheep pen next to the falls) and—farther along (next to the turnoff for road 48 to Þingvellir)—the low and beautiful **Laxá**. Unless it's fogged in, you'll be able to spot the metal smelters at Grundartangi on the far side of the fjord.

Ponder that until 1998, when the tunnel under Hvalfjörður was finished, this was the main road from Reykjavík to the north.
• *After about 35 minutes, you'll wind back to highway 1 near the south tunnel entrance, and turn toward Reykjavík, another 30 minutes away.*

Borgarnes

A pleasant town of approximately 2,000 people about an hour from Reykjavík, Borgarnes (BOHR-gahr-NESS) is the main hub of West Iceland. The town is set on a rocky peninsula jutting out into the estuary formed by the region's several rivers, which merge near here (calling it a "fjord" is generous). A bridge and causeway built in the early 1980s cross the mouth of the estuary. Across the water from town, Hafnarfjall mountain—

with its steep scree slopes—is an impressive sight.

Borgarnes was an important spot in the earliest days of Icelandic settlement. According to the sagas, this area was home to the early settler Skalla-Grímur Kveldúlfsson ("Grímur the Bald"). After a bloody feud with Norwegian King Harald Fairhair, Skalla-Grímur fled Norway and sailed to Iceland. His father died on the journey, and—following Viking Age custom—Skalla-Grímur dropped his casket in the sea, then built his settlement where it washed ashore...at a place now called Borg, on the outskirts of Borgarnes. Skalla-Grímur lived out his days here, where he raised his son Egill Skallagrímsson (pron. AY-ihtl). An even more dynamic figure than his father, Egill was ugly and passionate—equal parts battler and bard—and the protagonist of some of Iceland's most

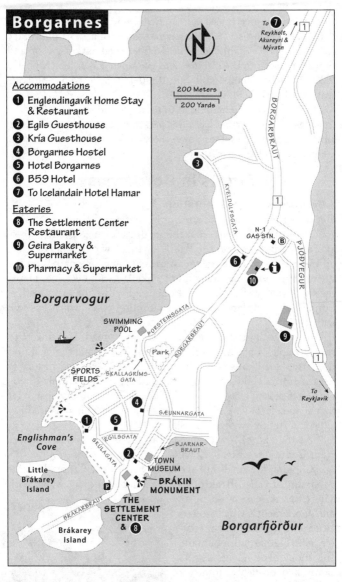

colorful Settlement Age stories (now recounted in the town's Settlement Center). For those intrigued by the sagas, Borgarnes is a fun place to visit.

Arrival in Borgarnes: As you cross the causeway, you'll pass the recommended Geira Bakery (Geirabakarí; on the left by the Bónus **supermarket**). Just beyond, at the town's main road junction, the N1 gas station also houses a free WC, the town's bus station, and an overpriced café and convenience store (long hours daily). Next door is a Nettó **supermarket,** with a Lyfja **pharmacy** (Mon-Fri 10:00-18:00, Sat 10:00-16:00, closed Sat off-season and Sun year-round, tel. 437-1168) and the town **TI** inside (Mon-Fri 9:00-18:00, Sat 10:00-16:00, Sun 10:00-14:00, closed Sat-Sun off-season; tel. 437-2214, www.west.is).

Turn left off the main road to reach the old part of town. The small park on your right has a few parking spaces. Better yet, drive another couple of minutes down the main road to the Settlement Center, which has a parking lot.

Sights in Borgarnes

▲Borgarnes Town Orientation

Get your bearings with this town orientation, either on foot or as you drive through. Start from the small park called **Skallagríms-garður** (Park of Grímur the Bald)—with a few picnic tables—just off the main road from the top of the old town. The park is on the site of a burial mound thought to be Skalla-Grímur's tomb. Down the side street next to the park (to the right from the main road) is Borgarnes' good, large, outdoor **swimming pool,** which has fine sea views.

Continue a little farther down the main road. If you were to veer a couple of blocks to the left (down Bjarnarbraut), you'd find Borgarnes' **local museum,** which tells the 20th-century history of Iceland from a child's perspective (1,200 ISK, summer daily 13:00-17:00, off-season closed Sat-Sun—but ask at the library upstairs if they'll open it for you, Bjarnarbraut 4—look for a big red building, tel. 433-7200, www.safnahus.is).

At the end of town—just before the bridge—is the **Settlement Center** (described below).

Capping the small hill above the Settlement Center, look for a monument called **Brákin,** which resembles a giant wheel with wings. It's an easy walk up to the monument, which offers nice views over the town, estuary, and Hafnarfjall mountain. The monument honors Egill's nanny and de facto mother, a Celtic woman named Þorgerður Brák. According to the sagas, when an adolescent Egill angered his father during a game,

Skalla-Grímur was about to beat the boy...likely to death. Brák stood up to Skalla-Grímur, who—now completely forgetting his son and furious with his servant—chased her to the end of the peninsula here, where she leapt into the water and tried to swim to the island just offshore. Skalla-Grímur threw a giant stone at Brák, killing her. Today the channel between the monument and the island is still known as Brákarsund.

From the Settlement Center, you can cross a bridge to the little island called **Brákarey,** home to Borgarnes's tiny harbor. Borgarnes is one of a very few coastal towns in Iceland that did not form as a fishing center, and remains home to a mix of services and light industry.

Between the Settlement Center and the Brákarey bridge, a little parking lot offers access to a pleasant waterfront **trail.** The path arcs around **Englishmen's Cove** (Englendingavík) on the sleepy back side of the peninsula, where Englishmen reportedly lived during the Middle Ages. After passing a nice beach (and a recommended hotel/restaurant), the trail eventually leads to the town's playing fields and swimming pool. From here, you'll enjoy glorious views of the island and the mountains beyond.

▲Settlement Center (Landnámssetur)

This modest yet thoughtfully presented sight is Borgarnes' best-known attraction and one of the prime places in Iceland to learn about the Settlement Age; for history buffs, it's worth ▲▲. The center has two exhibits: one (upstairs) explaining how Iceland was discovered and settled, and the other (downstairs) retelling the grisly Egill's Saga, which took place in and around Borgarnes. Each takes 30 minutes to see with separate, essential audioguides.

Cost and Hours: 2,500 ISK, includes both audioguides, daily 10:00-21:00, Brákarbraut 13, Borgarnes, tel. 437-1600, www.landnam.is.

Visiting the Museum: The upstairs exhibit ponders the questions of why and how Viking Age **settlers** first came to Iceland. The exhibit is interactive: As you listen to the audioguide, you'll press buttons to light up the locations where various settlers first arrived and carved farmsteads out of the wilderness, and stand on a Viking ship's prow as it rocks back and forth on the waves. It's thought that the ships could cross from Norway to Iceland in under 72 hours. Arriving in Iceland, the first settlers found a land with forested birch valleys and scrubby willows along the coast. The woodlands that covered over a third of Iceland's land area were cleared to make way for fields and grazing lands for sheep. A cooling climate and overgrazing made it difficult for the trees to regenerate, resulting in the nearly treeless land we see today.

The downstairs exhibition illustrates **Egill's Saga,** step by step, with interesting wooden figures and carvings by local artist Aðalheiður Eysteinsdóttir. Egill (c. 904-995) was a poet-warrior, mixing brutishness and sensitivity, who got into all sorts of trouble in both Iceland and Norway. He feuded with the king of Norway, wrangled with a witch, and married his foster sister (and brother's widow). After two of his sons died, Egill composed *Sonatorrek,* a moving lament that is among the most famous examples of Old Norse poetry. By the age of 80, Egill—now a sour old man—toyed with the idea of throwing his wealth of silver pieces into the assembled crowds at Þingvellir, simply to start a riot. Instead, like his father before him, he buried his treasure somewhere in the Borgarnes area...where today, some people still look for it. For more on Egill's story—and the rest of the sagas—see page 108.

Sleeping in Borgarnes

Borgarnes has several pricey business-class hotels, but I prefer these more affordable B&Bs. Kría Guesthouse is conveniently located on a bluff overlooking Englishmen's Cove, on the quiet back edge of town. Englendingavík Home Stay, Egils Guesthouse, and the hostel are right in the center.

$$$ Englendingavík Home Stay, above the recommended restaurant, offers 10 comfortable rooms, some with private bath, in a renovated 1880s-era building just steps from Englishmen's Cove (family rooms, rooms with shared bath have kitchen access, breakfast extra, hot tub, Skúlagata 17, tel. 555-1400, http://englendingavik.is/rooms, info@englendingavik.is, owner Margrét Rósa).

$$ Egils Guesthouse has two buildings in a wonderfully central location just up the stairs from the Settlement Center. Their Guesthouse Kaupangur, in an old family home, has five thoughtful rooms—some with private bath (breakfast extra at café, Brákarbraut 11, mobile 860-6655, www.egilsguesthouse.is, info@egilsguesthouse.is). Their South-Rock Apartment is a freestanding building closer to the water, just yards from the guesthouse (sleeps 6, kitchenette, washing machine).

$ Kría Guesthouse, in a residential area on the peninsula's northwest side, has two spacious rooms that share a bathroom and tangled garden leading down to the water (no breakfast, hot tub, kitchen access, chickens in the yard, next to a hair salon at Kveldúlfsgata 310, tel. 437-1159, www.kriaguesthouse.is, info@kriaguesthouse.is). They also rent cottages on the road to Deildartunguhver.

¢ The **Borgarnes Hostel** is in the old town center, not far from the Settlement Center (Borgarbraut 9, mobile tel. 695-3366, www.hostel.is, borgarnes@hostel.is).

Other Options: In a pinch, try one of these **$$$$** business-class hotels: **Hotel Borgarnes** (a few blocks from the Settlement Center, tel. 437-1119, www.hotelborgarnes.is); **B59 Hotel** (across from the TI, also runs an upscale hostel, Borgarbraut 59, tel. 419-5959, www.b59hotel.is), or **Icelandair Hotel Hamar** (on a golf course just off highway 1 north of town, tel. 433-6600, www.icelandairhotels.com).

Eating in Borgarnes

$$ The Settlement Center has the most appealing restaurant in town (just upstairs from the exhibit). You can eat here even if you don't visit the museum itself. At lunch, they offer a good-value vegetarian buffet (daily until 15:00). It's a substantial spread—soup, salads, pasta and potato dishes, and fresh fruit—and worth planning ahead for. At dinner, the restaurant has affordable main courses and expensive three-course fixed-price meals (restaurant open daily 10:00-21:00, same contact info as museum).

$$ Englendingavík (Englishmen's Cove) is a classy-feeling place that overlooks the beachy cove, with a few outdoor tables. It's pricey by local standards, but scenic (daily 11:00-21:00, Skúlagata 17, tel. 555-1400, www.englendingavik.is).

$ Geira Bakery (Geirabakarí), the first building on the Borgarnes side of the causeway, makes all manner of pastries, serves budget lunches—soup with bread, sandwiches, and the like—and has tables with great views of Hafnarfjall and the water (Mon-Fri 7:00-18:00, Sat-Sun 8:00-17:00, Digranesgata 6—look for the gray building next to the Bónus supermarket, tel. 437-2020).

Grábrók Crater

A half-hour north of Borgarnes, highway 1 curls around the pint-sized volcanic cone of Grábrók (GRAU-brohk, literally "Gray-pants"). In good weather, hiking up to its rim is easy, fun, and worth ▲▲.

Watch for the parking lot on the left, just after you pass the crater (free to park, no WCs). From here, wooden steps and board-walks lead up to the rim. You can climb to the top in about 15 minutes, and—if it's not too windy—stroll the gravel path that circles the crater rim, which takes about 10 minutes.

Grábrók was formed in an eruption about 3,200 years ago—around the time of the ancient Egyptians—but there was no one here to see it. The beautiful lava field that you drive through just

before reaching Grábrók flowed out in the same eruption. A thick layer of moss and lichen has grown on top of the lava, changing color with the seasons.

From the top, enjoy stunning panoramas of the crater and the surrounding area. The classically conical mountain to the north, formed 3.4 million years ago, is called Baula (BOY-la, which means "to moo"). Closer in, to the northwest, is a sinister, heavy-browed ridge called Hraunsnefsöxl. To the west, away from the road, is a second, similar-sized crater called Grábrókarfell. A third crater, Litla-Grábrók, was mined for gravel and is hard to make out. To the south (toward Borgarnes) is the campus of Bifröst, a small college originally founded to train managers for Iceland's network of cooperative stores (and here I was hoping to find the Bifröst of the sagas: the rainbow bridge leading to Asgard, home to the Nordic gods).

Just past Bifröst is Hreðavatn, a pretty lake with a managed forest at the far end. In the valley around you are both working farms and summer houses, some of them quite lavish.

As you descend Grábrók, look down along the slope to your left. You'll see an odd stone structure with many compartments, which looks at first glance like it might be an ancient ruin. It's actually a set of drystone pens built to hold sheep rounded up each fall, and it's still in occasional use (it's called Brekkurétt; *rétt* is the word for a sheep pen). You can walk through it if you'd like. If you continue farther north on the Ring Road, you'll pass more elaborate, modern pens.

Sleeping and Eating near Grábrók: A half-mile before Grábrók, the red-roofed **$$ Hotel Bifröst,** set in a tiny university hamlet, offers four simple rooms and a basic restaurant/bar (call ahead to see if restaurant is open, tel. 433-3030, www.hotelbifrost. is, info@hotelbifrost.is).

About minute or two past Grábrók crater, **$$ Hraunsnef** ("Lava Nose") country hotel is a working farm with cottages, a classy valley-view restaurant, and 15 straightforward rooms in various unassuming buildings (breakfast extra). As it's located just before the pass to the north, this place works well for those headed around the Ring Road. The hotel's fancy **$$$ restaurant** offers breakfast, affordable lunches, and pricey dinners (daily 8:00-10:00 & 12:00-21:00, call ahead to confirm, tel. 435-0111, www.hraunsnef.is, hraunsnef@hraunsnef.is).

Your only other eating option is to pack a picnic.

Reykholt and Nearby

These sights fill the broad, sparsely populated valley of the Hvítá (White River), which flows from the Eiríksjökull glacier and empties into the estuary near Borgarnes. I've listed these roughly in order from west to east. Fitting all of these into a single day is doable but challenging; you're better off being selective. As you drive, count the sheep and horses sprinkled across the pastures between red-roofed farmsteads.

▲Deildartunguhver Hot Springs

Located off highway 50 near Reykholt, Europe's most powerful hot spring gushes out almost 50 gallons of boiling water per second.

You'll see steaming fountains of hot water spurting up next to a colorful rock face. Signs warn you not to touch the water. The beige concrete building is a pumping station that sends the water through a big pipe to Borgarnes and Akranes for home heating. The water is about 200°F here; it cools naturally to about 170°F by the time it reaches Borgarnes (where it's mixed with cooler water for your shower). You might find tomatoes from nearby greenhouses for sale here from an honor box.

▲▲▲Krauma Geothermal Nature Baths

If you're looking for an Icelandic Zen garden, go no further. This spa-like bath, sharing a parking lot (and water source) with the hot springs, is uncrowded and peaceful. Limited to 130 bathers at a time, the goal here is relaxation. Melt into the five warm pools and two steam baths, order a poolside drink, get your blood going in the cold plunge, and linger before the fire in the small relaxation room. The upscale on-site restaurant serves dishes prepared with local vegetables (some grown in hothouses warmed by the springs) and meat from the nearby Háafell goat farm.

Cost and Hours: 3,950 ISK, towel rental-800 ISK, daily 11:00-23:00, off-season until 21:00, reservations smart in summer for both baths and restaurant, tel. 555-6066, www.krauma.is.

Continuing to Reykholt: From Deildartunguhver and Krauma, return to the main road, head a half-mile downhill on highway 50, and turn left on highway 518, following signs five minutes to Reykholt.

Reykholt

Reykholt, set bucolically in the center of the valley, is home to a religious and scholarly complex devoted to medieval studies. Those excited about medieval Iceland and the sagas rate it ▲ for the chance to see its historic church and tour its museum. Scholars come on retreats here to write and use the fine library.

For 35 years, Reykholt was the home of **Snorri Sturluson** (1179-1241)—one of the most prominent figures of Iceland's post-Settlement Age. A poet, historian, and politician, Snorri wrote some of the famous sagas, including—possibly—the locally set Egill's Saga. Snorri was also a chronicler for all of medieval Scandinavia: He wrote *Gylfaginning,* a tale about the pantheon of Norse gods, and *Heimskringla,* the earliest and most definitive history of Norwegian kings. Snorri was successful in the political realm, as well, serving two terms as the Alþingi's law speaker and hobnobbing with the king of Norway. In fact, his support of continued union with Norway made him plenty of enemies back home—enemies who killed him in a surprise attack, right here at Reykholt. To this day, Snorri is arguably more popular among Norwegians (whose history he chronicled) than among Icelanders; the statue of him in Reykholt was done by Norway's top sculptor, Gustav Vigeland.

Reykholt has two handsome **churches,** one small and traditional from the 1880s, the other large and modern from the 1990s (free). Underneath the modern church is the **Snorri's Saga exhibition** (Snorra Stofa). It's one large room, and is a bit dry (basically just posters), but modern and with good English—worth considering on a rainy day (1,200 ISK, daily 10:00-17:00, Oct-March closed Sat-Sun, audioguide-1,500 ISK, pay WCs, tel. 433-8000, www.snorrastofa.is).

The little outdoor hot pool, **Snorralaug** (Snorri's Pool), has been here since the 10th century (it's mentioned in the sagas). Look for it behind the old school building, and open the wooden door

in the hillside behind the
pool to see the first few
feet of a tunnel. This may
have led to the cellar of
a now-vanished building
that was part of the com-
plex in Snorri's day. (Such
tunnels were typical at the
time, and there's a similar
one at Skálholt, along the

Golden Circle.) Bathing in the pool is not allowed. As you circle
the school, you'll see the footprint of what may have been Snorri's
home.

Sleeping near Reykholt: About 10 miles east of Reykholt is
$$ Hótel Á (River), near the recommended Brúarás GeoCenter
Café at the valley's crossroads. It's an endearingly rural option run
by a local farmer's family. Perched on a ridge overlooking the wide
river valley are 25 surprisingly modern rooms with private baths
(pricey dinner available to guests, Kirkjuból 2, Reykholt, tel. 435-
1430, www.hotela.is, hotela@hotela.is, Raggi).

$ Fossatún (Waterfall Field) is a fun little compound along
highway 50 between Borgarnes and Reykholt, just where the road
crosses a small river, with a nice view over "Troll Falls." They have
12 modern rooms with private bath in the sod-roofed hotel/res-
taurant; six older, more rustic rooms with shared bath and kitchen
in the guesthouse; and 18 heated wood-clad "camping pods" that
share bathrooms and a kitchen (15 minutes from Reykholt, bed-
ding and towels available for pods, on-site Rock 'n' Troll restau-
rant—see below, tel. 433-5800, www.fossatun.is, info@fossatun.
is). The place is run by musician and writer Steinar Berg, author of
the Icelandic children's book *The Last Troll*.

Eating in and near Reykholt: Several tree-sheltered picnic
benches in Reykholt beckon on a nice day. At the back of the Snor-
ralaug complex is the sleek, modern Fosshotel Reykholt, with a
pricey **$$$ restaurant**—but I'd rather carry on east just a few min-
utes to the excellent **$ Brúarás GeoCenter Café,** the best place
to eat around here. In an angular, modern structure at the bridge
where highways 518, 519, and 523 meet (between Reykholt and the
waterfalls), it offers a brief but thoughtful menu of mostly locally
sourced dishes, including lamb soup, burgers, and big salads. The
café also serves as the area's unofficial TI (restaurant open daily
11:00-20:30, closed off-season, tel. 435-1270, www.geocenter.is).

Toward Borgarnes from Reykholt, the Fossatún, listed earlier,
also runs the **$$ Rock 'n' Troll** restaurant, with good soups and
view seating opposite the falls (daily 7:30-9:30 & 18:30-21:00, in
summer also 12:00-14:00).

▲▲Hraunfossar and Barnafoss Waterfalls

These two waterfalls are a 20-minute drive up the valley from Reykholt along highway 518. They're free and easy to see—just a few minutes' walk from your car (free parking, pay WCs).

The main river running through the valley here is called the Hvítá (White River, the same name—but not the same river—as the one that flows over Gullfoss waterfall on the Golden Circle). As you approach the falls, you'll see that the upper part of the valley is covered by relatively new lava. New lava is porous, and streams often sink into lava fields, flowing underneath the surface for considerable distances. At **Hraunfossar** (Lava Waterfalls), you'll look across the river and see rivulets of groundwater pouring out from under the striped layers of lava on the other side and falling into the stream, like many bridal veils.

A hundred yards upstream is **Barnafoss,** a more typical waterfall on the main stream. The name means "children's waterfall," and you can see what looks like the remains of a natural bridge spanning the falls here. According to legend, two children who were supposed to stay home while their parents were at church went out to play instead and drowned when they fell off the bridge; the mother destroyed the bridge so no other children would meet such a tragic fate. A pedestrian bridge over the river lets you get a closer look at the falls.

Eating at the Falls: By the waterfall parking lot is a small, basic **$ café,** with soup, snacks, ice cream, and coffee.

Húsafell

About 10 minutes past Barnafoss and the Hraunfossar, this hamlet is a service center for the union-owned cottages in the area that many Icelanders frequent. The area is anchored by a fancy hotel and campground, with a variety of eateries (from a swanky dining room to a basic café/shop), and is the departure point for the Into the Glacier tours to Langjökull (described later). The main reason to stop here is to enjoy Húsafell's surprisingly extensive **thermal swimming pool,** with multiple outdoor pools and a waterslide. Aside from the premium Krauma bath at Deildartunguhver, this is your best option in this part of West Iceland—and the most affordable (1,300 ISK, 400 ISK for kids ages 6-14, www.husafell.is).

▲Víðgelmir Lava Tube

Víðgelmir (VEETHE-GHELL-meer)—marketed as simply "The Cave"—is a lava tube formed about a thousand years ago during an

eruption in the Langjökull volcano system. The top of a river of lava crusted over, enclosing the molten part underground. When the lava stopped flowing, it left behind a hollow, mile-long, tube-like corridor, now below ground level. Today visitors can take a

guided walk through the lava tube and ogle its unusual formations: tubular lava stalactites shaped like strands of spaghetti, and formations that look like melted chocolate. While Víðgelmir requires a substantial commitment of time and money—and I've toured far more impressive caves in Europe—the volcanic spin makes this worth considering for rock nerds. Dress warmly—wear a jacket, hat, and gloves at any time of year; underground, the temperature hovers right around freezing.

Cost and Hours: 6,500 ISK, daily tours run hourly 9:00-18:00, fewer tours mid-Sept-mid-May—generally 4-5/day, confirm times before you go, mobile 783-3600, www.thecave.is. It's best to book and pay in advance online, rather than just show up. If you're running late for your tour time, they can normally switch you to a later tour on the same day.

Getting There: From Reykholt, it's a 30-minute drive east down a mostly unpaved road. Cross the bridge at highway 519, then head east along highway 523. You'll drive to the end of a rough gravel road in the middle of a lava field.

Visiting the Cave: Check in at a little shed, where you'll be issued a helmet and a headlamp. Then you'll walk across a petrified lava flow 300 yards to a hole formed centuries ago when part of the tube's roof collapsed. Here you'll climb down a wooden staircase and follow boardwalks through about a half-mile of the mile-long cave. You'll see multicolored layers of basalt lava, which built up over the course of the long eruption, and get a good, up-close look at some remarkable lava formations. Remember, this is different from a limestone cave: The "stalactites" and "stalagmites" weren't formed over eons by dripping water, but all at once, a thousand years ago, as the liquid lava cooled and hardened. Your guide will point out where they found evidence of humans living here (perhaps a Viking Age outlaw); let you (gently) handle a few samples of the delicate lava formations; and flip off the lights so you can experience total darkness.

▲Háafell Goat Farm

This is a one-family project by Jóhanna Þorvaldsdóttir and her clan, who idealistically set out a few years ago to breed Iceland's

nearly extinct goat stock—descended from animals brought by the first settlers. Now the family invites travelers to visit their rustic farm, meet (and, if you like, cuddle) some adorable baby goats, learn about their work, watch the goats butt heads playfully, and sample (and buy) the wide variety of products they make from their goats: feta cheese, ice cream, soap and lotions (from tallow), and goat-hide carpets and insoles. This is a fun, hands-on activity for kids. I consider the cost of admission worthwhile just to keep this Icelandic tradition alive.

Cost and Hours: Guided tour including coffee-1,500 ISK, 750 ISK for kids; June-Aug daily 13:00-18:00, Sept-May by appointment only; mobile 845-2331, http://geitur.is, haafell@gmail.com.

Getting There: The farm is on gravel highway 523, about midway between the junctions with highways 522 and 519, on the north side of the river Hvítá. It's about 20-25 minutes' drive from Reykholt, depending on which way you circle around.

Langjökull Glacier

At the far upper end of the valley, a four-wheel-drive track leads up to the Langjökull glacier—Iceland's second largest. If you're in the area (particularly if you're overnighting and have extra time), consider paying for a pricey tour that gets you close to all that ice. Note, though, that the tours are time-consuming, there's a lot to do in the valley on your own, and you can get close to glaciers more easily and cheaply elsewhere in Iceland (such as Sólheimajökull, on the South Coast).

The **Into the Glacier** tour takes you into a cave that has been bored into the snow and ice. You'll meet your tour at Húsafell and board an eight-wheel-drive super truck for the 30-minute transfer to the cave, where a guide will lead you around the tunnels. Bundle up—the temperature is generally around freezing (19,500 ISK, 2,000 ISK extra for four-wheel-drive shuttle, generally 4-7/day June-mid-Oct 10:00-15:30, fewer departures off-season, 2-4 hours total, also possible to combine with snowmobile trip or as an all-day excursion from Reykjavík, tel. 578-2550, www.intotheglacier. is).

SNÆFELLSNES PENINSULA

The long finger of land called Snæfellsnes (SNIGH-fells-ness), poking out of Iceland's west coast to the north of Reykjavík, offers an "Iceland in a nutshell" experience: an easy loop trip with glimpses of glaciers, black sand beaches, lava-rock landscapes, epic fjords, bridal-veil waterfalls, climbable craters, basalt sea stacks, and charming fishing towns. While Snæfellsnes is not necessarily the best place in Iceland to experience each of these features, it's perhaps the most convenient and compact place to get a little taste of everything.

Snæfellsnes means "Snow Mountain Peninsula"—named for Snæfellsjökull, the glacier-topped volcano that looms up at its tip. The peninsula enjoys an Iceland-in-miniature geography: Its northern coastline is ruffled with fjords, similar to Iceland's North and Eastfjords. Its southern coastline features bald mountains over tapering scree skirts, laced with gorges and waterfalls, with little farms tucked here and there—much like Iceland's South Coast. And its interior consists of rugged mountains. Best of all, Snæfellsnes is home to one of Iceland's most recognizable landmarks: the "green Matterhorn" mountain peak of Kirkjufell, an icon of Ice-

landic nature that rivals the Blue Lagoon as the poster child for tourism here.

Stunning natural sites aside, Snæfellsnes is deeply rooted in history as one of the earliest settled parts of Iceland. The air here is thick with the sagas— that mix of historical chronicle and fantastical legend. (Brush up on the sagas before you go by reading the sidebar on page 108; for Snæfellsnes-specific sagas, read the sidebar later in this chapter.) Snæfellsnes' main town, Stykkishólmur, is a pleasant harborside burg with some enjoyable sights and good hotels and restaurants. Taken together, Snæfellsnes is an appealing package, either as a day trip from Reykjavík or—better—with an overnight or two.

PLANNING YOUR TIME

Snæfellsnes demands a lot of driving to be seen in a single day (about 6 hours, not including stops). You'll need to be selective and plan on returning home to Reykjavík weary (and late).

If you have just a couple of days for sights outside the capital area, a satisfying solution is to spend a night or two somewhere on the Snæfellsnes Peninsula. Many visitors to Iceland either do day trips from Reykjavík, or commit a week (or more) to the Ring Road; Snæfellsnes represents the Goldilocks "just right" middle option. And Snæfellsnes' relative remoteness can be seen as an asset, as it gets you away from the tourist crowds that hew close to the capital.

Snæfellsnes is also a reasonable (overnight) add-on to the first leg of your Ring Road loop: From Borgarnes, head up here for a night or two, before rejoining highway 1 and continuing on your way around the island. Finally, Snæfellsnes is also a logical first stage on a journey up to the remote and rugged Westfjords—an easy ferry crossing away (see the next chapter).

On Your Own or with an Excursion: If you're day-tripping, given the long round-trip from Reykjavík, it's tempting to book an excursion and leave the driving to someone else. A typical itinerary takes 12 hours and costs around 15,000-17,000 ISK (depending on group size). This is a popular offering; you can go with any of the companies mentioned on page 164.

Snæfellsnes Drive

I've organized the sights of Snæfellsnes in a one-way, counterclockwise loop around the peninsula. If you're doing it all in one day, you'll need to skip some stops (I've noted which ones); with two days, you can squeeze in just about everything mentioned here.

PLANNING YOUR DRIVE

A visit to Snæfellsnes is more satisfying with an overnight. I've outlined your priorities for each option below.

Snæfellsnes as a Day Trip from Reykjavík

Here's a suggested whistle-stop schedule for those wanting to hit just the highlights of Snæfellsnes and get home in time for a late

The Sagas of Snæfellsnes

Snæfellsnes is one of the major locations featured in the Icelandic sagas. Here are a few of the sagas and other stories you're likely to hear about while in Snæfellsnes. (For more on the sagas, see the sidebar on page 108.)

The biggest name in this region is **Bárður Snæfellsás**, the protagonist of his own saga. Bárður was a towering man—said to be one-quarter giant and one-quarter troll. He brought his family from Norway to Snæfellsnes to settle the land. After his daughter was pushed onto an iceberg and floated off to Greenland, an enraged Bárður killed the boys who were responsible, then retreated to the snow cap of the Snæfellsjökull glacier. An icebound hermit, Bárður became a near-mythical guardian figure who prowled the land wearing a heavy gray cloak tied with a belt made from a walrus-hide rope. Bárður would appear from time to time to help people in need. The saga goes on to tell the story of his son, Gestr, and his journey back to Norway.

Stykkishólmur—one of Iceland's first settlements—is the backdrop for the **Saga of the People of Eyri** *(Eyrbyggja saga)*, telling the tale of Snorra Goði Þorgrímsson, who eventually left his pagan, Viking ways behind and embraced Christianity. This saga also includes the story of Styr the Slayer, and the two Berserkers who met a grisly end (see page 295).

The **Saga of the People of Laxárdalr** *(Laxdæla saga)* tells the story of people who lived along the Breiðafjörður (on the north coast of Snæfellsnes). The central narrative is a gripping love triangle: Childhood friends Kjartan Ólafsson and Bolli Þorleiksson fall in love with the same woman, the beautiful Guðrún Ósvífrsdóttir. Tragedy ensues.

Guðríður Þorbjarnardóttir is not a legend—she was a real Icelandic woman and an inspiration to any traveler. In the tenth and eleventh centuries, Guðríður traveled to Greenland, Vínland (today's Canada), England, and Rome. She was mentioned in two different sagas: The Saga of Erik the Red, and the Saga of the Greenlanders. You can read Guðríður's story and see her monument at her birthplace, near Hellnar (see page 307).

While not officially part of the sagas, **Axlar-Björn Pétursson** (1555-1596) is another folk figure you may hear about. This Snæfellsnes native is Iceland's only known serial killer (think "Jörgen the Ripper"). When he was just 15, Axlar-Björn was led by a dream to a mountaintop where he found an axe. He used it to slay a fellow teenager—the first of a lifetime of victims (as many as 18, some sources say). Axlar-Björn was eventually arrested, executed, and hanged, and his body broken on a wheel and dismembered. The stories of Axlar-Björn capture the imaginations of Icelanders, who, after all, live in a land with one of the world's lowest crime rates.

dinner. This is a highly selective plan, which skips many of the stops described in this chapter (or simply offers a quick glimpse as you whiz past).

9:00   Leave Reykjavík and head north on highway 1 to Borgarnes—a good place for a WC, coffee, and stretch-your-legs break

10:30   Carry on north, keeping an eye out for a peek at Gerðuberg cliffs; then drive over Vatnaleið Pass to the Bjarnarhöfn Shark Museum (skipping Stykkishólmur)

12:00   After touring the Shark Museum, carry on westward through fjord country to Grundarfjörður, stopping just beyond the town center at Kirkjufellfoss for a short waterfall hike and Kirkjufell photo op

13:00   Continue west through the towns of Ólafsvík, Rif, and Hellissandur, stopping for lunch where you like (best at Café Gilbakki in Hellissandur)

14:00   Enter Snæfellsjökull National Park and loop around the tip of the peninsula, stopping to climb Saxhóll Crater and/or to walk along Djúpalónssandur black sand beach (allow about 30 minutes each)

15:30   Pull over just past Malarrif lighthouse for a view of the Lóndrangar rock formations, then stop in Arnarstapi for a quick look at the seaside basalt formations (add an hour or more if you decide to tour Vatnshellir Lava Cave)

16:30   Begin the 2.5-hour drive back to Reykjavík; you could make quick stops en route to see Rauðfeldsgjá gorge, the Black Church in Búðir, Bjarnarfoss waterfall, or seals at Ytri-Tunga (each adds 10-15 minutes to your return)

19:00- Arrive back in Reykjavík; for an earlier dinner,
20:00   consider stopping in Borgarnes at the Settlement Center's fine restaurant (see page 277); from there it's about an hour's drive to Reykjavík

Snæfellsnes in Two Days

My preferred choice, this allows you time to linger and fit in more stops—and it lets you flex with the always-unpredictable weather. I've roughed out some possibilities below, which you can adapt according to your interests.

Day 1

In the morning, head from Reykjavík up to **Borgarnes** (1 hour); if you're intrigued by the sagas, you can tour this town's Settlement Center (see the Borgarnes & Reykholt Valley chapter). Carry on north, with a quick stop at the **Gerðuberg Basalt Cliffs.** Then take the Vatnaleið road to the north coast to visit **Stykkishólmur;** tour that town's Norwegian House and Volcano Museum, consider a boat trip, and have lunch if you haven't already. In the early afternoon, head to the **Bjarnarhöfn Shark Museum** for a taste of fermented shark. Then go west through Snaefellsnes' fjord country to **Grundarfjörður,** where you can snap endless photos of the landmark **Kirkjufell** mountain. Sleep in the Grundarfjörður area or in Stykkishólmur (or head back down to Snæfellsnes' south coast).

Day 2

Today is for Snæfellsjökull National Park. Head out westward along the north coast, perhaps stopping for a photo op at **Svöðufoss** waterfall (just before Rif). Entering the national park just past Hellissandur, stroll **Skarðsvík** yellow sand beach, climb to the top of **Saxhóll** crater, walk down to **Djúpalónssandur** black sand beach, and enjoy the views of the **Lóndrangar** rock formations. If you enjoy spelunking, consider touring **Vatnshellir Cave;** if you prefer a scenic coastal walk, park in **Arnarstapi** and do the two-hour round-trip hike to Hellnar and back (with views of basalt formations the whole way). From here, make good time heading back to Reykjavík (about 2.5 hours), considering quick stops to see **Rauðfeldsgjá** gorge, the **Black Church** in Búðir, **Bjarnarfoss** waterfall, and/or seal spotting at **Ytri-Tunga.**

Extra Overnight: Spending a second night is a particularly good plan if you'd enjoy a rewarding but time-consuming visit to **Snæfellsjökull glacier** (by snowcat or on foot), or a **boat trip on Breiðafjörður** from Stykkishólmur.

Snæfellsnes Tips

Choosing a Home Base: For those spending a night or two, I've recommended accommodations scattered around the peninsula. **Stykkishólmur** is a handy hub and has the most services, but feels a bit farther from the national park sights at the far end of Snæfellsnes (see "Sleeping in Stykkishólmur" near the end of this chapter). **Grundarfjörður** is a nice compromise: smaller but just big enough to provide needed amenities, about 30 minutes closer to the national park, and in a scenic setting with fantastic views of Kirkjufell peak (see page 297). And Snæfellsnes' sleepy **south coast** is a fine spot to settle into remote countryside, a bit closer to the main road back down to Reykjavík (see "Sleeping on Snæfellsnes' South Coast" at the end of this chapter).

Activities to Reserve: If you want to tour **Vatnshellir Cave**— the lava tube near the tip of Snæfellsnes—it's wise to book ahead in peak season; they suggest calling earlier the same day, or even the day before (see page 305). Also arrange in advance for a snowcat tour or hike on **Snæfellsjökull glacier** (see page 301).

Weather and Road Conditions: All the roads on my described route are paved (though many of the detours and side-roads are not). Still, in winter, any road can be icy. If you're here outside of summer (or anytime in inclement weather), check the road conditions map at Road.is. If the weather is questionable, it's even more appealing to take a bus tour.

Seasonal Closures: The farther you get from Reykjavík, the less "year-round" places are. And Snæfellsnes is far enough that many of its restaurants, and even some accommodations and sights, may be closed off-season. I've listed hours for high season, which typically runs from late May through early September; outside of this time, expect closures (and call ahead before making any long journey to a particular place).

Snæfellsnes Loop

Snæfellsnes makes for a long day from Reykjavík: Count on six hours of driving round-trip, not including stops (that's 130 miles each way to the tip of the peninsula and back). Below, I've linked the main stops with driving directions. My "Planning Your Time" itinerary suggestions, earlier, are designed to help you prioritize, depending on how much time you have. Pace yourself, be selective, and stop only at sights that appeal to you.

REYKJAVÍK TO STYKKISHÓLMUR (VIA BORGARNES)

Setting out from Reykjavík, take highway 1 north one hour to Borgarnes. (For details on the route, see page 266.)

▲Borgarnes and Northward

The endearing fjordside town of **Borgarnes**—facing a looming scree mountain from across its fjord—could be worth a quick visit, if only to tour its **Settlement Center** and enjoy the views from **Englishman's Cove** (page 275).

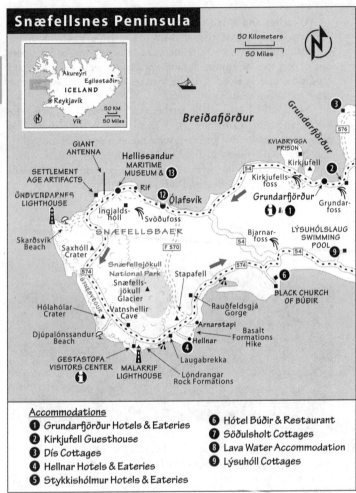

Snæfellsnes Peninsula

Accommodations
1. Grundarfjörður Hotels & Eateries
2. Kirkjufell Guesthouse
3. Dís Cottages
4. Hellnar Hotels & Eateries
5. Stykkishólmur Hotels & Eateries
6. Hótel Búðir & Restaurant
7. Söðulsholt Cottages
8. Lava Water Accommodation
9. Lýsuhóll Cottages

Leave Borgarnes north on highway 1. On the outskirts of town, turn left at the roundabout toward *Stykkishólmur*, on highway 54. You'll follow this north for about a half-hour (27 miles). This is a flat, desolate, not particularly pretty landscape, with bogs, lakes, and scrubby vegetation. Soon you'll see—looming up straight ahead, then on the left side of the road—the flat-topped **Eldborg Crater**, which rises nearly 200 feet above the surrounding lava field. With the evocative name "Fire Fortress," it last erupted around 6,000 years ago. (While climbable, it requires a long hike; save your crater-climbing energy for Saxhóll, later on this drive.)

Carry on past Eldborg. Where highway 55 splits off to the right (marked for *Búðardalur*), you'll carry on along highway 54 as

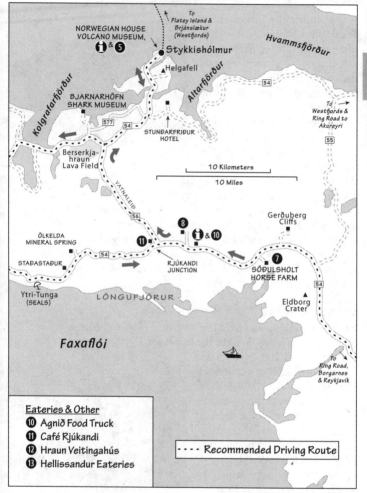

To
Flatey Island &
Brjánslækur
(Westfjords)

NORWEGIAN HOUSE
VOLCANO MUSEUM,
ⓘ & ⑤
Stykkishólmur

▲Helgafell

Hvammsfjörður

Kolgrafarfjörður

Altarfjörður

54

To
Westfjords &
Ring Road to
Akureyri

BJARNARHÖFN
SHARK MUSEUM

577 54

55

STUNDARFRIÐUR
HOTEL

Berserkja-
hraun
Lava Field

VATNALEIÐ

10 Kilometers

10 Miles

56

Gerðuberg
Cliffs

ⓘ ⑧ & ⑩

ⓘ⑪

ÖLKELDA
MINERAL SPRING

54

RJÚKANDI
JUNCTION

SÖÐULSHOLT
HORSE FARM ⑦

54

STAÐASTAÐUR

LÖNGUFJÖRÐUR

Eldborg
Crater

Ytri-Tunga
(SEALS)

Faxaflói

To
Ring Road,
Borgarnes
& Reykjavík

Eateries & Other
⑩ Agnið Food Truck
⑪ Café Rjúkandi
⑫ Hraun Veitingahús
⑬ Hellissandur Eateries

- - - - **Recommended Driving Route**

it bends to the left. Watch for the *Velkomin á Snæfellsnes* sign—of-ficially welcoming you to the region.

• *Soon, on the right side of the road, watch for the turnoff marked for Gerðuberg (and other places). Drive down this unpaved road about a mile to where you'll see gravel pullouts offering access to...*

▲Gerðuberg Basalt Cliffs

This is Iceland's longest chain of basalt cliffs: a volcanic formation of interlocking hexagonal pillars that gradually splinter away from each other. (This shape inspired the roofline of Reykjavík's land-mark church, the Hallgrímskirkja.) From the road, surefooted visi-tors hike up the short, steep, muddy trail for a close look. Reaching a height of 50 feet, this evocative curtain of basalt stands sentry, as if guarding the stronghold of Snæfellsnes. While you've just come through some flat terrain, this sheer wall of rock suggests that you've reached one of Iceland's tectonically, geothermally active zones.

Note: If you're in a hurry, you can simply keep an eye out for this low, rocky ridge on the right side of the road (far less impressive from a distance, but you can still make out its unique shape).

• *About 10 minutes (or 10 miles) beyond the cliffs, on the right, look for a little complex of tourist services: N1 gas pumps; a Snæfellsnes visitors center with pay WCs and free maps (daily 9:00-16:00, shorter hours off-season); and the handy* **$ Agnið food truck,** *serving good, basic grub.*

A couple of minutes farther along, you reach the turnoff on the right for highway 56 (marked Stykkishólmur *and* Grundarfjörður*). Turn right onto this road, which is also called...*

Vatnaleið Road

Before heading up and over the Vatnaleið pass, consider stopping off at the crossroads **$ Café Rjúkandi** for a coffee or lunch. The easygoing café has good cakes and a short menu of traditional light meals (daily 10:00-17:00); in the evening, their restaurant features more expensive meals (mid-May–mid-Sept daily 18:00-21:30, off-season until 20:00, mobile 788-9100).

Carry on over Vatnaleið, which takes you in just 15 minutes or so from Snæfellsnes' south coast to its north. On the ascent, you'll pass pretty streams and waterfalls; descending, you enter a jagged lava-rock moonscape with red hills and distant views of Breiðafjörður—the vast body of water that defines the peninsula's northern shore. Watch on the left for a viewpoint pullout, with picnic tables made from basalt columns—offering a stretch-your-legs view over this rocky landscape.

• *Coming down the far side of the pass, you'll reach a T-intersection with highway 54. To visit the town of Stykkishólmur, turn right and follow this road for about 15 minutes (11 miles). On your way into Stykkishólmur, you'll pass through a low-lying rocky terrain of inlets and lakes. A few miles before town, watch on the right for the picturesque, rocky hill with the white church at its base, next to a lake. Called Hel-*

gafell (Holy Mountain), this superstition-infused site played a role in the sagas, was later home to an Augustinian abbey, and remains dear to Icelandic hearts.

But if you're short on time (for example, you're day-tripping from Reykjavík) and want to focus on Snæfellsnes' natural sites, skip Stykkishólmur. Instead, turn left on highway 54, and pick up the tour below, under "Snæfellsnes' North Coast."

▲Stykkishólmur

Snæfellsnes' main town is little more than a smattering of historic houses facing a busy harbor, protected from the fjord's waters by a picturesque basalt islet. If you're staying overnight or taking the boat from here, Stykkishólmur is a fine place to spend time. And even if you aren't, the town is worth a stroll (unless you're in a rush). It enjoys a nice variety of restaurants, some worthwhile shops, and a pair of good museums: The **Norwegian House** is one of Iceland's best museums for getting a glimpse at upper-class historic lifestyles, and the **Volcano Museum** exhibits art inspired by volcanoes. For details on visiting Stykkishólmur, see the end of this chapter.

SNÆFELLSNES' NORTH COAST

• *From the T-intersection outside of Stykkishólmur, take highway 54 and follow it west, passing the turnoff for highway 56 (Vatnaleið). As you pass this junction, you'll begin driving through a spiky lava-rock landscape called the...*

▲Berserkjahraun Lava Field

This lunar landscape—draped with yellow lichen—was formed by volcanic eruptions around 4,000 years ago. Just off to the left is a legendary site known as Berserkjahraun, named for two doomed Berserkers—elite Viking warriors notorious for going into battle with no armor. (While today that word connotes a wild, uncontrollable attack, it comes from the Old Norse for "bear shirt," which was all that protected these fighters from enemies.)

According to the sagas, during the early Settlement Age, two Berserkers—Halli and Leiknir—traveled here from Sweden and came to work for a local man named Styr. Halli fell in love with Styr's daughter, but Styr would only give them permission to wed if the Berserkers completed what he thought would be an impossible task: building a bridle path through the middle of this lava field. Halli and Leiknir made short work of the job, and Styr was faced with the prospect of an objectionable son-in-law. So, when the Berserkers were done working, Styr offered them a break in a sauna, which turned out to be a trap...they were locked inside and boiled alive. History now knows the farmer as "Styr the Slayer." Like many Icelandic legends, this tale likely contains a kernel of truth: Archaeologists have discovered the remains of two large men buried under a cairn in this area.

• *Two miles after the junction with highway 56 (Vatnaleið), watch carefully on the right for the turnoff to road 577 (marked Helgafellssveit). If you're intrigued by Iceland's weirdest food, detour here to get a taste and to see how it's made: Turn off, then turn left at the sign for Bjarnarhöfn. You're heading for the little farm tucked at the base of the mountain. About two miles off the main road, you'll reach the...*

▲▲Bjarnarhöfn Shark Museum

At this family-run farm, brothers Kristján and Guðjon make Iceland's traditional "rotted shark" *(hákarl)*. When they're not hanging

fermented slabs of shark to dry in their barn, they enjoy showing visitors through a museum lovingly stocked with their family's traditional tools, exhibits on local bird life, and, of course, an education in fermented shark... plus a taste. The visit begins with an eight-minute slideshow presentation, where one of the brothers describes the process (for details on this dish, see the sidebar on page 497). You'll get to touch a shark's sandpaper-like skin and run your fingers over its sawtooth-like jawbone. Then you'll have the opportunity to taste a tiny cube of *hákarl*, mounted on a little slice of rye bread (to help cut the flavor). Pro tip: It smells worse than it tastes, but the chewy texture and ammonia flavor (with some salty notes) can be off-putting. After the tour and tasting, head out back to see (and smell) the sheds where slabs of fermented shark hang from the rafters to dry.

Cost and Hours: 1,200 ISK, daily 9:00-18:00, Oct-May daily 10:00-17:00, tel. 438-1581, https://bjarnarhofn.is.

Eating: The handy on-site **$ café** serves no shark but has a short menu of easy meals (burgers, fish-and-chips; open in summer only 11:00-17:00).

• *Back on highway 54, carry on west, through...*

▲▲Snæfellsnes' Fjord Country

The views over the next several miles are stunning, as you cross two fjords on bridges, with towering mountains on both sides of the road. All of these fjords are arms of the same big mega-fjord, called Breiðafjörður—the aptly named "wide fjord" that separates Snaefellsnes from the Westfjords, to the north. (What's the difference between a fjord and a bay? If its mouth is wider than it is long, then it's technically not a fjord. While it sure looks like a bay on maps, Breiðafjörður qualifies as a fjord.)

Crossing the first fjord, **Hraunsfjarðarvatn,** you'll enjoy a grand view of cascading mountain peaks lined up above the waterline. The second fjord, **Kolgrafarfjörður,** is famous for its biodiversity; arctic birds, seals, and even whales are spotted here.

After crossing a neck of land, you'll begin driving around the broad bay of Grundarfjörður—framed at the far end by the tent-shaped ridge of **Kirkjufell.** While you may not quite recognize it from this angle, you certainly will when you get to the far side of town.

As you start along the black sand beach toward the town of Grundarfjörður, watch on the left for **Grundarfoss**—one of many grand waterfalls in Snæfellsnes, this one plunging 230 feet from the cliffs. (You can park in front of the gate and walk across the fields for a closer look.)

• *Soon you reach the town of...*

▲Grundarfjörður

While this midsize-by-Icelandic-standards town (pop. 900) isn't much to see, it's one of the most popular spots on Snæfellsnes for the classic views it provides of the nearby Kirkjufell peak.

Grundarfjörður's proudest moment came three centuries ago, when Denmark designated it as one of Iceland's original six trading towns (in 1786). It cultivated strong trade connections with the French, who built a church in town. Today the main business is tourism: It's a hub for food, drink, and accommodations.

Driving through town on the main road, watch on the left for the **Saga Center,** which houses several services, including the **TI** info desk, the town library, pay WCs, and two exhibitions: a 10-minute slideshow of historic town photographs (called Bæringsstofa), and a modest museum displaying some town artifacts. The most interesting items are a French cannon that washed up here around 1720 (likely from a whaling ship), and a fishing boat dating from 1913. There's also a children's play area and a re-constructed shop from the 1950s (free, likely open June-mid-Sept daily 9:00-17:00, off-season 13:00-17:00 and closed Fri, Grundargata 35, tel. 438-1881).

Sleeping in Grundarfjörður: Two affordable guesthouses face the main road in the town center. **$$ The Old Post Office Guesthouse** (Gamla Pósthúsið) is just that: a family-run B&B filling a utilitarian, blocky building with 12 rooms, most with private bathrooms and some with Kirkjufell views for no extra charge (shared kitchen but no breakfast, Grundargata 50, tel. 430-8043, www.topo.is). **¢ Guesthouse 43,** across the street, is a simple budget choice. Sædís, who grew up in this house, has now turned it into a fine little B&B with three rooms that share a bathroom. She prefers bookings via Airbnb or Booking.com (Snæfellsnesvegur 43, mobile 888-0232).

Sleeping just Outside of Grundarfjörður: On the road leading into town—just a few minutes' drive away—are **$ Kirkjufell Guesthouse** and **Grund Guesthouse,** a family-run accommodations campus with 12 rooms in two different houses (some with shared bathroom), plus apartments. Communication can be tricky, but the price is reasonable, the facilities are modern, and the views across the fjord to Kirkjufell are grand (mobile 840-6100, grundguesthouse@gmail.com). **$$$ Dís Cottages** are eight freestanding, modern, boxy, well-equipped houses on a ridge with a view over the fjord and Kirkjufell Mountain. The location—about a 15-minute drive from town—is enjoyable for those who appreciate remoteness (small kitchenettes—B.Y.O. breakfast, Þórdísarstaðir 350, mobile 892-7746, www.discottages.is).

Eating in Grundarfjörður: There's only one good place for a real meal in town: **$$$ Bjargarsteinn** is a high-end *mathús* (house of food) occupying a charming 1908 house that was recently relocated from Akranes—85 miles away—to Grundarfjörður's waterfront. The interior is drawing-room cozy, with big views of the Kirkjufell mountain filing the windows, and in good weather, there are even better views from tables outside. The food is traditional Icelandic presented with just the right amount of modern panache. It's worth reserving ahead (daily 17:00-22:00, Sólvellir 15, tel. 438-6770, www.bjargarsteinn.is).

$ Láki Hafnarkaffi, down near the harbor and operated by a local tour company, has pizzas and other basics (daily 9:00-21:00, Nesvegur 5, tel. 546-6808).

In a pinch, you can grab a hot dog at the **Mæstro** food truck (summer only, across from the Saga Center/TI at Grundargata 33). Across the main road, the **Kjörbuðin** grocery is the village hub—it has a little café with basic food, as well as a pharmacy, post office, and liquor store (Mon-Fri 9:00-21:00, Sat-Sun from 10:00).

• *Just beyond Grundarfjörður's center, about a mile outside of town, you'll approach Iceland's most famous pointy peak. Watch for the small gravel parking lot on your left (just after a small lake)—likely jammed with cars. Park here and hop out for a better look at...*

▲▲▲Kirkjufell View from Kirkjufellsfoss Waterfall

This waterfall-with-a-mountain-backdrop has quickly become one of the most famous bits of scenery in all of Iceland. Immortalized in postcards, tourist brochures, the covers of guidebooks, and (under cover of snow) "North of the Wall" in *Game of Thrones,* this scene is a joy to immerse yourself in. At the end of the last Ice Age, receding glaciers carved this mountain to a razor point that resembles

a church steeple—earning it the name "Church Mountain" (*kirkju-fell*, pron. KIRK-yoo-fehtl). Notice how you can still see the stripes of rock that formed the land here over time, before it was eroded back down. Even though it's only 1,520 feet tall, Kirkjufell is undeniably majestic.

From the parking lot, walk about 10 minutes up the path on the right side of the waterfall. For the best views—with the waterfall in the foreground, and the peak towering behind—cross the bridge and circle around to the left, then look back down. Even when it's a human traffic jam—as it often is—this view is well worth the walk.

• *Back in your car, continue west on highway 54. Immediately after the waterfall parking lot, look to see if horses are gathered at the base of the mountain on the right. If so, pull off here—at the sign for Háls—for a postcard photo: Icelandic horse and iconic mountain.*

Along the North Coast

Now make good time continuing west for about 25 minutes (14 miles). First, you'll climb up to the headland, passing another dramatic castaway mountain on your right, connected at the far end by a narrow causeway. Tucked around the far side of this peninsula is the super-minimum-security **Kvíabryggja Prison,** which houses about two dozen inmates who are near the end of their sentences (with no fences—almost like a halfway house). Some of Iceland's corporate bigwigs who were convicted after the 2008 economic crisis did time here. A controversy broke out a few years back when these wealthy prisoners were found to have fancier bicycles than their poorer cellmates. And in 2015, there was a "jailbreak" when two prisoners didn't return from unstructured outdoor time by the appointed hour—the first escape in nearly 30 years. (They were captured the next day, several hours away at Þingvellir National Park.) The jail's biggest problem: Confused tourists routinely drive up to the building after mistaking it for a visitors center, which proves disruptive for inmates and guards alike.

Coming down on the far side of the headland, you'll follow a broad black sand beach, with lots of pretty waterfalls on your left. Look out over the broad Breiðafjörður for distant views of the Westfjords on the horizon.

• *When highway 54 splits off to the left, carry on straight as the road you're on becomes road 574 (signed for a trio of humdrum towns: Hellis-sandur, Rif, and Ólafsvík).*

Fishing Towns: Ólafsvík, Rif, and Hellissandur

Snæfellsnes' north coast is home to a series of humble fishing towns. You'll pass through three of them on your way to the national park. Each has a couple of intriguing landmarks, and taken together, they've scraped together a few good places for a meal.

Ólafsvík: First you'll see this little village, huddled under its giant mountain (Ólafs-víkurenni). Then you'll smell its fish-processing plants. That's a shame, since Ólafsvík's history goes way back—to 1687, when it received its trading charter. Today it's a humble, workaday community with a unique, modern church—look for its open-work, pointy steeple rising above town.

For a good meal here, consider **$$ Hraun Veitingahús,** filling a log cabin-type building on the main road. It has a charming, cozy, woody interior and an ambitious menu of Icelandic and international fare (daily 11:30-21:00, Fri-Sat until 22:00, Grundarbraut 2, tel. 431-1030, www.hraunrestaurant.com).

Between Ólafsvík and Rif: A bit past Ólafsvík, you'll curl around the mountain and reach a broad, flat expanse. Here is where (in good weather) you'll begin to get some views of **Snæfells-jökull**—the towering glacier-capped volcano that's the centerpiece of the national park (see sidebar). This is the needle around which this bulb of land spins. If it's socked in (as it often is), just keep an eye on your left—we'll be getting glimpses of this mountain from various angles during the rest of our drive.

About 2.5 miles out of Ólafsvík, watch on the left for a road leading to **Svöðufoss**—a waterfall that plunges 35 feet over a steep basalt cliff, with the Snæfellsjökull on the horizon behind it, creating a classic Snæfellsnes view. If the weather is clear and you have time for a closer look, you could turn off here and follow the unpaved road about a mile to a parking lot, where a 10-minute path leads through the lava field to the falls.

Rif: This tiny, humble town has only one claim to fame: **The Freezer,** a boutique hostel-slash-cultural center filling a cavernous old fish-processing factory a couple of blocks off the main road. They have dorm beds, unique themed rooms, a cozy lounge with mismatched secondhand furniture, and frequent cultural events, from live music and comedy shows to movie nights and karaoke (nightly events July-Aug, sporadically at other times). If you're

Snæfellsjökull:
"Snow Mountain Glacier"

The centerpiece and namesake of the national park—and the peninsula—Snæfellsjökull rises to 4,745 feet. Like many Icelandic glaciers, it sits upon an active (though currently quiet) volcano. This is where the characters in Jules Verne's *Journey to the Center of the Earth* discovered the entrance to the underworld. Believers in UFOs claim it has an extraterrestrial connection. And adherents of chakra believe it's one of the seven points on earth where that mystical power is most concentrated. Scientifically, it is possible that the volcano exerts a special magnetic pull—some visitors report having trouble sleeping in this area. Whatever the cause, Snæfellsjökull seizes people's imaginations.

While it's thrilling just seeing Snæfellsjökull from afar, adventure seekers can visit the glacier. The easiest and most popular option is a tour by **snowcat**—essentially a giant open-air pickup truck with tank treads. You'll meet at a designated point near the glacier (most companies are either near Arnarstapi, or up by the national park entrance near Hellissandur), load up onto the snowcat, and trundle across the ice for a close look at the glacier. Trips last about 2.5 hours, cost around 15,000 ISK, and run only from early May through late August (try The Glacier Tours, www.theglacier.is; Extreme Iceland, www.extremeiceland.is; and Summit Adventure Guides, www.summitguides.is).

You can also **hike** on top of the glacier. A three-hour hike—wearing crampons, tied up for safety with other hikers, and led by a guide—takes around three hours and costs about 15,000 ISK; a **snowshoeing** alternative is also available. Companies include Go West Eco-Tours (www.gowest.is) or Summit Adventure Guides (www.summitguides.is).

These tours are highly weather-dependent and can be cancelled; I'd skip it if there's bad weather or poor visibility.

---

staying in the area—and need something to do in the evening—check out what's on (Hafnargata 16, mobile 833-8200, www.thefreezerhostel.com). They also rent apartments in Hellissandur.

Immediately after Rif, a sign on the left points to **Ingjaldshóll**—a historic site (marked by a red-roofed church) a half-mile off the main road. History buffs may enjoy a quick stop in this place, where some say a young Christopher Columbus spent the winter of 1477 learning about the Icelanders' journeys—five centuries earlier—to the place called "Vínland"; later in life, Columbus would bring Europeans back to the Americas once again. (There's a painting of Columbus inside the church, which is often locked.) Near the church is a monument consisting of two stone pillars, honoring the poet and naturalist Eggert Ólafsson and his wife, Ingibjörg Guðmundsdóttur. If you look back toward the fjord between these rocks, you see the place (across the water, in the Westfjords) from where this couple set off on a journey in 1768...from which they never returned. The pillar is also inscribed with a poem by Eggert—a blessing upon Iceland—that every Icelander learns by heart.

Hellissandur: Like many remote Icelandic villages, Hellissandur has a surprising artistic flair. Take a quick spin through

town to see the **street-art murals**—including a huge painting of a ram near the bridge, done by two artists from Spain. Just beyond that is a cluster of humble homes spray-painted with murals every color of the rainbow. (A new information center for the national park may open somewhere around here by the time you visit—ask around.)

Hellissandur has one sight worth considering: The **Maritime Museum** (Sjóminjasafnið) is on the left side of the road, just past the main part of town. This modern museum features exhibits about sea life, geology, and local sea birds, and displays the oldest surviving fishing boat in Iceland (the *Bliki*, an eight-oared vessel from 1826). Outside are replicas of two interconnected sod-roofed fishermen's cottages—step inside to see how humbly fisherfolk once lived, and don't miss the stairs up to the sleeping loft in the attic. Surrounding the museum is a "Fishermen's Garden" strewn with labeled artifacts, including the skeleton of a sperm whale (1,300 ISK, June-late Sept daily 10:00-17:00, likely closed off-season, mobile 844-5969).

Eating in Hellissandur: This town has two excellent eating options—one for lunch, the other for dinner. On the right side of the main road, at the entrance to town, **$ Gilbakki Kaffihús** is an ideal place for a coffee, cake, or a light lunch, from delicious spicy fish soup to quiche. Charmingly run by sweet Anna—who built this house with her husband—it's a winner. This makes for a great "last chance pit stop" before entering the national park and circling around to the south coast; there's not much between here and Hellnar (June-Aug daily 9:00-18:00; May and Sept Thu-Mon 11:00-17:00, closed Wed; closed off-season; tel. 436-1001). The gray house perched on a ridge at the far end of town (on the left) is the dinner-only **$$$ Viðvík,** offering a fine-dining modern Icelandic menu that includes quality seafood. If staying nearby and in the mood for a quality dinner, it's well worth booking ahead (early

May-late Sept Tue-Sun 17:00-21:30, closed Mon and off-season, tel. 436-1026).

• *When you leave Hellissandur, you enter the official boundary of...*

SNÆFELLSJÖKULL NATIONAL PARK

The 65-square-mile knob of land that comprises Snæfellsjökull National Park (Þjóðgarðurinn Snæfellsjökull) is studded with many of the peninsula's best attractions. Continue along road 574 (called Útnesvegur) counterclockwise, circling the peninsula's glacier, Snæfellsjökull.

You'll pass rusted-metal *Velkomin* signs marking your entrance to the national park. Just past that, on the right, you can't miss the gigantic **radio antenna,** held in place by beefy cables. Towering at 1,350 feet, this is far and away the tallest structure in Iceland (and even taller than the Eiffel Tower). The tower is critical for maintaining communications with ships on rough seas.

Just past the antenna, you'll drive by the tiny settlement where some tours depart for trips up to the glacier (see the "Snæfellsjökull" sidebar, earlier).

• *About a mile after entering the park, watch for the sign on the right pointing to Gufuskálavör and Írskrabrunnur. These indicate the very scant remains of...*

Settlement Age Artifacts

Snæfellsnes settled early in Iceland's history—back in the late ninth century. And if you know what to look for, subtle artifacts of this period are all over. While the history is pretty obscure, historians can pull over here to stoke their imaginations. At the little fork, signs point to the left to the *Well of the Irish* (Írskrabrunnur)—the remains of a water supply dating back to the late 800s. Signs to the right point to *Gufuskálavör,* the ruins of a 14th-century fishing village. Across the main road is a stone shed where fishermen would hang their catch to dry (called *fiskbyrgi*).

• *Just a couple of minutes later, where the road bends to the left, take the little turnoff on the right marked* Öndverðarnes. *Follow this unpaved road about a mile through the black, chunky terrain until you reach...*

▲Skarðsvík Yellow-Sand Beach

This volcanic island has many black sand beaches...but a yellow one is rare enough to thrill Icelanders. This one is dramatically hemmed in by chunky black lava rock, which makes it very inviting to go for a stroll, listen to the surf, or take a break at the picnic table. On very sunny days, you may even see hardy locals swimming or sunbathing.

If you were to continue along this rough road past Skarðsvík, you'd eventually reach the **Öndverðarnes** lighthouse. However, it's a longish drive and you can't enter the building—I'd skip it.

• *Carry on south through the national park. After about four miles, on the right side of the road, you can't miss...*

▲▲Saxhóll Crater

This jagged red crater—rising nearly 360 feet above the flat terrain—is one of Iceland's most tempting to climb. If you have time for a hike, use the rust-red steps to hike up to the summit and peer down into the mouth of the crater—and enjoy the sweeping views of the surrounding countryside and sea, plus distant views of Snæfellsjökull. (Warning: The climb is much harder in windy weather.)

• *Back on the road, carry on another six miles. On the right, look for the turnoff for Hólahólar and Berudalur. If you'd like a peek at another crater, pull off here and drive about a half-mile down the unpaved road— which leads right into the middle of Hólahólar crater.*

Back on the main road, about 1.5 miles past the Hólahólar turnoff, watch on the right for Djúpalónssandur (also marked road 572). Turn off here and drive a mile or so down the road to...

▲▲Djúpalónssandur Black Sand Beach

This is a stunning opportunity to stroll on one of the best of Iceland's countless black sand beaches. Djúpalónssandur was once home to a thriving fishing station—one of the busiest on Snæfellsnes, 60 boats strong. But today it's entirely uninhabited.

From the parking lot (with WCs), follow *Til strandar* signs down to the beach—it's about a 10-minute walk all the way to the water. You'll hike through an evocative canyon of fanciful fairy chimneys—gnarled lava-rock towers reaching up to the heavens. You'll emerge onto the beach at an information plaque, explaining the four large stones lined up nearby. These **"lifting stones"** *(aflraunasteinar)* were used to prove the strength of would-be fishermen. They range from *fullsterkur* (full strength, 154 kg) down to *amlóði* (weakling), at 23 kg. To qualify for work, you'd have to be able to lift the *hálfsterkur* (half strength, 100 kg) onto a waist-high platform. This tradition continues today in Iceland, with "strongman contests" *(aflraunak-eppni)* similar to the ones at Scottish Highland Games.

Now turn your attention to some much smaller rocks: the beautiful, black lava "pearls" *(djúpalónsperlur)* that cover the beach. Feel these crunch under your feet. Bend down and pick up a handful, just to let them cascade through your fingers. But don't take any home—they're protected by the Icelandic government.

Hike across the lava pearls toward the surf. You'll notice that the beach is strewn with gnarled chunks of rusted metal. These are

the remains of the *Epine,* a British fishing trawler that washed up here in 1948. (Only five of the 19 crew members survived.)

Cresting the rise, you could walk downhill the rest of the way to the waterline. But stay well back from the surf, as this beach has a wicked tide and dangerous sneaker waves. (As at all Icelandic beaches, heed the warning signs that urge you to keep a safe distance, and never turn your back on the surf.) But do look left and right, appreciating the way that the jagged black sea stacks frame off the beach.

Head left along the beach, to find a smaller, second beach adjacent. The tall sea stack just offshore is called *Kerling* (Crone). And the row of jagged peaks on the left is called *Söngklettur* (Singing Rock). This is one of those places that some Icelanders believe are home to the "hidden people." Superstitious locals are careful to stay quiet in this area, and would never climb up on rocks like this. For more on these hidden people stories, see the sidebar on page 225.

• *Back on the main road, carry on two miles, where you'll see the building (on the left) that's the starting point for touring...*

▲Vatnshellir Cave

Famous for having inspired Jules Verne, this lava tube—formed during a volcanic eruption 8,000 years ago—can only be visited on

a 45-minute guided tour, which traverses about 650 feet of the cave, about 115 feet underground. The cave is chilly (always in the mid-30s Fahrenheit) and drippy, and requires climbing up and down about 130 slippery metal steps, plus navigating the

uneven terrain of the cave floor itself—it's best for the surefooted. Vatnshellir is less interesting to visit than some of Iceland's other volcanic caves (described on page 40), but if this is your handiest opportunity to see one, it's worth 45 minutes. You could try just showing up and taking whichever tour is available next (if you have time to kill, there's a lot to see within a few minutes' drive). But in peak season, it's smart to reserve ahead online—either earlier that same day, or the previous day.

Cost and Hours: 3,750 ISK, tours depart at the top of each hour daily in summer 10:00-18:00, additional departures possible in peak season, fewer tours off-season, mobile 787-0001, www. summitguides.is/tours. There are no WCs at the cave—the nearest are a few minutes' drive away, at the national park visitors center (see next).

Visiting the Cave: You'll be issued a helmet and a flashlight, then follow your guide to the metal spiral staircase you'll use to climb down into the cave. Exploring the cavern, you'll pass through three chambers. The first, uppermost chamber—called Bárðarstofa (Bárður's living room)—features a "table" and "chair" belonging to the mythical half-giant linked to this area. Then you'll carry on deeper, seeing various features—such as "lava stalactites" (formed in moments, rather than over eons), "shark's tooth" stalactites, and red (iron-rich) lava floes trapped in time. At the cave's lowest point, your guide will encourage everyone to turn off their flashlights—plunging you into absolute darkness.

• *About 1.5 miles after the cave, on the right, watch for the turnoff to Malarrif. Stop here for a visitors center with a WC, and for a look at the...*

Lóndrangar Rock Formations and Malarrif Lighthouse (Malarrifsviti)

This stretch of coast is named for an old fishing settlement here, **Lóndrangar.** The distinctive twin volcanic pinnacles (246 and 200 feet tall) are known as Þúfubjarg; the nearby hill with a sea cliff (home to many birds in summer) is called Svalþúfa.

At the Malarrif lighthouse, you'll find the **national park visitor center** *(gestastofa)*—the only real tourist information office in the area. This is a handy place to take a break, use free WCs, and peruse a fine exhibit about the park's geology (daily 10:00-17:00, tel. 436-6888). From here, you can walk about a mile each way to the rock formations of Lóndrangar (allow about 45 minutes round-trip; just walk with the water on your right, and as you do, keep an eye out for arctic foxes in the lava field and whales and seals in the water). In the summer, free ranger-guided walks depart from here daily at 13:00.

If you don't have time to hike out for an up-close view from

Malarrif, carry on past that turnoff. About three-quarters of a mile later, watch on the right for the easy-to-miss parking lot for a **viewpoint** (marked with a tiny *Svalþúfa-Þúfubjarg* sign). From here, it's a few minutes' walk to an overlook for a sweeping view.

• *Just past Lóndrangar, you exit the national park (góða ferð!). But there's still much to be seen along...*

SNÆFELLSNES' SOUTH COAST

You've rounded the bend and are headed back toward Reykjavík. Along the way, you'll pass dramatic rock formations in the sea, towering mountains, wide and sandy beaches, and a smattering of offbeat Snæfellsnes sights.

• *Immediately after leaving the park, you'll reach two towns offering opportunities to experience stunning...*

▲▲Basalt Sea Stacks, Arches, and Cliffs: Hellnar and Arnarstapi

This stretch of coast is blessed with breathtaking basalt formations. You can access them at two different towns, a couple of miles apart: Hellnar and Arnarstapi. If you're short on time, simply make a quick stop in this area for a peek (Arnarstapi's formations are better). But if you have a bit more time to invest in coastal scenery, it's well worth spending two hours on a gorgeous walk: Drive  to Arnarstapi; walk about 45 minutes (about 2 miles) back to Hellnar; have a coffee (or fish soup) at the Fjöruhúsið café; then walk back to your car.

• *Immediately before reaching the Hellnar turnoff—about three miles after the Lóndrangar viewpoint—pull off on the right to see...*

Laugarbrekka: This middle-of-nowhere spot features a small statue honoring Guðríður Þorbjarnardóttir—a remarkably well-traveled Icelandic settler who managed to see much of the world... despite having been born on this humble, remote spot in the year 980. She made eight long sea voyages in her lifetime, including multiple trips to Greenland and to Vínland (now known as North America). She counted Leif "The Lucky" Erikson as her brother-in-law. She gave birth to what's thought to be the first person of European origin born on American soil (her son, Snorri—whom she's holding on her shoulder in the statue). And then, later in life, she made a pilgrimage to Rome from her farmstead at Glaumbær (in Skagafjörður—see page 371). If you're an avid traveler, you can pay your respects to Guðríður as a kindred spirit.

• *Back on the road, it's just a half-mile farther to the turnoff (also on the right) toward Hellnar. You'll pass Bárðarlaug, a popular swimming pond (and supposedly the bathtub for the legendary giant Bárður Snæfellsás...more on him later).*

Hellnar: This tiny village is a natural seaport and was once a thriving fishing village. Home to nearly 200 people in 1700, tourism is today's main catch. Drive down to the parking lot on the bluff overlooking the sea, where you'll get a taste of the formations that stretch from here all the way to Arnarstapi.

Walk down to the **$ Fjöruhúsið** café, in a humble concrete shed burrowed into the hill, with a deck overlooking the cliffs. This is a prime spot for a coffee, snack, or basic meal. While simple—with a tight, cozy six-room interior—this place is beloved among Icelanders for their fish stew in a very scenic setting (also quiche and cakes; mid-April-mid-Oct daily 12:00-18:00, closed off-season, tel. 435-6844). The recommended **Fosshotel Hellnar** is above the port (see "Sleeping on Snæfellsnes' South Coast" at the end of this chapter).

Even if you're short on time, walk a few minutes on the trail just past Fjöruhúsið for a glimpse at some chunky basalt formations just offshore, which teem with sea birds in the summertime. Tucked back in all those jagged crevices is a natural cave called Baðstofa. If you were to follow this trail for about 45 minutes, you'd reach Arnarstapi.

• *To drive there, get back in your car, head back up to the main road, turn right, and carry on just one mile. You'll drive along the bottom of the pyramid-shaped peak called Stapafell, then turn off on the right and head into...*

Arnarstapi: This is another little community, once a trading post, that's tucked deep into a dramatic basalt landscape. Arnarstapi enjoys more grand views—this time of a perfectly formed volcanic sea arch.

On your way into town (road lined with tour companies and food trucks), watch on the right for the gigantic statue (built out of stacked rocks) of **Bárður Snæfellsás**—the legendary half-man, half-giant  who looms large in Snæfellsnes folklore. (For his story, see "The Sagas of Snæfellsnes" sidebar, earlier.)

From the parking lot by the statue, trek on the path a few minutes across the fields to the coastline. From here, you'll quickly find a natural arch rising up from the surf. Mind-bending basalt forma-tions ripple along the coastline in both directions from here. Walk along the coast as far as time and weather allow. For a shorter walk, turn left along the shoreline and walk about 10 minutes (each way) to the town's little harbor area, with a grand view of the towering Stapafell mountain peak. With more time, consider turning right and taking that longer walk (about 45 minutes one-way) all the way to Hellnar, then back again.

Warning: If the arctic terns are nesting (commonly in the early summer), they might dive-bomb you relentlessly. They pull up just before impaling you with their beaks...usually. To avoid escalating the standoff, do your best to avoid nesting areas.

• *Back on the main road, less than two miles after the Arnarstapi turnoff, on the left is...*

Rauðfeldsgjá Gorge

This volcanic gorge—carved by a river—is tucked back in the folds of the cliff. While it's visible from the road, curious visitors with time to spare can hike up about 15 minutes to the mouth of the gorge. While it's impressive to peer up into this narrow, steep space, you likely won't be able to go much deeper without wading through a river and hopping across stepping-stones; if time is short, just enjoy the view from the parking lot.

Like so many things on Snæfellsnes, this gorge comes with a legend: Bárður Snæfellsás (whom we met back in Arnarstapi) had a daughter who enjoyed playing with a neighbor boy, Rauðfeldr (Red Cloak). One day they were horsing around on the shoreline when Rauðfeldr pushed her onto an iceberg, which floated offshore and wound up drifting all the way to Greenland. Furious, Bárður threw Rauðfeldr into the gorge that still bears his name.

• *From the gorge, carry on east about 10 minutes (8 miles) through the lava field of Búðahraun. You'll pass lonesome farms, enjoy peeka-boo views of Snæfellsjökull on your left, and eventually head up over a bluff. Cresting the top of the bluff, watch for a pullout on the right offering grand views back over the basalt coastline, Stapafell mountain, and Snæfellsjökull. A plaque explains that this was the home to Axlar-Björn—Iceland's only axe murderer, who lived here in the 16th century (he's buried back near the Hellnar turnoff; for his story, see "The Sagas of Snæfellsnes" sidebar, earlier).*

Keep going; as the road flattens out, watch on the right for the op-tional turnoff to...

Búðir

Yet another charming seafront settlement, Búðir is famous for its landmark **black church** (Búðakirkja), picturesquely perched on a hill—all that's left of what was once a thriving trading post. This church, completed in 1850, is a favorite photo op that encapsulates the desolation of Iceland. While people enjoy snapping a photo, there's not much else to see here—it's skippable if you're running out of steam.

Along the road to the church, you'll pass the big and swanky **Hótel Búðir,** a popular site for weddings: Get married in the church...and your reception can be right next door. It's also a good, if expensive, place to stay—see "Sleeping on Snæfellsnes' South Coast" at the end of this chapter.

• *At this point, with Snæfellsjökull receding in your rear-view mirror, it's time to head...*

BACK TO REYKJAVÍK

Just past the Búðir turnoff, the road hits a T-intersection with highway 54. Turn right (east) and follow this back toward *Reykjavík* and *Borgarnes.*

As soon as you get on highway 54, watch on the left for the **Bjarnarfoss waterfall.** If you aren't waterfalled out, turn off on the small road (marked *Bjarnarfoss*) for a closer look. From the parking lot, a paved path leads about five minutes through the field to the foot of the falls.

About five miles along highway 54, the turnoff on the left to *Lýsuhóll* leads to a little farmstead (with recommended accommodations; see the end of this chapter). Deep in the settlement is the small **Lýsuhólslaug swimming pool,** fed by mineral-rich natural springs. This is a handy spot to unwind and splash in hot water after a long day's drive. Note that the pool has recently been closed for maintenance work, but should reopen soon—call ahead (when open, it's daily in summer 11:00-20:30, tel. 433-9917).

Back on highway 54, on the right, watch for the rock-strewn beach called **Ytri-Tunga,** which is known for the seals that bask here in summer (especially in June and July). (The sign may be missing, but look for the red house with the black roof.) Follow the unpaved road for about a mile to the little parking lot, where signs identify some of the seals that are often seen here. From the parking lot, it's a short walk to the sandy beach to see what you can spot.

The broad, sandy, golden-colored beaches along here—called **Löngufjörur**—are a popular place for horseback riding in cinematic scenery. If the weather's good, you can look back to grand views of the Snæfellsjökull glacier.

About 2.5 miles beyond Ytri-Tunga, on the left, are a red-steepled church and a small monument marked **Staðastaður**—once the residence of Ari Þorgilsson (1067-1148). "Ari the Wise" (Ari fróði), as he's called, was the author of the *Book of Icelanders*—a chronicle of the earliest settlers, and a cornerstone of the sagas.

There's not much to see here, but Icelandic history buffs can pay their respects at his giant, symbolic gravestone.

Two miles past Staðastaður, you reach (on the left) the small farm of **Ölkelda**. Pulling off here, look for the parking area in front of the *Welcome to the Mineral Spring* sign. Nearby, a little faucet sticking out of the ground dispenses naturally carbonated, iron-rich water that you can use to fill your bottle. Despite the metallic taste, the sign assures you it's very healthy—supposedly good for heart disease, lung disease, and diabetes. Notice the nearby ground tinted red by the heavy iron deposits.

Eight miles farther along, you'll reach the turnoff for highway 56 (Vatnaleið road) to the north coast—which we went down earlier. From here, you're essentially retracing your steps: Take highway 54 about 40 miles (approximately 45 minutes) to the northern outskirts of Borgarnes, where you'll turn right onto highway 1, head through the middle of Borgarnes, and continue about an hour to Reykjavík.

Or—if you've enjoyed Snæfellsnes enough that you'd like to extend your Iceland stay a week or so—turn left onto highway 1 and follow the Ring Road all the way around the island, 800 miles back to Reykjavík the long way. Why not?

Stykkishólmur

Snæfellsnes' main town may not quite be Iceland's most charming fjordside settlement...but it tries. (And it wins "most entertaining name" award.) The smattering of colorful, traditional shiplap houses that face its harbor echoes the scattering of islets, rocks, and skerries that fill the broad bay beyond. The bulky basalt islet called Súgandisey provides a natural harbor for Stykkishólmur, which originally put the town on the map for shipping and fishing (halibut and shellfish). Stykkishólmur has strong ties to Denmark, and still celebrates "Danish Days" each August.

Stykkishólmur (STIK-iss-HOLL-mur, pop. 1,195) has a critical mass of sights, accommodations, eateries, and services, making it a convenient home base and an enticing stopover. It has some

pleasant sights—including its lovely and intimate Norwegian House—and is also a popular springboard for heading out onto Breiðafjörður.

Orientation to Stykkishólmur

On the road into town, you'll pass several key landmarks. After a string of **gas stations,** watch on the right for the good town **swimming pool** (blue waterslide, set back from the road), then the only **Bónus supermarket** on the peninsula. (Turning right just before Bónus takes you up to the town's landmark church, the Stykkishólmskirkja.) Carrying on along the main road, you'll wind down into the town center and harbor area, where a few handy, small, free parking lots make it easy to stow your car and explore.

Tourist Information: While Stykkishólmur doesn't have a true TI, the **Seatours** booking office near the harbor hands out maps and answers questions (Smiðjustígur 3, tel. 433-2254).

Shopping: Stykkishólmur has some unique shops that may interest souvenir-hunters. On the way into town is a studio space with two artisans: **Leir 7,** a ceramic shop with unique designs that make use of local clay, and **Smávinir** woodworking (Mon-Fri 14:00-17:00, Sat until 16:00, closed Sun, Aðalgata 20). Closer to the town center, next to the Volcano Museum, the charming **Gallerí Lundi** has a nice, unpretentious assortment of local handicrafts (daily 10:00-18:00, shorter hours off-season, Frúargata 2).

Sights in Stykkishólmur

For such a little town, Stykkishólmur has some endearing and insightful museums. Note that the three main sights (Norwegian House, Volcano Museum, and Library of Water) are covered by a 2,650-ISK combo-ticket (buy it at any sight).

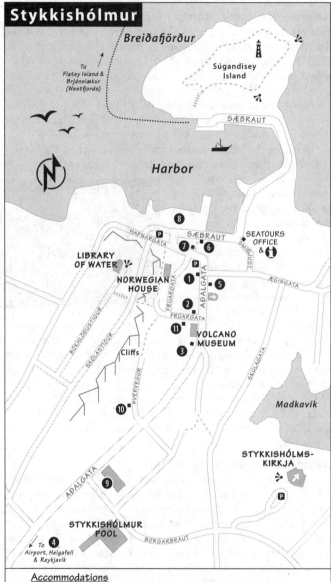

Stykkishólmur

Breiðafjörður

To Flatey Island & Brjánslækur (Westfjords)

Súgandisey Island

SÆBRAUT

Harbor

HAFNARGATA

SÆBRAUT

SEATOURS OFFICE &

LIBRARY OF WATER

NORWEGIAN HOUSE

FRÚARGATA

AÐALGATA

SMIÐJUST

ÆGISGATA

FRÚARGATA

BÓKHLÖÐUSTÍGUR

SKÓLASTÍGUR

VOLCANO MUSEUM

Cliffs

ÞVERVEGUR

SKÚLAGATA

Madkavík

STYKKISHÓLMS-KIRKJA

AÐALGATA

STYKKISHÓLMUR POOL

BORGARBRAUT

To Airport, Helgafell & Reykjavík

Accommodations
1. Hótel Egilsen
2. Akkeri Guesthouse
3. Hótel Breiðafjörður
4. To Stundarfríður

Eateries
5. Narfeyrarstofa
6. Sjávarpakkhúsið

7. Café Nú
8. Food Trucks
9. Grocery

Shopping
10. Leir 7 Ceramics & Smávinir Woodworking
11. Gallerí Lundi

▲Norwegian House (Norska Húsið)

This blackwood-clad home, a block up from the harbor, was the first two-story, wood-frame house in the country, and is still the oldest building in town (from 1832). Unusually intimate for a historical museum, this is worth ▲▲ for anyone who enjoys a time-travel experience.

Cost and Hours: 1,300 ISK; daily 10:00-17:00; Sept-April Mon-Fri 11:00-17:00, Sat 10:00-13:00, closed Sun; shorter hours in winter, Hafnargata 5, tel. 433-8114, www.norskahusid.is.

Visiting the Museum: The ground-floor ticket desk/gift shop is modeled after an old-timey store. Be sure to pick up the explanatory booklet as you enter, and invest some time reading its detailed explanations. Upstairs, the second floor is decorated exactly as it was when it was home to Árni Thorlacius (1802-1891)—a wealthy merchant and owner of a fishing fleet who imported wood from Norway to build this house. You'll feel like

his well-to-do clan invited you in to tour their home: the cabinet, where guests were greeted; the office, its desk strewn with handwritten notes and spreadsheets; the children's bedroom, with toys; and the music room, with a phonograph and small keyboard. It's all exceptionally well preserved and lovingly presented, with original furnishings and no barriers. The grandfather clock still ticks and tocks, and you can practically smell the *lefse* cooking. Don't miss the stairs up to the attic, with more historical bric-a-brac under heavy beams.

▲Volcano Museum (Eldfjallasafn)

In this country with many "volcano museums," this one takes a different tack: Its collection focuses on artistic depictions and other objects relating to famous eruptions from around the world, throughout history—from Vesuvius in ancient times, to Mount Fuji in Japan, to Tambora in Indonesia (erupted in 1815), to Parícutin in Mexico (emerged in the 1940s). You'll see a wide variety of paintings, illustrations, stained-glass windows, and other artistic and scientific representations of volcanic activity across time and cultures, plus a pile of volcanic rocks. This is the collection of highly respected Icelandic volcanologist Haraldur Sigurðsson, whom you can see interviewed in a National Geographic film about the 2010 eruption of Eyjafjallajökull, shown up in the loft. While most visitors are wowed by the Andy Warhol silkscreen print of Vesuvius, Haraldur insists that the collection's most important item is a tiny pile of tektites—tiny black glass pearls—that he discovered in Haiti, which suggested that it was indeed an asteroid strike that killed the dinosaurs (later confirmed by further study in Mexico).

Cost and Hours: 1,300 ISK; daily 10:00-17:00, Sept-April Mon-Sat 13:00-16:00, closed Sun; Aðalgata 6, tel. 433-8154.

Library of Water (Vatnasafn)

The modern, semicircular home that caps the rock above the harbor was the brainchild of American artist Roni Horn. Hike or

drive up and step into the minimalist interior, where you're greeted by sweeping views over the town rooftops and waters of the Breiðafjörður—all refracted through giant, vertical, transparent tubes. Each tube is filled with water from a different Icelandic glacier (an easy-to-miss legend in the hallway identifies them). It's a bit pretentious and may not be worth the cost of entry for some, but the views from the house—or for free, from the bluff nearby—are wonderful.

Cost and Hours: 700 ISK; May-Aug open daily 10:00-17:00 and you can head right up; shorter hours off-season (closed Sun-Wed), and you must first get a door-entry code at the Norwegian House or Volcano Museum; Bókhlöðustígur 19, mobile 865-4516, www.west.is/en/inspiration/services/library-of-water.

Town Church (Stykkishólmskirkja)

Stykkishólmur's dramatic, modern church (consecrated in 1990) caps a rocky bluff over town. Designed by architect Jón Haralds-

son, it seems inspired by the bleached vertebrae of a whale, stretching up toward the heavens. Step inside to appreciate its beautiful, austere, harmonious interior: Lights dangle down from the ceiling, a looming pipe organ fills one wall, narrow windows offer peek-a-boo views over Breiðafjörður, and above the altar is a hauntingly beautiful painting of an ethereal Virgin Mary holding the Baby Jesus (by Kristín Gunnlaugsdóttir).

Cost and Hours: Free, daily 10:00-17:00, at the top of Borgarbraut—just head up the road next to the Bónus supermarket.

Súgandisey Island

From the harborfront, you can't miss this little basalt island, which protects the town harbor from the bracing north wind. In good weather, it's fun to stroll (or drive) out to the base of the island, then climb up to its summit—marked by a little red lighthouse—for fine views back over town. From the top, a trail leads down to the seaward side of the island, then loops back to where you began. This is a great activity for passing the time while waiting for a ferry—which loads up right next to the rock.

Boat Trips on Breiðafjörður

Fanning out from Stykkisholmur's harbor is a bay speckled with islets that are, as locals like to brag, countless. This is part of Breiðafjörður, the vast body of water that separates Snæfellsnes from the Westfjords. If the weather's good and you're up for a boat ride, consider a variety of excursions offered by Seatours. The top option is their unique, popular **Viking Sushi cruise:** You'll go for a sightseeing cruise through the fjord's islands, then your captain pulls up a super-fresh catch of critters—mussels, scallops, sea urchins, and so on—which you'll eat raw, with chopsticks and wasabi (2.5-hour trip-7,800 ISK, in summer there's also a shorter 1.5-hour trip-6,300 ISK; tel. 433-2254, www.seatours.is).

Seatours also runs sightseeing trips to the tiny, remote island of **Flatey,** deep in the fjord. With year-round residents in the single digits, this tiny community (on an aptly named flat basalt rock) has a few colorful houses, a historic church, and—from about mid-July to mid-August—puffins and other sea birds. There's not much to do on the island other than wander, relax, and birdwatch...but that's just perfect for the travelers who choose to come here. Seatours offers trips to Flatey (either just for a peek, or to hang out on the island for a few hours); in summer, you can also spend several hours on Flatey on your way across to the Westfjords (for details, see page 320).

Sleeping in Stykkishólmur

$$$ Hótel Egilsen is a classy boutique hotel, filling a big, stately, red, 150-year-old house in the town center. Its 10 rooms are a tasteful mix of old style and modern amenities, and the main-floor breakfast room comes with a little library (breakfast extra, Aðalgata 2, tel. 554-7700, www.egilsen.is).

$$ Akkeri Guesthouse is a winner, with six modern, tidy, well-priced rooms in a cheery yellow house right in the town center (includes breakfast, Frúargata 1, mobile 844-1050 or 868-1406, akkeri@simnet.is).

$$ Hótel Breiðafjörður is a lesser value—more a simple

guesthouse than a "hotel," it has 12 basic rooms (all with private bathrooms) along the main road into town (Aðalgata 8, tel. 433-2200, www.hotelbreidafjordur.is).

Outside of Stykkishólmur: $$ Stundarfriður, a hotel on a remote ridge a 15-minute drive from town, is a good countryside option, with seven rooms with pleasantly woody decor, plus some small cottages (along highway 54 at Birkilundi 43, mobile 856-2463, www.stundarfridurehf.is). To get here, turn off to the south where the road forks into Stykkishólmur, and follow the unpaved road to Stundarfriður.

Eating in Stykkishólmur

$$$ Narfeyrarstofa is a grand, traditional, old-school place that feels like an aristocratic living room (that's what *stofa* means). They have a menu of traditional classics, plus a wide variety of burgers (daily 12:00-21:00, Aðalgata 3, tel. 533-1119, www.narfeyrarstofa. is).

$$ Sjávarpakkhúsið (Ocean Goods Warehouse) fills just that, with a simple menu of local favorites, including Breiðafjörður mussels, fish-of-the-day, and fish burgers. Their outdoor tables, facing the harbor, are the most enticing choice in town when the weather's good (daily 12:00-22:00, Hafnargata 2, tel. 438-1800).

$ Café Nú (Now), on the ground floor of the hostel a block above the harbor, is one of the coziest, most inviting cafés on Snæfellsnes. They have good coffee and a wide variety of treats, plus breakfast and lunch items such as quiche (daily 9:00-22:00, Hafnargata 4).

Food Trucks at the Harbor: You'll usually find a row of tempting food trucks along the harbor, offering good choices and lower prices in good weather (typically June-early Sept only).

Groceries: Bónus, on the road into town, is the best place on the peninsula to stock up on groceries (generally daily 11:00-18:00, Borgarbraut 1).

Sleeping on Snæfellsnes' South Coast

These are good choices for those who would enjoy settling deep into the countryside on the Reykjavík side of the peninsula. The first two are professional, big hotels, while the other three are more rustic—on family farms. For locations, see the "Snæfellsnes Peninsula" map near the beginning of this chapter.

$$$$ Hótel Búðir—in a gorgeous setting surrounded by water, with views to the southern mountains and all the way to the Snæfellsjökull glacier—is the posh choice. If money is no object, consider one of the 28 luxurious rooms. Its **$$$ restaurant**—open to nonguests—is also a fine spot for a high-end meal (daily 12:00-16:00 & 18:00-22:00, tel. 435-6700, www.hotelbudir.is).

$$$$ Fosshotel Hellnar—a remote outpost of the Iceland-wide chain—has 39 business-class rooms perching above the port of Hellnar. While quite expensive, this is a handy home base for those focusing on the coastline around Hellnar and Arnarstapi (tel. 435-6820, www.islandshotel.is).

$$$ Söðulsholt Cottages is a working horse farm run by Einar Ólafsson and his family. Tucked in the shadow of bulbous Hafursfell mountain where Snæfellsnes meets the mainland, they rent four modern cottages and also offer horseback riding tours (mobile 895-5464, www.sodulsholt.is). Look for the turnoff on the south side of highway 54, about two miles west of the Gerðuberg cliffs.

$$ Lava Water Accommodation is a tidy, cheery, family-run complex on a sheep-and-horse farm, with a variety of accommodations that mix classic and modern: simple, basic rooms with shared bathrooms in one of two houses, plus nine newly built, well-equipped cottages sleeping up to six people each. It's scenically set at the base of a mountain and comes with thoughtful touches such as laundry machines, a children's play area, and kitchens (mobile 893-3333, www.lavawater.is). To reach it from highway 54, find the turnoff for *Miðhraun* between the Snæfellsnes visitors center/Agnið food truck and the Vatnaleið road.

$$ Lýsuhóll is a horse farm with 12 small cottages. Homey and family-run, they also offer home-cooked dinner for guests and offer horseback rides (tel. 435-6716, www.lysuholl.is).

WESTFJORDS

Vestfirðir

If you wish you'd visited Iceland ten years ago, when it was still flying under the tourist radar...go to the Westfjords. Way up here, just shy of the Arctic Circle, you'll find towering bird cliffs, unpaved roads over stunning mountain passes, quirky offbeat sights, a proud fishing heritage, and hardscrabble communities squeezed between mountains and fjords—making a go of it on little sandy spits.

Dangling off the northwest coast of Iceland like a bunch of grapes, the Westfjords feel far from civilization. The entire population of this large region (8,600 square miles, a bit bigger than Connecticut) is about 7,300. This is an ideal destination for those who want to get a taste of rugged, less-touristed Iceland, but don't have the time to invest a full week on the Ring Road. It's the least volcanic part of Iceland, and the closest to Greenland—both geographically and in terms of weather. (It's usually chillier here than in Reykjavík—bundle up!)

Each of this region's many fjords and mountains has a slightly different character: wide, narrow, deep, sandbar-y, wall-like, broken.

Towns occupy the few flat patches—often on a spit of land *(eyri)* jutting out into the fjord. As the towns grew, newer houses were built on the "main" land—but the closer you build to steep fjord slopes, the more danger there is from avalanches and landslides.

The Westfjords were farmed

from early times—in fact, the sagas say that this was where Raven-Flóki set up the first-ever camp on Iceland (in 868)—but the region was never thickly settled. Still, by the early 20th century, the Westfjords had grown into a thriving fishing center, with about double its current population. Its main town, Ísafjörður, boomed, becoming home to a strong workers' movement. But as fish processing became more centralized, the area struggled to retain jobs and people. The Westfjords are also relatively untouristed, providing a welcome respite from the whistle-stop "layover tourism" farther south. Prime season here is shorter than in other parts of Iceland: Before early June and after early September, many businesses are closed up tight. Services are sparser here, too, so keep your gas tank full.

But don't wait too long to visit: Iceland's tourist authorities are determined to develop the Westfjords as the next big "undiscovered" destination. They're digging new tunnels and promoting this area as a far less busy road-trip alternative to the Ring Road. In fact, they're marketing the 530-mile loop around the Westfjords as "Ring Road 2." Visit soon—before all those "layover" visitors decide to extend their trips northward.

GETTING TO THE WESTFJORDS

Depending on how much time you have and what you want to see, consider some combination of the following:

Regular **flights** link Reykjavík's downtown airport to Ísafjörður in about 45 minutes. You can pick up a rental car at the Ísafjörður airport, making this an easy way to get a taste of the Westfjords in a hurry.

The opposite approach is to **drive all the way up from Reykjavík.** Figure at least six hours of driving time—not counting stops—from downtown Reykjavík to downtown Ísafjörður (highway 1, then highway 61). To begin in the Southern Peninsulas, you can drive from Reykjavík to there—also approximately six hours (highway 1, then highway 60; both routes described below).

A better plan—and the one I describe next—is to combine the Westfjords with Snæfellsnes, which is connected by **ferry to the Southern Peninsulas** (from Stykkishólmur to Brjánslækur). It's a similar amount of travel time to driving, but the ferry replaces tedious hours behind the wheel with a relaxed boat crossing.

By Ferry from Snæfellsnes (via Flatey)

With no stops, it's about a 2.5-hour drive from Reykjavík to Stykkishólmur, on the Snæfellsnes Peninsula (see page 291). From Stykkishólmur, the good ship *Baldur* carries passengers and cars across the vast Breiðafjörður to the dock at Brjánslækur on the Westfjords' southernmost peninsula (about a 45-minute drive from Patreksfjörður).

The ferry crossing takes about three hours, including a brief pause at the tiny, flat island of Flatey. The ferry is run by Seatours; it's smart to book ahead (5,760 ISK/person, plus 5,760 ISK for the car; typically runs 2/day in summer, 1/day off-season, check schedule on website; tel. 433-2254, www.seatours.is). The Breiðafjörður is somewhat protected, but the ride can still be rough any time of year. Fortunately, the ferry is big and designed to weather the waves.

Optional Flatey Stopover: The teensy, castaway islet of Flatey is a popular side-trip destination in its own right from Stykkishólmur (described on page 316). If you'd like to stop off on Flatey on your way to the Westfjords, ask about the option to leave your car on the ferry, get off in Flatey for a few hours, then hop on the next onward ferry to find your car waiting for you on the other side. This only works during the summer, when there are two daily ferries.

By Car from Reykjavík

Driving all the way up to the Westfjords from Reykjavík makes sense only if you're not also seeing Snæfellsnes. It's a pretty, though rather uneventful, sometimes quite desolate six-hour drive from Reykjavík to either Ísafjörður or Patreksfjörður. Both options are described below.

Driving from Reykjavík to Ísafjörður

I've outlined the only road route to the Westfjords that's fully paved and well engineered (about 280 miles). You'll branch off the Ring Road just north of Grábrók and can visit one or two West Iceland sights on the way as part of a day's drive (see the Borgarnes & the Reykholt Valley chapter).

Following highway 1 north from Reykjavík, go through **Borgarnes,** then, after **Grábrók crater**—well worth a stop—watch on the left for the turnoff for highway 60.

About 30 minutes farther (about 2 hours from Reykjavík), a turnoff on the right marked *Eiríksstaðir* leads 5 miles down a good gravel road to the spot that was once home to Erik the Red, before he went off to Greenland. A sod-roofed, Settlement Age longhouse has been reconstructed near the site of his farm. Costumed guides lead tours and explain life in the time of the Vikings (May-Sept daily 9:00-17:00, closed off-season, WCs, snack bar with sporadic hours, mobile 899-7111, www.eiriksstadir.is).

Just beyond that turnoff, you pull into **Búðardalur**—a good place for a break, with services and eateries. From Búðardalur, continue north about 30 minutes. After crossing a bridge over Gilsfjörður, veer right toward Hólmavík on highway 61 (over the pass called Þröskuldur—literally "Threshold").

In about 30 minutes, you'll descend to Steingrímsfjörður. When you hit the fjord, a brief detour to the right takes you three miles to a **Sheep Farming Museum**—a working farm with a good exhibit about this agrarian Icelandic industry...and baby lambs (June-Aug daily 10:00-18:00, closed off-season, tel. 451-3324).

North along the fjord is **Hólmavík** (Islet Bay)—the halfway point between Reykjavík and Ísafjörður. Hólmavík has eateries (Restaurant Galdur has a good reputation), a grocery store, and the Museum of Icelandic Sorcery and Witchcraft, which explains the real-life history of Iceland's witch trials, with borrowable English descriptions (Galdrasýning á Ströndum, daily 11:00-20:00, www.galdrasyning.is). Fill up your tank before leaving town—this is the last real gas station before Ísafjörður, 140 miles (2 hours) away.

Then you cross **Steingrímsfjarðarheiði pass** (summiting at 1,440 feet) and descend into the Westfjords. From here, you'll drive highway 61 around five fjords (count 'em)—a scenic but slow and tedious approach to the town of Ísafjörður. Each fjord is actually a narrow offshoot of one huge inlet—Iceland's largest fjord, called Ísafjarðardjúp. The five fjords are mostly unsettled, though you'll periodically pass a remote farm.

Confusingly, the first fjord you reach is also called **Ísafjörður** (Ice Fjord). At the point on its far end is the old school building at **Reykjanes**—on its own, bridged, minifjord called Reykjarfjörður. The school closed in 1995. It was built on the site of a hot-water source that has been used since the 1700s to evaporate sea water for saltmaking; you can stop at the shop to learn more (www.saltverk.com). The school building now houses the **$ Hótel Reykjanes,** with a casual, reasonably priced restaurant and a swimming pool (also a hostel and campground, www.reykjaneswestfjords.is); if you're in a pinch, there's also a gas pump.

A bridge spans the next fjord, **Mjóifjörður** (Narrow Fjord), so you don't have to drive all the way around it. On this remote fjord stands a remote guesthouse on a farm, **$ Heydalur**—a fine place to overnight if completely escaping civilization is your goal (www.heydalur.is; to reach it, turn left onto road 633 after crossing the bridge and drive six miles into the mouth of the fjord). They also have a restaurant, horseback riding, and thermal hot springs filling a rocky pool.

Between the second and third fjords is a farm called **Ögur,** with a café and car cemetery (www.ogurtravel.com).

Next up is **Skötufjörður** (Skate Fjord). Out in the mouth of this fjord is **Vigur** island—popular with puffin watchers during the summer months, when it's served by a boat from Ísafjörður.

Before the next fjord is **Litlibær,** a rustic, turf-roofed farmstead open to visitors. Run by the National Museum of Iceland, its historic interior has been preserved as a fine museum/café (mobile 695-5377, http://litlibaer.is).

Next, **Hestfjörður** (Horse Fjord) is actually two fjords, with the road skipping across a low pass from the main Hestfjörður into the smaller Seyðisfjörður to bypass the strikingly shaped mountain called Hestur (Horse). In Hestfjörður the road narrows to one lane, with passing places marked by *M* signs.

Finally, you'll curl around **Álftafjörður** (Swan Fjord). At its far side, you'll reach **Súðavík** (Slopes Bay)—an outpost of Ísafjörður, under a mountain with a distinctive cockscomb-shaped summit, and home to the Arctic Fox Center (see page 352). From here, it's another 20 minutes into a sixth fjord—**Skutulsfjörður** (Harpoon Fjord)—where the town of **Ísafjörður** lies. You made it!

Driving from Reykjavík to the Southern Peninsulas

If your goal is the Southern Peninsulas, you can drive from highway 1 around Breiðafjörður (about 240 miles). However, be warned that this does involve some unpaved stretches—which makes the Snæfellsnes ferry (described earlier) a tempting alternative.

Start by following the same route described above (highway 1 north from **Borgarnes;** turning left on highway 60; past Eiríksstaðir and through Búðardalur; then across the bridge over Gilsfjörður). Where highway 61 splits off to the right (to *Hólmavík*), instead stay on highway 60 (toward *Patreksfjörður* and *Reykhólar*).

Just a few miles after the highway splits, you'll reach the turnoff for **Reykhólar.** It's nine miles from the main road to this tiny town with a fine spa complex, called Sjávarsmiðjan, with hot pots and seaweed treatments (seaweed is processed in a nearby plant for use in cosmetics, www.sjavarsmidjan.is).

Carrying on beyond the Reykhólar turnoff, it's a long slog past (and, in some cases, in and out of) eight separate fjords that feed into the gigantic Breiðafjörður. Along here, you'll traverse some stretches of unpaved road; figure at least 2.5 hours of driving (120 miles) to Patreksfjörður. This is desolate country, with little settlement.

The next interesting point you'll reach is **Flókalundur,** named for Raven-Flóki—the original Icelandic settler—and home to a nature preserve. From here, it's best to turn south on highway 62 (toward *Brjánslækur*), which lets you stay on paved roads. You'll pass through Brjánslækur (where the ferry from Snæfellsnes arrives), then carry onward over the stunning Kleifaheiði pass to **Patreksfjörður**—the main town and home base for the Southern Peninsulas.

Westfjords Drive

The Westfjords gives you a remote, rugged corner of Iceland with stunning scenery. This huge area is slashed with dozens of fjords, forming a fringe of peninsulas big and small. Mentally, it helps to break the Westfjords down into four main sections (from south to north):

The **Southern Peninsulas,** centered around Patreksfjörður, are famous for the rugged Látrabjarg Peninsula and its thrilling bird cliffs.

The **Central Peninsulas**—the rugged zone between the Patreksfjörður and Ísafjörður areas—are essentially uninhabited and unpaved. This area, which encompasses the many small inlets of the sprawling Arnarfjörður, is home to spectacular scenery, including the dramatic Dynjandi waterfall.

The **Ísafjörður area** fans out from the Westfjords' main town—basically along the southern coast of the huge inlet called Ísafjarðardjúp (*djúp* means "deep"). This area includes the nearby towns of Flateyri, Suðureyri, Bolungarvík, and Súðavík.

The **Northern Westfjords** are almost entirely unpopulated. The terrain of hardy hikers and campers, this area can be subdivided into Snæfjallaströnd (Snowy Mountain Coast, partly accessible by road), Jökulfirðir (Glacier Fjords, accessible by boat from Ísafjörður in summer), and Hornstrandir (the Arctic-facing coast around Iceland's "Horn").

Most visitors focus on the Southern Peninsulas and/or Ísafjörður area, perhaps taking a quick excursion north to Hornstrandir.

Tourist Information: The region's excellent, informative website—Westfjords.is—is worth spending time with as you plan your trip.

Warning for Drivers: The Westfjords (especially between Ísafjörður and Patreksfjörður) have more unpaved roads than anywhere in this book. These roads are passable (slowly) with a two-wheel drive car, but a four-wheel drive and/or a bigger, higher-clearance vehicle is worth considering. The payoff is amazing scenery, an exciting end-of-the-world feeling, and a road trip you'll never forget. Long-term plans call for paving most of these roads; while this will take many years to complete (likely in the late 2020s), you may see construction underway, and roads I describe as "unpaved" may have been improved.

PLANNING YOUR DRIVE

To make the long journey up here worthwhile, the Westfjords deserve at least three days (not counting travel time up and back).

The Westfjords in Three Days or More

Assuming you're starting in the south and moving north, here's a good three-day plan. I've organized this chapter according to this approach.

Day 1: Patreksfjörður and Látrabjarg (Southern Peninsulas)

Based in Patreksfjörður, use this day for a scenic loop down to the tip of the Látrabjarg Peninsula—with its grand bird cliffs—and back again (total drive time: about 3-4 hours). Bring along a picnic, and take a detour to the Rauðasandur beach, ideally at low tide (check tide tables before heading out). Relax this evening in Patreksfjörður, with a dip at the town's exceptional fjord-view swimming pool.

Day 2: Patreksfjörður to Ísafjörður, via the Central Peninsulas

Today's your long, super-scenic driving day (pray for good weather; figure 3-4 hours on the road, not counting stops). Head north from Patreksfjörður and follow the fjords until the pavement runs out—then keep going, over rutted roads and through remote countryside. Stop at fjordside villages, remote hot pots, and scenic viewpoints that strike your fancy. If you're dawdling, have a fish-and-chips lunch in Bíldudalur; if you get an early start, do a picnic lunch at the spectacular Dynjandi waterfall, or a late bowl of soup at the Simbahöllin café in Þingeyri. Arriving this evening in the Ísafjörður area, settle in, and have a celebratory fish feast at the recommended Tjöruhúsið restaurant.

Day 3: Ísafjörður Area

Divide your time today between the humble sights in Ísafjörður itself, and side-tripping to your choice of nearby villages and sights: Arctic Fox Center in Súðavík, historic fishing station at Ósvör Maritime Museum in Bolungarvík, or historic bookstore in Flat-

Westfjords

Accommodations

1. Hótel Reykjanes
2. Heydalur Guesthouse
3. Patreksfjörður Hotels & Eateries
4. Breiðavík Hótel & Restaurant
5. Hótel Látrabjarg
6. Hnjótur Guesthouse
7. Melanes Campground
8. Bíldudalur Hotels & Eateries
9. Ísafjörður Hotels & Eateries
10. Flateyri Hotels & Eateries
11. Kirkjuból í Bjarnardal Rooms
12. Holt Inn

Eateries & Other

13. Litlibær Museum/Café
14. Franska Kaffihúsið
15. Café Dunhagi
16. Simbahöllin Café
17. Einarshúsið Restaurant & Rooms
18. Suðureyri Eateries
19. Kaffi Sól

eyri. Or, if you're feeling adventurous and the weather's good, take an excursion up to the remote Hornstrandir peninsula, or (closer) to Vigur island. To be super efficient, consider flying home to Reykjavík this evening.

Extra Overnight: To see it all and flex with the weather, spend another day in the Ísafjörður area.

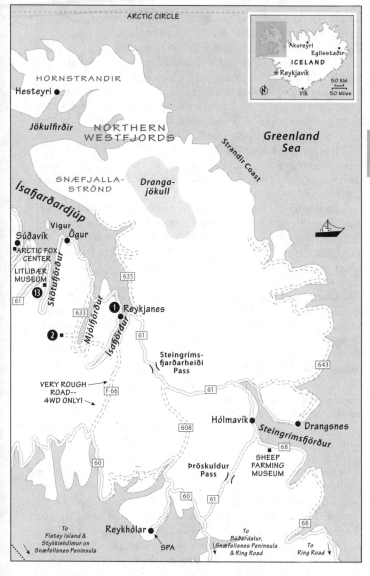

Itinerary Considerations and Strategies

There is a bewildering number of ways to fit the Westfjords into your itinerary. Here are some alternatives and tips to consider:

Combine with Snæfellsnes: This is my preferred option. Thanks to the handy Stykkishólmur-to-Brjánslækur ferry correction, the Westfjords are made to order to combine with the Snæfellsnes Peninsula. Spend a day or two doing Snæfellsnes, then take the ferry up to embark on my three-day plan, above, then head from Ísafjörður back to Reykjavík (by car or plane).

Combine with Ring Road: If you have plenty of time, splice in the Westfjords near the start of your Ring Road drive—as a very long detour between Borgarnes and Skagafjörður.

Long Drive Up and Back: If you love really, really long road trips, drive six hours from Reykjavík to Patreksfjörður; follow my suggested plan up to Ísafjörður; then drive six hours back (mostly via a different route) to Reykjavík.

Reverse the Loop: While I've narrated the Westfjords loop in a clockwise direction, you could reverse it—starting in Ísafjörður, then working your way down to Patreksfjörður. Just hold the book upside-down.

Ísafjörður Express Trip: Fly into and out of Ísafjörður's airport (from Reykjavík's downtown airport) for a day or two, and focus on that part of the Westfjords. You could even day-trip south along the Central Peninsulas as far as Dynjandi waterfall (about 2 hours each way); when open, the new, planned tunnel south from Ísafjörður will shave an hour off this round-trip.

One-Way Car Rental: For efficiency, consider a one-way car rental—for example, pick up your car in Reykjavík, drive up via Snæfellsnes and the Westfjords, and drop your car in Ísafjörður to fly back to Reykjavík.

More Westfjords Tips

For an overview on driving in Iceland—including common road hazards and a map with driving times—see the "Driving" section of the Practicalities chapter.

When to Go (and When Not to Go): The remote Westfjords have a very short tourist season. Prime time is exactly three months: from June 1 until August 31. (As one local told me, "Once the puffins leave...so do the tourists!") You have a week or two of buffer on either end, when most (but not all) businesses are still open. But before mid-May or after mid-September, expect most of what I've described in this chapter to be closed up tight. And the farther off-season you get, it's likely you'll encounter inclement weather and icy roads. I'd skip this region off-season. But if you're determined, do a strategic visit by plane into and out of Ísafjörður, and stick close by.

Two- or Four-Wheel Drive? The Westfjords are the one destination covered in this book where you may want to seriously consider a four-wheel-drive vehicle. While the route I've described is doable with a hardy two-wheel-drive vehicle (and a competent driver with lots of patience), the unpaved sections of road and many mountain passes are more comfortable with four-wheel-drive—if only for the added confidence it gives you.

Road Closures: Given the unpaved nature of many roads in this region, keep a particularly close eye on the road-conditions map at Road.is.

Fuel: Gas stations are few and far between, and many are unstaffed. It may be wise to invest in an N1 prepaid gas card in case your credit card isn't accepted. Given the scarcity of fueling opportunities, keep your tank full—top it off any chance you get.

WCs: Toilets are relatively rare between towns. Keep an eye out for remote countryside hotels or restaurants, some of which may charge a small fee for using the WC (unless you buy something). Given the limited opportunities to relieve yourself here, remember the old adage: Go when you can...not when you have to.

Other Driving Tips: Due to its remoteness—and the sheer amount of driving required—most of the tips for the Ring Road also apply to the Westfjords (see "Ring Road Tips" on page 365).

The Southern Peninsulas

The lonesome Southern Peninsulas—anchored by the teensy town of Patreksfjörður—offer a dramatic taste of the Westfjords. While the villages are humble and many roads are unpaved, this is an ideal spot to disconnect from civilization and commune with Icelandic nature. The big draw here is the Látrabjarg bird cliffs—one of the most spectacular natural sights in a country that's famous for them.

WESTFJORDS

WESTFJORDS

Brjánslækur to Patreksfjörður

The ferry from Snæfellsnes arrives at a place called Brjánslækur, on Vatnsfjörður, which is essentially just a ferry dock. From here, it's about a 45-minute drive to Patreksfjörður (all paved; just turn left onto highway 62 and follow it all the way to town).

Near Brjánslækur: Before heading to Patreksfjörður, consider a quick detour to a sight a few minutes' drive north of the ferry dock. According to the sagas, it was here—along Vatnsfjörður—that Raven-Flóki finally made it to Iceland at the conclusion of his long oversea journey from Norway, following a raven on the final stretch. Laying eyes on an iceberg-filled fjord, he dubbed this place "Ice-land." Today Vatnsfjörður is a nature reserve. The adjacent village is named **Flókalundur**—for Raven-Flóki. Along the road, watch for swimming pool signs to *Flókalaug,* a rustic but pleasant thermal pool overlooking the fjord, with a small lap pool and two hot pools (daily 10:00-12:00 & 16:00-20:00, closed off-season, also a campground with bungalows, www.flokalundur.is).

Onward to Patreksfjörður: This drive comes with a glorious introduction to Westfjords scenery. First you'll curl around the shoreline, past lovely coves and looming mountains. Then you'll begin to gain altitude as you climb over the pass called **Kleifa-heiði**—with stunning scenery across a desolate terrain of jagged rock. At the summit (1,325 feet), you pass a stony monument that seems to honor some great Viking Age warrior. In fact, this is simply part of a local tradition of road crews building a "stone man" upon completing a difficult project—and this road, when completed in 1947, was quite an accomplishment. Coming down the other side of the pass, you'll turn right and curl along the shore of the Patreksfjörður to the town of the same name.

Patreksfjörður

Patreksfjörður (pop. 675) doesn't have a lot of charm—but fortunately, it doesn't need it. While workaday, it's tidy, scenically set, and well cared for, with just enough tourist services to serve as a hub for the Southern Peninsulas—and an exceptionally nice thermal swimming pool, to boot. Like all Westfjords towns, Patreksfjörður is squeezed between its steep mountain and the waters of its fjord, with more buildings filling a spit that sticks out into the water. The town's name honors not St. Patrick, but

a Scottish bishop who provided spiritual guidance to one of this area's original settlers—a reminder of the often-forgotten Celtic influence in the settlement of Iceland.

Orientation: Most hotels and services line up either along the main road into town (Strandgata), or on a higher, parallel road just above (Aðalstræti). The "town center," on the spit, is quieter—home only to the TI and grocery store, and lots of nondescript houses and warehouses.

Tourist Information: The TI is operated by **Westfjords Adventures,** a private tour company. They hand out free maps and brochures, and offer helpful advice for independent travelers in addition to selling their own tours (Mon-Fri 8:15-17:00, Sat-Sun 10:00-12:00; off-season shorter hours and closed Sat-Sun; Þórsgata 8a, tel. 456-5006). Their excursions include trips to the Látrabjarg bird cliffs, Rauðasandur beach, and Dynjandi waterfall, plus boat trips (fishing, kayaking, whale watching) and super-jeep tours (for options, see www.westfjordsadventures.com).

Sights: The town's fine, modern **swimming pool** (Íþróttamiðstöðin Brattahlíð) is one of the nicest small-town pools you'll find—worth ▲▲. With a lap pool, a shallow simmer pool, two hot pools, and a sauna, it fills a glassed-in terrace overlooking the fjord, with grand views from hot water. If you've yet to sample an Icelandic swimming pool, let yourself be tempted to give this  one a try (1,000 ISK, mid-May-mid-Sept Mon-Fri 8:00-21:30, Sat-Sun 10:00-18:00, just before the church on the upper road through town, Aðalstræti 55, tel. 450-2350).

Sleeping and Eating in Patreksfjörður

Sleeping: $$$ Fosshotel Westfjords, at the entrance to town, is the biggest option (with 40 rooms) and the only real hotel in the southern Westfjords (Aðalstræti 100, tel. 456-2004, www.islandshotel. is). **$$ Hotel West,** filling a modern building between the lower and upper roads, has 18 rooms (all with private bathrooms); fjordview rooms cost the same (open year-round, Aðalstræti 62, mobile 892-3414, www.hotelwest.is). **$ Stekkaból Guesthouse** is tidy and stylish, though basic; its 19 rooms, in three buildings near the top of town, all have shared bathrooms, and many have grand views (Stekkar 19, mobile 864-9675, www.stekkabol.net). **$$ Ráðagerði Guesthouse,** a bit closer to the town center, is the simplest option and a lesser value, with 11 rooms, most with shared bathrooms (tel. 456-1560, www.radagerdi.net).

Eating: Options in this town are severely limited, but there is one solid choice: **$$ Stúkuhúsið** fills a cozy old house along the upper road with cramped tables, a well-stocked dessert cooler, and simple but high-quality local dishes, including several fish-of-the-day options. In good weather, they have an inviting deck with grand views over the fjord (Mon-Fri 11:00-22:00, Sat-Sun 12:00-22:00, closed Oct-April, Aðalstræti 50, tel. 456-1404, http://stukuhusid.is).

$$$ Fjall & Fjara, inside the Fosshotel Westfjords, is, well, a hotel restaurant—the space is far from charming, and the food is on the pricey side, but it's convenient and open when others are closed or full (daily, see hotel contact information earlier).

$ Vestur, at the N1 gas pumps at the start of town, has a simple menu of burgers and pizza. While nothing fancy, it's nicer than a gas-station restaurant really needs to be (daily, Aðalstræti 110, tel. 456-1515).

Groceries: Fjölval supermarket, near the TI/Westfjords Adventures in the town center, is bigger (Mon-Fri 8:00-19:00, Sat-Sun 11:00-18:00, Þórsgata 10). **Albina,** near the start of town (on the upper road just past the Fosshotel), is smaller but has a bakery (closed Sun, Aðalstræti 89).

Látrabjarg Peninsula

South of Patreksfjörður is a giant peninsula that's a pincushion of grand scenery and interesting sights. While "Látrabjarg" (LAH-tra-byerg) refers only to the famous seabird cliffs at the far-western tip, for convenience I'm using it to refer to the entire peninsula. This chunk of land—rated ▲▲—offers a full day of stunning scenery, white-knuckle drives, and offbeat attractions, and is made to order for a side-trip from Patreksfjörður.

Note: The Látrabjarg cliffs, at the end of this drive, are best when seabird life is in full fettle—that means roughly mid-June through mid-August. At other times, the drive is still scenic and worthwhile, but you'll see fewer birds. If you're near the edges of this prime season, ask around to find out which birds are currently roosting.

Planning Tips: Most of the peninsula's roads are unpaved, and some are quite rough (particularly near the bird cliffs). While it can be done—carefully—by a confident driver in a two-wheel-drive car, it's more comfortable with four-wheel drive, and it's wise for any driver to err on the side of caution and go slow. And gas up before you go—there's no fuel after you leave Patreksfjörður.

Rauðasandur is better at low tide, when you can see a much

broader and grander expanse of the beach. When planning your day, consider checking the tide tables (ask your hotelier or the TI) to decide when to visit; you'll pass the beach turnoff both in the morning (on your way out) and in the afternoon (on your way back).

LÁTRABJARG PENINSULA LOOP DRIVE

Driving from Patreksfjörður to the Látrabjarg bird cliffs is about 40 miles one-way and takes a bit over an hour at a fast but reasonable pace, not counting stops. (Give it 1.5 hours if you want to keep your fillings.) If detouring down to Rauðasandur beach, allow an additional 45 minutes of driving round-trip. The full round-trip requires at least three hours of driving time (more if you go slow on the rough patches).

• *From Patreksfjörður, head out of town east along the fjord on highway 62 (toward* Brjánslækur*). When you reach the fork at the base of the Kleifaheiði pass, bear right on road 612 toward* Látrabjarg*. After just two miles on this road, pull over at the rusted, beached ship.*

▲*Garðar* Shipwreck

In 1981, this Norwegian-built fishing ship was purposefully beached here after nearly 70 years in service. Today it still remains high and dry, and has become a favorite photo stop for visitors. The Westfjords—and particularly Látrabjarg—are notorious for their shipwrecks; we'll hear more about others as our day goes on.

• *Carry on along road 612. After two miles, on the left you'll see the turnoff for Rauðasandur beach (described next). If the weather's good, but might not last, you may want to get to Látrabjarg bird cliffs first. But if the tide's out at Rauðasandur, now's a good time to detour. (It takes about 45 minutes of driving round-trip, plus however long you spend at the beach.) If you're saving the beach for later, skip ahead to the next stop.*

▲Rauðasandur

This impossibly broad sandy beach—whose name means "Red Sands"—stretches virtually as far as the eye can see between dramatic rocks. At low tide, it's fun to stroll here, and this is one of the best places in the area to spot seals.

The unpaved road to the beach is about six miles one-way. You'll grind up through desolate rocky terrain, then crest a pass into a glorious striped canyon flowing with waterfalls and streams.

Soon the beach comes into view—filling the entire horizon. Reaching the bottom of the pass, you arrive at a fork in the road.

For the best beach access, turn left toward the recommended **Melanes** campground. After about two miles, you'll reach the campground itself, where you can park and pay to use the WCs. Tents fill a grassy field that stretches to the beach; a flock of sheep munch on the grass. From here, you can easily walk out onto the golden sands. If you have time and the tide's out, go for a little hike: Turn left as you face the beach, cross

the creek (there's a little footbridge and stepping stone), and head south—either along the beach itself, or along the rocky area above. You'll work your way toward some dramatic basalt cliffs and sea stacks that rise up from the beach. (You'll need to cross another stream at a makeshift log bridge to get all the way there.) Get as close as the tide will allow—keeping aware that the tide can come in fast, and sneaker waves are always a threat.

Back at the fork in the road, the other option is to head right, toward *Saurbæjarkirkja*. This takes you a mile or so along the beach toward a little black village church; just before it is the popular **$ Franska Kaffihúsið** (French Café), with coffee, waffles, and soup (open for a very limited season only—likely mid-June-mid-Aug, mobile 770-2161). While you can access the beach from this area, it's across a rough grassy area—for easier access, look for a small cove halfway between the café and the turnoff.

• *From the beach, return on road 614 to road 612, where you turned off. Carry on west along road 612. Very soon after the Rauðasandur turnoff, it becomes unpaved—which it will remain from here all the way to the end.*

Enjoy the road as it follows the coastline for about nine miles. You'll cruise past a big, beautiful beach; look down to see a long-abandoned airstrip; spot mussel farms out in the water; and enjoy views of Patreksfjörður town across the fjord. Weaving beneath dramatic vertical cliffs, you'll curl around headlands. Finally, you'll curve inland and pass right through the middle of the teensy settlement called...

Hnjótur

This miniscule community is home to an endearing **folk museum**—officially called Minjasafn Egils Ólafssonar að Hnjóti. (Look for the building with the two old fishing boats out front.) It's named for Egill Ólafsson, a local man who collected an extensive array of artifacts from the southern Westfjords. The heart of the collection includes tools, clothing, books, and an entire fishing boat. The newer section explains a rescue mission that took place when a British trawler ran aground at the Látrabjarg bird cliffs in December of 1947 (you can watch the 45-minute film, *Rescue at Látrabjarg,* that was made about the event). The museum also has pay WCs and a small café (museum entry-1,000 ISK, daily 10:00-18:00, shorter hours in shoulder season, closed Oct-April).

Next door to the folk museum, you'll likely see the remains of a **DC-3 airplane** in front of a hangar. Built in 1944, the US Navy

used this plane in Iceland in the 1970s (its base at Keflavík is now the main international airport) and even aided in the evacuation of the volcano-endangered Westman Islands in 1973. It was retired in 1977—after some 20,000 flight hours, from the Arctic Circle to the Antarctic Circle. So Egill Ólafsson brought it here as a memorial to all US Navy and Marine Corps troops who served in Iceland. Inside the hangar is another airplane—a Russian Antonov AN-2, built in 1967, which was damaged and landed in Iceland in 1993; if you'd like to see it, get the key from Kristinn, who runs the recommended Hnjótur Guesthouse (the brown house at the start of the village). Kristinn is Egill's son, and appreciates visitors who take an interest in his dad's work.

• *Continuing through the village of Hnjótur, in just about a mile you'll hit another crossroads. Keep following road 612 to the left, toward* Breiðavík *and* Látrabjarg. *(The only reason to turn right—toward* Kollsvík—*is to reach the recommended Hotel Látrabjarg, a few miles down this road.)*

From here, the road heads up over the rocky spine of the peninsula—you'll feel like you're on top of the world. Soon you'll start to see beaches on your right. You'll drop down to sea level, and—after about four miles—see signs on the right to...

Breiðavík Beach

This remote, sandy beach, while not as dramatic as Rauðasandur, is framed by big cliffs. Anchoring this area is the recommended Breiðavík Hotel; even if you're not sleeping here, you can stop off for a coffee or a meal in their big dining room.

• *It's seven more miles to the end of the road. You'll climb up over yet another headland, and finally drop down through a tiny village that really, really, really wants to you drive 30 kilometers per hour. From here, follow the low-lying rutted road through beach grasses, smelling sulfur. Just before the road climbs up to one more headland, keep an eye out—on your left—for the little, free WC (signed Brunna for a nearby spring). These are the closest WCs to the cliffs we'll be visiting next.*

Now head up one more steep road and pull into the parking lot for...

▲▲▲Látrabjarg Bird Cliffs

Látrabjarg is one of the world's most famous and most stunning bird cliffs. Even if it weren't for the birds, it would be an epic sight: gigantic cliffs looming up from the churning Atlantic, cast away at the end of the world. But in summer (roughly mid-June through mid-Aug), these cliffs teem with bird life—some 10 different species, an estimated one million birds in total. Even for those who can't tell a fulmar from a kittiwake, it's one of

those destinations that rewards the challenging journey. And as a bonus, it's also the westernmost point in Europe.

Látrabjarg is actually a chain of cliffs that's more than seven miles long, reaching heights of more than 1,400 feet—taller than the Empire State building (or, for Icelanders, six Hallgrímskirkjas stacked on end).

From where you park—near the boxy little Bjargtangar lighthouse—it doesn't seem too exciting. But head up the well-marked path and you'll soon enjoy sweeping views of these towering cliffs. Hike along the cliff-top trail as far as time, energy, and weather allow. The big, jagged cove just up from the parking lot—with views back to the lighthouse—is already quite thrilling. But the farther you go, the more cliffs you'll see. Consider going about a mile to the tall, pointy pinnacle of land that sticks way up, giving you grand views back on the cliffs you've just crossed over.

The best views are from up close to the edge of the cliff—a vertigo-inducing experience even for the very surefooted. Be very careful, as there are no barriers to keep you safe. The ground—with its many ruts and bulbous mounds—seems designed to trip you, and high winds can make it very dangerous to get too close to the edge. If it's not too soggy, you can lie on your stomach and slowly inch your way along the sod until your head is poking over the cliff face.

Once you do, you'll understand why Látrabjarg is so unique

and so important. If you designed a perfect habitat for sea birds, this would be it: A sheer rock cliff with plenty of ledges and alcoves for birds to take shelter and build nests, safe from predators. The walls of the cliff are streaked white, and the smell can be overpowering. Plug your nose and perk up your ears to the call of the different birds. Try to identify as many as you can: puffins, of course, but also guillemots, razorbilled auks, fulmars, and kittiwakes. Delicate little feathers are scattered across the grass, like flower petals after a wedding.

Peering down into the churning surf at the base of the cliffs, imagine the scene in December of 1947, when the British fishing trawler *Dhoon* crashed against these rocks. Local villagers—a volunteer rescue squad—flew into action and came to the cliffs with ropes and pulleys, staging a dramatic rescue and ultimately saving 12 of the crew members. Unbelievably, history repeated itself just a year later, when those original rescuers were re-enacting the event for a documentary. As they were filming the scene, a different British trawler (the *Sargon*) also ran aground on the rocks nearby—so the "actors" had to rescue those crew members, as well.

• *Our trip to the end of the world is complete. To get home, simply go back the way you came—it's about an hour to Patreksfjörður if you take it fast. Go slower for a less jarring ride (and to return your car in once piece).*

Sleeping on Látrabjarg Peninsula

The peninsula has a handful of accommodations options, all of them fairly basic and extremely expensive for what you get. Birders who want to be close to Látrabjarg may enjoy these choices, but I'd rather bunk in Patreksfjörður. All of these are closed off-season.

$$$$ Breiðavík Hótel, a short walk from Breiðavík Beach and a short drive from Látrabjarg, is the region's only real hotel. It has 44 rooms; half of them, in the big main building, are basic and old-fashioned, with shared bathrooms; the rest are in a long, low-lying, motel-like annex, all with views to the beach (tel. 456-1575, www.breidavik.is). Their **$$** restaurant serves lunch and dinner to guests and nonguests alike in a huge dining room (open May-mid-Sept daily 8:00-24:00).

$$$$ Hótel Látrabjarg is a humble little complex hunkered down on a ridge overlooking the fjord, about a 10-minute drive beyond the village of Hnjótur. The 12 rooms (all with private bath) are functional but cozy; you can pay more for grand views (open mid-May-mid-Sept, tel. 419-2810, www.hotellatrabjarg.com).

$$$ Hnjótur Guesthouse, the brown house at the start of the village, has 11 rooms and two cottages. The lodgings are basic and pricey for what you get, but well run by Kristinn (open May-late Sept, mobile 893-8024, www.hnjoturtravel.is).

$ Melanes Campground, stunningly located at the base of a cliff overlooking Rauðasandur beach, has a few camping cabins, plus showers, WCs, and a shared kitchen—a very tempting place to rough it (mobile 783-6600, www.facebook.com/campmelanes).

The Central Peninsulas

Patreksfjörður and Ísafjörður are little pockets of civilization on the otherwise untamed Westfjords. But the road between them is stark and desolate—and stunningly gorgeous. Settle in for a long day of driving, and you'll be rewarded with a panoply of scenery that's breathtaking (in every sense), ranging from mellow fjordside joyriding to high-altitude passes that put you on the rooftop of Iceland.

Beyond the crescendoing scenery, there's not much to see other than a few humdrum villages—and one of Iceland's most dramatic waterfalls (and that's saying something): Dynjandi. Those cascades alone would make it worth the long trip...even if this road weren't the only way to connect the northern and southern Westfjords.

Patreksfjörður to Ísafjörður

The drive from Patreksfjörður north toward Ísafjörður is long (about 110 miles) and slow—allow three to four hours of driving, not counting stops. Roads are paved only as far as Bíldudalur, followed by about 55 miles with no pavement whatsoever—sometimes over mountain passes—to Þingeyri, where you approach the more developed Ísafjörður area. Be patient and enjoy the scenery. Along the way are a few stops worth knowing about, listed in order as you move north, and linked with driving tips.

Tunnel Shortcut: Construction is underway on a tunnel near the northern end of this route, from Borgarfjörður near Dynjandi waterfall up to Dýrafjörður near Þingeyri. When open, this will likely cut 30 minutes or more from your journey. I've described the route assuming the tunnel isn't open, but if it is, you can decide whether you've had enough fjord scenery and cut up north quickly.

• *From Patreksfjörður, head north on road 63, across the headland to the next fjord. While you could detour to the left 2.5 miles here to reach the village of Tálknafjörður (described next), it's skippable if you're in a hurry: Carry on north (staying straight on highways 60 and 63, to* Ísafjörður *and* Bíldudalur*) and skip to the end of the Bíldudalur section.*

Tálknafjörður

This 300-person village is nicely wooded (a rarity in Iceland), and features a long, beachy spit that extends almost entirely across the fjord. The town center-piece is its hilltop modern church with a glass steeple; it also has N1 gas pumps and a nice swimming pool. The house next to the beached fishing boat, on the left side of the road in the middle of town, has a little self-service fresh fish shop that's fun to peruse.

Eating in Tálknafjörður: $$ Café Dunhagi, at the far end of town (near the swimming pool), is the best eatery here—either for coffee and cakes, or for a home-cooked meal; it also doubles as the village TI (Mon-Fri from 14:00, Sat-Sun from 12:00).

Rustic Thermal Bath: For a very rustic Icelandic bathing experience, carry on through town and continue about two miles on the (mostly unpaved) fjordside road. Watch on the right for a little white sign directing you to *pollurinn* ("the pool"). Here, perched on the hillside overlooking the fjord, you'll find a simple little bathing compound, with changing cabins, showers, and four small pools fed with geothermal water. No towels, no chemicals, no kidding (open 24/7, donation box).

• *Past the Tálknafjörður turnoff, follow highway 63 up over the headland between fjords. Cresting the pass, watch on the left for stunning views over several layers of fjords, with Bíldudalur in the foreground. This is the sprawling, many-armed Arnarfjörður. Notice how the valley has been carved into a perfect U-shape by glaciers.*

Descending to fjord level, you'll reach a junction. You can turn right on highway 63 for Ísafjörður—but first, consider bearing straight (on road 619) for a quick visit to...

Bíldudalur

This village of about 200 people is the last real population center you'll see for several fjords...so enjoy it. It's a hardworking town that does a fair bit of fishing (mainly prawns and salmon) and processes mineral-rich algae harvested in the fjord—you'll see these healthy products for sale all over town. But these industries aren't quite enough to sustain a thriving community, and Bíldudalur feels a bit ramshackle—especially down along its busy port. Still, it has gas pumps, an offbeat museum, a good place for a meal before a long drive (don't miss this, unless you're packing a picnic), and a fine little guesthouse—making it worth a quick stop.

The **Icelandic Sea Monster Museum** (Skrímslasetrið Bíldudal) fills a former factory with hyperbolic lore of the many weird creatures that have been spotted in Arnarfjörður. At once corny and bursting with local pride, it's a fun way to pass a half-hour; while there are a few big models of scary Icelandic creatures (including a seaweed-draped hedgehog called the "shore laddie"), the core of the exhibit are eyewitness accounts by local old-  timers (1,400 ISK, late May-mid-Sept daily 10:00-18:00, closed off-season, café, next to the town church—look for the big parking lot along the main drag through town, tel. 456-6666, www.skrimsli.is).

Sleeping in Bíldudalur: $$ Harbour Inn Guest House is surprisingly stylish, modern, and comfortable for a tiny, remote town, with 12 rooms—some with private bathrooms, and some with views over the fjord (also runs fishing tours on the fjord, open year-round, tel. 456-5005).

Eating in Bíldudalur: $ Vegamót Bíldudal has a tiny grocery store up front, and a cozy restaurant in back serving up burgers, sandwiches, and—the big draw—fish-and-chips. Consider this: If heading north, you won't see another real restaurant until Þingeyri, 60 long miles away. This is also where retired fishermen hang out in the morning, trading stories over coffee (summer daily 10:00-22:00, shorter hours off-season, tel. 456-2232).

• *From Bíldudalur, carry on along the fjord on highway 63. From here on out, you'll be driving along the shore of...*

▲▲Arnarfjörður

This gigantic fjord is shaped like a squid—and you'll be curving around its many tentacles for the next couple of hours. The

shape is appropriate, as Arnarfjörður is famous among Icelanders for its sea-monster lore. But for modern-day drivers, the scary part may be the roads: The next 20 miles or so are likely the roughest you'll encounter on this drive. While passable under normal circumstances, they can be quite rutted and potholed: Keep your speed reasonable and do your best to straddle big potholes and gnarly rocks. It's almost entirely unpopulated, so stock up on gas and food before moving on from Bíldudalur. (There are WCs here and there, most convenient at Dynjandi waterfall.) All along the way, you'll be immersed in spectacular Westfjords scenery. Settle in and remember to ease your grip on the steering wheel enough to enjoy it.

Leaving Bíldudalur, enjoy your last three miles of paved roads—ending around where you pass the town airstrip. (Yes, even this tiny little village has regular flights to Reykjavík—an essential lifeline for this remote community.)

Soon after the airstrip, you'll curl back to the apex of **Fossfjörður**—where a little farm perches under a churning waterfall (*foss-fjörður* means "waterfall fjord"). On your way out of this fjord, watch on the left for a little farmhouse with a distinctive pyramid-shaped roof—a fun fjordside photo op.

You'll cut around a headland, then back into the next fjord, **Reykjafjörður**—meaning "smoky fjord." Again, this is aptly named, because here you'll find a natural thermal spring feeding a big outdoor hot pool, called Reykjafjarðarlaug. This is a free place to swim and warm up (changing cabins and WC). Don't miss the smaller, natural stone hot pools, hiding just up the hill behind the giant blue pool.

You'll curl again around a headland, then dive back into **Tro-stansfjörður**. At the bridge at the fjord's apex, it's worth pulling over into the little picnic area for beautiful views of a waterfall that surges toward the fjord.

From here, you'll begin to ascend up, up, up to the plateau called **Dynjandisheiði** (over 1,600 feet) with stunning views back over the entire Arnarfjörður, all the way to where it opens into the North Atlantic. You'll find yourself up in the highlands, far above the fjords. Way up here, the Westfjords look like one big, flat plateau with great divots chipped away from its edges.

In the middle of this desolation, you'll reach a crossroads. Turning right (via highway 62) would take you down to Brjánslækur, where the ferry crosses to Snæfellsnes. Instead we'll turn left (toward *Ísafjörður,* on highway 60; also signed for *Þingeyri,* road 622) to carry on northward. From here, while still unpaved, the road is generally somewhat better—the worst of the potholes should be behind you. Enjoy the mountaintop lakes, rivers, waterfalls, and distant snow fields as you carry on along the top of the world.

Finally you'll begin your descent as you pass a *Dynjandi Conservation Area* sign. Twist your way down, following streams and waterfalls to the fjord. Soon you'll begin to see the gigantic Dynjandi waterfall on your left.

• *Just before you reach the water, turn off on the left and park in the lot for...*

▲▲Dynjandi Waterfall

Look up—way up, to the top of the cliff, where massive cascades pour over the edge of rock. *Dynja* means roughly "thunder," so this is essentially "Thundering Waterfall." It's the ultimate expression of Iceland's countless bridal-veil cascades.

But Dynjandi (DIN-yan-dee) isn't just one waterfall—it's several. You'll park near the base of the lowest one (big, free lot; WCs, donation requested), then hike your way up past a series of smaller falls. Each one is identified by name. A rocky, uneven, steep path leads all the way up to the biggest waterfall—hike up as far as you can. Standing at the plateau in front of the massive main falls, you feel the power—and the spray. Beneath you, water hurls itself through a chute of rock as it hopscotches down toward the fjord. From the top, you also enjoy grand views over the next fjord.

• *Back on the main road, follow the fjord around the headland, then back into* **Borgarfjörður.** *Near the apex of this fjord, they're building* *a tunnel through the middle of the mountain to the next fjord up; once complete (possibly in 2020, barring delays), this will provide you with a major shortcut—zip through the tunnel, popping out on Dýrafjörður near Þingeyri (at the end of this section).*

Until that tunnel is finished, you'll have to stick to the unpaved road along the north shore of Borgarfjörður. It's about 13 miles to our next stop, Hrafnseyri, at the base of the pass to the next fjord. Keep an eye across the fjord on your left, for distant views of Dynjandi waterfall.

Just before the road cuts up away from the fjord, watch on the right for the turnoff to...

Hrafnseyri

This isolated corner of the Westfjords (called "Raven Spit") was the birthplace of Icelandic founding father Jón Sigurðsson, who

lobbied the Danish government on behalf of independence during the 19th century. Today his birthplace is marked by a red-and-white church, a trio of turf-roofed houses, and a modern museum honoring this Icelandic hero—offering thoughtful exhibits and a break from your long drive (free, June-Aug daily 11:00-18:00, likely closed off-season, tel. 456-8260, www.hrafnseyri.is).
• *Just past Hrafnseyri, the road turns up away from the water—you're finally leaving Arnarfjörður behind as you twist up over the pass called...*

Hrafnseyrarheiði

This pass ("Raven Spit Heath") corkscrews up to more than 1,800 feet. While unpaved, the road is well-packed gravel, allowing fairly

good progress; the scenery is spectacular, though the lack of guardrails at certain twisty sections of road can inspire a death-grip on the steering wheel.
• *Winding down to sea level once more, you'll go over one more small rise, then return to civilization (and paved roads!) in the village of...*

Þingeyri

This small town (THING-yeh-ree, pop. 249) looks out over the Dýrafjörður from its commanding midfjord position. Its name (meaning "Assembly Spit") suggests this was one of the earliest population centers in the Westfjords, and the location of the area's *þing* (a smaller version of the Iceland-wide gathering at Þingvellir). Today it's yet another humble small town, worth a quick stop to gas up and grab a bite.

Eating in Þingeyri: $ Simbahöllin café, in an old general store from 1915, is one of the most appealing eateries in the Central Westfjords, and a great place to recover from a long drive. In addition to great coffee, they have good soup and a waffle iron cranking out fresh, crispy waffles. The café is rustic, charming, and modern all at once; you'll see it on the right in the town center, on the main drag (daily 10:00-18:00, until 22:00 mid-June-Aug, closed early Sept-mid-May, mobile 899-6659, www.simbahollin.is).

• *We're almost finished with the drive. From Þingeyri, head toward Ísafjörður on (paved) highway 60. You'll curl around the fjord, cut across its tip on a bridge, then head back up the other side—about 11 miles total. From here, highway 60 crosses up over the headland, passes two recommended accommodations (described under "Sleeping in the Countryside, near Flateyri" at the end of this chapter), then enters the tunnel to Ísafjörður and passes the turnoff to Suðureyri—all described in the next section.*

But before you head that way, consider one last detour: Just before the road leaves the fjord, watch for the turnoff on the left to Núpur. If you follow this four miles, on the right you'll reach...

Skrúður Botanical Garden

Directly across the fjord from Þingeyri, this little green patch is tucked up against steep cliffs. It's a "school garden" originally created in 1909 by a local parish priest to teach youngsters how to grow different types of plants. Form the parking lot, drop a donation in the box and let yourself through the gate into an inviting oasis of carefully labeled plants, gurgling fountains, and chirping birds. The small white greenhouse in the middle of the

garden has more information about the history of the place.

Ísafjörður

By Westfjords standards, Ísafjörður (EE-sah-FYUR-thur, meaning "Ice Fjord") is a thriving metropolis. While more functional
than charming, Ísafjörður has a spectacular setting—filling a broad
spit in the middle of a fjord—and pockets of historic charm, in the
form of colorful old shiplap houses. And it's the hub for transportation and services in this region...so you couldn't avoid it even if you
tried. Fortunately, it's a pleasant place to spend time. Time-travel
to the rustic early 20th century of weather-beaten fishermen at the
Westfjords Historical Museum, have lunch or dinner in an old tar
house, gaze up at the dramatic cliffs in every direction, and keep an
eye out for whales and puffins.

Orientation to Ísafjörður

With about 2,600 inhabitants, Ísafjörður is easily the biggest town
in the Westfjords. The main part of town fills a huge spit called
Eyri in the middle of Skutulsfjörður, with more homes clambering
up the base of the nearby mountain, and a few more neighborhoods
and services (including the big Bónus supermarket) strung along
the coastline to the west, toward the tunnel to points south. The
airport is across the fjord from the town center, a seven-minute
drive from town.

The main street into town has all of the major services (such
as the N1 gas station and Nettó supermarket)—but the next street
one block inland hogs all the charm. The main walking street
through town (Aðalstræti/Hafnarstræti) runs parallel to the main
traffic drag; that's where you'll find most of my recommended eateries and accommodations.

Ísafjörður anchors a small metropolitan area—known as Ísaf-
jarðarbær—that includes four smaller towns: Bolungarvík, Súðavík,
Suðureyri, and Flateyri. Each town is about 20 minutes by car from
Ísafjörður, and each has its own character and sights (explained at

the end of this chapter). The total population of this area is about 4,000—in other words, one out of every two Westfjorders.

Tourist Information: The very helpful TI hides at the far end of the big, gray, historic Edinborgarhúsið building on the main road into town (June-Aug Mon-Fri 8:00-18:00, Sat-Sun until 15:00; Sept Mon-Fri 8:00-17:00, Sat-Sun until 12:00; shorter hours off-season and closed Sat-Sun; Aðalstræti 7, tel. 450-8060).

ARRIVAL IN ÍSAFJÖRÐUR

Arriving in town by car, you'll follow the fjord's shore, then reach the big roundabout at the start of the town's spit (with the N1 gas station and modern church). Turn right here and follow the waterfront road into town; you can park near the TI (in the long, historic gray building on your left) or continue through the warehouse zone to park at the historic stand of buildings and the Westfjords Heritage Museum.

If arriving by **plane,** you'll find car-rental desks at the airport; it's a seven-minute drive around the fjord into town. A Flybus meets arriving flights to bring passengers to the Hótel Ísafjörður in the town center (1,000 ISK); buses return to the airport from the hotel about 50 minutes before flights depart.

Cruises dock in a warehouse zone along the east side of the town's peninsula; the TI and the historic houses at the Westfjords Heritage Museum are each within an easy five-minute walk (walk straight ahead from the ship; when you reach the busy waterfront road at the opposite side of the peninsula, turn right for the TI or left for the historic area).

Tours from Ísafjörður

Whale-Watching, Sightseeing Cruises, and More

This town is the jumping-off point for various activities around the Westfjords. Popular choices include whale-watching trips (either on traditional boats, or in a high-speed, rubber-hulled RIB); sightseeing cruises; and super-jeep drives up into the rocky highlands. Cruise passengers and people flying in for the day from Reykjavík find these tours a handy way to pack a lot in. The dominant companies are **West Tours** (next door to the TI, Aðalstræti 7, tel. 456-5111, www.westtours.is) and the more active **Borea Adventures** (a block away at Aðalstræti 17, tel. 456-3322, www.boreaadventures.com). Peruse your options online; it's smart to book ahead.

Tours to Hornstrandir

Both of the companies listed above also run ferry service and guided tours to Hornstrandir, the exceedingly remote nature-reserve peninsula at the northern fringe of the Westfjords. Hornstrandir has no towns or services—there's one guesthouse and lots of rugged camping—but in summer, it bursts forth with bird life. (Outside of May-Aug, it's off-limits without special permission.) The most efficient choice is to take a guided all-day **hiking tour** (including the boat ride there and back; options range from about 35,000 ISK to 50,000 ISK). Both companies also run transportation-only **ferry service,** typically used by people who are hiking in to do some camping. The nearest point (and most popular entry point), Hesteyri, is about an hour's ride from Ísafjörður. It's often possible to head over and back on the same day, but you may need to mix-and-match rides—check both companies' websites for full schedules. (A third company may begin operating boats from nearby Bolungarvík in the future—ask at the TI.)

Tours to Vigur

As a simpler alternative—but along similar lines—consider a boat trip to the tiny island of Vigur. It's closer, shorter, and in summer you'll see puffins (West Tours does a 3-hour round trip for around 12,000 ISK; see listing above).

Sights in Ísafjörður

▲Westfjords Heritage Museum (Byggðasafn Vestfjarða)

This humble yet exceptional museum—housed in a historic 1784 trading-post warehouse—strives to educate visitors about the unique Westfjords way of life, particularly as the region flourished thanks to the fishing industry in the early 20th century. The main-floor exhibit views history through the eyes of Karítas Skarphéðinsdóttir, who was born in this region in 1890, married a  much-older man at age 16, and later became active in the local workers' movement of the 1930s. Upstairs are eclectic exhibits about Westfjords life: tools for barrel-making and ship-building; a (stuffed) polar bear that drifted over on an iceberg from Greenland and was shot nearby in 1963; and a mesmerizing dramatized film about what it was like, a hundred years ago, to work on an open fishing boat out in the fjord. Together the exhibits do a fine job of presenting history through the fascinating stories of local individuals. Up in the attic are exhibits about how Westfjorders have taken full advantage of the region's sparse natural resources, from shellfish to driftwood to eider duck down.

Cost and Hours: 1,300 ISK, daily 9:00-17:00, closed Oct-mid-May, Neðstikaupstaður, tel. 456-3291, www.nedsti.is.

Nearby: The museum is part of a little ensemble of historic buildings called Neðstikaupstaður. However, only the museum and the recommended Tjöruhúsið restaurant, next door, are open to the public. The other two buildings are now the homes of local museum curators.

▲Ísafjörður Town Stroll

There's not much to see in this humble town, but this 20-minute stroll is designed to help you get your bearings.

Begin at the TI. Exiting, turn left, then left again to head down Aðalstræti—the town's historic main drag. The big gray building on your left, which houses the TI, is called Edinborgarhúsið—the "Edinburgh House," recalling when this was a warehouse engaged in long-distance trade with that Scottish city. Halfway down this building, duck in the door on your left to see old-timey photos of Ísafjörður from 1895, 1923, and 1966—illustrating the town's development. (There are also WCs on this hallway.)

Back out on Aðalstræti, carry on down the street—appreciating the **colorful old houses** on the right side, which are some of the town's most historic (notice the turquoise one marked *1816*), and still inhabited.

You'll pass several cute shops and historic buildings (watch on the right, one block away, for the chalet-style Ásbyrgi house from 1910). On the following block, on the left is the office for Borea Adventures, and on the right are two recommended cafés: hip Heimabyggð, then traditional Gamla Bakaríið.

At the end of the block is Ísafjörður's **main plaza**—with benches, the big Hótel Ísafjörður on the left, and the Iceland-wide Eymundsson bookstore chain straight ahead (in the rounded building, marked *Bókhlaðan*).

Bear left at the bookstore and head down the street (now called Hafnarstræti). Halfway down on the left is the endearing little **Museum of Everyday Life** (Hversdagssafn). The curators strive to showcase the quotidian experience of local community members—entirely based on actual interviews with local people. While the specific exhibits can change, they always shine a light on normal people's lives. For example, use the headsets to hear the stories of various shoes, flip through old photos with stories from the people who took them, or watch a series of films that elevate the everyday to a place of honor (700 ISK, June-mid-Sept Mon-Fri 10:00-17:00, Sat 11:00-14:00, closed Sun and off-season, Hafnarstræti 5, www.everydaylife.is).

Next door is the **Hamraborg** convenience store, the local favorite for a hot dog or soft-serve cone. Just beyond that, also on the left, is the big discount **Nettó** supermarket and post office.

Keep going a few short blocks past these modern buildings,

watching on the right for side streets with colorful historic houses (such as Mánagata); you'll also pass the recommended Húsið restaurant.

You'll wind up at Ísafjörður's can't-miss-it modern yellow **church** (Ísafjarðarkirkja). Built in 1995 to replace an old wooden church that burned down, it's still surrounded by the original churchyard. The church remains somewhat controversial both for its modern aesthetic (beige pebble Cubist-meets-Sydney Opera House?), and because its construction required the relocation of several old graves. It's sometimes open on weekdays; if so, step inside its serene, austere Lutheran interior, with a flock of red birds taking flight over the main altar.

Continue past the church, then cross the street to the **monument to fishermen** at the corner of the nearby lawn. The stately building behind the monument is the **Culture House**—today home to the town library and cultural center. It was built in 1925 as a hospital by state architect Guðjón Samúelsson, who designed buildings all over Iceland (including Reykjavík's  landmark church). Today it's open to the public who want to escape the rain and cold, use WCs and free Wi-Fi, check out some historic photos of Ísafjörður, and—at the top of the staircase—see old hospital equipment and an exhibit on the building's original use (free, Mon-Fri 12:00-18:00, Sat 13:00-16:00, closed Sun).

Our Ísafjörður walk is finished. You can head back the way you came, or duck uphill across the street from the Culture House for a stroll through the town's little, well-kept park.

Sleeping in Ísafjörður

Accommodations in this town are, generally speaking, unimpressive (as you'll see if checking online reviews). I've listed a few options here, though I prefer sleeping in the nearby countryside—see my "Sleeping in the Countryside, near Flateyri" options at the end of this chapter.

$$$ Hótel Ísafjörður is a big, sterile, business-class hotel right in the heart of town, with 36 rooms facing the main plaza (Aðalstræti 400, tel. 456-4111, www.isafjordurhotels.is). This hotel manages two other properties in town: **$$$ Hótel Horn,** a couple of blocks away, has 24 rooms for about the same price, with reception and breakfast at the main hotel (Austurvegur 2). **$$ Gamla**

Gistihúsið ("Old Guesthouse"), also nearby, has nine simpler rooms with shared bathrooms; in summer, they have their own reception and breakfast, but otherwise check in at the big hotel (Mánagata 5, tel. 456-4146).

$$ Gentlespace is a better-value choice, with a variety of apartments around town, plus three rooms that share bathrooms at their main guesthouse (Hlíðarvegur in the upper part of town, mobile 892-9282, www.gentlespace.is).

Eating in Ísafjörður

$$$$ Tjöruhúsið (Tar House) is a delicious and memorable, if touristy, dining experience at the historic tip of Ísafjörður. Inside a creaky old tar factory (from 1781) next to the Westfjords Heritage Museum, diners belly up to long, shared, rustic tables and dig into a smorgasbord of outrageously delicious fish dishes. Don't come here for an intimate, romantic meal—it's lively and convivial, and you're expected to get to know your tablemates. You'll begin with a bowl of delectable fish soup, then work your way through a buffet of intensely flavorful, freshly caught fish dishes, all served in sizzling skillets. The food is simply delicious, with a combination of traditional Icelandic flavors and palate-pleasing international ones. Although designed entirely for visitors, it's intimate and family-run, and both the historic atmosphere and the food quality are tops. While it's pricey and requires lots of waiting in line for the various dishes, it's worth the price and the wait. Reservations are required (3,500-ISK lunch buffet served daily 12:00-14:00; 6,000-ISK dinner seatings at 19:00 and 21:00; closed Nov-Easter; Neðstakaupstað, tel. 456-4419, www.tjoruhusid.is).

$$ Húsið, near the start of Hafnarstræti behind the N1 gas station, fills an old house with a welcoming atmosphere and reasonably priced burgers, pizzas, and fish of the day (daily 11:00-late, open year-round, Hafnarstræti, tel. 456-5555).

Bakeries: Two bakeries on the main street (Aðalstræti)—with entirely different personalities—offer good coffee, sandwiches, and sweets. **$ Heimabyggð** (meaning "a feeling of home") is the hip, youthful choice, with a short menu of delicious grilled sandwiches and comforting soup—all vegetarian—and a classic woody atmosphere (daily 8:00-18:00, Tue and Thu until 24:00, Aðalstræti 22b, mobile 697-4833). **$ Gamla Bakaríið,** a few doors down, is an old-school coffee-and-cakes shop that also has a variety of sandwiches (Mon-Fri 7:00-18:00, Sat until 16:00, closed Sun, Aðalstræti 25, tel. 456-3226).

Hot Dogs and Fast Food: $ Hamraborg is a locally beloved convenience-store-slash-fast-food joint, with typical Icelandic hot dogs, skippable pizzas, and a mean soft-serve toppings bar. With diner-like seating and a little slot-machine corner in the back, this feels like a perfect slice of small-town Icelandic life...like a 1950s soda fountain is to Americana (daily 8:00-23:30, Hafnarstræti 7, tel. 456-3166).

Brewpub Tasting Room: Dokkan Brugghús is not to be missed by beer lovers. This tasting room, hiding in a warehouse zone near the cruise terminal, has six beers on tap that are made on the premises (no food, tasting flights available, Mon-Fri 10:00-18:00, Sat-Sun from 13:00, may be closed Sun off-season, Sindra-gata 11, tel. 788-1980).

Supermarkets: Nettó supermarket is right on the main drag in the center of town (daily 10:00-19:00, Hafnarstræti 9), while a huge **Bónus** is a five-minute drive out of town (slightly shorter hours, near the turnoff for the tunnel to Flateyri/Suðureyri).

Towns near Ísafjörður

You'll quickly exhaust the town of Ísafjörður's sightseeing, but it's an easy and scenic 20-minute drive to any one of four neighboring settlements: Bolungarvík, Súðavík, Suðureyri, and Flateyri.

Collectively, this area is known as Ísafjarðarbær. All of these towns grew in the years around 1900, as they exploited the rich fishing grounds not far offshore. You'll sense this nautical vibe wherever you go in this region, and if you keep an eye out on the roads between fjords, you'll spot what look like big, open-air barns on the slopes near the sea. These are used for fishing equipment storage and to air-dry fish to create the Icelanders' beloved *harð-fiskur*—a sort of "fish jerky" that has been pounded flat and dried, then eaten with butter.

How to choose? Animal lovers flock to Súðavík's Arctic Fox Center. Bolungarvík is the best place to learn about traditional fishing lifestyles—and to walk through a sod-roofed fishermen's settlement. Flateyri has a historic bookstore and perhaps the most scenic drive—combining a trip through the region's tunnel (see sidebar) with one of the area's most scenic fjords (Önundarfjörður). Suðureyri is perhaps the least worth a visit—though it has a fine fish restaurant.

Getting There: Each town is in a different direction, but all are well signed from Ísafjörður. To reach Súðavík or Bolungarvík, you'll simply head around the headlands to the next fjord (the Bolungarvík road includes a standard tunnel); to reach Flateyri or Suðureyri, you'll use a somewhat unconventional tunnel—read the sidebar to be ready for it.

WESTFJORDS

Navigating the Ísafjörður-Flateyri-Suðureyri Tunnel

A unique tunnel was built in 1996 to string together these three remote fjordside communities. It's a bit tricky for novices—you could think of it as a "three-way, one-lane tunnel." But there's a clear and easy protocol for using it, and once you master it, it's a snap.

Coming from Ísafjörður, the tunnel begins as a standard two-lane road. But when you reach the fork (right for Suðureyri, stay straight for Flateyri), it reduces to one lane, with passing places. If you are driving from Ísafjörður *to* Flateyri or Suðureyri, you must give way to oncoming traffic by pulling right into the bays marked with a large lighted *M*. If you are **coming from Flateyri or Suðureyri,** you have priority and can drive straight through. However, it's polite to show consideration to oncoming cars who don't pull over in time—it can be hard to judge the distance accurately.

At the beginning and end of the one-lane sections are short curved stretches where you can't see oncoming traffic. In these places a sensor has been set up and a square, nonstandard red *STOP – bíll á móti* sign turns on if it detects a car coming the other way, directing cars traveling in the nonpriority direction to pull into the last passing bay.

It sounds tricky...until you do it, when you'll see that it's pretty straightforward. To avoid trouble, err on the side of pulling into a passing bay too soon rather than too late. If you make a mistake, the worst thing that can happen is that you might have to back up briefly. To see a video of what it's like, search for "Vestfirdir Tunnel" on YouTube.

Súðavík

This small town, with just 264 people, has few services but two crowd-pleasing sights. Facing out to the wide Ísafjarðardjúp, Súðavík feels more exposed than the other towns. The main thing it's known for, tragically, is a devastating 1995 avalanche that wiped out many buildings and killed 14 people (including eight children). The destroyed houses were rebuilt—but in a different, less avalanche-prone location. Look for a memorial to those killed in the avalanche, just below the Raggagarður playground.

Sights in Súðavík: The **Artic Fox Center** seeks to educate both Icelanders and visitors about this remarkable creature—Iceland's only native land mammal—which ekes out a challenging existence in some of the harshest conditions on earth. It's worth ▲▲ for those interested in animals. The exhibits, filling an old house, feature several stuffed foxes, adorable photos, thoughtful videos, and lots of information about how magnificently adapted the arctic fox is to its conditions (it has some of the thickest fur in the animal kingdom). The foxes thrive across the fjord on the remote Hornstrandir peninsula, where there's no human presence for most of the year; due to a scarce food supply, the mortality rate for these animals is about 80 percent. Upstairs, you'll learn about the tense relationship between Icelandic farmers and the foxes, who've been hunted going all the way back to the Settlement Age. While Icelanders think of the foxes as savagely attacking innocent sheep, the center's manager Sæmundur likes to point out that they're simply following their instincts and typically pick off only sick or weak lambs that wouldn't survive anyway. The highlight for most visitors is out back, where a pen holds live arctic foxes rescued from the wild—often young, orphaned foxes that would not have otherwise survived. While well worth a visit, be aware that there may not always be live foxes, and the center can be deluged from time to time by big bus tours—consider calling ahead to plan your visit accordingly (1,200 ISK, daily 9:00-18:00, May and Sept 10:00-16:00, closed Oct-April, tel. 456-4922, www.arcticfoxcentre.com). It's at the far end of town—watch for signs on the right.

Raggagarður—a big, fun playground (with WCs)—is Súðavík's other big draw. Watch for it up above the main road, on the right, in the center of town (look for the big swan-shaped arches).

Bolungarvík

This larger town (pop. 931) feels like the end of the world—facing towards the open Atlantic, and often bearing the full brunt of oncoming storms. While the town itself is a sprawl of characterless modern housing, the setting is striking, with giant mountains thrusting up from a black sand beach. The main reason to come here is for its interesting Ósvör Maritime Museum —the best place in the region to get a feeling for traditional fishing lifestyles. Bolungarvík also has a nice town swimming pool (you'll see its waterslide on the left on your way into town) and a pleasant natural history museum in the town center.

Sights in Bolungarvík: The **Ósvör Maritime Museum**—worth ▲—brings to life a time, not that long ago, when hardworking fishermen lived and worked here in practically Settlement Age conditions. The "museum" is an open-air collection of three sod-roofed buildings across the bay from the town center—as you exit the tunnel coming from Ísafjörður, immediately turn right (signed for *Ósvör*) and watch for them on the seaward side of the road, tucked along a rocky beach. Arriving at the open-air museum, you'll usually be greeted by a docent clad in traditional fishermen's gear, made of sheepskin, who can explain what you're seeing. Ósvör was a *verbúð* (seasonal fishing station) that was first set up here in the 1800s, when there were no towns in the

Westfjords. Farm laborers were sent here for part of the year. The station eventually fell into disuse but was rebuilt as a museum on the original foundations in 1988. The buildings include a fish-drying shed *(hjalli);* a fisherman's hut; and a salting house. You'll also see an open fishing boat down on the beach, and lots of equipment. If this place grabs your imagination, read Jón Kalman Stefánsson's *Heaven and Hell,* which is set here (1,200-ISK combo-ticket includes Natural History Museum, daily 10:00-16:00, closed Sept-May).

Bolungarvík's **Natural History Museum,** an afterthought to Ósvör, is worth a visit if you have time to head into the town center. Tucked upstairs from the Kjörbúð grocery store, it consists of a large, good collection of stuffed birds and animals (including a polar bear that was shot nearby); exhibits on minerals; the jawbone of a blue whale; and an explanation of the tunnel to Ísafjörður and its construction (covered by Maritime Museum ticket, Mon-Fri 9:00-17:00, Sat-Sun from 10:00, closed Sept-May, Vitastígur 3, tel. 456-7507).

Eating in Bolungarvík: $$ Einarshúsið, the big gray building just around the corner from the Natural History Museum, is a handy choice for a meal in town, with a cozy, old-timey interior (also houses TI and rents rooms, closed Tue, tel. 456-7901, www.einarshusid.is).

Nearby Hikes: If the weather's great and you'd enjoy a seaside stroll, you can walk along the **old coastal road**—now closed to traffic—that runs between Ísafjörður and Bolungarvík. From either end of the tunnel, turn off and drive around the headland until you can't drive anymore, then park and walk as far as you like (on the Bolungarvík side, it's just past the Ósvör Maritime Museum). But be warned: They dug the tunnel because of the many dangerous rockslides on this road, so keep your eyes open and ears alert as you walk.

Another popular choice (again, in good weather) is to head beyond Bolungarvík and up the unpaved road to **Bolafjall** mountain, with sweeping views over the region.

Suðureyri

Suðureyri ("South Spit," pop. 264) is a sleepy, pleasant-enough halibut-fishing town near the mouth of the long, narrow Súgandafjörður. While a fun drive for completists, it's perhaps the least appealing of the four towns near Ísafjörður.

The town's main attraction is **$$ Fisherman,** a trendy complex of hotel and restaurants that celebrate the local fishing tradition with modern style—big, black-and-white photos of grizzled old fishermen. They have 21 rooms—some with shared bathrooms (Aðalgata 14, tel. 450-9000, www.fisherman.is). They also have a small **$ café** with light fish meals (daily 11:00-23:00), and—across the street—a more serious (and pricier) **restaurant** with quality dishes made with fresh-caught fish (daily 18:00-21:00). If you're coming all the way to Suðureyri, you might as well combine it with a bite here—but call ahead, as they get busloads of visitors from Ísafjörður and can be unexpectedly slammed.

Flateyri

This town (its name literally means "Flat Spit," pop. 201) is the main settlement on Önundarfjörður. While it's a hardworking fishing village like the others, Flateyri has a bit more of an artistic bent.

The town's main claim to fame is the endearing **Old Bookstore,** family-run since 1914 and currently managed by Eyþór Jóvinsson (watch for it on the way into town—

marked *Bræðurnir Eyjólfsson*). Eyþór sells some old and some new books, and you can pay a small donation to tour the family's old apartment (daily mid-May-Aug 10:00-17:00, off-season typically open only Sat afternoons but you can call to see if Eyþór can let you in, mobile 840-0600, www.flateyribookstore.com).

The other interesting thing to see in Flateyri is the **berm** protecting the town from another avalanche (like Súðavík, the town was devastated by one in 1995—killing 20 people). From town, look up to the hillside and you'll notice this protective barrier.

Sleeping in Flateyri: $ Litlabýli Guesthouse is a charming little guesthouse right in the town center, elegantly run by Kristín and Ívar (Ránargata 2, mobile 848-0920, www.litlabyli.com).

Sleeping in the Countryside, near Flateyri: Considering the relatively low quality and value of accommodations in Ísafjörður, consider bunking in the countryside at one of these two places.

WESTFJORDS

About five minutes apart, they're both a 20-minute drive from Ísafjörður, but buried deep in bucolic fjordland scenery.

$$ Kirkjuból í Bjarnardal is along the pass leading from Flateyri toward Þingeyri. It fills a rustic old house with six cozy rooms, some with shared baths (tel. 456-7679, www.kirkjubol.is).

$$ Holt Inn is a bit closer to the fjord, filling an old boarding house with 11 rooms—all with private bathrooms. While the building feels a bit empty and the breakfast is uninspired, the serene countryside setting is enticing (tel. 456-7611, www.holtinn.is).

Eating in and near Flateyri: $ Bryggjukaffi, down by the harbor, is a good place for homemade soup (daily 11:30-18:00, weekends only off-season, Hafnarstræti 4, mobile 861-8976).

$$ Kaffi Sól is a charmingly no-frills local spot on a farm just as you turn off on the Flateyri road; they have coffee and sweets, plus home-cooked traditional dinners (daily 13:00-20:00, closed off-season, mobile 866-7706).

THE RING ROAD

THE RING ROAD

Hringvegurinn

Circling the Ring Road is the ultimate Icelandic road trip. You will see the country in all its moods: the deep valleys and fjordside hamlets of the north, the not-quite-bustling second city of Akureyri, the volcanic landscape around Mývatn, the desolate Eastfjords, the glacial landscape of the southeast, and the gentle, green South Coast. Be prepared for long days behind the wheel, but they'll deliver a marvelous payoff—all of Iceland's scenic highlights, in one big loop.

In this chapter, I outline the best five- to seven-day self-guided drive around the Ring, with plenty of suggestions for those with more time. Note that the South Coast, Borgarnes, and Reykholt Valley day trips described earlier in this book are basically part of the Ring Road, and two others—Golden Circle and Westman Islands—can easily be spliced into your Ring Road journey. And, with even more time and ambition, you could tack on a detour to the rugged and lonely Westfjords.

In theory, you could do the entire Ring and all the day trips in this book, and never set foot in Reykjavík. From Keflavík Airport, you could drive a couple of hours to one of the day-trip zones, spend a night there, and then continue along the Ring (for example, land at the airport, head straight to Borgarnes in West Iceland, and overnight there). However, most visitors stay in the Reykjavík area for a day or two before commencing the Ring. A week spent traveling Iceland's Ring Road is an epic journey unlike any other. Let's go!

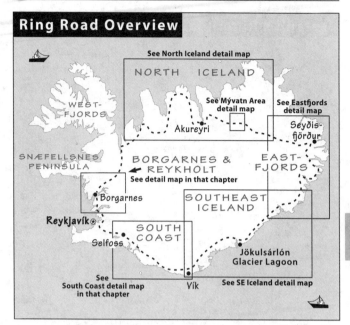

Ring Road Overview

NORTH ICELAND
See North Iceland detail map

See Mývatn Area
detail map

See Eastfjords
detail map

WEST-
FJORDS

Akureyri

Seyðis-
fjörður

SNÆFELLSNES
PENINSULA

BORGARNES &
REYKHOLT
See detail map in that chapter

EAST-
FJORDS

Borgarnes

SOUTHEAST
ICELAND

Reykjavík

SOUTH
COAST

Selfoss

Jökulsárlón
Glacier Lagoon

See
South Coast detail map
in that chapter

Vík

See SE Iceland detail map

RING ROAD

Ring Road Drive

Driving the Ring Road is a complex road trip that deserves serious planning. Use the day plans that follow as a guide as you custom-

ize your journey to match your interests, energy, and time. It's possible to do the loop in as few as five days (and four nights)—but that requires very long driving days. If you can, aim for seven leisurely days, even if they come at the expense of something else in Iceland.

PLANNING YOUR DRIVE

In the itinerary below, I've laid out a basic plan that takes you in five days—the absolute minimum—to the best-known sights, along with suggestions on where to overnight. With seven days or more, you can enjoy a saner pace, explore lesser-known destinations, avoid one-night stands, and really savor the trip. Be sure to read the Ring Road tips sprinkled throughout this chapter as you make your plans.

RING ROAD

Iceland's Ring Road

Greenland Sea

To Greenland

Denmark Strait

HORNSTRANDIR

Hesteyri

Ísafjarðardjúp

Bolungarvík

Ísafjörður

Dranga-jökull

Arnarfjörður

60

61

WEST-FJORDS

Patreks-fjörður

Breiðavík

Látrabjarg

Brjánslækur

Reykhólar

Flatey

Hólmavík

Drangs-nes

61

Breiðafjörður

Ólafsvík

Hellis-sandur

574

Snæfells-jökull

Grundar-fjörður

Búðir   Hellnar

SNÆFELLSNES

56

Stykkishólmur

Búðardalur

55   60

54

Hrútafjörður

Húnaflói

Skagaströnd

Blönduós

Hóp

Hvammstangi

STAÐARSKÁLI REST STOP

60

1

Skaga-fjörður

SKAGA-FJÖRÐUR

76

Sauðárkrókur

GLAUMBÆR MUSEUM   Hólar

Hofsós

Varmahlíð

NORTH

Blöndulón

KJÖLUR ROUTE 4-WHEEL DRIVE ONLY!

35

Grábrók Crater

54

Hraun-fossar

50

Reykholt

Hvanneyri

BORGAR-FJÖRÐUR

Borgarnes

1

Akranes

Faxaflói

Reykjavík

City

Reykjanesbær

Keflavík

43   Reykjanes Peninsula

Blue Lagoon

Grindavík

427

Hafnar-fjörður

Esja

36

36

Laugar-vatn

Þingvellir

GOLDEN CIRCLE

Geysir   Gullfoss

Viðgelmir Lava Tube

Langjökull

Reykholt

Flúðir

35

35

32

Hekla

1

Hveragerði

30

Selfoss

Þorláks-höfn

Hella

Hvolsvöllur

Seljalands-foss

26

Þórsmörk

Eyjafjallajökull

Skóga-foss

Vestmannaeyjar

Westman Islands

Surtsey

Landeyjahöfn

Heimaey

Dyrhólaey

SOUTH COAST

To Vínland

N

North Atlantic

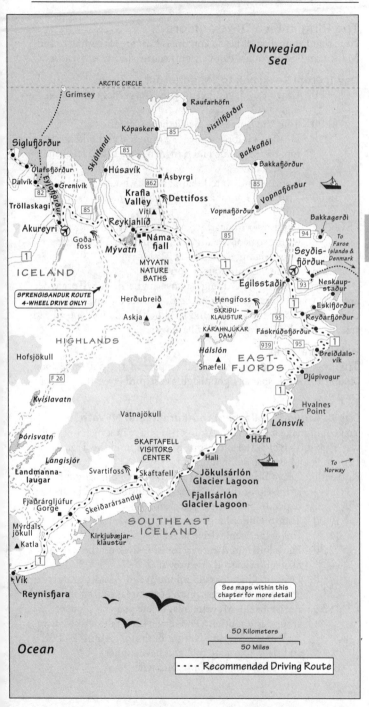

RING ROAD

Norwegian Sea

ARCTIC CIRCLE

Grimsey

Siglufjörður
Ólafsfjörður
Dalvík
Grenivík
Tröllaskagi
Akureyri

Skjálfandi

85

Húsavík

862

Krafla Valley
Viti
Reykjahlíð
Goða foss
Mývatn
Náma-fjall

MÝVATN NATURE BATHS

ICELAND

1

SPRENGISANDUR ROUTE
4-WHEEL DRIVE ONLY!

Herðubreið

Askja

HIGHLANDS

Hofsjökull

F 26

Kvíslavatn

Þórisvatn

Langisjór

Landmanna-laugar

Fjaðrárgljúfur Gorge

Mýrdals-jökull

Katla

1

Vík

Reynisfjara

Ocean

Kópasker

85

Raufarhöfn

Þistilfjörður

Bakkaflói

Bakkafjörður

85

Ásbyrgi

Dettifoss

Vopnafjörður

Vopnafjörður

94

Bakkagerði

To Faroe Islands & Denmark

Seyðis-fjörður

1

Egilsstaðir

93

Neskaup-staður

Hengifoss

SKRIÐU-KLAUSTUR

95

Eskifjörður

Reyðarfjörður

KÁRAHNJÚKAR DAM

Fáskrúðsfjörður

Hálslón

939

95

1

Snæfell

EAST-FJORDS

Breiðdals-vík

Vatnajökull

Djúpivogur

1

Hvalnes Point

Lónsvík

SKAFTAFELL VISITORS CENTER

Svartifoss

Skaftafell

Hali

1

Höfn

Jökulsárlón Glacier Lagoon

Fjallsárlón Glacier Lagoon

Skeiðarársandur

Kirkjubæjar-klaustur

SOUTHEAST ICELAND

To Norway

See maps within this chapter for more detail

50 Kilometers

50 Miles

- - - - Recommended Driving Route

The Ring in Five Days or More

Note that this plan and the closing times I list are for summer (mid-May to mid-Sept); hours can be significantly shorter off-season.

Day 1: From Reykjavík to Skagafjörður

9:00 Leave Reykjavík, heading for Borgarnes (1 hour) on highway 1

10:00 Tour the Borgarnes Settlement Center

11:15 Head to Grábrók crater (30 minutes) and hike to the top; have a picnic lunch there or eat at the Hraunsnef country hotel

13:30 Continue north to Glaumbær (2.5 hours)

16:00 Visit the Glaumbær open-air museum (closes at 18:00)

Evening Eat dinner in nearby Sauðárkrókur, then end your day with a soak at the Hofsós infinity pool (40 minutes from Glaumbær, closes at 21:00)

Sleep In the Skagafjörður countryside

Extra Overnight: Adding an overnight in the **Borgarnes area** lets you explore the sights in the Borgarnes & Reykholt Valley chapter (especially the area around Reykholt), and gives you a head start on the Skagafjörður and Tröllaskagi area.

With More Time...

True road warriors can add on all or part of the 530-mile loop around the wild, sparsely populated **Westfjords** (see the previous chapter).

Day 2: Around Tröllaskagi to Akureyri and Mývatn

You could make a beeline to Akureyri if you're in a rush (on highway 1); but it's worth the extra time to loop around the Tröllaskagi Peninsula and stop off in Siglufjörður.

8:30-9:00 Leave Skagafjörður area and drive to Siglufjörður, at the tip of the Tröllaskagi Peninsula (1-1.5 hours depending on where you sleep)

10:00 Tour Siglufjörður's Herring Era Museum

11:30 Enjoy the scenic drive to Akureyri (1 hour)

12:30 Have lunch in Akureyri (or in Dalvík on the way) and take a quick stroll downtown

14:30 Drive to Goðafoss (45 minutes) and view its grand waterfall, then press on to Mývatn lake (30 minutes)

16:30 Arrive in the Mývatn area, where you can sightsee around the southern end of the lake, take a restorative soak in the Mývatn Nature Baths (open until 24:00), and sleep like a log (oh, and have dinner)

Sleep In the Mývatn area or in Húsavík

Extra Overnight: If I were to add a night anywhere on this itinerary, it'd be in the **Mývatn area.** It's strategically situated about a third of the way through the Ring; extra time here helps you fit in more of the fascinating volcanic and geothermal sights around Mývatn, a visit to Húsavík (with a good whale museum and thermal bath), or a whale-watching trip from either Akureyri or Húsavík.

Akureyri, between Skagafjörður and Mývatn, is another candidate for an extra overnight. This buys you more time for the Tröllaskagi area (including the Hofsós Emigration Center) and for Akureyri itself (great municipal swimming pool and a wide choice of restaurants).

Day 3: From Mývatn to the Eastfjords

Morning   See any Mývatn sights you missed yesterday, including the baths and the geothermal sights just east of the mountains (or consider driving 45 minutes each way to visit the charming port town of Húsavík and its whale museum); whatever you do, eat lunch before heading out, as there's virtually nowhere to eat between Mývatn and the Eastfjords (your next destination)

12:30   Begin your drive east to Dettifoss (about an hour), and explore that spectacular waterfall

14:30   Continue toward the Eastfjords, stopping in Egilsstaðir (2 hours) if you need food or gas; then drive along one of Iceland's most scenic routes (45 minutes—including photo stops—over a breathtaking pass) to the appealing town of Seyðisfjörður

17:30   Arrive in Seyðisfjörður, enjoy dinner, and rest up for tomorrow's long Eastfjords drive

Sleep   In Seyðisfjörður (or Egilsstaðir, which saves some driving, but costs you spectacular scenery and a charming town)

Day 4: Along the Eastfjords to the Southeast

This is easily the most challenging—and most scenic—day of driving on this itinerary. Don't underestimate how long it takes to curve along all those beautiful fjords. Keep in mind that the most interesting sights are concentrated at the end of the day—you'll want enough time for them. Overnight options here span a two-hour stretch of road; the farther you go tonight, the less you'll have to drive tomorrow.

8:30   Leave Seyðisfjörður for the looooong drive along the Eastfjords to Höfn (nearly 4 hours without stops); break for WC/snacks in Djúpivogur (about 2.5 hours in)—your last chance before getting to Höfn

13:30   Late lunch in Höfn

15:00   Drive to the Jökulsárlón glacier lagoon (1 hour), ogle glaciers and nearby Diamond Beach, and consider a lagoon cruise (departures until 18:00)—or if sleeping nearby, do one first thing in the morning

Evening   With enough daylight and energy, consider an easy hike at Skaftafell National Park (45 minutes from Jökulsárlón), or linger at the glacier lagoon and beach before driving to your evening accommodations

Sleep   Near Höfn (better accommodations and restaurants), or near the Jökulsárlón glacier lagoon or Skaftafell (for hikers or those who want to shave off a bit of their Day 5 drive time); note that staying in Höfn adds about 1.5 hours to your Day 5 drive

Extra Overnight: Spending a second night in **Southeast Iceland** can help break up two long driving days. This is particularly tempting if you're interested in glacier activities or hiking at Skaftafell. But if you're *not* doing those things, you may prefer to overnight on the South Coast instead.

Day 5: Along the South Coast to Reykjavík

Before leaving—and if you're staying nearby—consider an easy nature hike at Skaftafell (or get up an hour earlier to hike all the way up to Svartifoss waterfall). Or, if you've slept near the glacier lagoons, do a cruise first thing this morning, before heading west.

Morning   Drive west to the town of Vík, on the South Coast, aiming to get there by lunchtime (about 3.5 hours from Höfn, 2.5 hours from Jökulsárlón glacier lagoon, or 2 hours from Skaftafell, including a few brief photo stops)

13:00   Lunch in or near Vík, then go 10 minutes farther to view the black sand beach at Reynisfjara

14:30   Drive to Seljalandsfoss (1 hour) and enjoy the waterfall

16:00   Continue to Hvolsvöllur (20 minutes) and visit the Lava Center (closes at 19:00)

Evening   Drive to Reykjavík (1.5 hours), having dinner en route or in the city (late)

Sleep   Collapse in Reykjavík. You did it!

Extra Overnight: Adding an overnight on the **South Coast** allows more time on the morning of Day 5 for glacier lagoon cruises and Skaftafell hikes, and lets you spread the South Coast sights over two days, breaking up the long drive back to Reykjavík. Other options include a Westman Islands side-trip (see Westman Islands chapter) or a Golden Circle loop (see Golden Circle chapter) on your way back to Reykjavík.

With More Time...

If you're adding time, and don't mind a series of one-night stays, I'd prioritize this way:

With a **sixth day,** add a second night in the Mývatn area.

With a **seventh day,** add a night on the South Coast.

With an **eighth day,** add an overnight in Akureyri.

With a **ninth day,** add an overnight in the Borgarnes area.

With **even more time,** spend a second night in one (or more) of these areas, listed roughly in order of preference: Southeast Iceland; Seyðisfjörður, in the Eastfjords; or the charming North Iceland towns of Húsavík and Siglufjörður.

Ring Road Tips

Here are some considerations as you plan your itinerary. For an overview on driving in Iceland—including common road hazards and a map with driving times, see the Practicalities chapter.

Time to Allow: The entire 800-mile circuit requires a minimum of about 20 hours of driving—but that doesn't account for the many places along the way that sit off the Ring. You'll drive an extra hour or two to reach some of the top sights (such as the best towns—Siglufjörður and Húsavík in the north, and Seyðisfjörður in the Eastfjords—or the most impressive waterfall, Dettifoss). To get a sense of the pace you'll need to keep, figure on about 30 driving hours, and divide by the number of days you've allotted (with five days, you'll average six hours a day behind the wheel).

Remember that you'll be stopping frequently en route for sightseeing, and sometimes hiking to a point of interest.

When to Go (and When Not to Go): The best time to drive the Ring Road is between mid-May and mid-September. Don't drive the full Ring anytime from November to March. April and October are chancy; with luck, you'll dance between the snowstorms, but it's just as likely that an icy or closed mountain pass will block your progress and derail your itinerary (in these months, prudent drivers should skip the Ring and stick closer to Reykjavík). Late September and early May along the Ring are fairly reliable, but you may encounter slippery roads or a freak snowstorm at higher elevations. Regardless of when you travel, keep a close eye on the road-conditions map at Road.is.

Two- or Four-Wheel Drive? In summer, rent a two-wheel-drive car; you won't need four-wheel drive if you're circling the island in a week. The entire Ring is paved, and the most rewarding detours are either paved or on gravel roads that are passable with two-wheel drive. Although four-wheel drive gives you a little more comfort and speed on unpaved roads, it's generally not worth the extra cost.

Clockwise or Counterclockwise? The Ring works well in either direction. I lean toward clockwise, which is how I've organized this chapter. The northwest quarter of the Ring is the least spectacular, so doing the trip clockwise lets you build to ever-greater highlights.

Sleeping Along the Ring: The trickiest part of your Ring itinerary is figuring out where to stay overnight. Depending on how many days you plan to spend on the Ring, you may end up with a string of one-nighters. **Book well ahead**—as far you can—as accommodations along the Ring fill up weeks (or months) in advance for summer. Be flexible on location; for example, when researching Mývatn accommodations, you might find better prices and availability in nearby Húsavík. With Iceland's geography and dispersed settlement in mind, I've highlighted general areas that work well for an overnight and recommended a few reliable establishments that I've checked out and like. Still, it's smart to look around on Airbnb or Booking.com, and consider well-rated alternatives.

Another option is to **camp,** either with a campervan or tent. With a campervan, every parking lot becomes a potential hotel; with a tent, you just need a campsite to pitch it in, and Icelandic campsites practically never fill up. Both options leave you free to change your itinerary on the fly (for more on campervans and camping, see page 488).

WCs: Though Iceland has made a concerted effort to add WCs at roadside sights, WCs can still be few and far between. Driving through the countryside, often your best (or only) WC option will be at a parking lot or café for a major sight. Some may be free, but most charge a fee (typically 100-200 ISK); some accept credit cards, but others require cash. Have a small amount of currency on hand for these situations. WCs at gas stations and eateries where you are buying food are typically free.

Not Enough Time to Drive? If you don't want to drive the entire Ring Road but want to get a quick look at the north, a good plan is to fly from Reykjavík City Airport to Akureyri (Air Iceland Connect flights depart 5/day and take 45 minutes, www.airicelandconnect.com) and home-base there for a few days, daytripping by rental car, public bus, or excursion to places like Siglufjörður and Mývatn (each less than 1.5 hours away). Egilsstaðir, in the Eastfjords, is also reachable by plane from Reykjavík, with rental cars available at its airport (one-hour flight).

Ring Road Excursions: If you want to do the Ring but don't want to drive it yourself, consider a guided bus tour. Family-run **GJ Travel** offers an eight-day Ring tour for about $2,200 (www.gjtravel.is); other reputable companies include www.nicetravel.is and www.seasontours.is.

West Iceland

Your Ring Road journey begins with a spin through West Iceland—the region called Borgarfjörður. This area has some fine sights and can be a satisfying side-trip from Reykjavík, but those doing the entire Ring Road will find more impactful sights, charming towns,

and dramatic scenery farther along. For that reason, Ring Road through-trippers should feel free to make short work of West Iceland—stopping only at its two most worthwhile sights: the Settlement Center in the beautifully set town of Borgarnes and the fun-to-climb crater called Grábrók.

Planning Tips: If you're doing the Ring Road at a more leisurely pace (with more than a week), this area can be a convenient first stop, especially if you're setting out on the Ring right after your Iceland arrival. It's a fairly straightforward 1.5-hour drive from the airport to charming Borgarnes, a fine place for your first night in Iceland before carrying on with the rest of the Ring.

Reykjavík to Skagafjörður

For more on this region—including a map, specific driving instructions from Reykjavík, and a complete rundown of the area's sights—see the Borgarnes & Reykholt Valley chapter. This leg takes about 4.5 hours without stopping.

• *Drive north from Reykjavík along highway 1, following signs for* Borgarnes, Akureyri, *and* 1n. *About one hour from Reykjavík, a bridge crosses into...*

Borgarnes

This fine town of 2,000 people perches on a little peninsula facing sheer scree cliffs. Borgarnes (BOHR-gahr-NESS) has some historical ties to the early Icelandic sagas (especially the colorful warrior-poet Egill); you can learn more about him and the earliest days of Iceland's habitation in the **Settlement Center,** which is well worth an hour (described on page 275).

Additional sights cluster about a half-hour east of Borgarnes, in the area near Reykholt (thermal springs and waterfalls, family-friendly goat farm, spa-like thermal pool, lava cave, important early Icelandic Christian sights—all described in the Borgarnes & Reykholt Valley chapter). But for those blitzing the Ring, all are skippable.

• *To continue directly along the Ring Road, head north from Borgarnes on highway 1. After about 30 minutes, along the road on your left, you can't miss the towering crater called Grábrók. The parking lot is also on the left, immediately after the crater.*

Grábrók Crater

Climbing to the top of Grábrók takes about 30-45 minutes round-trip and offers grand views over the region (for details on the crater and the lunch spots listed next, see page 277).

Lunch Options: Consider getting lunch near Grábrók before heading north over the mountains. Options include the **$$** bar/restaurant at the **Hótel Bifröst** and the more upscale **$$$ Hraunsnef**. Otherwise, two basic, roadside restaurants lie between here and Skagafjörður (described in the North Iceland section, later).

• *After visiting the crater, get back on highway 1 north, tracking the scenic Norðurá river.*

From Grábrók to Blönduós

As you approach the pass over **Holtavörðuheiði** (Hill-Cairn Heath), the farms thin out and the road climbs, finally cresting the pass at almost 1,400 feet.

Coming back down, you'll see the small Hrútafjörður (Ram Fjord) spread out before you. Just before the road meets the fjord, you'll hit **$ Staðarskáli**, a big rest-stop complex (free WC, burgers, Wi-Fi, long hours daily, tel. 440-1336, www.nat.is/stadarskali).

Stick with highway 1 as you skirt north along the fjord, then turn east. About 30 minutes in, watch on the right for a strange grouping of hillocks called **Vatnsdalshólar,** thought to be the result of a prehistoric landslide. Another half-hour of driving on highway 1 across a relatively flat landscape brings you to **Blönduós,** a small town along the Blanda river known to most Icelanders for its speed traps. There are a few restaurants here, including **$$ B&S** (daily 11:00-21:00, next to the big N1 gas station at the top of town, Nordurlandsvegur 4, tel. 453-5060, http://bogs.is).

From Blönduós to the Skagafjörður Area

As you make the trip over the mountain range from Blönduós to the Skagafjörður area, you'll be crossing into North Iceland. For this leg of the trip, you have a couple of route options.

Highway 744 to Sauðárkrókur or Hofsós (40 minutes/1 hour): If you're in a hurry to reach either of these towns, highway 744 is faster, lower in altitude, and nicely scenic.

Highway 1 Bypass to Varmahlíð (40 minutes): This equally scenic road follows the lovely Blanda river through a pastoral valley, then crosses Vatnsskarð pass to the hamlet of Varmahlíð (VAR-mah-HLEETH, Warm Slope, pop. 140), with a gas station, accommodations, swimming pool, and regional TI (in the sod-roofed wooden house at the highway junction, daily in summer, tel. 455-6161, www.visitskagafjordur.is).

About a mile before town is a turnoff to **Víðimýrarkirkja**, a "turf church" constructed of sod laid in a herringbone pattern. Although a church has stood here since the 12th century, this one dates from 1834 and is still used for weddings and Christmas Eve services (small entry fee, open daily in summer).

From Varmahlíð, you have several options. Turning left on highway 75 takes you to the area's most interesting sight, Glaumbær Museum (less than 10 minutes) and the town of Sauðárkrókur (20 minutes); the road eventually connects with highway 76, which runs through Hofsós (45 minutes from Varmahlíð) and the Tröllaskagi Peninsula. All of these are described in the next section.

Continuing along highway 1 from Varmahlíð leads to the bigger city of Akureyri (1 hour). Note that if you stay on highway 1, you'll bypass the Skagafjörður altogether. Unless you're in a huge rush, be sure to turn off and enjoy the Skagafjörður area.

RING ROAD

North Iceland

North Iceland is a delight, with beautiful fjords, the scenic Tröllaskagi Peninsula, Iceland's pleasant second city of Akureyri, and the country's most fascinating volcanic area at Mývatn. If this area were a bit closer to Reykjavík, it would be swamped with tourists. But it isn't...so it's not.

Planning Tips: Those without enough time to do the entire Ring could consider spending just a few nights in this area. But by car it's a long, six-plus hours one-way from Reykjavík. A more efficient plan is to fly from Reykjavík to Akureyri, rent a car there (or do excursions) for two or three days of side-tripping, then drive or fly back to the capital. The official tourism website, NorthIceland. is, offers a wealth of information.

Skagafjörður Area

Skagafjörður (SKAH-gah-FYUR-thur, Peninsula Fjord) is the name of this broad fjord and of the valley at its head. The Skagafjörður area has a pic-

turesque seaside setting, a few humble towns (Hofsós is the most interesting), and several intriguing islands just offshore.

There are enough attractions here to keep you busy for several hours—including one of Iceland's most interesting folk museums, at Glaumbær; the evocative Icelandic Emigration Center, in Hofsós; and a tranquil valley that was an important site in the early days of Icelandic

Christianity, at Hólar. The area also has several horseback riding options, and a rare Icelandic river suitable for rafting.

Planning Tips: The Skagafjörður area is sparsely populated and not well-developed for tourism. Compared to some of the country's more mainstream destinations, you may need to lower your standards somewhat. If you make good time getting to this area, a possible late-afternoon plan is to close down the Icelandic Emigration Center in Hofsós (open until 18:00 in summer); take a dip in that town's relaxing, thermally fed infinity pool overlooking the fjord (open until 21:00 in summer); then grab dinner on your way back to your accommodations.

Sights in the Skagafjörður Area

These sights are listed in the order you'll approach them on highways 75 and 76 from the main Ring Road. For directions, see "From Blönduós to the Skagafjörður Area" on page 369.

▲▲Glaumbær Museum

Inhabited until 1947 and a museum since 1952, this classic turf farmstead (pron. GLOYM-bire) shows how Icelanders lived for centuries, with limited access to timber for building and fuel. It's larger and better preserved than other similar farm museums in Iceland, and offers perhaps the country's most informative and intimate look at traditional Icelandic lifestyles. It

rates ▲▲▲ for those interested in Icelandic history.

Perhaps more stirring than the buildings you can see are those you cannot: The remains of an even earlier farm, from the 10th and 11th centuries, lie beneath the grassy field near the farmstead. This is thought to have been the farmstead of Guðríður Þorbjarnardóttir, also known in the sagas as Guðríður the Far Traveler, a Viking woman who ventured to the New World and Rome.

Cost and Hours: Free to wander the grounds, but well worth paying 1,700 ISK to enter the farmhouse complex; late May-late Sept daily 9:00-18:00; April-late May and late Sept-late Oct Mon-Fri 10:00-16:00, closed Sat-Sun; late Oct-March by appointment only; on highway 75 (less than 10 minutes north of highway 1 at Varmahlíð), tel. 453-6173, www.glaumbaer.is.

Eating: The sod houses sit between a modern church and two late-19th-century timber houses that were moved here in recent

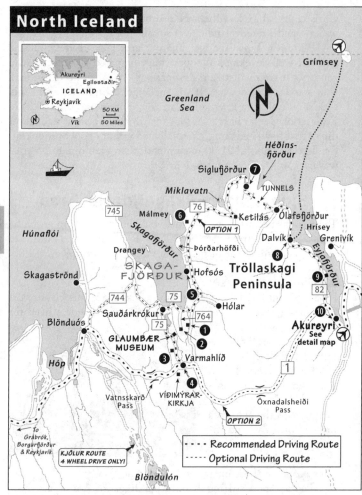

North Iceland

ICELAND
Akureyri
Egilsstaðir
Reykjavík
Vik
50 KM
50 Miles

Grímsey

Greenland Sea

Héðins-fjörður

Siglufjörður **7**

Miklavatn

TUNNELS

Ólafsfjörður

Málmey **6** 76 Ketilás

OPTION 1

Hrisey

Grenivík

Drangey Þórðarhöfði Dalvík **8**

Skagafjörður

SKAGA-FJÖRÐUR

Tröllaskagi Peninsula

Húnaflói

745

Skagaströnd Hofsós **5** **9** 82

744 75 Hólar

Blönduós Sauðárkrókur **10**

764 **1** Akureyri

75 **2** See detail map

GLAUMBÆR MUSEUM **3** Varmahlíð 1

Hóp **4**

Vatnsskarð Pass VÍÐIMÝRAR-KIRKJA Öxnadalsheiði Pass

OPTION 2

To Grábrók, Borgarfjörður & Reykjavík

KJÖLUR ROUTE 4 WHEEL DRIVE ONLY!

- - - - Recommended Driving Route
- - - - - Optional Driving Route

Blöndulón

RING ROAD

decades. In one of them, the cozy **$ Áskaffi** café offers soup, sandwiches, cakes, and a tasting plate of traditional Icelandic smoked and preserved foods "served in the manner of our mothers and grandmothers" (closed late Sept-April; tel. 453-8855, www.askaffi. is). The other house is a small gift shop.

Visiting the Museum: Because there were few trees left in Iceland, farmsteads were built from expertly cut chunks of sod. The corner posts and roof beams were wood—and were often an early settler's most valuable possessions.

Here the walls of the farm are made of sod and driftwood, with timber fronts and stone foundations. Study the alternating diagonal pattern used to pile up the layers of sod. The tops of the houses are covered with grass—the original roof garden. While the

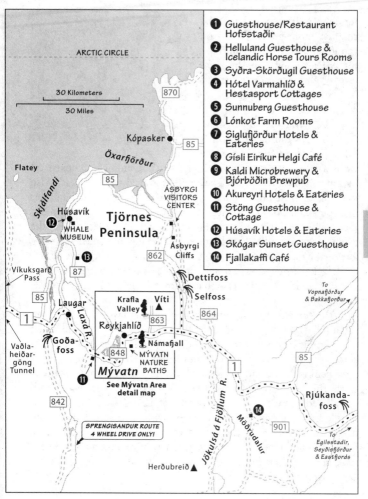

1. Guesthouse/Restaurant Hofsstaðir
2. Helluland Guesthouse & Icelandic Horse Tours Rooms
3. Syðra-Skörðugil Guesthouse
4. Hótel Varmahlíð & Hestasport Cottages
5. Sunnuberg Guesthouse
6. Lónkot Farm Rooms
7. Siglufjörður Hotels & Eateries
8. Gísli Eiríkur Helgi Café
9. Kaldi Microbrewery & Bjórböðin Brewpub
10. Akureyri Hotels & Eateries
11. Stöng Guesthouse & Cottage
12. Húsavík Hotels & Eateries
13. Skógar Sunset Guesthouse
14. Fjallakaffi Café

facades give the impression of separate buildings, inside the rooms are all connected.

Each room is explained in the English leaflet. At the front of the house are the nicest (and least troglodyte-style) rooms, reserved for guests. From there, a long, claustrophobic sod hallway connects the kitchen (with a fire fed by peat or dried sheep dung) with various pantries and storage rooms, where you'll see big barrels of animal innards and *skyr*—now a trendy yogurt-like snack, but back then a well-preserved staple.

At the back of the complex, you'll pop into the fascinating *baðstofa*—the communal living and sleeping room, lined with dorm-like beds where workers slept, two to a bed. Women—who did delicate spinning and knitting work—got the bunks with bet-

ter light, near the windows. The smaller, more genteel room on the left was for the farmer and his wife; the one on the right was for children (notice the loft bed, with a step for easier access).

Here you can understand why the Scandinavian words for "bed" come from the same word as the English "room." Each bed's opening is blocked off by a wooden panel (called a *rúmfjöl*) engraved with prayers. Also look for the little lidded pot above each bed; every person had their own personal pot *(askur)* from which they ate every meal. Imagine spending a long, dark, cold winter in here, huddled around the dim light of a candle. People stored personal items under their pillows—the only place that was strictly off-limits to everyone else.

Back outside, you can peek into a few more rooms that held farming tools. The farm even had its own little blacksmith's workshop.

You can either drive or walk up to the small wooden church on the hill beyond the farmstead. In the graveyard, look for the statue of Guðríður in a ship, carrying her son Snorri on her shoulder. According to the sagas, Guðríður (born near Hellnar on the Snæfellsnes Peninsula around the year 980) and her husband Þorfinnur Karlsefni Þórðarson followed Leifur Eiríksson's route to Vinland. They lived there for a time, possibly at L'Anse aux Meadows in Newfoundland, before returning here with their son, Snorri—the first European born in the Americas. Snorri was among the first Icelanders to adopt Christianity, and may have built a church here for Guðríður after she returned from a several-years-long pilgrimage to Rome.

Sauðárkrókur Town

The provincial center of Sauðárkrókur (SOY-thowr-KROH-kur, Sheep River Bend, pop. 2,500) enjoys a spectacular fjordside setting about 15 minutes north of Glaumbær, but the town itself is dreary. It's convenient for gassing up, grabbing a meal, or setting up bird-watching or sea-cruise excursions—but otherwise, I'd give it a miss.

Eating in Sauðárkrókur: Most of the limited options line up within a block or so along the main street, Aðalgata (a couple of blocks inland from the main highway). **$$$ KK Restaurant** (a.k.a. **Kaffi Krókur**) has a big, bright interior, offering a typical burgers-and-pasta menu at lunch and fancier options at dinner, most sourced from local farms (daily 12:00-22:00, Aðalgata 16,

RING ROAD

tel. 453-6454, www.kkrestaurant.is). **$$ Hard Wok Café** serves an acceptable approximation of Asian and Mexican dishes, plus pizza, in a pleasant setting (June-Aug daily 11:30-21:30, off-season closed 14:00-18:00 Mon-Fri, Aðalgata 8). **$ Sauðárkróksbakarí** is a popular main-street bakery with pastries and basic sandwiches, and inviting indoor seating (Mon-Fri 7:00-18:00, Sat-Sun 9:00-16:00, Aðalgata 5, www.saudarkroksbakari.net). There's also a supermarket in town.

Hólar Village

Hólar (HOE-lar, Hills), a pretty settlement at the upper end of a small valley, is a scenic detour if you have an hour to spare and an interest in Iceland's history (from highway 76, turn off on highway 767 for about 15 minutes/8 miles).

The center of Iceland's northern bishopric up until 1800, Hólar had one of the country's first printing presses and is now home to a small college (Hólaskóli), a historic church, a trio of little turf-roofed houses (not open to the public), and an exhibit on Icelandic horses (only in Icelandic; open June-Aug Tue-Sun, www.sogusetur.is).

Hólar was home to a colorful and important bishop, Guðmundur Arason (1161-1237). An orphaned, disabled ascetic, Guðmundur devoted himself to the poor and needy. After he became bishop of Hólar, Guðmundur gathered a motley crew of desperately needy people, whom he sustained with church wealth. He became known as "Guðmundur the Good." However, his unusual ways—and his assertion of the judicial powers of the Catholic Church—drew attention from the chieftains. The two factions came to blows, and Guðmundur was at various times imprisoned or sent into exile.

About 300 years later, another Hólar bishop—Jón Arason—was the main holdout against the Protestant Reformation. Jón was eventually executed at the headquarters of the other old Icelandic bishopric, Skálholt (on the Golden Circle).

Hofsós Village

On the east side of the fjord—about 40 minutes from Glaumbær, or 30 minutes from Sauðárkrókur—the village of Hofsós (HOFF-sohs, Temple Estuary, pop. 170) merits a stop, especially for anyone of Icelandic descent. A one-time summer trading center, it got its start in the 18th century, but never developed into a large town.

Today it's a village with a fine location perched on a bluff overlooking the fjord. (The late Icelandic-Minnesotan author Bill Holm, who some will remember from his appearances on *A Prairie Home Companion*, spent summers in Hofsós and wrote about the town in *The Windows of Brimnes*.)

The core of the village (with the swimming pool and recommended guesthouse) is separated from its old port by the outflow of the big Hofsá river. To reach the port area—with the main buildings of the Emigration Center—you'll either have to loop all the way around on the road, or park by the Sólvík restaurant and take the footbridge.

Icelandic Emigration Center (Vesturfarasetrið): This is the main sight in town—worth ▲, or ▲▲▲ if you have Icelandic ances-

try (1,700 ISK, June-Aug daily 11:00-18:00, Sept-May by appointment, tel. 453-7935, www. hofsos.is). It fills three historic buildings on the old port. The low-tech but thorough exhibits tell the story of the 20,000-some Icelanders who emigrated to the Americas from 1870 to 1914—a time when a series of volcanic eruptions, lower temperatures, and a general lack of prospects conspired to make life in Iceland very difficult, particularly in the northern parts of the island. In 1860, more Icelanders died than were born. At the same time, changes in Icelandic law made it possible for landless workers to leave traditional farming work in search of other opportunities. Those who left went mainly to Canada, where part of Manitoba became known as "New Iceland"; others wound up in the Dakotas, and a handful went to Brazil.

To see the museum, first tour the overview exhibit in the light green house, which includes a peek into a typical fishing shack—a *burrabúð* (dry house)—and, in the basement, a glimpse at life at sea and what the emigrants found when they reached the New World. The museum's owners also operate an Icelandic flag factory—take a peek in the room at the back.

In the big black house, a touching exhibit of photographs (made in 1890) lets you look into the brave faces of an Icelandic immigrant community in Manitoba. And across the footbridge, you'll learn about an Icelandic settlement in North Dakota. Visitors can also use the genealogy library.

Thermal Swimming Pool: Hofsós sports a fine, large municipal pool, which opened in 2010 as a gift to the village by two very wealthy Icelandic businesswomen. Entirely outdoors, the complex has both a big, warm infinity pool (with unobstructed views over the icy waters of the fjord) and a small hot pool. If you only have time for one thermal pool on your Ring drive, this is a good choice—small, user-friendly, scenic, reasonably priced, and in an area with few other evening diversions (1,000

ISK, generally daily in summer 7:00-21:00, tel. 455-6070, www. facebook.com/sundlauginhofsosi).

Eating in Hofsós: The only real eating option is the casual **$ Sólvík** restaurant, filling a cozy house down near the footbridge, with a short but appealing menu of fish, lamb, and burgers (daily 11:00-21:00, mobile 961-3463).

Sleeping in the Skagafjörður Area

The countryside near Skagafjörður is a good place to spend the night (accommodations in the fjord's main town, Sauðárkrókur, are gloomy). Another option is to carry on about 1.5 hours farther to sleep in Siglufjörður, near the tip of the Tröllaskagi Peninsula (with some excellent accommodations—see recommendations later in this chapter).

Overlooking the Skagafjörður Valley: $$$ Guesthouse Hofsstaðir is a cozy oasis perched on a postcard-perfect ridge, with cut-glass peaks in one direction and the broad estuary of the Skagafjörður valley in the other. Well-run by former chef Tóti and Guðný, they have 30 rooms in several log-cabin-like buildings (all with private bath and views) and a relaxing, upscale vibe (tel. 453-7300, www.hofsstadir.is, info@hofsstadir.is). Their good **$$$ restaurant,** open to all, has an appealing menu and sells homemade syrups and jams (daily 18:00-22:00, reserve ahead off-season). Coming from Sauðárkrókur on highway 75, turn right at the T-intersection with highway 76 (signed for *Reykjavík* and *Akureyri*); the guesthouse is a few minutes south.

$ Helluland Guesthouse has five simple but tidy rooms, all with shared bath, plus a bright and cheery breakfast room and a Swedish-influenced lounge. In a restored farmhouse overlooking the valley, it's a winner. Wake up early to watch them bring in the horses (mobile 853-3220, www.helluland.is, info@helluland. is). If you're in a pinch, their neighbor, **$ Icelandic Horse Tours,** has three even simpler rooms (also offers horse tours, mobile 847-8577, www.icelandhorsetours.com, info@icelandhorsetours.com, Lucca). To reach either, head east from Sauðárkrókur on highway

Islands in North Iceland

As you drive through North Iceland—if the visibility is good—you'll see a number of small islands scattered offshore. Ring travelers who aren't in a rush might consider a visit.

Drangey rises like a tabletop in the waters of Skagafjörður west of Hofsós. The steep cliffs of this uninhabited island are summer nesting grounds for seabirds (including puffins)—and a draw for birders. It's well known to saga readers as the refuge of the outlaw Grettir. In summer, you can visit the island with a tour from Sauðárkrókur (www.drangey.net). Farther north is **Málmey,** the fjord's other island, which was farmed until 1950 and is now home to a lighthouse.

Hrísey (Brushwood Island) sits in Eyjafjörður, near Akureyri. This was once Iceland's quarantine island for cats and dogs imported here from abroad—a more convenient quarantine is now near Keflavík Airport. A 15-minute ferry ride from Árskógssandur, near Dalvík, takes you to a small village (pop. 150) with a café and some pleasant, short hikes (www.hrisey.is).

Grímsey, the northernmost inhabited point in Iceland (pop. under 100), has two big draws: Its northern tip is *just* over the Arctic Circle, as if designed for people who want to say they've been there. And it's a good place to see puffins in summer. The island itself is pleasant (not stunning), and the small village with its little harbor is typically Icelandic. You can either take a ferry from Dalvík (3 hours one-way—prebook via Akureyri TI); an excursion boat from Akureyri (6 hours round-trip, including 2 hours on the island); or fly (30 minutes from Akureyri). Various North Iceland companies offer excursion packages. As flights and ferries run at most once daily, stay overnight if you really want to experience the island (www.visitgrimsey.is).

You can't visit **Kolbeinsey,** Iceland's northernmost point, which lies far beyond Grímsey. Now basically a sea rock, waves have eroded it to the point where it barely sticks up above the surface of the sea, and it's too small for a lighthouse. Not far back in the geological past, it was the top of an active volcano, probably similar to Surtsey in the Westman Islands. As it's important for establishing the bounds of Iceland's fishing zone, the government shored up the island with concrete to keep it from disappearing altogether.

Flatey is a pancake-shaped island in Skjálfandi bay. It was inhabited until the late 1960s, and some landowners still spend time there in the warmer months. There are occasional bird-watching tours to the island in summer.

75. After crossing the bridge, immediately turn right on highway 764 (marked *Hegranes*); the guesthouses are on the left after two miles (about 5 minutes on the unpaved road).

Near Glaumbær: On highway 75 just a few minutes south of the Glaumbær Museum, **$ Syðra-Skörðugil Guesthouse** offers five bright rooms with shared bath and kitchen access. They also run horse tours, including the option to ride from here to the museum (family rooms, hot tub, mobile 893-8140, www.sydraskordugil. is, info@sydraskordugil.is).

In Varmahlíð: At the junction of highway 1 and highway 75—a short drive south of Glaumbær—sits **$$$ Hótel Varmahlíð**. It's overpriced with 19 spacious-yet-old-school rooms, but it may have beds when others are full. It's convenient if you're skipping Skagafjörður and just need a place to sleep before continuing east (tel. 453-8170, restaurant open daily, www.hotelvarmahlid.is, info@hotelvarmahlid.is).

$$$ Hestasport Cottages (Horse Sport Cottages) rents seven well-kept cottages, each with private bath, circling a shared outdoor hot tub in a grassy meadow on the hill above the junction. Check-in is in a blue building off highway 1 before you reach the junction (look for *Hestasport* sign on the right, they also run horse tours, tel. 453-8383, https://riding.is/cottages, info@riding.is, Katja).

In Hofsós: The simple **$ Sunnuberg Guesthouse** fills a modern house right in the heart of the village (facing the little grocery/gas station). Its five basic rooms have private baths but are nothing fancy—no frills and no breakfast, though you can use the kitchen to make coffee (Suðurbraut 8, mobile 893-0220, www.sunnuberg. is, book by phone or email at gisting@hofsos.is).

Just North of Hofsós: **$$ Lónkot,** a remote waterfront farm with six practical rooms about 15 minutes north of Hofsós along the coast, is handy for those continuing around the tip of the Tröllaskagi Peninsula (cheaper rooms with shared bath, some rooms have ocean view, restaurant, Lónkot 76, tel. 453-7432, www. lonkot.is, lonkot@lonkot.is).

Skagafjörður to Akureyri

When you're ready to proceed from the Skagafjörður area to Akureyri, you have two choices: Drive inland on highway 1 over a mountain pass to Akureyri; or—my preference—invest a little extra time to take one of Iceland's classic scenic drives: north around the tip of Tröllaskagi Peninsula (Troll Peninsula).

Option 1, Tröllaskagi (about 115 miles, 2.5 hours): This route stays at lower altitudes as it hugs the northern coast through the towns of Hofsós, Siglufjörður, Ólafsfjörður, and Dalvík, before heading south along Eyjafjörður to Akureyri. The road is very scenic the entire way around and well worth the extra time. (For a detailed description of the Tröllaskagi route, see below.)

Option 2, Straight Shot on Highway 1 (about 60 miles, 1 hour): From Varmahlíð, highway 1 heads southeast over the Öxnadalsheiði pass (1,800 feet). The road is good, fast, scenic, and fun to drive, but can easily get snow in April and October (or even May and September). Near Akureyri, it broadens out into a fine green valley under jagged mountain peaks.

Which Route to Take? The decision depends largely on how much time you can spare. The faster inland route buys more time in Akureyri, and—if continuing onward the same day—gets you into the Mývatn area earlier (you'll be glad to have more time for its many wonderful sights). The attractive coastal route runs along the sea (and Siglufjörður will tempt you to stop), but you'll sacrifice some time in Akureyri and Mývatn. If you have a night in Akureyri, or a second night near Mývatn, the Tröllaskagi detour is easier to justify.

The choice also depends on your departure point in Skagafjörður. If you sleep as far north as Hofsós, continuing north around the coastal route is only about 30 minutes slower than back-tracking to highway 1 (not counting sightseeing stops).

Tröllaskagi Peninsula

The mountainous Tröllaskagi (TREW-tlah-sky-ee) is flanked by two fjords, Skagafjörður and Eyjafjörður. Drivers who opt for the scenic route around the penin-sula's tip will curve high above the sea and skirt deep glacial valleys. Along the way, you'll be tempted to stop for photographs (use the strategically placed, scenic picnic pullouts), and two of the towns—Hofsós and Si-glufjörður—have good muse-ums that merit an hour or two

of your time. The drive around the peninsula—from the heart of the Skagafjörður area to Akureyri—takes about 2.5 hours.

• *From Varmahlíð or nearby, head north to highway 76.*

Hofsós North to Siglufjörður

About 15 miles from the base of the fjord is the tiny village of **Hof-sós,** with its fine Icelandic Emigration Center and small but tempt-ing thermal swimming pool, overlooking the fjord. (For more on Hofsós, see earlier in this chapter.)

Continuing north, look out to the dramatic offshore islands:

In good weather, you'll be able to see the more distant **Drangey** island, a popular destination for birders. If it's socked in, you might pick out a pair of closer-in islands: the table-like **Þórðarhöfði** (technically a peninsula, connected to the mainland by a sandbar), then **Málmey.**

As the road curves right—heading around one of the peninsula's fingers—it alternates abruptly between paved and unpaved stretches, with isolated, hardscrabble farms. Steady as you go, carrying on through desolate, spectacular scenery.

• *As you approach the Miklavatn lagoon, at the scenic valley junction called Ketilás (with a small N1 gas station), you hit a T-intersection; turn left to stay on highway 76 (marked* Siglufjörður*).*

Curl up along the far side of the water, with nice views back on the mountainous coastline. As you reach the topmost part of the peninsula, look out to sea and realize that the next stop is the Arctic Circle. This is the northernmost point of this drive—and perhaps the farthest north you'll ever be in your life.

• *About 45 minutes after leaving Hofsós, the road winds along high bluffs over the sea before taking you through a short one-lane tunnel, then deposits you in the adorable town of Siglufjörður.*

▲▲Siglufjörður

The town of Siglufjörður (SIG-loo-FYUR-thur, Mast Fjord, pop. 1,200) is reason enough to tour Tröllaskagi. Tucked away from the sea at the end of a short fjord, and dramatically flanked by high peaks, it has a tidy charm and a pioneer spirit. The harborfront provides a lovely stroll, and colorful homes scamper up the hillside above town. There's a free parking lot right at the old

harbor downtown, next to the landmark Sigló Hótel and a short walk from the Herring Era Museum. Public WCs are at the adjacent campground, and a TI is in the library across the street (daily in summer, tel. 467-1555, info@fjallabyggd.is).

Fish is what put the town on the map. Practically no one lived here until the mid-19th century, when locals started to use the good harbor as a trading post and shark-fishing base. Later, herring took over, and the town boomed as a sort of "Atlantic Klondike" from about 1900 until midcentury, when overfishing caused herring stocks to collapse.

At its peak, Siglufjörður's harborfront was jammed with piers, bristling with boats, and fragrant with fish-processing stations; the

RING ROAD

population swelled to over 3,000. Salted herring—nutritious and well-preserved—was prized in many countries during the world wars, and for a time represented up to half of Iceland's total export income. In fact, the wealth generated by the herring operation here helped make Iceland financially independent—and, soon after, politically independent—from Denmark. But by the late 1960s, the herring shoals had disappeared for good, and Siglufjörður's population crashed. Today this burg is sleepy, with a little fishing and more and more tourism.

Herring Era Museum (Síldarminjasafn): Among Iceland's most engaging, this museum (worth ▲▲) has exhibits filling three large, historic buildings, right along the main road (just past Sigló Hótel toward Akureyri). It's well worth an hour (or more) of your time. I never knew the herring industry could be so fascinating (1,800 ISK, June-Aug daily 10:00-18:00, May and Sept 13:00-17:00, Oct-April by appointment, Snorragata 10, tel. 467-1604, www.sild.is).

Begin at the red building at the far end of the row—the **Salting Station** (a.k.a. Róaldsbrakki, from 1907). At the entrance,

notice the panoramic photograph of the embankment out front—now so sleepy—lined with hundreds upon hundreds of herring-filled barrels. This Norwegian-owned factory (one of 23 salting stations in town) could crank out 30,000 barrels of salted herring in a year. On the main level, peek into the offices of a typical herring company. Don't miss the creaky upstairs, with the living quarters for the "herring girls" who lived and worked here, 50 at a time, through the herring season. All summer long, the young women worked outdoors, rain or shine, cutting and salting herring. You'll see rows of dorm-like beds, with clothes still hanging from hooks and music playing on the radio. At the very top, in the attic, equipment hangs from the rafters. Exiting this building, find the warehouse down below, where the salting line and storage areas were.

Then head to the multicolor-fronted building next door, the **Fish Factory**—a jumble of heavy machinery where some of the catch was processed into oil or fishmeal (for animal feed). You'll see everything from an old hand press to motorized equipment powered by a huge diesel engine. The exhibits upstairs help tell the story.

Finally, enter the yellow **Boathouse,** where you can stroll through an impressive life-size re-creation of the jammed harbor at

RING ROAD

its peak. Step into shacks decorated with antique pulleys, lanterns, nets, buoys, and other tools. Walk around on the decks of the largest boat (the *Týr*), imagining this scene multiplied a hundredfold on the harbor out front.

RING ROAD

Sleeping in Siglufjörður: One of Iceland's most appealing high-end, fjordside hotels, **$$$$ Sigló Hótel** fills a picture-perfect building on the waterfront in the middle of town. Everything is done with class in its 68 harbor-view rooms and its stay-a-while atrium bar/lounge. If you're going to splurge on an Icelandic fjord, do it here (private hot tub and sauna, restaurant, Snorragata 3, tel. 461-7730, www. siglohotel.is).

$$ Siglunes Guesthouse, a few short blocks away in a residential zone, is a homey place (well-run by proud Hálfdán) with 19 rooms above a dark, retro-feeling lounge. It's a nice mix of antiques, modern features, and local artists' work. About half the rooms have private bathrooms (breakfast extra, Lækjargata 10, tel. 467-1222, mobile 659-9699, www.hotelsiglunes.is).

Eating in Siglufjörður: Sigló Hótel runs several eateries in the colorful sheds around the harbor. Of these, **$$ Hannes Boy** (in the yellow building) serves good fish, burger, and soup lunches, and has outdoor seating (daily 11:30-21:00, shorter hours off-season, tel. 461-7730, www.hannesboy.is). A block north is the little main square (directly under the church) and two good choices: **$ Fish & Chips,** a family-run shop serving fresh-caught fish (Mon-Fri 11:00-17:00, closed Sat-Sun, tel. 467-1172) and **$ Torgið** (The Square), a popular, casual bar/café with international cuisine (lunch and dinner served daily, likely closed for lunch off-season, tel. 467-2323, www.torgid.net). If you're around at dinnertime, venture a block farther to the recommended **$$ Siglunes** guesthouse, which serves an interesting Moroccan-fusion cuisine (closed Mon).

• *As you leave Siglufjörður, head south.*

South to Dalvík

From Siglufjörður, you'll drive up on a headland (scenic pullout on the left), then disappear into a long tunnel. After 2.5 miles, you'll pop out at a virgin lake, **Héðinsfjarðarvatn,** a good picnic spot.

From here, you'll immediately enter an even longer tunnel (4.5 miles), eventually surfacing above the town of Ólafsfjörður.

• *Passing through Ólafsfjörður, the road becomes highway 82 and follows alongside the fjord.*

Leaving Ólafsfjörður (picnic pullout on the left), you'll begin to gain altitude and go through an older one-lane tunnel with pullouts. Signs explain who must pull over (there's even an instructional YouTube video—search "Olafsfjardargong"). You'll emerge along the shore of Eyjafjörður (Island Fjord)—whose name is inspired by its resident island, Hrísey, which you can't miss ahead of you, just offshore. Wind down along the mossy, stony hillside to the flat plain below, flanked by a serrated row of snow-topped peaks.

• *Next stop, Dalvík.*

From Dalvík to Akureyri

Pulling into the town of Dalvík (Valley Bay), you'll drive along its busy harbor. Where the road bends right and heads inland, consider stopping at the **$ Gísli Eiríkur Helgi café.** This relaxed and inviting coffeehouse is named for three comically "backward brothers" of Icelandic lore (look for their odd tools on the walls and blacked-out dining room inside). The café has great view seating upstairs; sells good coffee, cakes, and sandwiches; and puts on an excellent lunchtime soup-and-bread buffet (daily 11:00-20:00 in summer, Grundargata 1, mobile 666-3399, Heiða and Bjarni also run a hostel and rent cottages).

• *Continue south on highway 82.*

Beer pilgrims might consider a short detour at **Árskógssandur** (Riverwood Sands, about 10 minutes past Dalvík). This is home to **Kaldi,** Iceland's oldest microbrewery (since 2006), which offers one-hour tours of its factory (2,000 ISK, includes samples and souvenir glass, tours on the hour Mon-Fri 11:00-15:00, call ahead at other times, tel. 466-2505, www.bruggsmidjan.is). A short drive away is their fancy brewpub, **Bjórböðin,** with tastings of locally produced beers, a limited menu, and an upscale beer spa—where for 9,900 ISK you can immerse yourself in the hoppy stuff (daily, reserve ahead for the spa, tel. 414-2828, www.bjorbodin.is).

• *Highway 82 dead-ends at highway 1 (the Ring Road proper), about 20 miles beyond Dalvík. From the T-intersection where highways 82 and 1 meet, it's six more miles to Akureyri.*

Akureyri

Akureyri (AH-kuh-RAY-ree; Field Spit), with just 18,000 people, still qualifies as Iceland's second city and the unofficial capital of North Iceland. In many ways, Akureyri is a mini Reykjavík. Its pint-sized, pedestrian-friendly town center has an artfully graffitied vibe, heart-shaped red traffic lights, and small outposts of big Reykjavík shops. There's a mini church designed by Guðjón Samúelsson (architect of Reykjavík's Hallgrímskirkja), a mini *Sun Voyager* statue along its waterfront, and even its own mini Pond (south of town, near the airport). On the hill above downtown is the botanical garden and city pool.

Like any second city, Akureyri has its own proud identity. The town is a jolt of prosperity and commerce wedged between the many sleepy Ring Road villages. And its setting, right along the deep Eyjafjörður, easily one-ups Reykjavík's. Arriving in this modest metropolis can be culture shock after a few days of small towns and tiny villages. The city's history is very short, as there was little settlement here until the late 19th century. Fishing is the mainstay of the economy, and there's also a small university and a hospital.

Though a perfectly pleasant place, Akureyri doesn't have a lot of sightseeing. On a quick trip around the Ring Road, it's best as a handy stop for a meal and a short stroll. With a little more time, poke into its striking church, wander its botanical garden, or enjoy its large thermal swimming pool complex (both the botanic gardens and the pool are open late). And if you're interested in whale watching, this is one of the places in Iceland to do it (though it's arguably better in Húsavík, a bit farther along the Ring, and easier in Reykjavík).

Orientation to Akureyri

Whether you're coming directly across the mountains from Skagafjörður, or around the top of Tröllaskagi, you'll approach Akureyri on southbound high-way 1. This main road carries you right through the center of town, and then turns to cross the fjord just by Akureyri's airport.

Tourist Information: You'll find Akureyri's TI in the Hof conference and cultural center, a striking, round, brown building—you can't miss it as you drive in. The staff is helpful and well-informed, and you can pick up brochures for all of Iceland (June-late Sept daily 8:00-18:30, late-Sept-May until 16:00, closed Sat-Sun in winter, Strandgata 12, tel. 450-1050, www.visitakureyri. is). Be sure to walk around the building to get a photo with the red-heart stoplight.

Parking: Lots in downtown Akureyri require that you put a little blue cardboard clock (called a *bifreiðastæðaklukka*, or *klukka* for short) on your dashboard showing the time you arrived (signs clearly indicate the maximum stay; enforced Mon-Fri 10:00-16:00). If you need a clock, ask at the TI, a gas station, or a bank.

Pharmacy: There's a handy **Apótekarinn** pharmacy on a main shopping street (daily 9:00-17:30, across from Backpackers Hostel at Hafnarstræti 95, tel. 460-3452, www.apotekarinn.is).

Sights in Akureyri

Town Walk

Begin by exploring the vest-pocket **town center,** a pleasant grid of not quite traffic-free streets lined with good restaurants and touristy shops (including branches of Eymundsson bookstore and clothing stores 66° North and Geysir). It takes just a few enjoyable minutes to wander here and get your bearings.

Up for a climb? In the town center, with your back to the water, you'll see steps leading up to the hill-capping Lutheran Akureyri **church** (Akureyrar-kirkja), with Art Deco lines and a crushed-volcanic-rock facade.

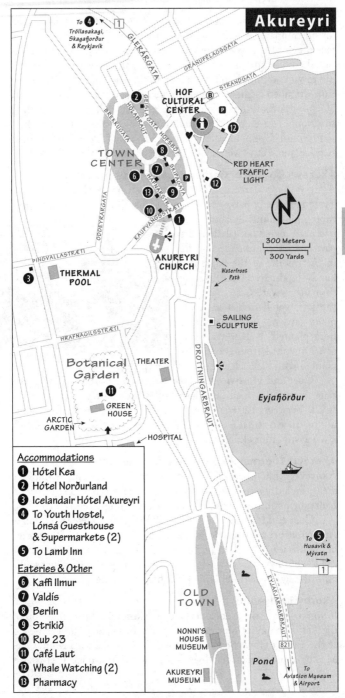

Akureyri

Accommodations
1 Hótel Kea
2 Hótel Norðurland
3 Icelandair Hótel Akureyri
4 To Youth Hostel,
   Lónsá Guesthouse
   & Supermarkets (2)
5 To Lamb Inn

Eateries & Other
6 Kaffi Ilmur
7 Valdís
8 Berlín
9 Strikið
10 Rub 23
11 Café Laut
12 Whale Watching (2)
13 Pharmacy

RING ROAD

With ample time and a desire to go for a long and level stroll (or on Sundays, when most shops are closed), head right (as you face the fjord) and walk along the waterfront path, past some traditional architecture, for about 20 minutes, all the way to Akureyri's **old town** and mini Pond, then loop back. Just before the Pond, the time-stamped original settlement of Akureyri stretches a few short blocks with traditional block houses and a few museums, including the Nonni Museum in the childhood home of beloved Jesuit priest Jón "Nonni" Sveinsson. (Sveinsson's *Nonni und Manni* books about two Icelandic boys were made into a TV show in the 1980s.)

Akureyri Botanical Garden (Lystigarður Akureyrar)

Akureyri's top attraction, especially on a sunny day, is its botanical garden. This city park—compact but smartly designed and impeccably maintained—showcases

northern plants (all labeled). Its pleasant, recommended café, in the middle of the park, is a handy landmark. Uphill (away from the waterfront) and to the left, you'll find a little alpine garden, with mountain flora planted in a pretty rockery. Downhill from the café is planted with lusher Icelandic and Arctic flora.

Cost and Hours: Free, June-Sept Mon-Fri 8:00-22:00, Sat-Sun from 9:00, facilities closed off-season but garden open to stroll, between Eyrarlandsvegur and Þórunnarstræti, free parking by the east (main) and west entrances, pay WC, tel. 462-7487, www.lystigardur.akureyri.is.

Akureyri Thermal Pool (Sundlaug Akureyrar)

Akureyri's fine thermal swimming pool has extensive outdoor areas, including an ambitious waterslide. If you have yet to try an Icelandic pool, this sprawling complex is a fun place to start.

Cost and Hours: 1,000 ISK, 250 ISK for kids ages 6-17, June-Aug Mon-Fri 6:45-21:00, Sat 8:00-21:00, Sun 8:00-19:30, shorter hours off-season, corner of Þingvallastræti and Þórunnarstræti at the top of town (east of the botanical garden), parking lot just south on Hrafnagilsstræti, tel. 461-4455, https://sundlaugar.is.

Akureyri Museums

If you have the time, consider one of Akureyri's museums. Top of the list is the **aviation museum** (Flugsafn Íslands), in a building at the airport (June-Sept Tue-Sun 11:00-17:00, closed Mon, Oct-May by appointment, tel. 461-4400, www.flugsafn.is). There's also a city history museum, an engineering museum, and a motorcycle museum. For details, ask at the TI.

Whale Watching, Island Hopping, and Other Excursions

Whale watching and other excursion boats line up at the waterfront. It's best to book ahead—well-established companies include **Elding** (www.elding.is) and **Ambassador** (www.ambassador.is). Expect to pay around 11,000 ISK for a classic three-hour cruise (double that for a two-hour high-speed RIB trip).

Akureyri is also a hub for day trips (by boat or plane) to the little island of Grímsey, just north of the Arctic Circle (see the "Islands in North Iceland" sidebar, earlier).

An excursion can make it easier to link up Akureyri with the worthwhile sights around Mývatn. **Star Travel** (www.startravel. is), **The Traveling Viking** (www.ttv.is), and **Saga Travel** (www. sagatravel.is) all run day tours (around 28,000 ISK).

Sleeping in Akureyri

You could do worse than sleeping in Akureyri, which feels like a return to civilization for Ring drivers. The town is also a good base for day trips: Head to lake Mývatn one day, to Siglufjörður the next, and so on.

In the Center: $$$$ Hótel Kea is a classic address with 104 business-class rooms right below the church steps, putting all of Akureyri at your doorstep. Rates are slushy but often land on the side of good deals (elevator, Hafnarstræti 87, tel. 460-2000, www. keahotels.is, kea@keahotels.is).

$$$ Icelandair Hótel Akureyri, with 99 well-designed rooms, offers big-hotel comfort in a hilltop location. It's in a residential zone, across from the swimming pool (breakfast extra, Þingvallastræti 23, tel. 518-1000, www.icelandairhotels.com, akureyri@icehotels.is).

$$ Hótel Norðurland, sister to Hótel Kea, has 41 comfortable rooms with private baths and a mod lounge just a few blocks off the harbor (no elevator, Geislagata 7, tel. 462-2600, www.keahotels.is, nordurland@keahotels.is).

¢ Akureyri's **official youth hostel** has 49 beds (Stórholt 1, tel. 462-3657, www.hostel.is, akureyri@hostel.is).

Cheaper Options Outside Town: In the idyllic countryside 10 minutes south of Akureyri, **$$ Lamb Inn** is on a working family farm called Öngulsstaðir. It rents 20 straightforward rooms in a converted cowshed, most with simple, prefab-like bathrooms (cheaper rooms with shared bath). They have a hot tub for guests, and a good dinner-only restaurant serving lamb raised right here (Öngulsstaðir 3, tel. 463-1500, www.lambinn.is, lambinn@ lambinn.is).

$ Lónsá, on the northern edge of town, is a basic but clean 13-room guesthouse with shared bath, guest kitchen, lounge, and laundry facilities. In old-fashioned Icelandic style, you get a better rate if you bring your sleeping bag—you get a pillow, pillowcase, and bottom sheet, and can pay extra for a towel. They also offer two cabins and a campground (breakfast extra, tel. 462-5037, www. lonsa.is, lonsa@simnet.is).

Eating in Akureyri

In the Town Center: To get a taste of Akureyri, window-shop menus at the dozen or so eateries—ranging from a hot-dog wagon or fish-and-chips to Tex-Mex or curry.

For a cozy, casual space, look for **$$ Kaffi Ilmur** (Aroma Café), filling an old house on a hillside a few steps above the main grid of streets (daily 8:00-21:00, outdoor seating in summer, lunch-only Oct-May, good-value lunch buffet, Hafnarstræti 107b, tel. 571-6444, www.kaffiilmur.com). Just up the street, **$ Valdís** dishes up creative flavors of ice cream from behind a counter in a tiny blue house (daily 10:00-23:00, tel. 537-7373).

$ Berlín, with a cozy, tight, hipster vibe, is popular for breakfast and lunch (cheap salads and sandwiches, daily 8:00-18:00, Skipagata 4, tel. 547-2226).

Nearby, you can ride an elevator to the top floor of a downtown high-rise (which, here in Akureyri, means just five stories) to **$$$ Strikið,** a modern Nordic bistro with an eclectic menu. While quite pricey at dinner, they offer good lunch specials with a view (daily 11:30-22:30, Skipagata 14, tel. 462-7100, www.strikid.is).

And for top-end dining, **$$$$ Rub 23** has a reputation even among Reykjavík urbanites for its grill-focused Asian-fusion food and sushi (Mon-Fri 11:30-14:00 & 17:30-22:00, dinner-only Sat-Sun, across the street from the church steps at Kaupvangsstræti 6, tel. 462-2223, www.rub23.is).

In the Botanical Garden: At the center of the garden is **$ Café Laut,** serving sandwiches, salads, and soup in a striking picture-windowed building (late May-late Sept daily 10:00-19:00, closed off-season, Eyrarlandsvegur 30, tel. 461-4601).

Supermarkets: Bónus is along the main road as you drive into town from the west (Langholt 1). There's also **Nettó,** in the Glerártorg mall, also along the main road.

Akureyri Connections

Akureyri is a transportation hub for the north and is well-connected to **Reykjavík** by **bus** #57 (2/day, 1/day on Sat, 6.5 hours to Reykjavík's Mjódd station, www.straeto.is). In summer you can also take cross-country bus #610 over otherwise inaccessible Highland passes (1/day, 10.5 hours, brief stops at Geysir and Gullfoss, www.sba.is).

In summer (June-mid-Aug), Strætó offers other bus connections, but they don't work for a same-day round-trip: Once daily, a bus leaves in the afternoon for **Mývatn** (3.5 hours), then continues on to **Egilsstaðir** (a hub for the Eastfjords, 5.5 hours). To reach the fun little fjordside town of **Siglufjörður,** in summer three daily buses allow for a same-day return (1.5 hours each way; for the best views, sit on the right on the way up, and the left on the way back).

Off-season, all bus schedules are reduced. Long-distance buses stop at the Hof conference and cultural center, by the TI.

You can also **fly** in less than an hour from Reykjavík City Airport to the Akureyri airport—you'll spot the runway in the middle of the fjord, about two miles from the center (car rental and taxis available; look for flights at www.airicelandconnect.com). Note that there are flights from Keflavík Airport to Akureyri, but they are timed to international arrivals and do not allow layovers; if you plan to visit Reykjavík first you'll want to fly from the city airport.

Akureyri to Mývatn

It's about 60 miles (75 minutes) from Akureyri to Mývatn.

Leaving Akureyri: From Akureyri, highway 1 crosses the fjord by the airport and turns north along the opposite shore (pullouts offer views across the fjord to the city). After about 20 minutes, immediately following the last pullout, you'll reach a roundabout and a choice: scenic pass or tunnel. Know what you're doing before you get here.

Option 1: If you follow signs to *Grenivík/Svalbarðseyri,* the road climbs steeply away from the fjord. Stay right at the Y onto highway 84 to cross the first pass of the day, **Víkurskarð** (1,100 feet), then rejoin highway 1. Víkurskarð is beautiful in summer but treacherous in snow.

Option 2: If instead you follow signs to *Egilsstaðir/Mývatn/ Húsavík,* you'll enter the four-mile-long Vaðlaheiðargöng **toll tunnel** and barrel straight under the mountain. There's no toll plaza: Rental-car drivers are expected to pay online (1,500 ISK in advance or within three hours, 2,500 ISK thereafter, easy to register in advance and pay at www.veggjald.is). In good weather, I'd take

RING ROAD

the scenic pass rather than paying for the tunnel, which only saves about 10 minutes.

• *It's about 45 minutes from here to our next stop, Goðafoss. Rejoining highway 1 (or emerging from the tunnel), you'll drive through lightly forested foothills that open into a valley. Just after a large lake (Ljósa-vatn—Mirror Lake—has pullout with WC), a turnoff on the left leads to Húsavík (highway 85). But we'll continue another five minutes across the rocky landscape to reach...*

Goðafoss Waterfall: This ▲ pretty, horseshoe-shaped water-fall on the Skjálfandafljót river is not so high (only 40 feet), but it is quite broad (100 yards). There are two parking lots, one on each side of the falls, with paved walkways and viewpoints along both sides. It takes just a couple of minutes to walk to the best views. The west parking lot has no services but gives you ac-cess to the tidepool-like rocks at the top of the falls, and perhaps

the best overall view of the cascades. The east lot is beyond the gift shop/café (pay WC). You can return to the highway to drive between the two, or use the pedestrian bridge that was once the main road.

This waterfall plays a role in the sagas. In 1000, the law speak-er of the Alþingi made a momentous decision: Þorgeir Ljósvet-ningagoði, whose home farm (Ljósavatn) was in this area, was as-signed to choose whether Iceland would remain pagan or (under great pressure from Norway) become Christian. Þorgeir chose to have Iceland convert, and to fully own up to his decision, he became a Christian, came home, and allegedly threw his carved pagan statues into this waterfall—giving it the name Waterfall of the Gods (Goða-foss). For more on Þorgeir, see page 195.

• *From Goðafoss, the road climbs over a low pass called **Fljótsheiði** (800 feet). You'll pass another turnoff for Húsavík (highway 845), then drop down to the small settlement of Laugar.*

Laugar to Mývatn: There's not too much to see in this sparsely populated countryside. You'll pass a few farms and drive along the shore of a desolate lake, then along a small river, **Laxá.** The river is famous as the site where, in 1970, almost two hundred locals took matters into their own hands and blew up a small, controversial dam they had opposed. Over a hundred individuals "confessed" to the crime and refused to say who did what, making prosecution difficult.

• *About an hour from Akureyri, you'll reach the junction of highways 1 and 848. Carry straight along on highway 848.*

You're just west of lake **Mývatn**. From here, follow highway 848 counterclockwise as it loops around the south and east shore of the lake, with several attractions (described next).

From Mývatn, it's a 45-minute detour north on highway 87 to the bayside town of **Húsavík** (described on page 404).

Mývatn

Mývatn (MEE-vahtn; *n* almost silent—literally Midge Lake, after the tiny gnats that thrive here) is one of Iceland's most impressive natural areas. The lake itself—about 14 square miles, broad and shallow—has an intriguingly ragged coastline, with lots of bays and islets. Better still, it's ringed by a delightful array of volcanic features, from bubbly pseudocraters to otherworldly pillars to a climbable volcanic cone.

A short drive away are even more sights, including a geothermally active valley and one of Iceland's best premium thermal baths. The entire area is ringed by striking flat-topped mountains, making it feel like the setting for an interplanetary science-fiction epic. With its accessible size, remote location, and diversity of easy nature hikes, Mývatn feels like Iceland's Yellowstone; many visitors call it their favorite area of all.

Note that the Mývatn area lacks a real town, but the appealing small town of Húsavík is just a 45-minute drive north. Húsavík is worth a detour (and can be a good place to stay, if Mývatn is full or if you're interested in whale watching; see page 405).

Orientation to Mývatn

Mývatn is the name of the lake, but also refers to the entire area (which Icelanders call Mývatnssveit). Sights are scattered around the lake, which is ringed by two roads. Highway 1 runs along the west and north side, with few sights other than Sigurgeir's Bird Museum. Highway 848, on the south and east sides, is more interesting, especially along the 10-mile stretch between the hamlets

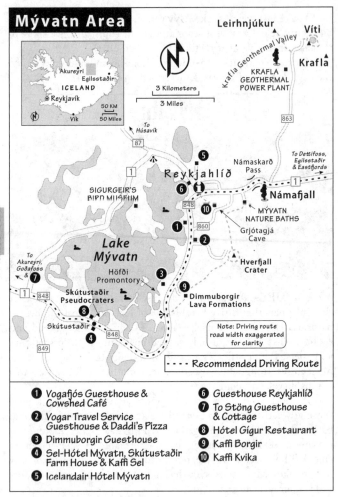

Mývatn Area

ICELAND
Akureyri
Egilsstaðir
Reykjavík
Vík

50 KM
50 Miles

3 Kilometers
3 Miles

To Húsavík

Leirhnjúkur

Krafla Geothermal Valley

Víti

Krafla

KRAFLA GEOTHERMAL POWER PLANT

863

To Dettifoss, Egilsstaðir & Eastfjords

Reykjahlíð

Námaskarð Pass

Námafjall

SIGURGEIR'S BIRD MUSEUM

848

MÝVATN NATURE BATHS

860

Grjótagjá Cave

Lake Mývatn

Höfði Promontory

Hverfjall Crater

To Akureyri, Goðafoss &

Dimmuborgir Lava Formations

Skútustaðir Pseudocraters

848

Skútustaðir

848

849

Note: Driving route road width exaggerated for clarity

- - - - Recommended Driving Route

RING ROAD

1. Vogafjós Guesthouse & Cowshed Café
2. Vogar Travel Service Guesthouse & Daddi's Pizza
3. Dimmuborgir Guesthouse
4. Sel-Hótel Mývatn, Skútustaðir Farm House & Kaffi Sel
5. Icelandair Hótel Mývatn
6. Guesthouse Reykjahlíð
7. To Stöng Guesthouse & Cottage
8. Hótel Gígur Restaurant
9. Kaffi Borgir
10. Kaffi Kvika

of Skútustaðir and Reykjahlíð. Another cluster of sights lines the stretch of highway 1 that runs east away from the lake, toward the Eastfjords.

Most settlement around the lake is on dispersed farms. **Reykjahlíð** (RAYK-yah-HLEETH, Steamy Slope), at the lake's northeast corner, is the closest Mývatn comes to a village, with about half of the region's population—a whopping 200 people. It has the nature reserve visitor center, small supermarket, bank, gas station, health center, and a few streets with houses. **Skútustaðir** (SKOO-tu-STAH-theer), on the southern shore, is just a church, a handful of hotels, and gas pumps, next to a farm.

Tourist Information: The **Mývatnsstofa Visitor Center** in

Reykjahlíð is staffed by knowledgeable park rangers and offers maps and hiking advice. A small but worthwhile exhibit explains the lake's geology and biology (daily in summer 8:00-18:00, shorter hours off-season, Hraunvegur 8, tel. 464-4460). The website VisitMyvatn.is is also helpful.

Navigation Note: Google Maps makes some errors in this area; supplement with printed maps or the local website Ja.is.

Tours and Activities: In the parking lot of Icelandair Hótel Reynihlíð, **Mývatn Activity** rents bikes and can arrange bike, hiking, and jeep tours as well as other activities (mobile 899-4845, http://hikeandbike.is). **Mýflug Air** runs sightseeing flights over the region (www.myflug.is). Various local companies offer **horseback riding** (Saltvík: www.saltvik.is; Safari Horse Rental: http://safarihorserental.com). If you stay longer in the region, several operators offer day trips to the giant **Askja** volcanic caldera, deep in the Highlands south of Mývatn, which you can reach only in a 4x4 vehicle (Fjallasýn: www.fjallasyn.is; Mývatn Tours: www.myvatntours.is).

Eating: This area has no real "destination" restaurants, but I've listed a few practical choices mixed in with the sights. Try to sample two local products that are often served together: sweet, dark-rye bread that's buried underground and baked with natural thermal heat, then topped with decadent, smoked lake trout.

Dealing with Midges: You may want to wear a net to protect yourself from midges flying into your nose, ears, or mouth (see sidebar). You can bring one from home or buy one locally (sold at area supermarkets). Don't bother using insect repellent: The bugs aren't out to bite you—they're just a nuisance.

Sights near Mývatn

AROUND THE SOUTH AND EAST SHORE

These sights ring the lakefront. I've listed them in the order you'll encounter them driving counterclockwise from Skútustaðir (southwest) to Reykjahlíð (northeast) along highway 848.

▲Skútustaðir Pseudocraters

At the tiny settlement called Skútustaðir, you reach the first of many striking volcanic sights at the lake. Park at the lot (next to the Hótel Gígur) and spend 20 minutes walking the half-mile "Crater Trail," between the road and the lake, through the pseudocraters (also called "rootless cones"). These grassy dimples are not real volcanic craters. They're all that's left of what had been giant bubbles in molten lava: Water under the lava boiled into steam, rose to the surface, and popped. A paved walkway leads to the top of the nearest crater, then continues as a gravel path. Metal stairs climb up to the rims of several of the craters. A longer path here (Bird Trail, 1.5 miles) takes an hour.

Eating at Skútustaðir: Next to the parking lot, **$$$ Hótel Gígur** offers lakeside views and a more upscale experience (daily, closed off-season). Across the street (no views), **$ Kaffi Sel** serves cheap,

simple meals and a handy, lunchtime soup-and-bread buffet (daily, tel. 464-4164, www.myvatn.is). The restaurant inside **$$ Sel-Hótel Mývatn** has a more substantial lunch buffet for about double the price (daily).

• *To continue around the lake, follow the lakeside road counterclockwise. Within a few miles you'll leave grassy rolling hills and enter a lunar landscape covered by an ancient lava flow. As you come up over a rise, watch on the left for a pullout overlooking a lagoon that's filled with serrated lava islands. As you look out over the water, notice the wooded peninsula to the north (on your right). This is...*

Höfði Promontory

For years, a local couple worked to reforest this small peninsula, and laid out sheltered walking trails with views of the lake and the lava columns that rise up from it. It has its own parking lot (just beyond the pullout mentioned above) and makes a nice 30-minute stop on a pleasant day, offering panoramic views over the region. If you come on a calm summer day, you may see more insects than you ever have in your life. Wear a net, or prepare to spit midges.

• *On the land side of the road, a little farther north (toward Reykjahlíð), watch for the turnoff for our next stop, which sits about a half-mile off the main road.*

▲▲Dimmuborgir Lava Formations

Literally the Dark Castles, Dimmuborgir (DIM-moo-BOR-geer) is a fantasyland of spectacular pillars and crenellated formations. It's the most satisfying place around the lake for an easy nature walk, and it's fun for kids—with a little imagination a rock easily becomes the face of one of the numerous trolls said to live here. Locals walk through reciting their favorite

The Geology, Flora, Fauna (and Midges) of Mývatn

Because Mývatn sits along the gap between the Eurasian and North American tectonic plates, the area is very active geothermally. Relatively recent volcanic eruptions—about 2,500 years ago—shaped the landscape here: A powerful eruption created the Hverfjall crater, and vast amounts of lava from a fissure (vent) eruption poured out, blocking a river (creating the lake), then flowing down the valley toward Akureyri.

The lake is protected as a nature reserve, and boating is restricted. The water is shallow and calm; ducks and other migratory water birds breed around the lake and its surrounding wetlands. Far from the sea, the area has slightly warmer, drier, and less windy summers than other parts of the country.

Unfortunately, these conditions make it a perfect home  for midges (mý), the aquatic insects after which the lake is named. They don't bite (this distinguishes them from the nasty midges common in Scotland, no-see-ums in the US, and sandflies in Australia). But Mývatn's midges (in the chironomid family) do swarm—in such numbers during the summer, especially in windless conditions, that locals sometimes wear nets over their heads to stop the little things from getting into their ears, mouths, and noses.

Mývatn is also home to black flies (Simulium vittatum), which do bite. Fortunately, these are mostly concentrated in the less touristed western end of the lake and the Laxá river, and with luck, you won't encounter them at all. (They're also found elsewhere in Iceland.)

Mývatn has plenty of biodiversity beyond its bugs and birds. The lake itself is rich in nutrients and has an abundance of aquatic life. Mývatn and a lake in Japan are the only places on earth known to support kúluskítur (marimo), an unusual algae that forms into lovable green, softball-size spheres. Unfortunately, the balls have mostly disappeared from Mývatn in the last few years, although one is tenderly cared for at Sigurgeir's Bird Museum.

folk tales, including that of Gammur, an eagle that's the guardian spirit of north Iceland.

The Dimmuborgir formations originated when everything here was underwater. From the lakebed, magma leaked upward and solidified, forming spiky, stalagmite-like columns. Well-marked, paved trails lead through Dimmuborgir; study the posted map to plan a route for the amount of time you have. The shortest walk takes only 15 minutes, but you could easily spend two hours here. A marker above the parking lot identifies the surrounding peaks. Entrance and parking is free (pay WC at the café), and if you visit early or late, it will be less crowded.

Eating at Dimmuborgir: Above the Dimmuborgir parking lot, **$$ Kaffi Borgir** has a soup-and-bread lunch buffet and a short menu of main dishes. Their "bread in a bucket" is baked in the ground for 24 hours. If you can handle the midges, their outdoor seating is atmospheric (daily 10:00-21:30, closed off-season, tel. 461-1144, www.kaffiborgir.is).

• *Returning to highway 848, continue north, watching for* Hverfjall *signs. A gravel road leads 1.5 miles to the parking lot for...*

RING ROAD

▲▲Hverfjall Crater

The vast, dry Hverfjall crater (KVER-fyahtl, sometimes spelled Hverfell) rises just east of the lake—you can't miss it. From the parking lot (free to park, pay WCs, info boards), a path leads up the gravel slope of the mountain to the rim, where there's an excellent view down into the broad crater and back toward the lake. The hike up is a good workout, but isn't too steep and takes about 20 minutes one-way. Allow another 1.5 hours to hike the crater's two-mile perimeter. In strong winds, the walk up isn't much fun, and the loose soil can start to fly around; otherwise, your effort will be rewarded.

Hverfjall is what's known as a tephra volcano—composed of volcanic ash and small debris, created in an eruption about 2,900 years ago. It's big: The cone-shaped mountain itself is over a mile wide and 550 feet tall, and the crater is a half-mile in diameter.

Eating near Hverfjall: Just north along the road toward Reykjahlíð is **$$$ Cowshed Café,** with a country-kitschy vibe and tasty farm-to-table cooking; it's my favorite choice for a meal in the area (it's part of the recommended Vogafjós Guesthouse). It's in a barn, with views of the lakeshore and mooing cows—you can see the milking area through a window (daily 11:00-21:30 in summer, closes earlier off-season, tel. 464-3800, www.vogafjosfarmresort. is).

• *The next stop is best reached from highway 1 (see complete directions below).*

Grjótagjá Thermal Cave

Tucked in the middle of nowhere a few minutes' drive from the lake is a hidden cave filled with natural thermal waters. It gets more attention than it deserves for being a filming location for *Game of Thrones* (the romantic retreat where Jon Snow and Ygritte, ahem, violated the oath of the Night's Watch). While skippable for most, curious *GoT* fans may find the brief detour justifiable. You'll park

next to a buckled ridge of lava, where extremely uneven, rocky footing leads down to a steaming pool. Watch your step—this is at your own risk, with no guardrails or barriers—and getting in the water is forbidden. Another path leads to the top of the lava formation, where you can see the crevasse stretching into the distance.

Getting There: Even though it's on road 860, Grjótagjá is most easily accessed from highway 1, just east of the lake but before the turnoff for Mývatn Thermal Baths; watch for the small *Grjótagjá* sign. From the turnoff, it's a quick 1.5-mile drive to the parking lot (portable WC, info board). Note that road 860 continues from the cave all the way to Mývatn's east shore (near Vogafjós Guesthouse); this can be a handy shortcut, but you may need to let yourself through a gate. It's also possible to hike here from Hverfjall and Reykjahlíð.

ON THE NORTHWEST SHORE
Sigurgeir's Bird Museum (Fuglasafn Sigurgeirs)

Mývatn is famous among birders, who have observed more than 115 species here (including 30 types of ducks)—making it one of the richest birding areas in the world. This museum, worth ▲ for birders, offers an opportunity to examine hundreds of taxidermy specimens up close (as well as an extensive egg collection). Display cases show off a striking diversity of birds, including nearly every bird found in Iceland and many that migrate here to breed. Webcams and telescopes let you observe live birds on the lake, and the staff loves to advise visiting birders. A second, smaller building displays a boat once used to ferry passengers across the lake.

The collection is named for avid birder Sigurgeir Stefánsson, who lived on this farm and collected most of the specimens you see (usually birds that were already deceased). Nature did not return his kindness, as at age 37, Sigurgeir drowned during a freak storm on the lake. But his legacy—and his passion—live on here.

Cost and Hours: 1,500 ISK, mid-May-Oct daily 12:00-17:00, shorter hours off-season, on-site café, on road 8735 at the farm called Ytri-Neslönd—signposted off highway 1, tel. 464-4477, www.fuglasafn.is.

RING ROAD

GEOTHERMAL SIGHTS JUST EAST OF MÝVATN

On and near highway 1 going east from the lake are several other worthwhile attractions—most of them related to the geothermally alive landscape. You might find it simplest to fit these in on your way from Mývatn to the Eastfjords, but it'd be a shame to rush them. Since they're all within 10 miles of the lake, you can easily double back if you're staying nearby.

• *Along highway 1, five minutes from Reykjahlíð (and before Námas-karð pass), watch for* Jarðböðin *signs on the right to reach...*

▲▲▲Mývatn Nature Baths (Jarðböðin við Mývatn)

This premium swimming pool is one of Iceland's most appealing thermal bath experiences. Imagine the Blue Lagoon, but a bit more modest, less crowded (maximum capacity is about 430), and about half the price. The baths' outdoor lagoon is beautifully designed: two big pools with natural contours, rocky walls, pebbly bottoms, and fine views over the volcanic countryside (black rock, steaming vents, and distant lake views). Like the Blue Lagoon, the water here is naturally heated excess from a nearby geothermal power station (at Bjarnarflag); unlike the Blue Lagoon, the water here isn't salty, has no silica suspended in it, is more white than blue, and has a slightly sulfurous odor. The nature baths are open late, making it an ideal way to unwind after a long day driving the Ring or exploring Mývatn. It's not quite luxurious or spa-like (no swim-up bar, no mud masks, no private shower cabins), but for many, these baths are a just-right Goldilocks compromise between the expense and pretense of the Blue Lagoon and the austere functionality of standard municipal pools. Locals enjoy it, too. The industrial complex across highway 1 (at the turnoff for the baths) is a former geothermal power plant.

Cost and Hours: 5,300 ISK, towel rental-850 ISK, daily late May-Sept 9:00-24:00, off-season 12:00-22:00, timed-entry tickets available online but unnecessary, often referred to as *Jarðbaðshólar* on maps and signs, tel. 464-4411, www.myvatnnaturebaths.is.

Visiting the Baths: The modern entry building has free parking, a nice café, free WCs even for nonbathers, and a view deck overlooking the pool. Buy your ticket (prepay for a drink bracelet, if you like), find your way to the simple locker room, shower, and stow your clothes. It's best to remove easily tarnished jewelry and glasses or other delicate lenses, which can be damaged by the water's minerals (for more on best practices at thermal pools, see page 42). Then head outside and lower yourself into the steaming water, which is highly alkaline and slightly milky. Temperatures range from 34°C to 41°C (93-105°F), with hot and cool spots around the pool. Explore, float, and relax. If you bought a drink, flag down an attendant to bring it to you. The two steam baths, in little sheds around the pools' perimeter, vent natural geothermal steam through the floor at a temperature of about 50°C (122°F).

Eating at the Baths: The complex has a good cafeteria, **$ Kaffi Kvika** (Magma Café), with indoor and outdoor seating overlooking the lively lagoon (no bath ticket required). As this is essentially your "last-chance lunch" (other than picnicking) between here and the Eastfjords, consider stopping on your way out of the area (open same hours as pool). You're not allowed to eat your own food on the premises.

• *Just past the baths, you'll crest the small Námaskarð pass. Watch on the right (after the steep initial climb) for a pullout with a commanding panoramic view over the entire Mývatn area. Coming down the other side of the pass, a turnoff on the right leads in a couple hundred yards to a parking lot for the...*

▲▲▲Námafjall Geothermal Area

The steaming, bubbling, brightly colored landscape of Námafjall (NOW-mah-fyahtl)—which is also sometimes called Hverir (Hot

Springs) or Hverarönd— is one of Iceland's most accessible and impressive geothermal areas. While it lacks a spouting geyser, it's more colorful and more interesting (and in a more impressive setting, ringed by mountains) than Geysir on the

Golden Circle—and it's far less crowded, with very few ropes and signs (use caution and stay on the trodden paths). Parking is free (no WCs).

Park and step outside—getting slapped in the face with pungent hydrogen sulfide fumes. Then plug your nose and explore this compact, astonishingly diverse landscape. You'll see fumaroles (like little stacked-rock ovens spitting steam), bubbling pools and mud pots, and a terrain brushed in a rainbow of vivid colors. The mountainside just beyond the plain also has steaming vents; with extra time, you can hike up the trail for a closer look and for views back over this landscape. The sulfur deposits in this area were once mined for gunpowder (*náma* means "mine").

• *A quarter-mile farther on, detour onto paved highway 863 (to the north). This five-mile-long road passes through a steaming landscape, linking several worthwhile attractions.*

▲▲Krafla Geothermal Valley

The volcano Krafla (KRAH-plah), at the end of this valley, was active as recently as the 1980s; now the valley is the site of a geothermal power plant (notice the pipeline and electric cables on your left).

• *As you head up the valley, keep an eye out on the right for a...*

Showerhead: Sticking up from the ground, a single showerhead stands lonely in the middle of a volcanic plain. It appeared overnight several years ago—perhaps as a prank or art installation—but it really is hooked up to natural thermal water. Stop and give it a try. (Someone added a sink the last time I was there; unfortunately it doesn't work.)

• *Continuing up the valley, you can't miss the simmering...*

Krafla Geothermal Power Plant: This plant taps into superheated liquid deep underground to generate electricity. Its modest, summer-only visitors center has exhibits and a brief film about Iceland's geothermal plants (free entry, WCs, and coffee; June-mid-Sept daily 10:00-17:00, closed off-season, www.landsvirkjun.com).

• *After leaving the power station,* there's a parking lot on the left at the head of a marked path that takes you across a lava field to the...

Leirhnjúkur Volcanic Cone: Meaning literally Clay Peak, this low volcanic cone formed during eruptions around 1980. Volcano buffs enjoy the full hiking circuit here—all the way around the mountain. It takes about three hours and includes colorful pools, still-steaming lava formations, and more. To get a quick feel for the place, walk out to the mountain and back (about 15 minutes each way, partly on boardwalks); you'll see some mud pots and fumaroles. The footing can be slippery—if you value your shoes (and feet), stay on the marked paths.

• *Continuing on the main road past the Leirhnjúkur parking lot, look for a pullout on the right with info boards and a stunning view back over the valley. Then drive to the end of the road and the...*

Víti Crater: This unearthly volcanic crater with a lake inside was formed during eruptions in the 1720s. You'll park and walk uphill to the rim, with fantastic views over the colorful walls and water. From here, a path leads all the way around

the crater (30 minutes). Víti (Hell) is big, wild, and an altogether powerful and forbidding sight. Don't go down to the water, which is hot.

Sleeping near Mývatn

While this is a delightful area to spend the night, reserve your rooms well ahead, as hotels can book up very quickly. If things are booked solid, stay in Húsavík—a pleasant waterfront town a 45-minute drive north (described later). You can also try checking back to see if you can fill a cancellation. Camping is allowed only at designated sites.

On the Eastern Shore: Near all the major sights, **$$$$ Vogafjós Guesthouse** is a family-run working farm with 26 good, tidy rooms with private baths in three newer wooden buildings. Reception is at the recommended Cowshed Café restaurant (tel. 464-3800, www.vogafjosfarmresort.is, vogafjos@vogafjos.is).

$$ Vogar Travel Service feels like summer camp. They run a basic guesthouse (20 rooms with shared bath, 8 rooms with private bath, breakfast extra) in several buildings, a campground, and a pizza joint. They'll do laundry for anyone—drop off in the morning to pick up 24 hours later (south of Reykjahlíð on highway 848, tel. 464-4399, www.vogartravelservice.com).

$$ Dimmuborgir Guesthouse has eight simple rooms (with private bathrooms and a shared kitchen) in a main building and several prefab wooden cottages (with private baths and kitchenettes). It's loosely run but family-friendly (2-night minimum in summer, no breakfast, Geiteyjarströnd 1, tel. 464-4210, www.dimmuborgir.is, dimmuborgir@emax.is).

On the Southern Shore, at Skútustaðir: Family-run but characterless, **$$$$ Sel-Hótel Mývatn** has 56 business-class rooms that feel designed for tour groups and conferences. It's across from the pseudocraters, with a shop, café, and restaurant on-site (elevator, tel. 464-4164, www.myvatn.is, myvatn@myvatn.is).

$ Skútustaðir Farm House, tucked behind the Sel-Hótel complex, is family-run, with 14 modern rooms (10 with shared bathrooms, 5 with private bathrooms) in a mix of old and new buildings, plus a standalone cottage (breakfast extra in cottage, shared kitchen, laundry facility, tel. 464-4212, www.skutustadir. is, book by email at info@skutustadir.is, Sofia).

On the Northern Shore, at Reykjahlíð: **$$$ Icelandair Hótel Mývatn** has 59 industrial-chic rooms, along with a friendly bar and more formal restaurant (pricey but hearty breakfast, elevator, tel. 464-4170, www.icelandairhotels.com). They also operate the older and cheaper nine-room **Guesthouse Reykjahlíð,** in the red-roofed house across the highway.

In the Countryside to the West: An authentic farm, **$$ Stöng Guesthouse and Cottage** is a couple of miles down an unpaved side road, on the way from Goðafoss to Mývatn. Their two dozen rooms are spread among a main building (from the 1920s), a motel, and cottage-style outbuildings on land that's been in the family since 1870. It's not as spiffy as other options, but it's less expensive and guests can use the two hot tubs. Older rooms in the main building have a shared bath; private-bath rooms are more modern but still basic (closed Nov-March, restaurant with traditional dinners, tel. 464-4252, mobile 896-6074, www.stong.is, stongmy@stong.is).

Húsavík

Húsavík (HOOS-ah-VEEK, pop. 2,200), north of Mývatn, is a pretty little burg with a nice harbor facing the fjordlike Skjálfandi bay. For visitors with time to linger, Húsavík offers a pleasant real-town vibe, a handful of appealing restaurants, two swimming pools, a colorful town church, a good whale museum, and some of Iceland's best whale watching. If you're enjoying long summer days and want to take a dinnertime side-trip, Húsavík is pleasant enough to warrant the drive from Mývatn. Húsavík is also a good fallback home base when rooms around Mývatn are all booked up.

Getting There: From Mývatn, Húsavík is about a 45-minute drive (35 miles) north on highway 87 from near Reykjahlíð. As you leave the lake area, you'll pass through a bulging volcanic landscape interspersed with hardy sheep farms; you can see clearly where the undulating lava buckled and bubbled as it cooled. Then you'll traverse a stark, desolate terrain, with few settlements and several stretches of unpaved road. Eventually you run into the picturesque

RING ROAD

The Other Circles

In the Mývatn and Húsavík area, you may notice references to the **Diamond Circle**. This tourist route—a would-be competitor to the Golden Circle closer to Reykjavík—is a suggested sightseeing route through northeast Iceland that connects Mývatn, Húsavík, the Tjörnes Peninsula, Ásbyrgi (a stunning set of cliffs and canyons formed by massive glacial flooding a few thousand years ago), and the Dettifoss waterfall (for specifics, see www.diamondcircle.is).

From Ásbyrgi (50 minutes northeast of Húsavík), partly gravel road 862 and all-gravel road 864 (open in summer only) lead along either side of the Jökulsá á Fjöllum river to Dettifoss; from there you can continue back to the Ring without backtracking through Mývatn. There's a one-pump gas station and a visitors center just off highway 85 at the head of Ásbyrgi canyon (visitors center open in summer 9:00-18:00, shorter hours off-season, WCs, tel. 470-7100, www.vatnajokulsthjodgardur. is, asbyrgi@vjp.is). You'll probably need four-wheel drive for these rough roads, though (check conditions at www.road.is and with locals before proceeding). While striking, Ásbyrgi is, for most visitors, a long and challenging drive. As roads improve in this area, Ásbyrgi will become easier to build into a Ring Road trip.

Some of the towns and villages on the Ring Road route are also part of what's known as the **Arctic Coast Way,** a 550-mile driving itinerary linking 21 small towns and five islands along Iceland's far northern coast. Promoted as a less-touristy alternative to the Golden Circle, if you're looking to really get off the beaten path, this is the way to do it. For details, see www.northiceland.is.

RING ROAD

Skjálfandi bay, turn right onto highway 85, and carry on into town. From Akureyri, you can reach Húsavík from highway 1 by turning north on highway 85 before Goðafoss, or highway 845 after the falls (about an hour and 80 miles either way).

Orientation to Húsavík: This little town is simple. The main road coasts downhill to the town center and a handy parking lot on the harbor. Everything I mention is within a five-minute stroll. The Húsavík Whale Museum ticket desk serves as a basic town **TI,** with maps and brochures (see www.visithusavik.com).

Sights in Húsavík

▲▲Whale Watching
Facing the Greenland Sea and about as far north as you can get in Iceland (next stop: Arctic Circle), Húsavík is one of Iceland's top whale-watching destinations, with the best likelihood of actually seeing a whale. Several well-established companies have sales kiosks

Whaling in Iceland

While early Icelanders did occasionally catch whales, using Moby Dick-style harpoons, they lacked the technology to exploit the sea mammals at any commercial scale. Whalers in the seas around Iceland came mostly from Europe: Basque sailors began whaling in the Atlantic in the 11th century, reaching Icelandic waters in the 17th century. They occasionally clashed with locals, and in 1615, Icelanders massacred 30 Basque castaways in the Westfjords in an event called the "Slaying of the Spaniards." In the late 17th century, Dutch whalers arrived, and Norwegians dominated the industry from about 1883 until overhunting led to a ban in 1915. Whaling resumed in 1935, with another ban in 1983. In 2006, Iceland controversially decided to permit commercial whale hunting, both of relatively abundant minke whales and of threatened fin and sei whales.

overlooking the hardworking harbor. Options range from classic old wooden boats to high-speed RIBs (rigid inflatable boats). A standard three-hour trip costs around 10,500 ISK. The main operators include North Sailing (www.northsailing.is), Gentle Giants (www.gentlegiants.is), and Salka Whale Watching (www.salkawhalewatching.is). But if your time in this area is

limited, consider whale watching from Reykjavík or Akureyri instead.

▲Húsavík Whale Museum (Hvalasafnið á Húsavík)

This thoughtful museum offers an informative look at the whales that fill the waters around Iceland. Though fairly dry and scientif-

ic, the exhibits are good, with miniature models of whales, an actual jawbone of a sperm whale, a display on seabirds, a one-hour *Giants of the Deep* film, and several good children's areas. But the museum's highlight is hanging from the rafters upstairs: the skeletons of 11 whale species, including narwhal, sperm, humpback, orca, and pilot. The biggest skeleton—in the side hall on the main floor—is an 80-foot-long blue whale. These specimens were not hunted, but washed up on beaches, then removed and processed by the museum. (Anytime a beached whale corpse appeared around Iceland, locals called the museum to come cart it away.) Rounding out the exhibits are art installations related to whales and an unapologetic overview of the history of whaling in Iceland, including a film with archival footage of workers processing and rendering slabs of blubber.

Cost and Hours: 2,000 ISK; daily May-Sept 8:30-18:30, Oct-April 10:00-16:00, closed Sat-Sun Nov-March; Hafnarstétt 1, tel. 414-2800, www.hvalasafn.is.

Húsavík Church (Húsavíkurkirkja)

Húsavík's unusually colorful and interesting town church dates from 1907 (you can't miss its pointy steeple along the main street as you come into town). Stepping inside, it's clear this church was designed by shipbuilders: Stout beams intersect in the middle of the ceiling, like perpendicular boat hulls, all painted in cheery colors. Rather than a pulpit, there's a simple lectern, shaped like an open book. Notice the c. 1930 painting over the altar depicting the resurrection of Lazarus...but set in Iceland (see the backdrop of lava rock).

Geosea Geothermal Sea Baths

Opened in 2018, this small but modern geothermal bath pipes mineral-rich seawater warmed by underwater vents into three outdoor pools (including an infinity pool) set high on a cliff overlooking the ocean. It's arguably the most scenic of Iceland's commercial thermal baths, and is limited to 160 bathers, making it much more intimate than the Blue Lagoon or baths at Mývatn.

Cost and Hours: 4,300 ISK, timed-entry tickets available but not necessary, towel rental-800 ISK, daily May-Sept 10:00-24:00, off-season 12:00-22:00, coffee shop, a 20-minute uphill walk (or 3-minute drive) from the harbor at Vitaslóð 1, tel. 464-1210, www.geosea.is.

Húsavík City Pool (Sundlaug Húsavíkur)

Less expensive (and more family-friendly) than Geosea, the Húsavík city pool has a large outdoor section, a smaller children's pool, hot tubs, sauna, and water slides (800 ISK, Mon-Fri 7:00-21:00, Sat-Sun 10:00-18:00, just north of the harbor at Laugarbrekka 2, tel. 464-6190, www.nordurthing.is).

Sleeping and Eating in Húsavík

Sleeping in Town: $$ Post-Plaza Guesthouse, in an official-looking building a block off the main drag, started life as the post office. Inside you'll find six bright-white rooms with glassy private baths and a mod shared kitchen and lounge area. The price includes a picnic-style breakfast (Garðarsbraut 21, mobile 777-2330, www.postplazaguesthouse.com, post.plaza.husavik@gmail.com).

$$$ Árból Guesthouse, a couple of blocks up from the harborfront, has 10 contemporary rooms with shared bathrooms in a fine, creaky old wood-frame house (Ásgarðsvegur 2, tel. 464-2220, www.arbol.is, arbol@arbol.is); they also have six studio apartments across the street.

Sleeping Outside Town: $ Kaldbaks-Kot, set in a hand-planted grove of trees, is a lovely little countryside compound of 17 jewel-box wooden cottages (sleeping 2-10 people, all with private bathrooms and mini kitchenettes). It's in a gorgeous setting, perched just above a private lake busy with birds a few minutes' drive outside Húsavík (breakfast extra, mobile 892-1744, www.cottages.is, cottages@cottages.is).

$$ Skógar Sunset Guesthouse, on a remote ridge along highway 87 (about 15 minutes south of Húsavík and 30 minutes north of Mývatn), has four tidy, well-constructed prefab rooms (with private bathrooms and kitchenettes) on a sleepy family farm (no breakfast, mobile 845-3757, ornsig66@simnet.is or book on Airbnb).

Eating in Húsavík: Overlooking the busy pier at the town's main harborfront, **$$$ Salka** is a good all-around choice for high-end Icelandic cooking in a bright setting (daily 11:30-21:00, Garðarsbraut 6, tel. 464-2551). **$$ Naustið,** a block up in town, fills a bright yellow house and has inviting outdoor seating, but no views (daily 12:00-22:00, Ásgarðsvegur 1, tel. 464-1520). I'd pick either of these over the sling-'em-out **$ Fish & Chips** or the pricey **$$$ Gamli Baukur,** your other waterfront options.

Mývatn to Eastfjords

It takes about two hours, nonstop, to drive the 110 miles from Mývatn to Egilsstaðir, the gateway to the Eastfjords. Though relatively short in terms of driving distance, this stretch takes you over a wild, uninhabited highland (at 1,700 feet) that can be snowy well into spring. The worthwhile detour to the impressive Dettifoss waterfall adds two more hours (one for driving, and another to hike around the falls). Coastal Seyðisfjörður, a more interesting place to overnight than Egilsstaðir, adds yet another 30-45 minutes of driving. So all told, expect about five hours en route from the shores of Mývatn to the shores of Seyðisfjörður.

Avoid the temptation to spend extra time taking the longer northern route (along highway 85) from Mývatn to Seyðisfjörður via Kópasker. Devote time to Iceland's far northeast corner only if you're spending several weeks here.

Be aware that blowing sand can sometimes kick up between Mývatn and Egilsstaðir; check the forecast before setting out.

Sights near Mývatn

• *From the lakefront settlements around Mývatn (last chance for gas!), head east, passing Mývatn Nature Baths (last chance for food!). Then head over Námaskarð pass. Once you leave the Krafla Valley, there are no services (and virtually no civilization) along highway 1 for nearly two hours (though there are portable toilets at the Dettifoss parking lot).*

If you haven't yet, consider stopping off at the fascinating **Námafjall** geothermal area (easy to see quickly) or drive up the **Krafla Valley** to see the geothermal sights there (takes longer)—both are described earlier in this chapter, under "Mývatn."

• *About 12 miles (15 minutes) east of Krafla, watch for the turnoff on the left for paved highway 862. The parking lot for the Dettifoss falls sits about 15 miles (20 minutes) off the main road. You'll drive across an arid moonscape scattered with rocks and occasional hardy plants.*

Note that there's a second turnoff to Dettifoss a bit farther east—highway 864—which heads up the opposite, east side of the river and falls. This affords a slightly better view, but is accessed via a rutted, slow-to-drive gravel road. There's no bridge across the river near the falls. If you're following your GPS, be sure it's directing you to your intended riverbank.

RING ROAD

▲▲Dettifoss Waterfall

Iceland's second-largest river, Jökulsá á Fjöllum (Glacial River in the Mountains), flows north 130 miles from the edge of the Vatnajökull glacier—Iceland's largest—to the Greenland Sea. Along the way it traverses some of Iceland's most dramatic canyons and waterfalls, including Iceland's most powerful, the thundering Dettifoss (DEH-tih-foss).

Dettifoss is both broad (340 feet) and high (150 feet), sending more than 130,000 gallons rushing over its parapets every minute. The gorge below the falls (Jökulsárgljúfur) was carved by a cataclysmic glacial flood. Like Gullfoss on the Golden Circle, you'll view Dettifoss from above.

From the parking lot (free, always open, portable toilets), you'll walk 15 minutes (about a mile) along a well-marked path to the overlook. The walk in—through a stony plain with basalt columns—is part of the fun. Finally you reach the falls, which rumble into their canyon, spitting up a misty cloud (often with a rainbow). There are two viewpoints: The lower one, reached via a metal staircase and trails across slippery rocks, gets you fairly close to the top of the falls. Retrace your steps, then follow the ridgeline trail up to the upper viewpoint, with boardwalks and a viewing platform, for the big-picture view.

A third trail leads to the right, to more viewpoints, then continues about two-thirds of a mile (10 minutes) upstream from

Dettifoss to a smaller waterfall called **Selfoss.** The walk rewards you with epic views of the strikingly wide Jökulsá á Fjöllum as it flows between the two falls. Glacial sediment can make the water seem milky or even muddy. The riverbanks are striped with bold, vertical basalt ledges—some of which are sloughing off—and a few black sand beaches are tucked between the rapids.

Downstream from Dettifoss is yet another waterfall, **Hafragilsfoss,** which is almost as broad and high as Dettifoss itself; it's difficult to reach without a 4x4 vehicle, and best skipped.

From Dettifoss to Egilsstaðir

• *Leaving Dettifoss, return to the main road and continue east. After a few miles, you'll cross a scenic, single-lane white suspension bridge across Jökulsá á Fjöllum—the river that flows over the Dettifoss waterfall.*

Just after the bridge, across from the turnoff for highway 85 north, is a last-chance pullout with portable toilets. From here, it's about 80 miles (1.5 hours) through a stark, almost lunar landscape, essentially Iceland's "Big Sky Country." This is a real Highland experience.

• *As you proceed, keep an eye on your right for the tabletop mountain called...*

Herðubreið: Iceland's answer to Norway's Pulpit Rock is a tuya—a steep, flat-topped volcano created when molten rock pushed up through a glacier. Just behind Herðubreið—but not visible from here—is Askja, a volcanic crater lake buried deep in Iceland's interior, and one of the country's most famous remote and scenic destinations.

A pullout on the left leads to a viewpoint looking back over the flats, with info boards explaining how an eruption changed the landscape from farmland to this barren plain.

If you're in a pinch, there is one place for refreshment between Mývatn and Egilsstaðir, but it's not directly on highway 1: About 24 miles (30 minutes) after the Dettifoss turnoff, watch on the right for road 901 to *Möðrudalur*. About five miles down this road is Fjalladýrð, a working farm with a campsite, guest rooms, a shop, views of Herðubreið, and the café **$$ Fjallakaffi,** known for its homemade *ástarpungar* (love balls)—a fried sweet dough with raisins (tel. 471-1858, www.fjalladyrd.is).

• *Continue along the desolate plain, with very little vegetation save for some parched, scrubby grasses.*

Jökulsá á Dal Valley: Finally you wind your way down a picturesque, lush green valley of the Jökulsá á Dal (Glacial River in the Valley). Enjoy the scenery, following the turquoise river with waterfalls all around, as you drop down from the Highlands into the Eastfjords. Only one of the waterfalls has a pullout: The 420-foot **Rjúkandafoss** (on the left) is worth a brief stop for the quick 10-minute hike to a viewpoint.

• *Where the road bends and crosses the river, stay on highway 1 and drive toward the panorama of snowcapped peaks, up over a rocky plateau, eventually crossing the wide Lagarfljót river to reach the large town of...*

Egilsstaðir (Egill's Farm): This functional hub and gateway to the Eastfjords has gas stations and some decent places to eat or spend the night in a pinch. But for even better scenery and a legitimately charming town, I'd continue on to **Seyðisfjörður.**

RING ROAD

From Egilsstaðir to Seyðisfjörður

Your drive is not quite over—you're 30-45 minutes from Seyðis-fjörður. (For more on both towns and a map of the area, see the next section, "Eastfjords.")

• *From Egilsstaðir's main intersection (at the N1 gas station), turn left to stay on highway 1 (marked* Reyðarfjörður*) and drive up through the residential part of town. After just a half-mile—as you crest the hill—turn left onto highway 93, marked* Seyðisfj *(with a ferry icon). After another half-mile, turn right to stay on highway 93 (also marked* Seyðisfj*).*

Over the Fjarðarheiði Pass: Here begins one of Iceland's most scenic drives—the stunning road that summits Fjarðarheiði (Fjord Heath), the pass leading to Seyðisfjörður. (Note: This road is frequently snow-covered and sometimes closed in April and October.) You'll curve up switchback after switchback, gaining altitude (and gasping at the lack of guardrails) be-fore disappearing into a mysti-cal landscape of mountaintop  ponds. Icebergs bob in the big Heiðarvatn (Heath Lake), even well into summer (a handy pullout on the left allows a lakeside photo op). You'll crest the pass at 2,030 feet, and then begin the slow, stunning switchback descent down to the fjord. The road wraps around on itself several times, tying neat little bows around craggy cliffs and gushing waterfalls (the Fjarðará river goes over nearly two dozen falls on its way down the mountain). It's often socked in, but when clear, this route offers breathtaking fjord-and-waterfalls views.

• *Returning to sea level, you pull into artsy* **Seyðisfjörður***—ready to explore.*

Eastfjords

Iceland's remote, sparsely populated east is as scenic as it is lonesome. Its coast is slashed with a dozen deep, steep fjords, with very few tunnels and no bridges to speed your progress. Wrapping around fjords is very slow going, making this the most tedious (albeit scenic) stretch of the Ring Road. You can easily drive for miles and miles without ever seeing another car.

The main tourist draw here is the charming fjordside town of Seyðisfjörður—the most interesting stop, by far, in eastern Iceland, and the no-brainer choice for an overnight. To get there, you'll pass through the practical population center of Egilsstaðir (lots of services and a possible place to sleep). The nearby long, skinny lake called Lagarfljót, with a few mediocre sights, may also be worth a stop. But with limited time, don't linger here: From this area, you'll turn south, tracing the long, jagged shoreline to Southeast Iceland and glorious glacier country.

Planning Tips: Seyðisfjörður, with its striking setting and excellent assortment of hotels and restaurants, is the best place to spend the night. Egilsstaðir is a good backup—and it cuts down on driving. Accommodations can be tough to find the night before the weekly Norröna ferry to Denmark departs from Seyðisfjörður (schedules at www.smyrilline.com)—but if you're here that night, you'll find these towns (especially Seyðisfjörður) particularly lively. The regional TI website, www.east.is, is good.

Egilsstaðir

The workaday community of Egilsstaðir (AY-ill-STAHTH-eer, pop. 2,500) lacks Seyðisfjörður's creative charm, but it enjoys a fine setting along the lovely Lagarfljót lake. It's the largest community in the east, with a big swimming pool, supermarkets, and other

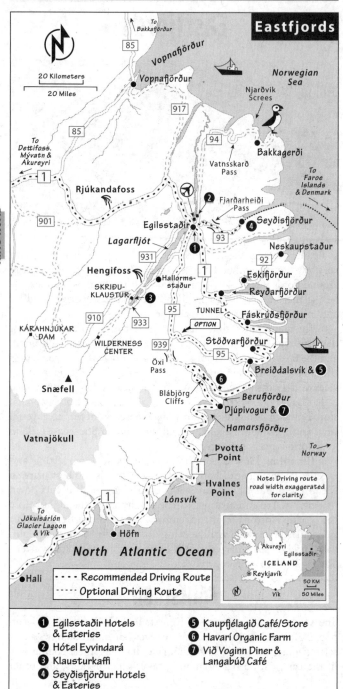

RING ROAD

Eastfjords

20 Kilometers
20 Miles

To Bakkafjörður

Vopnafjörður

Norwegian Sea

Njarðvík Screes

Vopnafjörður

Bakkagerði

To Dettifoss, Mývatn & Akureyri

Vatnsskarð Pass

94

917

85

Rjúkandafoss

Fjarðarheiði Pass

To Faroe Islands & Denmark

Egilsstaðir

Seyðisfjörður

901

Lagarfljót

Neskaupstaður

931

93

92

Hengifoss

Eskifjörður

Hallorms-staður

Reyðarfjörður

SKRIÐU-KLAUSTUR

95

Fáskrúðsfjörður

TUNNEL

KÁRAHNJÚKAR DAM

910

933

OPTION

WILDERNESS CENTER

939

Stöðvarfjörður

95

Snæfell

Öxi Pass

Breiðdalsvík & 5

Vatnajökull

Blábjörg Cliffs

Berufjörður

Djúpivogur & 7

Hamarsfjörður

Þvottá Point

To Norway

1

Hvalnes Point

Note: Driving route road width exaggerated for clarity

To Jökulsárlón Glacier Lagoon & Vík

1

Lónsvík

Höfn

North Atlantic Ocean

Akureyri

Egilsstaðir

ICELAND

Hali

- - - Recommended Driving Route
- - - Optional Driving Route

Reykjavík

Vík

50 KM
50 Miles

1 Egilsstaðir Hotels & Eateries
2 Hótel Eyvindará
3 Klausturkaffi
4 Seyðisfjörður Hotels & Eateries

5 Kaupfélagið Café/Store
6 Havarí Organic Farm
7 Við Voginn Diner & Langabúð Café

services—making it a good place to stock up before your long on-ward journey.

Tourist Information: Right along highway 1, you'll find a helpful regional TI (Mon-Fri 8:30-18:00, Sat 10:00-16:00, Sun 13:00-18:00, shorter hours and closed Sun off-season, shares a storefront with Hús Handanna art shop right at the town's main intersection, www.visitegilsstadir.is).

Sights near Egilsstaðir

Lagarfljót

This deep lake is so long and skinny that it can be thought of as a broad river—as reflected by its name (LAH-gar-flyoht, Lake River). Lagarfljót feels like Iceland's answer to Loch Ness. It even comes with its own Nessie-style legend: The Lagarfljót Wyrm. The story goes that a young girl placed a slug in a box with a golden ring, hoping it would increase her gold. But when the slug grew instead of the ring, she threw it into the water—where it got bigger and bigger, wreaking havoc on lakeside settlements. Finally the Wyrm was chained to the bottom of the lake, where it (supposedly) still sits.

For most travelers, glimpsing Lagarfljót as you drive through Egilsstaðir is enough. If you're on your way south along the Ring Road and have lots of driving ahead of you, I'd take a quick glance and move along. But if you're spending the night in Egilsstaðir, consider a drive along Lagarfljót.

Driving Along the Lake: It's about a 35-minute drive from Egilsstaðir to Skriðuklaustur, the settlement near the lake's south end. A few sights cluster here, but most are closed off-season—call or check in Egilsstaðir before heading out. From Egilsstaðir, drive seven miles south on highway 95, then split off on highway 931, which runs along the lake's east bank. You'll eventually drop down along the lakeshore, pass the national forest at Hallormsstaður (where they've successfully reforested 280 square miles), then cross a bridge over the lake, where you can choose among several sights. (You can also use highway 933 on the west bank, but it has several gravel sections.)

To reach the **Hengifoss waterfall,** turn right after the bridge (still on highway 931); you'll soon see the Hengifoss parking lot (free parking and WCs). It's a steep, 1.5-mile hike (about an hour one-way) up a gorge to reach the 390-foot waterfall; if the flow is light, you can walk around behind the fall (www.hengifoss.is).

To reach the little settlement of **Skriðuklaustur** (Landslide Monastery), turn left after the bridge (onto highway 933 south, on the west side of the lake) and drive five minutes. The sights here are a bit underwhelming: **Gunnarshús,** the home of author Gun-

RING ROAD

nar Gunnarsson (1881-1975), who made a name for himself in Denmark and Germany writing popular books about Iceland; the **Snæfellsstofa visitors center,** run by the nearby national park, with advice on hiking and other activities (look for boxy building on the left at the Skriðuklaustur turnoff, tel.

470-0840, www.vjp.is); and the scant remains of the **Skriðuklaustur monastery,** the final Catholic monastery built in Iceland before the Reformation (c. 1493). It's been excavated in recent years (look for information panels at the site), but there's not much to see.

For lunch consider the top-notch **$$$ Klausturkaffi,** downstairs in the Gunnarshús. This wonderful little spot is run by a mother-and-daughter team, who lay out a buffet of traditional, homemade Icelandic dishes. It's a filling, delicious, and memorable meal (June-Aug daily 10:00-18:00, coffee-and-cake buffet daily 15:00-17:00, shorter hours April-May and Sept-Oct, tel. 471-2992).

South from Skriðuklaustur: With even more time, you could continue south of town and up the valley, where there are some natural thermal pools, a museum about Iceland's Highlands, an abandoned farm with a crank-it-yourself cableway bridge, a closer look at Snæfell (Iceland's tallest mountain not covered by a glacier), and plenty of hiking options. For details, ask at the TI in Egilsstaðir, the Snæfellsstofa visitors center, or stop in at the Wilderness Center, a 20-minute (10-mile) drive on partly unpaved roads past Skriðuklaustur (tel. 440-8822, www.wilderness.is).

Other Day Trips from Egilsstaðir

If you stay an extra night in Egilsstaðir and are interested in environmental issues or dams, you could take a day to drive south to the big dam at **Kárahnjúkar,** in Iceland's reindeer country (though the animals don't always show themselves).

A better bet (in good weather) is the tiny coastal village of **Bakkagerði** (also called Borgarfjörður Eystri), a good hour to the northeast by car. The draw here in summer is the puffin colony at the old harbor, a five-minute drive beyond the village (free parking, WCs, enclosed viewing hut). Wooden steps take you up a rocky outcrop to see puffins up close. A boardwalk to the left leads to the enclosed viewing hut; continuing up the stairs to the right affords views of more puffins as well as nesting ducks and arctic terns.

The entire village comprises 50 homes (including a still-lived-in traditional turf house), 80 residents, a few guesthouses, and a grocery store. A popular music festival held in the dilapidated herring factory draws crowds in July (http://braedslan.is).

If you thought the drive to Seyðisfjörður was a fun challenge, you'll love getting to Bakkagerði: After an uneventful 20-mile drive across the plain on highway 94, you'll follow a series of unpaved switchbacks up, up, up to the crest of 1,400-foot Vatnsskarð pass (pullout with pay WC, trailheads, and expansive views—look for Dyrfjöll mountains with their glacier-cut "door"). From the pass you go down the other side...and *then* things get interesting, as you wind around the sheer fjord headland on a narrow track of loose rock below the Njarðvíkurskriður—the Njarðvík Screes. Look it up before you go.

Sleeping and Eating in Egilsstaðir

Sleep here only if Seyðisfjörður is full, you're in a rush, or the roads are questionable; Egilsstaðir spares you the challenging drive over Fjarðarheiði pass.

$$$ Gistihúsið Egilsstaðir, on the site of the original Egilsstaðir farm, is a big, functional, group-oriented hotel renting 52 rooms (near the lakefront just off the town's main intersection, tel. 471-1114, www.egilsstadir.com, hotel@gistihusid.is). Up above town—just before you head up the road to Seyðisfjörður—is **$$$ Hótel Eyvindará,** with 35 rooms and seven cottages in a rustic, forested setting (tel. 471-1200, https://eyvindara.is, eyvindara2@simnet.is).

Eating in Egilsstaðir: For an easy roadside meal, **$ Bókakaffi**—in Fellabær, right along highway 1—is a cozy bookshop/café that serves an inviting weekday lunch of soups and savory crêpes and a late afternoon coffee-and-cake buffet (Mon-Fri 11:00-18:00, closed Sat-Sun, watch for it below and to the right immediately before crossing the bridge into Egilsstaðir, on Helgafell, www.bokakaffi.is). Across the parking lot from the TI, **$$ Salt Café & Bistro** has standard café fare and is a good option on weekends, when Bókakaffi is closed (Mon-Sat 10:00-21:00, Sun from 12:00, Miðvangur 2, tel. 471-1700). The recommended Gistihúsið Egilsstaðir hotel also has a pricey but good restaurant, **$$$ Eldhúsið,** that's open to nonguests. You'll find a **Bónus supermarket** on highway 1, near the town's main junction.

Seyðisfjörður

The most appealing town in eastern Iceland, Seyðisfjörður (SAY-this-FYUR-thur, pop. 700) is a delightful hybrid. It's a gritty, workaday port, where the Norröna car ferry from Denmark injects Iceland with a weekly fix of international car-trippers (and the occasional big cruise ship overruns the place). But it's also, per capita, Iceland's most artistic corner, with a youthful, creative spirit. Fortunately, these two factions wear their peeling paint and rust equally well. Postindustrial decay just looks right in Seyðisfjörður.

The town—with a fine harbor at the innermost point of a 10-mile-long fjord—was built up by Danish merchants in the mid-19th century; it boomed around the turn of the 20th century thanks to Norwegian-run herring fisheries. Many fine buildings survive from this time, when Seyðisfjörður also became the terminus for the telegraph cable connecting Iceland to Europe. As herring stocks collapsed, the town went into slow decline.

Fortunately, the town took an artistic turn—largely thanks to German artist Dieter Roth (1930-1998), who moved to Iceland in 1957 and later founded an art academy here. Today, Seyðisfjörður's art programs attract young people from across Iceland and abroad, giving this tiny, remote community an unexpectedly cosmopolitan vibe. A top-notch sushi restaurant and a bustling microbrew pub face each other across the rainbow-painted mini main street.

While light on "sights," per se, Seyðisfjörður is an enjoyable place to simply wander and explore. The town has more than its share of services for travelers, thanks to the regular ferry traffic.

Tourist Information: The TI is inside the ferry terminal, but save yourself a trip by checking their excellent website (tel. 472-1551, www.visitseydisfjordur.com).

Sights in Seyðisfjörður

Town Walk

Get your bearings in this little burg with this brief spin tour and stroll. Begin just across the bridge from the supermarket and Hótel Aldan, by the black obelisk honoring Otto Andreas Wathne—a Norwegian entrepreneur who helped develop the town.

Spin Tour: Look out over the little lagoon (Lónið), and find the white tower and glass gangway for the Norröna car ferry, which runs weekly to the Faroe Islands and Denmark. The ferry, the town's main industry, is an important plot point for the popular Icelandic TV series *Ófærð (Trapped)*, which is set in Seyðisfjörður.

Look farther right and up the road, which runs along the fjord past the Hótel Snæfell and below a pretty waterfall. For some remote seaside beauty, you can walk (or drive) as far as you like along this road, which extends 10 miles to the end of the fjord.

Next, spin right to look up into the little town center. The gray-and-red blocky building is the town's fine thermal swimming pool. Standing out front is an abstract sculpture, called *Útlínur,* that represents the outline of the fjord. This sculpture, and the murals adorning the school building at the corner, are reminders of the importance of art in this remote hamlet. Uphill and just to the right of the swimming pool, the classic old red building—once the town hospital—is now its youth hostel. The little rust-colored marker across the street from you (by the Fjarðará river) identifies area peaks, and a signboard beyond that outlines local hikes.

Stroll: Now let's stretch our legs. Cross the bridge, turn right at Hótel Aldan, and walk up the pretty "rainbow street" toward the

town church. This colorful stretch captures Seyðisfjörður's creative spirit. Painted a few years back by civic-minded locals to simultaneously celebrate Pride month and brighten the town, it's become a beloved fixture. Tourists wear it out with their selfies, so every few months the pavement is washed down by the fire department and repainted, often by high school kids.

On the left you'll pass the local pub, which is *the* place in town to sample Icelandic microbrews. The next house, slathered in black-and-white graffiti, is a gifty boutique called Gullabúið. Across the way, the red house is an arts-and-crafts shop. At the end of the street is the photogenic, but often closed, Blue Church (Bláa Kirkjan), which hosts weekly concerts in summer (www.blaakirkjan. is). A block behind the church is *Snjóflóð (Avalanche),* a monument made with the mangled girders of a factory that was swept away by an avalanche in 1996. Scenic as they are, the steep mountain walls around Seyðisfjörður come with a steep price: the danger of being buried by snow.

From here, if the weather's decent, it's a pleasant 15-minute stroll around the lagoon—offering enjoyable looks at local homes and backyards. To extend the walk to the pretty little town waterfall (Búðaráfoss), when you reach the main road, turn left toward the ferry dock, and then look for the path just before the stream.

Artistic Sights and Museums

If you're lingering here, you can explore a variety of artistic sights. A 15-minute hike up a steep hillside (above the Brimberg seafood

RING ROAD

factory) is **Tvísöngur,** a "sound sculpture" made of interconnected concrete huts that resonate in a five-tone harmony. The **Skaftfell Center for Visual Art** often has free exhibitions on view. They also guide tours through the **House of Geiri,** the former home of a local artist (summer only, http://skaftfell.is).

The town is also home to the **Technical Museum of East Iceland,** housed in a machine shop, where you can learn about everything from town history to that original telegraph (1,000 ISK, summer only Mon-Fri 11:00-17:00, www.seydisfjordur.org).

Hikes, Bikes, Kayaks, and More

Ask your hotelier (or at the Hótel Aldan if you're just here for the day) for information on hikes, rental bikes and kayaks, boat tours, and fishing trips. It seems everyone in town has a side gig, and the lineup changes from year to year.

Avid hikers can attempt to climb the **Bjólfur** mountain, with stunning views over the fjord (1,970 feet; you can hike steeply up from the avalanche barriers on the Fjarðarheiði road), or the **Seven Peaks** that surround the fjord. An easy four-mile loop starts near the bridge and loops to the **Fjarðarsel** power plant and across the valley floor back to town.

Sleeping in Seyðisfjörður

Remember, Seyðisfjörður can fill up on the night before the weekly ferry leaves—book well ahead on those days. Hótel Aldan is the only of these listings to serve breakfast (a pricey buffet). It's open to nonguests and is where virtually every tourist in town winds up each morning. You can also buy breakfast items at the supermarket.

Hótel Aldan offers the town's only real hotel rooms, divided between two historic buildings. Check in at their reception building in the heart of town (can't miss it, by the bridge), and they'll direct you to one of two annexes: **$$ Hótel Snæfell,** a creaky old house on the waterfront with 12 contemporary-style rooms; or **$$$ The Old Bank,** with nine bigger rooms and more amenities, in a residential area (breakfast extra, served at the reception building at Norðurgata 2, tel. 472-1277, www.hotelaldan.is, hotelaldan@simnet.is). They also rent two apartments with kitchenettes.

$$ Við Lónið (By the Lagoon), well run by charming Maggý, has eight beautifully appointed, modern-minimalist rooms (all with private bath). It's right along the rainbow street facing the lagoon and fjord (fjord-facing rooms are quieter and have a balcony for a bit more, mobile 899-9429, www.vidlonidguesthouse.com, email through website to reserve). Maggý is proud of her town and happy to offer suggestions for dining and things to do.

$ The Old Apothecary rents three rooms with private bath in a c. 1885 house right at the main bridge in the town center. There's no reception—you'll check yourself in—but it's a good value, and owner Oliver is available if needed (no telephone, website, or email—book on Airbnb or Booking.com).

¢ **Hafaldan Hostel,** part of the Hostelling International network, runs a tight ship at its two branches: They have 34 beds in the wonderfully creaky old hospital building, and 18 more near the old harbor (reception at old hospital location at Suður-gata 8, private rooms available, mobile 611-4410, www.hafaldan.is, seydisfjordur@hostels.is).

Eating in Seyðisfjörður

Hótel Aldan has two pricey but excellent eateries in its reception building (at Norðurgata 2) in the heart of town: **$$$ Nordic Restaurant,** on the main floor, has a nicely rustic, casual atmosphere and modern Icelandic fare, including good salads (May-Sept daily 12:00-22:00, cheerful outdoor seating in good weather, tel. 472-1277). Upstairs, **$$$$ Norð Austur** (North East) has exceptional sushi and other Japanese-Icelandic fusion dishes in a cozy setting. The ingredients are fresh, the chefs are talented, and the ambience is top-notch. Let this place tempt you into a splurge (dinner only, June-Sept daily 17:00-22:00, mobile 787-4000, www.nordaustur.is).

$$ Bistro Skaftfell is a casual cellar bar below the Center for Visual Art, a short walk around the fjord from downtown. They have affordable pizzas at lunch or dinner, always with a vegan option. Order at the counter, then find a seat; feel free to grab a board game, relax in the outdoor beer garden, or head upstairs to see what's on in the gallery (daily 12:00-21:00, Austurvegur 42, tel. 472-1633). There's a TV room in back and an eclectic library of art books.

$ Kaffi Lára (named for the house's former resident)—also called **"El Grillo"** for the local beer on tap—is a boisterous bar right along the little main street, serving 20 types of beer and basic pub grub. On weekends, it's open very late and rollicking, with occasional live music (daily 12:00-22:00, Norðurgata 3, tel. 472-1703).

Supermarket: Stock up on picnic or breakfast supplies at **Samkaup Strax** (marked *Kjörbúðin*), right at the bridge in the center of town (open daily).

Eastfjords to the Southeast

Driving along the Eastfjords (from Seyðisfjörður) to Southeast Iceland is a long but scenic day. Following my recommended route, it's about 145 miles (3.5 hours nonstop) to the lighthouse at Hvalnes point, which marks the shift to the southeast landscape, and 175 miles (4 hours) to Höfn—the biggest town in the southeast region.

As you plan your day, note that you may want to continue beyond Höfn before stopping for the night. It's another 45 minutes to accommodations near the glacier lagoon at Jökulsárlón, and 45 minutes beyond Jökulsárlón to Skaftafell National Park. The farther you get tonight, the shorter tomorrow's drive will be.

Before leaving Egilsstaðir, it's smart to stock up on supplies, use the WC, and get gas. Services are extremely sparse for the rest of the day. From Egilsstaðir, you have two options for continuing south:

Option 1, Highway 95 (summer only): This inland route is shorter but less scenic than option 2 (my recommended route). It climbs up to 1,500 feet over an unpaved pass, descending to the coast near Breiðdalsvík. You could then take the shortcut along highway 939, called Öxi—a sometimes-steep gravel road with no guardrails that climbs even higher, to 1,800 feet. Taking Öxi shaves about 30 miles off the trip, but only a little time, as you'll need to drive slowly. (If you're weighing the choice, check out videos of driving Öxi on YouTube, and look at current road conditions at www.road.is.)

Option 2, Highway 1: The main route hugs the coast and is more scenic, paved all the way, adds about 30-45 minutes to your drive, and is the route I recommend (and detail next). From Egilsstaðir, highway 1 runs down to the sea at Reyðarfjörður; from there, the highway continues through a tunnel and along the coast.

From Egilsstaðir to Reyðarfjörður

• *From Egilsstaðir's main intersection (at the N1 gas station), take highway 1 (marked* Reyðarfjörður*) southeast. (Coming from Seyðisfjörður, you can bypass Egilsstaðir as you drop down from the pass.) You'll curve down a long, grooved valley, framed by craggy mountains rutted with tumbling waterfalls (scenic pullout on right as you near the valley floor). Finally you hit your first fjord at...*

Reyðarfjörður (Baleen-Whale Fjord): The fjord is home to an industrial town of the same name (pop. 1,100). When you're still a mile or so outside of town, watch on the right for the turnoff to stay on highway 1 (marked *Fáskrúðsfjörður* and *Höfn*). You'll cut across a few thin rivers, and enjoy views across the fjord on your left of the town of Reyðarfjörður. The aluminum smelter located here gives Reyðarfjörður a more diverse economic base than usual in a small Icelandic village, and more jobs—a key to keeping young people here.

• *From Reyðarfjörður, you'll go through a nearly four-mile tunnel, then drive down toward—but not through—the village of Fáskrúðsfjörður.*

Fjordside Villages

Long ago, **Fáskrúðsfjörður** (Austere Fjord, pop. 660) was a supply center for French boats fishing off Iceland, and honors its history with both Icelandic and French on its street signs.

• *At the fork as you approach town, turn right to stay on highway 1 (marked* Stöðvarfjörður*), crossing a single-lane bridge over a rocky riverbed.*

Now settle in for a looooong drive—a couple of hours, at least, cutting in and out of deep fjords and passing scattered farms. Highway 1 goes up and down and up and down, as you cross the various finger foothills of the mountains, then drops down into deep ravines formed by receding glaciers. Each fjord is anchored by a sparsely populated little village. These hardscrabble communities debate whether to keep schools open and services alive. Pull over as you like for photo ops—there are ample roadside waterfall and coastline views. If it's sunny, you'll be in heaven. If it's socked in... pretend.

First, dramatic **Stöðvarfjörður** (pop. 200) has a handy little **Saxa** guesthouse/café/gas station. The town also has a little museum (Steinasafn Petru) that displays the rock collection and garden of a dearly departed local woman (www.steinapetra.is).

Next, **Breiðdalsvík** (Wide-Valley Bay, pop. 140) is wider and less scenic—notice it's a *vík* (bay) rather than a *fjörður* (fjord). If you need a pit stop, turn left off highway 1 onto a spur to reach the town, nestled under a rocky outcropping (with the cozy, artsy **$ Kaupfjélagið** café/general store). This town is better developed for tourism than some, and even has some accommodations and a spiffy website (www.breiddalsvik.is). Note that at Breiðdalsvík, highway 95 rejoins highway 1.

You'll cross the bay on a long causeway, curve around the headland (good pullout at Streitisviti lighthouse), then follow the road, separated from the sea by pastures. Just as you enter the next fjord, watch on your right for the blink-and-you'll-miss-it organic farm **$ Havarí.** Tucked in the back of the barn is a little café run by a local artist/musician couple. They serve a vegetarian menu and host live music events every other week though the summer (daily, shorter hours off-season, they also rent a few hostel beds, www. havari.is).

After the farm, you'll enter **Berufjörður,** a long, skinny fjord with virtually no settlement at all and fish farms in the water below eroded peaks. On the left (just after Þiljuvellir farm), watch

RING ROAD

for **Blábjörg**—naturally blue cliffs that rise above a black pebble beach. A parking area and steps down to the beach let you examine the volcanic rock spotted with blue-green minerals.

Continuing around the fjord, geology buffs will want to make a quick stop at the **Teigarhorn** natural monument, where mineral rock formations known as zeolites were once mined (https://teigarhorn.is). Note that it is illegal to remove stones from the monument.

• *At the far end of Berufjörður, you'll pass the towering, pyramid-shaped Búlandstindur mountain, then reach...*

Djúpivogur

Djúpivogur (DYOOP-ih-VOH-ur, Deep Cove, pop. 500, plus a herd or two of reindeer in early summer) is considered the last town of the Eastfjords. With its harbor huddling under beautiful views of grand peaks, it's a natural place to take a break.

Drive down to the harbor, where **$ Við Voginn** is a diner-style eatery perched on a little hill with views over the fishing boats (burgers, fish-and-chips, tel. 478-8860). Steps away, **$ Langabúð** is a historic log building from 1790, housing a café and museum (the museum desk doubles as the town TI). A small Kjörbúðin **grocery store** and gas station sit on the main street, and an outdoor art installation called *Eggin í Gleðivík* rings the old fishing port with 34 giant **stone bird eggs,** representing each breed in the region (the largest belongs to the red-throated diver, the town's official bird; follow signs to *Gleðivík*).

If you feel like lingering, Djúpivogur is a haven for rock hounds, with tiny rock gardens and showrooms. Look for Jón Sigurðsson, who enthusiastically shows off his personal collection and **workshop** (Hammersminni 10, straight ahead between the hotel and recommended Við Voginn).

• *From Djúpivogur, you'll leave the fjords in your rearview mirror. It's another 45 minutes to Hvalnes point.*

From the Fjords to the Southeast

With the fjords behind you, you'll curl around two more wind-swept bays—**Hamarsfjörður** (Crag Fjord), where the angled layers of the mountains look like a sinking ship, then **Álftafjörður** (Swan Fjord, speckled with islands)—with stunning views of cascading mountains receding to the horizon.

At Álftafjörður, if you're lucky, you may spot some of its namesake migratory whooper swans. Near the end of the fjord you'll pass the little point called **Þvottá** where, in the tenth century, a missionary sent by the king of Norway first arrived to Christianize the Icelanders. This "Washing River" (as its name means) is where the missionary baptized his first Icelander.

Just after, you'll round the bend of the last of the Eastfjords, pass the Stapinn sea stack (with a good photo pullout), then reach the point of land marked by the **Hvalnes lighthouse.** Here the landscape begins to change. You're no longer in fjord country, but in Southeast Iceland.

To continue your drive to **Höfn**—the biggest population center for about 300 miles (about 30 minutes away)—and through the rest of the southeast, see the next section.

RING ROAD

Southeast Iceland

The rugged, 200-mile-long coastline of Southeast Iceland is shaped by Vatnajökull, Iceland's (and Europe's) biggest glacier. It is massive: By volume, Vatnajökull (VAHT-nah-YUR-kutl, Lakes Glacier) contains more water than Africa's Lake Victoria, and by area, it's larger than the state of Delaware. Greedy with its superlatives, Vatnajökull is also home to Iceland's highest peak (Hvannadalshnúkur, 6,900 feet). This is one big chunk of ice.

Throughout Southeast Iceland, the Ring Road tightropes between Vatnajökull and the open Atlantic. You'll cross many broad beaches of pebbles, ground up and washed out by glaciers, and get a good look at several glacier tongues, stretching down from the top of the big ice monster and lapping at the lowland valleys.

Southeast Iceland has a few widely scattered sights, including some spectacular natural wonders. The highlights are glacier lagoons, where icebergs bob in dreamy pools: the famous (and quite touristy) Jökulsárlón, and the lesser-known and smaller Fjallsárlón. Near Jökulsárlón is the so-called Diamond Beach, where glittering chunks of ice wash up on a velvety black sand beach.

To get up close to all that glacial scenery, the Skaftafell wilderness area offers hikes, from easy to strenuous. And the main town of this area, Höfn, is a practical, peninsular little burg whose restaurants specialize in the delectable local specialty, *humar* (langoustine).

Planning Tips: You'll likely want to spend a night in this area, to rest up between two long days of driving. Accommodations are sparse, so book well ahead. While Höfn is the only real town in Southeast Iceland—and has some good accommodations—it's at the region's easternmost end, so sleeping there makes the next day's onward drive that much longer. From a practical point of view, you may be better off dining in Höfn, then continuing farther west to your hotel. You'll find accommodations around Hali and Jökulsárlón, 45 minutes past Höfn (allowing you both a late-evening and early-morning look at the glacier lagoon), and in the Skaftafell area, another 45 minutes beyond that.

Glacier Activities: It's best to reserve ahead for many activities in this area, including boat trips on the glacier lagoons; hiking or snowmobiling across a glacier; or visiting an ice cave. For details on your options, see the Icelandic Experiences chapter. Do some homework and book your activity a few days ahead (as soon as weather reports become reliable), but before they sell out (most tour companies have online calendars that count down available slots). Consider booking your activity for the morning after you overnight in the southeast (avoiding a stressful drive to make a late-afternoon appointment). If you're especially interested in glacier activities, add a second overnight—either in this area, or along the South Coast.

Southeast to South Coast

Driving from where Southeast Iceland begins (at Hvalnes point) to Vík (which kicks off the South Coast) is about 200 miles—or about four hours of driving, nonstop. Some of Iceland's most impressive natural sights are here, but they're spread out, with long stretches of road in between. In this section I describe the drive between Hvalnes point and Vík. For detailed descriptions of the towns and sights recommended along this route, see the "Southeast Iceland Towns and Sights" section later in this chapter.

Sandstorm Alert: The most dangerous area for potentially car-damaging sandstorms along the Ring Road is the section between Skaftafell and Vík, where you'll pass through wide stretches of sand. If windy conditions are forecast, try to avoid this area.

Hvalnes Lighthouse: The first stretch—as you round the bend from the Eastfjords, at Hvalnes point—offers a glorious introduction to the glacial scenery of the southeast. The simple orange tower of Hvalnes lighthouse, barely visible from the road, welcomes visitors to this area. Notice the more intense surf here—crashing on the rocks—rather than the gentle lapping of Eastfjords waves.

Lónsvík Bay: Immediately after the lighthouse, there's a pullout at the end of an astonishingly long, far-as-the-eye-can-see, natural causeway along the bay of Lónsvík. Scrambling out on the pebbly footing provides a nice stretch-your-legs-after-the-fjords, welcome-to-the-southeast moment.

RING ROAD

Southeast Iceland

Kvíslavatn

Vatnajökull

26

Þórisvatn

26

Langisjór

Svartifoss

Skaftafells-
Jökull

▲Hekla

Landmanna-
laugar

Lómagnúpur▲

SKAFTAFELL
VISITORS
CENTER

⑬

MANGLED
BRIDGE
GIRDERS

F-210

Fjaðrárgljúfur
Gorge

⑧ Skeiðarársandur

Kirkjubæjar-
klaustur

⑨

Mýrdals-
jökull

208

⑤

Eldhraun

North

To
Skógafoss,
Hvolsvöllur
& Reykjavík

▲ Katla

204

1

Dyrhólaey
Promontory

Vík

Myrdalssandur

Reynisfjara
Black Sand Beach

Continuing around the bay, notice that the landscape has shifted from mossy cliffs and green fields to massive, sloping mounds of loose pebbles and flat, rocky expanses. Keep an eye out for bunkers on the right side of the road, which block rockslides. And notice the water changing colors, as mineral-murky glacial runoff mixes in shades of green, blue, and yellow.

Just past the settlement of **Stafafell** (where Iceland's first law speaker is said to have lived), you'll use a one-lane bridge to cross the first of many glacial riverbeds. These distinctive waterways—where centuries-old ice finally melts and runs off to the ocean—are always shifting.

• *At the far end of Lónsvík bay, you'll go between scree-sloped mountains and through a short tunnel. Popping out the other side, straight ahead you'll get your first glimpse of a glacier: the Hoffellsjökull tongue of Vat-*

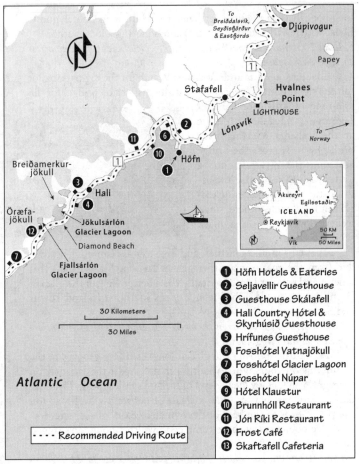

To
Breiðdalsvík,
Seyðisfjörður
& Eastfjords

Djúpivogur

Papey

Stafafell

Hvalnes
Point

LIGHTHOUSE

Lónsvík

To
Norway

2 Seljavellir Guesthouse

11

6

10

Höfn

1

Breiðamerkur-
jökull

1

3 Hali

4

Öræfa-
jökull

12

Jökulsárlón
Glacier Lagoon

Diamond Beach

7

Fjallsárlón
Glacier Lagoon

30 Kilometers

30 Miles

Akureyri

Egilsstaðir

ICELAND

Reykjavík

50 KM
50 Miles

Vík

Atlantic Ocean

1 Höfn Hotels & Eateries
2 Seljavellir Guesthouse
3 Guesthouse Skálafell
4 Hali Country Hótel &
Skyrhúsið Guesthouse
5 Hrífunes Guesthouse
6 Fosshótel Vatnajökull
7 Fosshótel Glacier Lagoon
8 Fosshótel Núpar
9 Hótel Klaustur
10 Brunnhóll Restaurant
11 Jón Ríki Restaurant
12 Frost Café
13 Skaftafell Cafeteria

- - - - Recommended Driving Route

RING ROAD

najökull. Soon after—about 15 minutes later—you reach the turnoff (on the left, highway 99) for the town of Höfn.

From Höfn to Hali: As it's the biggest population center for more than 100 miles in either direction, **Höfn** is good for a break—gas up, use the WC, and have a meal. For suggestions on places to eat in Höfn, see "Southeast Iceland Towns and Sights," later. Otherwise, there are a couple of options past town.

Beyond Höfn, the roadside guesthouse/restaurant **Brunnhóll** has a popular ice-cream counter and café (lunch and dinner; on the left). If you're passing through in the evening, for a better meal, carry on about a mile farther to the recommended **$$ Jón Ríki** brewery/restaurant (dinner only; on the right, at Hólmur farm).

Just after Jón Ríki, on the left after a bridge, a pullout offers good views of the not-so-distant glacier. About 35 miles (45 minutes) past the Höfn turnoff, on the left, is a building shaped like a long bookshelf, at the little settlement of **Hali,** with a hotel, guesthouse, cafeteria-like café, and museum honoring a local author.

• *About 10 minutes beyond Hali, sweeping glacial views open up across the desert-like plain.*

Glacier Lagoons and Tongues: Watch for the big parking lot (on the right, immediately before a white suspension bridge) for the stunning **Jökulsárlón glacier lagoon**—a must-stop to gape at the icebergs. Getting back on highway 1, cross the bridge and immediately turn left onto a gravel road to reach the just-as-dramatic (and often overlooked) **Diamond Beach,** where small icebergs wash up on a black sand shoreline.

About 10 minutes farther, and easy to miss (since it's not visible from the road), is another glacier lagoon, **Fjallsárlón.** This quieter and smaller lagoon actually has a better view of the glacier. Both lagoons are described later, under "Southeast Iceland Towns and Sights."

• *Back on highway 1, cut across the boulder-strewn flats between glacier-topped mountains and coastline.*

Take turns spotting the glacial tongues filling grooves in the mountains on your right. About 30 minutes past the lagoons, on the right, you'll enjoy ideal views of Iceland's tallest peak, Hvanna-dalshnúkur. Just beyond that, a small turnoff to a gravel road (on the right) leads to the base of the Svínafellsjökull glacier and dramatic ice boulders that have tumbled down the mountain's jagged face.

• *About 10 minutes past Hótel Skaftafell, just after a one-lane bridge, on the right, is the easy-to-miss turnoff for highway 998 and...*

Skaftafell National Park: About 1.5 miles off the main road, you'll reach the park's visitors center (with WCs and a cafeteria; for more on the park, see later in this chapter).

Almost immediately after the Skaftafell turnoff, on the left, watch for a pullout next to a pair of **mangled girders.** They're all that's left of a bridge that washed out in the fall of 1996: A volcanic eruption heated up a mountaintop lagoon of glacier water, which came rushing down the mountainside in a days-long flood that peaked at more than 10 million gallons per second. Such floods, called a *jökulhlaup,* are relatively common along Iceland's southern coast. That's partly why many of the bridges you'll cross on this drive are wimpy one-lane ones, which can be easily replaced. These bridges also sit slightly higher than the roadbed. If there's a flood, this makes it easier to cut out segments of the road to divert the rushing water and, hopefully, save the bridge.

• *Continuing west, you'll cross the extremely broad outwash plain called...*

Skeiðarársandur (Spoon-River Sands): The majority of meltwater from Vatnajökull drains to the Atlantic from this delta, which covers 500 square miles—the largest such glacial drainage delta in the world. (Geologists worldwide sometimes call an outwash plain a *sandur*—borrowing the Icelandic word). As you cross Skeiðarársandur, notice the extremely long one-lane bridge no longer in use. An eruption in 2011 caused the main watercourse to shift to the west (leaving this river a mere trickle), and forced construction of the two-lane bridge you're driving on now.

Approaching the end of the sands, you'll cross a long one-lane bridge at the base of the beefy peak called **Lómagnúpur.** Here the landscape shifts to chunks of lava—striking, sharp-edge cliffs with lots of waterfalls, interspersed with a handful of farms tucked into velvety hillsides.

All along the coast, you'll pass vast **purple fields** of Nootka lupine. In 1945, this flowering plant was introduced (from North America) to Iceland to combat erosion and to enrich the depleted soil. It's now the subject of controversy as it's become invasive in some areas, and threatens delicate native species—including Iceland's native bees and certain mosses. Just down the road, locals are actively destroying fields of lupine to protect what lies beneath.

• *Eventually, about 45 miles (nearly an hour) past the Skaftafell turnoff, you'll come to a roundabout. If you need a break, take the second exit to pull into...*

Kirkjubæjarklaustur: The lone point of civilization between Höfn and Vík, Kirkjubæjarklaustur (KEERK-yoo-bay-yahr-KLOY-stur; Church-Farm Monastery, pop. 120) is the place to gas up and grab some food. Exiting the roundabout, just follow the main street; you'll reach a little building housing the busy **$$ Systrakaffi café,** a little grocery store, and a liquor store.

• *Back on highway 1, a few minutes past Kirkjubæjarklaustur, there's a fine little natural area that's good for stretching your legs. To reach it, just after leaving town, watch for the turnoff marked* Holt *and* Fjaðrárgljúfur.

Fjaðrárgljúfur (Feather-River Canyon): An unpaved road

takes you in about 10 minutes to this gently scenic gorge of soft, rounded hills grooved by a deep river (parking lot with WCs and picnic tables). From here you can hike up along the upper rim of the 1.5-mile-long, 300-foot-deep canyon, peering down into its unique formations.

• *From Kirkjubæjarklaustur, it's about an hour (45 miles) to the next town, Vík.*

The Road to Vík: You'll pass through an alien landscape of bubbly lava rock blanketed with yellow moss—a world of mole-hills with pointy tops, alternating with purple lupine. Resembling a science experiment gone wrong, this is the **Eldhraun lava field**—at 218 square miles, the world's largest lava flow, created in the 1783-84 Lakagígar eruption. Also known as the Skaftár Fires, Laki surged out of a 16-mile-long row of fissures and craters, with deadly consequences in Iceland and Europe. Laki spewed ash and poisonous gas, destroying farmland and killing half the region's livestock. The years that followed were dubbed "the hardship of the haze." Almost a quarter of Iceland's population died from starvation.

Somewhere in there, you'll see a pointy-ridged mountain, **Hjörleifshöfði**—it looks a bit like a sleeping stegosaurus. And soon you'll begin to catch glimpses of the **Mýrdalsjökull** glacier on the horizon to your right.

Before long, you're crossing another broad *sandur* (Mýrdalssan-dur). The row of cliffs on the left marks your next stop: the town of Vík, the gateway to the South Coast.

Southeast Iceland Towns and Sights

You'll reach the following towns and sights as you drive south from Hvalnes to Vík via the route above.

▲Höfn

Höfn (pron. hurpn, with a nearly silent *n;* pop. 2,200) is the only real town in Southeast Iceland. Set on a narrow peninsula, this fishing-harbor town offers easy access to the Vatnajökull glacier, a supermarket, a good swimming pool, and some enticing places to eat. The harborfront, more practical than quaint, serves as a local tourism hub, with lots of restaurants, tour operators offering trips to the glacier, and a handy **TI/national park visitors center** called Gamlabúð (daily June-Aug 9:00-19:00, Sept and May until 18:00, Oct-April until 17:00, up the stone stairs at Heppuvegur 1, good glacier exhibit, tel. 470-8330, https://gamlabud.business.site). The promontory beyond the harbor is a nature reserve. Summer flights on Eagle Air link Reykjavík City Airport to the small Hornafjörður Airport at Höfn nearly daily in about an hour (www.isavia.is).

Sights in Höfn: Höfn's best sight is the Vatnajökull glacier across the fjord. But if you have time in town, consider a walk on the pleasant paved trail along the peninsula's east side. Walking north from the harbor offers views of the glacier across the mud-flats; walking south brings you to the Ósland nature reserve (great for birders). Keep an eye out for models of planets as you walk—they're part of a scale model of the solar system (the sun is on Ós-land). There's a simple Maritime Museum in an old Quonset hut near the harbor, and the town swimming pool has waterslides, hot tubs, and a steam bath (at Víkurbraut 9).

Eating in Höfn: This fishing town is crazy about the local delicacy, *humar* (langoustine—a smaller cousin of the American lobster), celebrating it with a weeklong festival in June and cook-ing it every which way. While you'll pay royally to sample *humar,* I consider it a justifiable investment.

Several seafood restaurants cluster near the harbor. **$$$$ Pakkhús Restaurant** has a lively dining room upstairs, a cozy pub and outdoor seating downstairs, and a menu of *humar* and other specialties. If you really want to settle in for a memorable meal at the end of a long day's drive, do it here (daily 12:00-22:00, Krosseyjarvegur 3, tel. 478-2280, www.pakkhus.is). For something simpler and cheaper, try the diner-style **$ Hafnarbuðin,** which sits in a little shack farther around the harbor. Order at the counter, then try to find a seat in the cramped interior. Their "langoustine baguette" is Iceland's answer to a lobster roll (they also serve fish-and-chips, burgers, and milkshakes—a rarity in Iceland, daily 9:00-22:00, Ránarslóð 12, tel. 478-1095).

$$ Íshúsið, a welcoming pizzeria right on the harbor, of-fers the standards, but their "Lobster Festival" pizza is tops (daily 12:00-22:00, behind Pakkhús at Heppuvegur 2a, tel. 478-1230, www.ishusidpizzeria.is).

Farther out, along the road toward highway 1, **$$$ Kaffi Hornið** is a convivial, reliable choice for comfort food in a log cabin (daily 11:30-23:00, Hafnarbraut 42, www.kaffihornid.is).

Eating near Höfn: A good dinner-only option, **$$ Jón Ríki** (Jón the Rich) is tucked at the back of a nondescript farming settlement called Hólmur, right along the Ring Road (about 20 minutes/17 miles west of the Höfn turnoff). This sociable, casual microbrewery/restaurant, in an artistically decorated barn, serves pizzas and local dishes (daily June-Aug 17:00-21:30, closed off-season, tel. 478-2063, www.jonriki.is).

RING ROAD

Sleeping in and near Höfn: See the "Sleeping in Southeast Iceland" section, later in this chapter.

Hali Farm

The 20th-century Icelandic author Þórbergur Þórðarson was born on this farm in 1888. Þórbergur is most remembered for his humorous, self-deprecating essays and *The Stones Speak*, a memoir of his childhood in this isolated place, where the glacial rivers weren't bridged until the 1970s.

The farm is now home to the **Þórbergssetur museum** (also called the Thórbergur Center), which is designed to look like a giant bookshelf containing Þórbergur's works. Inside, an audioguide takes you through scenes from the author's life. You'll learn about the history of the property and its famous resident, and you can step into a re-created *baðstofa* (main room of a traditional farmhouse) and bedroom. The exhibit makes Þórbergur and his writings meaningful to outsiders—and it's a good break from driving. (The building is also the reception for the recommended Hali Country Hótel—see "Sleeping in Southeast Iceland," later.)

Cost and Hours: 1,000 ISK, includes audioguide, daily 9:00-21:00, café, tel. 478-1078, www.thorbergur.is.

Glacier Lagoons
▲▲▲Jökulsárlón

This glorious sight is one of Iceland's best: a lagoon where giant, bobbing chunks of centuries-old ice float in dreamy tranquility, in front of a glacier backdrop.
The lagoon called Jökulsárlón (YUR-kurls-OUR-lohn, Glacier-River Lagoon) is also one of Iceland's youngest natural features. It first appeared around 1935, as a lagoon filled the deep chute gouged out by the receding Breiðamerkurjökull glacial tongue (which continues to re-

treat about a foot per day, a pace that has increased dramatically over the last decades). The lagoon now covers seven square miles and reaches a depth of nearly 900 feet. If Breiðamerkurjökull disappears altogether, it would leave behind a 15-mile-long fjord.

The lagoon's temperature hovers just above freezing. Saltwater from the nearby Atlantic backs up the short Jökulsá river into the lagoon, which helps prevent it from freezing over. (The ocean rarely goes above about 45°F.)

You can view the icebergs easily from the shore, or (better) take a tour of the lagoon by boat. Spot any wildlife? Occasionally

Visiting Glacier Lagoons in the Southeast

The glacier lagoon at Jökulsárlón is big and impressive, but for some visitors, it feels touristy and crowded. With multiple

boats cruising its waters at once, the experience can lose some magic. I'd stop off to ogle the dramatic lagoon (and the nearby Diamond Beach), then carry on 10 minutes for a more intimate boat trip at Fjallsárlón. This often-overlooked lagoon is just as spectacular.

Whichever lagoon you visit, be extremely careful. Tempting as it might seem, trying to step out onto an iceberg that drifts near the shore is a terrible idea. The ice chunks can flip over, trapping you underneath, immersed in near-freezing water.

Chunks of ice the size of buildings crack off the glacier with a sharp bang, like a gunshot. When they first calve off, the ice is a brilliant, deep blue. After just a few hours in the sun, the outer layer begins to melt, trapping tiny air bubbles and turning the surface white. Darker patches show where the ice dredges up sediments while grinding along the glacier bed. Because the grit stays put when the ice melts, icebergs grow darker as they age. All that sediment is what makes the lagoon's water murky.

Like icebergs at sea, these chunks of ice extend far beneath the surface. What you see floating is generally only one-tenth of the iceberg. Occasionally the melting patterns make an iceberg unbalanced, until it suddenly flips over with a thundering splash. Like a living organism, the lagoon is always changing, with icebergs bobbing and drifting around the still water. They slowly decrease in size until they're finally small enough for the current to carry them down the short Jökulsá river and out to the Atlantic.

RING ROAD

seals swim up the outflow river and can be seen basking on the ice chunks. And seabirds, including arctic terns, nest nearby in the early summer. If you happen to wander too close to a nest, you could get dive-bombed.

Glacier Lagoon Boat Trips: At Jökulsárlón, you have two options for getting out on the frigid water—a large, slow-moving "amphibian boat" (5,800 ISK, 45 minutes) or a smaller, faster RIB—rigid inflatable boat (9,900 ISK, 1 hour). Your captain/guide will narrate as the boat weaves between floating icebergs to reach the glacier wall at the end of the lagoon. If you're lucky you'll hear it creak or see a chunk of ice break off.

You'll be provided with lifejackets on either boat, and warm coveralls on the RIB. Either way, bundle up before heading out (close-fitting hat and gloves). Ideally, check the schedule and book online once you're fairly confident that the weather will justify the trip (tours run daily July-Aug 9:00-19:00, shorter hours off-season, no trips Nov-April, tel. 478-2222, www.icelagoon.is).

On arrival at the lagoon, go to the ticket kiosk to trade your emailed receipt for a ticket, then proceed to your boat's meeting point. Amphibian boats generally load close to the ticket kiosk; for the RIB you'll first be directed to a changing cabin to get outfitted, then walk with your captain/guide about 500 feet to a small dock.

Eating at Jökulsárlón: A too-small **$ café** is to the right of the boat ticket kiosk, offering soup, sandwiches, and hot drinks (free WCs in trailers nearby). In peak season, you may also find **food trucks** and picnic tables at the far end of the parking lot.

▲▲▲Diamond Beach

This dramatic sight hides down a gravel road just south of the bridge at Jökulsárlón (see page 430 for directions). Don't miss it.

Park (free, no WC), then walk up the shifting slope and down again to the shore. Glittering icebergs both large and small lie stranded on a fine black powder beach...like so many diamonds on display. By the time they reach these sands, many of the icebergs have been tumbled by currents and waves, leaving  them shiny and smooth. The beach changes constantly: Sometimes the "diamonds" are many, other times they're sparse. Sometimes they're transparent, other times white, occasionally blue, and often there's a mix of colors and sizes. Photographers can occupy themselves for hours.

Be extremely careful exploring this area. The Atlantic coastline here is notorious for its sneaker waves. If you turn your back to the ocean or wade into the (frigid) water here, you're taking your life in your hands. But even from a safe distance, Diamond Beach takes your breath away.

▲▲Fjallsárlón

Fjallsárlón (FYATL-sour-lohn, Mountain-River Lagoon)—the Back Door alternative to Jökulsárlón—is just seven miles farther down the main road (10 minutes), but tucked out of sight (watch for the big *Boat Tours* and red *Fjallsárlón* sign). From the parking lot—with a modern services building, including WCs, a good café, and boat-trip ticket offices—you can hike up onto a little ridge for great views of the Fjallsjökull glacial tongue, with the lagoon in the foreground. This lagoon started to form about 20 years ago as the glacier receded up the slope. It's smaller than Jökulsárlón (about one-fifth the size and one-third the depth), but that means you're up closer to the glacier itself.

Boat Trips: With Fjallsárlón's smaller size, the 45-minute RIB cruises here feel more personal. Boat trips run nearly hourly through the summer (6,900 ISK, hourly tours run April-mid-Oct daily 9:30-17:30, www.fjallsarlon.is). You can just show up and hope for an available slot, but it's more reliable to book online a day or two ahead.

Eating at Fjallsárlón: The modern, inviting **$ Frost Café** offers a soup-and-bread option, salad bar, and sandwiches (daily in summer from 11:30 to end of last boat trip, WCs free for customers).

Skaftafell National Park

Skaftafell (SKAF-tah-fehtl) is part of the larger Vatnajökull National Park (watch for the turnoff for highway 998 from the Ring Road). Within the park are Iceland's highest mountain, Hvannadalshnúkur (6,900 feet), and the mountain's Öræfajökull glacier, and the Skaftafellsjökull glacial tongue, which pokes down from Vatnajökull in the distance.

It's 750 ISK to park in the sprawling parking lot (which teems with hikers on nice summer days). You can pay at kiosks at the parking lot or at the visitors center (know your license plate number). A short walk on a gravel path brings you to the **visitors center,** with some small exhibits about the area, a short film in English, and plenty of advice about local hikes (maps for sale, info boards describe hiking routes, typically open daily 8:00-21:00 in summer, shorter hours off-season, camping available, free WCs, tel. 470-8300, www.vatnajokulsthjodgardur.is).

Eating at Skaftafell: A big, basic **$ cafeteria** with glacier views and outdoor seating serves uninspired salads, sandwiches, and main courses (daily 9:00-21:00 in summer, 10:00-19:00 off-season). There's also often a **food truck** in the parking lot near the campground.

RING ROAD

RING ROAD

▲▲Hiking at Skaftafell

Some people spend days hiking in this area, but even if you're just passing through, it's worth sampling one of the trails. Here are some popular choices, all of which begin from the Skaftafell parking lot (time and distance estimates are round-trip). Before heading out, be sure to get the hiking pamphlet (or ideas for other hikes) from the visitors center, and be aware of local weather conditions. The last three hikes require a stiff uphill

climb to the ridge called Skaftafellsheiði, which looms above the visitors center.

"Geology Trail" to Skaftafellsjökull (easy, 2.3 miles, 1 hour): The easiest and most popular choice, this loop hike (mostly over even and flat terrain, blue trail S1) takes you to the glacier tongue that runs off Vatnajökull. This is perhaps your best chance to get up close to a glacier without taking a lagoon cruise. (If you're planning to hike at Sólheimajökull farther along the South Coast, this trail may be somewhat redundant.) Rangers lead free guided walks on this route three times a day in season—if you'd like to join one, call ahead for the schedule or check the posted schedule for the next departure.

On your own or with a ranger, from the visitors center, you'll cut through a brushy "forest" of birch trees, cross a rocky field, walk along the base of a cliff, and go up the valley cut by the receding glacier. When you get to the glacier, conditions may allow you to walk up and touch it (but your path will likely be impeded by a river or pool of water). Don't attempt to climb the glacier without proper equipment, and don't be surprised by the glacier's brown or black appearance—it picks up a lot of grit as it grinds down its valley.

Svartifoss (moderate, 2-2.5 miles, 1.5-2 hours): While only about 60 feet tall, Svartifoss (Black Waterfall) enjoys one of Iceland's most dramatic waterfall settings, gushing over a cliff of basalt columns. While utterly spectacular, a visit requires a sturdy uphill hike (elevation gain of about 850 feet). Note that there are two routes to Svartifoss: Short and steep (red trail S2), or longer and more gradual (blue trail S2). Sort out your options at the visitors center.

Svartifoss-Sjónarsker-Sel (moderate, 3.5 miles, 2.5 hours): From Svartifoss, further hikes tempt those with more time and energy. One popular, moderate option links the waterfall to the fine viewpoint at Sjónarsker—overlooking the astonishingly broad

Skeiðarársandur glacial river delta—and a traditional turf house at Sel (blue trail S2).

Svartifoss-Sjónarnípa (challenging, 4.5 miles, 4-5 hours): More ambitious is the demanding trail from Svartifoss across to the hillside to Sjónarnípa, which rewards the effort with stunning views over Skaftafellsjökull. From Svartifoss, you'll take red trail S5/S6.

Glacier Walks and Ice Cave Tours

The parking lot at Skaftafell is busy with huts and vans for various companies leading tours onto the ice. Excursions range from an hour in length to all-day walks. For these up-close glacier experiences it's best to book ahead. The following companies offer one or both activities: Glacier Journey (www.glacierjourney.is), Arctic Adventures (www.adventures.is), and Extreme Iceland (www.extremeiceland.is). For glacier walks, these companies are more specialized: Icelandic Mountain Guides (www.mountainguides.is) and Glacier Guides (www.glacierguides.is). For more on glacier activities, see the Icelandic Experiences chapter.

Sleeping in Southeast Iceland

For locations, see the map on page 428.

In Höfn: The **$$$ Milk Factory,** along the road between Höfn and highway 1 (a long walk or short drive from the harbor), is a fun choice, renting 17 rooms in a former milk-processing plant with clean, tidy, modern style. Check out the photos in the lobby to see the factory in its heyday (Dalbraut 2, tel. 478-8900, reception@milkfactory.is).

$$$$ Charming but pricey **Hótel Höfn,** facing the ocean three blocks from the main road and recommended Kaffi Hornið, is a rewarding splurge with a chic nod to its retro roots in its 68 rooms. It's a 20-minute stroll to the harbor along the pedestrian promenade (no elevator, buffet breakfast, restaurant, Víkurbraut 20, tel. 478-1240, www.hotelhofn.is, info@hotelhofn.is).

$$$ Hótel Edda Höfn is the other big-hotel option in town, with a large, modern lobby and 36 rooms in a characterless building with glacier views. It's in a handy location just steps from the harbor (breakfast extra, Ránarslóð, tel. 444-4000, www.hoteledda.is, edda@hoteledda.is).

$$ Guesthouse Dyngja feels like you're staying at a friend's house. It's a reliable, cheerful place with seven updated rooms (some with shared bath) a few steps above the harbor (breakfast extra, family room with private entry, mobile 866-0702, www.dyngja.com, fanney@dyngja.com, Signy).

Just Outside Höfn: In a modern motel-style building,

$$$ **Seljavellir Guesthouse** offers 20 practical rooms in a farm valley a few minutes north of Höfn. Each room opens out to its own patio (mobile 845-5801, just off highway 1, www.seljavellir. com, info@seljavellir.is).

Between Höfn and the Glacier Lagoons: Tucked beneath a huge mountain about a half-hour from Höfn or Jökulsárlón, $$$ **Guesthouse Skálafell** is a simple, family-run compound with 13 rooms and three cozy cottages. Rooms in the older building share a bath (tel. 478-1041, www.skalafell.net, info@skalafell. net, Sindri). The guesthouse shares a parking lot with the national park's Hjallanes trailhead (1-mile, 3-mile, and 5-mile hike options).

$$$ **Hali Country Hótel** is big and functional, just a 10-minute drive east of the Jökulsárlón glacier lagoon by the Hali farm/Thórbergur Center (described on page 434). It has 39 rooms scattered through three buildings fronting the ocean (reception and breakfast at museum, laundry service, mobile 867-2900, www.hali. is, hali@hali.is).

$$ **Skyrhúsið Guest House,** in a tall and narrow building across the street from the Thórbergur Center, is more hostel than hotel. It offers 11 bright and basic rooms with shared bath (tel. 478-8989, https://skyrhusid.is, skyrhusid@gmail.com).

Between Skaftafell and Vík: Comfortable and well-run, $$$ **Hrífunes Guesthouse** is almost to the South Coast; some rooms have views, and some have private bathrooms. You'll meet your fellow guests at the good dinner served family-style (request dinner a day ahead, packed lunches available, laundry service, 15 minutes off highway 1 on highway 209, mobile 863-5540, www. hrifunesguesthouse.is, Hadda).

Big Chain Hotels: For less personality but plenty of beds, you'll find big branches of well-established Icelandic chains that cater mainly to tour groups. The Fosshotel chain has multiple branches (www.fosshotel.is): $$ **Fosshótel Vatnajökull** has 66 rooms just outside of Höfn (tel. 478-2555, vatnajokull@fosshotel. is); $$$$ **Fosshótel Glacier Lagoon** is a splurge with 104 rooms beside a waterfall between Jökulsárlón and Skaftafell (tel. 514-8300, glacier@fosshotel.is); and $$ **Fosshótel Núpar** has 60 rooms about 20 minutes north of Kirkjubæjarklaustur (tel. 517-3060). $$ **Hótel Klaustur** has 57 rooms in the village of Kirkjubæjarklaustur (Klausturvegi 6, tel. 487-4900, https://hotelklaustur.is, info@hotelklaustur.is).

RING ROAD

South Coast

Iceland's South Coast—stretching from Vík about 40 miles west to the Markárfljót river and Seljalandsfoss waterfall—is one of Iceland's most enjoyable corners. Within this hour-long stretch you'll encounter black sand beaches, scenic promontories, hikeable and touchable glaciers, a pleasant folk museum, and two spectacular waterfalls. On the way back to Reykjavík, there's less to see, though the Lava Center is a good stop to learn more about volcanoes.

Planning Tips: If you're rushing the Ring, you'll have a busy day of sightseeing and a late drive back to Reykjavík. Spending a night here allows you to linger at the area's attractions before returning to Reykjavík (or side-trip to the Westman Islands, an easy ferry ride from here, if the weather cooperates).

Vík to Reykjavík

For more specifics on the South Coast—including a map, sightseeing details, recommended eateries and accommodations, and strategic tips—see the South Coast chapter. Since that chapter is designed for day trips from Reykjavík, the sights are presented there from west to east—the opposite order for those completing a clockwise Ring tour. Below is a rough outline for visiting these sights, traveling from east to west.

The first part of the drive—from Vík to Seljalandsfoss waterfall—takes only about an hour (about 40 miles), but contains many hours' worth of sightseeing. (If you're very selective, you can have a satisfying visit to this stretch in about 3-4 hours.)

Once you leave Hvolsvöllur (and its Lava Center), it's a fairly straightforward 1.5-hour, 70-mile drive to Reykjavík, with fewer temptations en route.

From **Vík** (where you'll find gas stations and eateries), you'll twist up and over a mountain pass. As you descend, watch on the left for the turnoff to the **Reynisfjara black sand beach,** with fabulous basalt formations, scenic sea stacks, handy beach café, and dangerous sneaker waves (10-minute drive from the main road on highway 215).

Just a bit farther along on highway 1, the turnoff for highway 218 leads five minutes to **Dyrhólaey promontory,** with fine views and a lighthouse hike (skippable for those in a rush).

Continuing 25 more minutes, you'll reach the turnoff for **Sólheimajökull glacier** (a five-minute drive from the Ring Road on highway 221). From the parking lot, it's a 15-minute hike to the glacier; depending on conditions (and your own surefootedness), you can often walk right up and touch the glacier. But if you've already visited the glacier lagoons in the southeast, this is skippable.

Just past the Sólheimajökull turnoff, also on the right, is the settlement called **Skógar,** which has the striking Skógafoss waterfall and a fine folk museum.

From here, the road continues west in the shadow of **Eyjafjallajökull,** the volcano whose 2010 eruption famously disrupted European air travel. The roadside Katla Geopark Visitor Center covers the Eyjafjallajökull eruption and geological aspects of the region (but the Lava Center—coming up soon—does it on a grander scale). You'll enjoy great views of the **Westman Islands,** with teeth-like cliffs hovering just offshore (for details, see the Westman Islands chapter).

Around 25 minutes (18 miles) after leaving Skógar, turn off on the right to highway 249 and the parking lot for the long and lovely **Seljalandsfoss waterfall**—where you can actually walk behind its tumbling torrent.

Back on highway 1, you'll cross the Markárfljót river and curve inland—going through the humble communities of **Hvolsvöllur** (with its excellent Lava Center—a state-of-the-art volcano exhibit), **Hella,** and **Selfoss** (with the grave of chess legend Bobby Fischer). Highway 1 cuts north past **Hveragerði** (with a satisfying pizzeria/brewery—see page 209), then switchbacks up and across the volcanic, desolate **Hellisheiði** plateau. Before you know it, you're approaching the Reykjavík suburbs.

Your epic Ring Road odyssey is finally at its end. Well done!

ICELAND WITH CHILDREN

With relatively few museums and plenty of stunning natural wonders and other outdoor activities, Iceland is a great destination for kids. Icelandic culture prizes children. Many restaurants and museums have designated play areas, and every neighborhood has a playground. And Iceland's dramatic landscapes make for a road trip that rivals the great national parks of the US. Encourage your kids to learn about exciting geological features like volcanoes and glaciers so they can play tour guide. Figure out what their friends' names would be using the Icelandic naming system (I'd be "Rick Dicksson"). And challenge them to master the pronunciation of "Eyjafjallajökull."

Trip Tips

PLAN AHEAD
Involve your kids in trip planning. Have them read about the places that you may include in your itinerary (even the hotels you're considering), and let them help with your decisions.

Where to Stay
- In Reykjavík, hotels are pricey and can be cramped; renting an apartment or house can be cheaper and provide more room to spread out. The advantages of renting a home in Reykjavík's suburbs are substantial—you'll have more space and get a look at real Icelandic life. But be warned that short-term rentals might not be childproofed or fully equipped for small kids (unlike hotels, which are likely to have loaner cribs). Search for places with the amenities you'll need—or, if necessary, bring them along.
- Outside of the capital area, you'll find fun farmstay and cot-

tage options that are ideal for families (see the "Sleeping" section of the Practicalities chapter).

- Minimize moves by planning longer stays. From a home base in the Reykjavík area, you can spend days side-tripping to many of Iceland's highlights: Golden Circle, South Coast, Blue Lagoon/Reykjanes Peninsula, Borgarnes/Reykholt Valley, and more. If doing the entire Ring Road, budget enough time to spend multiple nights in places like Mývatn, Southeast Iceland, or the South Coast.
- Consider hotels with restaurants (on-site or nearby), so older kids can go back to the room while you finish a pleasant dinner.
- In most of Iceland, hot water is piped directly from geothermal sources. It can be scalding right out of the tap. Show your kids how to carefully test the water temperature before washing their hands or getting in a shower or bathtub. (Also reassure them that the sometimes-sulfurous odor of the hot water is perfectly natural and safe.)

What to Bring (or Not)
- Don't bother bringing a car seat—car-rental agencies usually rent them (but reserve in advance).
- Bring your own drawing supplies and English-language picture books, as these are pricey in Iceland.
- Pack a swimsuit, towel, and maybe goggles for fun in Iceland's many thermal swimming pools.
- With the unpredictable weather (even in summer), bring a waterproof jacket and plenty of layers to bundle up your child.
- If you're flying Icelandair, ask for the nice, complimentary box of items that kids under 10 will appreciate. And check out the airline's onboard video entertainment showcasing Iceland's many attractions that may help get your child excited about what lies ahead.

EATING
Iceland offers plenty of food options for children.

What to Eat (and Drink)
- Icelandic soups (especially the staple lamb soup, called *kjötsúpa*) are hearty, nourishing, and accessible for kids. The freshly made bread that accompanies most soups is a good bet for picky eaters.
- Most accommodations provide a hearty buffet-style breakfast (including cereals, breads, cheeses, juices, yogurts, fresh fruit, etc.) with enough options for kids to fortify themselves for a busy day of sightseeing.

CHILDREN

- Iceland's wide variety of yogurt-like treats (*þykkmjólk*, *jógurt*, and *skyr*) are tasty, but not as sweet as American-style yogurts. Try mixing in fresh fruit or topping it with granola.
- Pop into a bakery for heavenly scents and fresh-baked pastries. In Reykjavík, try the colorful Brauð & Co or Sandholt (with a larger selection). At Brauð & Co, you can even watch the bakers at work (for details, see page 147).

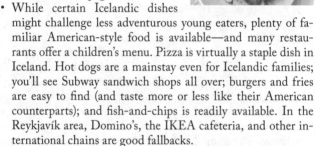

- While certain Icelandic dishes might challenge less adventurous young eaters, plenty of familiar American-style food is available—and many restaurants offer a children's menu. Pizza is virtually a staple dish in Iceland. Hot dogs are a mainstay even for Icelandic families; you'll see Subway sandwich shops all over; burgers and fries are easy to find (and taste more or less like their American counterparts); and fish-and-chips is readily available. In the Reykjavík area, Domino's, the IKEA cafeteria, and other international chains are good fallbacks.
- Most kids will enjoy sampling local sweets. Icelandic candy is tasty and unique. Licorice encased in chocolate is a specialty. Note, though, that a lot of Icelandic licorice is stronger than an American kid's palate is used to. And Icelanders love soft-serve ice cream. For a special treat, ask at an ice-cream store for a *bragðarefur*—an overflowing cup of soft serve with candy or sauces mixed in. Also look for familiar sweets in new packaging—for example, *Rís Buff* (puffed rice and marshmallow covered in chocolate). Kids also might like to try the local orange soda, Egils Appelsín.
- Adventurous older kids might get a kick out of trying some of Iceland's more exotic foods, such as whale, the infamous fermented shark, or other "hardship meats."

When and Where to Eat

- In Reykjavík, eat dinner early, when restaurants are less crowded.
- Skip romantic or super-traditional eateries. Try relaxed cafés (or fast-food restaurants) where kids can move around without bothering others. Many eateries have play areas.
- Picnics work well. Stock up on supplies at one of Iceland's budget supermarkets, Bónus and Krónan.

CHILDREN

SIGHTSEEING

The key to a successful Iceland family vacation is to slow down. Tackle one or two key sights each day, mix in a healthy dose of pure fun, and take extended breaks when needed.

Planning Your Time

- Lower your sightseeing ambitions and let kids help choose daily activities. Plan longer stays at fewer stops—you won't regret it.
- To make your trip fun for everyone in the family, mix heavy-duty sights with kids' activities—such as going for a swim or soak after tackling a museum or long hike.
- If you're linking destinations by car, be prepared for long stretches of arguably not much to see. Come ready with activities for kids to do in the car (you can only count so many sheep), plan ahead for meal and bathroom stops, and take advantage of scenic pullouts to stretch everyone's legs.
- Keep in mind that museums in Iceland can be very expensive. Even a fairly modest exhibit that takes less than an hour to see can cost $20 or more per person; younger children may get discounts. Weigh your sightseeing options and consider the investment each place requires...and remember that, for families with a car, most of Iceland's best attractions—in the great outdoors—are free.

Successful Sightseeing

- Older kids and teens can help plan the details of a sightseeing visit, such as what to see, how to get there, and ticketing details.
- Audioguides are great for older children. Many exhibits—such as the Wonders of Iceland exhibit at the Pearl in Reykjavík, or the Lava Center near the South Coast—offer interactive exhibits that will keep kids of all ages en-gaged. For younger children, hit the gift shop first so they can buy postcards and have a scavenger hunt to find the pictured items. When boredom sets in, try "I spy" games.
- Bring a sketchbook and encourage kids to select an object or landscape to draw. It's a great way for them to slow down and observe.
- Pick up a field guide to Iceland's flora and fauna and use it to identify unfamiliar birds and plants.

Making or Finding Quality Souvenirs

- Souvenirs tend to be extremely expensive. Parents may find it wise to give kids a budget and advise them to choose their souvenir carefully. Many of the same items are available for the same price at multiple locations.
- One of my favorite suggestions is to buy your child a trip journal where he or she can record observations, thoughts, and favorite sights and memories. This journal could end up being your child's favorite souvenir.
- For a group project, keep a family journal. Pack a small diary and a glue stick. While relaxing at a café, take turns writing about the day's events and include mementos such as ticket stubs from museums, postcards, or pinches of black sand from volcanic beaches.

WHAT PART OF
EYJAFJALLAJÖKULL
DON'T YOU UNDERSTAND?

- Younger kids may enjoy a typically Icelandic stuffed animal, like a cuddly puffin. An Icelandic flag is simple, colorful, and low-cost. T-shirts with unique Icelandic words or sayings are fun.

MONEY, SAFETY, AND STAYING CONNECTED

Before your trip gets under way, talk to your kids about safety and money.

- Give your child a money belt and an expanded allowance; you are on vacation, after all. Let your kids budget their funds by comparing and contrasting the dollar and the *króna*.
- Particularly outside of the capital area, Iceland's nature is untamed and can be quite dangerous. Anytime you're near the open ocean (especially along the South Coast), be aware of the risk of sneaker waves—which can suddenly deluge a beach, pulling people out to the open ocean. At any geothermal area, keep children very close at hand and ensure that they understand the extreme danger of straying from marked paths and into scalding springs. (Impress on your kids that the water is extremely

hot, not just warm...they shouldn't try to "test" the temperature with their finger.) And if you're walking up close to a glacier, don't go on top of the ice unless you are properly outfitted and with a guide. For a complete rundown about safe travel, see the sidebar on page 34.

- In town, if you allow older kids to explore a museum or neighborhood on their own, be sure to establish a clear meeting time and place.

- It's good to have a "what if" procedure in place in case something goes wrong. Give your kids your hotel's business card (or write down the address of your rental apartment), your phone number (if you brought a mobile phone), and emergency taxi fare. Let them know to ask to use the phone at a hotel if they are lost. And if they have mobile phones, show them how to make calls in Iceland (see the "Staying Connected" section of the Practicalities chapter).

- If traveling with older kids, you can help them keep in touch with friends at home with cheap texting plans and by email. Hotel guest computers and Wi-Fi hotspots are a godsend. Readily available Wi-Fi (at just about every business in Iceland) makes bringing a mobile device worthwhile. Most parents find it worth the peace of mind to buy a supplemental messaging plan for the whole family: Adults can stay connected to teenagers while allowing them maximum independence.

Top Kids' Sights and Activities

ATTRACTIONS AROUND REYKJAVÍK

For specifics, see the individual listings under "Sights in Reykjavík," page 91.

Reykjavík City Hall

The large 3-D map of Iceland will fascinate many kids and can be a nice prelude or postscript to your Iceland visit.

Laugardalur

This valley, just east of downtown, is where Icelanders spend time with their kids. It has a "family park" (including the city's biggest jungle gym and a few amusement-park rides), a zoo (with mostly farm animals), botanic gardens, and an indoor ice rink.

Árbær Open-Air Museum

Not far from Laugardalur, this very kid-friendly exhibit lets you walk through historic buildings from around Iceland.

Whales of Iceland

While this attraction is expensive, kids love wandering among the life-size models of majestic giants. Actual **whale-watching cruises** may bore kids; read my description in the Icelandic Experiences chapter before assuming yours will enjoy one.

Kolaportið Flea Market

Open weekends only, this downtown flea market is fun for the whole family to explore.

Hallgrímskirkja Lutheran Church

This architecturally striking church is an eye-catching symbol of the capital, which kids might enjoy seeing inside and out. If the line isn't too long, ascending its tower offers a fine view over the city's colorful rooftops. The statue of **Leifur Eiríksson** out front is a fun photo-op landmark (with a dramatic story).

The Pearl

The viewpoint here offers a farther-out, big-picture view of Reykjavík, and the **Wonders of Iceland** exhibit downstairs makes Icelandic nature fun for kids, with interactive exhibits and a walkthrough ice cave. Enjoy an ice cream with a 360-degree view of the city and surroundings.

The Pond

The small lake in the heart of Reykjavík has walking paths and ducks to feed—and if it's cold enough in winter, they may have a skating rink. At the northeast corner of the lake, find the sweet little "Mother's Garden" (Mæðragarðurinn)—designed in 1925 for moms to bring their kids to play (notice the touching statue, called *Motherly Love*).

Walking Paths

On a nice day, the paths along the south side of the Reykjavík peninsula make for a nice stroll and have lots of diversions. At low tide, you can walk down onto the rocks and sand (in the bay, there are no giant ocean waves to worry about). Start near the streets called Ægisíða and Faxaskjól (take bus #11).

Indoor Play Areas

High-energy kids can spend an afternoon doing tumbly activities at a couple of indoor facilities. The Kringlan shopping mall has the "Adventure Land" (Ævintýraland) supervised play zone where parents can pay to leave kids for an hour or two (ages 3-9); www.kringlan.is/aevintyraland. The giant IKEA has a small, supervised play area, called Småland, for kids ages 3-7 (free for up to an hour or so, may be a line to get in, www.ikea.is).

Saga Museum

Life-size mannequins enacting great moments of early Icelandic history help bring those tales to life. But some of the mannequins may be too graphic (violence and a little nudity) for certain kids; before buying tickets, flip through the picture book at the entrance to help you decide. At the end of the visit, kids have a chance to dress up like a Viking. Skip the audioguide—it's too dry for younger kids.

Harpa Concert Hall

Kids enjoy walking around the lobby of this bold concert hall—with its many multicolored windows—and walking out on the jetty just beyond it for views back on the sailboat harbor in front of the building.

The Settlement Exhibition

Older kids might enjoy seeing the actual remains of this Viking Age longhouse from the 10th century, well explained by interactive exhibits.

Icelandic Phallological Museum

Jaded, older teenagers (bored with every other museum in town) may show a spark of interest at this collection of preserved animal phalluses. In some ways, 12-year-old boys are the most fitting audience possible for this collection.

Viking World

Near the international airport in the town of Keflavík, this museum features a replica Viking boat and some interactive exhibits. For younger kids, the highlight is across the parking lot, in the Settlement Age petting zoo (summer only). While mostly underwhelming, this exhibit is a handy place to kill some time near the airport and Blue Lagoon (see page 181).

OUTDOOR AND WATER FUN

There are many remarkable things for kids to see in nature: glaciers, volcanoes, puffins, horses, and more. Most of these are equally suitable for kids as for adults, though some do have age restrictions. Below I've called out a few highlights for families. For an overview of these activities, see the Icelandic Experiences chapter.

Waterfalls

Iceland offers many opportunities to get up close to waterfalls, from Gullfoss (on the Golden Circle) and Seljalandsfoss and Skógafoss (on the South Coast) to Dynjandi (in the Westfjords) and Dettifoss (in the North). Each one's a bit different, but they're all thrilling. Surefooted kids particularly enjoy **Seljalandsfoss,** where they can walk behind the falls (see page 220). Be very careful at any waterfall when it's cold—the mist can make footing icy and slippery.

Basalt Columns

The black sand beach at **Reynisfjara,** on the South Coast, has seaside caves and stair-step basalt columns that kids enjoy climbing on (see page 230). But be very careful with kids at this beach, as this is one of the places prone to sneaker waves (see safety warning above).

Glaciers and Glacier Lagoons

All along the South Coast, you'll spot glacial tongues lapping down from giant, slow-motion rivers of ice. If you're doing a long road trip, the best place to see these is from the glacier lagoons in Southeast Iceland: **Jökulsárlón** and **Fjallsárlón** (see page 436). You can walk very near to a glacier at **Skaftafell National Park** (see page 437). And at **Sólheimajökull** on the South Coast, you can take a short hike along an iceberg-filled lagoon right up to the glacier's snout (see page 227). Older kids might enjoy walking (or snowmobiling) on top of a glacier, or touring an ice cave, both of which you can experience by joining an excursion. For more on these options, see the "Glaciers" section in the Icelandic Experiences chapter.

Volcanoes and Other Geothermal Areas

Iceland's volcanic landscape is fascinating to see and learn about. For more tips, see the "Volcanoes" section of the Icelandic Experiences chapter.

   Grábrók (near Borgarnes, see page 277) and **Hverfjall** (by

Mývatn, see page 398) are comparatively easy and safe crater experiences for small kids (they'll still need a bit of hand-holding at
the top). Less than an hour southeast of Reykjavík, the one-hour
guided tour of **The Lava Tunnel** (Raufarhólshellir) is an easy and
fun underground walk through a colorful 5,000-year-old lava tube
(see page 41). The most kid-friendly volcano museum is the **Lava
Center** in Hvolsvöllur, which you'll drive right by on a South Coast
day trip (see page 219). And the best all-around volcanic sight is
the **Westman Islands,** where you can walk up onto a lava flow
that partly covered the town in 1973, visit the excellent Volcano
Museum (called Eldheimar), and hike up to the still-warm summit
of Eldfell (see the Westman Islands chapter).

At places like **Geysir Geothermal Field** (on the Golden Circle), it's exciting for kids to walk through a bubbling, steaming,
spurting landscape of hot water (see page 200). But stay on the
trail!

The **Mývatn** volcanic area in North Iceland—with its many
unique land formations, steaming geothermal landscapes, and easy
nature walks—is Iceland's Yellowstone. The lava castles at Dimmuborgir are fun for kids and relatively safe. If you're setting up for
a few days of nature trips anywhere outside of the capital, Mývatn
is a good choice (see page 393).

Historic Sights

While its historical importance may be lost on younger kids,
Þingvellir, on the Golden Circle route, can still be fun. Although
the rocky outcrops and rushing river may make parents nervous,
children like the boardwalks and paths.

In the northern town of Skagafjörður, the open-air **Glaumbær Museum** does a fine job re-creating the lifestyles of medieval Icelanders. You can actually walk through several sod-walled
homes and better understand how people lived. While the museum
is not specifically aimed at kids, older children interested in local
folk culture enjoy it (see page 371).

Zoos, Farms, and Animal Activities

Slakki Zoo, just off the Golden Circle route, is a combination petting zoo and indoor minigolf complex whose core audience is kids under eight. Families could make this their main target for a Golden Circle day trip and manage to glimpse some of the better-known sights on the way (see page 207).

In the summer, try to find a place to look for **puffins.** You can spot these adorable seabirds all over—you're likely to have luck on a short cruise from Reykjavík, at Reynisfjara black sand beach on the South Coast (look above the basalt columns), or on the Westman Islands (on a minibus tour or at the town's Puffin Rescue Center). Farther afield, you may see puffins at Flatey island (north of the Snæfellsnes Peninsula), at Ísafjörður (in the Westfjords), or at Bak-kagerði in the northeast (off the Ring Road).

A number of **Icelandic farms** offer horseback riding, accommodations, restaurants, or areas where visitors can see animals and learn a bit about the workings of Icelandic farm life. Many of my accommodations outside of Reykjavík are on working farms. Good restaurants on farms include Efstidalur II and Friðheimar on the Golden Circle, and Fjósið on the South Coast (see those chapters for details). There's also Cowshed Café near Mývatn (see the Ring Road chapter).

The unique Icelandic horse—typically small and mighty—offers an enjoyable **horseback riding** experience for visitors old and young. Riding opportunities are plentiful around Iceland, including at horse farms (some near Reykjavík; see page 50). In the Reykholt Valley, kids love the family-run **Háafell Goat Farm,** which is working hard to revive the nearly extinct Icelandic goat. It's a fun visit—with hands-on goat encounters.

Thermal Swimming Pools

Iceland's thermal bathing scene is extremely kid-friendly—particularly at municipal swimming pools, which you'll find around the capital area and throughout the country. Many of the larger pools have colorful waterslides and other activities that are designed just for kids, and there's usually a shallow wading section for tiny tots. For tips on thermal pools—including the procedure for entering a pool complex—see the Icelandic Experiences chapter.

Iceland's upscale premium baths are less suitable for kids. For example, families may want to steer clear of the famous and expensive Blue Lagoon,

as it doesn't have any areas or activities designated for children, the mellow and spa-like atmosphere feels very grown-up, and its opaque water makes anything that slips under next to impossible to find. I also wouldn't take younger kids to the rugged natural thermal bathing experiences (like Reykjadalur); those landscapes are quite volatile, and it's easy to absentmindedly step into too-hot water. It's best to stick with the many municipal pools around Iceland.

Sledding

If you're in Reykjavík on a snowy winter day, you can borrow sleds and drive to the slope at Ártúnsbrekka in the eastern part of the city. It's off the street called Rafstöðvarvegur, near the Elliðaá River.

CHILDREN

ICELAND:
PAST & PRESENT

On the far northern fringe of Europe, surrounded by the open Atlantic, Iceland has an epic history that's been shaped by the sea. Here's a brief overview.

PREHISTORY
As the North American and Eurasian tectonic plates pulled apart, lava welled up between them. Over many millions of years of eruptions, Iceland was formed. Eruptions continue today in the middle of the island, along a belt running roughly from the north to the south and southwest. This belt, which passes close to (but not through) Reykjavík, contains Iceland's active volcanoes, as well as its hot springs and geothermal energy sources. The older lava has been pulled east and northwest by the spreading plates, meaning the western and eastern fjords are volcano-free (good) but also have little or no underground hot water for heating (bad). The sea's waves have eroded the rock to form steep cliffs in some parts of the island, while in others, glaciers flowing down from the Highlands have carved deep valleys and fjords.

For most of human history, Iceland was uninhabited. Egypt, Greece, and Rome rose and fell, but the only creatures here were birds, fish, foxes, and an occasional confused polar bear who drifted over on an iceberg from Greenland.

700-900: THE SETTLEMENT AGE
During the Viking Age, Celtic monks and Scandinavian seafarers began to explore the North Atlantic: first the Faroe Islands, and then Iceland. The innovation of a sturdier keel—spanning the entire length of a ship—allowed the early Scandinavians to sail with confidence on the open ocean. They pickled their foods in

Iceland Almanac

Official Name: The Republic of Iceland (Lýðveldið Ísland), but locals just say "Ísland" (EES-lond).

Size: 39,682 square miles, a little larger than Maine. With about 340,000 people, Iceland is one of the least-populated countries in Europe.

Geography: Iceland is oval-shaped, with three peninsulas extending from the west side. The coastal regions are green and grassy. The interior uplands are mostly wasteland—cold and snowy in winter—with glaciers and swift-flowing rivers.

Latitude and Longitude: Between 63° and 66°N and 13° and 25°W (similar latitude to Fairbanks, Alaska). The island is located between the Greenland Sea, the Norwegian Sea, and the open North Atlantic Ocean.

Biggest Cities and Towns: More than half the population resides in or around Reykjavík (the capital, with 216,000 people). Other "cities" include Akureyri (in North Iceland, pop. 18,000), Keflavík (15,000, including its sister town of Njarðvík), and Selfoss (7,000).

Economy: The Gross Domestic Product is about $18 billion, and the GDP per capita is around $52,000. The major money-makers for Iceland are tourism, fishing (40 percent of exports), and hydropower (from dams that generate electricity used for metal smelting). Iceland's unemployment hovers around 4 percent. About 2 percent of Icelanders work in agriculture, 4 percent in fishing and fish processing, 1 percent in metal processing, 15 percent in other industries, and 78 percent in services.

Government: The prime minister is the chief executive, and typically the head of the leading vote-getting party. The president has a mostly ceremonial role, but helps to form parliamentary coalitions and can refer legislation to a referendum. There are 63 legislators in the single-house parliament (the Alþingi), who sit for four years unless early elections are called.

Flag: The flag is a red-and-white Scandinavian cross on a blue field. Blue represents the skies, white represents glaciers and ice, and red represents volcanic fire.

The Average Icelander: The average Icelander will live 83 years. He or she has two children and goes through 18 pounds of coffee beans per year. Over two-thirds of Icelanders (238,000) are registered members of the state-supported Lutheran church. Legend has it that 1 in 10 Icelanders will publish a book.

fermented whey (to preserve valuable nourishment when far from home) and used birds and whales to help them navigate the seas.

No one knows exactly how, when, or where the first arrivals came to Iceland. Much of the country's early history was passed down orally over the centuries, then finally recorded for the first time in the "sagas"—a series of tales mixing historical fact and fanciful legend. (For example, one from the *Heimskringla* describes Iceland's four guardian spirits, now commemorated on its coat of arms: the eagle, bull, dragon, and giant.) While the sagas can't be taken as literal history, they are loaded with stories (rooted in who knows how much truth) that are deeply ingrained in the Icelandic national identity. For more on the sagas, see the sidebar on page 108.

According to the sagas, the discoverer of Iceland was Hrafna-Flóki Vilgerðarson, who released three ravens when he was under sail; the first two turned back to Norway, but the third flew in the opposite direction—eventually leading him to Iceland. He became known by the nickname Hrafna-Flóki—Raven-Flóki. The sagas say that Ingólfur Árnarson was the first permanent settler in Iceland, at today's Reykjavík, around AD 874. But archaeologists have found evidence of settlement dating much earlier than that.

Whoever came first, these settlers grew in number around the middle of the ninth century. Once they established a course they could follow with confidence, it took these early Scandinavians just 72 hours to cross from Norway to Iceland. Influenced by political events in Norway and Ireland, a mix of people from both lands brought their livestock and took up permanent residence in Iceland. Most were pagan, following the old Germanic religion of Thor (Þórr) and Odin (Oðinn), and spoke Old Norse.

Interestingly, geneticists believe that many of the female settlers were Celts, while more of the men were Scandinavian. It seems that Ireland and Scotland were good places for Scandinavian men to find wives (willing or unwilling) to bring on the journey. Today, the Scandinavian narrative dominates Icelandic history; only faint traces of Celtic culture survive.

Settlement Age Iceland had no towns; everyone lived on farms. The newcomers appreciated Iceland's abundant fresh water and grazing land for sheep. It was a challenging existence, but early Icelanders tamed the land and made it their own.

900-1300: THE ICELANDIC COMMONWEALTH

The settlers established a primitive government, in which several dozen local chieftains *(goðar)* held power. The chieftainships could be inherited or sold. As in other Germanic lands, they held regular courts and legislative assemblies (called a *þing*, like the English "thing"). Beginning around AD 930, an island-wide assembly—called the Alþingi (all-thing)—convened once a year, at Þingvellir.

Meanwhile, Icelanders began to explore farther and farther into the chilly North Atlantic. Around the 980s, led by an exiled outlaw named Eiríkur Þorvaldsson (Erik the Red), Icelanders settled on the west coast of Greenland, and eventually established over 300 farms there. These communities would last until the 1400s, when the weather turned colder. A few years after the settlement of Greenland, an Icelander named Bjarni Herjólfsson was blown off course on his way to Greenland, and sighted the coast of northeastern Canada. Leifur Eiríksson (son of Erik the Red) bought Bjarni's ship and explored the unknown continent. Another expedition, led by Karlsefni Þórðarson and his wife Guðríður Þorbjarnardóttir, settled there, possibly at L'Anse aux Meadows in Newfoundland, but the Icelanders' North American settlements did not last. (For more on Leif Erikson, as Leifur is known stateside, see page 89; for more on Guðríður Þorbjarnardóttir, see page 307).

Iceland maintained a diplomatic and trading relationship with Norway, whose King Ólafur Tryggvason (r. 995-1000) tried to introduce Christianity to his subjects. He also sent missionaries to Iceland, who succeeded in making some converts, but failed in Christianizing the entire island. To nudge the Icelanders further, the king detained some Icelandic traders. This kicked off a furious debate at the assembly in Þingvellir in the year AD 1000. The assembly chose to convert rather than engage in a devastating trade war with Norway, and the entire country accepted Christianity in one fell swoop. (For more on the legend surrounding this mass conversion, see page 195.) Privately, however, some Icelanders continued to follow their pagan faith. Icelandic culture features a blending of Christianity and Old Norse ways, and to this day, many Icelanders have two given names—one with Christian roots, and the other pagan.

Iceland's Neighbors: Greenland and the Faroe Islands

Iceland is just a short flight (1.5-2 hours) from east Greenland and the Faroe Islands, making it possible for travelers to combine a trip to Iceland with one of these two destinations (see map on page 11).

Iceland, Greenland, and the Faroes share a history of medieval Norse settlement and later, Danish colonial rule. Greenland and the Faroes have much smaller modern populations—both about 50,000 people—and were not large enough to declare independence as easily as Iceland.

Today, both remain part of Denmark, but manage some of their own affairs. Locals learn Danish in school and use it in some contexts, but prefer their own tongues (two related Inuit languages in Greenland; Faroese, which is somewhat similar to Icelandic, in the Faroes).

The Faroes are a relatively wealthy Nordic society with rich fishing grounds, like Iceland. In Greenland, the original Norse settlement was abandoned in the 1400s, and the population today is Inuit with some later Danish intermarriage. Greenland has great potential wealth, but also a legacy of social problems (similar to that experienced by native communities in Canada and the US).

It's easy to fly round-trip from Iceland to either Greenland or the Faroes, although fares are high. You can also travel from Iceland to the Faroes on the Norröna car ferry from Seyðisfjörður in eastern Iceland, which continues on to Denmark. Both Greenland and the Faroes are spectacular destinations—Greenland is icy, barren, and majestic; the Faroes green, wet, and steep.

The easiest way to visit Greenland from Iceland is to fly from Reykjavík to Kulusuk (pop. 250) in east Greenland. In summer, regional airline Air Iceland Connect offers a day-trip to Kulusuk, with four hours on the ground. Kulusuk is on a small island of the same name, and anyone staying overnight usually takes a 10-minute helicopter flight to the main town of Tasiilaq (pop. 2,000) on the larger island of Ammassalik.

Air Iceland Connect also flies via Akureyri to a less practical destination, the east Greenlandic airport at Nerlerit Inaat (also known as Constable Point), which serves the village of Ittoqqortoormiit (pop. 500, also known as Scoresbysund). Bear in mind that east Greenland is a world away from the capital of Nuuk (pop. 18,000), on the west coast facing Canada. The east and west coasts even have their own languages, about as different as Italian and Spanish. Flights from Iceland to Nuuk and other west-coast destinations take about three hours.

Skálholt (near Geysir and Gullfoss) became the religious center of south Iceland, and Hólar (in Skagafjörður) the religious center of the north. Small communities grew up at each place. Otherwise, there were still no towns in Iceland. Farmers who were rich enough built small churches on their property.

All told, there were about 4,000 farms in Iceland during this period. The weather was warmer then, allowing grain to grow. At first there were large stretches of woodland, and the grassy areas (not yet affected by overgrazing) extended far inland. But over a period of just a few centuries, the forests were hacked into oblivion—to be used as construction material and fuel, and to open more grazing and farming land. The settlers were pastoralists, living off their animals' meat, milk, and wool. They kept cattle, sheep, and pigs, and used horses for transport and herding. They also did some fishing at certain times of the year.

Although you'll often hear this period described as a golden age that was later "restored," and Iceland's Alþingi is sometimes described as "the world's oldest parliament," the commonwealth period was no modern democracy. Society was stratified, with property owners on top, tenant farmers a step down, then landless laborers and slaves at the bottom. Women kept to the home and were mostly shut out of the realms of power, politics, and frontier justice.

The sagas were first written down around the end of this period, in the 12th through 14th century. No one knows exactly why Iceland became such a center of literary activity. Some scholars have suggested that the Celtic element of Icelandic society brought a talent for storytelling.

During these years, the language spoken in Iceland was about the same as in mainland Scandinavia. The archbishop of Iceland was in Norway. Icelanders sometimes thought of themselves as Norwegian, but in some ways emphasized their distinctness. At first, they were not formally subjects of the king of Norway. This changed in the 1200s, as chieftains from different families and parts of Iceland warred against each other inconclusively for control of the country. After decades of fighting, they resolved their differences by swearing allegiance to the king, who was just then trying to consolidate Norwegian power over Greenland and Scotland as well. In 1262, at the annual assembly in Þingvellir, Icelanders agreed to what became known as the "Old Covenant"—unilaterally declaring themselves to be subjects of Norway. The esteemed Alþingi was reduced from a primitive "parliament" to, essentially, an appeals court.

1300-1600: MEDIEVAL TIMES

Although Iceland was part of Norway, it retained its own laws. Aside from a single Norwegian governor (who lived at the farm called Bessastaðir, near Reykjavík), local officials were all Icelanders. Norway, preoccupied by its relations with Sweden and Denmark, showed little interest in Iceland or Greenland. In 1397, Norway joined with Sweden and Denmark in the Kalmar Union. Sweden left the union in the 1520s; meanwhile, Norway (suffering from the cooling climate) effectively became a dependency of Denmark. Thus, it became faraway Copenhagen—rather than Trondheim, Bergen, or Oslo—that Iceland answered to.

During the 1300s, Icelanders began to export fish and set up fishing stations on the coast, where they lived temporarily in the springtime. Christianity, which allowed eating fish on fast days, created a strong market for dried cod in Europe.

But Icelanders were not allowed to live permanently on the coast. Icelandic law required any landless person to live on a farm, for one-year periods starting each May. The farmer had to provide food and shelter in return for labor. If the farmer sent the laborer fishing in the spring, he got all their catch. Landless laborers were not allowed to marry. It was possible for them to buy or lease a farm, but not always easy. This system, called the *vistarband*—similar in some ways to Russian-style serfdom (if less harsh)—persisted all the way up until the 1890s.

The plague known as the Black Death reached Iceland in 1402, about 50 years after it decimated Europe. Approximately one-third of the island's inhabitants perished. But because Icelandic society was so rural and isolated, the country was not as disrupted as many in Europe. In fact, the plague opened up more opportunities for upwardly mobile peasants to buy their own land.

In the 1400s and 1500s, English and German merchants began to fish in Icelandic waters and trade with Icelanders, and they tried to set up permanent settlements on the Icelandic coast. They were, however, kicked out by the Danish government, which slowly began to see Iceland as an economic asset...and wanted its trade for themselves.

Around 1540, the Protestant Reformation reached Iceland by royal decree. The only real resistance came from the bishop of the northern diocese at Hólar, Jón Arason, who saw the Lutheran faith as an unwelcome Danish imposition. He was captured, brought to Skálholt, and executed.

It was during these centuries that the mainland Scandinavian languages developed away from Old Norse, while Icelanders' speech remained the same. By the end of this time, mainlanders could no longer understand Icelandic—and Icelanders felt themselves more and more separate. After the Reformation, the Bible was translated into Icelandic for the first time and printed in Denmark.

1600-1800: DANISH MONOPOLY

In 1602, King Christian IV of Denmark decreed that only a few specific merchants from Copenhagen and nearby towns would be allowed to trade with Iceland. Twenty harbors around the Icelandic coast were set up as trading points, where these merchants would come each summer to sell grain, timber, fine cloth, and other goods in return for Icelandic fish and woolens, all at fixed prices. Icelanders who had something to sell had no choice but to deal with the local merchant, a similar relationship to the one between the Hudson's Bay Company and native Canadians.

During these years, Iceland had about 50,000 people—the number rising and falling with famines and epidemics. Since only property-owning men could marry, the rate of marriage was low, and illegitimacy was common—prefiguring Scandinavia's loose attitude toward marriage today. Infant mortality was high, partly due to the odd belief—prevalent in northern Scandinavia—that babies should be given cow's milk instead of being breast-fed. Iceland still had no towns and no schools. Children were supposed to learn to read the Bible from others on the farm, under the watchful eye of the local pastor. In the mid-1700s, about half the population was literate. Dancing was banned, and there were very few musical instruments. Pirate raids along the coast were a problem, and the authorities often suspected witchcraft among the population—and meted out punishments as stiff as those in Salem.

Up until the 1700s, Reykjavík was just a large farm, like many others around the country. But around midcentury, Skúli Magnússon, a high Icelandic official, got support from Denmark to set up several businesses in Iceland, including textile manufacturing. He chose Reykjavík as the location, as it was close to the country's administrative seat at Bessastaðir. A row of workers' houses was built in what is now downtown Reykjavík, and although Skúli's enterprises failed, they were enough to seed settlement at what became Iceland's capital.

Unfortunately, the late 1700s also brought natural catastrophes that demonstrated the fragility of settlement on this volcanic island. In 1783, on the heels of several cold winters, a huge eruption started along a fissure running southwest from Vatnajökull glacier, creating a set of craters now called Lakagígar. Strong earthquakes destroyed most of the buildings of the southern bishop's seat at Skálholt. The ash from the eruption was loaded with toxic gases and blocked the summer sunlight. Livestock died and famine struck the land, killing one-fifth of the population.

One bright consequence of the eruption was a loosening of the trade monopoly in 1787. Now any Dane (not just certain merchants with a license) could trade with Iceland. (Germans and English were still excluded.) As part of these reforms, in 1786 the Danish crown selected six Icelandic harbors, including Reykjavík, as official trading locations. That same year, Reykjavík received "town" status, and emerged as the logical seat of Iceland's religion (becoming home to both bishops), government (the annual Alþingi gathering), and education system. As Reykjavík took over as Iceland's administrative center, the Alþingi was abolished in 1800 (it was restored in 1844). Even as Denmark extended more rights to Iceland, change was in the air.

1800-1900: A NATION EMERGES

In the 19th century, Icelanders redefined their relationship with Denmark. They wanted to restart their own legislative assembly and have control over their own affairs, though within the Danish realm. They also wanted the freedom to trade with whomever they wanted—not just Danes—and at whatever price the market would bear. The leader of the fight for these reforms was Jón Sigurðsson, an Icelandic scholar who lived in Copenhagen (now honored by a statue facing Iceland's parliament). Through persistence, they reached both goals in the 1840s and 1850s. In 1874, the king of Denmark approved a written constitution for Iceland. Icelanders thus gained much more autonomy than their neighbors in the Faroe Islands and Greenland, which are still part of Denmark today.

Iceland remained very poor. As the century drew to a close, most Icelanders still lived in houses made with thick turf walls

and a grassy sod roof. The nicer rooms were paneled with timber. The houses often backed up against a hillside for support and insulation. You can see these sod houses today at Árbær Open-Air Museum, just outside Reykjavík; at Skógar, on the South Coast; and—best of all—at Glaumbær in Skagafjörður (north Iceland).

In the late 1800s, about 20,000 Icelanders emigrated to North America (principally Manitoba, Canada; for more on this story, visit the Iceland Emigration Center in Hofsós). Among those who stayed, about a quarter suffered from a debilitating tapeworm called echinococcus, acquired from living in proximity to dogs and sheep. Only in the 20th century was the parasite eliminated by banning meat processing on farms and by limiting contact between people and dogs. Laws against dog ownership in Icelandic towns have only recently been relaxed.

Fishing technology improved, and by the 1870s, Icelanders exported more fish than agricultural products. Defying age-old custom, Icelanders began to settle along the coast and gather into towns, where they built wood-frame homes with corrugated iron roofs.

In the 1880s, Icelandic farmers banded together in cooperatives to challenge the Danish merchants who dominated Icelandic commerce. Together, they had enough negotiating power to buy consumer goods and sell wool and lamb abroad on better terms than before. Up until about 1990, many of Iceland's shops still belonged to farmers cooperatives.

1900-2000: INDEPENDENCE AND MODERNIZATION

In 1902, the first boat motor came to Iceland—and within a couple of decades, the fishing industry was revolutionized. The country kept urbanizing, and by the 1930s, two-thirds of Icelanders lived in towns (including one-third in Reykjavík). But while the country slowly modernized, it remained poor. Roads were few and bad. Housing in towns was cramped, chilly, and heated with coal. Icelanders, accurately, saw themselves as country cousins to their Nordic relatives, who lived in cities with grand architecture, museums, and fine universities. The Great Depression hit hard, and at the outbreak of World War II, Iceland was one of the poorest parts of northern Europe.

Icelanders continued to chip away at Danish control. They created their own flag and currency, and developed their own political parties. In 1918, they negotiated a 25-year agreement to become a separate state under the Danish crown.

One morning in 1940, British soldiers landed in Iceland without asking permission—knowing that Germany would act if they didn't. The next year, the American and Canadian military relieved the British. Sixty thousand corn-fed North Americans arrived on the island, outnumbering the local men, who naturally saw them as a threat. (Meanwhile, some local women saw them as an opportunity, and wound up marrying soldiers and starting new lives in American towns.) Iceland didn't participate actively in World War II, but 230 Icelanders were killed—mostly on merchant ships sunk at sea. While that sounds minimal, it's almost the same loss of life, per capita, as in the United States.

For the most part, Icelanders didn't mind the wartime Allied "occupation," which left them with improved roads, bridges, and other infrastructure. For example, the Allies built Keflavík Airport and an adjoining base, which American troops ran until 2006.

In 1943 (while Denmark was occupied by the Nazis, and Iceland by the Allies), Iceland declared its complete independence. After the war, Iceland joined NATO (in 1949). The US base at Keflavík provided income and employment to Icelanders and influenced Iceland culturally. Only after Icelanders started tuning in to the base's TV station in the 1960s did the Icelandic state broadcasting service finally start a local television station of its own.

Icelanders had begun tapping geothermal sources for home heating with hot water in the 1930s. Slowly, coal disappeared as a fuel, and by the 1960s, all of Reykjavík was heated with water piped from underground sources in the countryside. This meant very low energy costs, still today one of the saving graces of living in Iceland. Meanwhile, rivers were dammed for power generation—and soon Iceland had an electricity surplus.

In the 1970s, the first metal smelters were built to make use of the electricity. The fishing industry prospered; each small town had a fishing fleet and freezing plant. Political parties dispensed jobs and mortgages to members in return for their fidelity.

Icelanders maintained close ties to the Nordic countries through the 20th century. By the 1990s, Denmark, Sweden, and Finland had chosen to join the European Union. Iceland and Norway stayed out of the EU—but they did join the European Economic Area (EEA), a looser alliance that makes Iceland subject to most EU regulations, but keeps local control over fishing, agriculture, and customs policy. Since then, Icelanders have started to see themselves as more European than Nordic.

THE 21ST CENTURY AND ICELAND TODAY

In the first two decades of the 2000s, it seemed like Iceland—so long ignored by the rest of the world—was constantly in the international news: First came its financial boom-and-bust cycle, culminating in the 2008 crisis; then the eruption of Eyjafjallajökull in 2010, which left European air travelers cursing this remote island;

and most recently its unprecedented tourism boom and vivid examples of climate change.

Starting around 2000, Iceland privatized its publicly owned banks. The banks grew tremendously, taking advantage of European rules to accept deposits from other countries. Icelanders flocked to work for the banks, and society prospered. Skeptics were silenced: When a politician questioned some of the government's banking policies on the floor of parliament, the then-finance minister, a trained veterinarian, famously quipped, "Guys, can't you see the party?" Driving their Lexuses around Reykjavík, Icelanders finally felt they had arrived; they were Nordic hillbillies no more.

But the "party" was an illusion. The banks didn't have enough assets to cover their debts, and collapsed in 2008 in one of history's largest bankruptcies—a cold shower for the entire country. The Icelandic *króna* crashed in value, and many people lost their jobs, savings, and homes. Some bankers, exposed as charlatans, received brief prison terms.

Tourism was a saving grace. A relatively minor player in Iceland's economy for many decades, after 2010 it started to boom. In 2015, tourism surpassed fishing as Iceland's top industry. In 2016, for the first time, more Americans visited Iceland than the number of people who live in Iceland. Icelanders scrambled to deal with the huge demand. It seems like every farm added short-stay cottages and every town a small museum. Nation-ally, Iceland responded by improving infrastructure and discussing what limits might need to be placed on visits to its natural wonders. Iceland also learned that while tourism may seem like easy money, it's very seasonal, and many tourism jobs are not lucrative. And tourism is not immune to economic disruption: After the sudden demise of Iceland's low-cost carrier WOW Air in early 2019, tourism took a significant hit and unemployment rose.

Iceland lags behind mainland Scandinavia in indicators such as educational achievement, press freedom, government transparency, and health care. Icelanders work longer hours but are less productive per hour than their Nordic cousins. It's difficult to attract international businesses, and many educated Icelanders leave for jobs in Europe's big urban centers (where they are free to settle due to Iceland's EEA membership). Many of the young people you meet in the tourist trade are not Icelandic, but rather recently arrived Eastern Europeans seeking adventure and higher wages. Some politicians say the way forward is to lower the cost of living, improve schools and health care, raise public-sector salaries for jobs like teaching and nursing, and make shopping easier. The vision is to make living in Iceland as appealing as living in Norway or Denmark or Germany (although these priorities often clash with the deeply ingrained interests of the agricultural and fishing lobbies).

The control of retail trade is also a key issue, just as it was in the 1700s and 1800s. Many of Iceland's wholesale companies are run by the descendants of those original Danish merchant families. Visitors often assume that the country's high prices are due to transport costs or the small size of the market. In fact, they have more to do with weak competition, protectionism, inefficient businesses, and government efforts to keep the Icelandic *króna* stable. Local retailers have successfully lobbied to make it hard for Icelanders to order from online retailers like Amazon. Many frustrated Icelanders fly abroad to shop, and bring home clothes and toys in their suitcases.

There are also unresolved political issues. Iceland's voting system overrepresents rural interests in parliament, and farmers have used their disproportionate power to lobby for import restrictions that inflate the price of meat and dairy products. The Icelandic constitution is outdated—much of it dates from 1874. A committee elected by referendum drafted a new constitution in 2013, but beneficiaries of the status quo blocked any change.

Locals and foreigners alike used to see Iceland as a very honest, transparent country. But since the banking mania ended, Icelanders have realized that what they once thought of as "keeping wealth in the family" or "helping out friends and political allies" could also be described as "corruption." Some would like Iceland to become a full member of the European Union, seeing regulation from Brussels as a professional, stabilizing influence on a small country that has limited local expertise. Others value Iceland's partial autonomy, and see the EU as burdensome, bureaucratic baggage.

Overall, though, Iceland today is a secure, peaceful, and fairly well-off country. Although Icelanders have plenty of guns for hunting, violent crime is rare, with fewer than two homicides a year. The 2017 murder of a young Reykjavík woman (by a visiting fisherman from Greenland) was shocking enough to prompt increased security measures including more surveillance cameras, long common elsewhere in Europe.

Among European teenagers, Icelanders drink the least of all, although alcoholism remains a problem, as elsewhere in northern Europe. Although many politicians sympathize with Icelanders who would like to be able to buy beer and wine in supermarkets, research shows that the state monopoly keeps alcohol consumption low, especially among young people.

Perhaps the most controversial issue for Icelanders today is

Who Are the Icelanders?

Iceland is the most sparsely populated country in Europe, with only about eight people per square mile. And yet, it has a seat in the United Nations, ambassadors, a flag, its own currency, and a president—who governs only about 340,000 people, but nevertheless hobnobs with the likes of Justin Trudeau, Angela Merkel, and Vladimir Putin.

Icelanders are sensitive to this irony. They know their nation's small size can bring them disproportionate (and some would say undeserved) prominence on the world stage. (Consider that Icelanders get their own Eurovision contestant, while similar-sized communities in Norway compete for the privilege.) Exaggerated tales of Iceland's small scale persist: You may hear that the president's home number is listed in the phone book, but that hasn't been true for years.

In some ways, Iceland is the most Scandinavian country, where the old common Scandinavian language survives best, and where historical narratives were first written down. In other ways, Iceland is the least Scandinavian—physically and linguistically distinct from the others, considerably influenced by American culture, and the least progressive in its education, health, and welfare systems.

Icelanders frequently criticize themselves as *kærulaus* (a

control over natural resources. Iceland's neighbor, Norway, has channeled much of its oil wealth into a fund that the country draws on for everyone's benefit and that secures Norway's prosperity into the future. In contrast, Icelandic fishing "quota" (the right to harvest fish from the sea) is in the hands of private investors who pay society little or no rent for it. Similarly, profits from Iceland's energy surplus go largely to multinational companies who buy electricity at cut-rate prices. Many Icelanders believe that more of this wealth should be channeled to the public good, and that investing in health and education would finally bring the country's standard of living up to a mainland level. Fishing-quota owners have also concentrated fish processing in fewer and fewer places. This is efficient, but has decimated jobs in some formerly flourishing small towns.

Environmentally, Icelanders struggle with the effects of hundreds of years of soil erosion and deforestation. The government has worked to increase forest cover and reseed barren land (recently

word which means negligent, careless, inconsiderate, or flippant). *Kærulaus* suggests that there are no rules; and even when there are rules, no one knows them; even when people know the rules, they don't follow them; when people break the rules, no one cares; and if anyone tries to enforce the rules, they will be laughed at. This doesn't apply in all situations (and doesn't mean you can start driving off-road or stealing from your hotel), but it does accurately describe the country's opportunistic, frontier mentality.

Another, more hopeful phrase that Icelanders like to use is *Þetta reddast* ("It'll work out"); this represents a conviction that your special needs can be accommodated, and that no one will be left behind. Icelanders are quick to make special exceptions and expect others to do the same for them.

Icelanders often project an image of unity and Mayberry-like innocence, and visitors sometimes come away with an idealized picture of the country, focusing on things like renewable energy and the low crime rate. But if you take the time to read and understand Iceland's complex political, social, and environmental issues, you'll find that the country is as contentious and competitive as any other.

One impressive thing about Icelanders is how gracefully they have handled the enormous influx of tourism to their sparsely populated homeland. Of course, there are grumbles and thoughtful criticism—including the worry that so many people passing through could spoil what's so special about this country. Few countries could manage such a drastic spike in tourism as well as Iceland has. One way or another...*þetta reddast.*

using lupine, whose purple flowers you'll see along roadsides in early summer). Another perennial environmental debate is whether to build more dams to harvest the country's remaining hydroelectric potential.

Iceland's government is taking climate change seriously, and aims to make Iceland carbon neutral by 2040 by promoting green energy production, cutting carbon dioxide emissions, reforestation, and allowing only clean-technology transportation after 2030. Scientists are also conducting research into ways to capture and store carbon dioxide emissions underground. The effect of climate change is especially obvious by the toll it is taking on Iceland's glaciers. In 2019, Icelandic politicians and activists held a "funeral" for the once thriving Okjökull glacier in western Iceland, now reduced to a patch of "dead," unmoving ice. Okjökull marked the first time a sizable glacier's demise was directly attributed to climate change, but it won't be the last; scientists predict that in 200 years, all of the country's glaciers will be gone.

Despite the unique challenges this remote island grapples with, one thing remains steady: Iceland's ability to impress its many visitors. Icelanders have come a long way from the millennium they spent as hardscrabble peasants on isolated farms. Against all odds, their plucky little country is prosperous, known and respected around the world, and enjoying its status as a favorite transcontinental layover.

PRACTICALITIES

This chapter covers the practical skills of Icelandic travel: how to get tourist information, pay for things, sightsee efficiently, find good-value accommodations, eat affordably but well, use technology wisely, and get between destinations smoothly. For more information on these topics, see www.ricksteves.com/travel-tips.

Tourist Information

Iceland's **national tourist office** offers practical information and trip-planning ideas on their website (www.inspiredbyiceland.com), which also links to good regional information.

In Iceland, a good first stop is generally the tourist information office (abbreviated **TI** in this book). While you can get plenty of information online, I still make a point to swing by the local TI to confirm sightseeing plans, pick up maps, and get information on transit (including excursion-bus schedules), walking tours, special events, and nightlife.

Anticipating a harried front-line staffer, prepare a list of questions and a proposed plan to double-check. Some TIs have information on the entire country or at least the region, so try to pick up maps and printed information for destinations you'll be visiting later in your trip. A useful **free booklet** is *Áning—Travel Guide*, which lists swimming pools, campgrounds, hotels, guesthouses, and bus routes. It's advertising-supported, but comprehensive and fairly neutral. Find it at TIs and hotels.

Travel Tips

Travel Advisories and Covid-19 Entry Requirements: You'll likely need to present proof of vaccination or a negative Covid-19 test result. For info on this and other health and safety conditions for your destination, check with the US embassy for Iceland (see below) and the travel pages of the US State Department (www. travel.state.gov) and Centers for Disease Control and Prevention (www.cdc.gov/travel).

Emergency and Medical Help: For any emergency service—police, fire, or ambulance—call 112. For simple illnesses, go to a pharmacist for advice. For more serious problems, ask at your hotel for the nearest medical services. Or dial 1770 to reach the after-hours Læknavakt medical service (www.laeknavaktin.is), available for free phone consults weekdays from 17:00 to 8:00 and around the clock on weekends. Non-Europeans can pay a reasonable fee to visit any of Iceland's state-run primary care centers (*heilsug.slust..*) during business hours.

ETIAS Registration: US and Canadian citizens may soon be required to register online with the European Travel Information and Authorization System (ETIAS) before entering Iceland (quick and easy process). For the latest, check www.etiasvisa.com.

Theft or Loss: To replace a passport, you'll need to go in person to an embassy or consulate (see next). If your credit and debit cards disappear, cancel and replace them (see "Damage Control for Lost Cards" on page 477).

File a police report either on the spot or within a day or two; you'll need it to submit an insurance claim for lost or stolen travel gear, and it can help with replacing your passport or credit and debit cards. For more information, see www.ricksteves.com/help.

US Embassy in Reykjavík: By appointment only Mon-Fri 8:00-17:00, tel. 595-2200, after-hours line for emergencies only—595-2248, Laufásvegur 21 (may move to Engjateigur 7 by the time you visit), http://is.usembassy.gov.

Canadian Embassy in Reykjavík: Mon-Fri 9:00-12:00 and by appointment, Túngata 14, tel. 575-6500, www.canadainternational.gc.ca/iceland-islande.

Time Zones: Iceland doesn't observe Daylight Savings Time (due to its far-north location, it's already often either light or dark).

In summer, Iceland is one hour behind Great Britain and four/seven hours ahead of the East/West coasts of the US. In winter, Iceland is on par with Great Britain and five/eight hours ahead of the East/West coasts of the US. The exceptions are the beginning and end of Daylight Saving Time: Europe "springs forward" the last Sunday in March (two weeks after most of North America) and "falls back" the last Sunday in October (one week before North America). During those weeks, Iceland is even with Great Britain and four/seven hours ahead of the East/West coasts of the US. For a handy online time converter, see www.timeanddate.com/worldclock.

As Iceland's clocks are set closer to Europe than the island's geography justifies, the sun doesn't reach its zenith in the sky until after 13:00, and rises and sets later in the day than you might expect. Expect very long days in summer (about 20 hours of "sunlight" a day from May to July) and very short days in winter (December averages about 4 hours of sunlight).

Business Hours: Shops in Iceland are usually open from 10:00 or 11:00 until at least 18:00, with no lunch break. Supermarkets, other large retailers, and tourist-oriented shops are mostly open long hours daily, with slightly reduced weekend hours. Small shops often close early on Saturday. Banks are generally open Monday through Friday from 9:00 to 16:00.

Watt's Up? Like continental Europe, Iceland's electrical system is 220 volts, instead of North America's 110 volts. Most newer electronics (such as laptops, battery chargers, and hair dryers) convert automatically, so you won't need a converter, but you will need an adapter plug with two round prongs, sold inexpensively at travel stores in the US.

Discounts: Discounts for sights are generally not listed in this book. However, seniors (age 60 and over), youths under 18, and students and teachers with proper identification cards (obtain from www.isic.org) can get discounts at many sights. Always ask.

Online Translation Tips: Google's Chrome browser instantly translates websites; Translate.google.com is also handy. The Google Translate app converts spoken or typed English into most European languages (and vice versa) and can also translate text it "reads" with your smartphone's camera.

Money

Here's my basic strategy for using money in Iceland:

- Upon arrival, head for a cash machine (ATM) at the airport and withdraw a small amount of local currency, using a debit card with low international transaction fees.
- Keep your cards and cash safe in a money belt.

PRACTICALITIES

Exchange Rate

120 Icelandic krónur (ISK) = about $1

Iceland uses the *króna* (meaning "crown"; plural *krónur*). To very roughly convert prices from Icelandic *krónur* to dollars, lop off the last two zeros and subtract 20 percent: 2,000 ISK = about $16; 6,000 ISK = about $48. Coins range from 1 to 100 ISK, and bills from 500 to 10,000 ISK. (Check www.oanda.com for the latest exchange rates.)

- Pay for most purchases with a credit card with low (or no) international fees.

PLASTIC VERSUS CASH

Icelanders rarely use cash; they pay with plastic even for small purchases such as parking meters and hot dogs. It's possible to get through an entire Icelandic trip without ever using local cash.

In Iceland, I use my credit card nearly exclusively, for everything from hotel reservations and car rentals to everyday expenses such as meals, gas, and sightseeing. While you could use your debit card for some of these expenses, keep in mind that you have greater fraud protection with your credit card. The card you use may depend on which one charges the lowest international transaction fees.

Exceptions to Iceland's all-plastic system are in-city buses (which can be paid by app), a scant few coin-operated parking meters, and unstaffed pay WCs at countryside sights—where you're asked, usually on the honor system, to put 100-200 ISK in a box (or the equivalent in US dollars). You could withdraw a couple thousand crowns and change them into 100-ISK coins for these WCs. Or just bring a handful of dollar bills to save a trip to the bank.

Don't withdraw or exchange more Icelandic currency than you need. Most merchants prefer plastic, and you'll scramble to spend unused crowns at the end of your trip. Consider any *krónur* you bring home with you a souvenir: It's bothersome to exchange *krónur* back to dollars even in Iceland, and impossible (or possible only at punishing rates) outside the country.

WHAT TO BRING

I pack the following and keep it all safe in my money belt.

Credit Card: Use this to pay for most items (at hotels, larger shops and restaurants, travel agencies, car-rental agencies, and so on).

Debit Card: Use this at ATMs to withdraw local cash.

Backup Card: Some travelers carry a third card (debit or credit; ideally from a different bank) in case one gets lost, demagnetized, eaten by a temperamental machine, or simply doesn't work.

A Stash of Cash: I carry $100-200 as a cash backup, which comes in handy in an emergency.

What NOT to Bring: Resist the urge to buy *krónur* before your trip or you'll pay the price in bad stateside exchange rates. Wait until you arrive to withdraw a minimal amount of money. I've yet to see a European airport that didn't have plenty of ATMs.

BEFORE YOU GO
Use this pre-trip checklist.

Know your cards. For credit cards, Visa and MasterCard are universal, American Express and Diners Club are less common, and Discover is unknown. Debit cards from any major US bank will work in any standard Icelandic bank's ATM (ideally, use a debit card with a Visa or MasterCard logo).

Know your PIN. Make sure you know the numeric, four-digit PIN for each of your cards, both credit and debit. Request it if you don't have one, as it may be required for some purchases in Europe (see "Using Credit Cards," later), and allow time to receive the information by mail.

Report your travel dates. Let your bank know that you'll be using your debit and credit cards overseas, and when and where you're headed.

Adjust your ATM withdrawal limit. Find out how much you can take out daily and ask for a higher daily withdrawal limit if you want to get more cash at once. Note that international ATMs will withdraw funds only from checking accounts; you're unlikely to have access to your savings account.

Ask about fees. For any purchase or withdrawal made with a card, you may be charged a currency conversion fee (1-3 percent) and/or a Visa or MasterCard international transaction fee (less than 1 percent). If you're getting a bad deal, consider getting a new credit or debit card. Reputable no-fee cards include those from Capital One, as well as Charles Schwab debit cards. Most credit unions and some airline loyalty cards have low or no international transaction fees.

IN ICELAND
Using Credit Cards
Despite some differences between European and US cards, there's little to worry about: US credit cards generally work fine in Iceland. I've been inconvenienced a few times by self-service payment machines that wouldn't accept my card, but it's never caused me serious trouble (I carry cash just in case).

European cards use chip-and-PIN technology; most chip

cards issued in the US instead have a signature option. Some European card readers will accept your card as-is while others may generate a receipt for you to sign or prompt you to enter your PIN (so it's important to know the code for each of your cards). If a cashier is present, you should have no problems.

At self-service payment machines (transit-ticket kiosks, parking kiosks, gas pumps, etc.), you'll likely need to know your PIN. If your card won't work at the machine, look for a cashier who can process your card manually or take cash. For more tips on paying for fuel, see the "Driving" section, later in this chapter.

Dynamic Currency Conversion

If merchants offer to convert your purchase price into dollars (called dynamic currency conversion, or DCC), refuse this "service." You'll pay extra for the expensive convenience of seeing your charge in dollars. If an ATM offers to "lock in" or "guarantee" your conversion rate, choose "proceed without conversion." Other prompts might state, "You can be charged in dollars: Press YES for dollars, NO for *krónur*." Always choose the local currency.

Using Cash Machines

European cash machines have English-language instructions and work just like they do at home—except they spit out local currency instead of dollars, calculated at the day's standard bank-to-bank rate. In most places, ATMs are easy to locate—in Iceland, ask for a *hraðbanki*. When possible, withdraw cash from a bank-run ATM located just outside that bank. Ideally, use the machine during the bank's opening hours, so you can go inside for help if your card is munched.

If your debit card doesn't work, try a lower amount—your request may have exceeded your withdrawal limit or the ATM's limit. If you still have a problem, try a different ATM or come back later—your bank's network may be temporarily down.

Avoid "independent" ATMs, such as Travelex, Euronet, Moneybox, Your Cash, Cardpoint, and Cashzone. These have high fees, can be less secure than a bank ATM, and may try to trick users with "dynamic currency conversion" (see above).

Security Tips

While Iceland is one of the safest places you can travel, from a petty-crime perspective, there are a few general guidelines to keep in mind anywhere:

Pickpockets target tourists. Keep your cash, credit cards, and passport secure in your money belt, and carry only a day's spending money in your front pocket or wallet.

Before inserting your card into an ATM, inspect the front. If anything looks crooked, loose, or damaged, it could be a sign of a card-skimming device. When entering your PIN, carefully block other people's view of the keypad.

Don't use a debit card for purchases. Because a debit card pulls funds directly from your bank account, potential charges incurred by a thief will stay on your account while your bank investigates the fraudulent use.

To access your accounts online while traveling, be sure to use a secure connection (see the "Tips on Internet Security" sidebar, later).

Damage Control for Lost Cards

If you lose your credit or debit card, report the loss immediately to the respective global customer-assistance centers. With a mobile phone, call these 24-hour US numbers: Visa (tel. +1 303/967-1096), MasterCard (tel. +1 636/722-7111), and American Express (tel. +1 336/393-1111). From a landline, you can call these US numbers collect by going through a local operator. European toll-free numbers can be found at the websites for Visa and MasterCard.

You'll need to provide the primary cardholder's identification-verification details (such as birth date, mother's maiden name, or Social Security number). You can generally receive a temporary card within two or three business days (see www.ricksteves.com/help for more).

If you report your loss within two days, you typically won't be responsible for unauthorized transactions on your account, although many banks charge a liability fee.

TIPPING

Iceland is emphatically a no-tipping country. That means that you should not tip at restaurants, in taxis, in hotels, or anywhere else. Since you'll pay for almost everything with plastic—and most people carry little or no cash—it's difficult to tip even if you wanted to.

Despite the no-tipping culture, guides on bus tours and other excursions in Iceland will sometimes suggest that you tip them. While you're free to slip them a little extra money (in any currency) for a job especially well done, you are neither expected nor required to. Icelandic labor law requires that employees receive a full basic wage, independent of any expected gratuities.

GETTING A VAT REFUND

Wrapped into the purchase price of your Icelandic souvenirs is a Value-Added Tax (VAT, called VSK or *virðisaukaskattur* in Icelandic) of about 24 percent. You're entitled to get most of that tax back if you purchase more than 6,000 ISK (about $50) worth of goods at a store that participates in the VAT-refund scheme. You

PRACTICALITIES

must ring up the minimum at a single retailer—you can't add up your purchases from various shops to reach the required amount. (If the store ships the goods to your US home, VAT is not assessed on your purchase.)

Getting your refund is straightforward...and worthwhile if you spend a significant amount on souvenirs.

Get the paperwork. Have the merchant completely fill out the necessary refund document. You'll have to present your passport. Get the paperwork done before you leave the store to ensure you'll have everything you need (including your original sales receipt).

Get your stamp at the border or airport. Assuming you're departing Iceland from Keflavík Airport, it's relatively easy to re-coup your VAT. Fill out the refund slip that the merchant gave you, and bring it to the VAT refunds desk on the airport's main level, across from the car-rental counters. Even if there's a line, it typically moves quickly. Have your passport and ticket available, as well as the credit card you want the refund to go to. Show them your purchases, receipts, and forms.

You're not supposed to use your purchased goods before you leave. If you show up at customs wearing your hand-knit Icelandic sweater, officials might look the other way—or deny you a refund.

Collect your refund. If you request on the form that you want your refund on your credit card, the VAT desk will simply file it for you. If you want cash, after getting your paperwork stamped, bring it to the bank in the airport's main hall; they are responsible for refunding VAT.

CUSTOMS FOR AMERICAN SHOPPERS

You can take home $800 worth of items per person duty-free, once every 31 days. Many processed and packaged foods are allowed, including vacuum-packed cheeses, dried herbs, jams, baked goods, candy, chocolate, oil, vinegar, mustard, and honey. Fresh fruits and vegetables and most meats are not allowed, with exceptions for some canned items. As for alcohol, you can bring in one liter duty-free (it can be packed securely in your checked luggage, along with any other liquid-containing items).

To bring alcohol (or liquid-packed foods) in your carry-on bag on your flight home, buy it at a duty-free shop at the airport. You'll increase your odds of getting it onto a connecting flight if it's packaged in a "STEB"—a secure, tamper-evident bag. But stay away from liquids in opaque, ceramic, or metallic containers, which usually cannot be successfully screened (STEB or no STEB).

For details on allowable goods, customs rules, and duty rates, visit www.cbp.gov.

Sightseeing

Sightseeing can be hard work. Use these tips to make your visits to Iceland's finest sights meaningful, fun, efficient, and painless.

MAPS AND NAVIGATION TOOLS

A good map is essential for efficient navigation while sightseeing. The maps in this book are concise and simple, designed to help you

locate recommended destinations, sights, and local TIs, where you can pick up more in-depth maps.

You can also use a mapping app on your mobile device. Be aware that pulling up maps or looking up turn-by-turn walking directions on the fly requires a data connection: To use this feature, it's smart to get an international data plan. With Google Maps or City Maps 2Go, it's possible to download a map while online, then go offline and navigate without incurring data-roaming charges, though you can't search for an address or get real-time walking directions. A handful of other apps—including Apple Maps and Navmii—also allow you to use maps offline.

For advice about maps for drivers, see page 512.

PLAN AHEAD

Set up an itinerary that allows you to fit in all your must-see sights. Sightseeing in Iceland is distinctive in that many of the things you'll want to see are natural wonders (volcanoes, geothermal areas, glaciers). Many are within striking distance of Reykjavík, but require a car or an excursion. You won't typically have to worry about opening hours or admission (see below), but you will need to plan how you'll get there. For advice, see the Beyond Reykjavík chapter.

For a one-stop look at opening hours in Reykjavík, see the "At a Glance" sidebar in that chapter. Most sights keep stable hours, but you can easily confirm the latest by checking with the TI or sight websites.

Don't put off visiting a must-see sight—you never know when a place will close unexpectedly due to bad weather, a holiday, or renovation. Some sights are closed or have reduced hours at least a few days a year, especially on holidays such as Christmas, New Year's, and Labor Day (May 1). A list of holidays is in the appendix; check online for possible closures during your trip. In summer, some sights may stay open late; in the off-season, hours may be shorter or sights may be closed completely.

If you plan to hire a local guide, reserve ahead. Popular guides can get booked up.

Study up. To get the most out of the sight descriptions in this book, read them before you visit.

AT SIGHTS

Much of the sightseeing you'll do in Iceland is outdoors—and almost all of that is free (there may be a charge for parking and WCs).

Icelanders have lately been debating if this can endure, given rising tourist numbers and the cost of upkeep. Tickets, passes, or local taxes may figure in the future for some popular natural sights.

At Outdoor Sights: Usually you'll park in a big, free parking lot (a few charge a fee). Near the parking lot, you'll often find WCs (some pay, some free); a small café or snack stand; and orientation panels with a helpful introduction to the sight. Bigger sights might have a staffed visitors center where you can get more information.

For some natural attractions, expect a walk (5-15 minutes each way) to reach the sight itself from the parking lot. Always stay on marked trails—both for your own safety and to avoid disrupting the beauty you came to see.

In general, be aware that Iceland's raw nature is as potentially dangerous as it is gorgeous. Read "The Many Ways Iceland Can Kill You" sidebar in the Icelandic Experiences chapter; carefully review sight-specific details in this book; and heed any warning signs posted at the sight itself.

At Museums and Other Indoor Sights: You may not be allowed to enter if you arrive too close to closing time. And guards start ushering people out well before the actual closing time, so don't save the best for last. If the museum's photo policy isn't clearly posted, ask a guard.

Audioguides and Apps: Many sights rent audioguides with useful recorded descriptions in English. Often, you'll download the audioguide for free to your own mobile phone, using on-site Wi-Fi. If you want to rent an audioguide device (where available), you'll pay a token amount; if you don't mind being tethered to your travel partner, you'll save money by bringing a Y-jack and sharing one audioguide.

Sleeping

Extensive and opinionated listings of good-value rooms are a major feature of this book's Sleeping sections. I like places that are clean, central, relatively quiet at night, reasonably priced, friendly, small enough to have a hands-on owner or manager and stable staff, and run with a respect for Icelandic traditions. I'm more impressed by a convenient location and a fun-loving philosophy  than flat-screen TVs and a fancy gym. Most places I recommend fall short of perfection. But if I can find a place with most of these features, it's a keeper. My recommendations run the gamut, from dorm beds to fancy rooms with all the comforts. You can also consider a short-term rental, or camping your way around Iceland in a campervan.

Book your accommodations as soon as your itinerary is set, especially for Reykjavík and on the Ring Road (where there aren't enough rooms to meet demand in the areas around Mývatn and Höfn). For the peak summer months, rooms can be completely booked up many months ahead. See the appendix for a list of major holidays and festivals in Iceland: Some—like Þjóðhátíð in the Westman Islands—merit reserving far in advance. For tips on making reservations, see the "Making Hotel Reservations" sidebar later in this chapter.

Icelandic homes and smaller hotels rely on geothermal energy for heat. There's usually no central thermostat, just individual controls on each radiator. Typically, if it gets too warm, Icelanders will open a window before they turn down the radiator. Hot water is often geothermal as well (you'll smell the sulfur). Many guesthouses and farmstays offer a shared hot tub to guests. These are not the chlorinated hot tubs you're used to in the US—they're filled daily with fresh hot spring water, with a minimum of chemicals.

Be aware that if you visit Iceland in June or early July, it will never get fully dark. Accommodations come with blackout curtains that try to darken your sleeping quarters; some travelers will also want to bring a nighttime eye mask.

RATES AND DEALS

I've categorized my recommended accommodations based on price, indicated with a dollar-sign rating (see sidebar). The price ranges suggest an estimated cost for a one-night stay in high season in a

PRACTICALITIES

Sleep Code

Hotels are classified based on the average price of a standard double room with breakfast in high season.

$$$$	**Splurge:**	Most rooms over 35,000 ISK
$$$	**Pricier:**	28,000-35,000 ISK
$$	**Moderate:**	20,000-28,000 ISK
$	**Budget:**	15,000-20,000 ISK
¢	**Backpacker:**	Under 15,000 ISK

Unless otherwise noted, credit cards are accepted, hotel staff speak English, and free Wi-Fi is available. Comparison-shop by checking prices at several hotels (on each hotel's own website, on a booking site, or by email). For the best deal, always book directly with the hotel.

standard double room with a private toilet and shower, including breakfast, and assume you're booking directly with the hotel (not through a booking site, which extracts a commission). Room prices can fluctuate significantly with demand and amenities (size, views, room class, and so on), but these relative price categories remain constant.

Room rates are especially volatile at hotels that use "dynamic pricing" to set rates. Prices can skyrocket during periods of peak demand, and be discounted deeply when demand plummets. Of the many hotels I recommend, it's difficult to say which will be the best value on a given day—until you do your homework.

Booking Direct: Once your dates are set, compare prices at several hotels. You can do this by checking Hotels.com, Booking.com, and hotel websites. After you've zeroed in on your choice, book directly with the hotel itself. Contact small family-run hotels directly by phone or email. When you go direct, the owner avoids the commission paid to booking sites, thereby leaving enough wiggle room to offer you a discount, a nicer room, or free breakfast (if it's not already included). If you prefer to book online or are considering a hotel chain, it's to your advantage to use the hotel's website—if it offers online booking. Some Icelandic hotels use Booking.com as their default booking engine and list prices in euros or US dollars; in these cases calling or emailing may net you a better rate.

Booking directly also increases the chances that the hotelier will be able to accommodate any special needs or requests (such as shifting your reservation). Going through a middleman makes it more difficult for the hotel to adjust your booking.

TYPES OF ACCOMMODATIONS
Hotels

Double rooms listed in this book range from $100 (very simple, toilet and shower down the hall) to $400 suites (maximum plumb-

ing and more), with most clustering around $200-250. Most hotels also offer single rooms, and some offer larger rooms for four or more people (I call these "family rooms" in the listings). If there's space for an extra cot, they'll cram it in for you.

In general, a triple room is cheaper than the cost of a double and a single. Three or four people can economize by requesting one big room.

In Iceland, hotels are usually large (big enough for groups), impersonal, and corporate-owned. If you want a more mom-and-pop feeling, look for guesthouses and farmstays (described later). An ample breakfast buffet is generally included.

Arrival and Check-In: If you're arriving in the morning, your room probably won't be ready. Check your bag safely at the hotel and dive right into sightseeing.

In Your Room: Most hotel rooms have a TV, telephone, and free Wi-Fi (although in old buildings with thick walls, the Wi-Fi signal might be available only in the lobby). Simpler places rarely have a room phone, but usually have free Wi-Fi.

More pillows and blankets are usually in the closet or available on request. Towels and linens aren't always replaced every day.

Checking Out: While it's customary to pay for your room upon departure, it can be a good idea to settle your bill the day before, when you're not in a hurry and while the manager's in.

Hotelier Help: Hoteliers can be a good source of advice. Most know their town well, and can assist you with everything from route tips to finding a good restaurant.

Hotel Hassles: Even at the best places, mechanical break-downs occur: Sinks leak, hot water turns cold, toilets may gurgle or smell, or the Wi-Fi goes out. Report your concerns clearly and calmly at the front desk.

If you find that night noise is a problem (if, for instance, your room is over a nightclub or facing a busy street), ask for a quieter room in the back or on an upper floor. To guard against theft in your room, keep valuables out of sight. Some rooms come with a safe, and other hotels have safes at the front desk. I've never both-

Using Online Services to Your Advantage

From booking services to user reviews, online businesses play a greater role in travelers' planning than ever before. Take advantage of their pluses—and be wise to their downsides.

Booking Sites

Booking websites such as Booking.com and Hotels.com offer one-stop shopping for hotels. While convenient for travelers, they present a real problem for independent, family-run hotels. Without a presence on these sites, small hotels become almost invisible. But to be listed, a hotel must pay a sizable commission... and promise that its own website won't undercut the price on the booking service site.

Here's the work-around: Use the big sites to research what's out there, then book directly with the hotel by email or phone, in which case hotel owners are free to give you whatever price they like. Ask for a room without the commission mark-up (or ask for a free breakfast if not included, or a free upgrade). If you do book online, be sure to use the hotel's website. The price will likely be the same as via a booking site, but your money goes to the hotel, not agency commissions.

As a savvy consumer, remember: When you book with an online booking service, you're adding a middleman who takes roughly 20 percent. To support small, family-run hotels whose world is more difficult than ever, book direct.

Short-Term Rental Sites

Rental juggernaut Airbnb (along with other short-term rental sites) allows travelers to rent rooms and apartments directly from locals, often providing more value than a cookie-cutter hotel. Airbnb fans appreciate feeling part of a real neighborhood and getting into a daily routine as "temporary Europeans." Depending on the host, Airbnb can provide an opportunity to get to know a

ered using one, and in a lifetime of travel I've never had anything stolen from my room.

For more complicated problems, don't expect instant results. Above all, keep a positive attitude. Remember, you're on vacation. If your hotel is a disappointment, spend more time out enjoying the place you came to see.

Small Guesthouses and Farmstays

In the countryside, $150-200 buys you a simple room with a shared bathroom in a small guesthouse or rural farm accommodation. For a private bathroom, you'll step up to the $250-300 range—but that may mean a bigger property that's less personal and charming. Even if you're disinclined to share a bathroom, consider compro-

local person, while keeping the money spent on your accommodations in the community.

Critics view Airbnb as a threat to "traditional Europe," saying it creates unfair, unqualified competition for established guesthouse owners. In some places, the lucrative Airbnb market has forced traditional guesthouses out of business and is driving property values out of range for locals. Some cities have cracked down, requiring owners to obtain a license and to occupy rental properties part of the year (and staging disruptive "inspections" that inconvenience guests).

As a lover of Europe, I share the worry of those who see residents nudged aside by tourists. But as an advocate for travelers, I appreciate the value and cultural intimacy Airbnb provides.

User Reviews

User-generated review sites and apps such as Yelp and TripAdvisor can give you a consensus of opinions about everything from hotels and restaurants to sights and nightlife. If you scan reviews of a restaurant or hotel and see several complaints about noise or a rotten location, you've gained insight that can help in your decision-making.

But as a guidebook writer, my sense is that there is a big difference between the uncurated information on a review site and the vetted listings in a guidebook. A user-generated review is based on the limited experience of one person, who stayed at just one hotel in a given city and ate at a few restaurants there. A guidebook is the work of a trained researcher who forms a well-developed basis for comparison by visiting many restaurants and hotels year after year.

Both types of information have their place, and in many ways, they're complementary. If something is well reviewed in a guidebook and it also gets good online reviews, it's likely a winner.

PRACTICALITIES

mising from time to time—not only to save money, but also to land at a more characteristic place.

While becoming less common, at guesthouses and farmstays you may see separate prices for "made-up beds" and "sleeping-bag space." Sleeping-bag space means that the guesthouse provides a mattress with sheet and pillow (no pillowcase); you bring your own sleeping bag. A made-up bed includes a comforter and duvet cover.

Guesthouses: Especially in Reykjavík and other towns, you'll find plenty of small guesthouses with five to 10 rooms and a mix of shared and private bathrooms. In general, guesthouses are cozier, cheaper, and have more character than hotels, but tend to come with simpler amenities and smaller breakfasts.

Farmstays: Many Icelandic farms rent space to travelers, ranging from a room or two in the main farmhouse to a string of prefab cabins set up elsewhere on the property. These can range from basic summer-camp style to very modern, with private baths and contemporary amenities. Aside from Reykjavík, Iceland had practically no towns until the late 1800s—staying in the countryside lets you experience Iceland as it was for centuries. Sheep are the most common livestock (they're up in the mountains during the summer), and some farms keep cows or horses; hay is the main crop. While farm families offer a cordial welcome, Icelanders tend to be reserved and you should mostly expect to be left alone. The Icelandic farm-tourism association, cleverly branded as **Hey Iceland,** has a helpful interactive map on their website that lets you pick a spot (www.heyiceland.is, tel. 570-2700). Member farms also tend to list at Airbnb, Booking.com, and similar sites (described below).

Cottages: Many countryside accommodations feature a mix of guesthouse rooms and private, small, stand-alone or duplex-style cottages. Not necessarily rustic and charming, these are often built quite recently (to accommodate Iceland's tourism spike) and can be more modern than the guesthouse rooms. A cottage can be a good investment for the added space, privacy/soundproofing, and amenities (usually a basic kitchenette); it's an especially good choice for families or groups traveling together—a cottage typically costs less than two rooms in the guesthouse. A few accommodations are cottage-only.

Short-Term Rentals

A short-term rental—whether an apartment, house, or room in a local's home—is an increasingly popular alternative, especially in expensive Iceland. Particularly in peak season, you can often find an apartment that costs approximately half what you'd pay at a hotel—likely with more space, a kitchen, and other features. You trade away the convenience of a staffed reception desk, readymade breakfast, and other hotel amenities, but the savings are substantial. And, while it varies dramatically, some short-term hosts are more helpful than any hotel receptionist. If you're willing to stay in a room in someone's home (rather than have an entire property to yourself), you can save even more.

Finding Accommodations: Websites such as Airbnb, FlipKey, Booking.com, and the HomeAway family of sites (HomeAway, VRBO, and VacationRentals) let you browse a wide range of properties. Alternatively, rental agencies such as InterhomeUSA.com and RentaVilla.com, which list more carefully selected accommodations that might cost more, can provide more personalized service.

Before you commit, be clear on the location. I like to virtually "explore" the neighborhood using the Street View feature on

Google Maps. Also consider the proximity to public transportation and how well-connected the property is to the rest of the city. Ask about amenities (elevator, laundry, Wi-Fi, parking, etc.). Reviews from previous guests can help identify trouble spots.

Think about the kind of experience you want: Just a key and an affordable bed...or a chance to get to know a local? There are typically two kinds of hosts: those who want minimal interaction with their guests, and hosts who are friendly and may want to interact with you. Read the promotional text and online reviews to help shape your decision.

Confirming and Paying: Many places require you to pay the entire balance before your trip. It's easiest and safest to pay through the site where you found the listing. Be wary of owners who want to take your transaction offline; this gives you no recourse if things go awry. Never agree to wire money (a key indicator of a fraudulent transaction).

Apartments or Houses: If you're staying in one place for four or more nights, it's worth considering an apartment or rental house (shorter stays aren't worth the hassle of arranging key pickup, buying groceries, etc.). Apartment or house rentals can be especially cost-effective for groups and families. Icelandic apartments, like hotel rooms, tend to be small by US standards. But they often come with laundry facilities and small, equipped kitchens, making it easier and cheaper to dine in.

Rooms in Private Homes: Renting a room in someone's home is a good option for those traveling alone, as you're more likely to find true single rooms—with just one single bed, and a price to match. Some places allow you to book for a single night; if staying for several nights, you can buy groceries just as you would in a rental house.

Other Options: Swapping homes with a local works for people with an appealing place to offer (don't assume where you live is not interesting to Icelanders). Good places to start are HomeExchange.com and LoveHomeSwap.com. Icelanders, who are the world's heaviest per-capita users of these sites, like traveling to North America and typically vacation abroad around the same time of year that Americans do (June-Aug). To sleep for free, Couchsurfing.com is a vagabond's alternative to Airbnb. It lists millions of outgoing members who host fellow "surfers" in their homes.

Hostels

A hostel provides cheap beds where you sleep alongside strangers for about $20-50 per night. Travelers of any age are welcome if they don't mind dorm-style accommodations and meeting other travelers. Most hostels offer kitchen facilities, guest computers, Wi-Fi, and a self-service laundry. Hostels almost always provide bedding,

Making Hotel Reservations

Reserve your rooms as soon as you've pinned down your travel dates. For busy national holidays and some festivals, it's wise to reserve far in advance (see the appendix).

Requesting a Reservation: For family-run hotels, it's generally best to book your room directly via email or phone. For business-class and chain hotels, or if you'd rather book online, reserve directly through the hotel's official website (not a booking website). Here's what the hotelier wants to know:

- Type(s) of rooms you want and size of your party
- Number of nights you'll stay
- Your arrival and departure dates, written European-style as day/month/year (18/06/21 or 18 June 2021)
- Special requests (en suite bathroom, cheapest room, twin beds vs. double bed, quiet room)

Confirming a Reservation: Most places will request a credit-card number to hold your room. If you're using an online reservation form, make sure it's secure by looking for the *https* or a lock icon at the top of your browser. If the hotel's website doesn't have a secure form where you can enter the number directly, it's best to share that confidential info via a phone call.

Canceling a Reservation: If you must cancel, it's courteous—and smart—to do so with as much notice as possible, especially for smaller family-run places. Cancellation policies can be strict; read the fine print before you book. Many discount deals require pre-

---

but the towel's up to you (though you can usually rent one for a small fee). Family and private rooms are often available.

Independent hostels tend to be easygoing, colorful, and informal (no membership required; www.hostelworld.com). You may pay slightly less by booking directly with the hostel.

Official hostels are part of Hostelling International (HI) and share an online booking site (www.hihostels.com). HI hostels typically require that you be a member or pay extra per night. Iceland has over 30 official hostels, more or less evenly distributed around the island. They're generally clean, well-run, and a great value for solo travelers on a budget. Many are open all year, though the more rural hostels typically close from November or December to February or March.

Campervans and Camping

In Iceland, you can rent a converted van or pickup outfitted with beds, which lets you drive around the island without needing to find a place to stay. Some campers even have four-wheel drive and high clearances that let you drive over the mountain roads in the interior. While a campervan rental isn't cheap, it can cost less than

From:	rick@ricksteves.com
Sent:	Today
To:	info@hotelcentral.com
Subject:	Reservation request for 19-22 July

Dear Hotel Central,

I would like to stay at your hotel. Please let me know if you have a room available and the price for:
• 2 people
• Double bed and en suite bathroom in a quiet room
• Arriving 19 July, departing 22 July (3 nights)

Thank you!
Rick Steves

payment, with no cancellation refunds.

Reconfirming Your Reservation: Always call or email to reconfirm your room reservation a few days in advance. For B&Bs or very small hotels, I call again on my day of arrival to tell my host what time I expect to get there (especially important if arriving late—after 17:00).

Phoning: For tips on calling hotels overseas, see page 504.

other forms of accommodation, and lets you be more flexible with your itinerary.

Campervan Rentals: A two-bed, two-wheel-drive campervan outfitted with basic cooking gear and bedding will run you about $175/day in summer ($110/day in shoulder season). Larger vans and those with four-wheel drive are more expensive. Major campervan outfitters (all located near Reykjavík) include Kúkú Campers (tel. 415-5858, www.kukucampers.is),  GO Campers (tel. 517-7900, www.gocampers.is), Cozy Campers (tel. 519-5131, www.cozycampers.is), and Happy Campers (near the Keflavík airport, tel. 578-7860, www.happycampers.is). You'll also find campervans advertised on Airbnb.

Arrange your rental period to cover only the dates when you'll be driving around the island: Begin and end your trip in the Reyk-

PRACTICALITIES

javík area—using public transportation or a rental car and sleeping in a regular bed—then pick up the camper from the Reykjavík suburbs.

Where to Camp: Once you're out in the countryside, it's generally OK to park discreetly overnight in any semipublic lot. However, Icelanders are increasingly concerned about the impact of tourism, so you'll often see signs at scenic spots specifically prohibiting camping. As for showering, that's what Iceland's municipal thermal pools are for: You'll pay a few extra dollars per day to clean up—and luxuriate—in endless hot water (an unofficial list of pools is at

www.sundlaugar.is). Or pay to use the facilities at a campground along your route (see next).

If you prefer a more formal place to overnight, you'll find inexpensive campgrounds *(tjaldsvæði)* all around the island. Most don't require reservations and are open from about mid-May to mid-September. For an unofficial list, visit https://tjalda.is. A 28-day pass that covers most campgrounds is sold at www.campingcard.is.

Car Camping: Camping while driving a regular rental car has many of the same advantages as a campervan, and is cheaper. If you bring your own camping gear, make sure it's suited to Iceland's high winds and chilly temperatures. Or rent gear in Iceland: **Iceland Camping Equipment,** in downtown Reykjavík, rents everything you might need at fair prices (Barónsstígur 5, mobile 647-0569, www.iceland-camping-equipment.com).

Eating

Traditional Icelandic cuisine isn't too far removed from its Viking Age roots—relying heavily on anything hardy enough to survive the harsh landscape (lamb, potatoes), caught in or near the sea (fish, seabirds), or sturdy enough to withstand winter storage (dried and salted fish). Today's chefs have built on this heritage, introducing international flavors and new approaches to old-style dishes. In recent years, Reykjavík has emerged as a foodie

destination—with both high-end, experimental "New Icelandic"

Restaurant Code

Eateries in this book are categorized according to the average cost of a typical main course. Drinks, desserts, and splurge items (steak and seafood) can raise the price considerably.

$$$$	**Splurge:** Most main courses over 5,500 ISK
$$$	**Pricier:** 4,000-5,500 ISK
$$	**Moderate:** 2,500-4,000 ISK
$	**Budget:** Under 2,500 ISK

In Iceland, a takeout place or soup-and-bread buffet is **$**; a sit-down café is **$$**; a casual but more upscale restaurant is **$$$**; and a swanky splurge is **$$$$**.

cuisine and a renewed appreciation for the country's traditional, nose-to-tail "hardship" cuisines. The capital offers a wide variety of dining options, but even in the countryside, you're never far from a satisfying meal.

Food and drink prices in Iceland are strikingly high, but it is possible to eat well here without going broke. There's no tipping, taxes are built into prices, and restaurants cheerfully dispense free tap water, making eating out more reasonable than the menu prices might initially seem.

Icelanders eat three meals a day at about the same times as Americans. Breakfast *(morgunmatur)* in homes tends to be oatmeal, cereal with milk, or bread and cheese, but hotels and guesthouses will lay out a good spread with eggs and cold cuts. Lunch *(hádegismatur)* is served between about 11:30 and 13:00, while dinner *(kvöldmatur)* usually starts at 18:00.

RESTAURANT PRICING

I've categorized my recommended eateries based on the average price of a typical main course, indicated with a dollar-sign rating (see sidebar). Obviously, expensive specialties, fine wine, appetizers, and dessert can significantly increase your final bill.

The categories also indicate the personality of a place: **Budget** eateries include street food, takeaway, basic cafeterias, bakeries, and soup-and-bread buffets. **Moderate** eateries are nice (but not fancy) sit-down restaurants, ideal for a straightforward, fill-the-tank meal. Many of my listings fall in this category.

Pricier eateries are a notch up, with more attention paid to the setting, presentation, and (often inventive) cuisine. **Splurge** eateries are dress-up-for-a-special-occasion swanky—typically with an elegant setting, polished service, and pricey and intricate cuisine.

RESTAURANT AND CAFÉ DINING

Not very long ago, it was unusual for Icelanders to eat outside the home or a workplace cafeteria, except on special occasions. But with the country's increasing wealth (and the influx of tourism) over the last decade or two, restaurants have become much more popular. All restaurants are smoke-free, and all restaurant staff speak English.

In Reykjavík, lunches are a particularly good value, as many places offer the same quality and similar selections for far less than at dinner. Make lunch your main meal, then have a lighter evening meal at a café. Many places offer a lunch special—typically a plate of fish, vegetables, and a starch (rice or potatoes) for 2,000-3,000 ISK.

Outside Reykjavík, the easiest lunch spots are roadside grills—often connected to a gas station and serving hamburgers, hot dogs, and fries, and possibly breaded fish. Any decent-sized town will also have a real (if small) café, restaurant, or bakery with better food (homemade soup, sandwiches, quiches, and so on).

The best and healthiest lunch option at a small café or bakery is often an all-you-can-eat soup buffet, which includes unlimited bread and butter. For about 1,700-2,000 ISK, this can make for a satisfying meal. Look for thick, homemade soups (such as lamb soup, *kjötsúpa*).

Paying: Icelandic restaurants are often very flexible about splitting the bill between several guests, and waiters will ask each person to recall what they ate and drank. There is no tipping at Icelandic restaurants, and credit cards are accepted everywhere. It's common even at quite respectable restaurants to order and pay at the counter and then sit down, or to stand up and pay at the counter after your meal.

ICELANDIC CUISINE
Seafood

In this island nation, you'll see fish *(fiskur)* on every menu, prepared just about every way you can think of—and some ways that might not have occurred to you. Many restaurants have a fresh, delicious, and affordable "fish of the day" offering that's always worth considering. Also look for fish-and-chips, smoked trout, fried balls o' cod, shrimp-on-a-sandwich, sushi, and hearty fish stew.

A common dish is *plokkfiskur* (mashed fish), traditionally made with whatever fish scraps were at hand. Today this fish gratin or hash is made from haddock or cod cooked with milk, butter, and chopped potatoes; it's a comfort food, sometimes topped with cheese and often eaten with sweet rye bread.

Icelandic fish is almost always very good. Don't get hung up on fresh versus frozen—here, both are fine (fish that's frozen at sea, right after it's netted, often tastes the freshest, although never-frozen fish has better texture).

Deboned fish filets are the mainstay of the Icelandic diet. Haddock *(ýsa)* is by far the most common, followed by cod *(þorskur)* and plaice *(rauðspretta)*. You'll also see more expensive salmon *(lax)* and arctic char *(bleikja)*, both of which are farm-raised in pens. You'll sometimes see cod cheeks *(gellur)*, and Icelanders eat the roe (eggs) of both cod and lumpfish. Lately, Icelanders have started to make fish chips, which look a bit like potato chips but are much more expensive.

One favorite Icelandic splurge is *humar*, which is typically translated on menus as "lobster" but is actually a 10-inch-long crus-

tacean that's somewhere between a prawn and a crayfish (a more precise name is langoustine, Norway lobster, or—in Britain—scampi). *Humar* is expensive and considered a delicacy; it's often made into soup, but you can pay royally to enjoy it baked or sautéed in butter and garlic. Tiny precooked and peeled Greenland shrimp *(rækjur)* are often added to sauces or eaten on open-face sandwiches.

PRACTICALITIES

Icelandic Whitefish

Most commonly, you'll see whitefish on Icelandic menus. These are all quite similar on the plate and differ more in texture than in taste. They are all mild in flavor and can all be steamed, pan-fried, or deep-fried.

Karfi: Atlantic redfish, also known as ocean perch

Keila: Cusk, distantly related to cod

Langa or *blálanga:* Ling, a long, slim whitefish

Lúða: Halibut, a large fish that's not widely eaten in Iceland (because it's expensive and high in contaminants)

Rauðspretta: Plaice, a small, very thin flatfish like flounder or sole, usually breaded

Skötuselur: Monkfish or anglerfish; only the firm-textured tail is eaten (and can substitute for lobster)

Steinbítur: Wolffish, also known as ocean catfish or Atlantic catfish (but very different from the catfish of the American South)

Þorskur: Cod; when preserved in salt, then rinsed, it's called *salt-fiskur* (this changes the taste and texture)

Ufsi: Pollock, related to haddock and cod and often fried

Ýsa: Haddock, the everyday fish in Icelandic homes

More Icelandic Fish

Grásleppa: Lumpfish, small and, yes, lump-like; its eggs are dyed red and black, and widely sold in Iceland as *kavíar*

Makríll: Mackerel, often smoked or canned

Síld: Herring, generally pickled and eaten with bread

Silungur: Trout, farm-raised and often smoked

Meat *(Kjöt)*

Don't miss the chance to try the excellent Icelandic **lamb** *(lambakjöt)*. Even if you don't normally like lamb, it's worth trying here. Icelandic sheep range free, grazing on wild grass, resulting in a lean and tender meat. You'll find leg of lamb, rack of lamb, and other top-notch preparations on menus. *Kjötsúpa* ("meat soup"), an Icelandic staple made with chunks of lamb and root vegetables, is a more traditional way to eat lamb that warms you

on cold days. *Hangikjöt,* smoked lamb, may be served warm or cold. *Svið,* an acquired taste, is a sheep's head that's been split down the middle; you eat the cheeks and, if you like, the eye and tongue.

Icelanders traditionally ate only modest amounts of **beef** *(nautakjöt)*, and almost no **chicken** *(kjúklingur)* or **pork** *(svínakjöt)*—but today the latter two make up more than half of local meat consumption.

Thanks to the Danes, **hot dogs** *(pylsur)* became a common snack in Iceland in the 20th century. Unlike the average American frankfurter, some Icelandic hot dogs contain lamb in addition to beef and pork—but you probably won't taste the differ-

Eating Whale in Iceland

Iceland is a rare country where you're likely to find whale offered in restaurants. Some travelers see this as an exciting tasting opportunity, but for others, it's offensive and unethical.

The whale on Icelandic menus is the relatively small minke whale *(hrefna)*, which is not endangered. Historically, Icelanders rarely ate whales; whale hunting proliferated mainly to export whale meat to Norway and Japan. Antiwhaling groups point out that tourists, thinking they're doing something "local," consume most of the whale meat sold in Iceland today.

A sizable minority of Icelanders would like to see their countrymen stop whaling, arguing that the practice serves no valid commercial or scientific need. The safety of eating whale is also debated. Toothed whales, which feed higher on the food chain, have high concentrations of mercury. Baleen whales, like the minke, are considered safer to eat, as they are filter feeders—the baleen in their mouths acting as big strainers. Still, Iceland's food-research institute recommends that pregnant and breastfeeding women limit their intake of minke whale meat.

More nationalistic Icelanders support whaling, seeing it as a symbol of their country's independence and power over its marine resources. It's fair to say that Iceland, Norway, and Japan continue to hunt whales more to make a political point than to supply a strong market for the meat (which, rumor has it, mostly winds up in Japanese school lunches).

ence. You'll find hot dogs sold at gas station grills and at stands around town, often near swimming pools and in shopping malls. Wieners come in a bun with your choice of condiments (mustard, ketchup, mayonnaise-based remoulade, chopped raw onions, and crispy fried onions are popular). To keep things simple, ask for "one with everything" *(eina með öllu)*. At about 300-400 ISK, this makes for a good fill-me-up on the go.

Whale, Puffin, and Other Novelty Meats

Restaurants here market nonendangered **minke whale meat** to tourists as a special experience. You'll see it offered both raw (like sushi) or grilled as steaks or on skewers. Some say it resembles beef—or, because it's a bit gamey, perhaps deer or elk. Ahi tuna is perhaps the best comparison, in terms of flavor and texture. Whale isn't a traditional Icelandic dish, and while some travelers enjoy the chance to sample it, others raise ethical concerns (see sidebar).

A few restaurants offer relatively expensive **seabird** dishes. You'll be eating a member of the auk family *(svartfugl)*—more likely a guillemot or murre than a puffin, as Iceland's puffin popu-

PRACTICALITIES

lations are currently low. These birds were, and still are, netted on seaside cliffs at certain times of year.

Iceland's **reindeer** population, introduced from Sweden in the 1700s, isn't large enough to support a commercial market. But you may occasionally see it on the menu of a restaurant with a private source.

Hardship Meats (Þorramatur)

In deep winter, when food supplies ran low on the farm, Icelanders traditionally reached down to the bottom of the barrel and ate the least appetizing parts of their livestock, which they had preserved in sour whey. In the 20th century, nostalgic urban Icelanders started the custom of serving these dubious delicacies at parties and buffets in January and February. They're known as *þorramatur*, after the Old Norse winter month of *þorri*.

The most commonly served dishes are pressed ram's testicles *(hrútspungar)*, which actually aren't bad; liver and blood sausage *(lifrapylsa, blóðmör,* and *slátur)*, somewhat similar to Scottish haggis; sheep's head (described earlier); and fermented Greenland shark, cut up into smelly little cubes *(hákarl)*. While a few restaurants sell (overpriced) tiny portions of "rotted shark" (as it's casually called), the most affordable way to sample this is to buy a tiny tub in the food section of Reykjavík's Kolaportið flea market. For more on this dish—which, like many strange foods, makes a lot more sense once you understand its history—see the sidebar.

Dairy Products

As well as regular **milk** *(mjólk)*, try thicker, fermented *súrmjólk* or *AB-mjólk* on your cereal. Protectionist policies make import-ed cheeses very expensive, and (perhaps because of the lack of competition) Icelandic **cheese** *(ostur)* is generally bland and undistinguished. The most fla-vorful hard cheeses are Óðals Tindur and Óðalsostur. Like other Scandinavians, Iceland-ers enjoy brown "cheeses" that are made from boiled-down,

slightly sweetened whey. The soft, spreadable version, called *mysin-gur* (similar to Swedish *messmör*) is much more popular in Iceland than the hard *mysuostur* (which resembles Norwegian *brunost*). Rice pudding *(grjónagrautur)* with cinnamon is a comfort food and com-mon snack.

Icelanders eat **yogurts** and other curdled milk products in endless varieties (plain, sweetened, low-fat, high-fat, sold with

Iceland's Infamous "Rotted Shark" (Hákarl)

The Greenland shark can live up to 400 years, grow up to 22 feet long, and weigh over 2,500 pounds. They began to be hunted in Icelandic waters back in the 14th century for their giant livers, which produced highly valuable oil that was lucratively exported to Europe. But that left Icelanders with 90 percent of the shark going to waste: Greenland shark meat, when fresh, is high in toxins.

And then, centuries ago, some very brave, very clever (or very hungry) Icelander figured out a solution: If you ferment the shark for about six weeks in very cold temperatures, through a natural process, lacto-bacteria break down the toxins into ammonia. (While originally the shark flesh was buried underground during fermentation, today it's simply stacked in wooden crates.) After a few months of drying, *voilà!*: The shark is edible. It tastes like ammonia...but it's edible. And on a frigid island perennially struggling to survive, that's a very good thing.

Icelanders don't eat much shark. It's so pungent, and so high in protein and omega-3s, that a little goes a long way—so it's consumed in small amounts, as a delicacy. If you're skeptical, they'll reassure you that *hákarl* is good for you: In fact, though, shark (which feeds at the top of the ocean's food chain) is full of mercury, and pregnant women should pass up any offers to try it.

Some restaurants sell tiny portions of *hákarl* for high prices. But most tourists just want a nibble (if that). For a free sample in Reykjavík, stop by the weekend flea market. Or, if you're headed to Snæfellsnes, visit the Bjarnarhöfn Shark Museum for a taste and to learn about how it's made (see page 296).

folding plastic spoons and caps full of muesli, and so on). Of the sweetened, flavored yogurts, the richest is called *þykkmjólk* (a real treat); a close second are the flavors sold as *Húsavíkur jógúrt*.

At the other end of the spectrum—and an Icelandic staple—is *skyr* (pron. "skeer"), a plain, no-fat product made from skim milk that's similar to Greek yogurt sold in the US. Though you'll hear *skyr* hailed as a magical low-fat discovery, Icelanders have long agreed that *skyr* tastes best mixed with cream and fruit. It's also good baked into cheesecakes.

Mysa is whey—the acidic liquid leftover from the cheese- or *skyr*-making process. Sold in cartons in the supermarket, it's become trendy as a probiotic beverage (think kombucha). The taste is a mix of sweet and sour.

Fruits and Vegetables

Icelanders have traditionally collected an edible lichen that grows wild here, called *fjallagras* (mountain grass). *Fjallagras* is added to breads and soups, and brewed into tea. The only fruits that grow easily in Iceland are berries—especially blueberries *(bláber)*, crowberries *(krækiber)*, and currants *(rifsber)*. Potatoes do well here, as do turnips (the main starchy root vegetable before potatoes arrived from the New World). Then there's rhubarb, often used in baking and jam.

Today, Icelanders also grow a range of vegetables—tomatoes, cucumbers, mushrooms—in massive, geothermally heated greenhouses, but even with the cheap energy here these are usually more expensive than imported equivalents.

Breads and Baked Goods

Most grain won't grow here, so all grains (except barley) are imported. Since rye was once the cheapest grain to buy, and lacking much wood or fuel, Icelanders learned to bake **rye bread** in makeshift ovens dug in hot spots in the ground, near geothermal springs. Today this dense, chocolate-brown bread, called *rúgbrauð*, is made with a little barley malt or other sugar, and baked slowly at a low temperature, making it slightly sweet and gingerbread-like. It's often served with *plokkfiskur* (fish gratin), topped with smoked fish, or just with butter for breakfast. Another traditional rye bread, *flatbrauð* is an unleavened, flat circle baked in a pan; it resembles a soft tortilla. It's typically buttered and topped with sliced smoked lamb.

The island's bakeries make several characteristic wheat-based **pastries,** many with Danish origins. *Vínarbrauð* (like a danish), sold at bakeries in long, wide strips, is usually filled with jam and topped with a stripe of sugary glaze. *Kleinur* are knots of deep-fried dough; sold fresh, singly, in bakeries or in bags in the supermarket, they go well with a cup of coffee.

A relic from earlier times is *laufabrauð* ("leafbread"), paper-thin circles of wheat-flour dough, which Icelanders, in the weeks before Christmas, inscribe with patterns and fry (traditionally in sheep tallow, these days more often in oil). You'll see round containers of factory-made *laufabrauð* on sale in supermarkets in December.

Sweets

Chocolate-covered **licorice** is the signature Icelandic candy. Supermarkets sell dozens of varieties on this theme, such as *Draumur* ("Dream") candy bars and bags of olive-shaped *Kúlu-súkk*—the name is a play on the words for ball *(kúla)*, chocolate *(súkkulaði)*, and the Greenlandic town of Kulusuk. By European standards,

Icelandic licorice is very tame, with little salt and a mild flavor. Some like *fylltar reimar*, hollow ropes of licorice stuffed with a sugary filling. Iceland's thriving candy industry (the islanders are still making up for centuries of deprivation) also cranks out lots of licorice-free sweets and chocolates, such as the inexpensive *Hraun* (Lava) bars, whose rocky surface resembles a lava field.

Like other Nordic people, Icelanders prefer **soft-serve ice cream.** When you order your cone, prepare to say whether, for a few extra krónur, you'd like it *með dýfu* (dipped into a chocolate sauce that hardens over the cold ice cream), *með kurli* (rolled in little chocolate beads), or both. At better ice-cream shops, a *bragðarefur* (literally "flavor fox") is soft ice cream blended with your choice of chocolate chunks, crushed candy bars, nuts, or other goodies (basically like a gigantic McFlurry). Ask for two spoons.

INTERNATIONAL CUISINES

Perhaps because so much of the country's food is imported (and many native dishes are so unpalatable), Icelanders are very open to other cooking traditions. A wave of Thai, Vietnamese, and Filipino immigrants came to the country in the 1980s, and now you can buy coconut milk, tofu, and fish sauce at supermarkets. Icelanders love pizza (though Italians here are few), and the American military presence has left behind a taste for Cheerios and Doritos. And in the last couple of decades, Polish immigrants have opened a couple of good supermarkets and started to produce fine sausage.

SUPERMARKETS AND OTHER CHEAP EATS

Travelers can save money, especially at dinnertime, by assembling a picnic at one of Iceland's supermarkets. The two discount supermarket chains, **Bónus** and **Krónan,** are the names to know. **Hagkaup** is more expensive, but carries a wider range, and some Reykjavík branches are open daily 24 hours. **Samkaup** is common in the countryside (but not particularly cheap). Steer clear of the extremely high-priced **10-11** convenience stores.

Hagkaup and other larger supermarkets sometimes have a hot-food counter with grilled chickens or roasted meats sold by weight. Supermarkets also sell prepared sandwiches, soft cheeses, shrimp and tuna "salads" that can be spread on bread, and plenty of cold cuts.

Other than **Subway** and **Domino's,** major fast-food franchises have only a slight presence in Iceland. (That means no McDonald's...and no Starbucks. You'll survive.)

BEVERAGES
Water, Coffee, and Other Nonalcoholic Drinks

Restaurants dispense the country's excellent tap **water** *(vatn)* for free, sometimes from a help-yourself table with pitchers and a stack of glasses. Buying bottled water is a waste of money here, unless you want it with bubbles—in that case, look for *kolsýrt* (carbonated) *vatn* or *sódavatn*. Blueberry is the country's only native **juice** (*safi* or *djús*), an expensive delicacy produced in small quantities in the fall.

Icelanders are among the world's biggest **coffee** *(kaffi)* drinkers. (Blame the dark, cold winters.) Many cafés and restaurants offer free refills. For other hot beverages, look for tea *(te)* or hot chocolate (*heitt súkkulaði* or *kakó*).

Icelanders love **malt soda** *(malt),* a sweetened and carbonated beverage made from yeast, malt, and hops just like beer, but with little or no fermentation. Egils Maltextrakt is the best-loved brand. Though thought of as nonalcoholic, Icelandic *malt* reportedly contains about 1 percent alcohol, which is not mentioned on the label. That means you'd need to drink practically a six-pack of *malt* to get the same effect as from one beer. At Christmastime, Icelanders like to mix *malt* fifty-fifty with orange soda; they call the result *jólaöl* (Yule ale).

Wine, Beer, and Spirits

All **wine** *(léttvín)* in Iceland is imported. Light **beer** (*bjór;* 2.25 percent alcohol) is sold in supermarkets, but for anything stronger you'll need a state-run Vínbúðin store (or a bar or restaurant). Prices are high, especially for wine and spirits. If you plan to seriously imbibe during your visit, make a point of stopping at the airport duty-free store on your way into the country, before you retrieve your luggage. Airport prices are 20-50 percent lower than in Reykjavík, and the limit is generous. (You can plan your purchases, and check the current allowances, at www.dutyfree.is.)

In recent years, many small craft breweries have sprung up in Iceland, offering interesting alternatives to the major Scandinavian and local beer brands like Tuborg and Viking. There's even a holiday dedicated to beer—Beer Day, on March 1, marks the 1989 end of the country's 74-year prohibition of beer.

The local hard **liquor** industry has also diversified, and produces a range of vodka, gin, and even local single-malt whiskey. You'll also see liqueurs made with local berries. Björk is a liqueur flavored with birch and even comes with a birch twig in the bottle. The most traditional strong spirit, called *brennivín* (and marketed as "Black Death"—you've been warned!) is aquavit, made from fermented potatoes and flavored with caraway.

Tips on Internet Security

Make sure that your device is running the latest versions of its operating system, security software, and apps. Next, ensure that your device and key programs (like email) are password-protected. On the road, use only secure, password-protected Wi-Fi hotspots. Ask the hotel or café staff for the specific name of their Wi-Fi network, and make sure you log on to that exact one.

If you must access your financial info online, use a banking app rather than accessing your account via a browser. A cellular connection is more secure than Wi-Fi. Avoid logging onto personal finance sites on a public computer.

Never share your credit-card number (or any other sensitive information) online unless you know that the site is secure. A secure site displays a little padlock icon, and the URL begins with *https* (instead of the usual *http*).

Staying Connected

One of the most common questions I hear from travelers is, "How can I stay connected?" The short answer is: more easily and cheaply than you might think.

The simplest solution is to bring your own device—mobile phone, tablet, or laptop—and use it just as you would at home (following the money-saving tips below, such as getting an international plan or connecting to free Wi-Fi whenever possible). Another option is to buy an Icelandic SIM card for your US mobile phone. Or you can use Icelandic landlines and computers to connect. Each of these options is described next, and more details are at www.ricksteves.com/phoning. For a very practical one-hour talk covering tech issues for travelers, see www.ricksteves.com/mobile-travel-skills.

USING A MOBILE PHONE IN ICELAND

Here are some budget tips and options.

Sign up for an international plan. To stay connected at a lower cost, sign up for an international service plan through your carrier. Most providers offer a simple bundle that includes calling, messaging, and data. Your normal plan may already include international coverage (T-Mobile's does).

Before your trip, call your provider or check online to confirm that your phone will work in Iceland, and research your provider's international rates. Activate the plan a day or two before you leave, then remember to cancel it when your trip's over.

Use free Wi-Fi whenever possible. Practically all of Iceland

PRACTICALITIES

The Icelandic Language

Pretty much all Icelanders speak English comfortably, although usually not with the accent-less fluency typical of mainland Scandinavians. Locals will visibly brighten when you know and use some key Icelandic phrases such as *takk* (thanks) and *skál* (cheers; for more, see the "Icelandic Survival Phrases" on page 537). Don't try too hard, though; many of the tourism employees you'll encounter are immigrants who don't speak much Icelandic either.

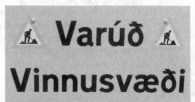

If you know Norwegian, Danish, or Swedish, you'll be able to pick out some words on signs and menus, but Icelandic vocabulary and grammar are different enough that the other Scandinavian languages aren't of much practical help.

A thousand years ago, all Scandinavians—from Greenland to the Baltic—spoke the same language. In the Middle Ages, many Germans settled in Norway, Sweden, and Denmark. The residents of those countries borrowed many words, and their grammar and sound patterns changed. But isolated Icelandic changed far less over the centuries. Modern Icelanders can learn to read the sagas—recorded in the 13th and 14th centuries—with only a little more difficulty than English speakers learning to read Shakespearean English. Modern Icelandic, like English, preserved the original Germanic unvoiced and voiced "th" sounds (spelled þ and ð; capital Þ and Ð). And like German, Icelandic still has four cases and three genders.

The hardest thing about modern Icelandic is the pronunciation. Several Icelandic sounds are rare in the world's languages. Among these are the voiceless versions of *l, r,* and *n,* often spelled *hl, hr,* and *hn.* To make these sounds, put your tongue in position, then breathe out. Another unusual sound is a sort of breathy *h* that Icelanders make before the double consonants *pp, tt,* and *kk* (*stoppa,* "to stop," sounds like *stohpa*). Then there's the Icelandic *ll,* which is usually pronounced *tl.* Yet another quirk: you'll often hear Icelanders say "yes" (*já*) while breathing in, instead of breathing out. It sounds like a little gasp. (Try it yourself.)

Several common sounds are absent from Icelandic, notably those spelled *sh, ch, zh, j,* and *z* in English (they pronounce Cheerios "Sirius"). And a few exotic consonant clusters can create confusion: *fl* and *fn* are pronounced like *pl* and *pn* (so Keflavík and Hafnarfjörður come out sounding like "Keplavík" and "Hapnarfjörður"). But *pt* sounds like *ft,* and *kt* like *cht* (with the *ch* of "loch"), so the Icelandic names for the ninth and tenth months of the year sound like "Seftember" and "Ochtober." After a consonant at the end of a word, *l* and *n* turn into the sounds written *hl* and *hn,* so the *n* in the word *vatn* (water) sounds almost silent to foreign ears.

Like the other Scandinavian languages, Icelandic tacks the definite article onto the end of a word: it comes in several forms, including *-inn, -in,* and *-ið,* all of which mean "the." So *hús* means "house," and *húsið* means "the house."

Abstract and technical words, which in other languages tend to take an international form, are often unrecognizable in Icelandic. That's because 20th-century Icelanders put a lot of effort into creating old Norse-based words for new inventions: Today, all Icelanders call a telephone *sími,* a radio *útvarp,* and a computer *tölva.* But Icelanders completely rejected the invented word *flatbaka* in favor of the word *pítsa*—which, heresy of heresies, they tend to spell *pizza.*

If you'd like to try tackling Icelandic pronunciation, the list below shows the most common sounds. The stress is always on a word's first syllable, although longer words may have a secondary stress. For a breezy, humorous introduction to the language, pick up Alda Sigmundsdóttir's *The Little Book of Icelandic.*

Letter	Sounds like:
Þ/þ	unvoiced th, like "breath"; the letter is called thorn
Ð/ð	voiced th, like "breathe"; the letter is called eth
hl, hr, hn	unvoiced versions of *l, r, n* (blow the sound out)
j	*y* in *you*
hj	*h* in *hue*
hv	*kv* in *kvetch*
ll	*tl* in *butler*
á	*ow* in *how*
é	*ye* in *yet*
í, ý	*ee* in *seen*
ó	*oa* in *road*
ú	*oo* in *soon*
a	*a* in *father*
e	*e* in *set*
i, y	*i* in *sit*
o	*o* in *not*
u	the German *ü* ("oo" with pursed lips)
ö	the German *ö* ("oh" with pursed lips)
au	*ö* followed by *i*
ei, ey	*ay* in *may*
æ	*ie* in *pie*

How to Dial

International Calls

Whether phoning from a US landline or US mobile phone, or from a number in another European country, here's how to make an international call. I've used one of my recommended Reykjavík hotels as an example (tel. 514-6000). Note that Iceland does not use area codes.

Mobile Tip: With a mobile phone, the "+" sign can replace the access code (for a "+" sign, press and hold "0").

US/Canada to Europe

Dial 011 (US/Canada access code), country code (354 for Iceland), and phone number.

▸ To call the Reykjavík hotel from home, dial 011-354-514-6000.

Country to Country Within Europe

Dial 00 (Europe access code), country code, and phone number.

▸ To call the Reykjavík hotel from Germany, dial 00-354-514-6000.

Europe to the US/Canada

Dial 00, country code (1 for US/Canada), and phone number.

▸ To call from Europe to my office in Edmonds, Washington, dial 00-1-425-771-8303.

Domestic Calls

To call from one Icelandic landline or Icelandic mobile phone to another, simply dial the phone number.

▸ To call the Reykjavík hotel from Akureyri, dial 514-6000.

More Dialing Tips

Icelandic Phone Numbers: Icelandic phone numbers are all seven digits long (except for special services like weather and directory information). Iceland's land lines start with 4 and 5; mobile lines start with 6, 7, and 8 and cost substantially more to dial.

has high-speed cellular service, but unless you have an unlimited-data plan, you're best off saving most of your online tasks for Wi-Fi. You can access the internet, send texts, and make voice calls over Wi-Fi.

Most accommodations offer free Wi-Fi, and many cafés have free hotspots for customers; look for signs offering it and ask for the Wi-Fi password when you buy something. You'll also often find Wi-Fi at TIs, major museums, public-transit hubs, airports, and aboard some buses.

Minimize the use of your cellular network. The best way to make sure you're not accidentally burning through data is to put your device in "airplane" mode (which also disables phone calls and texts), turn your Wi-Fi back on, and connect to networks as

Toll and Toll-Free Numbers: It's generally not possible to dial Icelandic toll or toll-free numbers from a US mobile or landline (although you can sometimes get through using Skype). Look for a direct-dial number instead.

More Phoning Help: See www.howtocallabroad.com.

European Country Codes			
Austria	43	Ireland & N. Ireland	353 / 44
Belgium	32	Italy	39
Bosnia-Herzegovina	387	Latvia	371
Croatia	385	Montenegro	382
Czech Republic	420	Morocco	212
Denmark	45	Netherlands	31
Estonia	372	Norway	47
Finland	358	Poland	48
France	33	Portugal	351
Germany	49	Russia	7
Gibraltar	350	Slovakia	421
Great Britain	44	Slovenia	386
Greece	30	Spain	34
Hungary	36	Sweden	46
Iceland	354	Switzerland	41
		Turkey	90

Drop an initial zero when dialing a European phone number—except when calling Italy.

PRACTICALITIES

needed. When you need to get online but can't find Wi-Fi, simply turn on your cellular network (or turn off airplane mode) just long enough for the task at hand.

Even with an international data plan, wait until you're on Wi-Fi to Skype, download apps, stream videos, or do other megabyte-greedy tasks. Using a navigation app such as Google Maps over a cellular network can take lots of data, so do this sparingly or offline.

Limit automatic updates. By default, your device constantly checks for a data connection and updates apps. It's smart to disable these features so your apps will only update when you're on Wi-Fi. Also change your device's email settings from "auto-retrieve" to "manual" (or from "push" to "fetch").

Use Wi-Fi calling and messaging apps. Skype, WhatsApp, FaceTime, and Google Hangouts are great for making free or low-cost calls or sending texts over Wi-Fi worldwide. Just log on to a Wi-Fi network, then connect with any of your friends or family members who use the same service. If you buy credit in advance, with some of these services you can call or text anywhere for just pennies.

Some apps, such as Apple's iMessage, will use the cellular network for texts if Wi-Fi isn't available: To avoid this possibility, turn off the "Send as SMS" feature.

Buy an Icelandic SIM card. If you anticipate making a lot of local calls, need a local phone number, or your provider's international data rates are expensive, consider buying a SIM card in Iceland to replace the one in your (unlocked) US phone or tablet. The most efficient way to buy an Icelandic SIM card is either on the plane (Icelandair flight attendants sell them) or at Keflavík Airport (before you claim your bags, detour into the duty-free store; after you exit, visit the 10-11 and Elko convenience stores in the arrivals hall). If you wait until you're in Reykjavík, you can find phone-company stores in the Kringlan and Smáralind shopping malls. The two companies to consider are Síminn (www.siminn.is) and Vodafone (www.vodafone.is); they offer comparable starter packages for about 2,000-3,000 ISK, depending on how much data is included. If you need help setting up your SIM card, buy it at a mobile-phone shop.

WITHOUT A MOBILE PHONE

It's less convenient but possible to travel in Iceland without a mobile device. You can make calls from your hotel and check email or get online using public computers.

Most **hotels** charge a fee for placing calls—ask for rates before you dial. You can use a prepaid international phone card (sold at supermarkets, convenience stores, and gas stations). These cards offer a cheaper rate if you access the system by calling the landline, and a higher rate if you call the toll-free number.

Some hotels have **public computers** in their lobbies for guests to use; otherwise you may find them at public libraries (ask your hotelier or the TI for the nearest location). On an Icelandic keyboard, use the "Alt Gr" key to the right of the space bar to insert the extra symbol that appears on some keys. If you can't locate a special character, simply copy and paste it from a web page.

PRACTICALITIES

MAIL

You can mail one package per day to yourself worth up to $200 duty-free from Europe to the US (mark it "personal purchases"). If you're sending a gift to someone, mark it "unsolicited gift." For details, visit www.cbp.gov, select "Travel," and then "Know Before You Visit." The Icelandic postal service works fine, but for quick transatlantic delivery (in either direction), consider services such as DHL (www.dhl.com).

Transportation

Your options for linking destinations in Iceland are tourist-oriented excursion buses, unguided do-it-yourself excursion buses, public buses, rental cars, and short-hop flights. (Iceland has no rail system.)

If you're staying in Reykjavík and plan only a few brief forays outside the city, you can get by without a car. But most visitors find that renting a car gives them maximum flexibility for getting out into the Icelandic countryside. You won't find convenient public transportation options for reaching some sights (including the biggies—the Golden Circle and South Coast); instead you'll likely need to rely on pricey excursions. For this reason, renting a car can be more cost-effective than it initially seems.

For an overview of public transportation in Iceland, see http://publictransport.is. For general information on transportation throughout Europe, see www.ricksteves.com/transportation.

EXCURSION BUSES
Guided Excursion Buses

You can select from a full menu of guided bus tours to get into the countryside. You're paying a premium for a guide and a carefully designed experience, but these excursions take the guesswork out of your trip. For more on this option, see the Beyond Reykjavík chapter.

Do-It-Yourself Excursion Buses

In summer months, several private companies offer direct, regularly scheduled bus transport to many popular outdoor destinations, especially spots off the Ring Road and in the interior, such as Þórsmörk and Landmannalaugar. These buses are unguided, with routes intended to get hikers and campers to popular outdoor destinations, but anyone can use them to reach some of Iceland's most spectacular sights.

For example, you can leave Reykjavík early in the morning, spend a couple of midday hours taking a short hike in Þórsmörk or Landmannalaugar, and return to the city for a late dinner; you could also overnight in a tent or cabin and get picked up the next day. These buses can come in handy for day-tripping from Akureyri to Dettifoss, or from Skaftafell to the Lakagígar craters.

Companies to consider include Reykjavík Excursions (under the name Iceland On Your Own, www.re.is/iceland-on-your-own), Sterna Travel (www.icelandbybus.is or www.sternatravel.com), and Trex (www.trex.is). Confirm your departure location in Reykjavík; there may be several options. Reykjavík Excursions, Sterna, and Trex buses stop at the BSÍ bus terminal, which is within walking distance of downtown. Note that several of these companies also offer guided trips to some of the same destinations.

Highland Route to the North: An exciting bus journey is to travel from Reykjavík to the north (Skagafjörður, Akureyri, or Mývatn) through Iceland's interior Highlands, over either of two passes—Kjölur or Sprengisandur. The trips run only when the passes are clear—usually from late June to early September. The route, which can't be driven in a normal rental car, gives you a look at some of Iceland's most desolate and remote scenery. (The high-clearance buses have large tires that can cope with the rocky roads...be prepared for a very bumpy ride.)

East Iceland: Reykjavík Excursions and Sterna also run one daily bus in each direction around the east end of the island, between Akureyri and Höfn.

Circle Passes: The bus companies offer passes (about 40,000 ISK) that allow you to circle the island, stopping wherever you like (early June-early Sept only). If you're planning to loop through several parts of Iceland by bus, one of the "passport"-style fares can be handy—they're essentially hop-on, hop-off tickets covering a specific route and cheaper than paying for individual journeys.

PUBLIC BUSES

Iceland has a good network of scheduled public buses (painted yellow and blue and called *strætó*), run as a single system by city and local governments (www.straeto.is). The Strætó system doesn't cover the country's sparsely populated eastern edge (from Egilsstaðir to Höfn), but a privately run bus service fills in the gaps.

Although the Strætó network is more geared to locals than visitors, it can be useful to those traveling from one town to another, such as from Reykjavík to Selfoss or Akureyri. Reykjavík city buses are part of the Strætó network and use the same tickets and fare structure.

For long-distance trips, you can pay by credit card or through a Strætó app (see page 64). Strætó's buses also accept cash (although no one pays this way) and little brown paper tickets (sold only in 20-ticket strips). From Reykjavík, Strætó's long-distance buses leave from a terminal in the suburbs called Mjódd, which is linked to downtown by frequent city buses (ask driver for a free transfer ticket).

RENTING A CAR

Car rental makes a lot of sense in Iceland, unless you're traveling solo. Two people splitting the cost of a rental car and gas will save a lot over the cost of bus excursions, while enjoying the flexibility of stopping whenever and wherever they want. Driving is easy here—the hardest part is navigating the round-abouts of suburban Reyk-javík, but even that is a breeze once you've had a

little experience. Once out in the countryside, traffic is extremely light. The Ring Road is practically made for road trips with friends. (For a Ring Road trip, also consider a campervan rental—see page 489.)

It's cheaper to arrange most car rentals from the US, so re-search car rentals before you go. Consider several companies to compare rates. Most of the major US rental agencies (including Avis, Budget, Enterprise, Hertz, and Thrifty) have offices in Ice-land. Also consider the two major Europe-based agencies, Europ-car and Sixt. Iceland's smaller, homegrown rental agencies may offer cheaper used vehicles (beware that some of these cars are real clunkers—read carefully before booking). Or consider using a consolidator such as Auto Europe (www.autoeurope.com—or the sometimes cheaper www.autoeurope.eu), which compares rates at several companies to get you the best deal.

Wherever you book, always read the fine print. Check for add-on charges—such as one-way drop-off fees, airport surcharges, or mandatory insurance policies—that aren't included in the "total price."

Rental Costs and Considerations

Figure on paying roughly $350 for a one-week rental in summer, and $50-100 less in spring or fall. Allow extra for supplemental insurance, fuel, tolls, and parking. To save money on fuel, request a diesel car. And don't pay extra for air-conditioning: Even on sunny summer days, rolling down the window is enough to cool things down.

Manual vs. Automatic: Almost all rental cars in Iceland are manual by default—and cars with a stick shift are generally cheaper. If you need an automatic, request one in advance.

Age Restrictions: Some rental companies impose minimum and maximum age limits. Young drivers (25 and under) and seniors (69 and up) should check the rental policies and rules section of car-rental websites.

Four-Wheel vs. Two-Wheel Drive: Many tourists think of a trip to Iceland as more of an "expedition" than it really is, and shell out for a high-clearance SUV when they would do just fine with a teeny two-wheel-drive car. You won't need four-wheel drive for the itineraries in this book in summer, or for a quick winter stopover if you stick to Reykjavík. (The one exception is the Westfjords, which does have some rougher, unpaved roads; the routes I've described are doable in a two-wheel-drive car, but may be more comfortable with four-wheel drive.) A more rugged vehicle makes sense only if you're planning to traverse Iceland's interior Highlands (not covered in this book), drive outside the capital area in winter, ford unbridged rivers (such as on the road to Þórsmörk), or spend lots of time on mucky, rutted dirt roads in the countryside.

Off-Limit Roads: Be clear on where you can drive your rental car. Normal two-wheel-drive vehicles are fine for well-maintained unpaved roads. But rental cars can't be driven on roads in the interior, which cross unbridged rivers and can be very rough. (If you want to drive on these roads, rent a four-wheel-drive vehicle.) Consider any road designated with an "F" on maps or road signs to be off-limits. Highway 35 (over the Kjölur pass) and highway 550 (called Kaldidalur) are also off-limits even though they don't have an F—this should be stated on your rental agreement.

Picking Up Your Car

Most visitors to Iceland pick up their rental car either at Keflavík Airport or at a rental company's Reykjavík office. It's generally easiest to pick up and drop off at the airport, which has the widest selection of on-site agencies. It's also possible to pick up in Reykjavík and drop off at the airport (or vice-versa). This is considered a one-way rental, with a small extra charge (but often less than the airport bus fare). Car rental in Akureyri and some smaller towns is also possible.

Always check the hours of the location you choose: Off-airport, many rental offices close from midday Saturday until Monday morning and, in smaller towns, at lunchtime.

When selecting a location, don't trust the agency's description of "downtown" or "city center." In Reykjavík, rental offices are all either at the domestic airport or in industrial areas on the outskirts of the city—a long, costly taxi ride from the center. Before choosing, plug the addresses into a mapping website.

Before driving off in your rental car, check it thoroughly and make sure any damage is noted on your rental agreement. Rental agencies in Europe tend to charge for even minor damage, so be sure to mark anything not already noted. Find out how your car's gearshift, lights, turn signals, wipers, radio, and fuel cap function, and know what kind of fuel the car takes (diesel vs. unleaded). When you return the car, make sure the agent verifies its condition with you. Some drivers take pictures of the returned vehicle as proof of its condition.

Car Insurance Options

When you rent a car, the price typically includes liability insurance, which covers harm to other cars or motorists—but not the rental car itself. To limit your financial risk in case of damage to the rental, choose one of these options: Buy a Collision Damage Waiver (CDW) with a low or zero deductible from the car-rental company (roughly 30-40 percent extra), get coverage through your credit card (free, but more complicated), or get collision insurance as part of a larger travel-insurance policy.

Basic **CDW** costs $15–30 a day and typically comes with a $1,000-2,000 deductible, reducing but not eliminating your financial responsibility. When you reserve or pick up the car, you'll be offered the chance to "buy down" the basic deductible to zero (for an additional $10-30/day; this is sometimes called "super CDW" or "zero-deductible coverage").

If you opt for **credit-card coverage,** you must decline all coverage offered by the car-rental company—which means they can place a hold on your card for up to the full value of the car. In case of damage, it can be time-consuming to resolve the charges. Before relying on this option, quiz your credit-card company about how it works.

If you're already purchasing a **travel-insurance policy** for your trip, adding collision coverage can be an economical option. For example, Travel Guard (www.travelguard.com) sells affordable renter's collision insurance as an add-on to its other policies; it's valid everywhere in Europe except the Republic of Ireland, and some Italian car-rental companies refuse to honor it, as it doesn't cover you in case of theft.

Car-rental agencies may encourage you to spend upwards of $25/day for supplemental insurance to cover damage from sand-storms (blowing sand can ruin a car's finish and gravel can break windows). Depending on where you're driving, this is usually not necessary (sandstorms are most likely to occur between Vík and Skaftafell on the Ring Road)—check the forecast to see if extremely high winds are expected where you're going. You may also be offered insurance against damage from volcanic ash. Unless there's an active eruption, the risk from ash is very low.

For more on car-rental insurance, see www.ricksteves.com/cdw.

Navigation Options

Navigating in the Icelandic countryside is a breeze. Signage is good (though the lettering on signs can be quite small), there's only one Ring Road (though many side roads), and free paper maps and/or downloaded maps on the device of your choice are usually enough to get you around. If you'll be navigating using your phone or a GPS unit from home, remember to bring a car charger and device mount.

Your Mobile Phone: Most of Iceland is well covered by high-speed cellular service. The mapping app on your phone works fine for navigating Iceland's roads, but for real-time turn-by-turn directions and traffic updates, you'll need mobile data access.

Driving all day can burn through a lot of very expensive data. Unless you have unlimited data, consider downloading maps in advance from Google Maps, City Maps 2Go, Apple Maps, Here WeGo, or Navmii, giving you turn-by-turn voice directions and maps that recalibrate even though they're offline. You must download your maps before you go offline—and it's smart to select a large region. Then turn off your data connection so you're not charged for roaming. Call up the map, enter your destination, and you're on your way. Even if you don't have to pay extra for data roaming, this option is great for navigating in areas with poor connectivity.

GPS Devices: If you want the convenience of a dedicated GPS unit, consider renting one with your car ($10-30/day). These units offer real-time turn-by-turn directions and traffic without the data requirements of an app.

A less-expensive option is to bring a GPS device from home. Be sure to buy and download the maps you'll need before your trip.

Paper Maps and Atlases: Even when navigating primarily with a mobile app or GPS, I always make it a point to have a paper map, ideally a big, detailed regional road map. It's invaluable for getting the big picture, understanding alternate routes, and filling in if my phone runs out of juice. The free maps you get from your car-rental company usually don't have enough detail. Look for the free *Big Map* (www.bigmap.is), which has a map of Reykjavík, including suburbs, on one side, and on the other, a serviceable map of the whole country. The free *Around Iceland* booklet includes maps of each region and of small towns. You could also buy a better map of the country in advance (they're cheaper in the US—Michelin #750 is good), or pick one up (for a hefty 3,000 ISK) at a gas station, convenience store, or bookshop in Iceland.

Navigational Websites: Google Maps covers Iceland about as well as Europe or the US. The Icelandic telephone directory website, www.ja.is, has more precise maps, but it's less user-friendly; you can't download the data, and it sometimes expects you to search for place names in an unusual format.

DRIVING

Exploring Iceland by car is a pleasure. Most of the main roads are paved and (outside Reykjavík) relatively uncrowded. In recent years the country has invested heavily in improving its public infrastructure with more paved roads, better signage, and roadside bathrooms. But driving in Iceland does come with unique customs and hazards you should know about. A large percentage

of serious car accidents in Iceland involve foreign tourists. The website www.drive.is has a helpful (if overlong) video introducing the basics. Remember to pack sunglasses for driving: The sun stays low in the Icelandic sky all year.

Road Rules: Be aware of typical European road rules; for example, Iceland requires headlights to be turned on at all times (usually an automatic feature in Icelandic cars), and forbids using a mobile phone without a hands-free headset. In Iceland, you're not allowed to turn right on a red light, unless a sign or signal specifically authorizes it, and on expressways it's illegal to pass drivers on

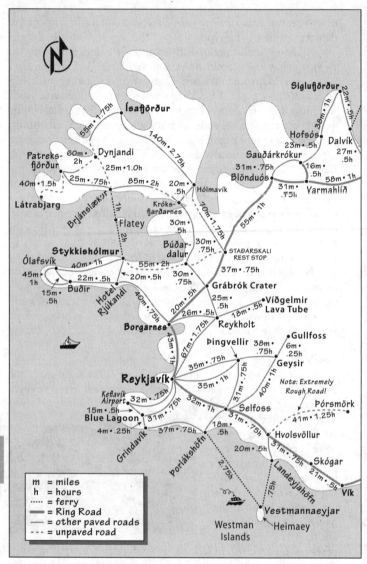

the right. Even major highways like highway 1 are predominantly two-lane, so pass with care. The police may stop you for a routine check (keep your rental paperwork close at hand).

Ask your car-rental company about these rules, or check the "International Travel" section of the US State Department website (www.travel.state.gov, search for the country in the "Learn about your destination" box, then click on "Travel and Transportation").

Speed Limits: Speed limits are by road type and often aren't

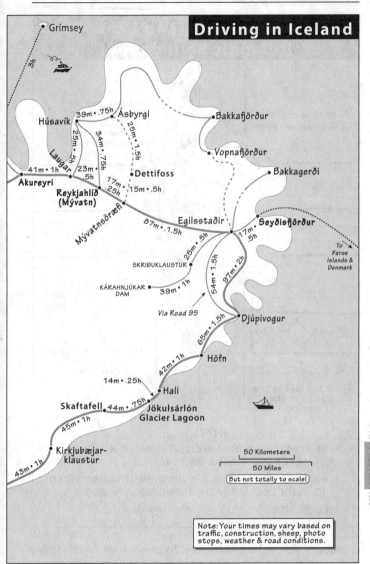

Driving in Iceland

Grímsey

3h

Húsavík 39m•.75h Ásbyrgi Bakkafjörður

25m 34m•.75h 25m•1.5h Vopnafjörður

Laugar .5h 23m Dettifoss Bakkagerði

Akureyri 41m•1h .5h 17m•.25h

Reykjahlíð 15m•.5h
(Mývatn)

Mývatnsöræfi 87m•1.5h Egilsstaðir 17m•.5h Seyðisfjörður

To Faroe Islands & Denmark

25m•.5h

SKRIÐUKLAUSTUR 54m•1.5h 97m•2h

KÁRAHNJÚKAR 39m•1h
DAM

Via Road 95 65m•1.5h Djúpivogur

42m•1h Höfn

14m•.25h Hali

Skaftafell 44m•.75h Jökulsárlón
Glacier Lagoon

45m•1h

Kirkjubæjar-
klaustur 50 Kilometers

43m•1h 50 Miles

But not totally to scale!

Note: Your times may vary based on
traffic, construction, sheep, photo
stops, weather & road conditions.

PRACTICALITIES

posted. Generally, the speed limit in rural Iceland is 90 km/hour
(or about 55 mph) on paved roads and 80 km/hour (50 mph) on
gravel roads. In towns, the limit is 50 km/hour (about 30 mph;
often lower in residential neighborhoods). The tunnel under
Hvalfjörður has a 70 km/hour (45 mph) limit. Speed cameras are
widely used and limits are enforced with high fines (you might get a
ticket by mail after you return home). To give you a chance to slow
down, cameras are always marked in advance with a blue *Löggæs-*

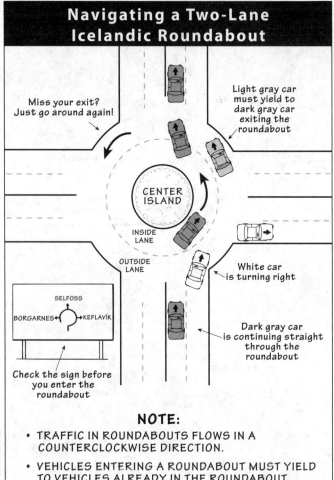

Navigating a Two-Lane Icelandic Roundabout

Miss your exit? Just go around again!

Light gray car must yield to dark gray car exiting the roundabout

CENTER ISLAND

INSIDE LANE

OUTSIDE LANE

White car is turning right

SELFOSS
BORGARNES — KEFLAVÍK

Check the sign before you enter the roundabout

Dark gray car is continuing straight through the roundabout

NOTE:
- TRAFFIC IN ROUNDABOUTS FLOWS IN A COUNTERCLOCKWISE DIRECTION.
- VEHICLES ENTERING A ROUNDABOUT MUST YIELD TO VEHICLES ALREADY IN THE ROUNDABOUT.
- LOOK TO YOUR LEFT AS YOU MERGE ! ☺

lumyndavél sign with a camera icon. In towns, solar-powered *þinn hraði* (your speed) signs flash a green, happy face when you're at or below the speed limit; a red, sad face means you're going too fast.

Roundabouts: The rules at double-lane roundabouts (traffic circles) in Iceland differ from those elsewhere in Europe. Here, the car in the *inner* lane of the circle has the right of way when exiting the roundabout. That means that cars in the outer lane that want to continue around the circle must yield to cars in the inner lane that want to exit. If you're in the inner lane, you have priority, but still use your right-turn signal when you want to exit.

Here's some good advice for double-lane roundabouts: If you're going straight through or left, stay to the left when approaching and enter the inner lane. If you're turning right at the roundabout, stay right and enter the outer lane, because you'll be exiting immediately anyway. If you're in the outer lane and don't want to take the next exit, put on your left-turn signal to show that you'll be continuing around. In all cases, drive defensively (keeping in mind that there may be a tourist in the outer lane who isn't used to the local rules).

The above advice applies only to double-lane roundabouts, which you'll find mostly in Reykjavík and larger towns. Once in the countryside, the vast majority of roundabouts are single-lane, which work the same as anywhere. Remember that at any roundabout, all cars already in the circle have priority over cars entering, in any lane.

Fuel: Gas is around $7 a gallon; diesel is a bit cheaper. Be careful to use the right fuel: Unleaded gas is called *bensín* and sometimes identified with the octane rating *(95 okt)* and has green pumps; diesel is *dísel* and has black pumps.

Although unlikely, there's a small chance that your US credit and debit cards may not work at some Icelandic gas stations—especially unstaffed pumps. Be sure your card has a chip, know your PIN, and be prepared to move on to another gas station if necessary. Especially in rural areas, don't let your tank get too low. Buy fuel during the day, when stations are open and have a cashier on hand. If you have trouble buying gas at the pump, go inside the gas station and ask the cashier to process your card manually. You can also try asking inside the gas station for a prepaid gas card (which you should be able to purchase with any US card), or pay with your emergency cash. Those driving in remote areas can plan gas stops in advance: Major fuel providers N1, ÓB, Orkan, and Olís list their pump locations online.

Street Signs and Signage: Conveniently, street names in the same neighborhood in Icelandic cities and towns all end with

the same element. For example, Faxaskjól, Sörlaskjól, Granaskjól, and other streets ending with *"skjól"* are all next to each other in Reykjavík; to find them, follow road signs reading *"Skjól."*

On highways, yellow signs point in the direction of the named town. The highway number is in white on the left, and the distance (in kilometers) is on the right. Red signs point to sights, which are also indicated by

AND LEARN THESE ICELANDIC ROAD SIGNS

Speed Limit (km/hr) · **Speed Camera** · **Ring Road (Highway 1)** · **Pullout** · **No Passing**

Gravel · **One-Lane Bridge** · **One-Lane Tunnel** (EINBREID GÖNG) · **End of Paved Surface** (MALBIK ENDAR) · **Caution: Livestock**

Blind Hill (BLINDHÆÐ) · **One-Lane Road** (EINBREITT SLITLAG) · **4WD Only** (ILLFÆR VEGUR) · **Very Rough Road–Even for 4WD** (TORLEIÐI)

Point of Interest · **WC** · 1 Mosfellsbær 7 — Destination (middle), road number (left), distance in kilometers (right) · **No Entry** · **Peace**

a loopy symbol in a blue box. Signage is less prevalent than in other European countries. Turnoffs can come up with very little advance warning, and signs tend to be quite small—keep your eyes peeled. Yet when you turn off onto local roads, you'll often encounter almost comically detailed signs showing the location of every local sight and farmhouse.

Parking: Paid parking zones in Reykjavík are marked with a blue-and-white sign with a large "P" and the number of the zone (for a map, see www.bilastaedasjodur.is/gjaldskylda/gjaldsvaedin). Don't assume it's free—check around for meters or ticketing machines. In downtown Akureyri, you'll need to put a "parking clock" *(bifreiðastæðaklukka)* in your car window showing the time you arrived; time limits are posted at each lot. For more specifics, see those chapters.

Driving Hazards

Weather and Road Conditions: Always check the weather forecast and road conditions before you drive. The Icelandic Road Authority (Vegagerðin) website (www.road.is) shows up-to-date snow, ice, and wind conditions on all the major roads in the country. Visiting this site is a must before setting off on any car trip, even in summer. Learn the colors: Green means the road is totally clear, orange means there are a few icy patches, light blue means that the road is definitely slippery, and dark blue means that you should just stay home. White means snow cover. Closed roads are in red.

Regional maps let you click on weather stations to see a read-out of the latest wind-speed measurements, so you know whether things are getting worse or dying down. Clicking on the individual measurement stations lets you see webcams, wind-speed data, and the number of cars that have passed by in the last ten minutes and since midnight. If no one else is driving a particular stretch of road, don't let yourself be the first. To speak to a real person about road conditions, call the Icelandic Road Authority's hotline at tel. 1777 or 522-1100 (daily in summer 8:00-16:00, in winter 6:30-22:00). They also have recorded information at tel. 1778.

Once you're on the road, giant electronic signboards with information on temperature and wind conditions are set up along routes leading to mountain passes and notoriously windy spots. These post real-time information you need to decide if winds are too strong or road conditions otherwise too dangerous to continue.

One-Lane Bridges, Tunnels, and Roads: There are more than 30 one-lane bridges on the Ring Road alone (most in the southeast), and many more on side roads. They're announced with an *Einbreið Brú* sign and an easy-to-understand picture. The car that reaches the bridge first has priority, but before dashing across, slow down and make sure the other driver has judged the situation the same way.

Iceland also has several one-lane tunnels, cutting beneath mountains and between fjords, and announced with an *Einbreið Göng* sign. Passing places inside the tunnel are marked with a big letter *M*. If the pullout is on your side, you're required to pull

over and let oncoming traffic pass you. Sometimes you can't see oncoming traffic; in those cases you'll encounter either a standard red stoplight or a dual-language *Stop: Bíll á Móti (Stop: Oncoming Cars)* sign.

One-lane roads are marked *Einbreitt Slitlag*. The same rules apply: You'll see the same *M* signs, indicating pullouts to allow oncoming traffic to get by.

Blind Summits: Signs saying *Blindhæð* warn you that you're about to crest a rise where you can't see oncoming traffic (or sheep in the road). Slow down and stay to the right. Blind summits are especially common on unsurfaced roads in the countryside.

Unsurfaced Roads: In rural areas, side roads and driveways are usually dirt or gravel, and you'll likely encounter unpaved stretches of small highways. The "Road info viewer" at www.road. is shows which roads are paved: Click on "Layers," then "Names" to show place names.

Be especially careful at the points where the pavement ends and gravel starts (marked with a *Malbik endar* sign). Speed limits on unsurfaced roads (which can be pocked with deep potholes) are lower (80 km/hour—about 50 mph), and you'll usually want to go even slower than that. Driving on a good gravel road in a two-wheel drive car is nothing to be afraid of, but don't try to force your car down a muddy road that's a mess of puddles and ruts. Drive to conditions, and do your best to straddle the biggest potholes and surprise rocks.

Banked, No-Shoulder Roads: Many roads in Iceland have narrow to nonexistent shoulders and are banked up above the surrounding terrain. Be vigilant to possible hazards in your lane: bicyclists, slow-moving farm equipment, tourists who stop for photos (see next), and wayward sheep. Be especially careful in icy or slippery conditions: If your car slips off the road, it will likely roll over. (Another good reason to wear your seatbelt.)

Photo Stops: With no shoulders and few pullouts, it's tempting to stop in the middle of what seems like a deserted road to take a photo. Don't. Even if it means missing a great shot, find a spot where you can pull over safely. The mouth of a farm driveway often works.

Marshy Shoulders and Fields: In the spring, poorly drained, unpaved surfaces can be marshy. If visiting isolated sites in the countryside, think twice about where you park to avoid getting stuck.

Off-Road Driving: This is strictly forbidden and looked on very unfavorably. You can help protect Iceland's natural beauty and ecosystem by staying on official roads.

Wind: High winds occur all year and present real danger to drivers. Two notoriously windy spots are just north of Reykjavík along the Ring Road, at Kjalarnes (before the Hvalfjörður tunnel) and at Hafnarfjall (across the estuary from Borgarnes). An average sustained wind speed of 15 m/s (meters per second—that's about 35 mph) is enough to make you tighten your grip on the steering wheel, while anything from 20 m/s (45 mph) on up can get dangerous quickly. Gusts, measured separately, can be much stronger. The effect is worst if you're driving a long, high, or flat-sided vehicle, and slippery roads magnify the risk. In some parts of the country, high winds can damage your car by blowing sand and even gravel onto it (see "Sandstorms," later).

If you're caught in high winds, slow way down, keep two hands on the wheel, don't pass, and keep an extra-safe distance from other vehicles. If things turn very bad, pull over and stop—though ideally not somewhere with loose, blowing soil. When opening and closing car doors in windy weather, especially when parked next to other cars, never let go of the door. If you can, park facing into the wind. This prevents a sudden strong gust from flinging your door open and breaking its hinges.

In addition to the Icelandic Road Authority resources described earlier, the Icelandic weather service (http://en.vedur.is) can give you a general sense of the expected wind conditions around the island.

Sandstorms *(sandfok):* If you stay in the southwestern part of the country, there's very little danger of sand damage to your car, because there are no extensive sandy areas near roads. There are, however, several places along the Ring Road where blowing sand is common in windy weather: along the South Coast where the road crosses the Markárfljót river; between Vík and Skaftafell; and in northeast Iceland, between Mývatn and Egilsstaðir. Avoid these stretches when high winds are forecast.

Livestock: In early summer, stay alert for free-ranging sheep on countryside roads. Typically, a ewe and her lambs will be on opposite sides of a road, and as a car approaches, the lambs will run to their mother for safety. If you hit a sheep, you are liable for damage to both your car and the sheep. If you see sheep ahead, slow to a crawl, stop if needed, and wait for them to regroup before slowly continuing on. Unsurfaced roads often have cattle grates at crossings.

Other Drivers: Aggressive driving and speeding are common in Iceland. In addition, tourists here are sometimes inexperienced drivers or unfamiliar with local conditions. Drive defensively and watch out for distracted or confused motorists.

Winter Driving: I don't recommend driving outside Reykjavík and the airport area at all during the winter months (roughly Nov-March). In Reykjavík, winter snowfall tends to be fairly light, and when there is a storm, city streets are cleared fairly well. The road to the airport is also usually kept in decent shape.

Outside the city, though, roads can be a

PRACTICALITIES

sheet of ice for weeks at a time, especially at higher elevations (for example, on parts of the popular Golden Circle daytrip from Reykjavík). In winter, Icelanders only navigate these roads with studded tires and all-wheel-drive cars, and that's what you should do, too, if you absolutely must drive in the countryside at this time of year.

FLIGHTS

To compare flight costs and times, begin with an online travel search engine: Kayak is the top site for flights to and within Europe, easy-to-use Google Flights has price alerts, and Skyscanner includes many inexpensive flights within Europe. To avoid unpleasant surprises, before you book be sure to read the small print about refunds, changes, and the costs for "extras" such as reserving a seat, checking a bag, or printing a boarding pass.

To Iceland

International visitors to Iceland almost always arrive at **Keflavík Airport** (see page 154).

Flying from North America to Iceland: Start looking for international flights about four to six months before your trip, especially for peak-season travel. Off-season tickets can usually be purchased a month or so in advance. Icelandair dominates US routes; Delta also has a few flights to Keflavík.

Stopovers: Many people visit Iceland as a stopover on their way between North America and Europe. Icelandair's hub-and-spoke operation makes this easy, and the extra cost is negligible (usually just a few dollars in extra taxes).

Plan your visit to minimize jet lag. Visiting Iceland on the way from the US is doable, but tends to make jet lag tougher (landing in Iceland early in the morning after an overnight flight from the US, staying two or three days, then continuing on to mainland Europe on an early-morning flight). For a more relaxed stopover, visit Iceland on your way back (leave Europe on an afternoon flight to Iceland, stay for a few days, then continue to the US on a late-morning or afternoon flight).

Flying from Mainland Europe to Iceland: Especially in summer, Iceland is served by a huge range of flights from many different companies. These include legacy airlines, especially Icelandair, but also SAS, Lufthansa, and British Airways, as well as discount airlines such as Wizz Air, EasyJet, and Norwegian.

Within Iceland

Icelanders fly frequently within the country. Domestic flights are hassle-free (with no security checkpoints), reasonably priced (by Icelandic standards), and a good option for tourists—especially in winter (when roads are icy) or to make the best use of limited time. Purchased in advance, the 45-minute flight from Reykjavík to Akureyri is not that much more expensive than the much-longer bus ride. The 45-minute flight to Ísafjörður offers an easy peek at the Westfjords without a six-hour drive each way. The 20-minute flight from Reykjavík to the Westman Islands is a great time-saver. Iceland is very scenic from the air on a clear day. But note that in very windy weather, flights are delayed or cancelled.

Most internal flights leave from the "domestic" **Reykjavík City Airport** (code: RKV), just south of downtown (for details, see page 157).

Air Iceland Connect (tel. 570-3000, www.airicelandconnect. com) serves Akureyri, as well as Egilsstaðir, Ísafjörður, some smaller towns, and the Faroe Islands and Greenland. Their terminal is on the west side of the domestic airport (city bus #15, Reykjavíkurflugvöllur stop). From Keflavík Airport, there is also service to Akureyri, restricted to passengers connecting to or from an international flight.

Eagle Air (tel. 562-2640, www.eagleair.is) uses smaller planes and serves the Westman Islands, Höfn, and Húsavík. Their terminal is on the east side of the domestic airport, next to Icelandair's Hotel Natura (city bus #5, Nauthólsvegur stop).

TO ICELAND BY SEA

Smyril Line's **Norröna car ferry** sails between Hirtshals in Denmark and Seyðisfjörður in eastern Iceland once a week (tel. +298-345-900, www.smyrilline.com), stopping at its home port of Tórshavn in the Faroe Islands en route. The trip takes 48 to 60 hours, depending on the season. In summer you can add a two- to three-day stopover in the Faroe Islands. Consider this approach: Fly from the US to Europe, sail as a one-way foot passenger on the ferry from Denmark to Iceland, rent a car for your Iceland explorations (either in Seyðisfjörður or after flying or going by bus to Reykjavík), then fly home from Keflavík (this works fine in reverse, too).

Several **cruise lines** visit Iceland, often as part of North Atlantic sailings that include European and North American ports as well as Greenland, Svalbard, or the Faroe Islands—a scenic approach that links Iceland to other northern lands that share its maritime history.

PRACTICALITIES

Resources from Rick Steves

Begin your trip at RickSteves.com: My mobile-friendly **website** is *the* place to explore Europe in preparation for your trip. You'll find thousands of fun articles, videos, and radio interviews; a wealth of money-saving tips for planning your dream trip; travel news dispatches; a video library of my travel talks; my travel blog; and my latest guidebook updates (www.ricksteves.com/update); and my free Rick Steves Audio Europe app. You can also follow me on Facebook, Instagram, and Twitter.

Our **Travel Forum** is a well-groomed collection of message boards where our travel-savvy community answers questions and shares their personal travel experiences—and our well-traveled staff chimes in when they can be helpful (www.ricksteves.com/forums).

Our **online Travel Store** offers bags and accessories that I've designed to help you travel smarter and lighter. These include my popular carry-on bags (which I live out of four months a year), money belts, totes, toiletries kits, adapters, guidebooks, and planning maps (www.ricksteves.com/shop).

Rick Steves Tours, Guidebooks, TV Shows, and More

Small Group Tours: Want to travel with greater efficiency and less stress? We offer more than 40 itineraries reaching the best destinations in Europe. Each year about 30,000 travelers join us on about 1,000 Rick Steves bus tours. You'll enjoy great guides and a fun bunch of travel partners (with small groups of 24 to 28 travelers). You'll find European adventures to fit every vacation length. For all the details, and to get our tour catalog, visit www.ricksteves.com/tours or call us at 425/608-4217.

Books: *Rick Steves Iceland* is one of many books in my series on European travel, which includes country and city guidebooks, Snapshots (excerpted chapters from bigger guides), Pocket guides (full-color little books on big cities), "Best Of" guidebooks (condensed, full-color country guides), and my budget-travel skills handbook, *Rick Steves Europe Through the Back Door*. A complete list of my titles—including phrase books; cruising guides; travelogues on European art, history, and culture; and more—appears near the end of this book.

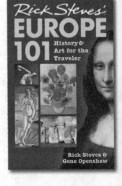

TV Shows and Travel Talks: My public television series, *Rick Steves' Europe*, covers Europe from top to bottom with over 100

half-hour episodes—and we're working on new shows every year (watch full episodes at my website for free). My free online video library, Rick Steves Classroom Europe, offers a searchable database of short video clips on European history, culture, and geography (http://classroom.ricksteves.com). And to raise your travel I.Q., check out the video version of our popular class on Iceland (as well as other talks covering travel skills, packing smart, cruising, tech for travelers, European art, and travel as a political act—www.ricksteves.com/travel-talks).

Radio: My weekly public radio show, *Travel with Rick Steves,* features interviews with travel experts from around the world. It airs on 400 public radio stations across the US, or you can hear it as a podcast. A complete archive of programs is available at www.ricksteves.com/radio.

Audio Tours on My Free App: I've produced dozens of free, self-guided audio tours of the top sights in Europe. For those tours and other audio content, get my free **Rick Steves Audio Europe app,** an extensive online library organized by destination. For more on my app, see page 30.

APPENDIX

Holidays and Festivals

This list includes selected festivals plus national holidays observed in Iceland. Many sights and banks close on national holidays—keep this in mind when planning your itinerary. Before planning a trip around a festival, verify the dates with the festival website, the national tourist office (www.inspiredbyiceland.com), or my "Upcoming Holidays and Festivals in Iceland" web page (www.ricksteves.com/europe/iceland/festivals).

Jan 1	New Year's Day
Jan 6	13th Day of Christmas (bonfires, fireworks)
Mid-Jan-mid-Feb	Þorri (Old Norse midwinter celebration)
Feb	Carnival Week (special foods, costumes): starts Feb 15 in 2021; Feb 28 in 2022
April	Easter: April 4, 2021; April 17, 2022

April	Aldrei Fór Ég Suður music festival in Ísafjörður, Westfjords (Easter weekend, www.aldrei.is)
Late April	Old Norse first day of summer (parades, sports): April 22, 2021; April 21, 2022
May 1	Labor Day
May	Ascension Day: May 21, 2020; May 13, 2021
May-June	Whitsunday and Whit Monday: May 31-June 1, 2020; May 23-24, 2021
Early June	Seaman's Day, Reykjavík (first Sun, www.hatidhafsins.is)
June 17	Icelandic National Day (parades, theater)
Mid-June	Viking Festival in Hafnarfjörður (www.fjorukrain.is): June 11-15, 2020; June 10-14, 2021
Early July	Goslok festival in Vestmannaeyjar (commemorates end of 1973 volcanic eruption): weekend following July 3
Early July	Icelandic horse convention (even years only, www.landsmot.is): July 6-12, 2020
Early Aug	Commerce Day, a.k.a. "Shop Workers' Day Off" (first Mon)
Early Aug	Þjóðhátíð National Festival in Herjólfsdalur, Westman Islands (first weekend; fireworks, bonfires, and singing; www.dalurinn.is)
Late Aug	Culture Night in Reykjavík (free admission to museums; www.menningarnott.is): Aug 22, 2020; Aug 21, 2021
Sept	Réttir—sheep roundups in the countryside
Late Sept-early Oct	Reykjavík International Film Festival (www.riff.is)
Oct 9-Dec 8	Lighting of Imagine Peace Tower, Viðey Island, Reykjavík (www.imaginepeacetower.com)
Late Oct-early Nov	Iceland Airwaves music festival, Reykjavík (www.icelandairwaves.is)
Dec 23	St. Þorlákur's Day (Christmas shopping, evening strolling, traditional meals of skate)
Dec 24-26	Christmas holiday
Dec 31	New Year's Eve (bonfires and fireworks)

APPENDIX

Books and Films

To learn more about Iceland past and present, check out a few of these books and films. Some of these books may be difficult to access outside Iceland, though you may find used copies at online retailers.

Nonfiction

Bringing Down the Banking System (Guðrún Johnsen, 2013). A finance scholar and banking regulator explains Iceland's colossal 2008 bank failure in layman's terms.

Does Anyone Actually Eat This? (Nanna Rögnvaldardóttir, 2014). Iceland's best-known food writer reviews the country's food traditions.

Exploring Iceland's Geology (Snæbjörn Guðmundsson, 2016). This concise guide explains the geology behind 50 of Iceland's most popular natural sights.

The Far Traveler: Voyages of a Viking Woman (Nancy Marie Brown, 2008). Brown uses archaeological and scientific evidence to examine the Icelandic saga of Gudrid the Far-Traveler. Brown's other books include *Song of the Vikings: Snorri and the Making of Norse Myth* (2014) and *Ivory Vikings: The Mystery of the Most Famous Chessmen in the World and the Woman Who Made Them* (2016).

The History of Iceland (Gunnar Karlsson, 2000). This well-written general history of the country also comes in a condensed version, called *A Brief History of Iceland.*

The Indian (Jón Gnarr, 2015). Iceland's best-known comic actor—and recent mayor of Reykjavík—recalls his childhood, during which he was bullied and sent to a boarding school. Two sequels, *The Outlaw* and *The Pirate,* carry on his story.

Lake Mývatn: People and Places (Björg Árnadóttir, 2015). This is a friendly introduction to the popular Lake Mývatn region.

The Little Book of the Icelanders (Alda Sigmundsdóttir, 2012). An Icelander returns home after living in America and explains Icelandic culture with a critical and sometimes cynical eye.

Names for the Sea (Sarah Moss, 2013). A British academic writes about the year she spent in Iceland with her husband and kids.

The Ring of Seasons (Terry Lacy, 2000). An American and long-term Iceland resident describes an idealized year in the life of an Icelandic family.

Ripples from Iceland (Amalia Líndal, 1962). In 1949, a young woman from Boston marries an Icelandic student, moves to Reykjavík, and starts a family.

Viking Age Iceland (Jesse Byock, 2001). Byock provides a good introduction to the society and politics of Iceland in its earliest years, from settlement through the 13th century.

Wasteland with Words: A Social History of Iceland (Sigurður Gylfi Magnússon, 2010). This book focuses on 1870 to 1940, when Iceland grew from a shivering, impoverished colony to a land on the brink of prosperity and independence.

The Windows of Brimnes (Bill Holm, 2007). Minnesotan writer and poet Bill Holm, who spent several summers in a cottage in Skagafjörður near the home of his ancestors, reflects on the differences between Iceland and the US.

Fiction

Angels of the Universe (Einar Már Guðmundsson, 1993). An intelligent young man descends into mental illness in 1960s Reykjavík.

The Blue Fox (Sjón, 2003). In this short, poetically written fable a 19th-century Lutheran pastor hunts an arctic fox.

Burial Rites (Hannah Kent, 2013). Kent writes a fictionalized account of the final months of Agnes Magnúsdóttir, whose 1830 beheading (for taking part in a murder) was the last time the death penalty was used in Iceland.

Frozen Assets (Quentin Bates, 2011). This book is one in a series of gripping crime novels starring Gunnhildur "Gunna" Gísladóttir—a shrewd policewoman who, in the course of a murder investigation, uncovers corruption at the highest levels.

Heaven and Hell (Jón Kalman Stefánsson, 2015). Stefánsson, a poet, brings his lyrical prose to this novel of a fishing accident and a young boy's search for meaning in remote Iceland in the early 20th century.

Independent People (Halldór Laxness, 1934). Nobel Prize-winning Laxness' best novel tells the story of Bjartur, a farm laborer who jumps at the rare chance to have his own farm. In his single-minded quest to take charge of his destiny, he destroys everyone around him.

The Sagas of the Icelanders (edited by Robert Kellogg, 2001). These classic stories, still fresh after 800 years, are set appealingly amid the Icelandic landscape.

Film and TV

These films and shows are generally available for streaming in the US.

101 Reykjavík (2000). This comedy is set in downtown Reykjavík in the 1990s—before tourism took over—when it was still bohemian. Hlynur lives with his mother and is having problems committing to his girlfriend. He winds up involved with Lola, who is his mother's friend—in fact, more than her friend.

Devil's Island (1996). This film highlights the adventures of a lower-class Reykjavík family living in abandoned WWII barracks. It includes gangs, an Elvis soundtrack, and a main character aptly named Baddi.

Life in a Fishbowl (2014; Icelandic title: *Vonarstræti*). Three lives intersect during Iceland's financial collapse: an alcoholic writer, a young unmarried mother who has turned to prostitution, and a morally compromised banking executive.

No Such Thing (2001). This bizarre American-Icelandic indie film, with its *Beauty and the Beast* theme, stars Sarah Polley as a journalist who tries to tame the beast—who incidentally killed her fiancé.

Nói the Albino (2003). In this portrait of small-town adolescence, Nói lives with his grandmother and alcoholic father in the Westfjords, and falls for a girl at the local gas station.

The Seagull's Laughter (2001). In the 1950s, shapely Freyja returns to Iceland from America, where she has been living with her soldier husband, and stirs up all kinds of trouble.

Trapped (2016; Icelandic title: *Ófærð*). As the car ferry from the Faroe Islands arrives one day, a body is found floating in the fjord. The pass is snowed in, so none of the passengers can leave town, and investigators from Reykjavík can't arrive. Whodunit?

The remaining films may be harder to find (check www. icelandiccinema.com).

Angels of the Universe (2000). Páll descends into mental illness after being dumped by his girlfriend.

Children of Nature (1991). A man and a woman, once childhood friends, meet again when they move into the same senior citizens home. They decide to escape together and go on a car trip into the countryside.

The Icelandic Dream (2000). Tóti tries everything he can to get ahead, but keeps messing up. This dark, realist, somewhat-amateurish comedy explores class differences in Reykjavík and the effects of the former American military presence.

Mr. Bjarnfreðarson (2009). This black comedy stars Jón Gnarr as a sadistic misfit, damaged for life by his mother's left-wing activism and trying to regroup after serving prison time for an "accidental" murder.

Remote Control (1992; Icelandic title: *Sódóma Reykjavík*). Axel goes in search of his mother's lost TV remote and gets mixed up with a gang of mobsters. This low-budget comedy with a hard-rock soundtrack has been called Iceland's equivalent of *The Big Lebowski*.

When the Raven Flies (1984). An Irish boy travels to Iceland to take revenge on Vikings who killed his parents.

Conversions and Climate

Numbers and Stumblers

- Europeans write a few of their numbers differently than we do. 1 = 1, 4 = 4, 7 = 7.
- In Europe, dates appear as day/month/year, so Christmas 2021 is 25/12/21.
- Commas are decimal points and decimals commas. A dollar and a half is $1,50, one thousand is 1.000, and there are 5.280 feet in a mile.
- When counting with fingers, start with your thumb. If you hold up your first finger to request one item, you'll probably get two.
- On escalators and moving sidewalks, Europeans keep the left "lane" open for passing. Keep to the right.

Metric Conversions

A **kilogram** equals 1,000 grams (about 2.2 pounds). One hundred-dred **grams** (a common unit at markets) is about a quarter-pound. One **liter** is about a quart, or almost four to a gallon.

A **kilometer** is six-tenths of a mile. To convert kilometers to miles, cut the kilometers in half and add back 10 percent of the original (120 km: 60 + 12 = 72 miles). One **meter** is 39 inches—just over a yard.

1 foot = 0.3 meter	1 square yard = 0.8 square meter
1 yard = 0.9 meter	1 square mile = 2.6 square kilometers
1 mile = 1.6 kilometers	1 ounce = 28 grams
1 centimeter = 0.4 inch	1 quart = 0.95 liter
1 meter = 39.4 inches	1 kilogram = 2.2 pounds
1 kilometer = 0.62 mile	32°F = 0°C

Iceland's Climate

First line, average daily high; second line, average daily low; third line, average days without rain. For more detailed weather statistics for destinations in this book, check Iceland's English-language website http://en.vedur.is, and for both Iceland and the rest of the world, www.wunderground.com.

	J	F	M	A	M	J	J	A	S	O	N	D

Reykjavík

35°	37°	37°	41°	47°	52°	55°	54°	49°	44°	38°	36°
27°	29°	29°	33°	39°	44°	47°	46°	41°	36°	31°	28°
10	13	12	12	14	15	15	14	11	9	11	10

Akureyri

34°	35°	36°	42°	49°	56°	58°	57°	50°	43°	37°	34°
22°	24°	24°	35°	36°	43°	46°	45°	38°	31°	27°	23°
20	20	21	24	26	24	24	24	22	20	19	20

Westman Islands

38°	39°	39°	42°	46°	50°	53°	53°	49°	44°	40°	39°
31°	32°	32°	35°	40°	44°	47°	47°	43°	38°	33°	31°
13	11	14	14	17	16	18	17	14	12	14	13

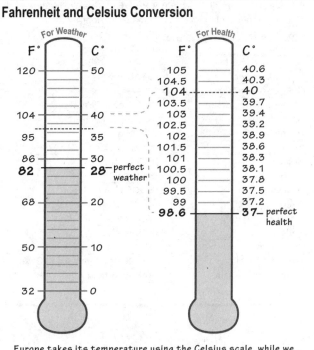

Fahrenheit and Celsius Conversion

Europe takes its temperature using the Celsius scale, while we opt for Fahrenheit. For a rough conversion from Celsius to Fahrenheit, double the number and add 30. For weather, remember that 28°C is 82°F—perfect. For health, 37°C is just right. At a launderette, 30°C is cold, 40°C is warm (usually the default setting), 60°C is hot, and 95°C is boiling. Your air-conditioner should be set at about 20°C.

APPENDIX

Pronunciation Guide for Place Names

For more help in pronouncing Icelandic words, see "The Icelandic Language" sidebar on page 502 and "Icelandic Survival Phrases" later in this chapter.

Akureyri	AH-kuh-RAY-ree
Baula (mountain)	BOY-la
Borgarfjörður (fjord)	BOR-gar-FYUR-thur
Borgarnes	BOHR-gahr-NESS
Dettifoss (waterfall)	DEH-tih-foss
Dimmuborgir (craters)	DIM-moo-BOR-geer
Djúpivogur	DYOOP-ih-VOH-ur
Dyrhólaey (promontory)	DEER-hoh-la-AY
Egilsstaðir	AY-ill-STAHTH-eer
Eldfell (volcano)	ELD-fehtl
Eyjafjallajökull (glacier volcano)	EH-ya-FYAH-tla-YUR-kutl
Fjallsárlón (glacier lagoon)	FYATL-sour-lohn
Geysir (geyser)	GAY-seer
Glaumbær	GLOYM-bīr
Gljúfrabúi (waterfall)	GLYOO-vrah-BOO-ee
Grábrók (crater)	GRAU-brohk
Gullfoss (waterfall)	GUTL-foss
Hafnarfjall (mountain)	HAHP-nahr-FYAHTL
Hafnarfjörður	HAHP-nar-FYUR-thur
Heimaey	HAME-ah-AY
Höfn	hurpn (n almost silent)
Hofsós	HOFF-sohs
Hólar	HOH-lar
Húsavík	HOOS-ah-VEEK
Hverfjall (crater)	KVER-fyahtl
Jökulsárlón (lagoon)	YUR-kurls-OUR-lohn
Keflavík	KEP-la-VEEK
Kerið (crater)	KEH-reethe
Kirkjubæjarklaustur	KEERK-yoo-bay-yahr-KLOY-stur
Kirkjufell (mountain)	KIRK-yoo-fehtl

Kleifarvatn (lake)	CLAY-vahr-VAHT
Krafla (geothermal valley)	KRAH-plah
Lagarfljót (lake)	LAH-gar-flyoht
Laugardalur	LOY-gar-DA-lrr
Laugavegur	LOY-ga-VEH-grr
Mjódd	MEE-ohd
Mývatn (lake and area)	MEE-vahtn (n almost silent)
Námafjall (thermal field)	NOW-mah-fyahtl
Nesjavallaleið (mountain pass)	NESS-ya-VAHT-la-layth
Reykjadalur (thermal valley)	RAYK-yah-DAL-lrr
Reykjahlíð	RAYK-yah-HLEETH
Reykjanes	RAYK-yah-NESS
Reykjavík	RAYK-yah-VEEK
Reynisfjara (black sand beach)	RAY-nis-fyah-rah
Sauðárkrókur	SOY-thowr-KROH-kur
Seljalandsfoss (waterfall)	SELL-yah-lahnds-foss
Seyðisfjörður	SAY-this-FYUR-thur
Siglufjörður	SIG-loo-FYUR-thur
Skaftafell (national park)	SKAF-tah-fehtl
Skagafjörður	SKAH-gah-FYUR-thur
Skógafoss (waterfall)	SKOH-gah-foss
Skógar	SKOH-ar
Skútustaðir (pseudocraters)	SKOO-tu-STAH-theer
Snæfellsnes	SNIGH-fells-ness
Snæfellsjökull (glacier)	SNIGH-fells-YUR-kutl
Sólheimajökull (glacier)	SOHL-HAY-ma-YUR-kutl
Stykkishólmur	STIK-iss-HOLL-mur
Þingvellir	THING-VET-leer
Þórsmörk (mountain ridge)	THORS-murk
Tröllaskagi	TREW-tlah-sky-ee
Varmahlíð	VAR-mah-HLEETHE
Vatnajökull (glacier)	VAHT-nah-YUR-kutl
Vestmannaeyjar	VEST-mah-nah-AY-ar
Víðgelmir (lava tube cave)	VEETHE-GHELL-meer

Iceland Packing Checklist

Whether you're traveling for five days or five weeks, you won't need more than this. Pack light to enjoy the sweet freedom of true mobility.

Clothing

- ☐ 5 shirts
- ☐ 2 pairs pants
- ☐ 5 pairs underwear & socks
- ☐ Waterproof shoes
- ☐ Sweater or warm layer
- ☐ Rainproof/windproof jacket with hood
- ☐ Fleece hat, gloves
- ☐ Swimsuit & swim accessories (eyeglass strap, bathing cap, or goggles; small towel)
- ☐ Sleepwear/loungewear

Money

- ☐ Debit card(s)
- ☐ Credit card(s)
- ☐ Hard cash ($100-200)
- ☐ Money belt

Documents

- ☐ Passport
- ☐ Other required ID: Vaccine card/Covid test, entry visa, etc.
- ☐ Driver's license, student ID, hostel card, etc.
- ☐ Tickets & confirmations: flights, hotels, trains, rail pass, car rental, sight entries
- ☐ Photocopies of important documents
- ☐ Insurance details
- ☐ Guidebooks & maps

Toiletries

- ☐ Basics: soap, shampoo, toothbrush, toothpaste, floss, deodorant, sunscreen, brush/comb, etc.
- ☐ Medicines & vitamins
- ☐ First-aid kit
- ☐ Glasses/contacts
- ☐ Face masks & hand sanitizer
- ☐ Sunglasses (esp. if driving)
- ☐ Sewing kit
- ☐ Packet of tissues (for WC)
- ☐ Eye mask (for sleeping)
- ☐ Earplugs

Electronics

- ☐ Mobile phone
- ☐ Camera & related gear
- ☐ Tablet/ebook reader/laptop
- ☐ Headphones/earbuds
- ☐ Chargers & batteries
- ☐ Phone car charger & mount (or GPS device)
- ☐ Plug adapters

Miscellaneous

- ☐ Daypack
- ☐ Sealable plastic baggies
- ☐ Laundry supplies: soap, laundry bag, clothesline
- ☐ Small umbrella
- ☐ Travel alarm/watch
- ☐ Notepad & pen
- ☐ Journal

Optional Extras

- ☐ Second pair of shoes
- ☐ Travel hairdryer
- ☐ Water bottle
- ☐ Fold-up tote bag
- ☐ Small flashlight
- ☐ Mini binoculars
- ☐ Inflatable pillow/neck rest
- ☐ Tiny lock
- ☐ Insect head net (if visiting Mývatn area)
- ☐ Strap-on ice cleats (winter only)

APPENDIX

Icelandic Survival Phrases

Icelandic has some unique letters, most notably Ð/ð (the voiced "th" sound in "breathe," represented by "th") and Þ/þ (the unvoiced "th" sound in "breath," also represented by "th"). The letter á sounds like "ow" (rhymes with "now"). The long i in "light" is represented by "Ī."

English	Icelandic	Pronunciation
Hello (formal)	Góðan daginn	GOH-thahn DĪ-ihn
Hi / Bye (informal)	Hæ / Bæ	HĪ / bĪ (as in English)
Do you speak English?	Talarðu ensku?	TAHL-ar-thoo EHN-skoo?
Yes. / No.	Já / Nei.	yow / nay
I (don't) understand.	Ég skil (ekki).	yehkh skeel (EH-kee)
Please. / Thank you.	Vinsamlegast. / Takk.	VIN-sahm-lay-gahst / tahk
Excuse me.	Fyrirgefðu.	FIH-ree-GEHV-thoo
No problem.	Ekkert mál.	EHK-kert mowl
Super	Fínt	feent
OK	Allt í lagi	ahlt ee LAH-yee
Goodbye (more formal)	Bless	bless
one / two	einn / tveir	ayt / tvayr
three / four	þrír / fjórir	threer / FYOH-rir
five / six	fimm / sex	fim / sex
seven / eight	sjö / átta	syur / OWT-tah
nine / ten	níu / tíu	NEE-oo / TEE-oo
hundred	hundrað	HOON-drahth
thousand	þúsund	THOO-sund
How much is it?	Hvað kostar þetta?	kvahth KOHS-tar THEHT-tah?
Is it free?	Er þetta ókeypis?	ayr THEHT-tah OH-kay-pis?
Is it included?	Er þetta innifalið?	ayr THEHT-tah EEN-nee-fah-lith?
(Icelandic) crowns	(íslenskar) krónur	(EE-slehn-skar) KROH-nur
Where is...?	Hvar er...?	kvar ayr...?
...the toilet	....klósettið	...KLOH-seht-tith
men	karlar	KAHT-lar
women	konur	KOH-noor
left / right	vinstri / hægri	VIN-stree / HĪ-grih
straight	beint	baynt
opening hours	opnunartími	OHP-noo-nar-tee-mih
At what time?	Hvenær?	KVEH-nīr
Just a moment.	Augnablik.	OOG-nah-bleek
now / soon / later	núna / bráðum / seinna	NOO-nah / BROW-thoom / SAYT-nah
today / tomorrow	í dag / á morgun	ee dahkh / ow MOR-goon
Cheers!	skál	skowl

INDEX

INDEX

MAP INDEX

Our website enhances this book and turns

Explore Europe

At ricksteves.com you can browse through thousands of articles, videos, photos and radio interviews, plus find a wealth of money-saving travel tips for planning your dream trip. And with our mobile-friendly website, you can easily access all this great travel information anywhere you go.

TV Shows

Preview the places you'll visit by watching entire half-hour episodes of *Rick Steves' Europe* (choose from all 100 shows) on-demand, for free.

ricksteves.com

your travel dreams into affordable reality

Radio Interviews

Enjoy ready access to Rick's vast library of radio interviews covering travel tips and cultural insights that relate specifically to your Europe travel plans.

Travel Forums

Learn, ask, share! Our online community of savvy travelers is a great resource for first-time travelers to Europe, as well as seasoned pros.

Travel News

Subscribe to our free Travel News e-newsletter, and get monthly updates from Rick on what's happening in Europe.

Classroom Europe®

Check out our free resource for educators with 500+ short video clips from the *Rick Steves' Europe* TV show.

Audio Europe™

Pack Light and Right

Gear up for your next adventure at ricksteves.com

Light Luggage

Pack light and right with Rick Steves' affordable, custom-designed rolling carry-on bags, backpacks, day packs and shoulder bags.

Accessories

From packing cubes to moneybelts and beyond, Rick has personally selected the travel goodies that will help your trip go smoother.

Shop at ricksteves.com

Experience maximum Europe

Save time and energy

This guidebook is your independent-travel toolkit. But for all it delivers, it's still up to you to devote the time and energy it takes to manage the preparation and logistics that are essential for a happy trip. If that's a hassle, there's a solution.

Rick Steves Tours

A Rick Steves tour takes you to Europe's most interesting places with great

with minimum stress

guides and small groups of 28 or less. We follow Rick's favorite itineraries, ride in comfy buses, stay in family-run hotels, and bring you intimately close to the Europe you've traveled so far to see. Most importantly, we take away the logistical headaches so you can focus on the fun.

Join the fun

This year we'll take 33,000 free-spirited travelers— nearly half of them repeat customers—along with us on 50 different itineraries, from Athens to Istanbul. Is a Rick Steves tour the right fit for your travel dreams?

Find out at ricksteves.com, where you can also request Rick's latest tour catalog. Europe is best experienced with happy travel partners. We hope you can join us.

See our itineraries at ricksteves.com

A Guide for Every Trip

BEST OF GUIDES

Full-color guides in an easy-to-scan format. Focused on top sights and experiences in the most popular European destinations

Best of England
Best of Europe
Best of France
Best of Germany
Best of Ireland
Best of Italy
Best of Scotland
Best of Spain

COMPREHENSIVE GUIDES

City, country, and regional guides printed on Bible-thin paper. Packed with detailed coverage for a multi-week trip exploring iconic sights and venturing off the beaten path

Amsterdam & the Netherlands
Barcelona
Belgium: Bruges, Brussels, Antwerp & Ghent
Berlin
Budapest
Croatia & Slovenia
Eastern Europe
England
Florence & Tuscany
France
Germany
Great Britain
Greece: Athens & the Peloponnese
Iceland
Ireland
Istanbul
Italy
London
Paris
Portugal
Prague & the Czech Republic
Provence & the French Riviera
Rome
Scandinavia
Scotland
Sicily
Spain
Switzerland
Venice
Vienna, Salzburg & Tirol

HE BEST OF ROME

ne, Italy's capital, is studded with
an remnants and floodlit-fountain
es. From the Vatican to the Colos-
, with crazy traffic in between, Rome
nderful, huge, and exhausting. The
s, the heat, and the weighty history

of the Eternal City where Caesars walked
can make tourists wilt. Recharge by taking siestas, gelato breaks, and after-dark
walks, strolling from one atmospheric
square to another in the refreshing evening air.

*f Pantheon—which
st dome until the
ly 2,000 years old
y over 1,500).*

*f Athens in the Vat-
fies the humanistic
e.*

*ediators fought
nother, entertaining*

*Rome ristorante.
e at St. Peter's*

Rick Steves books are available from your favorite bookseller.
Many guides are available as ebooks.

POCKET GUIDES
Compact color guides for shorter trips

Amsterdam	Paris
Athens	Prague
Barcelona	Rome
Florence	Venice
Italy's Cinque Terre	Vienna
London	
Munich & Salzburg	

SNAPSHOT GUIDES
Focused single-destination coverage

Basque Country: Spain & France
Copenhagen & the Best of Denmark
Dublin
Dubrovnik
Edinburgh
Hill Towns of Central Italy
Krakow, Warsaw & Gdansk
Lisbon
Loire Valley
Madrid & Toledo
Milan & the Italian Lakes District
Naples & the Amalfi Coast
Nice & the French Riviera
Normandy
Northern Ireland
Norway
Reykjavík
Rothenburg & the Rhine
Sevilla, Granada & Southern Spain
St. Petersburg, Helsinki & Tallinn
Stockholm

CRUISE PORTS GUIDES
Reference for cruise ports of call

Mediterranean Cruise Ports
Scandinavian & Northern European
  Cruise Ports

Complete your library with...

TRAVEL SKILLS & CULTURE
*Study up on travel skills and gain
insight on history and culture*

Europe 101
Europe Through the Back Door
Europe's Top 100 Masterpieces
European Christmas
European Easter
European Festivals
For the Love of Europe
Italy for Food Lovers
Travel as a Political Act

PHRASE BOOKS & DICTIONARIES
French
French, Italian & German
German
Italian
Portuguese
Spanish

PLANNING MAPS
Britain, Ireland & London
Europe
France & Paris
Germany, Austria & Switzerland
Iceland
Ireland
Italy
Scotland
Spain & Portugal

Credits

For help with this edition, Rick relied on...

RESEARCHERS
Jennifer Davis

Raised in Eastern Oregon, Jennifer spent her childhood exploring the back roads and mountain trails of the Pacific Northwest. Her first trip east of the Rockies was a direct flight to Paris— still her favorite European city. Now managing editor for guidebooks at Rick Steves' Europe, Jennifer is grateful that travel led her family to reconnect with its Italian roots. Jennifer lives north of Seattle with her husband, Steven, and daughter, Madeline.

Glenn Eriksen

A solo backpacking trip across Europe and Scandinavia back in the '70s turned out to be Glenn's first step on the road to Rick Steves' Europe. Today, as a guidebook editor and researcher, he indulges his love for the Old Country while helping Rick's readers "keep on travelin'." When not on the road, Glenn lives in Seattle with his wife, Kathy, and enjoys hiking, photography, and staying in touch with his Norwegian roots.

Acknowledgments

The authors wish to say *"Takk!"* to the following people for their travel savvy and expertise: Angela Walk, Kevin Williams, Dave Hoerlein, Shawna Hewitt, Jens Ruminy, Kendra Willson, Austin Yuill, Yorick Harker, and Robyn Stencil.

Photo Credits

Avalon Travel
Hachette Book Group
1700 Fourth Street
Berkeley, CA 94710

Printed in Canada by Friesens.
Second Edition. Fifth printing June 2023.

ISBN 978-1-64171-231-6

For the latest on Rick's talks, guidebooks, tours, public television series, and public radio show, contact Rick Steves' Europe, 130 Fourth Avenue North, Edmonds, WA 98020, 425/771-8303, www.ricksteves.com, rick@ricksteves.com.

Rick Steves' Europe
Managing Editor: Jennifer Madison Davis
Assistant Managing Editor: Cathy Lu
Special Publications Manager: Risa Laib
Editors: Glenn Eriksen, Tom Griffin, Suzanne Kotz, Rosie Leutzinger, Jessica Shaw, Carrie Shepherd
Editorial & Production Assistant: Megan Simms
Editorial Intern: Bridgette Robertson
Researchers: Jennifer Davis, Glenn Eriksen
Contributors: Cameron Hewitt, Ian Watson
Graphic Content Director: Sandra Hundacker
Maps & Graphics: David C. Hoerlein, Lauren Mills, Mary Rostad
Digital Asset Coordinator: Orin Dubrow

Avalon Travel
Senior Editor and Series Manager: Madhu Prasher
Editors: Jamie Andrade, Sierra Machado
Copy Editor: Maggie Ryan
Proofreader: Patrick Collins
Indexer: Stephen Callahan
Production & Typesetting: Lisi Baldwin, Rue Flaherty, Jane Musser
Cover Design: Kimberly Glyder Design
Maps & Graphics: Kat Bennett, Mike Morgenfeld

COLOR MAPS

Reykjavík Center • Iceland • Southwest Iceland

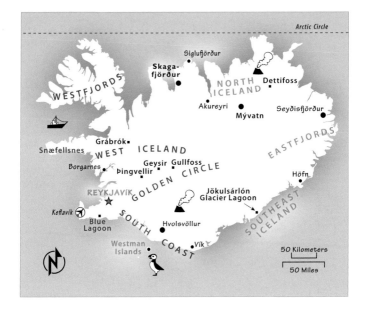

Arctic Circle

Siglufjörður

Skaga-
fjörður

NORTH
ICELAND

Dettifoss

Akureyri

Mývatn

Seyðisfjörður

WESTFJORDS

EASTFJORDS

Grábrók

Snæfellsnes

WEST ICELAND

Borgarnes

Geysir Gullfoss

Þingvellir

GOLDEN CIRCLE

Höfn

REYKJAVÍK

Jökulsárlón
Glacier Lagoon

Keflavík

SOUTHEAST
ICELAND

Blue
Lagoon

Hvolsvöllur

SOUTH COAST

Vík

Westman
Islands

50 Kilometers

50 Miles

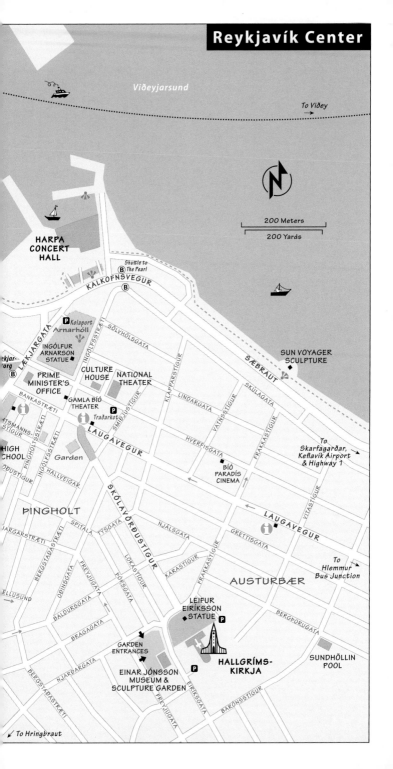

Iceland

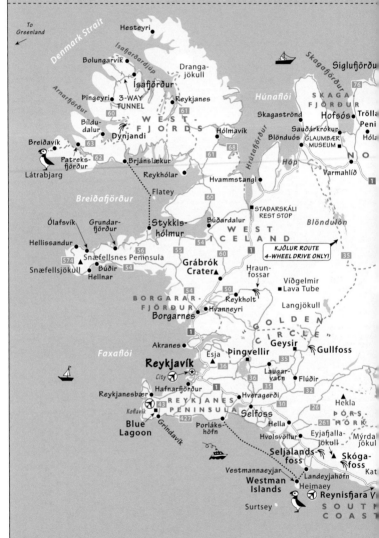

Greenland Sea

To Greenland

ARCTIC CIRCLE

Denmark Strait

Hesteyri

Bolungarvík

Ísafjarðardjúp

Drangajökull

Ísafjörður

Reykjanes

Skagafjörður

Siglufjörður

76

Húnaflói

SKAGA-FJÖRÐUR

Skagaströnd

Hofsós

Trölla-Peni

Arnarfjörður

Pingeyri

3-WAY TUNNEL

WEST-FJORDS

61

Saudárkrókur

Blönduós

GLAUMBÆR MUSEUM

Hóla

NO

Bíldu-dalur

Dynjandi

Hólmavík

Hrútafjörður

Varmahlíð

1

Breiðavík

Patreks-fjörður

62

Brjánslækur

61

68

Hóp

Látrabjarg

Reykhólar

Hvammstangi

Flatey

60

Breiðafjörður

Búðardalur

STAÐARSKÁLI REST STOP

Blöndulón

Ólafsvík

Grundar-fjörður

Stykkis-hólmur

WEST ICELAND

1

KJÖLUR ROUTE 4-WHEEL DRIVE ONLY!

35

Hellissandur

56

55

54

60

Snæfellsnes Peninsula

574

Búðir

54

Grábrók Crater

Hraun-fossar

Snæfellsjökull

Hellnar

BORGARAR-FJÖRÐUR

54

50

Reykholt

Viðgelmir Lava Tube

Langjökull

GOLDEN

Hvanneyri

Borgarnes

1

Akranes

Esja

Pingvellir

36

Geysir

Gullfoss

CIRCLE

Faxaflói

Reykjavík

City

Hafnarfjörður

35

Laugar-vatn

Flúðir

32

Reykjanesbær

1

REYKJANES PENINSULA

36

Hveragerði

30

26

Hekla

Keflavík

43

427

Selfoss

ÞÓRS-MÖRK

Blue Lagoon

Grindavík

Þorláks-höfn

Hella

261

Hvolsvöllur

Eyjafjalla-jökull

Mýrda-jökull

Seljalands-foss

Skóga-foss

Vestmannaeyjar

Landeyjahöfn

Kat

Westman Islands

Heimaey

Reynisfjara V

Surtsey

SOUTH COAST

To Vinland

North Atlantic

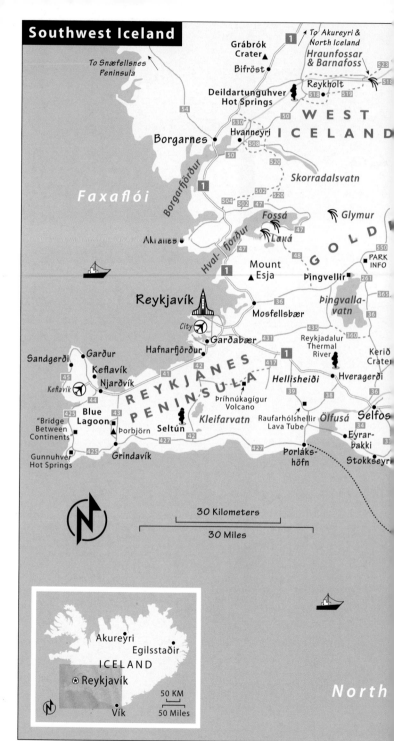

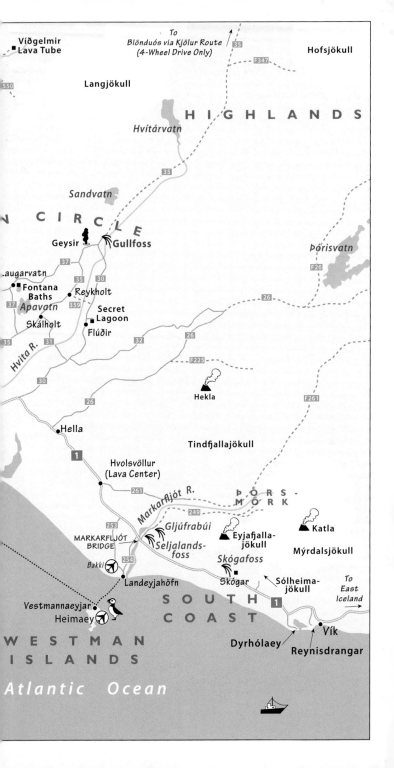

Let's Keep on Travelin'

Your trip doesn't need to end.

Follow Rick on social media!